Ladies

AND NOT-SO-GENTLE

Women

Ladies
AND NOT-SO-GENTLE
Women

ALFRED ALLAN LEWIS

VIKING

VIKING

Published by the Penguin Group
Penguin Putnam Inc., 375 Hudson Street,
New York, New York 10014, U.S.A.
Penguin Books Ltd, 27 Wrights Lane, London W8 5TZ, England
Penguin Books Australia Ltd, Ringwood, Victoria, Australia
Penguin Books Canada Ltd, 10 Alcorn Avenue,
Toronto, Ontario, Canada M4V 3B2
Penguin Books (N.Z.) Ltd, 182–190 Wairau Road,
Auckland 10, New Zealand

Penguin Books Ltd, Registered Offices:
Harmondsworth, Middlesex, England

First published in 2000 by Viking Penguin,
a member of Penguin Putnam Inc.

1   3   5   7   9   10   8   6   4   2

LIBRARY OF CONGRESS CATALOGING-IN-PUBLICATION DATA
Lewis, Alfred Allan.
Ladies and not-so-gentle women / Alfred Allan Lewis.
p. cm.
ISBN 0–670–85810–2
1. Marbury, Elisabeth, 1856–1933.   2. De Wolfe, Elsie,
1865–1950.   3. Morgan, Anne Tracy, 1873–1952.   4. Vander-
bilt, Anne Harriman, 1862?–1940.   5. Literary agents—United
States—Biography.   6. Theatrical producers and directors—
United States—Biography.   7. Interior decorators—United
States—Biography.   8. World War, 1914–1918—War work—
France.   9. Philanthropists—United States—Biography.
10. Women—United States—Biography.   11. Female
friendship—United States.   I. Title.
CT3260 L48   2000
920.72'0973—dc21   99–055217

This book is printed on acid-free paper. ∞

Printed in the United States of America
Set in Minion
DESIGNED BY BETTY LEW

To
Ralph
❖

$\mathscr{A}$CKNOWLEDGMENTS ❧

My gratitude to all of the curators and librarians at the research centers, museums, and libraries without whom writing this book would have been impossible, with special thanks to David Wright of the Pierpont Morgan Library, Kenneth Craven of the Harry Ransom Humanities Research Center of the University of Texas, Veronique Wiesinger of the Chateau de Blerancourt, Saundra Taylor of the Lilly Library at Indiana University, Hutton Wilkinson of the Elsie de Wolfe Foundation, Lola L. Szladits of the Berg Collection of the New York Public Library, Fiorella Superbi Gioffredi of Villa I Tatti, Janet Duncan of the University of Virginia, and Katherine Martinez of the Cooper-Hewitt Museum. Mention must also be made of the remarkable treasures to be found in the library of the New-York Historical Society. My appreciation extends to Peter and Diana Marbury, who allowed me access to the only surviving letters that Elisabeth Marbury wrote to members of her family. It likewise goes to Anne Morgan's nieces, Carolie Woods Noble and the late Mabel Satterlee Ingalls, as well as to Jane S. Smith, Elsie de Wolfe's commendable biographer, who so generously shared her research materials, to Didi D'Anglejan-Chatillon, who opened the world of Anne Morgan's Blérancourt to me, and to Frank Liberman, who allowed me to see the Marbury-de Wolfe Versailles guest book that revealed who was at Villa Trianon and when. I must also mention Samuel Stevens Sands Jr., Brendan Gill, Roddy MacDowell, Eugene Von Braun-Monk, Radie Harris, Marta Linden Emery, Ernest Samuels, Leon Edel, Tony Duquette, Pauline C. Metcalf, Lilla Pennant, Cleveland Amory, George Eels, R. W. B. Lewis, Margaret L. Moser, Mrs. N. M. Martin, Rae Corsini, Mary Lee Fletcher, Jessica Mitford, Nigel Nicolson, Angela P. Supplee, Jean Bach, Betty Kern Miller, the Reverend Anthony dalla Villa, Ann Tanneyhill, Mildred Hall, Sister Marguerita Smith, Marlene Rajakrishnan, James B. Pendleton, George

Durenberger, Tom Beaton, Carmen Lopez, James H. Heineman, Edward Cazalet, Addie Herder, Eileen Finletter, Gloria Jones, and Marshall De-Bruhle. I am forever in the debt of my editor, Jane Von Mehren, who kept the faith, Beena Kamlani for her Herculean editorial job, and Jessica Kipp for her editorial assistance.

Acknowledgments

$\mathscr{C}$ONTENTS ॐ

$\mathscr{I}$NTRODUCTION ❧

Until the mid-twentieth century, with the exception of a few female monarchs, political history was made by men while social history was created by women. Men dictated the shape of the world in which we lived while women fabricated the style in which we inhabited it. Such was the case of the woman who was arguably the most influential monarch of the last two centuries, Victoria of England. It was her ministers and generals who formed the British Empire of the nineteenth century, but it was Victoria's rules of conduct and constricting morality that dictated the way in which the entire English-speaking world deported itself for almost a century after her death. So persuasive was her message that it is still mistaken for Christianity by a large segment of the religious right in the United States.

Paradoxically, it was in the Victorian era that women experienced the greatest forward thrust toward their own liberation in the Western world's history. They may not have gotten the vote, but the vote was intrinsically of little worth in the nineteenth century. Only a numerically insignificant minority of men had it and, of that group, a still smaller number had the power to institute change. What women did receive was an unprecedented control of their own property. It was imperfect, but it was no longer a given that what belonged to a husband was his and what belonged to his wife was equally his. As Victoria's reign lengthened, ladies were finding divorce an increasingly acceptable alternative to misery.

Women were going to universities and entering fields from which they previously had been barred. Their numbers in law, medicine, and commerce were slight compared to present times. But the difference between none and a few is far greater than that between a few and many. The improvement in their literacy was illustrated not only by the sudden plethora of women novelists but also, more significantly, by the number of books written specifically for women readers.

Living in an age already named for a woman might have added a psychological component to what began in the middle of Victoria's reign. Women began to wonder about their civil rights, to question their traditional roles in society, and, once having questioned, to rebel against them. Some did it stridently, literally chaining themselves to the pillars of society in an attempt to bring them down. Theirs were the names rattling through history, the mothers immaculately giving birth to a women's movement.

There were other women who also rebelled, but it was a much quieter, more subtle revolution, one more in keeping with their traditional roles. They worked within the strictures of the middle and upper classes to which their families belonged and radically modified their traditional roles in it. In so doing, they also made permanent changes in what was deemed socially acceptable behavior for all members of their sex. Elisabeth (Bessy) Marbury, Anne Tracy Morgan, Elsie de Wolfe, and Anne Harriman Vanderbilt were among them. They did not find prominent places in the posthumous histories of their times but were much better known and more influential during them than many who did. Their likenesses and opinions were on the front pages of the nation's newspapers. In an era when print was the only medium of communication, they were profiled, quoted, and photographed, often writing articles explaining themselves in the leading periodicals of the day.

They belonged to that generation of women who were born and became adults during the reign of Victoria. The deepest sentiments of Victorianism were, if anything, stronger in the United States than in England and helped to shape their values: intellectual, sexual, and psychological.

Elsie de Wolfe and Elisabeth Marbury had grown up and spent their adult lives in or on the periphery of New York society, which was arguably the most Victorian in the world. They decided to live together, but not as an act of rebellion against the prevailing social system. They had grown up and were comfortable in it. They simply desired acceptance, to extend its confines to include them as they were.

Sexual freedom was something with which, as Victorians, they were not overly concerned. No diaries or intimate letters have survived, and at what level of intimacy Bessy and Elsie lived can only be surmised. Had they begun their relationship a decade earlier, it would have been classified as a "Boston marriage," an arrangement in which two women shared a domicile, expenses, and every intimacy of marriage short of sexual intercourse. As they and their intimacy survived Victoria and lasted long into the new patriarchy of the twentieth century, it was surmised they were "gay," a term applied to sexually active female homosexuals long before it was to their male counterparts, who were then considered chronically if not clinically "sad."

In the Boston marriage, social historians of all political persuasions seemed to feel more at ease negating the possibility of sexual fulfillment. It would probably be closer to the mark to evaluate the terms of the Boston marriage as no different from those of any other Victorian marriage. In both same-sex and heterosexual relationships, middle- and upper-class women of the period frequently found difficulties dealing with their own sexual needs and responses. They had been trained to have difficulties, and many were proud of those difficulties. They considered their sexual inhibition one of the things that set "ladies" apart from women of the lower classes. Of course, in their own minds, it was decorum rather than inhibition.

There was no way of ascertaining whether the passion Bessy and Elsie shared was genital. None of their contemporaries ever reported any confessions by either of them. When they first set up housekeeping together, they were known as "the bachelorettes," not in any pejorative sense suggesting homosexuality, indeed, as the antithesis of that. It absolved them of the accusation of sexual intimacy. They were like two old bachelors sharing digs who might be a bit "old-maidish" but were never "pansies"—a "pansy" was something *other*—just as Bessy and Elsie were something other than tribadies. The former might smoke—but never cigars or a pipe—and the latter was a frilly little filly—no neckties for her!

They would live together through another generation for whom they would become a sapphic legend, thereby exchanging one set of tired banalities for another. It was reasoned by their juniors that the two old girls could not have lived in loving intimacy for so many years without "doing it." They *had* to be dykes—any other modus vivendi would have been too complex to contemplate.

What was their sexual truth? Of what importance was it to them at the time: of what significance is it to us now? Elisabeth and Elsie loved each other and, for more than thirty years, had a rare camaraderie in which they commingled on every level that was significant to them. The same could be said for only the rarest of unions in which sexual intercourse played the dominant role.

The twentieth century brought changing sexual and social attitudes. The working woman was no longer an oddity, and the successful professional female was looked upon with respect that almost, but not quite, equaled residual male resentment of her. Richard Freiherr von Krafft-Ebbing had already written *Psychopathia Sexualis* and Henry Havelock Ellis had begun to publish his seven-volume *Studies in the Psychology of Sex*. A profusion of previously unimaginable information about same- and opposite-sex possibilities began to appear in popular magazines. There was speculation about what couples of all sexes did. At the same time, the once-unassailable phalanx of formidable females who had ruled New York society began to be weakened by divorce.

Were it only that they shared a life, there would have been little to record about Bessy and Elsie beyond that unexceptional fact. What was extraordinary was that they had to invent a life before they could share it. Actually, several lives. Bessy Marbury was the first woman writers' agent. In addition to opening the profession to women, her revolutionary concept of her function gave writers greater control over their own work while infinitely increasing the amount of money they could expect to earn from it. Among those who benefited from her representation were George Bernard Shaw, Oscar Wilde, Victorien Sardou, Edmund Rostand, W. Somerset Maugham, Clyde Fitch, Edith Wharton, Alexandre Dumas *fils,* Theodore Dreiser, Rachel Crothers, and Eugene O'Neill.

Perhaps her most significant contribution to theatrical history was, as P. G. Wodehouse maintained, the invention of the modern American musical comedy. She produced the musicals that made Jerome Kern the best-known composer of his generation and discovered Cole Porter as well as producing his first musical.

Although never a suffragette, she came from a long line of involved Democrats and, once women won the vote, became one of the earliest female political power players in the Democratic party. Her early support of Franklin Delano Roosevelt promoted his career and made her one of his trusted advisers.

A majority of their contemporaries believed Bessy's greatest invention was Elsie. She recognized the latter could not merely be her "wife," that she had to make something of her life. Using her new theatrical power, and despite Elsie's lack of real talent, Bessy turned her dear partner into a well-known Broadway actress. When this did not lead to stardom, Elsie became restless. Bessy opened another door for her that led to Elsie's career as an interior decorator and the lasting fame that was as meaningful as her great success, for she was among the first to put a value on celebrity for its own sake.

Elsie played at being a suffragette once it became a fashionable cause among her socialite friends, but her one undeniable contribution to the liberation of women was giving them a profession in which they would become leaders. She may not have been the first interior decorator, but she was the first female in the profession and made it one in which women could follow her and still remain what society termed "ladies."

*E*lsie was not the only woman whose life was changed by an intimacy with Bessy Marbury. The latter may not have inspired sexual passion in the former, but there can be little doubt she did in Anne Morgan, whose life changed radically because of it. Anne was the youngest child of J. P. Morgan and more acceptable to some members of New York society than her often overbearing father. Many eligible men vied for the hand of this tall, handsome daughter of one of the world's richest and most powerful men but none appealed to her. Her boundless energy was displaced in athletics and acting as her father's hostess on his annual trips to Europe.

Bessy changed all that. She awakened a dormant social conscience that turned her into one of the country's most influential advocates for the rights of often-abused and always underpaid working women. She used the Morgan name, a symbol of the excesses of capitalism, to help its disenfranchised victims. While remaining true to her father's Republican party politics, she underwrote women who played powerful roles in the establishment of some of the most radically left-wing unions in the country.

During her life, Morgan was passionately involved with several women. The most intimate of these relationships was with Anne Harriman Vanderbilt. The latter came from a family that used its charm, good looks, and financial success to make a place for itself in New York society. A dutiful Victorian daughter who, through successive widowhoods, married better and better, she became increasingly wealthy and powerful but knew little happiness until late in her life. A woman of her position was expected to play the role of Lady Bountiful, but her philanthropies were of a higher order than those of the majority of women in her privileged world of Vanderbilts and Astors. She was responsible for the first program to combat drug addiction. The apartment development she built for indigent tuberculars was considered a model of inexpensive housing that would let the same light into the homes of the poor with which Elsie de Wolfe was flooding the mansions of the rich.

During World War I, the Annes, Morgan and Vanderbilt, were leaders of that army of courageous American women who served in France long before any American men were in the conflict. Theirs was not primarily a political statement but a humanitarian one. Often risking their own lives, they were there to nurse the wounded and to help the innocent civilians, many of whom lost what little they had during the battles. They remained to alleviate the pain and loneliness suffered by the American boys when their country entered the war. Although the U.S. government did nothing to recognize their service, the French bestowed their highest honors on them.

*I*n 1920, after the death of her husband, Anne Vanderbilt had no desire to live in his ostentatious Fifth Avenue mansion. Bessy was also looking for a new home, and Anne Morgan finally decided to move out of the Morgan mansion. All three opted for an unfashionable, somewhat disreputable neighborhood on the edge of the East River. Elsie was not only to decorate their houses but also to help them to select an architect, Mott B. Schmidt. The result was the only cluster of homes in New York built largely by and for women. Bearing no relationship to the overblown grandeur of the mansions of their husbands and fathers, Sutton Square can still lay claim to being the loveliest and most graceful square block in the entire city. It was the perfect illustration of what Elsie had written a decade earlier.

> I . . . wish to trace briefly the development of the modern house, the woman's house, to show you that all that is intimate and charming in the home as we know it has come through the unmeasured influence of women. Man conceived the great house with its parade rooms, its *grand appartements* but woman found eternal parade tiresome and planned for herself little retreats, rooms small enough for comfort and intimacy. In short, man made the house: woman went him one better and made . . . a home.

With the exception of Susan B. Anthony and Carrie Chapman Catt, these four women knew almost every American woman of significance during the hundred years that spanned their lives. Their story encompasses the lives of many of these women. Among the latter, only Alva Belmont could be considered one of the revolutionaries of the women's movement, but they were all participants in or witnesses to the most significant changes of their times in the attitudes of both sexes.

Neither rabble-rousers nor conformists, they were the pragmatists who helped to adapt revolutionary principles in ways that made them palatable to the public. In the course of achieving this formidable goal, they ventured into areas seldom explored by women and, in the process, redefined themselves. They were not unlike the current women leaders who had taken the doctrines of the firebrands of the Seventies liberationists and made them feasible in an increasingly complicated world.

They had dash, wit, intelligence, and industry. Without actually discovering anything new, they had the courage to transform much that was stagnant. There is a case to be made for ingenuity and a gift for orderly change also being tools of a revolution.

Ladies

AND NOT-SO-GENTLE

Women

Names

In the many books written since her death, Elisabeth Marbury has been given the sobriquet Bessie. However, in her letters to her family, she signed herself Bessy, and that is what she will be called in this book. The confusion may have started early on, when she was so occupied with getting people to spell her first name, Elisabeth rather than Elizabeth, that she did not want to further confuse the issue by correcting Bessie to Bessy. By the time she could, she was simply too famous to make the change.

Anne Vanderbilt likewise preferred Anne, although her first wedding announcement and many early legal documents called her Anna while one of her husbands addressed her as Ann. In accordance with her own wishes, she will be Anne in this book.

CHAPTER ONE ❧

Gasping for air and gulping down large hunks of land in one great inhalation, the greedy new metropolis was stretching north along the twin arteries of commercial Broadway and stately Fifth Avenue. By 1850, New York's middle-class strivers had moved uptown to the third of the great residential squares that had been inserted in Manhattan's rectangular grid of streets. Madison Square spread leafily east from their one point of intersection where, with Twenty-third Street, they formed a six-pointed "Etoile" that New Yorkers boasted compared with any Paris might have to offer. But the days of private and gracious habitation in that verdant oasis were numbered even as they began. Within ten years of the construction of the Square's first townhouse, in 1853, Franconi's Hippodrome appeared on the northwest corner of Twenty-third Street and Broadway facing the Square. It could seat ten thousand, under a canvas roof stretched over brick walls, and was built to house spectacles. This grandest edifice in all of New York City took two years to build and cost an unprecedented two million dollars. The enterprise was a failure, and a scant three years later the building was torn down to make way for a magnificent white marble palace of a hotel. The old Hippodrome had wanted a racy theatrical connotation, and its address was on Broadway. The new hotel on the same site, a so-called Renaissance palazzo striving after elegance and dignity, was significantly named the Fifth Avenue Hotel. From the Fifties onward, no more private homes were built on the Square.

In the same year the great hotel was opened, Elizabeth McCoun Marbury gave birth to her fifth child, on June 19, 1856. This second daughter was born at home, at 76 Irving Place, and named for her mother. She would later claim that her name always had been spelled as she spelled it as an adult, Elisabeth, and that it was a family name and spelling. There were many Elizabeths among the McCouns as well as several in the Marbury family, but there was not one recorded Elisabeth. It was the earliest of the many myths she invented about herself while living a life that was itself mythical enough to have won a place in Bulfinch.

Another myth had it that she came from "an old New York family" with all that the phrase implied. Her father, Francis F. Marbury, actually had emigrated from Maryland, while her maternal McCoun relations were an "old" Oyster Bay family only in the chronological sense of having long been established in the rural Long Island community. John McCoun (originally Mackholme), of Aberdeenshire, Scotland, was the first of his line to set foot in the American colonies. He had been a loyalist soldier in the army of the Stuart king until taken prisoner by Cromwell's forces, on September 3, 1651, at the Battle of Worcester. On November 11 of that year, John and David Mackholme were among 276 healthy young Scottish prisoners shipped to the Massachusetts Bay Colony and sold into indentured service for six to eight years. Far from being the adventurous younger son of a grand and distinguished lineage, as the legend of so many old New York families would have it, the first American McCoun was little better than a white slave.

Samuel and William, John's sons by the second of his three wives, migrated to Oyster Bay. Both prospered in the manner in which young men of no particular fortune did prosper in those days: they married the daughters of comparatively well-to-do landowners. The McCouns continued to rise socially and economically through marriages with members of prosperous New York families such as the Phelpses and the Townsends.

A talent for politics and an instinct for placing oneself on the side of the winners was Bessy Marbury's legacy from the McCouns. What she did not inherit was their ability to marry well. Grandfather McCoun improved her future standing with the Colonial Dames and Daughters of the American Revolution when he married Emma Jackson, a member of a distinguished Huguenot family whose mother had been on the reception committee for the first great independence ball, held in New York City, in honor of the Marquis de Lafayette.

When young William Townsend McCoun came to New York to study law, in 1804, it was still an affably small city "which clustered about the Battery and overlooked the Bay, and of which the uppermost boundary was indicated by the grassy way-sides of Canal Street." The aspiring attorney knew and thought little of old John Jacob Astor, a fur merchant who had to be watched carefully, for he was as likely to skin a customer as a beaver. In the summer he would buy fresh watermelons off Cornelius Vanderbilt's boat anchored in the harbor.

McCoun was soon recognized as a man with a great future at the bar. By

1812, he was doing well enough to marry and set up house in then fashionable Warren Street. He continued in private practice until 1831, when he was appointed vice chancellor of the First Circuit Court. He remained in that position until forced to retire in 1846, having reached sixty, which was the age prescribed by the court as the limit of judicial service. His wife had died the year before, and though lonely he was still too vigorous to settle for retirement.

By a special provision of the court of 1846, the vice chancellor was elected justice of the Supreme Court of the Second District. It was a position he held with distinction until 1853, when he officially retired to his estate in Oyster Bay, if retirement was the right word for it: at the age of sixty-seven, he took up the dual positions of overseer of highways and town commissioner, which he held almost until his death at the age of ninety-two, in 1878.

*I*n 1844, a brilliant young man of excellent Maryland family applied to Vice Chancellor McCoun for the position of law clerk in his chambers. It may have been the name, Marbury, that drew the vice chancellor's immediate approbation. William Marbury was a famous name in the history of American jurisprudence and the cousin once removed of Francis F. Marbury, the young applicant standing before him.

When Thomas Jefferson's secretary of state, James Madison, withheld William Marbury's appointment as justice of the peace for the District of Columbia, which had been made by President John Adams shortly before his term expired, he sued. The case, *Marbury* v. *Madison,* was brought before the Supreme Court in 1803. It was Chief Justice John Marshall's first great case. In it, he confirmed the Supreme Court's right of judicial review. That proposition was at the heart of the vice chancellor's legal philosophy, and it tickled him to have a Marbury in his office.

Francis F. Marbury was a remarkable young man. He had entered Amherst College at the age of thirteen. Upon graduating, he taught high school, in Hudson, New York, to boys not much younger than himself. He continued at that until he had saved enough from his earnings to move to New York and pursue his studies of the law. It was after passing the bar, in 1837, that he entered the employ of the vice chancellor.

A dapper fellow of slim, elegant proportions, he had a taste for all those good things that were well beyond his means. His affable southern charm masked a ruthless ambition. It was not long before he realized that both his ambition and his tastes could be satisfied by paying court to his employer's plain but handsomely dowered daughter. On his part, the vice chancellor was well aware that his Elizabeth could do far worse than a man with his young clerk's promise. The chap's suit was no crime in his court. The junior and senior attorneys met; the terms were agreed upon; the suit was adjudicated.

The Marbury family first appeared in English history at the time of the Magna Carta. The name derived from the hamlet of Miribirie, in Cheshire, which had been confirmed by King John to William de Miribirie. By the fifteenth century, the family included several generations of successful Marbury lawyers and clergymen as well the odd physician cropping up every now and again.

Francis's direct forebear, Thomas Marbury, passed the bar at Gray's Inn, London, in the beginning of the seventeenth century. He migrated to Virginia and married into the Isham family. Through the Ishams, Nevilles, Fitzhughs, and John of Gaunt, Bessy Marbury was in direct descent from King Edward III.

An Elizabethan Marbury, an earlier Francis, was rector of St. Pancras, in London, a friend of Sir Francis Bacon and himself a true Renaissance man. While in prison for accusing the bishop of London of choosing men for the priesthood too ignorant to give spiritual guidance, he wrote a spirited comedy, *The Contract of Marriage between Wit and Wisdom,* which was performed successfully in the lively Elizabethan theatre. A copy exists in the British Museum. This made him the first and only theatrical Marbury until Bessy came along almost three centuries later, unless one counts his grandnephew by marriage. (Francis's wife was Bridget Dryden, the great-aunt of the poet-laureate dramatist John Dryden.)

Francis had twelve children, the most famous of whom was Anne Marbury Hutchinson. Anne had a sister Elizabeth Marbury as well as a stepsister Elizabeth Marbury. Rector Francis educated Anne with the books from his own library. The New York Francis, almost three centuries later, would do the same with his daughter. Although Bessy went to school, she always claimed that her real education came from the books in her father's library and law office.

After her marriage, Anne Marbury Hutchinson had emigrated to the Massachusetts colony, where her espousal of a liberal church and freedom of worship brought her into direct conflict with Governor John Winthrop and John Cotton. She and her followers moved on to Rhode Island. After her husband's death she migrated again, believing she would have more freedom in the Dutch colony of Pelham on Long Island Sound. It was a lonely spot later known as Anne's Neck, near a river later named the Hutchinson River. The year was 1643 and the Algonkians, displaced by the white settlers from their Manhattan homeland, set upon the party, massacring Anne and her whole family. It was one of the tribe's rare acts of aggression. The irony was that Hutchinson was among the few émigrés who had refused to contribute arms, or the money to purchase them, if her compatriots intended to use them to exterminate native Americans.

Anne Marbury Hutchinson was one of the first American civil libertarians and the first woman to win a place in the history of the nation. Bessy must have been unaware of this extraordinary collateral ancestor, for she never mentioned the connection and was not one to have hidden anything that might have reflected so favorably upon her. The sad fact was that singular, independent women were often omitted in the oral family histories handed down from generation to generation.

*T*he marriage of Francis and Elizabeth McCoun Marbury was not unlike many of the period. If there was no grand passion, there was an amiability and congress of interests that outlasted passion. This mutuality was fundamental to the solid unions of the period.

Theirs was a time in which good manners were a very important constituent of education for both sexes, and that instilled politesse extended to the rest of their public and private lives. There were exceptions, but couples generally were not rude to each other. It was a defined society: marital roles were assigned, played, and respected even when the performance fell short of perfection. If there was boredom, it was not damned as the eighth deadly sin, and recrimination seldom was mistaken for communication.

*W*ithin a decade of entering the bar, Francis had fulfilled the promise his father-in-law had seen in him. He had provided two grandchildren with a third on the way and purchased a townhouse, at 76 Irving Place, close to fashionable Gramercy Park. The second half of the century was borning, and he was well positioned to be one of its inheritors. The United States was becoming a maritime power, and one of his specialities was maritime law. The country was on the brink of the era of the great investment bankers, and one of his clients was the New York Stock Exchange. As the freedom of the continent was being constricted in a web of railroad tracks, he represented one side or the other in the many large suits brought by one king of the rails against another in the never-ending battle for supremacy of turf. As the century aged, the former colony grew closer to the mother country as a major trading partner and ally: Francis Ferdinand was counselor to the New York consulate of Great Britain.

*E*lisabeth's earliest memories were associated with what she later deemed her most unattractive traits: "cowardice, gluttony, and mendacity." She pointedly described herself as a "chubby little person." It was only as she matured that her more attractive qualities emerged: compassion, loyalty, a gift for friendship. Once she made a friend, it was an eternal commitment. She had no time for enemies: that was a waste of people who might one day prove useful. The adult Bessy would constantly amaze, infuriate, and delight by proving a rare combination of Pollyanna and Reynard. Why not? Paradox was a survival mechanism for many women of her generation.

During the Civil War, a grateful client presented Francis Marbury with a stalk laden with green bananas. This fruit was little Bessy's "strongest passion." Her eyes widened as they followed the unripened stalk's progress downstairs to the kitchen and out to the pantry. That was on a Wednesday evening. The child grew feverish devising and discarding schemes for getting her hands on them, and by Sunday she could stand it no longer. They had to be hers!

As the rest of the family prepared to go to church, little Bessy began to cough, and sneeze, and wheeze, and hold her throbbing head. The poor child showed every symptom of coming down with some dreadful illness. The servants also went to services. There would be nobody in the house except the cook, who would be down in the kitchen preparing the dinner. Perhaps her mother should stay home to look after the invalid. No, no, the child protested, fearing she might have overdone it, she'd be fine by herself, all she needed was some rest.

It seemed forever before they were dispatched. Bessy got out of her bed in the nursery on the top floor and crawled down four flights of stairs to the basement kitchen. Getting by Cook did not pose a problem, for she was up to her elbows in poultry and flour, rapt in her artistry.

In the pantry at last, the pudgy little body sank to the floor and, forgetting all biblical injunction, caressed her forbidden fruit. As Sigmund Freud and she were born within a month of each other, she had no idea of the gesture's symbolism beyond a biblical admonishment. "I had Adam and Eve discounted, for I ate *six* green bananas at one fell swoop."

That afternoon, a worse illness overtook her than the one previously feigned. The pains in her stomach were real, as was the perspiring fever in her brow. Neither her frantic mother nor the family physician could find the source of the malady, and little Bessy refused to explain. If the doctor was trying to put the fear of God in her when he said her hours were numbered, he succeeded. The combination of theatrics and religion, which would later play so large a part in her life, took over.

> Then all the Sunday school threats of eternal damnation flashed before my eyes. Hell fire was sizzling. Red devils were dancing. Three-pronged forks were pricking. I was broken at the wheel. My spirit groaned, my flesh was conquered, my soul cried out. I confessed—not through remorse, but through fear. I had lied through fear. I was truthful through fear.

At that time there were more serious problems in the Marbury household than who ate the bananas. They colored Bessy's memories of the period. Although she was unable to recall exactly what had happened, it was something at once smaller and more subjective than the war that caused the traumatic response she ascribed to it. "Hatred replaced love. War drove out peace. . . . I began to realize that revenge and disaster went hand in hand."

Like her family and most of their friends, Mrs. Marbury was pro-Union. A letter was circulated in 1860 addressed to "the women of New York and especially to those already engaged against the time of wound and sickness of the Army," inviting them to a meeting at Cooper Union, where they would "appoint a General Committee with power to organize the benevolent purposes of all into a common movement."

It was signed by some of the most influential women in New York society, including Mrs. Hamilton Fish, Mrs. William B. (*the* Mrs.) Astor, Mrs. James J. Roosevelt, several of Edith Wharton's Jones aunts, Mrs. Abram Hewitt, Mrs. Lewis Morris Rutherfurd, Mrs. William Cullen Bryant, Mrs. Cyrus W. Field, as well as an assortment of Stuyvesants, Potters, Bayards, and Auchinclosses. The fact that Bessy's mother was among the signatories was one of the few recorded indications that, as she later claimed, the Marburys were associated with the old New York families.

The Women's Central Association of Relief was formed at that meeting, and despite having to care for five children, Mrs. Marbury committed herself to large-scale volunteerism on behalf of the Union cause. It was the overt source of the schism between the Marbury parents that so colored Bessy's memories of the period. Often called the war between brothers, this was a war between husband and wife in which the national conflict displaced their personal differences as the root of their problems. Francis was a southerner, descendant of generations of southerners. His allegiance was naturally to his family and background. He was also a Democrat, and many Democrats considered the war between the states a Republican altercation.

His fellow member of the distinguished men's club the Century Association and his Gramercy Park neighbor, the diarist George Templeton Strong, castigated Marbury as one of the treacherous "Copperheads" who should be drummed out of the club. The term was first used by James Gordon Bennett in his New York *Herald,* on July 20, 1861, to liken the anti-war group to copperhead snakes, which struck without warning. "A rattlesnake rattles, a viper hisses, an adder spits, a black snake whistles, a water snake blows, but a copperhead just sneaks."

Like many Democrats, Marbury turned it into a symbol of defiance by wearing "copperhead badges" made of one-cent copper pieces cut away so that only the head remained with the word *liberty* written across the brow. With an irony Marbury would have appreciated, for he was no traitor despite his familial allegiances, the current one-cent copper is adorned with the head of Abraham Lincoln.

*A*fter the Draft Act was passed in 1863, it became apparent that it was not only well-to-do men like Marbury, with biases based on political and regional loyalties, who were against the war. The terms of the new act made it possible for any man with three hundred dollars to buy a less fortunate youth to take his place in the army. Young John Pierpont Morgan purchased a poor northern laborer to fight and die for him. It proved a wise investment. Morgan's war profiteering made him much richer by its end than he had been at its start.

Karl Marx had published what could come to be known as his *Communist Manifesto* fifteen years earlier, but it already had spread its message to radicals around the world. In *the* Mr. Astor's New York slums, not two miles distant from *the* Mrs. Astor's ballroom, which could only hold four hundred, the scene was very different.

> [They were] packed 290,000 to the square mile in a density more choking than Bombay or Canton, and they listened to flaming tribunes ... who cried that if they must fight, let them fight against their oppressors, the capitalists.

Riots broke out in the streets of New York City. The mobs set fire to draft offices, gutted newspaper pressrooms, burned the tenements to which they had been condemned, and lynched blacks because, as far as the rioters were concerned, they were the cause of the war. Urged on by rabble-rousers, the city's needy poor armed themselves with stolen weapons and paving stones ripped up from the streets. It took three days for the police and volunteer militia to bring them under control. By then, it was estimated that one thousand people had been killed on both sides.

The Marbury family altercation seemed to have inflamed a world beyond its doors, and when Lincoln was assassinated, Bessy was so overwrought she remembered every detail of the day for as long as she lived. For four years her mother had been terrifying her with stories of southern atrocities. Now all she could think was, with the president dead, "the awful rebels . . . would surely pour into New York and kill us, each and every one."

She had to escape from her warring parents and hid in a seldom-used cedar closet. Sitting on a steamer trunk, she shivered with fear and waited. She could hear them calling for her but remained silent. Later, she heard her mother's sobs and the anxiety in her father's voice. It could be a trick. They were not to be trusted, and she remained silent. At length things grew hazy. It was almost as if the earth was slipping away beneath her. She had to get out, but the latch had slipped and the door was locked from the outside. Try as she might, she could not open it. With her last bit of strength, she cried out and pounded on it. The door was flung open, and the child fainted across the hall floor.

*T*he Marburys apparently did not subscribe to governesses. When Bessy was old enough, like her brothers and sister before her, she was sent to a day school. Many acceptable establishments were within easy walking distance of her home. As kindergarten toddler, she likely attended a coeducational school for very young children that was at Irving Place and Sixteenth Street. Bessy went on to spend several years at a "fashionable" girls' school not unlike Miss Graham's Academy for Young Ladies, at Fifth Avenue and Thirteenth Street. No book bags heavy with scholarly tomes for Miss Graham's students; posture took precedence over intellectual curiosity.

Bessy had little regard for what was considered a suitable education for a young lady. She considered her real education to have begun when her father started to teach her from the first Latin grammar. That was when she was seven. By the time she entered adolescence, she was able to read and discuss the works of Horace, Tasso, the Greek and Roman dramatists, Shakespeare, Dr. Samuel Johnson, Plutarch, and "a score of other classics." What would eventually prove most valuable was going down to his office and rummaging through his law library. Miss Marbury learned all of the fine points of drawing up a contract long before she ever thought she would need to compose one. She also acquired a knowledge of what was within the law, if only by the subtlest shaving of the facts.

The only lifelong friend Bessy made at that time was Sarah (Sally) Hewitt, the daughter of her father's friend, the latter mayor of New York City, Abram Hewitt, and granddaughter of the industrialist-educator Peter Cooper. It was not merely the closeness of their families that made Sally and Bessy best of friends. They were alike in many ways: both too boisterous in a demure age, too smart in a period of feminine fear of being thought clever, given to obesity when delicacy was the valued girlish charm, not interested in boys, indeed, sexually ambivalent. There was every reason for other girls to withhold their intimacy. As adolescents they had enough to cope with without these two. Puberty and menstrual cycles were mysteries inadequately explained by mothers who themselves inadequately perceived them.

Gramercy Park was a wonderful neighborhood in which to grow up. The park was actually a private square for the exclusive use of the inhabitants of the neighborhood. Unlike insecure, ostentatious nouveau riche Fifth Avenue or snobbish old-family Washington and Stuyvesant squares, it was a relatively new development that was both a quiet backwater of the city and a lively place inhabited by young professionals with a sprinkling of successful artists to give it a jaunty, slightly Bohemian air.

Despite her weight, Bessy was a natural athlete, and Gramercy Park was a paradise for any child who loved sports, until Samuel J. Tilden and Cyrus Field formed a committee that forbade any games in the park that endangered its "ornamental character." It marked the end of glorious afternoons of lawn tennis, croquet, and baseball—the latter, of course, the girls of that day were permitted to enjoy only as spectators.

Any spectacle, religious or secular, that appealed to all of her senses at the same time not only captured and held Bessy but also tempted her to become a part of it. It started at Mr. Barnum's circus, which would set up its canvas country tent each spring opposite the Academy of Music, at the foot of Irving Place and East Fourteenth Street. The color, the spectacle, the lights, the costumes, the music, even the pungent odors—it was everything that was both holy and worldly to her.

The Marburys believed the theatre was a part of education, and weekly attendance on Friday evenings began when Bessy was very young. For the child the theatre was a case of love at first sight. That love would change her life and remain a potent force in it until the day she died.

The first dramatic performance she could recall attending was at the ubiquitous Mr. Barnum's Museum at Broadway and Ann Street. It burned down in 1865, which would make her nine years old or younger. Barnum, who once boasted that there was a sucker born every minute, liked to pass

*L*adies and Not-So-Gentle Women

his establishment off as an educational institution. After buying their tickets, the audience was detained for some time in the museum before being permitted to enter the lecture hall, which actually was a theatre of three thousand seats. It specialized in vaudeville and evenings of minstrelsy alternating with runs of lurid melodramas, the most popular having been *The Drunkard*, which ran for one hundred performances, setting a long-run record for the period.

In his memoir *A Small Boy and Others,* Henry James also fondly recalled the Barnum's Museum of that era:

> —the weary waiting in the dusty halls of humbug, amid bottled mermaids, "bearded ladies" and chill dioramas, for the lecture room, the true centre of the seat of joy, to open: vivid in especial to me is my almost sick wondering if I mightn't be rapt away before it did open. [And when it did] . . . the stuffed and dim little hall of audience smelling of peppermint and orange peel, where the curtain rose on our gasping but rewarded patience.

Bessy was far more attracted to the men in her family than to the women. She admired her mother and tolerated her sister, but she adored her father and brothers and loved her grandfather most of all. The vice chancellor doted on his stocky, earnest child, some seventy years his junior, with fair hair pulled tightly back in a pigtail and large, deep-set blue eyes that seemed to look clear inside him to be sure he was telling the absolute truth when answering her endless questions.

With her small hand grasped by his large, ancient paw, they were boon companions exploring the city. It was the old gentleman's leave-taking, a farewell to the scenes and friends of his youth, and the little girl's introduction to places she would not ordinarily have visited, a hearing of tales of times and deeds that made the town and her grandfather both seem venerable. Even the place where he lived was filled with the excitement of history for the little girl. The vice chancellor had brought her grandmother as a bride to that very same narrow Federal house in Warren Street. That was when George Washington was still president. One of their neighbors was another descendant of the Huguenot émigrés, Major General Ebenezer Stevens, a hero of the Revolutionary War. Years later, Bessy would be the sometime friend and literary representative of the general's great-great-granddaughter Edith Wharton.

The pair had an annual ritual that lasted until the commercial part of the city totally overwhelmed McCoun's house on Warren Street, and he sold it in disgust to retire permanently to his Long Island farm. On the first bright day of early spring, he came by for her in his carriage to take a drive out into the country. They went north on the Post Road and turned east to the river along the country lane the city planners had designated as Fifty-seventh Street. Their destination was the greenhouses belonging to her grandfather's old friend Thomas Hogg. These were on the embankment a short distance to the north and could be seen from the distance as the visitors approached them. It was a thrilling sight to the little girl, those glittering glass domes reflecting the sunlight ricocheting off the clear sparkling water of the East River.

They had come so that McCoun might make his annual selection of new plants for the family homestead in Oyster Bay. In these transactions the old man became a wily country lad again and would not be hurried. Hogg knew this could take the better part of an afternoon and was thoughtful enough to have a diversion planned for the child. The fish ran fast and plentiful and could easily be caught from the rocky escarpment. Hogg always had a little rod and some worms ready for her. More than sixty years later, the memory was still fresh. "I can recall the joy I felt sitting over the water, my little fat legs dangling while I, feverish with excitement, would catch the small fish with which the river abounded."

Bessy's favorite time of the year was the summer holiday in Oyster Bay. The railroads were in their infancy, and trips to the rural neighborhoods of Long Island were taken by boat. They embarked at the Fourteenth Street pier on the East River and sailed north between Blackwell's Island and Mr. Hogg's glittering greenhouses, through the treacherous Hellgate, past Mr. Astor's and Mr. Gracie's Yorkville summer houses, and into the Long Island Sound.

At Glen Cove, the boat landing for Oyster Bay, old McCoun would be waiting with a team of stout farm horses harnessed to a wagon usually used for hauling farm goods. Wisps of hay and the odors of ripening vegetables and manure clung to the vehicle, conspiring to tell them they were in the heart of the country.

Her grandfather was a serious gentleman farmer on land that had been in the McCoun family for two centuries. Bessy recalled: "His livestock was my delight, and I remember how I trudged joyfully with him over every acre of his property, growing daily more and more familiar with the complexities of crops and fruit trees."

Francis Marbury was a successful attorney who earned very handsome fees, but he was also a compulsive speculator in real estate and the stock market. The devaluation of the dollar and his refusal to profit from the misery of his native South left him in a financially delicate position. Elizabeth McCoun Marbury was unable to prevent her husband's irresponsible speculation, but she permitted no public display of their circumstances. The world in which they moved continued to see them as the upper middle-class family they always had been. She was a formidable household accountant. The ability to keep both books and appearances was as valuable a legacy as the intellectual curiosity Bessy inherited from her father.

CHAPTER TWO

Starting with the first interview she ever gave, Elsie de Wolfe was a myth-maker carefully shaping Elsie de Wolfe into the legend she became, bringing her to the point of perfection at which all traces of the original woman ceased to exist. And why not? It was a national mania. Americans of her generation were constantly inventing and reinventing themselves, as they laid claim to titles and lineage that were not their own, to airs and fancies that were not their own, indeed, to lands that were not their own. They wantonly replaced homespun simplicity with manifest destiny, which was the ultimate myth. For all the years she spent in Europe, this was why Elsie remained quintessentially American. It was both her greatest charm and, as she knew better than anybody else, the secret of her success.

Her own most original creation, in shaping herself Elsie had what every artist longs for: the freedom to remodel, refine, redefine. The verifiable facts about her birth were her parentage and that she was born in New York City, on December 20; the year proved elusive, subject to her iron whim. In the early stages of Elsie's relationship with Bessy Marbury, both agreed that it was 1865, but when she was filling out the questionnaire for her inclusion in the 1924 edition of *Who's Who*, she claimed to have been born in 1870. She stuck to that when she married Sir Charles Mendl in 1926. Sir Charles gave 1872 as the date of his birth (which it was and remained in all official documents throughout his life). His unblushing bride claimed to be a mere two years his senior. She frankly admitted to all of her nearest and dearest that she'd modestly shaved a decade off her age, because she did not want to embarrass the darling old duffer. Saddling him with a wife a dozen years his senior might smell of fortune hunting on his side and title hunting on hers:

Alfred Allan Lewis

both odors were pungent enough to smack of the truth. This confession, quoted as gospel by her best friends, gave still another natal year, 1860, which actually came close to the truth. Eighteen seventy can easily be discounted as vanity: she wanted to be in her mid-fifties rather than closer to seventy. If that was her wish, there was no reason that she should not gratify it. Her first face-lift had taken twenty years off her age, at least in her photographs, which would be seen by many more people than actually saw her face and would continue to be seen for years after her death, thus becoming historic truth.

By June 1936, she had reversed herself and decided it was chic to be old. She told a *Time* magazine interviewer that she was eighty, placing her birth in December 1855, and making her older than Bessy Marbury. Eighteen fifty-five could also be chalked up to Vanity claiming to be eighty while looking sixty. When her attorney, Sol Rosenblatt, offered her will for probate on August 11, 1950, one month after her death, the documentation attendant upon it flatly stated that she was born in 1858, when the family was living at 159 West Twenty-second Street (first listing in the 1860 *Directory*). Elsie described the street as "fashionable," which was another myth. New York addresses were fashionable according to how far east or west of Fifth Avenue they were; the De Wolfes always lived a bit too far west for fashion. The address and a subsequent one on the same street, 227 West Twenty-second, were in a comfortable but undeniably middle-class neighborhood known as Chelsea.

The neighborhood had grown up around a seminary and was almost an independent small village of unpretentious cottages and row houses until that decade before the Civil War, when the developers had encased it in the brownstone uniformity that joined it to the rest of the city. Some of the aura of what once had been clung to parts of the area, as can be witnessed by Edith Wharton's description of it in *The Age of Innocence:*

> . . . Newland Archer rang the bell of the peeling stucco house with a giant wisteria throttling its feeble cast-iron balcony, which she had hired, far down West Twenty-third Street. . . . It was certainly a strange quarter to have settled in. Small dress-makers, bird-stuffers and "people who wrote" were her nearest neighbours; and further down the dishevelled street Archer recognised a delapidated wooden house, at the end of a paved path. . . .

That first 1860 listing had to have been placed in 1859, and the De Wolfes could well have been in residence there on the day of Elsie's birth, December 20, at the very end of the previous year. Before that momentous leap to

Chelsea, the De Wolfes had moved, as newlyweds, to déclassé Beach Street, where Elsie's older brother, Leslie, was born; and then, with the need for larger quarters, up to modest Greene Street, in Soho. The imminent arrival of Elsie must have been one of the motivations for the move to Chelsea, where a family could find a brownstone not unlike the ones found in the more prestigious blocks nearer to Fifth Avenue.

This restless movement was a way of life for many young families in Jamesian mid-nineteenth-century Manhattan. To this day nothing has changed very much. When Arthur Townsend spoke of taking a house, in *Washington Square,* his attitude could still be applied to life in the city or, for that matter, in the nation.

> "It doesn't matter . . . it's only for three or four years. At the end of three or four years we'll move. That's the way to live in New York—to move every three or four years. Then you always get the last thing. It's because the city's growing so quick—you've got to keep up with it. It's going straight up town—that's where New York's going. If I wasn't afraid Marian would be lonely, I'd go up there—right to the top—and wait for it. Only have to wait ten years—they'll all come up after you. But Marian says she wants some neighbors—she doesn't want to be a pioneer. . . . I guess we'll move up little by little; when we get tired of one street we'll go higher. So you see we'll always have a new house; it's a great advantage to have a new house; you get all the latest improvements. They invent everything all over again about every five years, and it's a great thing to keep up with the new things. I always try and keep up with the new things of every kind. Don't you think that's a good motto for a young couple—to keep 'going higher'? What's the name of that piece of poetry—what do they call it?—*Excelsior!*"

This very American attitude would eventually make Elsie de Wolfe first inevitable, and then rich. This was what all well-brought-up American women of her vintage wanted: inevitability and riches. It was Elisabeth Marbury who demonstrated for her that inevitability need have nothing to do with men, and riches still would ensue. It seemed as if Bessy knew that from the beginning.

One of Elsie's favorite anecdotes recounted growing up on the spot that would one day be part of R. H. Macy's department store. Rowland Macy had established his original dry-goods store on Sixth Avenue and Fourteenth Street in 1858, the likely year of Elsie's birth. The secret of the merchant's instantaneous success was a fixed price on every item and underselling the competition. Admittedly, these two policies would always be anathema to Elsie, but she would heartily have endorsed his strictly-for-cash, no-credit system.

Macy's moved up Sixth Avenue to Thirty-fourth Street in 1902. Within a relatively few years, because of Elsie de Wolfe's small revolution in the American way of life, the store had both an interior decorating service and a "corner shop" specializing in decorative antiques of occasionally dubious authenticity. It went to the heart of Elsie's rule on antiquities: decorativeness above either quality or provenance.

Putting her childhood in the middle of the store made such good telling, Elsie would have placed veracity last among her considerations. During that brief first period when the family lived on West Thirty-fourth Street, it was at 234 West Thirty-fourth, which was on the south side of the street (Macy's was on the north) and a full unfashionable block farther west.

The De Wolfe family did not return to West Thirty-fourth Street for another twenty years, and by any reckoning of birth year, Elsie was hardly still a little girl. It was in 1885 that they moved to a house at 139 West Thirty-fourth Street, on part of the site that would become the department store. That year she had come home from her first wonderful trip abroad, and to what had she returned? A narrow, ugly brownstone overstuffed with furniture and overcrowded with her autocratic father, long-suffering mother, and dreary, boring siblings. The entire period of that return to Thirty-fourth Street must have been one of the most traumatic of her life. She never discussed it with anybody except, perhaps, Bessy, who by then had entered her life and showed promise of becoming her salvation.

The obliteration from memory was never complete. No matter how far she traveled in her life, she would never completely be able to free herself of the memories of what had happened to her in that street. It was as if the scars left by her painful past were part of a never-to-be-completed monstrous work of art that constantly had to be reshaped into a more palatable form. She might mold it into an anecdotal myth involving her and it and Macy's, but that did not bring oblivion. She had to keep mentioning it in other contexts as if that could vanquish the defeat, the humiliation of returning to the father from whom she was never to be released except by his death.

When she finally got around to writing the airy soufflé of half-truths she called an autobiography, it was almost a half-century later, but the house on West Thirty-fourth Street appeared in the very first paragraph. It was cast in a traumatic context—but a child's trauma, one in which the little girl's sensibilities were wounded not emotionally but aesthetically. In the book it was not what they did to her that was so unnerving: it was what they did to a room. Her father remained a villain; her mother did not escape complicity for never having rearranged their lives with any greater success than she did their rooms. She spoke of herself in the third person, further removing Elsie from involvement.

> She was not pretty. She was ugly. Mother had said so often. Once Father had said to Mother, "I wonder, Georgiana, how you and I ever came to have such an ugly child." Just what ugly was she did not know. From the way it came out of the mouths of grown-ups she was sure it meant something very unhappy.
> Now she was to know.

In the book her mother had redecorated the drawing room. The child's reaction in the account was undoubtedly a disguised and heightened version of what the adult Elsie must have felt upon returning to live again under her father's roof and domination after her spurt of freedom in beautiful London, the center of the world in those days. She never before had been in the house in which she greeted her family after the years of separation. Her situation was suddenly as hopeless as the room in which she found herself. "Something terrible that cut like a knife came up inside her." At length, she caught her breath and cried out repeatedly, "It's so ugly! It's so ugly!"

She admitted that she recalled little of her early life, but that there was much pain in what she did remember. She added cryptically that in "going back" for the book, the pain had "lost its poignancy in appreciation." Without it, she claimed, her ambition might never have been awakened; she might never have so boldly sought change from the preordained order of her life as a conventionally brought-up Victorian young lady.

If at all noticed in New York society, the De Wolfes would have been looked down upon as provincials coming from, of all places, Nova Scotia, even if their hometown in that province, Wolfville, had been named for the family. It remained an area of Canada known by the Fifth Avenue parvenu only for the salmons smoked in accordance with methods brought over by its Scottish settlers. Longing for kinship to something a bit more distinguished than smoked fish, Elsie claimed that the name De Loup, which had belonged to the family in the distant European past, was that of its original settlers on this side of the Atlantic, "French Huguenots who came over to Acadia (Nova Scotia) in the same exodus as the people in Longfellow's *Evangeline*." It was another of her charming myths. Had she known the truth, it would have been one of those rare instances in which she would not have deviated from it, for it outclassed her invention. The American branch of the family descended from Frederick de Wolf, a baron of the Holy Roman Empire who in 1535 resided near Ghent on lands conferred upon him by the Holy Roman Emperor Charles V.

Elsie designed her own coat of arms. It was not necessary, for the family had an authentic and grander one of its own. Three wolf heads rested on a shield on the breast of the imperial double-headed eagle beneath the coronet of a baron of the empire, out of which a demi-wolf sprang, clutching a fleur-de-lis. Emblazoned upon the shield was the family motto: *Vincit qui patitur* (He conquers who waits or endures). The motto could have been written for Elsie, although she preferred the more flamboyant "Never complain, never explain," an adage purloined from her good friend Noel Coward.

The founder of the American line was Balthazar, the younger son of Baron Ariste de Wolff. He first appeared in the American records as De Wolf, in Hartford, Connecticut, in 1656. Elsie's great-grandfather Nathan de Wolf graduated from Yale and was a lawyer, justice of the peace, and registrar of probate before emigrating to Nova Scotia in 1761. His cousin Simeon, having already moved there and prospered, urged him to do the same. Nathan was forty-one at the time, and it was then or never if he was to make his fortune. The right honorable gentleman left the law in his native land and did very well as a Nova Scotia shopkeeper, so well that his son, Elsie's grandfather Stephen Brown de Wolf, was able to build a mansion on the main street of Wolfville, add a grandiloquent *e* to the end of his name, and marry a Miss Ruggles, who came of a good Tory family that had fled to Canada from New York during the American Revolution. Elsie inherited characteristics from this welter of De Loups, De Wolffs, and De Wolfs that were to provide the solid underpinnings for her own success. The legacy amounted to an amalgam of courage, an instinct for the main chance, and the successful shopkeeper's calculated affability: it would enable her to "get on" by ingratiating herself with those in power.

Elsie's tall and darkly handsome father, Dr. Stephen de Wolfe, received his medical degree from the University of Pennsylvania in 1845. Nova Scotia held little for this self-indulgent and cruel young man, who had what his daughter was to describe as a "baffling charm which permits those who possess it to have their way with a minimum of resistance." The place for him was New York City, where there were limitless opportunities: amusements to suit the most fastidious or possibly bizarre tastes, exciting games of chance, and heiresses who would surely fancy a good-looking, fairly well-born young professional man. This last was no negligible consideration, for he was the youngest son in a family of ten children and not likely to have much in the way of an inheritance. The cost of his education was apt to have been the limit of his expectations.

Somehow he failed in that all-important quest. It was surprising, for this was the age before the frenzy for titles, and he had all of the attributes considered important by well-to-do parents in search of husbands for their daughters. There must have been many who looked him over, but there were no takers. The fathers may have been crude and uneducated by Stephen's standards, but they were shrewd self-made men who had succeeded on an intuitive grasp of the strengths and weaknesses of others: they could see clear through suave, rather arrogant men like the young Canuck physician.

He was forced to return to Nova Scotia to find a bride. His family was well connected and dispersed through the province. It was likely one of his relatives had heard of the young woman, residing in the provincial capital of Halifax, who was in need of a husband and sufficiently dowered to be of interest to the prospective groom. Georgiana Watt Copeland and Stephen de Wolfe had one immediate thing in common. They both came of families that had earned *e*'s in emigration. The Coplands became Copelands in transit from Scotland to America. They were a prosperous family of the professional class with connections that reached into high places. Georgiana's paternal grandfather had been a professor of philosophy in Aberdeen. Her father, Alexander, was an attorney who had come to Canada to seek his fortune and found it, and her mother, nee Anna Anderson, was the sister of a baronet.

Except for her substantial *dot*, Georgiana stood high among the women least likely to be selected as a wife for Stephen de Wolfe. She was more austere than comely and had a personality totally devoid of humor or fancy while being overendowed with those traits traditionally considered part of the Scottish character. "Thrifty and with her feet well set on the ground, she saw life only in solid dimensions." She had an "uncanny intuitiveness," which was manifested in a penchant for prophesying gloom and doom. Her life with Stephen de Wolfe too often proved her a gifted clairvoyant. Elsie later described her father as "the rod of her [Georgiana's] chastening." He was as "extravagant and impractical" as she was "thrifty and practical . . . as gay as she was austere. A constant gambler, he liked to live as dangerously as she did securely."

Stephen returned to New York with his bride. Throughout their married life they were to move, and move, and move still again with the fluctuations of his fortunes. He made a good living as a skilled physician, a specialist in treating pulmonary conditions and the then prevalent and often fatal tuberculosis. If the family had been allowed to live on the income derived from his professional skills, there would never have been any financial problems, but like Francis Marbury, he was a speculator in the market. He was also a gambler, a man who preferred the high wire to the more mundane transportation available when his feet were on the ground. The household money drained through his fingers. Time and again, he appeared in the doorway—shoulders sagging, eyes glazed, nervous fingers fleeing through his hair—making the announcement Elsie could recall verbatim seventy years later: "We can't keep this up any longer. The servants must be paid off. And we must move to a smaller house. I'm a ruined man."

Fortunately, the situation was often soon reversed. A horse would come in—a flyer in copper might unexpectedly pay off in a big way. There were presents for everybody, and more extravagances, and more evasions of creditors. Alas, just as often they would have to move, and never any closer to the fabled Fifth Avenue of Elsie's daydreams. Ugly house was succeeded by uglier house, for Georgiana had no taste, only a sense of what was fashionable at the time. Victoria reigned in all of her many homes during the last half of the nineteenth century.

*H*is daughter's lack of distinction was perplexing to Stephen de Wolfe. There was never a moment this peacock did not make her aware of her homeliness. It was not only that he was not gentle; he was far worse, never attempting to hide a pity so untainted by love or compassion that it constantly reminded her of how distasteful she was to him.

By the time she was ten years old, she had developed into a competitive tomboy; anything the boys could do, she could do as well if not better. One afternoon a few of them climbed up onto the stone foundation of the iron grille fence in front of the De Wolfe house. Elsie thought it would be great fun to follow. As she ran along behind them, she lost her footing and fell to the slate pavement, breaking off half of one of her front teeth. She carefully picked up the piece and took it into her house to her father. He was a doctor; surely he could mend it. Stephen looked at his daughter and shook his head sadly. "You poor child. You certainly have finished yourself. Your teeth were your only decent feature."

With that, he put on his hat and left the house.

It seemed as if her mother also felt there was no way to make this child look attractive, and rather than vainly attempt to, she sensibly turned her into an object of economy in that improvident household. Her sensible little shoes were protected by large, awkward, heavy gaiters. The adult Elsie would later assemble a collection of the most gorgeous and fragile antique shoes.

The girl's dresses were made of inexpensive, coarse linsey-woolsey fabrics. To spare the awful frocks any unnecessary wear, Georgiana attached ungainly high white-linen cuffs that could be laundered separately.

Between the cuffs and a physician for a father, it was no wonder she was called "Butcher Sleeves" by the elegantly attired girls at Mrs. Macauley's School for Young Ladies, which she attended until she was fourteen. The establishment was on East Fortieth Street and Madison Avenue and considered one of the better girls' schools of the day. Girls could be cruel to a schoolmate as badly dressed as she was plain. But Elsie was a fighter. If she could not be beautiful, she was going to be charming. It was a resolution that strengthened her with a different kind of vanity, one that enabled her to rise above many of the petty humiliations inflicted upon her.

Her imagination provided a sanctuary. In that private place within her, she was no longer ugly but one of those beauties driving along Fifth Avenue in their smart equipage. When her mother was out, she would ransack her wardrobe for the plumed hats and beaded dolmans that in her fancy would turn her into a great lady like *the* Mrs. Astor, who though ugly was the most powerful, imperious, haughty woman in New York.

The latter half of 1869 brought one of those "black" days that were to rock the American stock market periodically over the years to come and almost always during the aptly named fall season. It was Jay Gould's speculation in the gold market that caused the panic of Black Friday, on September 24 of that year. Of course, Gould sold short and made a killing; the small-time investors lacked inside information and did not stand a chance.

The country was only beginning to recover when the worldwide depression of 1873 brought about a recession that lasted for the rest of the decade. De Wolfe was evidently affected adversely. The De Wolfes moved into the narrow brownstone that he hitherto had used exclusively as his office, examination rooms, and surgery. He never had intended to live in such cramped quarters with his rather large family of wife and five children, including an adolescent boy and girl, not to mention the servants that a man in his position could not do without. The house, at 138 West Thirty-seventh Street, was in the heart of the disreputable "tenderloin" district across the Sixth Avenue frontier of middle-class residential acceptability. Things eventually improved, and they were again able to make a home away from his office, but he was never to move his family across that invisible border.

It was in the house on West Thirty-seventh Street that Elsie became aware of some beauty in her surroundings, and it was her father who was responsible for it. Had her mother had her way, there would have been far less elegance in those crowded quarters. Because her father's office was at home, Stephen had prevailed and was able to indulge his artistic sensibilities in matters of texture and color. The woodwork was a light oak always beautifully waxed by hand rather than being stained one of the dark, somber tones then in fashion. He also ordered red velvet carpeting in place of the vapid florid Brussels carpet that was then the rage. Elsie became aware of the quiet elegance with which he had decorated his office. The furniture matched the paneled woodwork. On his desk there was a silver bowl of shiny red apples and a crystal vase of fresh red roses that, along with the apples, were in perfect harmony with the red plush floors. Elsie always believed she inherited her love of beauty and sense of color from her father. What she discovered in her father's office was the importance of harmony in color and textures. It would later become the signature and foundation of her decorative style.

Completing the lovely picture of her father's chambers was a huge white Persian cat who reclined sensually on the table before him and reached over to paw his arm, demanding and receiving affectionate stroking. It was something she also longed for but did not dare to demand, or request, or even beg for. For the rest of her life she loved all animals except cats: she never could stand cats.

The beautiful crystal vase on her father's desk was the "barometer of the family fortunes. When it was foul weather it held one rose. When it was fair there were dozens of roses which he always insisted upon arranging himself." At the end of June 1872, there was a single rose, although roses were blooming in profusion all over the city. Elsie was permanently taken out of school. She did not look upon it as a tragedy, for she had never enjoyed any of her subjects except history and English, nor had she liked any of her better-dressed, better-off schoolmates. Always best able to learn visually, she was soon to behold a place and style that would prove so exhilarating, memories of it would remain with her forever, marking one of the turning points in her life.

As in all of her most telling personal recollections, her vulnerability was displaced to a reaction to decor: that was the only area in which she could openly display her sensitivity to joy or sorrow. Elsie would never be able to deal with emotions except in terms of surfaces and the appearance of things. It was elation this time. Of the whole family, her father had selected her as his companion on a voyage home to Nova Scotia. This was a singular event in several ways. In all of her fourteen years, the family never had gone back to Wolfville, not even for her paternal grandmother's funeral two years earlier; her father always had felt alienated from his mother. It was likely Stephen was making the trip at this point in search of a loan from his family.

He probably had opted to take Elsie along because he found her the most pathetic of his offspring, thus the most likely to elicit sympathy.

There were many De Wolfe and Copeland relatives spread between Wolfville, which was in the valley of the Grand Pré, and Halifax, and Elsie was ostensibly paraded before all of them. Of the lot, it was her aunt, Augusta, whom she most adored. Augusta de Wolfe was Stephen's older sister and had brought him up. The fact that he had felt abandoned by his mother and was the youngest son of a father old enough to be his grandfather did much to explain his coldness, his inability to express love, his lack of compassion.

Elsie must have been aware that he expected her to appear a pitiful thing in need of charity, for when Augusta gave no indication that the girl's appearance was painful, she was able to forgo suspicions and open up to her aunt and to this new land. Again, the happiness she found in being with this maternal woman was expressed in terms of decor.

> In the Valley of the Grand Pre . . . I came to my first real knowledge of what constituted beauty. I was fascinated with the old French house and its period furniture. It had a feeling of space and symmetry entirely new to me. There was a peculiar rhythm in the wide green spaces of the fields and meadows rolling up to dark trees against a pale sky.

Many years later, that rhythm of dark green against the white northern skies would be echoed in her famous forest-green rooms.

The social climber in Elsie received a "tremendous thrill" upon learning that Queen Victoria's father, the Duke of Kent, had been housed in her old family home during a state visit to the valley in the early part of the nineteenth century. After all, she later explained, adding the coup de grâce of snobbism, dukes were then "something more than they are today."

She wept when she had to say good-bye to Augusta. It was the only time in her life she would ever admit to being moved by the loss of a loved one. Her aunt had been the first person to accept her for what she was. If Dr. de Wolfe received any financial help from his family, it could not have been much. His own fortunes, and those of his wife and children, did not improve for the remainder of the decade.

It was not until the early 1880s that Georgiana de Wolfe finally was able to amass the money to do something for her only daughter. How she did it—begged or borrowed or saved—is not known, but it was done. Elsie was already in her early twenties and neither pretty nor well educated. She had never made a formal debut in society: where would Georgiana have held the party—downstairs in her husband's surgery?

There were two choices. The money could have been used as a dowry, but the young woman had not evinced the slightest interest in boys nor was there a likelihood of attracting a desirable candidate given the modest sum and her comparably modest endowments. Georgiana had a better idea, with which her daughter heartily concurred. Elsie's cousin twice removed was the wife of Dr. Archibald Charteris, Queen Victoria's personal chaplain during her long stays at Balmoral Castle. Elsie would be dispatched to Edinburgh for a prolonged visit with these well-connected, if distant, relatives. By the time she came home, Ella Anderson de Wolfe would surely be somebody else, somebody truly remarkable. Mother and daughter were as one in that resolve.

CHAPTER THREE

Elizabeth McCoun Marbury and Georgiana Copeland de Wolfe, though very different women, were both devoted mothers who shared the virtues of thrift, domesticity, and fidelity to husbands often undeserving of their excellence. Their daughters Elisabeth and Elsie were undoubtedly paradigms of filial devotion who honored their mothers without having any desire to emulate them. They were part of a small group of adolescent girls who in the latter half of the nineteenth century had begun to look around and find few if any role models for the women they wanted to become. Bessy and Elsie both had to improvise and borrow bits and pieces from the scant examples in their world.

By the time they accomplished what they had set out to achieve and were no longer accountable to anybody, their stories, invented or purloined, had become a part of the myths of these legendary women—so delicious to their friends, so malicious to their enemies, so titillating to those who only read or heard about them. There was no way of denying these stories nor was there any desire to do so. Bessy and Elsie were artists who were their own masterpieces, and the craft that had gone into their creations of self had become as intimate a part of them as their skins.

They knew what was possible for intelligent women with no particular talents or looks. The idea of becoming schoolteachers or dependent upon

Ladies and Not-So-Gentle Women

the largesse of their brothers was no more attractive than joining the National Woman's Suffrage Association or the Woman's Christian Temperance Union. What they wanted was similar to what was desired by their better-endowed contemporaries. They wanted to be accepted by society—*good*, rather than high, society: talented, stimulating people who did things and said things that were at least quotable and possibly meaningful.

In 1872, Bessy's parents allowed her to take her first trip to Europe with a group of young people and, of course, the proper chaperons. Typical of those "Grand Tours," the principle was to cover as much geography as possible in as short a period as permissible. Bessy's group doggedly "did" the British Isles, Switzerland, the Rhine, Belgium, and France. The treks between stops were tedious, often dangerous, involving carriage rides in rugged terrains that had to be taken at a snail's pace with the brakes constantly applied to the steaming flanks of sweaty, reeking horses. Bessy concluded that "to tour Europe as part of one's early education was no light task. We were crammed with historical details which . . . I never digested."

Her most vivid memories centered on her first visit to Paris and neighboring Versailles, which would one day become a second home to her in which she would spend some of the happiest times in her life. That first visit took place a year after the Commune, that desperate uprising of the people of Paris after the Franco-Prussian War. Still visible was the destruction the besieged defenders had visited upon their own city.

The voyage was not all enlightenment and contemplation. What would a trip to Paris be without a Paris frock to show off at home? Not being the daughter of a millionaire, Bessy would not have dared to set foot in M. Worth's establishment, but the rue de la Paix abounded with excellent couturiers. They were all eager for new customers in that first year after the Commune, and all took oaths that they had made clothes for the wildly fashionable, maddeningly extravagant, sadly exiled Empress Eugenie.

Bessy selected a green camel's-hair dress that swept the floor, her first to dip below the tops of her boots. After it was delivered, she impatiently tore away its wrapping and put it on. The rest of the afternoon was spent in getting the feel of being a grown-up lady, entering rooms just to get the hang of gracefully lifting the long skirt so that it would not be caught as the doors closed behind her. For Bessy, the exciting, the creative, part of any show would always be the rehearsal.

The New York to which Bessy returned and the society into which she was about to be formally introduced were on the verge of revolutionary change, though much of the old New York world remained for a few years longer as it had been during her childhood, a place where a man's position was more likely to be measured by the size of his library than by the size of his ballroom. Within a few years, the United States would celebrate its centennial, and her native city was 150 years the nation's senior, more than enough time for it to have developed an upper class made up of professional and leisured gentlemen who prided themselves on being thoughtful and civilized if not intellectual. It was an attitude epitomized by her father and the other members of the Century Association. Via the manipulations of Caroline Schermerhorn Astor and her minion, Ward McAllister, who with only a partial sardonic deviation from truth were known as "the queen and her prime minister," a cataclysmic change was about to take place that would shape the social attitudes and aspirations of the metropolis well into the next century. It was during the winter after Bessy's return from Europe that the matriarchy took over New York society. It conquered, in the gender-flattering name the Patriarchs, a committee of twenty-five of the most prominent men in the city supposedly selected by Ward McAllister, who proclaimed they "had the right to create and lead Society." This group was to sponsor a series of subscription balls, at Delmonico's, to which each Patriarch would be permitted to invite four ladies and five gentlemen. Each list of guests would have to be submitted for the unanimous approval of the membership.

The Patriarchs was a shrewd compendium of the old order, represented by such men as Lewis Morris Rutherfurd, De Lancey Kane, and Alexander Van Rensselaer, and the new, including both John Jacob and William Backhouse Astor, William R. Travers, and the greatest gate-crasher of them all, McAllister himself. On the surface it appeared to be male business as usual. That was Caroline's (henceforth *the* Mrs. Astor) brilliant illusion, her sleight of hand, for it was she who actually had chosen the original group, allowing her creature, McAllister, to release her selections to the press as if they were his own. Using the voice of McAllister, she would create a new Knickerbocker society with a pivotal role in it for herself.

There had been great and gracious hostesses before *the* Mrs. Astor. These women were renowned for the charm and pleasure of their entertainments in a way she would never be, pleasure and charm being among the least of considerations at an Astor ball or dinner party. After the exaltation of being invited and knowing that those who were not asked knew that one had been, everything else was as dull, insignificant, and predictable as the food she served.

As a Schermerhorn, Caroline was old New York, but the Astors were a part of the new breed, although hardly arriviste, for the family was in its third generation as moneyed and landed gentry. In what might have been an attempt to keep his Astor patroness in her place, McAllister had said: "In my opinion, *four* generations of gentlemen make as good and true a gentleman as forty."

It was the massed weight of those oft-quoted aphorisms that would eventually crush him. For the most part they served *the* Mrs. Astor's purposes, and on the few occasions when they offended her, she ignored them. The Astors might only go back three generations, but when her husband's grandfather, the first John Jacob, died in 1848, he left a fortune of $22,000,000, which at the time represented one-fifteenth of all of the money in the whole of the United States. Never again would one American possess a personal fortune of that size in proportion to the national wealth.

When Caroline Astor met Ward McAllister in 1872, the time was right for both of them. Perhaps because she had been failed so dismally by a husband who elected to spend most of his time on his yacht with other women, her children—especially her four daughters—became the most important things in her life. It was only when her ambitions for them coincided with McAllister's social aspirations that she provided the means to his success. A man was necessary, if only as equerry, if she was to carry out her plans for launching her daughters into society. Either too clever or too proud ever to utter a word publicly against her philandering husband, she nevertheless knew he could not be depended upon. On the rare occasions he was at home, he was drunk or abusive, often both. McAllister was the perfect substitute. Without being sexually threatening, he was both amusing and flirtatious but, most important, he executed what she demanded of him with an excellence that met her exalted expectations.

Caroline's worldly husband might easily marry one of the girls off to some foreigner with a title. That was not to be countenanced. She wanted the *right* match for each of the girls, the right *American* match. McAllister understood that "a man with the aspirations of a Duke and the fortune of a footman" was beneath her consideration. His word became social law. When he said the limit of "ins" was four hundred, which was said to be the number that could fit comfortably in his patroness's ballroom, it caught on with the press, and they soon were, and still are, called the Four Hundred. He amplified for the benefit of the press (*the* Mrs. Astor would never deal directly with them, which certainly set her apart from most of her social rivals and all of her successors).

> Why there are only about four hundred people in fashionable New York Society. If you go outside that number you strike people who are either not at ease in a ballroom or else make other people not at ease. See the point? . . . When we give a large ball like the

last New Year's ball for eight hundred guests, we go outside of the exclusive fashionable set, and invite professional men, doctors, lawyers, editors, artists, and the like.

It was that latter group, combined with civilized gentlemen of leisure, that had formed the best circle in old New York before the reign of Queen Caroline, part of whose mission would be to make certain that intelligence, education, and talent were no longer countenanced in Fifth Avenue society. Her dominion would last for twenty-five years. Its decline was heralded by the publication of a Charles Dana Gibson satirical drawing with a caption dividing New York into "the Bohemian set, all brains and no style, Society proper with a fair amount of each, and the Four Hundred, all style and no brains."

The Marburys belonged in Gibson's second group, with a love of the arts that gave them access to the first. It was in this world that Bessy took her first independent social steps during that same winter as the launching of the Patriarchs' balls, to which she neither wanted nor received invitations. She would later reminisce about her initial steps into adult society but seldom mentioned a guest in the Marbury home. Her memories were of the parties she attended elsewhere and of the people she met at them. While her father spent freely, entertaining himself and others at his club and in restaurants, a strict economy was the norm where his family was concerned. His daughter thought twice before inviting anybody to a meal despite the occasional encouragement of her mother, who apparently had a homily for every occasion: "Ah, daughter, where there is room in the heart, there is always room on the hearth."

But reassurances aside, she had to keep within the budget. A party was once proposed that would have cost more than their "usual modest expenditures." Her mother's response was, "Why sacrifice a year's hospitality for one evening's entertainment?"

Her mother's tiresome adages sank deeper than her father's reputedly "brilliant witticisms." She could remember none of the latter, but recollection of those maternal precepts would become a source of income half a century later, when they found their way into a series of monthly magazine features for which she was paid quite handsomely. She also fell back on them whenever the paternal legacy of wit failed her during an interview.

With the polarization initiated by Ward McAllister, the society of literate men and women contracted to a few very hospitable houses where the mode was not elaborate spectacles but informal gatherings of artists, writers, actors, and the more literate professional men of the city. In describing that world, the Marbury world of the Seventies and Eighties, she could not resist a bit of condescension to *the* Mrs. Astor as well as to the multitude of women who would later make Elsie's fortune.

> Hostesses used to create their own atmosphere. They did not depend upon professional decorators. They gave as well as did their guests. They were not crushed by the weight of their magnificence. They were adequate and articulate in themselves. There was no suggestion of that mental vacuum which undigested wealth generally fails to fill.

Although she appeared to be having a grand time, Bessy would later describe those years as a period of "divine discontent." She had become "a polite philanderer reveling in the joy of living," but she had brains enough to know there was something infinitely better waiting for her, if she would only take the time to discover what it was. The manic activity continued. Her newly acquired calling cards were dutifully left at the doors of the appropriate hostesses. She joined the literary clubs of Gramercy Park, volunteered for social work, and even taught Sunday school. Her evenings were often expended in the rituals of the debutante of the period, proceeding from reception to dinner party, from dinner party to ball.

On the weekends there was fishing, riding, hunting, and tennis, often at Ringwood, the country home of the Hewitts, whose three daughters had been among her dearest friends since early childhood. The oldest, Amelia ("Miss Amy"), was exactly Bessy's age. Although she had a harelip and was the least attractive, she was the only member of the group to marry. The prettiest, young Eleanor ("Miss Nelly"), was also the best athlete, numbered in the small upper-class army who later claimed to have brought lawn tennis over from England to America. After coming into her own money years later, she was said to have amassed one of the largest collections of erotica in the country, which her brother threw into the East River after her death. The mannish clothes she affected had to be of the finest fabrics (for the Hewitt girls, fabrics were a passion) and made by Paquin or Worth.

Although two years older, Bessy was closest to Sarah ("Miss Sally") Hewitt. They were so alike in so many ways that a friend's description of Sally could serve as a description of both young women. "She was enormous and amusing. . . . a law unto herself and would have done anything she chose. Fortunately, she didn't choose to do anything outrageous."

The friends may not have been beauties, but infectious high spirits, fine, unblemished complexions, and bright eyes hinting of mischief made them by no means unattractive. They were heavy but not too much more than permitted in an era in which Lillian Russell's voluptuous figure set the standard for what was considered most sexually desirable in a woman.

The Hewitt family shared a mansion, at 9 Lexington Avenue, with Mrs. Hewitt's father, Peter Cooper. The old man was a self-made multimillionaire whose dream was to found an institution that would offer free technical training to young people of all races and creeds who could not otherwise obtain it. In 1853, he laid the cornerstone for the Cooper Union for the Advancement of Science and Art. A facility for women had been part of his plan from the beginning. In a message to the state legislature he wrote:

> In order that females may share in the benefits of this institution, the subscriber intends to set apart suitable rooms in the said building for an academy of design in which the art of engraving and design will constantly be taught with the further applications of science and art as the best calculated to widen the sphere of female employment.

He later added it would keep women from being forced to marry bullies out of economic desperation or having to resort for their livelihoods to occupations that were "revolting to the purity and sensitiveness which naturally characterize the female mind." It might not have been the ideal feminist doctrine, but for the 1850s it was remarkably enlightened.

The stream from which Gramercy Park got its name, the Cromarsie-Vly, ran through the Cooper-Hewitt property, which was one block north of the park and corresponded to the Marbury property one block south of it: the five Marbury children and the six Hewitt children, forming lifelong relationships, met and played in that common ground between. Beyond being neighbors, their fathers were friends and colleagues in the progressive wing of the Democratic party, founded by another Gramercy Park resident, Samuel J. Tilden, to rid the party of the excesses of Tammany Hall and "Boss" Tweed. The political disturbances of the Seventies were neighborhood affairs, and through her father's involvement Bessy had an intimate view of them. It was the beginning of a fascination with politics and dedication to the Democratic party that would endure for the rest of her life.

All of the reform Democrats adored Thomas Nast's brilliant satirical cartoons of Tweed and his gang, which had begun to appear regularly in the influential *Harper's Weekly*, in 1871. It was a literal example of bringing down the house with laughter. The affirmative response to the lampoons encouraged Tilden to seek indictments of the politician on charges of larceny and forgery that had defrauded New York City of thirty million dollars. Tweed was convicted in 1873, and the reformers were in the ascendancy. The next year, Tilden won the governorship of New York State, and Hewitt was elected to the House of Representatives. The days of castigation as a Copperhead were over; Bessy's father was on the side of the new political angels.

During that period Bessy did not find meeting politicians and inventors as thrilling as meeting writers, actors, and painters, which was much more likely to happen in the unique domicile of the newlywed Helena de Kay and Richard Watson Gilder than in the Cooper-Hewitt mansion. It was an age in which periodicals had the place in middle-class homes currently occupied by television sets; and a literary magazine such as the *Century,* which Gilder edited, was *Masterpiece Theatre* with a touch of *60 Minutes.*

In addition to serializations of the works of the best of the Victorian novelists (making it lucrative for writers to spin their books out to often excruciating lengths), the readers of the *Century* could look forward to controversial editorials, interviews, and articles by political, social, and academic scientists, as well as the work of the best of the contemporary essayists and poets, rounded off with illustrations by popular artists. The creators of this vast array of material could be found almost any evening in the Gilder home. A charming converted stable on Fifteenth Street between Irving Place and Union Square, it was called "the studio," because Helena, who was an artist, worked as well as lived there. Coincidentally, it was next door to the clubhouse of the Century Association, to which Gilder's magazine bore no relationship except that he and many of the men he published were members.

Gilder considered Walt Whitman, Henry James, Mark Twain, and William Dean Howells the greatest American writers (in the early months of 1885), the *Century* was simultaneously serializing James's *The Bostonians,* Twain's *The Adventures of Huckleberry Finn,* and Howells's *The Rise of Silas Lapham*), and on an evening when they were in the city, Bessy was likely to have met any or all of them there. One of the last times Twain and James ever met was twenty-five years later, when Helena de Kay had them to tea in London.

Those evenings at the studio must have inspired dreams in Bessy of becoming a hostess to similar groups of fascinating men and women. Bessy could envision no escape from the strained atmosphere at home except marriage. Her friends and family all thought she would marry young and well. She claimed that she had expected to become a wife and mother, that it was the most rewarding role for a woman. At sixty-six, after a lifetime of professional and political power and passionate relationships, she would still maintain marriage was the best career for a woman.

She had an ample figure, bright China-blue eyes, and a clear rosy complexion, and it had come as no surprise to her family when a serious, well-to-do young Bostonian began to exhibit a romantic interest in her. He was a most eligible suitor, and his courtship merited serious consideration. Francis Marbury encouraged his attentions by inviting him to join the family on a trip to Philadelphia for the Centennial Exposition. Alas, Bessy's beau was a heavy-handed, admirably practical bore. His suit was so unattractive to her that two trivial incidents were sufficient to put an end to it.

The young couple were passing an exhibit of the latest in heating appliances. Bessy was struck by the ugliness of the bulky new stoves that protruded well into the room and expressed a preference for those modeled after the old Franklin stove. Her would-be husband cut her off. The new models were much more efficient, and after he was married, he would insist on having none other in his home. How interesting, she thought, as whatever heat existed between them was instantly lowered.

A short while later they came upon a home furnishings exhibit. Bessy remarked upon the attractive textures and patterns of the new upholstery fabrics. Her swain again interrupted, this time declaring he would have nothing but horsehair in his home, as it wore so well and could be kept clean with so little effort. That did it. As soon as she could get her father alone, she told him the young man was hopeless, and any attempt to persuade her otherwise would be a wasted effort.

From the age of ten on, she claimed, she was always falling in love albeit conveniently in vain. The longest of her crushes was on a "fascinating gentleman, Byronic and Saturnic in appearance." This passion endured for four years and was rendered as hopeless as the others by his possession of a perfectly sound, abundantly rich wife who was his "generous provider." Fifty years later he became a vehicle for her wit when she described his declaration of "intense admiration" while never coming "within a thousand miles of suggesting a more compromising intimacy." She was forced to conclude she was only "orange juice to him; healthful and refreshing."

Whether he actually existed or was only another autobiographical device used to mask the true nature of her passions, the portrait she painted was of a man as sexually safe as any of the homosexual gentlemen with whom she later became intimate. Nevertheless, she persisted in claiming the reason she never married was not for lack of interest, but because she never met the right man.

If the men who presented themselves were not very appealing candidates, the alternative of sharing a life with another woman was becoming increasingly attractive. It was much more rewarding than loneliness or the acrid drudgery of becoming a spinster dependent in some "kindly" relative's home, a home that she would never be able to call her own. From an economic point of view, two could live more cheaply than one if they shared expenses. And then there was the closeness, the affection: two women could be demonstratively affectionate with each other in a way a man and woman seldom could be or desired to be even when married. There was no hint of sexual deviation in the display. The word *lesbian* was not yet in the vernacular, and female homosexuality was unheard of in that time and place. What women shared was friendship, a friendship that could be condescended to and condoned by men, for it did not threaten them. After all, they reasoned, what kind of a sex act was possible without a penis?

When Bessy was thirteen, *The Friendship of Women* by William Rounseville Alger was published. The book was so successful that it went through twelve editions, remaining in print for over twenty years, and could not have escaped Bessy's attention or that of any of the women to whom she was attracted. It was the sort of book passed from one girl to another, especially if the receiver was a crush. It was unlikely to have been confiscated or proscribed, as the author was a clergyman with a romantic as opposed to sexual view of feminine sensibilities. Reverend Alger was the chaplain of the Massachusetts House of Representatives as well as a popular lecturer and essayist.

There were chapters devoted to the nature of the relationships of wives and husbands, brothers and sisters, mothers and sons, fathers and daughters, and women with women. The most titillating chapter for girls of Bessy's generation was undoubtedly the one entitled "Pairs of Female Friends," which drew a revealing analogy between female bonding and the good clergyman's ideal of male affections:

> Friendship lies within the province of women as much as within the province of men; that there are pairs of feminine friends as worthy of fame as any of the masculine couples placed by classical literature in the empyrean of humanity; that uncommon love clothes the lives of its subjects with the interest of unfading ro-

mance; that the true dignity, happiness, and peace of women—
and of men, too—are to be rather in the quiet region of personal
culture and the affections than in the arena of ambitious publicity.

Among the female friendships Alger investigated was that of the plain but
brilliant Mme de Staël and the gorgeous, though not quite so brilliant, Mme
Récamier, who has come down to us as a piece of furniture named in her
honor: the chaise on which she flirtatiously posed for a highly regarded portrait by David. The Duchess of Devonshire, another of Récamier's fervent
female admirers, was quoted by Alger on the object of her affections: "At
first, she is good, then she is intellectual, and after this, she is very beautiful."
The letters Mme de Staël wrote to her are among the greatest examples of
epistolary art in French literature. They were loving, often extravagantly so,
but never was the feeling delineated in them sexually ambiguous. This was a
great asexual love affair between two women with only a revisionist hint of
homoeroticism when viewed from a late twentieth-century perspective.
The letters could only have thrilled Bessy, who one day would build a
brilliant career on a taste for the dramatic verbal elegance of the French. But
it was not an exchange of letters that would ever satisfy her innermost
needs. What she craved was something closer to what Alger described in his
biographical sketch of the ladies of Llangollen.

In the mid- to late eighteenth century, two young women of
wealth and social position, Lady Eleanor Butler and Miss Sarah
Ponsonby, formed such a deep attachment they wanted to forsake
the world and devote their lives to each other. They departed for
an obscure region deep in the country, but their relatives found
them and forced their return. They were not to be deterred and
soon eloped again, this time successfully to the valley of Llangollen, in Wales, where they settled permanently. . . .
Their charming cottage was furnished with great taste and
filled with every conceivable comfort. Here, surrounded by their
books and excellent pictures, they enjoyed no society better than
their own. Tales of the idyllic nature of their lives spread through
England bringing the most celebrated people of the period to
enjoy their hospitality and marvel at the depth of their attachment. Lady Eleanor and Miss Sarah lived together for sixty years
and, for a quarter of a century, never spent more than twenty-four
hours at a time out of the valley.

Years later, Bessy would attempt a variation on their way of life but with a partner for whom that intense intimacy was unthinkable.

To Bessy, who adored talent and clung to it as if it was something she hoped might be contagious, "the studio" offered exhilarating opportunities to come down with the creative fever. Although this was also available at other salons she frequented, what set the Gilders apart were the qualities of the women of the family. Richard's sister, Jeanette Leonard Gilder, only seven years older than Bessy, was already the literary editor of the New York *Herald,* to which she also contributed drama and music reviews. By the end of the Seventies, two of her plays had been produced by reputable stock companies in Philadelphia and her first novel published. With another brother, Joseph, she was arranging for the publications of a new magazine, *The Critic,* which would become an influential review of the arts. In 1890, she helped to effect the social downfall of Ward McAllister either accidentally or willfully, when she ghostwrote his book, *Society As I Have Found It,* in which she published in his name all the pompous, passé, and ridiculous aphorisms that made him the laughingstock of the society to which they were directed.

Jeanette's formal education had been sketchy at best, culminating in two years at a female seminary. When she was fifteen years old, the Gilder children were left fatherless by the Civil War. The unchallenged rule of the day placed greater value on the schooling of boys, and this gifted girl went to work so that her five brothers need not interrupt their studies to help support the family. It would later occur to her that there was something wrong with the accustomed order of things. This large and formidable woman, handsome in the mannish clothes she affected, was undoubtedly the first woman Bessy ever met to whom marriage was neither a logical choice nor a viable alternative to independence.

Still more alluring was the beautiful Helena de Kay, Richard Gilder's artist wife, who insisted on retaining her maiden name professionally at a time when even actresses became *Mrs.* Siddons, or *Mrs.* Kemble, or *Mrs.* Campbell, to say nothing of the most popular novelist of the period, *Mrs.* Humphry Ward. The De Kays were themselves an extraordinary family— Newporters in that period when the people who frequented the resort were either artists or, at the very least, possessed of an artistic sensibility. Helena's sister, Katherine Bronson, later lived in a Venetian palazzo, where she presided at a literary salon distinguished by the attendance of her close friends Henry James and Robert Browning. Her niece, Edith, Contessa Rucellai, would similarly preside in Florence, where Edith Wharton was her intimate friend and stellar attendee. Charles De Kay, the literary and art critic of *The New York Times,* founded the National Arts Club, which would later be located in Samuel Tilden's old Gramercy Park mansion. In a revolutionary move for its time, he included women among its charter members, but as brother to Helena and kin to Jeanette he could do no less in a club devoted to uniting the arts and bringing artists together with their serious patrons.

Always referred to by her colleagues as *the* Miss De Kay, who shared the studio with her husband, Mr. Gilder, Helena joined with other young artists to form the Society of American Artists as a "party of reform" against the National Academy of Art, the conservative old-guard association of artists quite distinct from the above-mentioned National Arts Club. The group of rebels included some of the great young names in all of the arts: the architects Stanford White and Charles F. McKim; the celebrated Polish actress Mme Modjeska; the painter John La Farge; and Walt Whitman. They were a part of the lively society Bessy found at the De Kay–Gilder ménage.

While providing no competition to the Fifth Avenue world of *the* Mrs. Astor (those who frequented one society would be neither welcome nor comfortable in the other), circles such as the one formed around *the* Miss De Kay did provide substantial evidence that upper-class New York offered social and intellectual alternatives (largely ignored in the fiction of the social critics Edith Wharton and Henry James) that helped to shape Bessy's notion of what constituted good company. It was also in the De Kay–Gilder household that she first became aware that a depth of passion and intimacy between two women could be not only tolerated but also recognized as an important if not indispensable part of female life within the Victorian family.

Women like Helena de Kay opened a world of possibilities for Bessy, demonstrating how liberated a woman could be within the accepted constraints of her society, city, and country. It was no secret that before she married Richard Gilder, Helena and the illustrator Mary Hallock Foote had been so deeply in love they wanted to live together for the rest of their lives. They met at some time between 1864 and 1867, when both were students at Peter Cooper's Institution of Design for Women. Their attraction to each other was almost immediate. They began to spend time exploring the city together and testing each other's reactions to the same things. The similarities were striking. What started as an adolescent crush—Molly, as Mary was called, was only seventeen in 1864 and Helena, somewhat younger—deepened rather than passing with the years. By 1869, they were both beginning to make a living at their art, and began to speculate about the possibility of a shared life of intimacy and work. They went off alone for a winter holiday and put the notion to the test. Upon their return, Molly wrote to her "dearest Helena" summing up her reactions to the time they had spent together away from their customary world.

> I have not said to you in so many or so few words that I was happy with you during those few so incredibly short weeks but surely you do not need words to tell you what you must know. Those two or three days so dark without, so bright with firelight and contentment within I shall always remember as proof that, for a time, at least—I fancy quite a long time—we might be sufficient for each other. . . . Imagine yourself kissed many times by one who loves you so dearly.

Her closing could be attributed to the sentimental excuses of the period but for the fact that the rest of the letter, including its charming reticences, was written by a woman in full command of the language who knew precisely how to say and imply what she wanted conveyed without a hyperbolic trace. Her subsequent letters became still more explicit with descriptions of nights spent entwined in each other's arms, of passionate kisses, of anointing each other's body.

> Imagine yourself kissed a dozen times, my darling. Perhaps, it is well for you that we are far apart. You might find my thanks so expressed rather overpowering. . . . We shall meet so soon and forget in that moment that we were ever separated.

There could be no doubt they were lovers; the only thing Molly left unwritten and obscured with time was whether the affair was sexually consummated. Curiosity might have been served in the more forthright Helena's letters, but unfortunately they were not preserved. Her daughter published a collection of her father's letters but apparently did not find it worth the effort to assemble those her mother wrote.

In 1873, the physical part of the affair between Helena and Molly came to an end, when the Hallocks insisted their daughter live at home. She apparently came from a far more conventional background than the De Kays. Molly would be twenty-six in November of that year; it was time she gave up her adolescent passions and concentrated on getting a husband. Dutifully, she found a suitor; pathetically, she could not bear to give up Helena, who was furious and, for a while, refused to see her. After they did meet, Molly wrote that she had wanted to say, if Helena had let her, that she loved her "as wives do love their husbands as friends who had taken each other for life," and that she believed in her as she believed in God.

Helena would not relent. If Molly believed in her as she believed in God, it would be an Old Testament God exacting an Old Testament vengeance. If Molly had a beau, Helena would have a fiancé—not simply any old fiancé, but her lover's benefactor and editor, Richard Watson Gilder. It must have seemed to onlookers like Bessy in that small Gramercy Park–Irving Place world that hell might indeed have no fury like a goddess scorned.

After the engagement was announced, a despairing Molly admitted she did not think her feeling for Helena had been the "noblest" kind of love. She told Gilder she believed his bride had loved her almost as girls love their lovers, and she had felt the same way, adding scornfully, "Don't you wonder that I can stand the sight of you?"

The friendship persisted in somewhat altered form. Molly was married the following year to Arthur D. Foote, a mining engineer, and went west, where she found a second career as a novelist. Predictably, her first book, *The Led-Horse Claim,* was originally published, in 1883, as a serial in Richard Watson Gilder's magazine. It was probably fortunate for their marriages that they lived a continent apart, for twenty-five years after they met, Molly could still feel passionate enough to write to her beloved friend: "It isn't because you are good that I love you—but for the essence of you which is like perfume."

An essence like perfume was something a woman could feel only for another woman. No man had that quality; it was at the heart of femininity. Bessy Marbury heard the stories women told about their friendships and those of women like Helena and Molly. She listened and yearned to experience such a relationship. She soon would, and would learn that the essence like perfume could linger for a lifetime and, indeed, have nothing to do with being good.

CHAPTER FOUR

The De Wolfe and Marbury families remained ensconced in the old established neighborhoods that centered around Gramercy Park and the squares. Bessy and Elsie would seldom have reason to venture above Forty-second

Ladies and Not-So-Gentle Women

Street until after the turn of the century. But the strivers continued to turn their attention ever northward along Fifth Avenue and a few key side streets. Fifty-seventh Street was among them. In 1837, it had been cut through from the embankment above the East River to the shores of the Hudson River at the sizable public expenditure of $11,310. Double the width of the neighboring east–west streets, it was intended someday to be a grand boulevard, but only a few visionaries could imagine the street, then stretching through farms, ever becoming a thoroughfare. A Mr. Mason, then president of the Chemical Bank, was among them. In 1825, well in advance of the city planners, he had spent $1,500 of his own money to purchase the length of what would become the eastern side of Fifth Avenue extending from Fifty-seventh to Fifty-eighth Street, to add to a Fifth Avenue parcel he already owned from Fifty-fifth to Fifty-sixth Street. He left these properties to his daughters, Mary and Rebecca, who had married two of their Jones cousins. That was the traditional way with the Masons and the Joneses, intermarrying to keep the Chemical Bank in the family.

The property and the neighborhood lay fallow until 1867, when his daughter, Mary Mason Jones, commissioned the architect Robert Mook to build what would become known as "Marble Row" on the block from Fifty-seventh to Fifty-eighth Street that her father had bequeathed to her. Although in the French Beaux Arts style, it was modeled on the English concept of terrace housing, which combined several townhouses in one unifying style. She made certain that she would have some family in the still-rural area by convincing her sister, Rebecca, to build the Colford Jones row on her Fifth Avenue property a block to the south.

Mary Mason Jones selected as her own residence the grandest mansion in her row, at the Fifty-seventh Street corner. She waited, knowing it would not be for long. In *The Age of Innocence,* her niece, Edith Wharton, nee Jones, depicted her as the crusty but extremely kind Mrs. Manson Mingott.

> It was her habit to sit in the window of her sitting-room on the ground floor, as if watching calmly for life and fashion to flow northward to her solitary doors. She seemed in no hurry to have them come, for her patience was equalled by her confidence. She was sure that presently the hoardings, the quarries, the one-story saloons, the wooden green-houses in ragged gardens, and the rocks from which goats surveyed the scene, would vanish before the advance of residences as stately as her own—perhaps (for she was an impartial woman) even statelier; and that the cobblestones

over which the old clattering omnibuses bumped would be replaced by smooth asphalt, such as people reported having seen in Paris.

By the late Seventies, West Fifty-seventh Street was well on its way to becoming a fashionable extension of Fifth Avenue. The William C. Whitneys had bought the townhouse at the southwest corner. The future president Theodore Roosevelt's father and uncle were in residence in two houses, 4 and 6, with Auchinclosses, Rothschilds, Wertheims, Oelrichses, Schiefflins, and Juilliards on their way.

In 1875, another of those wealthy visionaries, Effingham Sutton, had bought one of the new brownstones at the northwest corner of Fifth Avenue. He sold out a few years later to Cornelius Vanderbilt, who replaced the simple brownstone with the most ostentatious of the Vanderbilt mansions that were beginning to proliferate along Fifth Avenue below Central Park.

Sutton had a dream of an upper-class residential neighborhood along the East River. It was considered insane at the time but would become a reality still thriving over one hundred years later, long after the obliteration of all of the vainglorious Fifth Avenue monuments to the Vanderbilt family's regal aspirations.

When he first envisioned it, the woman largely responsible for the future Sutton Place was a young girl whose family was about to move into a house just across Fifty-seventh Street from him. By the time Anne Harriman made Sutton's dream come true, he would be long dead and she would be a Vanderbilt.

In 1875, the Oliver Harrimans purchased the double lot, 24 West Fifty-seventh Street, which measured 40 by 100 feet. It was considered a most impressive piece of property at a time when people were building their brownstones on lots as narrow as 14, 16, and 20 feet. The Harrimans built a four-story red brick with a garden in the rear and a basement for servants' rooms, the laundry, and the kitchen. The double size was necessary to accommodate a family with eight children ranging from Herbert, the baby, who was eleven, to James Low, the eldest, who was twenty-one.

The family had outgrown the house at 14 West Twenty-fifth Street, where Laura Low Harriman had moved as a bride and given birth to all of her children. When they bought the house, living near the edge of Madison Square was considered the last word in residential elegance. That was before the Hoffman House Hotel, which had Bouguereau's notorious painting "Nymph and Satyrs" hanging over its bar, was built on their corner. When the hotel decided to expand west along Twenty-fifth Street and made the Harrimans a substantial offer for their house, they snapped it up and bought the property on Fifty-seventh Street. By the time the family moved, the neighborhood had changed radically. There were no less than six houses of prostitution one block west along Twenty-fifth Street. The shops of the Ladies' Mile were marching right up to the entrance to Madison Square Park, and Mr. Vanderbilt was building his railroad yard on its eastern boundary.

The right people had begun to follow Mary Jones uptown. It was in that group that she would find the kind of men she was determined to have as husbands for her three daughters. She would not have them follow her example. Times had changed since Laura Low was a girl and had done what was then considered the proper New York thing. If a young woman could not find a husband from within her own set, the perfectly acceptable old-family solution was to marry one's daughter to a promising associate in the family business. She could only acquiesce when her beloved father had pushed the union with Oliver Harriman, who was not only a good-looking, affable young fellow but an indispensable asset to the firm. It had turned out well enough. He had proven a loving, devoted husband and father. Nevertheless, she was quick to acknowledge that she had married beneath her station.

The first American Harriman, Oliver's grandfather William, did not arrive in New York City until June 3, 1795, after a harrowing two-month sea voyage from England. Seven of his eight sons had perished before they reached America. His descendants claimed that he had been a prosperous dealer in stationery in London, who had ventured forth because he wanted the social advantages of doing well in the new republic. It was highly unlikely, for in those days nobody left London for America in search of social advantages. But he must have had capital, because when he moved to New Haven, Connecticut, he was known to his neighbors as "the rich Englishman." After chartering a number of sailing vessels, he began to engage in the West Indies trade. By 1800, he was doing well enough to move back to New York.

Although William never became a wealthy man, he did leave a comfortable estate to his surviving son, Orlando, who was becoming prominent in that commercial world. Anything was possible in the booming city. His friends were already beginning to marry into the old, good families. They were creating a New York social hierarchy, which, then as now, had more to do with bank balances than breeding.

Orlando married and had three fine sons, Orlando Junior, Edward, and Oliver. He was sufficiently affluent to afford to give the oldest, his namesake, to the church. Possibly, it was the lack of business sense as much as his piety that prompted this generous bequest, for Junior would continue to make decisions, in matters not ecclesiastic that spelled financial ruin for his family. His son, Edward Henry, would more than compensate for his failings in that area. But that would not occur until many years in the future.

In the early 1830s, the world was a truly wonderful place for the Harriman patriarch. He was following the lead of the Astors by investing most of his assets in real estate. Visions of millions of dollars would dance before his eyes as he raced around the area on and below Wall Street buying, often on credit, all the buildings on which he could lay his hands.

When the great fire of 1835 started, it was in precisely that area of lower Manhattan where Harriman had his holdings. It spread, taking with it most of his buildings. What remained standing was possessed by the holders of the mortgages on what had been destroyed. He was ruined, but so were many other men. Just when recovery seemed within reach, the second disaster struck. All that he had managed to recoup was swept away in the great financial panic of 1837. Harriman was never again able to retrieve what had been lost.

His son, Oliver, and his nephew, Edward Henry, were determined to succeed in the city in which their family had failed. Oliver's success came first. Of a gentler nature, he lacked both the ruthlessness and financial genius of his nephew; and though eventually wealthy, he was never the fabled tycoon E. H. Harriman would become.

Laura Harriman would never fully credit her husband for the business acumen that enabled him to succeed well enough to stake his nephew to a seat on the Exchange as well as to move his family to grander quarters on Fifty-seventh Street. It was equally difficult for her to admit it was his good manners and sweetness of disposition as much as her social ambition that won them a position among the old families denied the middle level of wealth, a position reserved for either those born to it or of such extraordinary new wealth it would be foolhardy to exclude them.

It was Laura Harriman's great good luck that her daughters were beauties, each with an individual charm that set her apart from her sisters. Emmeline, the oldest, had "a beautiful soothing voice . . . like a bit of music . . . a soft voice . . . to match her lovely face."[3]

The middle girl was named for her paternal grandmother, Anne Ingland Harriman, the daughter of a well-to-do family that, like the De Wolfes, had emigrated to New York from Nova Scotia. Anne was the most strikingly good-looking of the Harriman girls. She was fair and tall with a carriage that was almost regal. Beneath a surface sweetness made palatable by a sense of humor, there was a reticence approaching the enigmatic, a sense of some mysterious part of her not yet—perhaps never to be—revealed.

Lillie, the youngest, was a hoyden who laughed and dared and was to live her life with a devilish egocentricity that was every bit as dazzling as her looks.

The sisters were blessed with their father's compliant good nature, which was to prove a blessing to their mother. It enabled her to shape them to her will, which may or may not have been their own, but that was never a consideration, free will being something unheard of in dutiful Victorian daughters.

On the morning of December 6, 1879, Emmy's wedding day, Laura Low Harriman was the first to rise. Let the bride sleep on. After all, she had no more to do than to put in an appearance and look beautiful. Weddings were a mother's show, her day most of all, and she could not waste a moment of it. The rules of what was expected of her were so well ingrained, she might have written them. Thus it was known to her precisely how far beyond them she might go to make her party memorable without violating the sensibilities of the many and mottled arbiters of good taste who would be guests in her home. More than a few of the most prominent of them would be visiting the Harriman mansion for the first time. The reception would be held there after the church ceremony. From the beginning the refreshments had been a problem: no wines could be served—a wedding without Champagne!—in deference to the groom's grandfather, William Earl Dodge, Sr., who was president of the National Temperance and Publication Society. There was little, no matter how irritating, Laura would not do in deference to Mr. Dodge, co-founder with his father-in-law of the firm of Phelps, Dodge, the largest importers of metal in the United States.

The family agreed the florists had outdone themselves with the decorations for the church and house, which had never looked prettier. A spacious canopy of white roses had been erected under which the bridal couple would greet their guests. There were flowers everywhere. If it was excessive, it must be recalled that this was 1879, and more was quite definitely more.

It was the first wedding in the family. When it was time to leave for the church, the Harrimans and their five sons were not disappointed by the vision of the three girls in their bridal-party finery, which had been designed and made for them by Courbay, in Paris. Anne, one of her sister's bridesmaids, was dressed in a white satin gown that artfully outlined her slim, elegant figure. On her bosom she wore one of the pins of diamond butterflies crested with pearls that were her sister's gifts to her attendants. The long train of grenadine over satin was draped over her arm as she descended the stairs. How wise of Laura to have selected a wreath of white flowers that set off the classic features of this, her most beautiful child! Her assets had to be carefully put on display, for now that Emmy was profitably disposed of, Anne would be the next offering in the marriage marketplace.

Carriages waited at the door to take them scarcely more than two blocks to the Fifth Avenue Presbyterian Church, at the corner of Fifty-fifth Street, which had moved uptown from Nineteenth Street in the same year they had moved up to Fifty-seventh. Although the Harrimans were Episcopalians, the Lows were Presbyterians, and that was the faith Laura had imposed upon her children, particularly fortuitous on this day as abstemious Grandfather Dodge was an almost fanatically devout member of that denomination and one of the city's largest contributors to its charities and missions.

As Anne came slowly down the aisle, the eyes of at least two adoring males were focused upon her. One of the ushers, Elliott Roosevelt, with or without her consent, was spreading the word that they were engaged. In the congregation the handsome and eligible young sportsman Samuel Stevens Sands, Jr., had been invited by Laura Low Harriman. He had been assured by his hostess that her middle daughter was *not* engaged to young Roosevelt and would be more than receptive to his own suit.

A Dodge wedding brought out a distinguished gathering through which the Harriman hosts would be able to ascend a few rungs up that golden ladder. Among the guests were Mr. and Mrs. Bradley Martin, Mr. and Mrs. William H. Vanderbilt and their daughters, former governor and Mrs. Marshall Jewell, the Reverend James McCosh, president of the groom's alma mater, Princeton College, and Elliott's mother, Mrs. Theodore Roosevelt, Sr. Her husband had died earlier that year, and she and her daughter, Anna, were still in mourning. The unadorned severity of their black gowns stood out amid the opulently festooned crowd of peacocks like ominous harbingers of something unsuited to a wedding.

The Roosevelts were neighbors of the Harrimans on Fifty-seventh Street and had been close friends of the Dodges for years. Unlike Mittie Roosevelt's older son, Teddy, who was away at Harvard, Elliott was a wild and troubled boy who at nineteen already had a drinking problem. If the sensible, lovely Anne returned her son's ardor, she might prove his salvation. Laura Low Harriman was equally aware of the young man's problems and determined that her daughter would not throw away her life on him. Roosevelt was too adolescent, too unpredictable, and too unpromising. Sands was her candidate. The oldest of ten children, the handsome young man belonged to all the right clubs and was a partner in his father's successful Wall Street brokerage firm which would one day be his. The match might not be as brilliant as the one Emmy was making on that day, but it was not without distinction. The original family name was Sandys, which it remains in England. The first of their line to achieve distinction was Edwin, created Archbishop of York by Elizabeth I, in 1576. By the middle of the seventeenth century his American descendants were called Sands. A direct ancestor of Samuel had married the granddaughter of Bessy Marbury's collateral ancestor Anne Hutchinson. The New York branch of the family settled on the north shore of Long Island in an area still known as Sands Point. Samuel's great-great-great-grandfather was the first president of the New York chamber of commerce and the founder of the Bank of New York. His grandfather was a rear admiral in the United States Navy.

None of Laura Harriman's strategies, in what she considered were her daughter's interests, went unappreciated by Elliott Roosevelt's sister, Anna (Bamie to her intimates), the oldest and most intelligent of the four Roosevelt children. She was plain of countenance and left almost hunchbacked by a childhood case of Pott's disease. More perceptive than the brother who would become the president of the United States, she would one day be the source of love and inspiration to Elliot's daughter Eleanor.

*T*he Harrimans announced the engagement of Anne to Mr. Samuel Stevens Sands, Jr., during the winter of 1880. The wedding took place at four o'clock on April 7, 1880, a lovely early-spring afternoon. Although it was not the brilliant affair Emmy's wedding had been, just four months before, *The New York Times* called it "a fashionable marriage ceremony in a Fifth Avenue church," and described the throng as "not less than a thousand people, embracing representatives of our best society." Elliott had sent his sincere regrets, but Bamie was one of Anne's bridesmaids. The church was again the Fifth Avenue Presbyterian and the minister again the Reverend Dr. John Hall, whose wedding addresses were deemed "proverbial in Presbyterian circles." Many of the same guests were present at both weddings, but Laura had forgone an elaborate reception. Only family and a few friends were invited back to the house after the ceremony.

With full cognizance that this was her big moment, Anne gracefully approached the altar in stately steps, her hand resting lightly on Oliver Harriman's arm. The sighs of the enormous assemblage were drowned out by the great swelling hosanna of the wedding march played by the brilliant amateur organist Robert Pell. At the exact moment that Dr. Hall lifted his hand to pronounce the benediction, something extraordinary happened, something unparalleled that widened the eyes and lifted the aggregate heads that had been lowered in prayer.

The sexton threw a switch flooding the loft interior for the first time with the brilliant light of the new electricity. A new age had begun, although the bride was as unaware of it as her guests and probably more concerned with the coming first night of her honeymoon and the long ritual of married life radiating from it.

On the evening after the wedding, Bamie Roosevelt exchanged her role of bridesmaid for that of co-hostess with her mother at a family reception in honor of the beautiful Alice Lee's engagement to Teddy. It is not unlikely that Bessy Marbury was one of the guests. The McCouns and Roosevelts were Oyster Bay neighbors. She was the same age as Bamie, with whom she shared a bond of self-protective uninterest in boys; and only two years younger than Teddy, who had inspired her to raise English mastiffs. During the summer of 1881, when young Roosevelt was preparing to run for the State Assembly, he would try out his speeches on Bessy, but she was to prove a disappointment.

> One evening, he appeared with a bulging manuscript in his pocket, a speech he was to deliver the following night in the Jamaica Town Hall. It was pretty long and fairly dull. I fell asleep, and when he turned to me, eager for comment, I was dead to the world and to him.

Exactly one year and two days after the Dodge-Harriman wedding, on the evening of December 8, 1880, the home of Mrs. Theodore Roosevelt, at 6 West Fifty-seventh Street, was ablaze with the diffuse glow of gaslight. Mrs. Roosevelt was giving a party in honor of the debut of her youngest child, Corinne, who had been the recipient of over one hundred nosegays in honor of the occasion.

Six hundred guests would dance to the music of Landers's society orchestra and partake of one of M. Pinard's most delectable suppers. As one would expect of Mittie Roosevelt, once one of the fairest belles of antebellum Georgia, the festivities were in the best style the period had to offer. The library had been cleared for dancing and contained little more in the way of decor than a remarkable arrangement of every conceivable variety of pink carnations on the mantel over the welcoming warmth of the coal fire. Little baskets of roses were centered on the myriad small tables set up for the repast in a dining room rendered almost giddily spare by the removal of its customary massive and somber furnishings.

To the side of the flower-decked fireplace, Mrs. Roosevelt, flanked by Corinne and the new young Mrs. Theodore Roosevelt, nee Lee, greeted the distinguished group. Bamie was relegated to one side, where she could oversee the details of the party. From that day on, she would be the unmentionable spinster who made certain all ran smoothly, while her mother, her sister, and her beautiful sisters-in-law played the gracious hostesses.

From where she stood, Mrs. Samuel S. Sands, Jr., could see her sister Mrs. William E. Dodge III, in whose honor, two evenings before, there had been a first anniversary party at the Harriman mansion just down the street. Anne might have been ambivalent about having become one of the matrons while still in her debutante year had she not discovered that she already was expecting her first child. The knowledge permitted her to condescend to a ritual that so recently had been of such importance. The debutante year, what did it actually signify? It was no more than a sweet period of transition through which a girl passed so swiftly. Boisterous Douglas Robinson was hovering near the reception line, obviously smitten with Corinne, who seemed far from indifferent to his suit, which meant she was another deb who in all probability also would be a matron before her coming-out year was concluded. It was the way of the world, their world, the pretty wellborn young lady's world, which was not about to change.

CHAPTER FIVE

John Pierpont Morgan was no self-made man of the ilk of Jay Gould, Edward H. Harriman, or Andrew Carnegie. It would be more accurate to describe him as a self-aggrandizing man. If he looked down upon the others from a high-busted posture of Episcopalian rectitude, there was some justice in his lofty attitude. After all, the first Morgan had landed in this country in January 1636. It was sixteen years after the arrival of the *Mayflower* but several years before the arrival of Jan Aertsen, an illiterate Dutch peasant from De Bildt Utrecht, who came as an indentured servant. With a grandiloquence later reserved for their mania for mansions, Jan's progeny took advantage of the Bilt connection and fancied themselves Vanderbilts.

During those Jacksonian years, halcyon for a man with his eye on the main chance, Pierpont's grandfather Joseph Morgan opened a coffeehouse in Hartford, Connecticut, modeled on the eighteenth-century Lloyd's of London coffeehouse. His success eventually led to a directorship in the Aetna Insurance Company. His son, Junius Spencer, was a tall young man possessed of the good manners, conservatism, and dignity concomitant with careful if unimaginative New England breeding. Being the heir to what had become a considerable fortune did much to compensate for a lack of humor. It was said young Morgan's one error was marrying Juliet Pierpont, not that the girl was unattractive or of an undistinguished family: her lineage was far superior to his. The Pierponts could trace their way back to the Norman Conquest. Her father had graduated from Yale, which had been founded by one of his ancestors, but he was to be the scourge of his conservative son-in-law's life for as long as he lived.

The Reverend John Pierpont, of Boston's Old Hollis Street Congregational Church, was an impassioned preacher, an abolitionist and fiery orator of unyielding liberal convictions that to nineteenth-century Bostonians sounded uncomfortably radical. The antagonism erupted with his outspoken "heretical" espousal of Unitarianism. There were only two things completely unacceptable to these children of the Puritans: a denial of the sanctity of the Holy Trinity and a denial of the sanctity of property rights. Pierpont questioned both of those fundamentals.

He became estranged from his wealthy Morgan in-laws, to whom the righteous old pastor was a source of embarrassment until he died in poverty, unmourned by them. His most prominent physical characteristic was a large nose that turned an angry red whenever his zeal became inflamed. The acne rosacea was apparently all his grandson inherited from him: his great-granddaughter Annie Tracy would be the first of his line to inherit his dedication to the rights of the disenfranchised.

*J*ohn Pierpont Morgan was born on April 17, 1837, in Hartford. It was the year of one of the great financial panics that would periodically plague the American economy, bringing with it questions about the validity of the proposition that the capitalistic system was a boon to a majority of the people. In later years Pierpont would often be richer after a financial crisis than he had been at its onset, and that evoked more questions. His name became synonymous with all that was wrong with the system. It was a tribute to his success but a paradoxical one, for of all the men profiting from the system, he was possibly the least corrupt, the one who played the game with a degree of integrity that approached honor, which, as each new generation has reaffirmed, was deemed a liability on Wall Street.

The most salient thing about him was not that he was a capitalist but that he was a collector, an obsessed, acquisitive, and passionate man. His was a passion for business, a passion for power, a passion for objects, a passion for the gratification of all of his senses with an abundance of sex, food, drink, tobacco, alcohol. Passion was his closest approach to human love, which was something he gave freely only once in his whole life, and that was to his first wife, Mimi. Strangely enough, that union would be without gratification of any of his senses. Another paradox in his often paradoxical life.

Mimi Morgan, nee Amelia Sturges, was no beauty and somewhat older than her husband. She already was suffering from tuberculosis at the time they were married. Pierpont virtually had to hold her up during the ceremony, and she was too ill to attend the wedding breakfast. It was October 1861, and many cynically dismissed the hasty marriage as an expediency to keep him out of the Civil War, to get him out of the country at a time when the government was starting an investigation into war profiteering. There was more to it than that. One of his biographers, Andrew Sinclair, observed: "J. Pierpont Morgan had a Puritan conscience and an Episcopalian sense of sin."

It was nothing so purely pragmatic as escape from war duties that had motivated Morgan's first marriage. Taking Mimi as his wife was an act of passionate Puritan zeal demanding a sexual abstinence that more than atoned for past sins. Here was a sensual young man who was deeply in love and unable to consummate the marriage for fear of worsening his bride's physical condition. He gave up everything to care for her, literally carrying her aboard the ship that would take them on a winter honeymoon in North Africa and on the southern coast of France, where it was hoped the sunny, warm climate would provide the miracle cure. But there were no Protestant miracles. Despite his selfless ministrations, she died in Nice four months later, in February 1862. Whatever expiation the heartbroken young man needed for having survived her took the form of devoting himself to business. His practical God was merciful, and the business prospered beyond his dreams, indeed to the point of a begrudging paternal approval that always had been more difficult for him to attain than the grace of his Father in heaven.

Pierpont did not make the mistake of marrying for love a second time. When it behooved him to take another wife, he selected the handsome, somewhat aloof Frances Tracy. They were married in May 1865. Fanny was one woman on whom little of his sensual passion was ever expended, nor apparently did she expect, demand, or desire it of him. She did her part by producing children as required. Within a year of the wedding, Louisa was born, and, a year after that, the hoped-for son and heir, John Pierpont Morgan, Jr. (Jack to the family), made his appearance. The boy's father (Pierpont to the family) kept up his end of the marital bargain by weathering the panic of 1869 with no diminution in the Morgan lifestyle.

By the time Fanny became pregnant for a third time, in 1871, Morgan had moved the family into a handsome townhouse at 6 East Fortieth Street. That same year, he also bought a country estate, Cragston, in Highlands-on-the-Hudson, just south of West Point. The house was comfortable but had none of the ostentation of the millionaires' retreats in neighboring Rhinebeck and Hyde Park. He would have none of that, just as he would never live on Fifth Avenue. He found it all symbolic of the men in his business for whom he had no respect, those who found their identity in a vulgar display of wealth. Money never had been Morgan's chief incentive. As any good craftsman might, he respected it for what it always was to him: a tool of his trade.

It also enabled him to take up the social responsibilities that came with his new position in the community. He started to play a larger part in the charitable and institutional activities of his church, St. George's, in Stuyvesant Square. Joining the editor William Cullen Bryant, the publisher George Putnam, and the lawyer Joseph P. Choate, among others, in 1871 he became one of the first patrons of the Metropolitan Museum of Art.

By the time his second daughter, Juliet, was born in July, he should have been among the smuggest of men. That was not the case. He had begun to eat and smoke to excess and was becoming morbidly sensitive about the acne rosacea that continued to afflict his bulbous nose. With his meals, as with everything else in his life, he was the first at the table to consume everything on his plate. His physicians warned him to slow down; the incurable skin condition was probably caused by his chronic dyspepsia and could only be helped by stricter attention to his digestive system, but nobody had the power to curtail J. P. Morgan's appetites.

Annie Tracy Morgan, named for the most beautiful of her mother's sisters, was born at Cragston, on July 25, 1873. Pierpont may not have welcomed but did not appear to mind a third daughter. When he took the time to think about it, four females in his house gave him pleasure. He loved ministering to the women in his family, as he had to Mimi. He adored selecting their houses and furnishings, not simply the objets d'art but everything down to the last swag on the least significant window treatment. Above all, he loved to select their clothes. The majority of men visiting a Paris fashion house were more conscious of the *vendeuses* and the beguiling *mignonettes* who served as models or fitters than they were of the clothes. Not so with Morgan. Those piercing eyes were concentrated on the frocks to the exclusion of all else in the world.

It was different with his mistresses. He seldom went shopping with them for clothes or jewels. The fear of revealing the sensual gratification he derived from female things (almost more than he derived from the females themselves) made him choose more sensible commodities as presents. Stocks and bonds were male things that could not be held up to ridicule by a

*L*adies and Not-So-Gentle Women

spurned mistress. The feminine side of his nature was safe only with his family, which would never question the maleness of its head.

Business was the aura in which Morgan was best able to express his masculine half. Ruthless commercial success became the armor for many of these modern hollow men who were more ancient in their inner longings than ever they suspected. As time passed, his art collection was more and more where his feminine self would find its most satisfying release. A woman like Elsie de Wolfe openly gave way to her passion for beauty, and it was dismissed as a part of "her decorating." Fearful of revealing that it was the same feminine impulse stemming from the same delicate source, Morgan masked it behind the bluff facade of the latest millionaire power ploy, the game of collecting important art. The exalted level of his taste and the complexity of his motivations distinguished him from other tycoons playing the game. The most profound distinction between Elsie and Morgan in this area was the extent of financial resources each could devote to the creation of their monuments to self. They were twins dividing their identical gall in three parts: vanity, commercial genius, and an exquisite sensibility.

Sensualists, male and female, often have an androgynous area with borders obscured by unresolved sexual yearnings, patches of distilled eroticism that are undiluted by designation of a specific gender: so it was with Morgan. In other periods and cultures, or in a less religiously constrained man of his own times, this might have led to bisexual resolution. Contemporaries, biographers, and certainly family were loath to deal with Morgan's homoerotic impulses. They chose to neutralize them by implying that so long as they were acted upon in business, and he simultaneously kept a number of mistresses, they were "all right."

Although he undoubtedly did nothing physical about the homosexual side of his nature, its existence cannot be denied. Extreme good looks was an unspoken requirement for a partnership. He turned his bank, the place to which he was more passionately devoted than any other, into a house of Adonises from which all women were forever barred except once a year, when Fanny came down for the annual Christmas luncheon. Morgan adored beauty above all other things in men, in women, in art, and was equally ardent about all three. Whether it was a male, a female, or a painting he was after, he desired it passionately and would outbid all of his rivals to possess it.

The bright young men, the ones who swiftly made their way up in his employ, were almost exclusively WASP beauties, the confections that fed the fantasies of starved Victorian maidens and, in his subconscious, those of Morgan. It did not go unremarked, and one Wall Street wag quipped,

"When the angels of God took unto themselves wives among the daughters of men, the result was the Morgan partners."

If one had to be a clever and personable prostitute to make good in the world of finance, Morgan's was the best little house on Wall Street. The banker kept his boys close to him and worked them hard. If they were strong enough and ruthless enough to use the old man as he used them, the rewards were incalculable. If not, being one of the boys in the House of Morgan could be emotionally devastating.

Robert Bacon was undoubtedly the perfect example of a Morgan beau ideal. Intellectually brilliant, a star athlete, and breathtakingly handsome, Bacon was the crush of many a man's man. Theodore Roosevelt was one of his classmates at Harvard, and after becoming acquainted with him, wrote home: "Bob Bacon is the handsomest man in the Class and as pleasant as he is handsome."

Another classmate, Dr. Henry Jackson, was more effusive. "He was singularly blessed by nature with a superb physique to which was added a manly beauty; he may well be chosen as a type of the perfection of manhood at its best."

Morgan wooed and won this beauty, and he joined the firm as a partner. Another Morgan partner observed, "Mr. Morgan had fallen in love with Mr. Bacon and insisted upon having him near always."

Fortunately, Bacon had married a strong, sensible woman, Martha Waldron Cowdin, who was there for him whenever he craved some affirmation of his manhood. His need was strongest when the pressures of being Morgan's favorite became too much for him. A nervous breakdown forced him to resign from the firm and come home to her tender care. Like so many other deserted lovers, Morgan never forgave Bacon on a personal level while continuing to avail himself of professional favors made possible after Bacon embarked upon a new career in government.

By the time Bacon recovered from his breakdown, his old friend Theodore Roosevelt was in the White House and offered him a job in Washington as assistant secretary of state under Elihu Root. Once again the relationship with a powerful man became more important than wife and children. To Bacon, Root was always "my master." And again the feeling was returned by the stronger man. On the night before his protégé left Washington, Root wrote a note to him: "Until tonight, I have not permitted myself to realize you are to leave . . . and I feel as if I were marooned on a desert island. . . . Your brave-hearted cheerfulness and power of friendship and steadfast loyalty have been noble and beautiful. I am sure you have a still more distinguished career ahead of you for all who love you to rejoice in."

Despite the ambiguity of "all who love you," there can be little doubt Root himself was the lover to whom he was referring. The weaker but more beautiful Bacon was the beloved of Morgan, Jackson, Root, and Roosevelt. It was the nature of male relationships of the period. Much more than possible sexual consummation, love was the striking element, as it would be in the later delicately balanced relationships of Bessy Marbury and Elsie de Wolfe, and Bessy and Annie Tracy Morgan. If this was called a "Boston marriage" when it existed between women, Morgan's involvement with his beautiful partners might as aptly be termed a "Wall Street marriage."

The difference between the sexes was that men were as threatened by this love of female for female as they would have been by facing the implications of their own love for other men. Women, usually better able to accept their love for each other, often handled love between males with an admirable delicacy. Martha Bacon was one of scores of strong wives who refused to be intimidated by the asexual male lovers of their husbands. Rather than castigate, they were there to help put back together their weaker men when they were shattered by events (masking emotions) they dared not comprehend.

It might seem that Fanny Morgan was never placed in a position similar to Mrs. Bacon's, that her husband was the breaker in these relationships with men rather than the broken. It was not true. Morgan was often emotionally shattered and had to remove himself from the banks and the boys for months at a time.

Some declared Fanny was the one person in all the world who could not be broken by him, because she cared more about her position as Mrs. J. Pierpont Morgan and the mother of his children than she did about the man. One thing was certain: she seldom if ever wore the Worth gowns he brought home from Paris. Fanny much preferred taking the carriage and going down to New York's Ladies' Mile, where she made her own choices from its fashionable shops.

The year of Annie Tracy's birth brought the first public recognition of many characteristics by which he would be marked for the rest of his life. Morgan earned a reputation as one of the shrewdest and most ruthless bankers by not only weathering the great panic of 1873 but also managing to make money for his clients, partners, and, of course, himself. His secret was to remain in a fluid holding position and play a waiting game. Whether or not he had been unfaithful earlier in his marriage, this was the year in which his close associates first became aware of the infidelities that would grow with time. It was also the year in which his behavior began to reveal the hypocritical underpinnings of his pious, if arrogant, Protestant devotions. He sought a posture of public morality and, perhaps, one of private expiation in accepting Anthony Comstock's invitation to become one of the founding members of the New York Society for the Suppression of Vice.

Like many psalm-singers, Comstock made a more substantial living from denouncing vice than most of the pornographers he condemned did from their work. In that busy year of 1873, he was so responsible for enactment of federal legislation prohibiting the distribution of contraceptive information and "obscene material" through the mails that the bill became popularly known as the Comstock Law. He was primarily interested in the interdiction of commercial pornography, occasionally flexing his muscles by attempting to have a literary classic, such as *Tom Jones,* banned from the mails and often from public libraries on the grounds that "morals, not art or literature" was the only criterion for what was fit to read. He was, after all, an executive of the Young Men's Christian Association with the responsibility for cleansing minds of prurient thoughts and displacing all that sexual energy into sports, locker rooms, and showers. His special bête noire was the "libertine," and he took joy in boasting of the number of people he had driven to suicide. Of course, those suicidal libertines did not include the philanthropic libertines who gave him both financial backing and political power.

Morgan ruled his private household with the same autocratic high-handedness with which he ruled his banking house. Fanny; his son and heir, Jack; and the two older daughters, Louisa and Juliet—all shuddered at the raising of an eyebrow, let alone his voice. Only the youngest, Annie Tracy, ever dared to speak up in defiance. She was a long, thin child, not particularly attractive, with the face of a pixie. Her most striking features were piercing blue eyes that seemed to see right through the artifice with which people in her upper-class world masked their privileges. It was later noted that entire defense systems were known to crumble under her gaze. Those penetrating eyes came from her father, as did so many of her strengths. One of Pierpont's grandchildren observed that had the old man left the fortunes of the House of Morgan in this youngest daughter's control rather than in his son's, the family would be very much richer, to say nothing of more powerful.

By the time Annie was becoming cognizant of such things as relationships, her parents were maintaining no more than the facade of a marriage. It was rather like one of those follies so favored in English country houses, which from a distance appeared to be a bridge or summerhouse but up close was only two-dimensional. At one of the dinner parties with which the couple indulged in their folly of togetherness, young Annie Tracy was brought down by her nurse for the dessert course. The guests were amused by this funny-looking little thing, until she announced without so much as a by-your-leave that she had no intention of ever getting married. Some of those nearby may have observed that considering the example set by her parents' union, it was no wonder. Her father was not amused. "Well, then," he challenged, "what do you intend to be when you grow up?"

She turned those penetrating eyes on her father and discomfited all who were present by replying in a voice that filled the room with no less clarion clarity than his own: "Something better than a rich fool anyway."

*B*y the end of the Seventies, Morgan had decided the house on East Fortieth Street was too confining. More space was needed for the burgeoning art collection, the equal but separate lives shared by his wife and him, and the demands of children approaching adolescence. He was not about to march in the millionaire parade moving up Fifth Avenue to build their self-aggrandizing, overblown mansions in the fifties and sixties. He turned downtown to look for an already existing house that would suit his needs, observing pointedly, "I have no wish to add to the architectural monstrosities corrupting our skyline."

Morgan settled on a large brownstone mansion at 219 Madison Avenue. It was one of three built in the 1850s by Bessy Marbury's distant cousins, the Phelps family, which stretched along the east side of the avenue from Thirty-sixth to Thirty-seventh Street. The banker would eventually own all three but started by buying the one at Thirty-sixth Street and renovating it. His first alteration was to move the entrance around the corner to Thirty-sixth Street in order to accommodate an oversized bay window taking up most of the Madison Avenue frontage. Morgan may have inveighed against the excesses of the period, but within the comparative simplicity of its brownstone shell, the interiors of his home compared favorably with the immoderation of Fifth Avenue.

In October 1878, Thomas Alva Edison had formed the Edison Light Company with Drexel, Morgan as bankers. The most remarked-upon feature of Morgan's mansion was that it was the first house to be entirely illuminated by electricity. The newspaper reportage on the housewarming truly launched Mr. Edison's company, which contributed handsomely to the banker's growing fortune. The extra money would come in handy, for the house had brought into Morgan's life a man who would spend his money almost as rapidly as he earned it and, in the process, help the banker to amass one of the greatest private art collections in the world.

"Uncle" Henry Duveen was embarking upon his career as New York City's preeminent art dealer. His ability to provide works of art on the scale Morgan demanded forced the latter to overcome his inherent anti-Semitism and almost greater aversion to thick Dutch accents. At first, all he wanted

*A*lfred Allan Lewis

was good examples of the kitsch so popular with the Fifth Avenue crowd, but his acquisitiveness was coupled with innate good taste, and he soon recognized these works for what they were. Two events occurred at this point that would help to produce the breathtaking Morgan collection. Junius Morgan died, freeing his son of the last emotional and financial constraints on his artistic buying spree. Uncle Henry's nephew Joseph, the future Lord Duveen, entered the business, bringing with him polish and vision as well as the instincts of an imperial plunderer. Despite his being Jewish, these qualities made him the ideal agent for Morgan, for they were the same qualities Morgan had brought to banking with the same stunning success.

The family took up residence in the new house in the autumn of 1882. Annie Tracy was a stubborn, bright nine-year-old more interested in athletics than in the things that were supposed to interest little girls. She was far less concerned with feminine charm than her sisters were and far less concerned with feminine finery than her father was. It was as if she instinctively knew the price her mother had paid for cultivating those fluttery wiles that were supposed to guarantee a good life to a woman, and had already rejected that course for herself. A school for young ladies, specializing in teaching those very things for which she had no use, would obviously be a dismal failure for her. She continued to be educated at home, with a good teacher replacing her governesses. Morgan probably reasoned it was for the best: Lord knew what undesirables she might meet at a school.

Nevertheless, she had to have some companions and could not be permitted to pursue her lessons in isolation. He set up a private school for Juliet and Anne on the first floor of his new mansion in what was known as the Black Library. The room was named for its rich black Santo Domingo mahogany wainscoting. Whether or not the families of the other girls who were asked to join them in private education at the Morgan mansion were aware that they, too, were "off-horses" is not known, but no more fortuitous grouping could have been conceivable. Among them were Florence (Daisy) Jaffray Hurst and Ruth Morgan (no relation), with whom Annie Tracy formed lifelong friendships. Ruth was the peacemaker. Whenever the tomboys among them, led by Annie, would rough up an unpopular girl and lock her in the closet during the recess hour, it was she who would cry, "Oh, don't, don't! Do let her out." It was prophetic, for the young pacifist years later would become chairperson of the Committee on International Cooperation to Prevent War.

Those three would later become active in women's causes, but while they were still schoolgirls, the manifestation of feminism that most astonished and titillated them came from Clara Spence, who journeyed down from Boston weekly to give them elocution lessons. She was the first woman they ever saw who did not wear "a pair of the medieval steel-stays" that were considered a feminine necessity at the time. She left them off, she said, on principle! Ten years later, in 1892, Miss Spence started her own school in a brownstone, at 6 West Forty-eighth Street, admitting both boarding and day students. Although moved uptown, it still offers one of the best educations available to young upper-class New York City females.

s Grace Church was the religious center of the old New York families, and St. Thomas's was becoming the Vanderbilt church, so St. George's Church, in Stuyvesant Square, was Morgan's private religious domain. He ruled it, as senior warden, with the same high-handed imperiousness with which he ruled his bank and his home. Whenever they were in residence in the city, attendance at its Sunday school was compulsory for Annie Tracy and the older Morgan children. The devotion to the parish instilled by their father was so unshakable that it remained the family church long after the neighborhood around it had deteriorated.

In 1882, when a new rector was required for St. George's, Morgan took personal charge of selecting the new clergyman. His choice, William S. Rainsford, was as much a beau ideal of religion as his protégés Robert Bacon and Charles Schwab were of banking. The difference was in moral strength. Rainsford's belief in his God, Jesus Christ, provided a clear sense of right and wrong that would enable him to stand up to any of Morgan's challenges. Bacon and Schwab's god, Mammon, offered only material wealth, often breaking them as they pursued it, always humbling them before Morgan, who could bestow it.

Rainsford was a robust reformer with a gift for oratory. If his fiery eloquence did not persuade a drunk or reprobate to repent, he had no qualms about using his athletic physique and powerful fists to bring the sinner to his knees. He was likened to an "Anglo-Saxon Saint George" riding out to slay his dragon even if that dragon turned out to be his own benefactor. Recognizing the changing nature of the neighborhood, he realized that his church was doomed if it served only the diminishing number of privileged parishioners. His mission was to serve all of the people of his parish, including the poor and homeless. He constantly battled Morgan on these issues, and most of the time he won.

Over Morgan's vehement protests, the rector saw to it that pews were abolished so there was no distinction by rank or wealth inside the church; the number of vestrymen was increased to include representatives of the underprivileged in what had become their neighborhood; and the church facilities were expanded to serve their needs. He realized that religion was something Morgan would have "laid aside in disuse, rather than passed from man to man." His righteous indignation appealed to the Pierpont in Annie Tracy. Almost as important to her was the fact that he was the only person she ever saw stand up to her father and win.

As the situation between her parents deteriorated, she could look to Rainsford and his wife for comfort. She found her own Saint George in whose image she could grow. He provided her with an armor of righteous indignation to protect her when she set out to do battle against the swarm of social injustices she saw looming all around her. His words were a validation of her own feelings.

> The dangerous men are not the masses; but often men we know and dine with; men prominent in religious and philanthropic enterprises who are all the time trying to buy something that the law does not allow to be bought and that enlightened public opinion knows to be wrong: these are the men who do not trust the people—the great lawyers, great corporations, great insurance people—men who are always trying to do something that the law does not quite allow.

Annie Tracy Morgan had found her path. As she had proclaimed while still little more than an infant in her nurse's charge, it was to be "something better than a rich fool anyway."

CHAPTER SIX ❧

It was an age in which only three occupations were permissible for a well-brought-up young lady of a good but not wealthy family: she could become a schoolteacher, work in a shop, or attempt to earn a living as a writer. By 1880, Bessy Marbury, twenty-four and without a husband, had begun to sell short articles to newspapers and magazines, but was at best an indifferent journalist whose talents would never make her fortune. The most enjoyable thing about writing was the company of writers.

In the spring of that year, within weeks of Anne Harriman's fashionable wedding to Samuel Steven Sands, Bessy's father and she took the ferry to Hoboken to embark on a Cunard liner, destination, Liverpool. The idea was

*L*adies and Not-So-Gentle Women

to be in London in time for the season, which traditionally began the week after Easter and extended until just after the American ambassador's Fourth of July party. Francis Marbury may well have been following in the steps of so many other well-to-do American parents of the period with marriageable daughters who could not be marketed at home. The English upper class was overstocked with younger sons set adrift by primogeniture. These feckless young men were not averse to American wives with families that could give them a leg up in the new world, and Marbury, as the American counsel to the crown, would have been well positioned to make a deal. Whatever her father's motives were, the important thing to Bessy was that he had selected her to be his traveling companion. He was a charming, dapper man with connections extending beyond the London society in which she had little interest. Francis shared his daughter's appreciation of artists. As a member of the Century Association, he knew most of the English literary and intellectual celebrities from having played host to them during their visits to New York City.

On disembarking in Liverpool, the Marburys proceeded to London's Euston Station. Following their porter through the overwhelming Doric portico out into the street, they were shaken by a shattering, clattering, rattling din and pace that reduced memories of New York City to a recall of tranquillity. Here was the richest city in the world, the capital of an empire said to be so vast that the sun never set on it, although the great town's fogs made many visitors suspect the sun never rose on it.

For less than a shilling, a hansom cab carried them through Hyde Park, across the Palladian Georgian splendors of Belgravia, around cumbersome, unattractive Buckingham Palace to the lodgings they had booked in one of the red-brick chambers buildings on Jermyn Street, which ran parallel to and one street south of Piccadilly in the fashionable West End. It was just north of stately Pall Mall with its great clubs, including a Hellenic temple that housed the literary Athenaeum, where, as a member of the Century, Marbury enjoyed reciprocal privileges.

The American ambassador to England, James Russell Lowell, an old friend of Bessy's father, proposed that he be allowed to arrange for the young woman to be presented at court. Miss Marbury politely but firmly demurred, later commenting, "This held no attraction for me. Then, as all through my life, I escaped the lure of titles." She preferred to listen quietly to the stimulating conversations of her father and Lowell. The ambassador kept a liberated household: these discussions often took place over after-dinner cigars, and the young woman was not expected to withdraw from the table as females were in that period, a custom persisting in some British circles to this day. She savored their discussions of life at Brook Farm, that lofty if doomed Bostonian experiment in communal living. As a member of the inimical Brahmin caste of patrician intellectuals, Lowell was intimate with all of its Transcendentalist founders but of far too practical a bent to have ever himself become a member. Indeed, he once dismissed a leader of its educational system as having found his proper calling in the establishment of a "bureau for governesses."

The idea of the Farm began in 1840 with Elizabeth Peabody and Ralph Waldo Emerson fulminating in equal measure against the excessive materialism of the Industrial Revolution and the failure of the Unitarian Church and the Harvard Divinity School to offer either a practical or a spiritual alternative. Their objective was to form a self-sufficient model community of workers, teachers, and students producing what was necessary to live without excess. Its motto could be found in the words Elizabeth Peabody inscribed in bold letters:

LEISURE TO LIVE IN ALL THE FACULTIES OF THE SOUL.

Their idealism resulted in a combination of spiritual vigor and economic ineptitude that doomed the Farm to failure within six years of its founding. Nevertheless, through those who went forth from it, the ideals of Brook Farm continued to have an intellectual life in New York for years after its physical demise in New England. Horace Greeley, the publisher of the *New York Tribune,* was a champion of transcendentalism and hired many of its advocates as reporters and critics. Charles Dana, who founded the *New York Sun,* had been a teacher at Brook Farm. But it was with the women of Brook Farm that Bessy felt a natural kinship, sharing, as she did, their dual natures: half romantic idealist and half pragmatist. Forty years before she was to begin her own pursuit of meaningful work, there existed this group of extraordinary women who *did* things. Elizabeth Peabody, an educator and writer, was also the first American female publisher. She not only published the latest European and American books and publications of the romantic, Unitarian, and transcendental movements, but also opened her own bookstore to make them available. Her shop was the meeting place of Boston's intellectual community almost from the day she opened it. Preferring cerebral stimulation to physical passion in her relationships with men, she never married. Her sisters, almost as gifted as she, were more conventional in their emotional needs. The exceptional men the Peabody sisters married considered their brains fully the equal of their bodies: Sophia became the wife of Nathaniel Hawthorne, and Mary, of Horace Mann.

Margaret Fuller was the most intriguing of the Brook Farm women. She was the author of the classic feminist book *Woman in the Nineteenth Century,* one of the earliest calls for both political and emotional equality. It was published by Horace Greeley, who had hired her as the literary critic for the

Tribune, in 1844. He subsequently made her the first American woman foreign correspondent. In a more perfect world, Greeley would be better known for having sent the brilliant Fuller east to Europe than for having advised some unremarkable young man to go west.

Although she did marry and have a child, she never denied the possibility of passion between women. The awakening of sexual desire occurred when she was thirteen and fell madly in love with an older Englishwoman who accepted any exhibition of the young girl's adoration short of physical consumation. Fuller admitted that the nature of a later relationship with another woman was "conjugal" and described what she knew was possible for one woman to feel about another:

> It is so true that a woman may be in love with a woman and a man with a man. It is pleasant to be sure of it, because it is undoubtedly the same we shall feel when we are angels, when we ascend to the only fit place for the Mignons, where *sie fragen nicht nach Mann und Weib* (they ask nothing about man and woman). It is regulated by the same laws as that of love between persons of different sexes, only it is purely intellectual and spiritual, unprofaned by any mixture of lower instincts, undisturbed by any need of consulting temporal interests; its law is the desire of the spirit to realize a whole, which makes it seek in another being that which it finds not in itself. Thus, the beautiful seek the strong, the mute seek the eloquent; the butterfly settles on the dark flower. . . . How natural is the love . . . of Madame de Stael for Recamier, mine for_____! I loved for a time with as much passion as I was strong enough to feel. Her face was always gleaming before me; her voice was still echoing in my ear. All poetic thoughts clutered around the dear image.

Bessy was fascinated by these impassioned Boston women. The intimacy with which two women could live together (with or without sexual fulfillment) was already known as a Boston marriage. In 1886, Henry James would use the term as a double-entendre in the title of his novel *The Bostonian,* which was intended to be "a study of one of those friendships between women which are so common in New England," similar to one in which his own sister, Alice, was passionately involved. Many modern critics consider the book a study of repressed lesbianism. Much to Lowell's distress, Elizabeth Peabody was caricatured in the book as Miss Birdseye. After the turn of the century, a gifted member of the ambassador's own family, the poet Amy Lowell, was to live happily for years in such a marriage with the actress Ada

Dwyer. It was doubtful if Lowell fully understood or adequately described the intimate circumstances of the lives of so many of his female friends, but Bessy must have guessed. Intuition was keen in a young woman disturbed by "unnatural" desires and searching for others who, like herself, were possessed of a distinction that provided its own rationale for being "different." She sensed a oneness with their capacity for feeling an unprofaned love for another woman, while at the same time admiring the courage with which they pursued professions from which women previously had been barred.

$\mathcal{D}$uring earlier visits to England, Francis Marbury's charm and intelligence had won the friendship of many of the most distinguished intellectuals of the Victorian age: men such as Charles Darwin, John Tyndall, Thomas Henry Huxley, and Herbert Spencer. These agnostic scientists were challenging the myths of creation set forth in the Bible. Man was not created in the image of God but was simply the result of natural selection and what Spencer called "the survival of the fittest." It was fascinating, bewildering, certainly more than a little disturbing to Bessy, who, for all of her intellectual curiosity and omnivorous reading, was in many ways a religious naïf.

Almost as disquieting as the scientists was her one meeting with George Eliot, which occurred toward the end of her stay in England. Her father took her to one of Miss Eliot's Sunday at-homes, at 4 Cheyne Walk, on the Chelsea Embankment. That spring, the sixty-one-year-old writer had married John Cross, who was twenty-one years her junior, after having lived for twenty-four years happily and without benefit of clergy with a married man, George Henry Lewes. Bessy found her "rather austere and frightening," with an unattractive, angular face "redeemed in great measure by her wonderful eyes." What was impressive was the passion and honesty with which this homely woman had gone her own way until the marriage to Cross, which her admirers dismissed as "a common-place concession to public opinion; a sort of social aftermath which to them was colorless and unconvincing." Bessy could only have wondered if a woman like herself, a good deal less than a genius, would be allowed to live her life with an equal measure of honesty if not passion.

During the season of 1880, there was a notable loosening in the tight grip of middle-class morality in which Queen Victoria until then had confined her people. The roving eye of the Prince of Wales was making what came to be known as the "professional beauty" a creature to be reckoned with in London society. At the theatre and parties she attended with her father, Bessy's appreciation of the charms of these ladies was on a par with that of the heir to the throne. The sensation of that year was a young woman who was married to a man of neither social nor financial distinction. With beauty as her only asset, Lillie Langtry was determined to become the first among many in the future king's esteem. How well she succeeded is apparent in Bessy's description of her initial impact.

> I saw her for the first time at the opera. She came in rather late, when immediately all eyes were turned in her direction. The stage was forgotten. She stood for a moment wondrously fair and symmetrically slim. Her gown was of black net with tulle sleeves. There was neither paint nor powder on her face. Her complexion was literally like roses, the softest shade of pink and white. Her arms were very beautiful, in fact as she stood there, the target of concentrated admiration, it seemed to me that I had never seen anyone before who was quite so lovely.

Bessy found among the glorious English roses an assortment of American beauties to whom the prince often showed a marked preference: Lady Randolph Churchill (nee Jennie Jerome), Mrs. Arthur Paget (nee Minnie Stevens), and Lady Mandeville (nee Consuelo Yznaga). These young women originally had been sold into a socially acceptable form of white slavery. Contrary to the less acceptable varieties, it was the slaves who paid for their loveless bondage in contractually arranged large dowries. This was compounded when they found favor with the prince. Having little sexual use for them, the husbands happily made their brides available to Edward in exchange for such favors as invitations to the regal residence at Sandringham, commissions in the right regiments, the social prestige of being a part of the Prince of Wales set, or, best of all, a knighthood. The women experienced no retaliatory revenge for cuckolding their compliant mates, who obviously mistook the horns for some sort of royal decoration akin to the Order of the Garter.

Among Bessy's most memorable London evenings was attendance at a performance at the Lyceum Theatre, the home of the company of the most controversial actor-manager of his time. In the play performed on that memorable evening, Charles Reade's *The Lyons Mail,* this most contentious actor, Henry Irving, was appearing in the dual role of Dubosc and Lesurques. The controversy over Irving was not over whether he was a genius; even his severest critics were willing to grant him that. Francis Marbury could be counted among those detractors who did not think his genius justified bad diction and irritating mannerisms. His daughter was to be found in the opposing camp. She found the acting so overwhelming, so spellbinding, that Irving's eccentric elocution, peculiar gait, and the bizarre intonation of a not very powerful or musical voice actually contributed to the greatness of the performance. She was to see him in most of his great roles and eventually to work with him professionally. Her esteem for his histrionic powers never lessened even when they quarreled. On the other hand, she was never able to change her father's opinion that Irving was nothing more than an idiosyncratic ham. Another of Bessy's future clients, George Bernard Shaw, agreed with him.

Bessy returned home that autumn with no idea of what to do with the rest of her life. She could go on occupying the small hall bedroom on the third floor of her family's comfortable old house on Irving Place, but she had grown tired of doing nothing.

> I had the germ of independence in my system. Besides, my father, like thousands of others, had caught the get-rich-quick microbe. I wanted to have my own life-saver, in case of financial disaster, so I thought an anchor to the windward would be advisable, in other words, an individual bank account.

During her childhood holidays on her grandfather's farm, she had learned what there was to know about raising chickens and thought, here was an easy way to earn some money. Her plan may well have been inspired by the success of her good friend Sally Hewitt, who managed the family farm at Ringwood, New Jersey. Although their pursuits were dissimilar, the two young women were alike in the competence they brought to whatever they attempted. Sally was already a musician of close to professional skills, a crack shot, and a coachwoman of surpassing skill with the four-in-hand. In Bessy's case, the excellence was only beginning to be recognized.

The expanse of the McCoun-Marbury family acreage in Oyster Bay was a far cry from Bessy's cramped hall bedroom in Irving Place. The invention of the incubator solved her problem. There was just enough room at the foot of her bed for the one in which she invested her small capital. Her business was started in a freezing February in 1882. Having become a passionate devotee of John Ruskin during her stay in England, she regulated the temperature of the eggs in the incubator while devouring the pages of his *Sesame and Lilies*. The frost became so intense she carried the cumbersome incubator from room to room in search of sufficient warmth. When Bessy decided the only permanently warm place was against the steam housing in the one bathroom in the house, the collective temper of her family was frayed to the tearing point. No amount of tears or threats succeeded in persuading her to move the infernal contraption until after the first cheeps were heard. From one hundred eggs placed in the incubator, eighty-seven chicks survived and, when old enough, were carefully transported to the brooder waiting to receive them on the family farm. The initial good luck of the enterprise made her react "like the hayseed who first plays poker." On borrowed money that was eventually paid back, elaborate poultry yards were constructed, and in due time she was running what was considered a substantial poultry plant.

Her strong competitive streak found an outlet in exhibiting at poultry shows. At one show, out of thirteen entries she took nine first prizes and special awards. Her success at breeding chickens also bred romance. A few days after the show closed, a proposal of marriage was made by a forty-year-old widower who was a prosperous Connecticut breeder. Initially attracted by her success with chickens, he remarked that she looked to be a healthy young woman with a keen business sense who would make a practical help-mate for him. It was not exactly love's young dream, and she turned him down, later rationalizing: "Like many another girl over-confident of her charm, I thought I could marry whenever the spirit seized me. . . . More fool I! It was the last [proposal] that ever came my way."

She claimed that she never drove through a certain part of Connecticut without thinking she might have ended her days as a happy grandmother had she not been so "cock-sure" of her prospects. When real love came in the form of Elsie de Wolfe, she had no qualms about using her "keen business sense" to become "a practical helpmate."

CHAPTER SEVEN ॐ

As already has been observed, Elsie de Wolfe covered her tracks so well in accounts of her life, accurate chronology would always pose a problem. The calendar of the British court definitely placed Elsie in London in the spring of 1885 for her formal presentation to the queen. She claimed to have spent three years in Scotland prior to that and to have left the United States at the end of a summer, although her stint in amateur theatricals suggests that she left for Europe in the autumn of 1883.

Spending two years living with relatives abroad was more than sufficient for anything her mother had in mind. Her first stop in Scotland was a visit with her mother's uncle, Sir Alexander Anderson, who had been vice provost of Aberdeen before retiring to his country home some forty miles north, in Fraserburgh, where she went to spend a few weeks with him. Her only recollection was of "the garden where, because of the damp sea air, the heliotrope grew into the trees or clambered up to the very tops of the houses."

To hear Elsie tell of it, things barely improved when she journeyed south to stay with Sir Alexander's daughter, Catherine, and her husband, the Reverend Dr. Archibald Hamilton Charteris, who held the Chair of Biblical Criticism and Biblical Antiquities at Edinburgh University. He had earned his master's degree in his eighteenth year and was awarded an honorary degree of Doctor of Divinity before his thirty-third birthday. A year later, in 1868, he was named one of the royal chaplains ministering to Queen Victoria during her frequent stays at Balmoral Castle in Scotland. It was a singular honor. As he said: "It is a great thing to have upon the throne of this kingdom and empire, a sovereign who appreciates the Presbyterian service and loves the Church of Scotland. She is the first sovereign of whom this can be said."

Adding a melodramatic flourish to her Elsie-as-Cinderella act, Elsie would remember "the rectory was cold and gloomy." In point of fact, the Charterises never lived in a rectory, for the good doctor was not attached to a church but to the university. They lived in a detached house, at 1 Salisbury Road, "Grecian in style" and surrounded by a garden. It stood in a prosperous suburb at the corner of the South Road, the main thoroughfare into Edinburgh and less than two miles from the city's fashionable center.

Her recollection of the two or three years she spent in the Scottish capital was of a time of bleak austerity, of a cold, unrelenting dreariness. Obviously, she failed to notice that the beauty of this city, so exemplary of the classic style of Robert Adam, influenced her own taste for the rest of her life. The Adam designs were considered by many experts to be the inspiration for the Louis XVI furnishings she would later urge on her clients.

In truth, it was not the city but her hosts who were apposite to her inclinations. She dismissed them as "kindly people but austerely Scotch [sic]. Life . . . was a hair shirt, storing up recompense in a remote heaven." She was not completely wrong. As if to underscore his distaste for all his cousin-in-law reveled in, the evangelical reverend had proclaimed during the same year she arrived under his roof: "*Materialism* may be taken as the basis or the source of all the opposition with which Christianity has to contend in our day."

There was, however, much more to the Charterises than the well-intended dourness that Elsie deplored in them. Duncan Campbell, one of

Archibald's students, observed that his lectures "breathed a delightful spirit. . . . He is amazingly young in appearance, is quite boyish, indeed . . . I think his appointment must have attracted a good number of students. . . ."

Duncan's impressions of a visit to 1 Salisbury Road were also at odds with Elsie's recollection of "hair-shirt" humorlessness:

> Dr. and Mrs. Charteris were both very pleasant under their own roof-tree. His manner is exceedingly suave, Mrs. C. is very smart and lively. She is always poking fun at her husband, whom she styles "Archibald," "Professor," "dear child," indiscriminately. Mrs. Charteris is one of those women who can make themselves agreeable without an effort.

The Charterises were childless. There had been a series of young women who over the years had played the role of adopted daughter. This might explain why they had agreed to have Elsie for what was an exceedingly long stay even in those days of extended visits. Catherine Charteris was an amiable woman, and her new charge intuitively knew the art of ingratiation; they must have gotten on exceedingly well. Elsie had an almost chameleon-like gift for adaptability. In the Charteris home she took up religion as a discipline leading to conformity if not salvation. She would later claim a major reason for her spiritual awakening to the glories of the Church of Scotland was one she shared with the queen of England: a fascination with Dr. Archibald Charteris, who was "handsome beyond any adolescent's dream of a romantic hero."

Charteris was by no means an unworthy object of the adoration of a young woman who must have been considering a future of alternatives to marriage. In his own way, he was a feminist. Elsie surely took part in the Young Women's Guild organized under his guidance as the equal of the Young Men's Guild. It was his idea to make the deaconesses the peers of the deacons.

> We do not suggest mere honorary ranks and names; but we seek to associate an office with actual service. . . . It is proved in the experience of Christendom in our day that as helpers of their ministers in parochial work, women do far more than men; and there is a practical need of recognizing and organizing what the church thus thankfully accepts. . . . Every minister working among a large population would be overwhelmed if the female members of his congregation did not come to his aid.

Had the man who made those statements been alive one hundred years later, he would surely be among those endorsing a ministry open to women. In his own time, he inveighed the Presbyterian Church to train women as missionaries exactly as it trained its men. How Elsie's imagination must have been fired, when this Christian Adonis espoused his belief that "every minister who has ever sought to engage a Bible-woman must have longed for one who could be certified as having proved herself as competent in a field similar to his own"!

Visions of herself as a dedicated missionary more than likely prompted Elsie to write to her mother during this period, "A few more years of my frivolous outlook in life and I would have been a ruined woman."

The thought of her daughter spending the rest of her life among the savages would certainly have been enough to arouse Georgiana de Wolfe to remove her daughter from the handsome doctor's influence. She prevailed upon Catherine Charteris to urge her husband to arrange that Elsie be presented at the last court Queen Victoria would ever hold in London. Catherine would have to accompany her, as it was necessary for somebody previously presented to the monarch to present the new honoree.

Georgiana forwarded enough money to give Elsie a season in London before the girl was too old for it to make a difference. The elegant shops of Princes Street awaited, and in them the gorgeous paraphernalia that would replace the woolens as well as the existence that had made her twitch for so long.

> My days were a whirl from shop to shop . . . silk stockings for evening wear, and fine lisles for every-day. There was handkerchief linen underwear and a real corset of white brocade, and Swiss embroidery corset-covers and voluminous petticoats starched until they could stand alone, and dresses of silk and satin and mousseline de soie and soft cashmere, tucked and ruffled and shirred in the styles of that day. There were hats, too, for every hour, and high-heeled shoes of kid and satin, and boxes of kid gloves of different lengths.

Elsie summed up the whole glorious change in two simple words: "Life began."

*E*lsie's presentation did not take place until May 13, 1885, which represented a financial saving for her mother. By then the social season was almost half over, reducing by that much the considerable expenses of even the most modest of entries into society. No ball would be given in her honor nor would a house, servants, and equipage be engaged. Mrs. Charteris rented modest chambers in a respectable neighborhood convenient to Mayfair and Belgravia, the areas where most of the great entertainments took place.

The thirteenth was mercifully cool and overcast. Elsie was up well before seven on the memorable morning. It would take at least two hours to dress, and the coach was called for nine, anticipating two hours of crawling traffic on the short but snarled official processional route that ran from the Admiralty Arch down the Mall, along St. James's Park, to Buckingham Palace.

The actual costume worn for a presentation at court was as ritualistic as the ceremony. A recent bride traditionally wore her wedding dress, which went well with the elaborate and expensive bouquets all honorees were required to carry. By the time one of the official court hairdressers arrived, Elsie had bathed and was wearing a wrapper over the heavily boned corset into which she had been laced, nipping in her waist and plumping up her breasts to give the illusion of more cleavage than she thought possible considering her modest endowment. The maid did up the dozens of hooks and eyes on her white satin gown, trimmed with seed pearls and having yards of heavy train trailing behind it. Finally she was ready for the crowning touch. The traditional three white ostrich plumes, symbolic of the Prince of Wales, were attached by a jeweled band to the back of her head, with a white tulle veil cascading down from it to become one with the train of her dress.

Before departing for the palace, Elsie gazed at her image in the pierglass. It was a moment of transcendent joy. She could scarcely believe it. The reflection was not of a great beauty. But for the first time her heart could fairly sing: "I am not ugly. I need never be ugly again!"

At the palace the women bearing the deadweight of heavy trains were herded like so many overdressed oxen through a succession of rooms known as "the pens." At length, they approached the door to the Drawing Room. A gentleman-in-waiting lifted the train from the arm of a bedazzled Elsie and splayed it behind her. The gentleman passed her card to the lord chamberlain, who in roaring tones splashed her name over the murmuring, undulating crowd.

"Miss Ella Anderson de Wolfe."

And in she floated amid a glittering panoply of fabulously garbed, bejeweled women and men in a bewildering array of uniforms representing the staggering number of companies in the empire's service; all this under the flickering glare emanating from a parade of enormous candlelit crystal chandeliers in a vast chamber shrouded against the day by drawn damask draperies. There were 392 men and women presented on that dreary Wednesday. With varying degrees of accuracy, most would remember for the rest of their lives this event that consumed at most two minutes of one morning.

On a raised dais at the far end of the room sat "a little fat queen in a black dress and a load of jewels, with a wide blue ribbon across a wide bosom, smiling and nodding on her throne." It was doubtful the queen recognized the name as that of her beloved Scottish chaplain's cousin, or that anybody else took any note of the girl a bit past her prime and not of noteworthy family or looks.

*E*lsie's love of acting started when she was a child and continued until the end of her long life. When a stage wasn't available, a living room would do. Her performing was born neither of a need for artistic expression nor of uncluttered exhibitionism: it would always be her means of access. Soon after her presentation at court, auditions were called for an amateur charity production of Douglas Jerrold's comedy *The White Milliner* at the Criterion Theatre, in Piccadilly Circus. Trying out was a chance worth taking and would tend to substantiate the claim that she did indeed have some experience with performing in New York. She got the part; it did not matter that it was not a great part, for it was neither a great play nor a great production. The significant thing was that her colleagues came from the upper echelons of society. The door opened a little. Her gift for ingratiating herself, coupled with an innate style, was sufficient to allow her to squeeze through.

In an example of social water seeking its own level, the only lasting friendships she made were with two other American women, playing the same game but far more successfully. One, Mrs. Paran Stevens, was richer and better connected, but the other, Mrs. James Brown Potter, was much more beautiful. Leaving Elsie in the care of these two married and well-connected women, Mrs. Charteris returned to Scotland, deeming her responsibility for the young woman at an end.

Elsie had used all of her considerable gifts to insinuate herself with Stevens and Brown Potter, social gifts summed up in what would become one of the guiding principles of her life: Be pretty if you can, be witty if you must, be attractive if it kills you.

CHAPTER EIGHT ❧

Marietta Reed Steven's husband, Paran, was the man who was responsible for turning the Fifth Avenue Hotel into the grandest hostelry in New York City, and for as long as he lived, she was the queen of that commercial palace. So brassy was her hair, so handsome her profile, so gregariously vulgar her wit and generous her nature, it was little wonder legends grew up around her. She was less than half Paran's age and rumored to have been one of his chambermaids before he married her.

Marietta was actually the daughter of a fairly well-to-do greengrocer of Lowell, Massachusetts. Maintaining a townhouse at 244 Fifth Avenue, as well as a cottage in Newport, Marietta crashed into society.

Farther up Fifth Avenue, Mary Mason Jones was surely a Jones with whom it was worth keeping up. In the case of real estate, these women actually had greater insight into the residential needs of the middle and upper classes than many of the booming city's larger landowners. Within a year of her marriage, in 1817, Mrs. Jones was speculating by building a house, at 122 Chambers Street, which was the first to use gaslight and featured the brazen innovation of a permanently installed bathtub. It was sold at a great profit, which she parlayed in building investments ever upward, both financially and geographically, during the more than half-century that followed.

Marietta Stevens and Mary Mason Jones appreciated the city for what they could get out of it. In ways tempered by their different backgrounds, they were enthusiastic players of the New York game but neither mistook it for the *only* game on earth. Giving the lie to the generally held perception that it was only the nouveau riche who went after titles for their heiresses, the socially entrenched Mary Mason Jones acquired one for her daughter, and one of her granddaughters married the Comte de Maleisaye, which leads to an interesting piece of literary gossip.

Mrs. Jones's niece Edith Jones Wharton depicted Mary Mason as Mrs. Manson Mingott, and Marietta as Mrs. Lemuel Struthers, in her novel *The Age of Innocence.* The novelist must have recognized the similarities between the two women, for she substituted the background of Mrs. Stevens for that of her aunt in the book's portraits of them. Parenthetically portraying the reaction of "old New York" to the rise of vulgarians, represented by Mrs. Struthers, the central plot revolved around the return of the American-born Countess Olenska to live with her ancient and ailing grandmother, Mrs. Manson Mingott. In their real lives just as in the novel, the Comtesse de Maleisaye came home to stay with her dying grandmother, Mary Mason Jones.

*T*he novels of Edith Wharton and Henry James were largely responsible for inventing the myth of "old and "new" New York. The writers were seeking some American equivalent of the provincialism rampant in the upper or titled classes of Europe in which Napoleonic titles sought to invade the bastions of the ancien régime and the newly ennobled English industrial revolutionaries bought the estates of Tudor baronets. Ensuing social historians have grasped the Jamesian and Whartonian fictions as truths in their search for standards by which to judge the amorphous town. New York was of much too recent a vintage: it took centuries for European provincialism to become entrenched, and it festered best inland, away from the coast. The new city was a great seaport open to the influences from every corner of the earth, and thus much too worldly not to keep evolving. As the waves of the Atlantic daily altered parts of its shoreline, so the waves of immigration daily changed its social structure.

Wharton was like all the great New York women since its founding. She invented herself and her background by implying that her Rhinelander, Schermerhorn, and Jones relations were "old" New York, which they were only in the sense of having been in the city for three or four generations, though not in its society for that length of time. In the 1780s the Schermerhorns were ship chandlers and the Rhinelanders ran a German bakery. During that period, who was "in society" was determined by whose names appeared on Mrs. John Jay's "dinner and supper list." There was neither Schermerhorn nor Rhinelander, although there was one Jones, who may or may not have been related. The former did not appear until a Schermerhorn became *the* Mrs. Astor, and her minion, Ward McAllister, compiled his list of the Four Hundred, which included Edith's brother and niece. That was a century later.

*I*n 1871, Marietta's daughter, Mary (Minnie) Stevens, turned eighteen and was ready to make her debut. It was the event toward which all of her mother's conniving and pushing had been directed. The girl had everything going for her to make a brilliant match: striking beauty, charm, grace, wit, and intelligence, to say nothing of a handsome dowry. Her mother was ready to swing into action when her father became seriously ill. Good taste mandated a postponement of the formal festivities. This was the first of a series of catastrophes that would have daunted a lesser person.

When Paran Stevens finally did die, in 1872, the loss was of greater consequence than that of a husband and father. The loss was of a prime piece of real estate. For all the years he ran it, he held only a lease on the Fifth Avenue Hotel, which was canceled at his death. The premises were no longer available to Marietta for a great ball to introduce her daughter to society.

In the years immediately preceding his death, Stevens had speculated so heavily in real estate, there were not sufficient funds in the accounts to cover his wife's legacy. She was the leading creditor as well as the executrix of his estate. In that dual capacity, she took charge of the administration of the considerable Stevens properties.

In 1869, Richard Morris Hunt was starting his illustrious career when Rutherfurd Stuyvesant commissioned him to design the first New York building of French flats, or apartments. The Stuyvesant Apartments were located at 142 East Eighteenth Street, and within a short time they were a success, renting to some very distinguished people, including the actor Edwin Booth and the publisher George Putnam, many of whom had wearied of brownstone living. Soon after, Paran Stevens commissioned the architect to design something similar for a parcel he had assembled running from Fifth Avenue to Broadway, along the south side of West Twenty-seventh Street. The Stevens Flat House was completed only a short time before his death.

When the widow took charge of the flat building, she found the apartments were not renting quickly enough to pay expenses, much less satisfy her need for quick cash. Something had to be done. It occurred to her that many single women and widows, to say nothing of bachelors, found the thought of any kind of housekeeping odious. Why not offer them the alternative of what could be called an apartment-hotel? As in apartment buildings, the flats would be furnished by the lessees and include a salon, dining room, library, bedrooms, and bath, but in place of a kitchen there would be a service pantry. A first-rate restaurant would be on the premises, and meals could either be taken there or be ordered up to be served in one's suite. There would also be maid service available for the housekeeping chores.

The building was renamed for another formidable woman, the Victoria Apartment-Hotel. From the outset, it was a rousing success. Mrs. Paran Stevens had invented a style of urban living that would retain its popularity until the end of World War II.

Marietta was ready to make her next move. The first order of business was to get her twelve-year-old son, Harry, out of the way. He was a delicate child and would only be an encumbrance. She entered him in St. Mark's School, probably rationalizing that the hearty life led by its students would give him some necessary fiber. That child disposed of, she could turn all of her attention to the other, her beloved, beautiful Minnie, whose lustrous green eyes were not yet hard, but, with her mother's connivance, soon would be.

London was the logical place to begin. She had a powerful contact dating back to 1859, when the Prince of Wales had stayed at her husband's Fifth Avenue Hotel during his New York visit. At the time Marietta had been a handsome young woman who had made herself agreeable and quite possibly available to him. The connection with His Royal Highness had been kept alive through the years. The Stevens women arrived in London in time for the season of 1872, and word went out from the palace that the royal personage would deem it a personal favor if they were invited to all of the festivities. With sprays of shimmering jet and jeweled embroidery, M. Worth turned their mourning garb into gowns of glittering allure.

Minnie became the first of a string of American beauties who would captivate the prince. When and if she became his mistress remained a subject of conjecture. Beyond doubt was the fact that she retained his loyalty and affection for as long as he lived. Wanting to keep her where he could literally or figuratively lay his hands upon her, he nominated his subaltern and friend Captain Arthur Paget as a matrimonial candidate. He was officially the keeper of the prince's game and turf books and unofficially rumored to be his panderer and bookmaker.

Marietta Stevens would have none of it. Arthur was a good-looking, amiable enough young fellow but hardly what she had in mind for her beautiful daughter. He was the son of General Alfred Lord Paget, which sounded better than it was. The general was a life peer. The title did not pass down. Arthur was also the grandson of the Marquess of Anglesey, but that title would pass to the young man's uncle and cousin. Without a title in sight, the only other thing to recommend him would have been a fortune. Alas, the Pagets were all fortune hunters. Arthur's brothers Almeric and Sidney would both marry New York heiresses, respectively Pauline Whitney and Marie Dolan. Even his uncle, the future Marquess of Anglesey, would marry the Georgia heiress Minna King, also know as Minnie. A third marriage for him and second for her, it did not take place until the day after he officially assumed the title. Minnie King was no fool; if she was buying a title, she wanted to make certain she got it.

Mrs. Stevens paraded her daughter through the courts of Europe. It was to no avail. Minnie wanted Arthur Paget and only Arthur Paget, just as he wanted only her. It was that Victorian novelty: a love match. Despite being desperately in need of a rich wife, he had remained unattached and faithful to his sweetheart for six long years, before her mother finally relented and allowed the engagement to be announced.

There was little choice. Her daughter was twenty-five and, for all her natural endowments, in danger of remaining a spinster unless permitted to marry the only man she really wanted. Minnie had her own income, and after Mrs. Stevens paid for the initial expenditures for a house, furnishings, and carriage, the couple would have to live on it, for the groom was hopeless about augmenting it beyond the occasional gambling win, which was more often than not offset by the occasional gambling loss.

Ever resourceful, the young (as a wife, she was still young; as a single woman, she was not), beautiful Mrs. Paget had learned a great deal about negotiating with titled prospective husbands from watching her mother's maneuvers. She decided to put that knowledge to good use and went into the matchmaking business in an unofficial way, using her popularity as a hostess to cover her tracks. Her home became famous as a place for well-born but impoverished British layabouts to meet American heiresses in search of husbands or, in some cases, lovers. If the desired result was achieved, Minnie received a commission in the form of an expensive gift that could readily be converted into cash. Another source of revenue was the procuring of a presentation at court or introduction to the Prince of Wales, arrangements with which dear royal Bertie went along; it provided such an inexpensive way of indulging the lovely and probably compliant Minnie. His little darling's entrepreneurial ventures were so successful she could soon afford to pay her bills at Worth and her husband's debts and take a house in Belgrave Square, one of the most fashionable addresses in London.

Throughout this period, the beleaguered Marietta Stevens was having to cope with another problem. Her only son, Harry Leyden Stevens, had contracted tuberculosis and could no longer be kept at school. Occupied with marrying off Minnie and unable to go to him, she sent for him to come to England. By one knows not what stratagems, this extraordinarily resourceful woman managed to get an adolescent not yet out of prep school accepted at Oxford. His health did not permit that to last for long. She wasted no time in shipping him off to Switzerland for a stay at one of the many Alpine sanitariums devoted to the cure of tuberculars.

When Harry returned to England in 1879, Marietta reappraised her son. The sickly youth was gone; in his place was a robust, strikingly handsome young man. His new athletic prowess was evident in the skill with which he mastered lawn tennis at his sister's country house. Bringing the necessary equipment home with him, he introduced the game to Newport on a court he set up on the grounds of his mother's cottage. It was one of the few sports young men and women could play together and an immediate success.

That summer of 1880, Harry met and fell in love with young Edith Jones, who seemed to reciprocate his feeling. It was a good match from the point of view of the Joneses, who were hardly wealthy enough to support their airs, let alone their heiresses. The one hitch was Harry's high-spirited and pushy mother. Lucretia Rhinelander Jones was simply not secure enough in her own position to accept Marietta Reed Stevens. In any contest in assertiveness, the mothers would have been on a par. With a vulgarity equaling Marietta's, Lucretia liked to fancy herself *the* Mrs. Jones in competition with her husband's first cousin, *the* Mrs. Astor. They also shared the bond of having married for money rather than for love. In matters of taste in clothes and decor, both opted for the extravagantly ostentatious rather than the elegantly discerning. Lucretia, with her passion for cheap novels, was if anything more the Philistine than Marietta, who genuinely loved good music. Both ladies cruelly tried to break their daughters' spirits if not their hearts. They were too much alike to have been compatible in-laws, but that was not the real reason that the engagement of Harry and Edith was broken before it was officially announced despite the fact that the young people were obviously in love. The breakup was attributed to Mrs. Stevens, Lucretia Jones having been won over by the gentle Harry's solicitude at the time of her husband's death.

Some said the Joneses and Rhinelanders had been rude to her one time too many, and she was determined not to allow her son to be allied with them. But she was much too skilled a player to allow a slight to stand in the way of a good match that could only advance her social standing with *the* Mrs. Astor.

Money was also mentioned as a motive for her hostility. She retained control of the income from her son's inheritance of over $1,250,000 until he either married or turned twenty-five, whichever happened first. Undeniable as it was that Marietta was constantly in need of money, she seemed to have been able to extract sufficient funds to support her glamorous lifestyle from her position as executrix of the entire trust, without ruining her son's future happiness. Harry was slightly less than two years short of twenty-five, and she would surely not have stood in his way for such an insignificant extension of the period of her financial control over him. If it was only that, she could have made up for the time lost by insisting on a long engagement.

She was aware of something his physical appearance belied: Harry remained a seriously ill young man who should not marry unless the young woman was made aware of the situation, and he apparently never had informed the Joneses, or things would not have gone as far as they did. Tuberculosis was very much in the news during that year of 1882. Robert Koch was making headlines all over the world with his discovery of the cause of the disease. The many stories underscored how easily it was transmitted, that there was no cure, and that early death was almost certain. Fear of contagion became so widespread that landlords would not rent houses to the families of victims. Marietta undoubtedly informed the Joneses of her son's condition, and marriage to Edith became out of the question.

Harry Stevens died in Newport less than three years later. It would have been highly romantic to attribute his passing to a broken heart, but it was more accurate medically to call it what it was: the incurable tuberculosis of his youth. His estate passed to his mother and sister, neither of whom was with him at the time of his death. By then, Edith Jones, already married to Edward R. Wharton and far away, embarked upon the incessant travel that marked Edith Wharton's married life, as if, in the words of Tennessee Williams, she was "attempting to find in motion what was lost in space."

On a lovely spring day in 1885, Mrs. Paran Stevens was out in her victoria for a ride around Washington Square when she happened upon pretty young Cora Brown-Potter. It was no news that Mrs. Potter's marriage was on the verge of collapse. The older woman was about to depart for London and the pleasures of its social season. It occurred to her that the charming and gifted amateur actress would make a wonderful traveling companion. Cora demurred, explaining she had no money of her own for travel nor could she get any from her husband or his family. That was no problem: she would be taken on the trip as Mrs. Stevens's guest. With her marriage in a shambles and nothing to keep her in New York, the young woman gratefully accepted the invitation.

When Elsie de Wolfe began to court them during her London season, Stevens and Brown-Potter were staying at the Berkeley Hotel at the bottom of the Green Park end of Piccadilly, which was still a fashionable residential street lined with the townhouses of the aristocracy. It was not long before she was spending more time in their rooms at the smart hotel than in her own modest chambers.

One of the traits that would be immeasurably helpful throughout her future professional life was her ability to get along with difficult and spoiled women, especially the great beauties, knowing when and how to flatter them. Aware of her own comparatively modest endowments, she allowed herself to be used as the measure by which their beauty was enhanced. Like any good supporting actress, she knew precisely when to exit, leaving the star alone bathed in the becoming baby-pink spotlight.

In an example of that quid pro quo with which social climbers often help each other along, Mrs. Stevens helped Cora to have a brilliant season in London. In return, luster was added to her patroness's position when the younger woman met and conquered the Prince of Wales. She turned that trio of beauties—Jennie Churchill, Consuelo Mandeville, and Minnie

Paget—into a quartet of American mistresses to the future English monarch. It was then that Cora made up her mind never to return to her husband again. With the prince's patronage, Cora made her professional debut the following spring as the star of Wilkie Collins's play *Man and Wife*, at the Haymarket Theatre in London.

With all of this going on, it was no wonder Mrs. Stevens could not tear herself away simply because her son was dying, nor could Cora waste any time worrying about the infant daughter she had left behind in New York. Spring lapsed into summer. Elsie and Cora did not sail for New York until the end of August. Elsie must have wondered what awaited her at home. She was a very different woman from the one who had left, more poised and sophisticated, with a much higher degree of self-esteem. She had learned a great deal from her traveling companion about the strategies to which a woman might resort when forced to make her way in the world equipped with only one asset—herself. On the long voyage across the Atlantic, she was being prepared to take over the small place Cora had made in New York's social world, now that the latter was moving on to the world of the professional theatre. In that, too, Elsie would be learning from her, watching from the wings to see how she fared, how society reacted to one of their own becoming an actress.

Elsie needed to make her way in the world. By then it was clear there would be neither legacy nor advantageous match for her. Cora could give some advice, but their situations were not analogous. Elsie would not be leaving behind a husband and child. She would never receive the royal patronage her stunning colleague had. Her talent, if there was any, would have to suffice.

CHAPTER NINE ॐ

Both Bessy Marbury and Elsie de Wolfe returned to New York from Europe at the end of that summer of 1885. Bessy had been away only on a comparatively short holiday and saw no change in the city. Elsie had been gone for three years and was far more sensitive to the looks of places and what they indicated about the people living in them.

If Mary Mason Jones had pioneered the return to white marble with her Row, the Willie K. Vanderbilts' château clearly heralded the death of the brownstone age. With the uniform drabness beginning to lift from her native city, perhaps a concomitant flexibility was loosening its caste strictures sufficiently for Elsie to find a place "in society," which at that time seemed to be her ultimate goal. How she thought she would maintain that place, once achieved, is a matter of speculation.

Elsie's new mentors, Marietta Stevens and Cora Brown-Potter, insisted a marriage to or liaison with a man of wealth and/or position was the key to how high a woman could rise in the only world that counted for them. Where relationships with men were concerned, they implied love was a nice dividend, but capital investment was the certain way for him to increase a woman's status. If her man had only wealth, as was the case with Marietta Reed, Elsie would have to use her unflappable gall to make a social position for them. If he had only position, her ingratiating charm would be necessary to maintain it as well as use it to their advantage. Cora took the lead in guiding her along what everybody agreed was the right path.

The De Wolfes were then living in the narrow, overdecorated, over-crowded brownstone on West Thirty-fourth Street over which Elsie had wrongly claimed to have had a fit of hysterics as a child. The hysteria, if displayed overtly, was over returning to this insufficient home that stood practically in the shadow of the soot-strewing Sixth Avenue Elevated Railway and with the Thirty-fourth Street trolley clattering by on the cobblestone street night and day, so that the noise of her growing brothers inside was matched by the noise of train and trolley outside. The only oasis of quiet could be found in the drab brown Presbyterian church across the street, in which the family worshiped.

Far removed from the ambience of the Charteris house in graceful Edinburgh or London's elegant Berkeley Hotel, it possessed the one questionable advantage of being only little more than one block removed from *the* Mrs. Astor's mansion on Fifth Avenue. This was closer than the family ever before had lived to the city's best address, but they were still across Sixth Avenue in the tawdry Tenderloin district. In Europe, Elsie had found her champions, and she intended to use them to move to that world away, east of the El.

Cora Brown-Potter was returning to London almost immediately to try her luck in the professional theatre. She had no intention of coming back to New York except as a star. Like an abdicating queen naming her successor, she designated Elsie to take her place as the leading lady of the amateur theatre. Her protégée's talent and style made Cora's job easy, and Miss de Wolfe rapidly established herself as one of the best known of the amateur performers.

The amateur theatre of that time had a charm related to but different from the legitimate stage. Another of its leading lights, Rita Lawrence, later recalled its special magic.

> We rehearsed at night after the professional plays were over. Oh, the beauty of the night rehearsals! One sat up waiting until the audience had left, and then while the theatre was full of the throb and atmosphere of the professional life, the real art that we were dimly copying, we began our rehearsals.

Cora knew that if Elsie was to get on, something more than an amateur production was required. Married or single, a young woman of no means needed a prominent older protector if she was to succeed in the business of high society. Mrs. Brown-Potter had learned that lesson the hard way, from personal experience.

*B*y the time James Brown-Potter had brought the New Orleans beauty Cora Urquhart to New York after their honeymoon, it was clear to her that marrying him had been a terrible mistake. The only thing worse than her husband's weakness was his lack of fortune.

A patron had to be found, and quickly. She scanned the horizon, and it was not long before she was cruising New York Bay aboard Pierre Lorillard III's yacht, the *Reva*. The Lorillard family was so rich from tobacco and snuff that the word *millionaire* had been coined to describe the first Pierre, the grandfather of Cora's Pierre.

By the end of 1885, having found her Prince of Wales, she was ready to move on and had anointed Elsie as her successor with Lorillard. The piquant face of the charming newcomer may not have been as pretty as

Cora's, but it was fresher, and the still vigorous middle-aged man was not uninterested in his mistress's intimation that Elsie was prepared to become her replacement. Becoming an older millionaire's young protégée meant no less then than it did subsequently. In almost all instances she became his mistress. Elsie was probably a virgin when she first met Lorillard . . . and by no means an impatient one. Years later, Elsie confided to her friends James Amster and Robert Moyer that she always had been frigid. She told Moyer: "The one thing I've always loathed above all else is to be touched by somebody. I can't stand being handled like an object." Her eyes twinkled as she added, "Even an objet d'art."

Lorillard was an autocrat and, at the time they met, in the process of completing what could be considered his own demesne, Tuxedo Park. His architect, Bruce Price, described his intractable ways: "He talked rapidly and thought twice as fast as he talked and wished his orders carried out with a speed that equaled the sum of both."

Elsie had no doubt he was a "a dictator in his own right." As lord of the manor, he would more than likely insist upon his droit du seigneur. His "cold and exacting eye" put her off, but he could be the one who would escort her into the world she longed to enter. Ultimately, she might have no other recourse than to accept Lorillard while longing for a protector of a different sort.

*C*ora later claimed the idea for the club was hers. Lorillard, who hated assets that were not increasing in value, was complaining about not knowing what to do with a large parcel of land he owned in the Ramapo Hills, in Orange County, New York. It was later alleged to be anywhere from 6,000 to 600,000 acres, depending upon who was doing the reporting. The actual size was a little over 2,300 acres, which was big enough for any spread that close to civilization, larger than most European duchies and some principalities. It included a sizable and picturesque lake called Tuxedo, which was as close as the Anglo tongue could get to the Indian name Ptuck-sepo.

Cora asked, "Why not turn it into a fashionable and exclusive club?"

"What a sound idea," Lorillard replied. "It is more than an idea: it is an inspiration." Sound was the operative word. Sound as a dollar. The shrewd young lady had hit upon the only thing to do with the worthless property that would make it profitable: turn it into a club so exclusive people could not afford to not join. Next, Cora had to help him make it a success by signing up the men she originally had met through him and the many more she subsequently had met through them. She wrote to 150 men she knew intimately enough to invite them to become members, and before the first tree was felled, Lorillard had a membership described as "a guide to Who is especially Who in the Four Hundred."

In return for her help, Lorillard made Cora a present of a plot of land on which to build her own house. Her husband, Jim Brown-Potter, was not about to play the cuckold publicly by allowing people to surmise the house was a return for favors his wife had granted to Lorillard. He insisted the house and land be put in his name, and that he be made a charter member of the club. The house remained his even after the divorce, and on his death was left to his second wife. Cora sighed, "All my work for the Tuxedo Club went for nothing."

She had made a fool of her husband offstage and a spectacle of herself onstage, which resulted in her receiving no settlement or alimony at the end of her marriage, but she did not do badly. By the time she retired from her labors both on- and offstage, she had a handsome villa overlooking the Mediterranean, in Beaulieu-sur-Mer, and a more than ample amount in her bank account. How this could be accomplished was what her apt protégée, Elsie, wanted to learn.

The clubhouse was the pride of Tuxedo. Its crowning glory was the circular ballroom. It owed one striking feature to the insistence of Cora Brown-Potter. Opposite the entrance was a stage as well equipped as that of any small legitimate theatre. It was intended for amateur performance in general and specifically dedicated to the glorification of Cora's histrionic art. Unfortunately, she made her professional acting debut, in London, before the Tuxedo Club was ready for her.

The first play performed on it was a popular piece entitled *A Cup of Tea*. As Elsie was not only Cora's successor but already had performed her role in an Amateur Comedy Club production of the play, it was logical that she repeat it at Tuxedo.

During that autumn, Elsie was to become a fixture at the club, and her name began to appear regularly in the columns of *Town Topics,* which was devoted to the activities of society and might accurately be described as a popular *if* salacious combination of the contemporary *People* magazine and the *National Enquirer.* The publication gathered its dirt by bribing servants and tradesmen with cash, or by bribing fringe social characters with frequent and favorable mentions. It needed an informant at the new resort, and it is quite probable that Elsie got the job: there is no other reason why such a socially obscure amateur actress suddenly should begin to receive so much attention from the scandal sheet. Her new patron had placed her in a position to hear the latest dirt, and her well-guarded disdain for her new friends provided the rationalization for betraying them. As she later put it, perhaps being more autobiographical than intended, "It was at Tuxedo that I had my first glimpse of the ends to which women, and men too, will go to get into society."

What Elsie did in order to make a name for herself was not unusual. To this day it is the accepted way to get mentioned for those people nobody ever heard of except in "also present at" laundry lists in gossip columns, where their names appear as payment for the item.

$\mathcal{B}$essy Marbury was twenty-nine years old when she returned from Europe that autumn of 1885. Given her lack of means or striking looks, in addition to her independent spirit, there was little likelihood of her ever finding a husband or male lover if indeed she ever had wanted either. The pressure from her parents must have abated as they resigned themselves to the spinsterhood she was beginning to enjoy. All that remained was to find some means of earning a living that provided more than chicken feed and was more challenging than feeding chickens. She would then be free to shape her own life, or as free as a Victorian woman could be, which in one way was freer than contemporary women competing in the male work market. Having no access to that market, the Victoriennes were forced to invent whole new fields of endeavor for women, as Bessy and Elsie would do, or as Elizabeth Arden did a few years later by inventing a new industry. In their own businesses they would be second to nobody of either sex in authority and income.

These alternatives were not yet apparent in 1885, when Bessy began looking around for an occupation. Women could obviously make careers as actresses. They might go on to manage their own companies, if they had courage and intelligence as well as an adoring public. She knew she had what it took to be a manager but not the gift for acting, which seemed to be the only way a woman could achieve that end. It was galling. The frustration would remain until she was in a position to change that custom and in the process revolutionize the American theatre. In the meantime, she had to survive. Her father could be of little financial help, for until the day he died, he would believe a penny earned was tuppence spent. As did so many others of her class and generation, Bessy found an outlet for her love of the theatre in amateur productions. Her natural talents led to management and direction; it was in these capacities that she first met Daniel Frohman, who, along with his more famous younger brother, Charles, would contribute largely to the shape and success of her career.

In 1885, Daniel took over the Lyceum Theatre, which had been built that year on Fourth Avenue between Twenty-third and Twenty-fourth streets.

For a theatre to be successful in that era, it had to develop a regular audience of socially prominent patrons who, by their newsworthy presence at openings, would make it a place to see and be seen. He allowed Bessy to use his new theatre to stage amateur charity benefits on the assumption that the news would make the social columns, which were more important than the drama columns for the purpose of making the Lyceum fashionable. What Frohman could not have anticipated was the young woman's genius for "dressing a house" and turning an opening into a newsworthy event that could overshadow less than favorable reviews. It was a gift for which she would become legendary over the next forty years. One of Bessy's afternoons netted nearly five thousand dollars, which was considered a phenomenal take at the box office. Box office being a greater theatrical aphrodisiac than the mythical casting couch, Frohman became her champion.

*B*essy Marbury was staying at Tuxedo with her friends the Hewitts on the weekend on which *A Cup of Tea* was presented. Having sprained her ankle while dancing earlier that evening, she missed the performance. Elsie de Wolfe's own description of the high point would indicate she had not missed much. "In one scene, I had to faint on the sofa. In doing so, I took a double back roll onto the floor. This was considered very fine acting—"

The next day, the Hewitts could not stop talking about the new young actress. Along with the rest of Tuxedo, they probably also speculated about her relationship with Lorillard. It was all too much for Bessy. She had to get a glimpse of the paragon and insisted that a wheelchair be found to move her to the clubhouse that evening.

Bessy waited. Her considerable wit had garnered a circle of admiring females in which she was holding court. Suddenly, there was "a buzz of excitement when a slim, graceful young woman passed through the ballroom." Her slender appearance, her air of "French" distinction, were not the qualities to attract Bessy. To sum it up, Elsie was that worst of all things to the taste of a well-brought-up New York woman: she was continental. Bessy remarked: "I can't see anything to rave about in that lanky, black-eyed, black-haired little creature. Maybe, she can act, but—"

The two women did not get to know each other until Sally Hewitt invited both of them to a luncheon party she was giving, at the Cooper-Hewitt home on lower Lexington Avenue, in honor of Caroline Duer, who had just published a slim volume of sonnets. Caroline was one of the three remarkable Duer sisters who could trace their lineage back to Lord Stirling, one of the few noblemen in the original colonies. Following in the footsteps of

*L*adies and Not-So-Gentle Women

their poet mother, Elizabeth, all of the Duer women were "literary" and, for the time, "liberated." Elizabeth's granddaughter Alice Duer Miller became a very successful writer and wrote one of the very few narrative poems ever to become an international best-seller, *The White Cliffs of Dover,* which sold 125,000 copies in the United States alone. Caroline herself would later "suffer" a rather chic best-sellerdom via *Vogue's Book of Etiquette,* which she wrote after becoming a Condé Nast editor. Sister Katherine would marry the very rich but socially inferior Clarence Hungerford Mackay and become among the first New York society matrons to embrace the suffrage cause. When her daughter, Ellin, married Irving Berlin, the family was endowed with a good and astoundingly successful poet.

Elsie was asked to recite some of Caroline's poems. They dealt, if somewhat ambiguously, with what Lord Alfred Douglas later termed "the love that dared not speak its name." The verse that Elsie declared had aroused Bessy's interest began, "Sleep, tired eyes, the tender flame has fled." In it the narrator of undefined sex is crying out to a lover of equally undefined sex that their guilty love is worth it even if it means eternal damnation.

Elsie described the impression she made: "Elisabeth Marbury was pleased with the ardor with which I read it, and asked me to come and see her. Through her, I met many distinguished and important people and was in demand for private theatricals."

CHAPTER TEN ॐ

Many social historians have implied there was a revolution in New York City society in the early 1880s. What actually occurred was no more than a changing of the guard. A different set of women was issuing the most sought-after invitations, but the supporting cast to whom they was sent remained very much the same. The Paris-educated Beaux Arts architects Richard Morris Hunt and Stanford White were the architects as well as the interior decorators of choice. Worth continued to provide most of the costumes and Maryland went on shipping up its well-iced terrapin.

If the Seventies was the decade of the Astors, the years between 1883 and 1895 were the era of the Vanderbilts. Their dozen years of social greatness were bracketed by the great ball given by Mr. and Mrs. William K. Vanderbilt and their divorce. At the dawn of their era, when society and the women who ruled it were at their most virile, Alva Smith Vanderbilt, Willie K.'s wife, was positioning herself to become the new power in town. For a social leader she was rather young, only thirty-two, which was a novelty at the time. Her supporters spoke of her Paris education and her aristocratic, antebellum southern roots. With equal verity, her detractors pointed out that her mother ran a boardinghouse on déclassé West Forty-fifth Street between Broadway and Eighth Avenue. The most extraordinary thing to friends and foes alike was that this rather stocky, often ill-tempered pug-featured girl had managed to snare one of the world's most eligible young men. William K. Vanderbilt's father was called William H., and the son would be Willie K., both the best-looking and the most charming of all the Vanderbilts.

Alva married Willie on April 20, 1875, in James Renwick's Calvary Episcopal Church, which is still standing at Twenty-first Street and Park Avenue South. From that day forward, her prime objective was to change the way the Vanderbilts lived and conducted their affairs. One of her first steps was to take the role of Moses parting the Red Sea of Fifth Avenue to lead the Vanderbilts into the promised land of society. By the beginning of the 1880s, it was starting to look as if the family had decided to turn the west side of Fifth Avenue from Fifty-first Street to the entrance to Central Park into a Vanderbilt preserve. The two oldest daughters, Mrs. William B. Webb and Mrs. Hamilton McKown Twombly, led the way by purchasing two new brownstones at 680 and 684, respectively, next door to St. Thomas Episcopal Church and at the corner of Fifty-fourth Street. Located in the heart of that part of the avenue soon to be called Vanderbilt Row, St. Thomas's would replace St. Bartholomew's as "the Vanderbilt church" and be richly endowed by it in the same way St. George's had become wealthy as "the Morgan church."

As soon as his father, the old commodore, died, Alva's father-in-law, William Henry, bought the entire west side of Fifth Avenue between Fifty-first and Fifty-second streets, and commissioned John B. Snook, who recently had designed the first Grand Central Station for the family, to build a series of enormous brownstone mansions for himself and his two younger daughters, Mrs. Elliot F. Shepard and Mrs. William Sloane. Their massive stolidity made it clear the architect was more at home designing train stations than homes.

The race was joined between the two socially ambitious daughters-in-law, Alva and Cornelius II's wife, Alice. The small New York social world watched to see which would build the largest and most elegant Fifth Avenue mansion. The older son purchased several houses, including Effingham Sutton's brownstone, at the northwest corner of Fifty-seventh Street. With George B. Post as his architect, he planned to demolish them to erect his grand residence. Alva and Willie K. bought the land on the northwest corner of Fifty-second and Fifth, and with Richard Morris Hunt as their designer planned to build their château on it. Both wound up with houses that would have been more at home in the Loire River valley of France than the Fifth Avenue ravine of Manhattan. They split the honors in their race, with Alva's limestone by far the more elegant and Alice's red-brick and marble the larger. It would eventually grow to encompass the entire block to Fifty-eighth Street. By then, Alice had conceded taste to Alva and hired her sister-in-law's architect to design the extension.

Henceforth, Hunt would be the Vanderbilt architect of choice. The Vanderbilt name repeatedly cropped up in conversation and newspapers as the city watched, in awe, the gradual unfolding of the limestone colossus at 660 Fifth Avenue. Construction was started in 1880. Three years and more than three million dollars later, it was completed.

In January 1883, with her controversial mansion almost ready to be unveiled, Alva's social ambitions reached their closest approach to fulfillment. The Vanderbilts were the guests of *the* Mrs. Astor's chamberlain, Ward McAllister, at one of the series of ultra-exclusive Patriarch balls he had inaugurated at Delmonico's. He already had indicated to his patroness that the time of the Vanderbilts had arrived. The formidable lady had not been particularly receptive. What social distinction could come from building a vulgar white elephant of a house? It was an uncomfortably familiar pattern.

When the department store magnate Alexander T. Stewart built his elephantine white marble mansion across the street from her own more modest brownstone mansion, it was suggested the Stewarts had arrived. Not at *the* Mrs. Astor's doorstep, they hadn't! The merchant's social ambitions were forever squelched when that lady observed, "Just because one buys one's carpets from a man doesn't mean one has to allow him to walk upon them."

Alva prepared to strike back. Not only did she want to be on a par with *the* Mrs. Astor, she wanted to eclipse her, to become *the* Mrs. Vanderbilt. It was obvious from the curiosity they evinced at the Patriarch ball that most of the other social leaders were longing to get a peek at the inside of her new house. The William Kissam Vanderbilts would give a party to introduce it to them. More than a mere party, it would be an event to put to shame all others before it, the first of a series of balls that would fabulize the city's social history over the next eighty-three years. The last would be Truman Capote's black and white ball in 1963. Unique among McAllister's many successors in having an enduring talent that transcended a gift for gossip, Capote's great, malicious soul would have found in Alva's one of its true mates.

It became apparent by mid-January 1883 that the mansion would be ready to be viewed by mid-March. Nothing could be better, and Alva selected Monday evening, March 26, as the night for her party. No ball in the city's history had ever received so much coverage. It is not too much of an exaggeration to claim Alva invented modern social press agentry by freeing it of the snobbism imposed upon it by McAllister.

Receiving with the Vanderbilts would be their guest of honor, who was likewise worthy of several hundred yards of newsprint. In that town where the select few were spending the vulgar most on attempting to purchase the best European titles for their daughters, Lady Mandeville, whose husband was heir to the duke of Manchester, was an irresistible success story. Born Consuelo Yznaga, she belonged to a wealthy southern Cuban-American family and had been Alva's childhood friend. The relationship had been strengthened when Alva's sister, Jeanne, married Consuelo's brother, Fernando. In addition, the Vanderbilts' only daughter was Lady Mandeville's goddaughter and namesake.

By the time all of the expenses were totaled, the cost of the party came to $250,000, excluding help. At a very conservative evaluation, in contemporary currency this still makes it among the most expensive private parties in history. Was the enormous outlay of cash worth it to the host who was the often-overlooked hero of the occasion? One must hazard a guess that it was. Until that evening, he had been second among the Vanderbilt sons, a position that would eventually have proven financially punitive because of the family's tradition of primogeniture. After that triumphant evening, he was first among the Vanderbilts in New York society and the peer of his older brother, Cornelius, in his father's eyes, a fact that the old man officially acknowledged when he broke with family tradition and divided the bulk of his estate equally between Willie and Cornelius rather than leaving the lion's share to the latter.

The Vanderbilt guest list evinced a practicality with which Bessy Marbury would have empathized. Alva was a woman worth watching because she never lost touch with her aspirations. A fundamentally political person who was capable of changing with the times—it was this that set her apart from her adversaries. Ulysses S. Grant provided an example. He was among those she greeted respectfully despite being a southern woman whose father had been ruined by the general's victory.

As the daughter of a southerner with Copperhead sympathies, Bessy would have done no less. The man might have been an undistinguished drunk while in office, but he had been president of the United States. Despite the fact that *the* Mrs. Astor did not invite persons elected to *public* office because democracy simply did not fit into her scheme of things, having held the highest office in the land counted for something with the rest of New York society. Indeed, some of her closest friends went so far as to ignore all of Caroline's past annual balls and declare New York's last great party before Alva's was George Washington's inaugural ball.

Bessy must have heard all of the negative things said about Alva Vanderbilt. They were mostly by men railing against a woman who did not necessarily find them the preferred sex. There had to be something grand in a female about whom a multitude of men would find so many malicious things to say over a period of so many years. More noteworthy than male spleen was the fact that other women seldom found anything bad to say about Alva, including those with good reason to malign her. Even *the* Mrs. Astor would ultimately become one of her dearest friends and greatest champions.

 **CHAPTER ELEVEN** ৯৯

Samuel Stevens Sands, Jr., and his beautiful young wife Anne were a part of society without actually being *in* it. With the emergence of the new wealth, Ward McAllister found it convenient to split society into two necessary groups. The "nobs" were the wealthy old families who could trace their lineage back to the first settlers, while the "swells" were the new millionaires storming the social reefs on a rising tide of excess. McAllister believed a fusion of the two was what gave society its energy on the one side and elegance on the other. The Sands family had all of the qualifications necessary to be deemed nobs, while as swells the Oliver Harriman family made up in good looks and an inherent grace for what they lacked in the truly *big* money of the Vanderbilts and Anne's cousin, the new young railroad star Edward H. Harriman.

In 1881, the year after their marriage, Anne gave birth to their first son, George Winthrop, and the couple moved to the fashionable suburb of Riverdale, a wooded, hilly terrain offering magnificent views of the Hudson

River and Palisades. In those days it was the southwestern corner of West-chester County. Before the century was over, it would be incorporated into the Bronx and New York City.

The Harrimans had a summer place there when it was still a bucolic re-treat far from the city. Anne had lovely memories of childhood holidays along the Hudson, so much simpler than the vulgar ostentation of Newport, where her parents recently had bought a cottage.

It was the Vanderbilts who had turned Riverdale into a commuter's sub-urb. After they consolidated their New York Central Railroad with the Hud-son River Railroad, it became easily accessible to the city. The combination of clear, fresh air on its palisade and the verdant expanses tumbling down to the river offered a salubrious ambience in which to raise their families. The one drawback was that Sam Sands, an ardent equestrian, found the region too rugged to be good horse country. It did not offer that broad, flat expanse necessary for hunting or steeplechasing.

In 1884, Sam and Anne moved from Riverdale to Garden City, in Queens County, later Nassau, Long Island. The community had been founded in 1869 by the eccentric visionary Alexander T. Stewart, and would be the model for garden cities all over Europe, notably the one in north London. That was a remarkable year for the department store magnate. Construction was completed on his new block-long emporium from Ninth to Tenth Street on Broadway, as well as on the enormous white marble mansion at the corner of Fifth Avenue and Thirty-fourth Street that had drawn *the* Mrs. Astor's wrath down upon him.

Before 1869 was over, Stewart announced plans to build the first hotel in the country exclusively for working women. He knew the plight of his female employees and the awful conditions in which they were forced to live as women alone in the city. His intention was to establish a club-like atmosphere in which a sense of individuality and dignity could be fos-tered in fifteen hundred single working women at a fixed cost of two dol-lars a week including meals. Although a large part of the construction already had been completed, the depression of 1873 brought unprece-dented losses to the retail business, causing the project to be postponed in-definitely.

Stewart died in 1878, just as his hotel was finally being completed. His executor deliberately put the price of a room beyond the reach of most working women and closed it after less than two months of operation. He reopened it as the fashionable Park Avenue Hotel, boasting superior accom-modations for both men and women. The justification for going against the legator's expressed wish was that it was foredoomed to failure. Women wanted to associate with members of the opposite sex, and the restrictions imposed by a hotel for women discouraged even those few who might have wanted to live in that kind of communal atmosphere.

The abandonment of the women's hotel brought forth a storm of protests from leading feminists. A meeting was called at Cooper Union, where they signed pledges not to buy anything at the Stewart store for five years and to transfer their accounts to other stores. In sympathy with the cause, thousands of women from every conceivable background joined the first feminist boycott. They were so successful that Stewart's was out of business within four years.

*O*n Tuesday afternoon, February 16, 1888, Anne came to town on the new Long Island Rail Road trunk line. Sam and she had been invited to the housewarming that Mayor and Mrs. Abram Hewitt were giving at their residence, 9 Lexington Avenue. "Housewarming" was perhaps a misnomer, as the mansion actually had been built in the early 1850s by Mrs. Hewitt's father, Peter Cooper. The party was for the unveiling of the elaborate renovations that had been designed by the most promising young architect of the day, Stanford White.

The guests included Bessy Marbury and Elsie de Wolfe, along with the ubiquitous array of Vanderbilts, Fishes, Harrimans, Jays, Roosevelts, and Schermerhorns: the names that increasingly defined the society of the day. What greeted them as they alit from their carriages was an architectural revelation that would make a lasting impression on Elsie de Wolfe. She later took credit for innovating what she saw for the first time on that February afternoon, fifteen years before it occurred to her that she might become a decorator.

White had not only swept away the traditional brownstone high stoop but had also moved the entrance to the center of the mansion. The residence was entered on the street level through an etched glass panel door set in a portal of Doric columns. These simple changes converted a dour Victorian double brownstone into a graceful Georgian townhouse.

The afternoon's entertainment was provided by the Ladies Amateur Orchestra, organized by the Hewitt daughters. Although Reinhard Schmelz was the conductor and the one man among the thirty-two musicians, there was no doubt it was the first violinist, Miss Sally, who was the real leader of the band. Miss Nelly played the viola and was content to follow whoever led. Each of the socially prominent musicians wore a blue satin sash with a diamond ornament at the shoulder. One of the reporters present observed:

"The pretty girls composing it looked more than usually pretty with their violins tucked under their dimpled chins."

The Old Stager, in *Town Topics,* singled out Miss Sally for "her clearness of attack and the *brio* with which she colored the Magyar variations." He went on to wish each of the "blue-sashed angels more power to her wrist and a Stradivarius on her next birthday."

The next week, on Thursday afternoon, February 23, many of the same guests, including Anne Harriman Sands, were present for the first of two performances the orchestra gave for the benefit of the New York Skin and Cancer Hospital and the Sheltering Arms infirmity for poor children. On that occasion the New York *Press* was somewhat less flattering about the musicians: "As you got close to them, some of them did not look nearly so young or so pretty as they did on the stage, and as for their playing—well, that was for charity, and you know what charity covers."

Bessy was responsible for the show. It was she who had persuaded her good friend Miss Sally to allow her orchestra to give its first theatrical performance, ostensibly for the worthy causes noted. But Bessy's real purpose was to provide a showcase for Elsie's histrionic talents in a play that she had written for her. The social position of the women in the orchestra guaranteed great coverage of the event in the newspapers.

Bessy's play was a new version of an old French one-acter, *Je dîne chez ma mère,* by Decourcelle and Thiboust, which she retitled *Contrast.* In the program she claimed her work was "adapted from the French" rather than merely translated. It was the sort of piracy of French drama Bessy would almost single-handedly be responsible for stopping within a very few years.

Before embarking upon the production, Bessy had asked Daniel Frohman for the use of his Lyceum Theatre, on Fourth Avenue between Twenty-third and Twenty-fourth streets, for two matinees. She must have been extraordinarily persuasive, for he not only lent her the theatre but also donated the services of two of the leading actors in his stock company, Herbert Kelcey and W. A. Faversham.

What most impressed Frohman was the five thousand dollars Bessy raised for the charities. A self-made workaholic, slow to praise others, he was filled with admiration for her accomplishment. She had written the play, selected the cast, overseen the set and costumes, and convinced the orchestra ladies to appear in a public theatre, which was almost grounds for social ostracism. There was no aspect of the production that she had not overseen: superintending every rehearsal, assigning the dressing rooms, writing and placing the newspaper advertisements, and soliciting sponsors for the benefit theatre program. The New York *Press* further announced:

"Frohman is still puzzling his brain to find out her method of procedure. He says that if she would only accept a position in the business department of a theater, she should have the best place in the Lyceum."

The Brooklyn *Eagle* described her at that period as "a character in her way. Short, stout, and handsome, extremely clever and endlessly energetic." *Contrast* was not Bessy's first effort as a dramatist. The year before, she had written a satirical monologue, *An Afternoon Tea,* that had been given very successfully at another society matinee. But never before had she been so totally involved in a theatrical production.

In the year since the afternoon when Elsie gave her recital at the Duer home, Bessy and she had become best friends. Their intimacy was such that Bessy had visions of a professional as well as personal partnership in which she would write and produce vehicles that would make a star of her beloved friend. Writing, theatrical management, acting—these were among the very few occupations offering women handsome incomes and equality with their male colleagues.

Elsie's professional ambitions were also noted by the man from the *Eagle:*

> Miss De Wolfe's progress in that direction is marked, and it grows more rapid and decided day by day. It is so similar to Mrs. Potter's career that it looks as if the younger woman was setting her feet in the footprints left by Mrs. J. B. P. in her pilgrimage to the footlights. . . . I now undertake to assert that within the next twenty-four months, Miss De Wolfe will either have made her debut on the professional stage or be on the eve of doing so.

*L*ike many of the women in her set, Anne Sands probably had heard about a little volume entitled *Manners,* released later that year by the New York branch of the English publishers Cassell & Company, Ltd. It was the kind of book that might have been given as a present and handbook to the adolescent Annie Tracy Morgan. In a sober, soft binding and containing only 106 pages, it could easily be slipped into a lady's reticule and carried around for discreet referral. An index made it easy to locate the solution to any problem of politesse that might arise. A circumspect appeal to those with social ambitions was made by the endorsement printed in the flyleaf:

> The following ladies find this little handbook so carefully compiled and so accurate in detail that they find no hesitation in giving their support and endorsement. Mrs. Abram S. Hewitt, Mrs.

S. L. M. Barlow, Mrs. Chauncey M. Depew, Mrs. Theodore Roosevelt, Mrs. William Lane Booker, Mrs. Donald Cameron, Mrs. Burton N. Harrison, Mrs. Arthur M. Dodge.

Its discretion was so utter, no author was given credit. In its place appeared the following sly note:

> The publishers are not at liberty to mention the name of the writer, but they may say that she is a member of New York's most exclusive social circles and that her name is a guarantee for the authorative character of this handbook, which is not a mere compilation but is written from the author's own experience as a woman of society and fashion.

It was certainly no secret to her wide circle of friends and acquaintances that Bessy Marbury was the book's author. The only mystery was why she, who was the last to seek anonymity in any of her endeavors, should not have insisted that her name appear upon it. The slight volume would not have discredited its creator. Written in a breezy style, it was filled with all kinds of useful information for the social neophyte of the day. Among its many headings were *Bills, Breakfast, Cards, Calls or Visits, Carriages, Clubs, Chaperones, Christenings, Coats of Arms, Courtships and Weddings, Mourning, Dinners, Flowers, Garden Parties, Invitations, Letter Writing, New Year's Day, Private Theatricals, Theatre Parties, Toilet for Ladies, Toilet for Gentlemen,* and *Visiting in Country Houses.*

The rules of etiquette in Victorian New York society were as rigid and formal as those of life at the court of Louis XIV. Bessy's instructions were precise and easy to follow. The striver could consult the book to learn what was expected in a given circumstance. Starting first thing in the morning, she could learn to instruct her servants in the proper service and number of courses for breakfast. A little cosmopolitan note was added on "late breakfast in imitation of the French which in our country is usually called 'lunch'," and could be either formal or informal.

For Sam Sands, the presence of the Meadow Brook Hunt Club was what made Garden City more desirable than Riverdale. The club had leased land from the Stewarts in 1877 and four years later was incorporated as a private club whose primary purpose was foxhunting. Sam was a singularly bold horseman who loved the infinitely more dangerous steeplechasing as much as he did hunting. His fearlessness in the saddle was well known and a cause of great concern to his family, especially his passion for the steeplechase, one of the few races in which the skill and training of the horse and rider must be equal as well as complementary. There was an ever-increasing number of nasty, sometimes fatal falls among gentlemen equestrians whose courage outdistanced their skill and whose horses were often not sufficiently schooled in the subtleties of the sport.

If Anne voiced any qualms about her husband's hazardous pastime, it was in the well-modulated tones characteristic of her family, charming but incapable of giving proper emphasis to the concern she might have felt. The gentler foxhunt was certainly more to her liking, and she often joined him in riding to the hounds, cutting a handsome figure mounted sidesaddle on a thoroughbred hunter, wearing the flattering nipped-waist, long-skirted traditional habit. From its inception the Meadow Brook was a gathering place for fashionable sportsmen and their ladies. Its first president was William B. Travers, who was known as the greatest wit in New York despite his pronounced stammer.

Anne did not lack admirers, for among the stewards were Elliott Roosevelt and young Winthrop Rutherfurd, whose brother Lewis also put in appearances and who was already being singled out in *Town Topics* as "handsome, a champion racquet player, actively interested in all sporting matters, and a very good fellow."

Early in March 1889, Sam developed a cold to which he paid no attention. This was characteristic of the Victorian sportsman, who, using some half-digested evolutionary rationale, insisted he was the fittest and could ignore all ailments, as he was destined to survive them. Anne was too occupied to protest very vehemently. Plans were being made with her mother and Emmy for the two family weddings scheduled to take place less than two weeks apart, in November. Her brother, Bordie, would be marrying Annie Tracy Morgan's good friend Daisy Hurst, and twelve days later, the wedding of Lillie to Bill Travers, Jr., would also take place.

The wedding plans helped to relieve some of Anne's anxiety when Sam's cold was complicated by early symptoms of pneumonia. He reluctantly gave way to the doctor's insistence that he remain in bed, but not without protest. It did not matter what was wrong with him, he maintained, nothing on earth would keep him from riding in the first Meadow Brook meet of the season.

Anne and Sam could find some sickroom diversion in the scandalous controversy being waged in the press over plans for the Washington centennial ball scheduled to take place at the end of April. What occurred might be termed the coda to the orchestrated social change that had begun with the Vanderbilt ball.

The centennial committee was an all-male one, including Willie K. Vanderbilt, Stuyvesant Fish, Elbridge T. Gerry, William Jay, Robert Goelet, William Waldorf Astor, and, of course, Ward McAllister. McAllister, most experienced at organizing a ball, was designated secretary of the entertainment committee. He though of this grand occasion as his *chef-d'oeuvre,* his last blazing triumph before a gracious retirement from society.

> I have seen this Centennial Ball in my mind, and pictured even its smallest particulars. I saw its surging masses, never quiet, for I meant to put champagne on one side and refreshments on the other to keep the kaleidoscope moving. . . . I saw the opening quadrille in its every movement—a magnificent thing, as magnificent to the eye as to the fancy—and last of all the great cotillion.

It was the quadrille d'honneur that was his undoing. The old party-giver's vision was a dance executed by an assemblage of the most graceful and best-looking members of the old colonial families. That disqualified Mamie Fish on two of the three counts: grace, and looks. Her husband, Stuyvesant, who was a member of the centennial committee, placed his own list in motion, which naturally included most of his colleagues' wives and daughters. It was dismissed with an imperiousness that could only have been equaled by McAllister's patroness, *the* Mrs. Astor.

McAllister's complacency was shaken when Fish was seconded on the quadrille affair by another committee member, Elbridge T. Gerry. This gentleman's grandfather, a signer of the Declaration of Independence, was immortalized for having invented the nefarious system that bears his name, gerrymandering, which ultimately had a greater effect on the way politics were played in this country than the distinguished document to which he had affixed his signature.

When Astor, Vanderbilt, Jay, and Goelet lined up behind Fish and Gerry, the secretary of the entertainment committee had no recourse but to resign, and the war of the press release was on. On one day, McAllister took aim and fired: "Neither Fish nor Gerry has the slightest idea of how to get up a ball. . . . Gerry says that it makes no difference if you have nothing better than pork and beans as long as you have a crowd. That's his idea of a great ceremonial ball."

On the next day, Fish, who actually was blue-blood old New York, counterattacked: "The whole thing in a nutshell is that McAllister is getting pretty well advanced in age, and the committee is not one that can be bossed by any demagogue, big or little, young or old."

Old McAllister's reposte was, "That man, Fish! I do feel a little stronger on balls than a mere railroad president. All this, you know, is Fish's doing. Fish wanted to turn the whole thing into a Republican jubilee . . . I put a spoke in his wheel, and he got very angry."

His great mustaches bristling, Fish drew himself up to his patrician height and delivered the *coup de maître*. "Who is Ward McAllister anyway? McAllister does very well as the manager for a small ball like the Patriarchs [it still rankled that no Fish had been among the original members], where all he has to do is to say to Delmonico, 'Give us red shades instead of pink this time, and say, let's have some different sorts of wine, don't you know.'" He concluded with the deathblow: "McAllister was our major domo, our master of ceremonies, our caterer. As such, he was not acceptable to us, and we told him his services were no longer required. McAllister is a discharged servant. That is all." With that statement, the new music swelled to a deafening crescendo. The old boy was finished in New York society.

On the morning of March 19, Sam Sands insisted he was well enough to join the hunt. Perhaps Anne should have been more implacable, but the day was so fine that her protests were less strong than they might have been. The horses were brought around from the stables, and he mounted his strong, spirited steed, while Anne was contented with a much gentler filly, one that was probably no more keen on the event than she was. With the sound of the horns and the cry "Tally ho!" they were off, with Sam in the vanguard and out of sight almost before her foot was firmly in the stirrup.

The hunt had barely started when shrieks filled the air. Sam was hurt. His horse had stumbled and thrown him. It was like a macabre dream in which death happened faster than the speed of life. His illness had left him without the resources to fight. First, the injuries were more serious than suspected. Then his condition worsened at a breathtaking rate. And then he was dead. It was that quick. A few days passing like hours, then hours limping by like an eternity.

The obituary in *The New York Times* summed it up: "Having always been counted a singularly fearless horseman, this fatal result from what was almost his first mishap in the hunting field is as astonishing as it is sad."

Anne's mother always had said a lady had her name in the newspapers three times—when she was born, when she was married, when she died. Mama need have no fears. Anne's reputation was intact. Her name appeared nowhere. The paper briefly identified her as the second daughter of Mr. Oliver Harriman before passing on to an account of the hunting events that would be canceled in Sam's honor. It was as if she neither existed nor had any deep connection to what had happened. The next day, a follow-up account in the *Times* was devoted to the "severe blow" his death would be to steeplechasing, with no mention of the blow to her or to her two young sons. She was twenty-seven years old, and her life was over, the center cut away, and it was of less significance to the world than the canceling of a hunt breakfast.

Sam had left enough for the essentials: she would never be in want. Beyond that, both her father and his were honorable men who could be depended upon for the niceties. When Samuel Sands, Sr., died three years later, he left what would have been his late son's share of his legacy to be divided between the fatherless grandsons. Fifty thousand dollars each was a handsome sum in those days.

The legacy would provide the boys with a very comfortable start at whatever they chose to do with their lives. In the spring of 1889, their mother's problem was what to do with hers. The options were so pitifully few.

The rules of mourning allowed no leeway for family ties. Public appearances were strictly proscribed during the first year. Anne Harriman Sands could not be present in St. Thomas's Church on Fifth Avenue on Wednesday afternoon, November 13, 1889, when her brother, Bordie, married Florence (Daisy) Jaffray Hurst. She was not alone in her grief, for as suddenly as Sam had been taken from her, death had taken Billy Dodge from Emmy, leaving her also with two children. They were at home while the fashionable crowd gathered in the church, with Astors mingling with Vanderbilts and both gingerly exchanging polite bows with the newly acceptable Goulds. The J. Pierpont Morgans were also in attendance, accompanied by their three unmarried daughters.

Still an adolescent but already being singled out as a great heiress, the youngest, Annie Tracy, was far too serious to be overly impressed by the lavishness of the festivities. Watching her girlhood friend march down the flower-decked aisle, she surely felt some curiosity about whether the same fate lay in store for her. She was only sixteen, and there was more than time enough to look around to see if there might not be something better to do with one's life.

The following week, on Monday, November 25, Anne Sands's sister Lillie was married to William B. Travers, Jr. The ceremony took place in the privacy of her parents' home to allow the mourning Anne and Emmy to attend. The strikingly handsome sportsman Winthrop (Winty) Rutherfurd was an usher, and his equally stunning older brother, Lewis (Lewy), was among the guests. Amid the celebrants, Anne stood out as a tall, pale, and gauntly beautiful figure garbed in severe black silk that brought out the intense violet-blue of her eyes. Her two sons would have made angelic page boys had it not been for the black bands slipped over their jacket sleeves, signifying that they, too, were in mourning. She seemed to cling to them as if they might be her reason for living. But Anne had found another, more compelling reason. When nobody was watching, her eyes undoubtedly searched for Lewy Rutherfurd and found him gazing back at her.

CHAPTER TWELVE ঽ৹

The successive weddings of Annie Tracy Morgan's older siblings only served to affirm what was expected of her: nothing short of a traditional marriage. Should she fail to accept a husband (there would be many to choose from for the daughter of J. P. Morgan), her father would punish her in the way that would most effectively hurt her without wasting any of his valuable time: economically.

In April 1890, Annie Tracy's grandfather Junius Spencer Morgan was killed in an accident on the Riviera. Before the year was out, on December 11, 1890, the Morgan family was in attendance at the Arlington Street Church, in Boston, for the wedding of young Jack to Jane Norton Grew. The young woman was the product of impeccable Brahmin inbreeding. It was possibly because the arrangements were traditionally in the hands of the bride's family that the ceremony was simplicity itself, as was the reception following it in the Grew Beacon Street residence.

Fanny Morgan would miss her darling boy, but he had to get away from Pierpont for his own sake. He was twenty-three, and this eminently suitable match would give him somebody who would belong to him, somebody to compensate for the feelings he expressed to Fanny, vis-à-vis their mutual position with his father: "There certainly are some drawbacks to belonging to a busy man . . . as I believe you have sometimes found out."

Annie Tracy made her official debut during the following year. Given the young lady's lack of real interest, her mother's lack of energy, and her father's disdain for the rituals of what passed for society in New York, it may well have been similar to Edith Wharton's recollection of coming out:

> The New York mothers of that day usually gave a series of "coming-out" entertainments for debutante daughters, leading off with a huge tea and an expensive ball. My mother thought this absurd. She said her daughter could meet all the people she need know without being advertised by a general entertainment. . . . I

was . . . put into a low-necked bodice of pale green brocade, above a white muslin skirt ruffled with rows and rows of Valenciennes, my hair was piled up on top of my head, some friend of the family sent me a large bouquet of lilies-of-the-valley, and thus adorned I was taken by my parents to a ball. . . .

Annie had become a tall, handsome young lady with sufficient grace and popularity to be the only member of her family listed as part of McAllister's Four Hundred the following year. Ludicrous as the list was, it was a small peace offering. Pierpont never had expected any of his family to be included, but McAllister needed powerful new friends after the disaster of the Centennial Ball.

Later that year the handsome and decadent young French fortune hunter Count Boni de Castellane appeared on the scene. Annie Tracy was fluent in French and much better informed culturally than the typical American heiress. Years later, Grace Bigelow reminisced about the courtship with Clarence W. Barron: "Anne Morgan has one of the brightest minds I've ever known. And she admires brains. Her father was afraid that Count di [sic] Castellane would get her as Castellane is very brainy but not in good standing. However, one's standing made no difference with Anne Morgan."

One of the great drawbacks for her was that Boni could tolerate nothing more exhausting than spending other people's money while she was an avid sportswoman who adored tennis, sailing, swimming, and running. Although amused and stimulated by the dandy, Annie was far too intelligent to take him seriously.

Poor little rich sallow-faced Anna Gould was neither intelligent enough nor fluent enough in his language to get the count's drift. She adored him. When her father, Jay Gould, died, leaving $100,000,000 in trust for his children, her affection was returned. In fact, she became irresistible. Morgan was relieved when the French challenge was blunted. He could defer worrying about the youngest daughter until after the older ones found husbands. The example of his generosity to them, their *rewards* for doing the right thing, would surely inspire her to behave in a similar fashion.

The wedding of his middle daughter, Juliet, gave Morgan an opportunity to display his wealth and power. If there had been any doubt in Anne's mind that this was the tribal ritual for which he intended all of his daughters, it was dispelled by the relish with which her father took charge of the one at hand.

The groom, William Pierson Hamilton, a descendant of Alexander Hamilton, was a handsome, unexceptional young man whose major asset was that he was as acceptable to the bride's father as he was to her. Over three thousand invitations were dispatched to addresses in New York, Boston, Philadelphia, Washington, and London by the all-male secretarial staff at Drexel, Morgan.

The ceremony was called for three-thirty on Thursday afternoon, April 12, 1894, at the Morgan church, St. George's, in Stuyvesant Square. The bride was beautiful in a gown of the richest white satin trimmed with point lace ruffles and bodice. Juliet had done her duty, and her father rewarded her with a dowry of one million dollars, to which was added a mansion opposite his own, on East Thirty-sixth Street.

Six years would pass before the next Morgan wedding. To the surprise of many of the family's friends, it was the marriage of Pierpont's oldest and favorite child, Louisa. At thirty-four, she was considered a bit over the hill, and her ways were those of a spinster preferring her charities and domestic life to the busy social whirl of the young and booming city.

Many wondered how the old man would manage without her. For many years she had replaced her mother as his hostess and favorite traveling companion. They need not have been concerned. In this case the old saw held: My son is my son till he gets him a wife, my daughter's my daughter for the rest of my life.

The prospective bridegroom, Herbert Livingston Satterlee, was a prominent attorney and a member of one of the city's finest families. He respected his fiancée's intelligence and moral rectitude but was mad about her father, as was evidenced in the eulogistic biography he later wrote. Pierpont was gaining a son instead of losing a daughter.

With the Satterlee wedding, it almost seemed as if Morgan was at last making an effort to enter New York society and increase the odious Four Hundred by one. Among the 2,500 guests were all of its leaders, old and new, ranging from *the* Mrs. Astor through a slew of Vanderbilts, Whitneys, Tiffanys, and Goelets, and including old Ward McAllister's daughter; Anne Harriman's brothers Bordie and Ollie Junior, and their wives; Edith Wharton's sister-in-law and niece; as well as Bessy Marbury's distant cousins the Phelpses and Stokes. Still more surprisingly, the list also included several of the banker's business adversaries, most notably Andrew Carnegie, with whom he was having difficulties at that very moment over the formation of United States Steel; and Anne's cousin Edward H. Harriman, with whom he had been at war for years over railroad deals. Nobody declined despite a generation of Morgan's insults, snubs, and ruthless rivalries. Such was the remarkable personal power of a man who symbolized all that was both best and worst in American capitalism.

CHAPTER THIRTEEN

While it superficially seemed as if there were parallels between the life of Elsie de Wolfe during those years immediately following her return from Europe and that of Lily Bart, the prototypical heroine of Edith Wharton's *The House of Mirth*, they did not exist. Lily was beautiful and connected by birth to the oldest New York society; Elsie was neither. Whereas Lily was fundamentally headstrong, proud, and passionate, Elsie was basically calculating, accommodating, and cunning. The traits they shared were a love of luxury, of the kind of beauty created by and for wealth; and a concomitant loathing of the meanness that might be foisted upon them by the truth of their economic situations. Lily was destroyed by them, when her knight-savior, Seldon, "failed to reach the height of his opportunity." In Elsie's case, the question was, would the fair damsel allow herself to be rescued, would she resist the temptations of following where Cora Brown-Potter led and surrendering to her own desperate, all-consuming need to be a part of the haut monde? Elsie would always be attracted to women who were stronger, or more attractive, or more socially acceptable than herself and would find ingenious ways to become attractive to them. Although she was seldom a loser in these relationships, there was often some expense in accepting the hand-me-downs of her benefactresses. It was only with Bessy that she would have pride of choice and deal only in spanking new merchandise lovingly and freely given to her. But that was not to come to pass until a few years later.

In 1886, the question for Elsie had been how best to use Cora's cast-offs, the most appealing of which was her position as first lady of the amateur theatre. Elsie had no trouble assuming that mantle. In the season following her first appearances, she played leading roles in a series of best-forgotten plays with such titles as *Sunshine, The Hunchback, Circus Rider,* and *The Mouse Trap* (not to be confused with Agatha Christie's play of that title, which, though the longest-running play in the history of the English theatre, has not been running that long).

An investigation of what use Elsie and Pierre Lorillard made of each other must lead to only one conclusion about their relationship. From *Town Topics* to newspapers as far afield as the Paris *Herald Tribune,* the press continually coupled their names with Victorian insinuation that did not quite say but coyly implied a romantic liaison. The photographs of Elsie at the time reveal a woman who, though not quite pretty, was, to use a popular adjective of that day, winsome and already in possession of the wit, the flair, the sense of style and taste, that would one day make her fortune. It added up to as much as if not more than a wily older man such as Pierre could have wished for in a mistress.

That Lorillard was charmed by her was apparent from the beginning. He opened the doors of society as much as he could. By providing a stage at his club, he also encouraged her theatrical ambitions. Most important of all, there was the question of money. To enter the world to which she aspired cost a great deal of it. There was the cost of maintaining a wardrobe. For a stay at Tuxedo, there would have to have been morning dresses, luncheon outfits, afternoon frocks, riding and tennis clothes, tea gowns, and evening gowns, a different assortment for each day and all having to come up to an estimable level of extravagance. Some of the wardrobe must have been promoted. Dressmakers were always happy to lend things to women who traveled in the highest circles and wore clothes with distinction. Even so, if one did not have a personal maid to look after them, one had to be hired for the duration of the visit—that, plus tips for the other servants. There were other expenses such as the stakes at card games—which all but ruined poor Lily Bart—and Elsie was an avid cardplayer throughout her life. A house gift was also often in order. Even what was deemed a trifle by those hostesses would have cost far more than the average person could afford.

Where did the money come from to support Elsie's rather expensive way of life? It was impossible that it came from Bessy at that point in their lives. It was improbable that it came from her father. Within a few years, Dr. De Wolfe was to die in a financial state very close to bankruptcy. He had three sons to educate and start off in life and was unlikely to have been able to indulge the costly caprices of a daughter already past her first bloom. Elsie later claimed to have educated Charteris, the youngest of her brothers, by sending him to Groton. The boy was born around 1870, so would have been in prep school during the years that Elsie was making her way as an amateur actress. If there was any validity to her assertion, somebody had to have given her the money for his tuition. She assuredly was not earning it on her own.

With almost no assets beyond her wits, Elsie was managing to succeed. Her only possible source of financial backing was Pierre Lorillard, whose wife seemed to have faded into the background much as Annie Tracy Morgan's mother had. In all of the reams of publicity devoted to Tuxedo Park and her husband's sporting and social pastimes, Emily Taylor Lorillard was rarely if ever mentioned, despite not having been an invalid, indeed having been hardy enough to outlive her husband by several years.

The spring found Elsie sailing for Europe with her mother as chaperone.

It was probable that they were the guests of Lorillard. The owner of the first American horse to win the English Derby, he subsequently sold his stables but still traveled to Europe every spring to follow the horses of his friends in the big European races in England and at Longchamp, in Paris.

That London season of 1887 was one of the most exciting in years. It was Queen Victoria's Golden Jubilee, and the city was draped in bunting and flags. Shopwindows were festooned with streamers echoing the popular sentiments of the day: "God Bless Her," "The Mother of Her People," "1837 to 1887. Victoria the Good." This last slogan appeared on an array of souvenirs from marmalade jars to cricket bats, flooding the shops of the West End. There were also balls, and parades, and galas of every description, and all of Elsie's good friends of the previous season—Mrs. Paran Stevens, Cora, Jennie Churchill, Minnie Paget, and Consuelo Mandeville—could be relied upon to see to it that their charming American compatriot received her share of the most sought-after invitations.

From the point of view of her future, a more important thing happened while Lorillard and she were in Paris for the racing season at Longchamp. She was due to star in Bessy's new play, *Contrast,* the following season, and, probably at the playwright's suggestion, she began to take acting lessons from the great star of the Comédie Française, Mme Julia Bartet. It was the first but would not be the last time the distinguished French actress tried to help her. If she had no intention of turning professional, there would have been no reason to do anything in Paris more strenuous than visiting the couturiers who were always included in her itinerary.

So many Americans were visiting and living in Paris that year that the New York publishers Brentano Brothers announced plans to open an American bookstore in the city. Americans were taking up residence all over Europe. Complaining that London was "fast becoming an American city," Henry James quixotically fled from his countrymen in the British capital only to join his American friends in Florence.

*S*oon after Elsie returned to New York at the beginning of August, an invitation arrived to spend part of the month in Newport. With what alacrity she must have accepted! Anything was better than midsummer on Thirty-fourth Street, where the only respite from the white heat was to be found in the cindered shade of the El at the corner. Her hostess was Mrs. Isaac Townsend Burden. Neither old Boston nor old New York, the Burdens were second-generation Troy ironmongers but very, very rich; and rich, then as now, was the name of the game at Newport. They came along quickly in society by marrying up. The Townsend part of the name came from an alliance with that old family, who were kin to Bessy Marbury on the McCoun side. One of the Burden sons would later marry Willie K. Vanderbilt's niece Adele Sloane, which was dynastical in the sense that Burden iron made the tracks for Vanderbilt railroads.

It was probable that Lorillard had arranged for Elsie's invitation. Although he did not own one of the big "cottages," Newport was in its way as much a Lorillard town as Tuxedo Park. Just as they changed the way resort men dressed for dinner dances with their championing of the tuxedo, so they would change the beat to which they danced when, a few generations down the line, one of the Lorillards helped to found the Newport Jazz Festival.

Whoever was responsible for opening the Newport door for Elsie, she knew precisely what to do once she set foot across that gilded threshold: make friends with the press. This was facilitated by one of Lorillard's connections. He had been a yachting crony of James Gordon Bennett, Jr., the owner of the New York and Paris *Herald,* and both papers described Elsie as "the chic dancer of the evening" at the subscription ball at the Casino that climaxed the gayest week of the season.

Newport was a triumphant performance for Elsie, but the part of her summer that would have greatest significance for the rest of her life was yet to come. As the end of her visit with the Burdens approached, bringing with it the prospect of returning to her family in still-steaming Manhattan, she suggested to Bessy Marbury that they share a cottage for what remained of the season in Lenox, Massachusetts, which was just beginning to become fashionable and had not yet traded its simple rustic pleasures for the frenetic desperation of Newport. As Bessy later recalled: "We found just what we wanted, a little cottage, not too impractical nor uncomfortable. There was a certain 'picnic' atmosphere about it all which being young we really enjoyed."

In the Berkshires the intellectual colony outnumbered the millionaires. There were only thirty-five great summer cottages, the grandest being Shadowbrook, which belonged to yet another set of Bessy's distant cousins on the McCoun side, the Stokeses. They were related by marriage to the Phelpses, who in turn were connected to the Dodges, one of whom had married Anne Sand's sister Emmeline in that small New York world in which old families were almost exclusively partnered with other old families.

The Stokes house was named for the stream that ran by Nathaniel Hawthorne's cottage, Tanglewood. Artists and the arts pre-dated society in the Berkshires and would always find a congenial home there. When Edith Wharton built a summer place of her own, it was in Lenox rather than the Newport of her girlhood.

For Elsie, it was a place where there were no Lorillards, and Bessy was becoming an increasingly fascinating companion. The women of the community vied with the men for excellence in athletic as well as intellectual pursuits. One old-timer enthused about the ladies' baseball team a half-century after the fact. "We slid the bases, too—in long skirts and picture hats."

It must have been during that golden September that the two women realized they could share a rational life, that commitment to each other was the best of the few alternatives open to single women with no particular craving for a husband. Elsie discovered her first and only "great and enduring friendship." It was to enrich her life with "a devotion lasting over forty years."

In addition to Elsie's "proverbial generosity," Bessy thought it was their shared sense of the ridiculous that was to sustain her love for the rest of her life.

> We both had a keen sense of humor, which has never deserted us in all the years of our intimacy. Many a domestic storm has thereby been averted. . . . When two people can laugh together, there is less room for tears, and when they can see a joke at the same moment, catastrophe is often prevented. A sense of humor is probably the one saving grace in the world.

The one important thing remaining to grace their union was the financial freedom to sustain it. The money Bessy earned from her hatcheries was literally chicken feed when it came to setting up house in a style that would be acceptable to them. The idea that Elsie might turn professional actress must have seemed increasingly feasible, especially when coupled with her friend's notion that she could write plays that would make a star of her. Theirs would be an equal partnership professionally as well as emotionally, as she hoped would be demonstrated by the production of *Contrast*.

The singular component of their relationship that made it different from those of other women of the period sharing a Boston marriage was that at no time did it occur to Elsie that they would be unacceptable as a couple to society. She was not about to give up the position she had worked so hard to establish and live in a world of unfashionable bluestocking spinsters.

On Thursday evening, December 8, the Assembly, the oldest and most prestigious social club in New York, held its Christmas ball at Delmonico's.

Lorillard, though on the committee, was not permitted to have "that distinguished amateur" Elsie de Wolfe as his guest, presumably because she had appeared in public theatre, albeit for a worthy cause. Many of the more prominent ladies had issued a "her or us" challenge. He was forced to acquiesce but not before warning these too grandes dames that any attempt to embarrass Elsie would result disastrously for future cotillions. The *Herald* added: "Of course, Mr. Lorillard's set did not hesitate for a moment to throng the Lyceum and pat their gloved hands in applause of Miss de Wolfe's exquisite work."

She was never one to shrink from a challenge. Within a month of the Assembly debacle, she notified the Paris *Herald* that she would appear at the Lyceum again and in a social satire again, which might strike still closer to home with the grandes dames, as it was being written for her by the sister of Mrs. Cornelius Vanderbilt. It never came off. Instead, she appeared in Bessy's play.

At the same time Elsie was being rejected by the Assembly ladies, she in turn was rejecting an offer to play the leading female role in the opening production of the Amateur Comedy Club. There was no reason that she should have appeared with them simply because they asked her. Membership was barred to actresses. They were permitted to perform only as guests at the gracious invitation of the club. Elsie obviously did not deem that the most signal of honors and demanded the same privileges that were extended to the male membership: approval of what she would appear in and with whom she would act. It was not asking too much, since the club would be capitalizing on her reputation and the following she had developed.

There undoubtedly was an element of self-importance that had crept into Elsie's demeanor at about this time. Many of her friends observed it. Bessy and her mother took a bemused view of their darling's grandiloquence. On one occasion, when Mrs. De Wolfe was reproaching her daughter for a rude gaffe, Bessy tilted an eyebrow and remarked, "Oh, remember, dear Mrs. De Wolfe, that the star must be handled carefully."

Georgiana de Wolfe replied, "She's no star to me."

Elsie's sense of humor saved the day, and the two younger women began to laugh uproariously. As with people who live intimately, they developed a private vocabulary, and Georgiana's line became part of it. It would be repeated whenever Elsie got too hoity-toity and had to be brought down to earth.

An incident occurred during the Christmas festivities at Tuxedo Park that fueled the rumors about Lorillard and Elsie and must have served to intensify her desire to be free of him. He had donated the grand prize of an expensive diamond pin to a charity grab bag. To nobody's surprise or delight,

Elsie reached in and grabbed it out. The snickers about her "elderly benefactor" had to have been humiliating. The whole thing was a quirk of luck and chance; there was no way she could have known which anonymous package contained the pin. It made her more desperate than ever to prove her independence, her charisma as herself alone and not as his "protégée."

Her many efforts to get invited to one of the Patriarch balls bore fruit when a guest of Mrs. Edward Cooper dropped out at the last minute, and Elsie was asked to stand in. It is likely that Mrs. Cooper's niece Sally Hewitt, knowing of her aunt's dilemma and her good friend's desperation, had a hand in it. What should have been a moment of small triumph turned to yet another humiliation.

When Elsie appeared, looking and feeling radiant, her name was not on the list. There was a great to-do about examining tickets to make certain her invitation was legitimate. Time had been so short that Mrs. Cooper had neglected to inform the overseers, who had to approve of the substitution. It was an understandable oversight. The hostess had no reason to suppose that an intimate of Sally Hewitt's would be unacceptable.

The incident was magnified in repetition. The mortification must have been intense, and one of her friends stepped in to save her face. She was legitimately asked to the next ball by her hostess of the previous summer, Mrs. Isaac Townsend Burden. Even this small vindication was spoiled when the next issue of *Town Topics* appeared on January 26, 1888, and told the world Mrs. Burden had pressured the overseers to approve Elsie's invitation on the grounds that "Miss de Wolfe had been her guest at Newport, had recited in her drawing room, and she felt under social obligation to her."

Her salvation would not be found by simply being *in* society, or among the feckless hypocrites who habituated it, until she was as desirable to society as it was to her. The theatre was her last, best hope. Its people were much more attractive and, for all the artifice of their trade, much more natural. Among her friends in that world was George Alexander, a handsome young English actor then having a New York success in support of Sir Henry Irving and Ellen Terry on their American tour. On a card engraved with the names *Mrs. de Wolfe and Miss de Wolfe,* ignoring the existence of the father and husband, Dr. Stephen de Wolfe, Elsie wrote to her good friend and fellow amateur actress Alice Lawrence:

> Chere amie, I have been intending to send you a line for a week, but you may fancy how full my time has been [she was to open in *Contrast* on the next afternoon]—will you come to us to meet George Alexander (Faust) on Sunday evening next at nine-thirty. I have only asked a few as our rooms are so tiny. Yours cordially,

All of Elsie's efforts to become independent were to little avail. As late as July of the following year, *Town Topics* was still making nasty insinuations about her liaison with Lorillard. "Everybody who knows anything, indeed, knows where the de Wolfe money comes from."

CHAPTER FOURTEEN

Bessy was thirty-one years old when Elsie and she shared the Lenox cottage. If she ever had given any serious consideration to a conventional marriage, that September "picnic" put an end to it. She had known almost from the beginning, on that memorable afternoon at Sally's house when Elsie had recited so passionately, that she wanted to find a way to share the rest of her life with her. On what terms remained to be defined. It surely posed a great problem to a spinster, approaching what was then considered early middle-age, to want to change her life for another woman. What is unknown is how much this had to do with her turning to the Catholic Church in search of a measure of peace as well as answers to the questions beginning to torment her. Catholicism must have been very difficult for her beloved Quaker-Presbyterian-Huguenot family to accept, if indeed they ever did.

Her father was a trustee of the Madison Square Presbyterian Church, at the corner of Twenty-fourth Street and Madison Avenue, which had been founded two years before her birth. Bessy would later claim: "I owe much of any stability of character which I may possess and any self-restraint which I may exercise to this early training in the Presbyterian Church."

Bessy was so calculatedly vague about her conversion. It was almost as if one day she was Protestant and the next, Catholic. Her comments on the subject were invariably evasions.

> I have always strenuously objected to personal stories of conversions. They savor too much of the camp meeting and of the revival stock taking. Suffice it therefore to say that when I eventually determined to become a Catholic it was the result of adult conviction uninfluenced and spontaneous. An earnest desire to honestly understand what those of an opposing creed really do believe often leads to a change of faith, and to find in a world reeking

with stultifying selfishness the actual practice of sacrifice is as salutary as it is inspiring. Penance is the soul's best lubricant.

Describing the salient components of her Catholicism in terms of "practice of sacrifice" and "penance" was revealing when taken in the light of the contradictions in the nature, as well as of the ambiguities in the personal relationships, of this determinedly high-spirited, complex woman. For most Catholics, born or converted, more meaningful qualities of their faith would surely be grace, expiation, forgiveness. One point on which there can be no ambivalence: her conversion could only be described as a "spontaneous" act.

Bessy was experiencing doubts about the salvation of her soul, but there were none about the keenness of her mind. There was an iron optimism about her belief in her own ability to accomplish anything she thought worth doing: the question was what that would be. It had to be extremely lucrative if she was to compete with the likes of Pierre Lorillard for the favors of Miss De Wolfe. She knew her love's tastes ran to the extravagant, and that the girl was single-minded in gratifying them. Her first ambition was to make her fortune as a writer, ideally a playwright, with Elsie as her muse and star.

Bessy would always take pleasure in extending her support to anybody who needed it, but she was a born agent and would never have any qualms about exacting her commission for that aid. With Elsie, she became a vulnerable romantic gratefully accepting approximately 10 percent of her love in return for all she did for her. It was probably clear from the start this was all the aspiring actress would ever be capable of giving.

*S*ix weeks after the young women returned from Lenox, on November 19, 1887, Bessy received some tragic news. One of her good friends, Emma Lazarus, had died at home, at 18 West Tenth Street, after a prolonged and agonizing battle with cancer. Emma's first volume of verse had been published when she was only seventeen, and by the time she died, she was a world-renowned writer whose work was admired by George Eliot, Browning, Turgenev, James Russell Lowell, and Emerson. Seven years older than Bessy, she gave the younger woman her "first impetus toward the higher things of life." Like a gushing fan, Bessy declared, "To be with Emma Lazarus produced a stained glass effect upon one's soul."

How different this was from the effect produced in her by Elsie, who was, in every way, Emma's opposite! Unlike the De Wolfes, the Lazaruses were wealthy. Their ample brownstone was one of the best residences in the best part of Greenwich Village. Despite the luxury of her home, Emma's room was a whitewashed, sparsely furnished cell in which she slept on a plain iron bedstead. It took little imagination to envision what Elsie would have chosen for herself had she been born to similar ease. As Elsie would later claim that her opulent surroundings were good for her professionally, so Emma claimed that this severe simplicity was good for her work. Bessy was "inclined to applaud her [Emma's] wisdom," as she would also later endorse most of Elsie's choices.

Emma's last work, *By the Waters of Babylon,* was published in the *Century* just before she died. Possibly, Bessy was introduced to her by Richard Watson Gilder, for they met and became friends during that period at the beginning of the Eighties when she first began frequenting the Gilder salon. She was the first Jew with whom Bessy ever became friendly, and she had to admit her introduction to "this great race was made under remarkable guidance." She acquired "a respect and love for the Jews which otherwise . . . might have been denied." It was a fortuitous response, for her sympathetic association with the Jews in the American theatre would lead to much of her later success.

Although couched in terms of race, it was obvious that what Bessy felt for the poet was one of her earliest approaches to rapture for another woman.

> Through Emma Lazarus, I understood the beauty and simplicity of Ruth standing breast high amid the corn; and Rebecca at the Well was revealed to me as a woman full of the poetry and the pathos of her people.

Bessy also entered a world of Sephardic aristocracy that was new to her. Along with the Henricks, Baruch, Gomez, Nathan, and Cardozo families, the Lazaruses had arrived in New York on the *St. Charles,* "the Jewish Mayflower," in 1654, only forty years after the first Dutch settlers and twenty after Anne Marbury Hutchinson arrived in New England. They helped to finance the American Revolution and both sides of the Civil War, depending upon which area of the country was native to them. So well assimilated were they that Emma's father, Moses Lazarus, was one of the founders of the exclusive Knickerbocker Club as well as a member of the Union Club. He never recovered from the shock when both became restricted in the years during the great anti-Semitic mania that swept New York society with the arrival of vast numbers of Ashkenazi German Jews at the end of the Civil War. *The* Mrs. Astor was in the vanguard of those insisting New York society close the doors of its clubs and homes to them. There were rumors that the Astors had Jewish blood, and some said Caroline's anti-Semitism was her way of stilling them. Pierpont Morgan unsuccessfully tried to keep the German Jews out of Wall Street. In his case, it may well have been largely a case of vanity. He could not bear the fact that German-American Jewish bankers, notably Jacob Henry Schiff and the Seligmans, were his only true peers in New York, and that in Europe the Rothschilds not only surpassed him but also had been ennobled by the monarchs of three countries: England, France, and Austria.

If Moses Lazarus was saddened by these new manifestations of prejudice in people he always had considered his friends, Emma was incensed by it. The feeling was intensified when she saw the condition of immigrant infants in the settlement houses on the Lower East Side. She began to immerse herself in the new Zionism and exhibit a militant Judaism.

The French people raised the money to commission the sculptor Auguste Bartholdi to create a huge statue, "Liberty Enlightening the World," as a gift to the American people commemorating the friendship of the two countries and the centennial of their freedom. In November 1883, as the statue was nearing completion, money had to be found to erect the pedestal upon which it would rise, on Bedloe's Island, in New York Harbor. The nation's Republican administration and financiers were apparently uninterested in erecting a statue dedicated to liberty, and the committee made an appeal to artists. The best-known writers were asked to contribute original manuscripts that could be auctioned to raise the funds. Among those who did were Mark Twain, Longfellow, Whitman, and Emma. She submitted the text of a new sonnet, "The New Colossus," expressing her feeling about what the statue must symbolize if it was to have any meaning at all. It indicated she had not completely lost faith in her country and city.

> *Not like the brazen giant of Greek fame*
> *With conquering limbs astride from land to land;*
> *Here at our sea-washed, sunset gate shall stand*
> *A mighty woman with a torch, whose flame*
> *Is the imprisoned lightning, and her name,*
> *Mother of Exiles. From her beacon-hand*
> *Glows world-wide welcome; her mild eyes command*
> *The air-bridged harbor that twin cities frame.*
>
> *"Keep, ancient lands, your storied pomp," cries she*
> *with silent lips. "Give me your tired, your poor,*
> *Your huddled masses yearning to breathe free,*
> *The wretched refuse of your teeming shore.*
> *Send these, the homeless, tempest-tost to me.*
> *I lift my lamp beside the golden door!"*

*L*adies and Not-So-Gentle Women

After reading her poem, James Russell Lowell wrote to Emma: "I liked your sonnet about the Statue much better than I like the Statue itself. Your sonnet gives its subject a *raison d'être* which it wanted before quite as much as it wanted a pedestal. You have set it on a noble one, saying admirably just the right word to be said, an achievement more arduous than that of the sculptor."

When the statue was dedicated, on October 28, 1886, Emma was already dying and making a farewell tour of Europe with her sister Josephine. She read about the ceremony in the Paris *Herald,* and if it evoked any feelings, they were not recorded. Her poem was not inscribed on the pedestal nor were there any plans to place it there.

Emma returned to New York on July 31, 1887, shortly after her thirty-eighth birthday, and went directly to the family home on West Tenth Street. It was unlikely Bessy saw her before her death, for she was in great pain and saw very few of her friends. Emma's sister Anne Lazarus Humphreys-Johnston was named her literary executor. Anne, a Catholic convert, suppressed her diaries and for many years did not allow the reprinting of her Judaic and Zionist poems. Emma may have been thinking of her sister when she commented, "Converted Jews are probably not only the most expensive of all marketable commodities, but also the most worthless after they are purchased." It was not until 1903 that an admirer, Georgina Schuyler, got Emma's "verse about the huddled masses" inscribed in loving memory to her.

*I*n 1888, while still residing with her parents at 76 Irving Place, Bessy gave the *New York City Directory* her first independent listing, designating her profession as "author," which was how it would also appear in the next edition. Nevertheless, she could have had no illusions about the possibility of establishing financial independence with little books like *Manners* or plays written for amateur productions. All she wanted in this world would come to her through the theatre, but not in a way she could then anticipate. Her heretofore unimagined future began with that production of *Contrast* at Daniel Frohman's Lyceum Theatre, when Frohman was so impressed by her work that he advised her to go into theatrical management.

At about that time there was an announcement of the American production of Frances Hodgson Burnett's adaptation of her own near-classic *Little Lord Fauntleroy.* Bessy later claimed to have "heard indirectly that Mrs. Burnett knew little about the stage," so it occurred to her to offer her services as a business manager. A mutual friend gave her a letter of introduction that she promptly presented, making such a favorable impression that she was invited on the spot to attend rehearsals. She never left the author's side over the next two weeks. The only problem with her story was that Burnett did not know "little about the stage": she knew a great deal about it, and probably provided an invaluable education to Bessy.

It was undoubtedly Daniel Frohman who introduced the two women. His first association with Mrs. Burnett was when he produced *Esmeralda,* which William Gillette, the matinee idol, and she adapted from one of her stories. The play opened on a rainy Saturday evening, October 29, 1881, at the Madison Square Theatre on West Twenty-Fourth Street at the rear of the Fifth Avenue Hotel. Once out of the inclement weather, the audience found themselves in an "exquisite interior in which no color seemed to prevail at the expense of others." They were treated to a "charming, enjoyable play," in a drawing room atmosphere that George Odell described as "giving an effect of rich, simple elegance hitherto unknown in New York theatres."

In addition to the beauty of the playhouse, everything about the enormously successful 350-performance engagement was a joy for Mrs. Burnett, up to and including the gallantry of her collaborator, who insisted she had done most of the work.

Frohman's most recent association with the author was a good deal less happy. In 1887, he had produced Augustus Thomas's adaptation of her story, "Editha's Burglar." Mrs. Burnett may have been delighted to pocket her share of the royalties but was decidedly unhappy with both the producer and the playwright when neither sought her permission to do the adaptation.

Mrs. Burnett was miffed about the adaptation of "Editha's Burglar," but her full fury was not felt until several months later. One E. V. Seebohm informed her that he had made an adaptation of her most valuable property, *Little Lord Fauntleroy,* without so much as a by-your-leave. Despite her protests, he could see no reason why she should not be happy with accepting 50 percent of the play royalties and went ahead with plans for a production. It opened on February 23, 1888, at the Prince of Wales Theatre, in London. In the meantime, she wrote her own adaptation, *The Real Little Lord Fauntleroy.* Her English publishers, acting on her behalf, instituted suit against Seebohm for infringement of copyright. Under the law enacted in 1842, the adaptation of a book was permissible and could be presented onstage without the author's consent, but there could be no copies made of it if it contained any portion of the original work. As the play contained large portions of dialogue taken directly from the book and at least one copy had to have been made (Seebohm admitted to four) and deposited with the Lord Chamberlain in order to obtain permission for a production, the court judged entirely in her favor. Frances Hodgson Burnett's own adaptation of her novel was produced within days of the judgment and proved an enormous success. It was this version that the American producer Henry French intended to produce in New York. His reputation was not notable for a sense of honor or integrity. Should the play equal its London success, she would need somebody to look after her interests in New York, as she lived with her husband and sons in Washington, D.C. Thus, it was because she knew quite a bit about the theatre and its practitioners and not "little," as Bessy later claimed, that she was casting about for a representative.

Working with Mrs. Burnett was the start of Bessy's career, a career upon which she embroidered with such skill that many believed she had invented play agentry. This was no more true than the later claim that Elsie had invented interior decoration. Play brokers had been around for several years before she entered the field. They received their percentages in the same way the brokers of any other commodities were reimbursed by their clients. What Bessy Marbury did was to redefine the relationship between the writer and his or her agent. In so doing, she led her sex into a new profession. Women would always be preeminent as writers' agents, especially for playwrights. The most superficial as well as most frequently given explanation of their success was that their maternal instincts worked so well when dealing with their temperamental and sometimes childish clients.

Bessy surely had a motherly side, but it was among the least significant of the qualities contributing to her success. More important was what she had learned about international contracts and copyright law from her father and the books in his library. Most important was her shrewdness in dealing with publishers and theatrical management, her ruthlessness in protecting the rights of her clients. She and her female colleagues were often described as midwives in the birth of plays, but that was only because it was unheard of to think of "ladies" as obstetricians. She later said she would have become a lawyer if she had been a man "or lived in Arizona," and described the secret of her success as "a limitless capacity for taking pains."

> My clients leave everything to me. They never even talk business . . .
> [or have] anything to say to a manager . . . I attend to everything
> and leave the author free to work. A man will sometimes think he
> can do better himself and go around and peddle his plays, and
> then he comes to me finally, when generally I have to do the work
> all over.

Bessy was hired by Mrs. Burnett in November, when the New York production of *Little Lord Fauntleroy* was being set up in the new Broadway Theatre, which was boldly uptown, at West Forty-first Street, across the street from the five-year-old Metropolitan Opera House. The inevitable replacements had to be integrated into the company; adjustments had to be made in the performances to accommodate the needs of the much larger theatre. It was all fascinating to a young woman whose previous experience had been with amateur productions, and she never left her new employer's side during those two weeks of rehearsal. By the evening of the New York opening, December 3, the cast was playing brilliantly, and Frances Hodgson Burnett had the greatest triumph of her life. *Little Lord Fauntleroy* started the theatrical march uptown to what would later be called Times Square. Beginning with its phenomenal opening, the period in which Madison and Herald Squares were entertainment centers drew to an end.

The nature of Marbury's initial functions for Burnett remains a bit obscure. In the beginning she did not draw up her contracts, for the writer's husband was very adept at that. By her own admission, she spent several years as Mrs. Burnett's "private secretary and business agent," which was close enough to the mark. Nevertheless, the demands made upon Bessy were beyond those any writer, no matter how successful, would have dreamed of making on her play broker. Burnett insisted that Bessy come down to Washington every weekend to report on her activities. There was so much to discuss and no telephone to pick up. She never missed a visit, refusing to deviate from the routine even when suffering from tonsillitis and running a fever of 101 degrees.

Under Bessy's supervision, second, third, and even fourth companies for cross-country tours had to be swiftly organized and sent out before stock companies had a chance to knock off the play. "In those days, piracy was facilitated by our very lax interstate laws."

She was at last earning a living in the theatre, but she clung to the dream of becoming a writer. Despite her busy schedule, she found time to collaborate on a play with her friend Mrs. Charles Doremus. A benefit performance of their farce, *A Dead Shot,* was given at the Lyceum on Saturday afternoon, February 2, 1889. Except by Bessy's friends, it was forgotten by the end of the weekend and had no perceptible effect on the direction of Bessy's new career.

There is strong evidence that Bessy did not go abroad that summer. She adored world fairs and later recalled having "personally enjoyed four of these official amusement parks," which she designated as the Philadelphia Centennial, in 1876; Chicago's White City, in 1893; the Paris Exposition, in 1900; and the San Francisco Fair, in 1915. Had she been in Europe, she assuredly would have visited the Paris Exposition of 1889. Her first view from M. Eiffel's tower would not have gone unremarked, nor would she have neglected to mention the formidable exhibition of American painters, many of whom were friends she had made at the parties in the Gilders' studio. Wyatt Eaton's portrait of Helena de Kay Gilder was among the pictures on view.

Except for trips to Washington and to check on the road companies of *Little Lord Fauntleroy,* travel was out of the question that year, because she was busy establishing her career. Writing may have remained her first love, but she was far too practical to ignore the advantages of agentry. It would be unwise to rely entirely on Mrs. Burnett, no matter how profitable the relationship. The woman was too quixotic and often imperious. Bessy discreetly began to acquire additional clients and started treating herself as if she were among them. Miss Elisabeth Marbury, the distinguished new literary agent, was delighted to be representing Miss Elisabeth Marbury, the promising author of *Manners, Contrast,* and *A Dead Shot.*

A letter to J. B. Lippincott & Co., Philadelphia, dated August 30, 1889, provides an example of the tandem in which she harnessed both careers. The handwriting was Palmer-perfect, the spelling without error. It was addressed to "Dear Sirs," indicating that she was still so new at the game she did not have personal contacts among the editors at the more important magazines and publishers.

The first paragraph requested permission to submit a story (her own) of some 22,000 words for publication in their magazine. With a combination of good manners and shrewdness, she politely awaited the reply that would give her the all-important name to whom future submissions could be addressed.

The second paragraph did the selling. "The story has been very well thought of by several prominent publishers here—so much so that I have had three excellent offers for it—but as I would much prefer to have it brought out in your magazine, I must await your verdict before placing it elsewhere."

Her description of the story left little doubt that Elsie was the inspiration for her heroine of "A Gentle Adventuress." She was described as a young girl who was "a victim of fashionable society." Bessy added emphatically: "I do not think my heroine . . . either vulgar or ridiculous."

Enough said about her own work, she also had a manuscript to place by Miss Frances Courtenoy Baylor, the author of "On Both Sides" and "Juan and Juanita." Perhaps because she felt no more was necessary to introduce the work of a successful writer, her selling job on Miss Baylor's piece was exactly one sentence long. "This story runs about 50,000 words, and is exceedingly clever & interesting."

*T*he old dream of a playwright-actress partnership lingered until the afternoon of February 2, 1890, when the bill of an amateur benefit performance was split between them. The first half was devoted to Bessy's newest play, *A Wild Idea,* and the second filled by Elsie with a revival of one of her great successes, *A Cup of Tea.* It was the last time either of them would ever be associated with the amateur theatre.

Bessy could no longer ignore the fact she was on the threshold of a great future that was being made independently of her friend. As for Elsie, she did not know what she wanted. Her thirty-first birthday had been celebrated in December, and if there ever had been any dreams of making a successful marriage in society, they were fast fading. She also was getting a little too old for the role of a *demimondaine* even with a basically good-natured rake such as Pierre Lorillard. Where to turn was probably the subject of many intense heart-to-hearts with Bessy, conversations saved from the maudlin only by their wit. But the problem was a real one and Bessy, one of the world's great Miss Fix-its, must have ached to find a solution.

Elsie was not one of those fools who stood their ground as it was slipping out from under them. It was February, one of the roughest months in which to cross the Atlantic, yet she managed to persuade her mother once again to desert the boys and accompany her to Europe. It is doubtful Lorillard was still on the scene. This time they planned to put up in modest pensions that were a good deal less expensive than comparable digs at any of the fashionable resorts.

The friends arranged to meet in Paris, and Bessy sailed the following month. She was going to make a great deal of money with which she surely intended to come to Elsie's rescue. It was the culmination of a scheme that began sometime the previous year when a silken theatrical producer leased the Australian rights to *Little Lord Fauntleroy.* He put together a company to take over for a long tour. The play had never failed, and it seemed to Bessy a certainty that it would repeat its success down there.

She was to prove her father's daughter or, as she reasoned, exactly like anybody else who ever had anything to do with the theatre: unable to resist "a sure thing." When she was offered a 25 percent interest in the production, she grabbed it, although the investment took all of her savings.

The production was predictably profitable, as she discovered when the weekly statements passed through her hands on the way to Mrs. Burnett. The producer was careful to remit the royalties to keep his franchise, but Bessy never saw penny of profit or return on her investment. He was a slick and devious fellow who answered her queries with another offer she could not afford to turn down. Possibly because it dovetailed with Elsie's plans, he had no trouble persuading her to parlay her investment by booking passage for France to produce the play there. He promised a deposit of five hundred dollars would be waiting for her in Paris, plus fifty dollars a week for expenses, plus 50 percent of the profits. She should have realized there were too many pluses. It would prove the first and last time Miss Elisabeth Marbury was ever cast as a babe in the theatrical woods.

There are two stories told about the ensuing events. According to Mrs. Burnett, she paid for Bessy's passage and expenses not for her personally to produce the play but to find a French producer for it. Bessy's version was by far the more colorful one.

CHAPTER FIFTEEN

Bessy sailed for France in March, taking three hundred dollars with her, all she had left after her investment and her steamship fare. It was a "tempestuous voyage, cold and dreary."[1] They arrived in Le Havre in the middle of a blizzard. Not realizing it was only a summer resort and dismal in the winter, she had booked into the Hôtel Frascati. A few insufficient twigs burning in a small fireplace were the only source of heat in her room, and they had cost extra.

While she was feeling utterly depressed a cable arrived. She tore it open, hoping for news that would lift her spirits. Instead, it brought word that the producer had absconded. He had sent her abroad only to buy enough time to transfer the tour's profits beyond her legal reach.

She kept warm by pacing up and down through a chilled, sleepless night, wondering whether it would not be the wiser course to abandon her plans and return to New York. But that would have been confessing failure, an admission of fallibility her pride would not permit. And there was, after all, a commitment to Mrs. Burnett, to say nothing of Elsie.

By the next morning, the sun was shining brightly, and the temperature had climbed some twenty degrees. She opened her shutters to a view of glistening beach and bright blue sea. Her optimism returned, and she knew with everything in her that she would triumph. Paris and Elsie lay ahead.

> Exhilarated by these reflections, I paid my bill at the hotel, proceeded to the railway station, bought a second-class ticket and took the eight o'clock express to Paris. I felt with Monte Cristo that the world and all its treasures were mine.

Soon after Bessy joined the De Wolfes in their Paris pension, word came from New York that Dr. de Wolfe was gravely ill in New York. Elsie elected to remain in Paris with her friend rather than return to the States with her mother. As she had studied with Julia Bartet of the Comédie Française, her French was, at the very least, serviceable. Their first few weeks alone together were devoted to improving Bessy's skills in the language, which until then were admittedly "meagre [sic] and only connected with a classroom." Elsie did her tutoring well, and her friend acquired a certain colloquial fluency that earned her a reputation for always making herself absolutely understood. That, as Miss Marbury put it, "is an essential in business."

The new linguistic facility was a necessary part of Bessy's plan: she had to be able to communicate. French adaptations were consistently among the most successful plays on Broadway and went on to make additional fortunes from touring and stock companies. The original playwrights usually saw little of these profits, for their works were often bought outright for a fraction of their eventual worth, or they were cheated by an unscrupulous manager just as she had been. Her scheme was a simple one. She would represent the foreign authors in all contracts and dealings in the United States. Their work would only be licensed on a royalty basis, which was the most profitable arrangement and one they understood from dealings in their own country. Adaptations and casting would be conducted under her supervision. There would be visits to theatres to see that the houses were in line with the management's claims. The weekly statement would be forwarded to her office, along with the author's share of the gross, where they would be checked for any discrepancies. All this Bessy would do for a modest percentage of the writers' incomes. How would they ever be able to resist such a dream deal? She knew neither the French theatrical game nor any of the key players, and her big problem was how to gain entry to present it.

It was April in Paris, and despite the lyric, chestnuts would not be in blossom for at least another month. American women, however, were in full bloom. Mistress, wife, actress, heiress—their rank or profession was of no significance. So long as it provided a good income, they could generally be found queued up at M. Worth's establishment at 7 rue de la Paix, hectoring Charles Frederick or his sons, Gaston and Jean-Philippe, for the wardrobe necessary for the encroaching London social season, or the summer in Newport, or even for wear in the backstreets tucked away behind Fifth Avenue. Worth was unique among male couturiers in having sons and, after them, grandsons, as heirs that would keep his fashion house in one family for nearly one hundred years.

Among the women Bessy found shopping along that fashionable boule-

*L*adies and Not-So-Gentle Women

vard was Kate Forsythe, "a rather conspicuous actress on the American stage." She once had been taken to her New York apartment to see her remarkable bed. Enshrined on a platform some eight inches high, it was made entirely of repoussée silver. Miss Forsythe had claimed that she invested in some silver mines that had been such bonanzas the directors considered her "their mascot" and presented her with the bed. It was doubtful whether other investors were similarly rewarded.

It developed that Miss Forsythe had a heart of gold tucked away under the covers in that bed of silver. She had been negotiating for the rights to a French play and was only too happy to share her information with Bessy. To gain access to the inner circle of successful Parisian playwrights, who were all members of La Société des Gens de Lettres, the French society of authors which acted collectively for them, the would-be agent had to obtain the organization's endorsement, which could be granted only by its president, Victorien Sardou, probably the most successful playwright in the world at that time. His great hits in America included *Diplomacy, Divorçons, Fedora,* and *La Tosca.* The royalty system was used in France, but like all of his colleagues, he sold these great moneymakers outright in the States for a fraction of what they earned for their producers.

Forsythe gave her Sardou's address but could be of no help in setting up an appointment. For what seemed endless days, Bessy's "haunting and hopeless preoccupation" was searching for a way to get an interview with the writer, looking for somebody who might have his ear. There were no intermediaries available to her. She would have to write the kind of note that would arouse his curiosity, and in as few words as possible. The few words were due to the modesty of her endowments in written French and a shrewd suspicion that a man as busy as Sardou would have little patience for long-winded pitches.

By the end of the nineteenth century, the postal service had become a thing of joy all over the world. She posted her letter on Friday and by Monday had received his reply, saying he would accord her fifteen minutes of his time at 9 A.M. on Tuesday.

She arrived early and waited in an antechamber. Instead of producing anxiety, the knowledge that she only had fifteen minutes in which to rouse his interest had the reverse effect of clarifying her thinking. She was "perfectly cool and collected." As the clock struck the hour, the door to his study swung open, and a little man with a soft body and a contrastingly angular face came forward to greet her affably. Atop thinning neck-length hair, he wore a little black velvet biretta, for he lived in mortal fear of drafts. A loose coat, baggy trousers, felt slippers, soft shirt, and flowing cravat completed an outfit that suggested total comfort and which she later learned was what he wore to work as unfailingly as a French laborer wore his field-of-blue coveralls.

She was shown into a book-lined room with a long desk covered with pamphlets and papers sorted in neat, precise stacks. This was a compulsive man incapable of disorder and demanding clarity from those with whom he dealt. He asked her to be seated and literally ordered her to come immediately to the point. Fifteen minutes was what she had been granted, and fifteen minutes was what she could expect.

She plunged right in, telling him she wanted his help in revolutionizing the way French plays were sold in the United States, thereby making much more money for their authors. His own arrogance might have lost him a great deal of money on the American production of one of his greatest hits, *La Tosca*.

The play had opened in Paris on the same night Elsie had done her controversial *School for Scandal* in Tuxedo Park. It would later serve as the source for Puccini's perennially popular opera. Even before it went into rehearsal, Sardou had been inundated with offers for the British and American rights.

He directed all of the original productions of his plays. While he was staging *La Tosca*, Fanny Davenport bought the American rights to the play. After Davenport's great success in *Fedora*, another play Sardou had written for Sarah Bernhardt, she never again played a role that the French star had not originated. This latest indignity was too much for the divine Sarah. The play not only was written for her, but the tempestuous actress Flora Tosca had also been modeled on her. It had been her intention to introduce it to American audiences on her next tour of that country. And now this Davenport was again spoiling it by playing *her* parts in America before she did. Davenport! What, after all, *is* a davenport? A daybed! Aha! That explained everything. Very well! If she could not be the first to play it in the United States, she would not play it in Paris either. That meant the production would be canceled, for what actress in the world could ever replace *La Divinité*?

The writer was well aware of the Tosca in Bernhardt, and vice versa, and knew exactly how to soothe her. The play went forward and was a triumph for all concerned—including Fanny Davenport. As another America star, Otis Skinner, observed: "Miss Davenport was a handsome woman, her business sense keen and her industry untiring. To these qualities rather than her acting she owed the great success in which she accumulated a fortune in her productions."[7]

A great part of her fortune emanated from Sardou's plays, and he did not share in it. That was his arrogance in thinking he was shrewd in demanding top prices for the rights. Compared to what Davenport earned on his plays, whatever he asked was a bargain. That same year, she had done it again, when she bought the rights to his latest collaboration with Bernhardt, *Cléopâtre*.

At first, he was upset and then paradoxically comforted to hear from this young woman how, given the opportunity, she would insist La Davenport come up with his just share of the box office receipts in the future, and be on the spot to make sure there was no flimflam. Bessy could tell that her "mental machinery was working with regularity and at top speed."[8] At the end of her quarter-hour, she thanked him for his time and promptly rose to leave. As she reached the door, he called her back, saying he found he had another fifteen minutes to spare. She recalled complacently: "I knew then that my battle was won."[9]

He asked her to return the next day. That afternoon Bessy purchased a map of the United States and brought it along to the next meeting. She spread it out before Sardou and pointed out the large cities, giving their populations, rattling off the distances between them, naming the smaller towns along the way in which a company could play a split week or one-night stand. In those days theatre was the most significant form of entertainment in the world, and a successful play could have four companies all touring at the same time and selling out for months on end, occasionally for years. Her experience managing Mrs. Burnett's interests in the many companies of *Little Lord Fauntleroy* enabled her to estimate the author's income from them. Beyond that, he would not be giving up all of the purchase money he was accustomed to receiving up front. A good portion of that could be demanded as an advance against his future royalties. The more Sardou heard, the more appealing he found the rosy countenance of this plump little lady with the bright blue eyes.

Sardou took her around Paris to introduce all of his colleagues. Elsie sometimes came along, and the playwright was charmed by her style, ease of manner, and wit—traits so intrinsically un-American they were surely inherited from some French ancestor. This new relationship would play a part in changing Elsie's life much sooner than anybody could have supposed during that lovely late spring in which her friend was the one who became a star.

Bessy thought her "victory was complete" on the day she was taken around to the office of La Société des Gens de Lettres and recommended to Georges Pellerin and Gustave Roger, who managed the Society. Within three weeks, it was evident they intended to make her the sole American representative of the Society as, one by one, she was introduced to the members under the official aegis of Pellerin and Roger. They were accepting her on faith, but she was wise enough to know that quality was far more ephemeral in down-to-earth business dealings than it was in the ethereal realm of God. A recommendation from an eminent person would solidify their good opinion. Francis Marbury's good friend Whitelaw Reid was the American ambassador to France. Reticence was not among Bessy's noteworthy traits. She requested and received a reference.

*I*t was essential to her future that the first French play she handled in New York be a big success. The greatest hit in Paris that season was *Feu Toupinel* by Alexandre Bisson, who was among the few writers she had not yet met. An appointment was set up with the play's manager, Albert Carré. By the end of a week, Bisson agreed to give her a chance.

Feu Toupinel was hers. The first step was to have a literal translation made. It was partially to find a translator or adapter that the two women began to travel back and forth between Paris and London late that spring. Bessy wanted to try to duplicate her success with the French writers among their British colleagues. Her credentials were sufficient to induce a Dutch theatrical business manager residing in England, Jacob T. Grein, to allow her to represent his British clients in the United States, while he would do the same for her Americans in England. Bessy got the better of the deal, for, among others, he represented two of the most successful playwrights in London, Henry Arthur Jones and Arthur Wing Pinero. With these two added to her French list, she would automatically be among the most important play agents in the United States, though yet to earn a nickel from her exalted new position.

*W*hile Bessy was conducting business, Elsie was renewing old friendships. She was invited on June 11 to a reception the French-born Lady Wallace was giving for Prince Louis Philippe, the pretender to the French throne. She signed the guest book as Elsie Anderson de Wolfe, deeming the Anderson connection of some importance in Great Britain. Wallace lived in Hertford House and had the most noteworthy private art collection in London. The paintings were dazzling, but most memorable for Elsie was the unparalleled array of priceless eighteenth-century French furniture.

It was common knowledge Lady Wallace intended to give her collection to the empire. Elsie mentioned that Bessy's friend Isabella Stewart Gardner had also amassed a great collection and was building a grand residence in which to install it. Like Wallace, Gardner ultimately intended to give her house and collection to the people. Elsie was invited to bring her friends to view the collection the following week. Bessy could not help being struck by the magnificence of what she viewed, but for Elsie it was a transcendent vision, though it would take years before its power was manifested.

The intimate relationship of Bessy and Elsie did not go unnoticed in New York. On June 19, Bessy's birthday and the day after their visit to Hertford House, *Town Topics* enlightened their readers on the subject.

> The tender firm of Marbury & De Wolfe has its sign out in London just now, having returned to that city after a smart trip to Paris. It was not always deemed admirable for two unmarried women to sweep across the earth without parental guidance, but it now seems quite correct if one only possesses the audacity to assert so. Miss Marbury and Miss De Wolfe may be exceptionally secure and capable ladies ready to shed the blood of the masculine thing that refuses to observe at the first glance their unusual chastity and wisdom, but there are a few of us left who do not like them the more because they are so powerfully equipped. If there were something of old-fashioned timidity and incompetency in their make-up I think we should applaud them with greater zest. Miss Marbury is a hustling, painfully adequate woman of tact and business, and not young enough to need leading strings, therefore we may not sensibly deplore her scorn of maidenly habits; but how about Miss De Wolfe? Is she also a woman of business? I was thinking that she was something else—a society actress, or something resembling one. Whom does she belong to, and why is she skipping through London and Paris with Miss Marbury?

The innuendo and scorn could hardly be missed. By their behavior, Bessy and Elsie indicated they had decided upon the course their lives would take and would not pander to gutter gossips. Summer was upon them. London and Paris would soon be as empty and unpleasant as New York during that time of year. Nothing more could be accomplished professionally until the autumn. No amount of talk was going to stop them from going *en vacances,* their first *tour de France,* which appropriately enough would take place on bicycles.

Neither was rich in what Bessy termed "worldly goods." By her reckoning, they put together a common budget of six francs a day; only five, according to Elsie. Whoever was correct, it was a modest sum even then. The official rate was twenty cents to the franc, but a translation into value in contemporary currency cannot be made. What it purchased in small, homely inns and bistros in 1890 has no equivalence in our own times. They managed to acquire the bikes and the cycling outfits, which had a certain androgynous chic with their straw boaters, tailored shirtwaists with stiff detachable collars and cuffs, narrow cravats, and blazers. What an incongruous pair they made! One tall, and hard sharp angles; the other short, with soft round curves. They were two unlovely spinsters in their thirties. Their lives should have been grinding down into a dull, hopeless routine; instead, they were embarking upon what promised to be a wonderful holiday. "Off we started," Bessy said in the tone of a high-spirited, adolescent lacrosse player, "and I very much doubt whether any girls ever had a better or a healthier time than ourselves."

They strapped the "iron donkeys," as the French called their vehicles, to the exteriors of third-class railroad cars and set off to explore parts of France that were fresh to them. It was an ideal time for cyclists. Automobiles were almost unheard of, the first in France having been sold only three years earlier, when one of Carl Benz's three-wheelers was sold to a Parisian named Emile Rogers. They seldom passed a coach, as they avoided the main roads and kept to the country lanes, where traffic was limited to the occasional cart or horseman.

They went south from Paris to the Loire Valley and Touraine, because it had the advantage for novice cyclists of being "flat so that there would be no hill-climbing." Elsie took notes on everything, from the scene of a bloody assassination to the size of the portions in an inexpensive bistro. They pedaled from one great Renaissance château of that dynasty to another: Azay-le-Rideau, Chambord, Blois, Chenonceaux, Amboise, Talcy. Bessy summed it up: "We saw them all." They wheeled along "the hot dusty roads . . . delighting in everything . . . amused with every obstacle. . . . It was indeed a holiday."

Eventually, they came to rest at the little out-of-the-way inn of Mère Julia, in Pont-Aven, on the Atlantic coast. Despite its estimable drawbacks, they lived well within their budget, "if you could dignify our monotonous 'eats' as food." Every meal included some form of sardines. Yet the ambience at Mère Julia's was most congenial. Several artists were also staying there who, like Elsie and Bessy, were seeking atmosphere and beauty on a shoestring. "And many a merry outing did we all have together."

Perhaps it was simply as a respite from riding her bicycle that Bessy recalled the place so fondly, but something makes it seem as if it may have been far more meaningful. If the two women ever did consummate their relationship sexually, it may well have been at that inn. It could explain why almost thirty years later, when Elsie was about to break up their ménage to live permanently in Europe, the more sentimental Bessy went far out of her way to revisit Pont-Aven, and the little inn where she had spent "such happy days." Mère Julia was still alive, and all was as it had been—"the same disorder, the same sardines."

There is no way of telling whether Elsie had returned to New York City by midnight, September 24, when Stephen de Wolfe died. While her brothers were dismissed anonymously as "three sons," the *New York Times* obituary identified Elsie as his daughter who had achieved "an enviable reputation as an amateur actress." Unusual as it was that a daughter rather than the sons should be identified by name, there was no mention of her being at his bedside or in the house when he died. Her own memoir dismissed his death in a few lines, and, oddly, she placed his death a year earlier than it actually occurred.

It was quite likely Georgiana had informed her daughter of the seriousness of his condition. Elsie's feelings about her father were ambiguous at best, and she preferred not to allow his illness to terminate the pleasures of her French holiday with Bessy. It was a callous choice, which she probably regretted over the years to the point of reversing it by changing the year of his death to one in which she was at home and could have been at his bedside.

By the time Dr. de Wolfe's debts and medical expenses were cleared away, between two and three thousand dollars was all that remained to be divided among the mother, daughter, and three sons. This amounted to destitution for people who never had worked a day in their lives. Something had to be done and quickly. Elsie took charge. No matter what her social friends and *Town Topics* thought, there was no alternative to becoming a professional actress, but not in some modest role. Hardly a beauty in the Cora Brown-Potter or Lillie Langtry mold, she would, nevertheless, settle for nothing less than stardom if only the way could be found to attain it. Fortunately, Bessy was on her way and would carry Elsie along with her. That always had been the plan. Although it was not to be as playwright to her actress, it would work well. She could count on her Bessy to see to that.

CHAPTER SIXTEEN

Victorian New York set rigid rules governing a widow's conduct, which a *young* widow in particular had to obey or be forever cast out of good society. Knowing she could not control her own destiny at home was but one of many things that pushed Anne Harriman Sands to her first act of defiance, her decision to move far away from New York. Of the other reasons, the most obvious was simply to escape, to be gone from a place where she was no longer happy and had few prospects of future happiness. There was a more practical motive. At the time he so unexpectedly died, Sam Sands had neither come into his inheritance nor made his own fortune. With the fifty thousand dollars her father had put in her name at the time of her wedding and the rent from the Garden City property, she had been left in adequate but severely reduced circumstances. On her diminished income, the young widow decided that life would be far more comfortable in England. There was also the question of her physical allure, for Anne was striking in mourning. The unrelenting black of her Worth gowns was the perfect setting for her opalescent skin, her large sapphire eyes, her golden hair. Suitors began to appear much sooner than was considered seemly. Among them, Lewy Rutherfurd attracted her in equal measure to her attractiveness to him. It was a relationship that would be more decorously explored at some distance from the strictures of New York society.

Anne may occasionally have been homesick in London, but she was never lonely. Everywhere there were acquaintances dating back to her childhood, some on the prowl for titled husbands and others already married to them. Most of all, there was the first secretary at the American embassy, Henry White, and his accomplished wife, Lewy's sister Margaret, nicknamed Daisy. They were among the few Americans in a set known as "the Souls," which was made up of the brightest young people in London, including two future prime ministers, Asquith and Balfour, as well as a future viceroy of India, Lord Curzon, who would soon marry the American heiress Mary Leiter. The White residence was one of the places where the wealthiest and most attractive Americans mingled with the most intelligent and influential Britishers. Of most lasting importance to Anne, it was where Lewy and she could meet in a setting that did not compromise her.

By any measure, Lewis Morris Rutherfurd, Jr., was the beau ideal, combining wealth, extravagant good looks, charm, and athletic prowess. He was also exceedingly wellborn, descending maternally from Peter Stuyvesant. Although long since sold off by the family, the paternal ancestral estate, Morrisania, once had spread over a good portion of what would become the south Bronx. That line of wealthy landowners included Lewis Morris, one of the signers of the Declaration of Independence, and John Rutherfurd, the first senator from the state of New Jersey and a member of the committee that had designed the grid plotting the streets of Manhattan above Fourteenth Street. Both gentlemen appeared in the first social register in the United States, Mrs. Jay's *Blue Book.*

Lewy's father, Lewis Morris Rutherfurd, Sr., was one of the original Patriarchs and would later appear on McAllister's list of Four Hundred. He was a man of remarkable achievement rendered singular by his having been born with everything and thus having no need to accomplish anything. He was a dilettante astronomer and photographer, and his work was the equal of many professionals. His photographs of the moon surpassed all others in clarity and are still preserved in fireproof vaults by Columbia University, along with his pictures of the sun, the solar spectrum, and various star clusters.

In 1858, after being elected to the board of trustees of Columbia College, he set up its department of astronomy as well as expanding the curricula in mathematics and the other sciences. In Edith Wharton's *The Age of Innocence,* the character of Professor Emerson Sillerton was an affectionate portrait of him. For all of his considerable accomplishments, he remained a modest man. His associate Dr. B. Gould observed: "His dislike of ostentation and show was a conspicuous trait. . . . He was never known to wear any one of the many decorations . . . conferred upon him."

Lewis Morris Rutherfurd, Sr., sired seven children. So handsome was this brood that Rutherfurd was soon as famous for the looks of his children as he was for his scientific research. Lewis and his younger brother, Winty, were underachievers from their father's point of view but were the playboy charmers of the world to everybody else.

The Rutherfurds had a summer cottage next door to the Joneses on Harrison Street in Newport. Edith Jones Wharton had a crush on Winty and described the beauty of the Rutherfurd men as "proverbial." Years later, she told the story of an Englishman and American strolling down Piccadilly comparing the physiognomies of their respective compatriots.

"I'll grant you," the Brit said, "that your women are lovely; perhaps, not as regularly beautiful as ours, but often prettier and more graceful. But your men—yes, of course, I've seen very good looking American men; but nothing—if you'll excuse my saying so—to compare with our young Englishmen of the public school and university type, our splendid young athletes: there, like these two who are just coming toward us."

The two young "British" Adonises to whom he gestured were Winthrop and Lewis Morris Rutherfurd, Jr.

By the end of 1889, Anne and Lewy Rutherfurd were engaged. It was a whirlwind courtship, and the lovers were to be in England when it became official. The reaction of Victorian New York to the betrothal of a young woman less than a year into her widowhood must have been something so prodigious it could barely be moderated by the combined social prestige of the Harrimans and the Rutherfurds. The prospective groom complained to his father: "I have heard people at home are talking about Ann [sic] and me. Have you heard anything? If so, I should like to know what was said and by whom. I wish people would mind their own affairs."

There was a respite in their passions when Lewy took leave of her to accompany his mother, Margaret, to Cannes, where she could pass her winter in the milder climate of the South of France. The lovers could not bear to be separated for long, and shortly after the beginning of the new year, Anne arrive in Cannes chaperoned by her brother Jim and her sister Emmy. The party checked into a suite of rooms at the Hôtel des Anglais, a few blocks north of the Croisette and sheltered from the sometimes raw winds off the Mediterranean.

Lewy and Margaret Rutherfurd were at the Hôtel Californie, which was in the hills above Cannes. Although it was somewhat remote, they had chosen to stay there for its splendid views of the city and sea. Anne came up to call on her future mother-in-law on the very afternoon she arrived. The splendid impression Lewy's "fiance" made was conveyed in a letter to Daisy White in London, from Mrs. Dunfalls, her mother's paid companion.

"Mrs. Sands came up this afternoon to see her [Mrs. Rutherfurd]. She is very charming, so natural and unaffected, and seems so sensible. I am sure she will be a delightful addition to your family circle."

The "sensible" part of Anne's nature could not be stressed too strongly. It was hoped by Lewy's family that she would provide a moderating influence over him. The headstrong Lewy was already agitating for his infirm mother to move to the Des Anglais so he could be nearer to his sweetheart. Margaret Rutherfurd relented but not so far as to stay at the Des Anglais. To have the lovers housed in the same hotel would simply add to the scandal. They would take rooms at the Prince des Galles, which was closer to the city and a short distance away from the Harriman party. The pleasure Lewy took in his intimacy with Anne was manifest in a letter he wrote to his father a week after her arrival.

> Dear Governor,
>
> I am sitting in Ann's drawing room which she has made most comfortable and attractive with palms, flowers and all the little things women like to have about them. Yesterday, she, Mrs. Dodge, and their brother, Jim, and I went by rail to Nice, lunched at the Restaurant de Paris and then drove to Monte Carlo. Neither of the women had ever been there before and of course enjoyed every thing proportionately. We gambled a little and strange to say, won, had a good dinner and came home . . . I have not heard a word from Winty and only one letter from Stuyvie . . . I am economizing so as to have more next summer when it will be needed.

Once Lewy's betrothal to Anne was a *fait accompli,* the Rutherfurds' unequivocal acceptance of the match was a rare thing in the times and circumstances. It was manifest in a letter his brother Stuyvie wrote to his mother toward the end of January, although he could not resist a touch of his characteristic acerbity. "It is nice to see Lewy so happy and to think he has chosen so well. Give my love to him and to Mrs. S. if she cares to have it."

Stuyvie's acceptance was soon so unrestricted, he gave full sway to his acid wit when referring to the lovers. The attitude might well have stemmed from a subconscious resentment. He had married right out of college to one of the Morgans' Pierpont cousins. It had been a childless union that within a decade terminated in his widowerhood. Toward the end of February, in a letter to his mother, Stuyvie observed:

> What wonderful long walks Lewy is taking! It is surprising what changes the tender passion will make in a man. Generally, it is the head and the heart that are affected but in Lewis' case, it seems to have gone to his legs. I think he is doubly to be congratulated in having found a partner who has the health and strength for so much exercise.

The wedding was fixed for June 16, 1890, scarcely fifteen months after Sam Sands's fatal accident. The decision to marry in London was obviously made by the desire to be three thousand miles away from the censorious *tsk-tsks* of New York society. Anne's brother Jim came over from Paris, where he was living, to give the bride away. Aside from her sons, the only other members of Anne's family in attendance were her sister and brother-in-law Lillie and Bill Travers, motivated more by his being one of the groom's best friends than by the family connection. Daisy White was the matron of honor, and Winty, his brother's best man, in the Anglican service at St. George's Hanover Square, which was well known for its fashionable weddings—Shelley, Lady Hamilton, Disraeli, and George Eliot having been among those who had preceded Lewy and Anne down its aisle. A wedding breakfast followed at the Whites' residence at 9 Grosvenor Crescent. Anne was radiant and so much in love that the meager turnout of American friends and family could not have mattered less to her.

When they returned to New York, the newlyweds set up housekeeping at 246 East Fifteenth Street, a red brick Federal mansion at the corner of Second Avenue, six blocks north of the old family home at 175 Second Avenue, in which Lewy had grown up.

Like the Second Avenue mansion, the one on Fifteenth Street was part of the legacy left to Lewy's older brother Stuyvie by their uncle Peter Gerard Stuyvesant. It made him the wealthiest member of the family. The childless Peter feared the Stuyvesant name would die with him. To forestall this, he offered to make his sister's oldest son the heir to his considerable fortune on condition that his name be changed from Stuyvesant Rutherfurd to Rutherfurd Stuyvesant. Lewis Morris Rutherfurd could not stand between his son and such riches and allowed the name to be changed.

Old Peter could not have chosen more wisely in his quest for an heir. Rutherfurd Stuyvesant proved an excellent businessman who enhanced the value of the family real estate holdings, thus increasing his inheritance many times over. At only nineteen, he had commissioned Richard Morris Hunt to design the city's first apartment dwelling on East Eighteenth Street. When his parents left New York he added another story to the Second Avenue house he had allowed them to use as their residence and converted it into the Rutherfurd Apartments.

Lewis and Winthrop Rutherfurd were established in the L. & W. Realty Company, at 51 Liberty Street, presumably managing their brother's properties. It freed Stuyvie to pursue his new passion for collecting antiques and works of art, particularly the medieval armor that would later form the nucleus of the formidable Metropolitan Museum collection. His younger brothers did not have the characters of tycoons to whom business was a passion; to them it was merely a pastime. They did not allow the real estate business to interfere with the more pleasurable pursuits that placed them among New York's most popular young sports.

*M*argaret Chanler Stuyvesant Rutherfurd's death in 1891 was the first of a series of misfortunes that would beset the family during that year. It must often have seemed to Anne, as time passed, that she was a Jonah preceding death wherever she went. Even the birth of her daughter, the first of her generation to be named for her imposing late grandmother, Margaret Stuyvesant Rutherfurd, did not lighten her duties to the mourners. On January 6, 1892, she wrote from Tranquility to her father-in-law: "The last two days I have been going over the house and everything in it. . . . There are a number of things that need doing. May I give the orders for what I consider really necessary?"

Anne requested permission to redo her mother-in-law's room for the new baby. Always, she was tactful. Always, she was aware of her position as a mere woman, a daughter-in-law, a guest in the house that was supposedly her home. She assured him that she would do nothing, if he preferred to leave things as they were. She responded to his suggestion that she buy the baby a gift from him: "Would you mind my buying a carriage. . . . A good one is very expensive, and I can think of nothing she needs as much." She closed apologetically, "Please, excuse this disgraceful letter."

Lewis Morris Rutherfurd, Sr., died on May 30, 1892, at Tranquility. The bulk of his estate was left to Lewis Junior and Winthrop. There was no need to look after Stuyvie or Daisy, who had a very rich husband. He did leave Edgerston, his Newport house, to her, because she always had loved it more than the others. Because Stuyvie was the only one who could afford its upkeep, the seven-thousand-acre Tranquility was left to him with the proviso that his brothers could build houses on the property and have the use of it for as long as they lived.

Although not wealthy in Stuyvie's class, the young Rutherfurds were now able to do almost anything they wished. Their new affluence allowed Lewy and Winty to pursue the pleasures of the leisured life, spending still more time at Tranquility, breeding fox terriers and English pheasants, and less at their real estate office. It was an era that suited them perfectly, one in which the wealthy amateur athlete was something of a popular icon.

CHAPTER SEVENTEEN

Upon returning to Paris after the bicycle tour, Bessy Marbury got some disturbing news about the American prospects of *Feu Toupinel*. Most of New York's leading producers had been over to see the play and rejected it on the grounds that they believed the plot would prove too risqué for American audiences. In classic French farce tradition, it revolved around a man caught lying to both his wife and mistress.

With a facility for which she would become famous throughout her long career, Bessy improvised a solution. Why not make it two wives, instead of a wife and mistress, and kill off the hero before they discover his mendacity? Americans might have problems with a man having a mistress, she reasoned, but bigamy and widowhood were both acceptable to them, and thus *"Frantic" Toupinel* could become *Mr. Wilkinson's Widows.*

Of the New York managements, Bessy's best connections were the Frohman brothers. Daniel had been her original mentor, and Charles she considered the most promising manager on Broadway. The latter already had seen the play and rejected it. She wired him outlining her proposed revisions and asking him to reconsider. His return cable instructed her to draw up the contracts.

These professional shenanigans only served to confirm Victorien Sardou's original high opinion of her. His new play, *Thermidor,* was scheduled to go into rehearsal at the Comédie Française in December for an opening in late January. With what combination of charm and persuasiveness one can only begin to imagine, Bessy and Elsie de Wolfe convinced the most successful playwright in France to allow Elsie, an amateur, to play the leading role in a professional New York production. The women probably had the assistance of Julia Bartet, who was to play the part in the Paris production. Having replaced Sarah Bernhardt as the reigning actress of the Comédie Française, and considered by many to be her equal, she previously had accepted Elsie as a private student: it must be assumed that a performer of her stature gave lessons only to those in whose talent she genuinely believed. Bessy's largest problem would be to find a New York management that would agree to take a chance on her beloved friend. This was not to prove as difficult as at first it might have seemed.

The American theatre of 1890 was so vast, its appetite for new playscripts so voracious, that when Miss Marbury—which was how she would be addressed professionally for the rest of her life—arrived home as the exclusive representative of every dramatist in Paris as well as a number of the more important ones in London, she was in a fair way to name her own terms. Officially, she could draw up contracts dictating advances, royalties, and conditions of production. Her unofficial condition was a career for Elsie de Wolfe. Charles Frohman wanted only one thing out of life: to be the king of Broadway producers. Miss Marbury's formidable list of clients made it clear that pleasing her would contribute to the achievement of his own ambitions. Any management would have regarded a new play by Sardou as money in the bank. When she offered *Thermidor* to him, she must have added that the playwright wanted Elsie de Wolfe to play the lead. There could be worse choices on several counts. She was a highly regarded actress in the amateur theatre, which was still being given serious consideration by the public and press. A few seasons before, Cora Brown-Potter had made the transition from amateur to professional with great box office, if not critical, success. Elsie had a society following, which had to interest a man who had taken over Proctor's Twenty-third Street Theatre for his new company and would profit from having them on his subscription list.

An acceptable adapter had to be found for *Feu Toupinel.* Frohman opted for William Gillette, the well-known actor-writer whose play *All the Comforts of Home* he had produced the year before with some moderate success. The new play was a great hit that earned for M. Bisson an imposing fifty thousand dollars in royalties and, as Bessy was the first to boast, an equally imposing reputation for her. "Of course, my successful manipulation of this farce gave me a prestige beyond words. It was a clear case of money having talked."

For Gillette's part, he so admired the skill with which Bessy had dealt with the producer that he asked her to become his agent. Her list of successful American writers was expanding very nicely. As her client, Gillette was to write and star in two of the greatest successes of their day, *Secret Service* and *Sherlock Holmes.* She would also handle his successful star turns in plays by other clients: *Too Much Johnson, The Admirable Crichton,* and *Dear Brutus.*

With her mother along, Elsie returned to Paris at the beginning of December. Sardou had arranged for her to attend the rehearsals of *Thermidor* at the Comédie Française. Each morning, she hurried down the narrow, fashionable rue St. Honoré, undoubtedly often distracted by the appealing objects in the shopwindows, to the theatre in the Palais Royale. She learned the play in French before tackling it in English in order to understand the nuances of what she was observing. The leading man, Benoît Constant Coquelin, was arguably the greatest actor in France if not the world. When he was not wanted onstage, he would sit beside her and dictate suggestions for her to take down in the notebook that had become a necessary appendage. After the painstaking hours of rehearsal were over, she would rush over to Mme Bartet's flat, where the actress would take the time to coach Elsie in giving a line-by-line imitation of her own performance. Whether or not she would be successful in translating this mimicry into English remained to be seen.

Thermidor opened in Paris on January 24. The first-night audience sat through it in what appeared to be a polite sopor. The Paris newspaper accounts spoke of the play's reactionary anti-republicanism, and on the second night the audience rioted. The police had to be called in to eject a group of rowdy rebels who were throwing anything they could get hold of at the actors. The final curtain came down to rousing cries of *"A bas Sardou!"*

Ordinarily, such a passionate response would have been sufficient to create a *succès de scandale* and have the Parisians clamoring for admission, especially to a production at the Theatre of France distinguished by the names of Sardou, Bartet, and Coquelin. But word was also out on the ennui inspired by the play, and for all the sensationalism, no ticket buyers queued at the box office. Elsie later claimed that the play was banned after its first performance, which, though not true, put a good face on failure.

With the artifice endemic to the inspired agent handling an indifferent product, Bessy managed to convince Frohman not to abandon his production of *Thermidor* despite its failure in Paris. Sardou was one of the most successful and prolific writers in the world. *Thermidor* was the first of his plays with which Frohman was involved; given the right circumstances, there could be many more in the future. The producer renewed his option.

Bessy returned to Paris that spring for a holiday with Elsie. After having turned a French hit no American producer had wanted into a bigger New York hit and secured a first-rate Broadway production for a Comédie Française flop, she was the toast of La Société des Gens de Lettres. She had "a prestige beyond words." Even those writers Bessy knew in only a casual way spoke of her almost reverentially. The only time she ever met Alexandre Dumas *fils* was at Sardou's estate, at Marly-le-Roi. The Master, as people called Sardou, an avid vegetable gardener, was bending over his melon patch when Dumas came along. After being introduced to their shared agent, Dumas, whose "black moments" were famous, turned back to his host and sighed, "How I envy you who can feel such enthusiasm over a mere melon."

Sardou, who was as chronically optimistic as his colleague was pessimistic, replied, "How I pity you ... who are incapable of such a sentiment."

After that one meeting and several successful negotiations for American productions of his plays, the normally dour Dumas warmed up when Bessy's name came up in an interview he was giving to the Paris magazine *Gaulous:* "She is one who Balzac would have added to his gallery of sympathetic characters."

They arrived in New York aboard the *Gascogne,* on August 2. Frohman, as great a manipulator of the press as was Elsie, saw to it that she was met by a horde of reporters, one of whom observed that she was accompanied by "Miss Elisabeth Marbury and an enormous aggregation of luggage."

The new Broadway star was able to announce that the production of *Thermidor* would be first-rate in every way. The gifted English matinee idol Johnston Forbes-Robertson had been engaged as her leading man, and the scenery would be designed by Mr. Hunt, of the Metropolitan Opera. As for the clothes, though she was playing a peasant washerwoman, they had been made by Worth, and she had to say that her second-act gown was a knockout.

> There we were, then, two young women with very little money and very big dreams, wanting to find a home which would give us room for growth and where, when our busy day was over, we could find both rest and diversion. . . .
>
> The fashionable residence districts—Washington Square, Fifth Avenue, Madison Avenue, Central Park West—were all beyond anything we could afford. Gaily we pursued our way, sure that at the right moment the right house would present itself. We had exhausted—or thought we had—all of the desirable neighborhoods, when we thought of Gramercy Park—a spot hallowed in history, closed in from the outside world, and where the oldest and most interesting families had their homes. Here, too, rentals were high. Just two blocks away we happened upon a sleepy, shabby but adorable little house at the corner of seventeenth street and Irving Place. From the moment we saw it we felt no peace until the lease was signed.

As Elsie told it, the tale had the charm of youth and discovery, but, unfortunately, also some inaccuracies. It was unlikely it took them a great deal of time to think of Gramercy Park, or that Irving Place presented any surprises, as the Marburys were among the old and interesting families living in the neighborhood. They still resided in the Irving Place townhouse one block south of the Park in which Bessy had been born. The little house the women "happened upon" was three, not two, blocks away from Gramercy Park; it was two blocks away from Bessy's home. If, as they so often reputed, Washington Irving, the man for whom the street was named, actually had lived in that house, it would have been at just about the time of Bessy's birth.

Bessy and Elsie did rewrites on themselves for as long as they lived. It is probable they enlarged upon a neighborhood fable to add color to an otherwise quite drab house they would make famous during the period they shared it. So persuasive was their mythmaking that it prevailed long after their celebrity had faded away, attested to by the plaque at 122 East Seventeenth Street incorrectly informing passersby that it was the former residence of Washington Irving, while no medallion identifies the two women who lived there presiding over a salon in the Parisian tradition that was among the first to commingle the city's social and artistic worlds.

The red-brick house, with its iron-grille porch, was built in 1840 and numbered 45 East Seventeenth Street. Three years later, it became 73 East Seventeenth, which it remained until after the Civil War, when it finally was registered as 122. It is extremely unlikely that the bookish Bessy did not know that New York's most celebrated writer had never lived there. The legend about Irving probably arose from the fact that its first owner was his nephew Edgar. The only Washington Irving ever to have lived there was Edgar's son, who was named for his uncle.

*B*essy's achievements as a play broker had not yet fully displaced her dreams of becoming a popular writer. That would not happen until the evening of March 14, 1892, when Daniel Frohman produced *Merry Gotham* by Elisabeth Marbury at his Lyceum. The failure of her play was so complete he had another production, *The Gray Mare*, ready to open at the theatre within a month.

The end of Bessy's dreams of literary triumph gave her the freedom to devote all of her time to something that would prove of greater significance. By becoming the most important literary agent in New York, she opened a new profession to women in which they would remain a dominant force through the end of the next century. Two elements combined to make her preeminent in her field: the contractual skills she learned from studying the law books in her father's office; and the ability to think like a writer, which would enable her to advise her clients from a point of view akin to their own.

Her only change of address was the additional listing of an "office" at 21 West Twenty-fourth Street. Her play brokerage had outgrown her bedroom in Irving Place, just as her chicken hatchery had. That first office was one small room that she shared with her stenographer-typist, whose salary was ten dollars a week. When she added it to the rent of fifteen dollars a month, Bessy felt "bowed down by the sense of this responsibility. Commissions might come in slowly," and then where would she be?

But fortune was on her side with the success of *Mr. Wilkinson's Widows*, the options on *Thermidor* and her own play, *Merry Gotham*, Frohman's road tour of a revival of Sardou's *Diplomacy*, and the production of Mrs. Burnett's new play, *The Showman's Daughter*, as well as international companies of *Little Lord Fauntleroy* and the successful Broadway premiere of Henry Arthur Jones's *The Dancing Girl*. Within a month she had to lease the adjoining large room, with an increase of rental to thirty-five dollars. Her young employee was so busy typing contracts that Bessy began to think of hiring a personal assistant. Then, when it was still a daring new profession for a woman, the assistant proudly, defiantly called herself "a private secretary," a position previously filled exclusively by a male, as it continued to be for some time into the future at "old boy" firms such as Drexel, Morgan.

Fortune did not bless Elsie de Wolfe's first sally into the professional theatre. From the start of rehearsals, it was evident that there would be problems with *Thermidor*. It was something lacking in the play, rather than political opposition, that had caused its failure in Paris. An amateur actress, no matter how appealing, could not be expected to give a performance that compensated for dramatic flaws that one of France's greatest actresses, in the same role, had been unable to conceal.

For the opening of *Thermidor*, Miss Marbury did what she would become celebrated for doing better than anybody else in the New York theatre, what first had brought her to Daniel Frohman's attention: she orchestrated the audience. It was important to outdo herself for Sardou, Frohman, and Elsie, each of whom would be an essential part of the future that seemed more and more within reach. On the evening of October 12, the carriages stretched down Twenty-third Street as far as the stairs leading up to the Sixth Avenue El. The first-night curtain rose before the most socially prominent and glamorous assemblage in Proctor's history. If only the evening had ended with her contribution, it would have been triumphant. What followed was one of the few things on which Bessy and Elsie disagreed. The former said firmly, "The success of this drama was *nil*"; while the latter, admitting it was "not a money-maker," termed it "an artistic triumph." Elsie recalled that the critics were "most generous with me, applauding my efforts and setting me down as an actress of real promise."

The truth was that even Bessy's good friend Edward A. Dithmar, the critic on *The New York Times,* who offered a minority opinion by actually liking the play and Frohman's production of it, described the leading lady as "an error in judgment such as the best managers often make."

The *Dramatic Mirror* had praised many of her performances in amateur theatre but had to admit that her bearing was still "amateurish," and concluded that her resources as a professional actress were "decidedly limited."

Frohman had to fulfill his contracts with theatres across the country by providing them with "first-rate" productions and, despite the disappointing run, he sent Elsie and *Thermidor* on a long tour. She was to find her first theatrical tour "a miserable adventure." Too much already has been written about the dismal traveling arrangements, the seedy accommodations, that appalling food that even the greatest stars had to endure when touring in the United States until well into the first half of the twentieth century. It must have been close to intolerable for somebody as fastidious as Elsie. To lighten the ordeal, she brought her mother along with her for company, and whenever it proved feasible, Bessy came out to join them for a weekend. Nevertheless, the situation became so unpleasant that Georgiana de Wolfe wanted her daughter to give up and go home. Elsie would have complied were it not "for my gratitude to Charles Frohman and our own need for money."

During her years of cultivating the theatrical press to garner whatever mentions she could for her amateur productions, Bessy kindled genuine friendships with the two most important critics in New York, Dithmar and William Winter, of the *Tribune.* Until the end of the 1920s, it was not unusual for critics not only to fraternize with those they were hired to review but also to participate in theatrical productions. The famous Round Table at the Hotel Algonquin included the most successful writers and actors of the day as well as the most influential critics. It was unremarkable for a critic like Alexander Woollcott to write his review of a production and then dash off to join in the festivities at its opening-night party. In an extreme instance, George S. Kaufman served simultaneously as dramatic editor of *The New York Times* and co-author of some of Broadway's biggest hits.

Critics were often hired to rewrite scripts and do adaptations during the period when Bessy started her business. If they were not in fact consulted about casting, their deep friendships with certain actors made it likely that managements would hire them. There were instances when critics acted as unofficial representatives of artists they particularly favored. Such was the case of Dithmar and Winter with the young writer Clyde Fitch. After seeing a Boston production of one of his earliest efforts, *Betty's Finish,* they urged the actor-manager Richard Mansfield to commission him to write a vehicle for him. The result, *Beau Brummell,* was one of the star's greatest hits, remaining in his repertory until his death seventeen years later.

Fitch was properly launched as a playwright but improperly compensated for his work. He had been so eager to have Mansfield produce and star in a play of his that he had sold him all the rights for fifteen hundred dollars. When the young man complained that the actor was getting richer with each performance while he was earning nothing, his critic sponsors pointed him in the direction of Elisabeth Marbury.

Fitch knew from his first visit to Bessy's office on West Twenty-fourth Street that he would be able to rely on her "for future guidance so that never again would he be so foolish . . . this was the first and last time that Clyde Fitch ever sold a play for a fixed amount," and the first of many duels she would have with the pugnacious Mansfield over the rights of her clients. But she was too shrewd to underestimate his value to them, which was why she continued to submit plays to him. Fitch and she might have been aggravated every time they found him playing *Beau Brummell* to a full house from which they reaped no financial benefit, but they knew how much it contributed to the writer's new prominence. Bessy was too realistic not to acknowledge "the value of the publicity due to Mansfield's superb performance and stupendous success."

Clyde was a parent-ridden child who had been very nearly crushed between a permissive, magnolia-scented southern belle mother and a rigid professional soldier father. The captain could never understand how he had sired this effete boy, so sissified that as an Amherst undergraduate he had played all of the female leads in the plays put on by the college dramatic society. Although his heart was always in theatre, his parents would not countenance any thought of a career in it. His second love was the style in which people lived, and he originally went to New York to become what his father thought was an architect, and his mother knew was an interior decorator.

As surely as she filled a special role in his professional life, Bessy filled a special role in the emotional life of her new twenty-five-year-old client. She was the loving mother strong enough to protect him against the transgressions of his avuncular producers. It was extraordinary how often those who knew her best described her as possessing archetypically feminine characteristics. Her clients almost universally described her as protective, maternal, nurturing, compassionate. The producers, exposed to her tough side, had to admit that even at her most obdurate, Miss Marbury was "a lady." That was not to say she was without cunning and a certain obliqueness: she could not have succeeded so brilliantly without them. Poised on the blurred line between the deceitful and the devious, a line that her male colleagues so often purposely failed to see, she was never ruthless.

$\mathcal{A}$t the same time that Bessy agreed to become Fitch's agent, Charles Frohman signed the matinee idol John Drew to an exclusive contract and was looking for a good vehicle for him. *The Masked Ball,* a play by Bisson and Carré, would be perfect, and her new client was the ideal choice to adapt it. When she broached Frohman about it, he was not completely sold on what he termed "your pink tea author," but she needed only to point out the box office receipts of *Beau Brummell* to change his mind.

The Masked Ball was a great success, but Bessy had no illusions about the gifts and nature of her first successful American client. "His characterizations of women were as a rule more convincing than were those of men, for there was no use blinking at the fact that his own nature was a composite one. . . . This commingling of the masculine and feminine is very common in artists. . . . The mind of a man with the heart of a woman makes an ideal exotic that should not be despised. . . . They go hand in hand where artists are concerned."

At the end of the tour of *Thermidor,* Frohman did not renew Elsie's contract. Bessy was far too realistic to have pressed too hard on her friend's behalf. Her affection did not blind her to how negligible the talent was, but nevertheless neither Frohman nor she could deny the novice had a presence, an authority. Those were qualities Elsie would have in abundance throughout her life.

Elsie managed to obtain a position with Ramsey Murrey's touring company. Rehearsals were not scheduled to begin until the autumn, and when Bessy made her annual combination business and holiday trip to Europe that spring, Elsie accompanied her. Before Paris, they stopped in London, where Bessy was eager to renew her acquaintance with Oscar Wilde, whom she had met in New York during his American lecture tour ten years earlier, in 1882. Her wish to reacquaint herself with him was motivated by a desire to handle his play *Lady Windermere's Fan,* which was the biggest success in London.

When the agent and her prospective client met again, they were in many ways different people from the ones who had first been introduced in New York. Bessy had become almost as rotund, extroverted, and epigrammatic as he, and Wilde had become almost as good a businessman as she. When the actor-manager George Alexander reacted favorably to his first reading of *Lady Windermere,* he had asked how much the manager would give him for it and was offered one thousand pounds. The writer's reaction was "A thousand pounds! I have so much confidence in your excellent judgment, my dear Alec, that I cannot but refuse your generous offer—I will take a percentage."

The result was he earned seven thousand in the first year alone. When he heard Bessy did not believe in selling plays outright and always held out for royalties based on the weekly gross, he was happy to go with her. The business relationship developed into a close friendship. Like so many before her, she fell "under the thrall of his gifts as a conversationalist and could listen with delight to the brilliancy of his talk." She found that "his wit scintillated incessantly," but was not blind to an egotism "so obvious as to be beyond comment."

Wilde, his wife, and two sons lived in an extraordinary house at 16 Tite Street, in Chelsea. It was decorated in collaboration with the architect-decorator Edward Godwin, more as a conversation piece and setting for the most famous aesthete of his time than as a home. Its innovations influenced many future decorators, including Elsie and Syrie Maugham. The former decorated a portion of the Irving Place drawing room in a style reminiscent of the library in Tite Street, "variously described as Turkish, Moorish, and North African." Much later, the striking forest-green walls in the Wilde drawing room would be recalled and help to revive her career after her safe beiges and chintzes had become clichés.

It was with clients such as Wilde and Clyde Fitch that Elsie truly became Bessy's helpmate. They were obsessed with interior ornament, which was of little interest to Bessy, and Elsie could joyously discuss it with them for hours on end as if it were all that mattered in this world. Bessy had no patience with all that chichi. One of her clients, George Middleton, recalled: "She was always more interested in talking about ward politics than my scripts."

After a financially promising stay in London, the women crossed to Paris, where Sardou greeted them with the same warmth he always had displayed. He placed no blame on Elsie for the failure of *Thermidor,* which, after all, had never been a success in any production. Moreover, he expected that Bessy would go on making a lot of money for him and, with French nonchalance, reasoned that whither Bessy goeth, so goeth little Elsie.

Her French clients inundated her with scripts—good, bad, and indifferent. They unreasonably expected her to get productions for all of them, and astonishingly she very nearly did. She had a trunk load of these works to sort through and translate by the time Elsie and she sailed for New York.

*B*essy was becoming a wealthy woman. Within a year's time, she would be handling one huge success after another, including *The Masked Ball,* Gillette's *Settled Out of Court,* Brandon Thomas's classic farce *Charley's Aunt,* and William Lestocq's London hit *Jane,* to say nothing of the endless productions of French adaptations that were the mainstay of repertory companies both in New York and on the road.

Alfred Allan Lewis

To her surprise, Charles Frohman did not buy *Lady Windermere's Fan* despite its perfect roles for John Drew and young Maude Adams. She sold it instead to A. M. Palmer, who opened a successful New York run on February 6, 1893, with Julia Arthur and Maurice Barrymore, father of Ethel, John, and Lionel. Wilde was so pleased that he forwarded his latest play, *A Woman of No Importance,* before the month was out. He hoped she would like it and, more important, that Frohman would like it. He closed with: "With many thanks, believe me your sincere friend and admirer."

Despite the ego-enriching admiration of artists such as Oscar Wilde, she missed Elsie quite dreadfully during the months she was on the road with Ramsey Murrey's company. Bessy was hoping she would be home in time to help her decorate the offices she had taken in Frohman's new Empire Theatre building, at the corner of Broadway and Fortieth Street.

*W*ith no work in view for Elsie until the autumn and so much work for Bessy to do abroad, there was no reason for them not to leave on their annual trips early enough to be at the London opening of *A Woman of No Importance,* at the Haymarket Theatre on April 19. They both must have recognized that Lady Caroline Pontefract, though not the lead, would be an ideal role for Elsie. If Frohman were to take the play, would he not give her a second chance, especially if Bessy and Mr. Wilde backed her for the part? Their first move was to secure the playwright's endorsement. Bessy set up an audition, and he must have approved of her reading for he became Elsie's champion.

Frohman again declined a Wilde play, as did Palmer, but Bessy did sell it to the Anglo-American star Rose Coghlan, who was looking for a starring vehicle for New York. True to his word, Oscar wired Miss Coghlan when she started to cast her production that autumn: "Hope you will be able to get Elsie de Wolfe for comedy part in my play. She would be very good." He confirmed his action in a second wire to Bessy: "Have wired Coghlan to secure Elsie de Wolfe." Despite their combined efforts, Miss Coghlan did not cast Elsie in her production, leaving Elsie no recourse but to sign with Murrey for another season.

*E*lsie came into her own when she stopped trying to be a star in roles that either were too young for her or required a display of passions with which she had no familiarity, and became a character actress playing variations on the one character she ever created: herself.

Frohman rehired her to play Lady Kate Fennell in *The Bauble Shop.* If she

*L*adies and Not-So-Gentle Women

did well, it would undoubtedly lead to her being engaged as a permanent member of the Empire Stock Company. The producer did not want Elsie simply to please his most important source of new plays. He was aware of her recent favorable notices and had his own agenda for her. Elsie was to fill a very special niche in his company. There were actresses in it who were stunning stars, better performers, more beautiful, possessed of greater presence, but none had her special elegance. Onstage she was a lady. Very few actresses projected that quality with her seeming effortlessness. But very few had devoted most of their lives, as she had, to studying every gesture of those in society, so that she passed for one of them when passing among them. In a theatre company, in which drawing room comedies and society melodramas were the staples of the repertory, this was a precious asset.

Elsie was in Paris when Frohman wired her about the job. A line in the cable, "Bring these dresses, reception, dinner, carriage," reaffirmed how much her costumes always had contributed to her success. Frohman did not give her total carte blanche to select her own costumes and charge them to him no matter what they cost. He was in Paris a short time later to give his approval and apparently had no problem with her choices. It was as if he, too, was aware of what she was about to become and reckoned it worth the price.

Life seemed complete to Elsie when Frohman finally invited her to become a member of his stock company. She would probably never be one of its great stars with her portrait gracing the walls of the Empire Theatre, but she had become a dependable and competent "second woman." Moreover, she was collecting a small following of her own among the matinee goers, who appreciated her clothes and ladylike demeanor. The producer would do his share to increase her appeal by allowing her to spend more money on her costumes than anybody else in his company.

Two nights after *The Bauble Shop* opened in New York, Richard Mansfield opened his starring production of *Arms and the Man*, the first American presentation of a George Bernard Shaw play. The play had opened the previous spring in London as part of a repertory season that was not expected to be commercial and which lived up to that expectation. Mansfield had slipped in to see a performance of the Shaw play. Recognizing a superb vehicle, he decided to do it in the United States. When the actor and playwright met in Mansfield's rooms at the Langham Hotel, "an invigorating antipathy sprang up between them." They were equally matched in arrogant know-it-all stances, but each recognized the other had something that would be of value. On June 9, they signed a contract, drafted by Shaw, for an American production. The speed with which the actor-manager agreed to its terms made Shaw suspect he might not have asked for the best terms and the contract should be revised. With typical Shavian paradox, he asked Mansfield to recommend an American agent to protect him against Mansfield, whom he did not trust.

Recalling how he had bested her over Clyde Fitch, the actor suggested Elisabeth Marbury. Bessy also remembered and was determined it would not happen again. She renegotiated the contract, demanding the best possible terms for the playwright. Mansfield was forced to capitulate. Bluntschli was a magnificent part for him but would be equally good for John Drew, and if he did not agree to her demands, Bessy would give the play to Frohman. When the play was a great success, she went over every item in the weekly statements to make certain that Shaw received every penny due him. The result was the first real money he ever made.

*L*ife was going at an exhilarating pace for both Bessy and Elsie. In November, William Gillette gave Bessy another big hit when he adapted one of the French plays she was representing, *La Plantation Thomasin,* as a starring vehicle for himself and retitled it *Too Much Johnson.* Elsie was earning a very decent salary and at last could afford to send her mother and brothers off to live someplace else, if only Bessy would take over the lease on the Irving house. It was more than rent and more than not wanting to live alone: she wanted to live with Bessy, and Bessy wanted to live with her. But for all her business audacity, Bessy could not stand up to her family and say she wanted to move a mere two blocks away in order to live with another woman.

On March 5, Francis Marbury died. There was no longer any excuse, but still she apparently hedged. How could she leave her mother alone in her time of bereavement? Elsie undoubtedly observed that Mrs. Marbury was the responsibility of *all* of her children and not merely of the one single female.

It was at this crossing of dilemma and sorrow that, according to Elsie, Bessy declared she had become a Catholic. There were those who might have attributed her alleged conversion to the solace the church offered for the loss of a beloved parent. A second explanation existed for Bessy's professed conversion. This new faith must have helped to provide her way out, her way two blocks south to that new life she had been longing for. It was more than likely the rigid Elizabeth McCoun Marbury would not have countenanced a "Papist" under their roof and told her daughter she would have to choose between her home and the Roman church. With what relief the apostate made her choice and signed the papers making her the mistress of the Irving house and the mate of the dear creature who already lived there.

With the great changes in her personal life and her involvement with her clients, there was little time for mourning. The forever cantankerous Mansfield was trying to convince Shaw to leave her. In early 1895, Mansfield asked Shaw to send him *The Philanderer* but requested that he not have to deal with Bessy should he want to produce it. Shaw replied on February 25, reminding the actor it was on his recommendation he had selected her as his representative in the first place, adding that despite his sometimes impossible demands, she had remained "interested in my peculiar ways" and had never given him "the faintest cause for complaint." He was aware she could get him much better terms for his work with either of the Frohmans than he got from Mansfield, but she had never pressed them upon him. He underscored that Bessy had been scrupulously fair in respect to the actor, insisting he had done everything that could be done for *Arms and the Man,* that his performance had been superb, and that he had sacrificed more profitable business to give it every possible chance to succeed.

A nettling point for Shaw was that Mansfield performed the play in repertory with his old warhorses, *Prince Karl, Beau Brummell,* and *Dr. Jekyll and Mr. Hyde.* At the height of its success, people in London were asking why he had not given it to Frohman, who would have run it for three consecutive months in New York and then put it on a long road tour. The only person who had refrained from discussing it with him had been the "scrupulously fair" Bessy. Were he to send *The Philanderer* to her, she would offer to sell it to Frohman for a big advance on which she would earn a handsome profit. Shaw added: "If she didn't, I should begin to doubt her business ability."

If Mansfield did not want to deal with Bessy, they could make their own deal as they had on *Arms and the Man,* which was done before she became his agent and which he had regretted until Bessy got it amended. He declared: "I always make my own contracts and deal directly with managers. An agent's commission would be sheer loss to me."

This was classic Shavian twaddle. At the time he wrote it, the man had but one success in his whole career (the one Mansfield had given him, on which Bessy had looked after his interests) and, were it not for his wife's money, he would still have had to write theatre and music reviews to support himself. The managers with whom he dealt were the London equivalent of Off Broadway who could afford only limited and modest engagements. Two decades later, he would begin to do what he claimed always to have done. Until then, Miss Marbury would continue to look after all of his interests outside Britain, and so well that it would bring him both artistic and commercial success in America and Germany long before it came to him in England. To maintain that Bessy would do this and deal with his admittedly "peculiar ways" without collecting a commission for her labors must have sounded as inane to Mansfield as it would have to anybody who ever had negotiated with her, especially when at that stage of his career there was so little recompense for so much effort on her part. Ego rampant, the writer persevered: "This limits Miss Marbury to her business of relieving you of the trouble of remitting me my royalties and of getting me good exchange."

To suggest that she would even do that much without her customary commission was incredible, nor was it probable that Mansfield believed him. It was only after this flight of fancy that Shaw finally got down to his real point in regard to Bessy: "If you don't like *The Philanderer,* which I think extremely probable, it would suit me very well to have the fact of its existence known to Frohman. So by all means continue to send the supplies through her."

With his Bessy position defined, Shaw turned to what he really wanted from the star in a superb piece of ego manipulation. "Now let me ask you whether you can play a boy of eighteen—a strange creature—a poet—a bundle of nerves—a genius—and a rattling good part. The actor-managers here can't get down to the age."

The part was Marchbanks, in his latest play, *Candida.* The canny Shaw's next appeal was to the well-known parsimony of the actor, evoking visions of a great profit on the small investment. "*Candida* is the most fascinating work in the world. . . . in three acts, one cheap scene, and with six characters . . . By the way, there's probably money in the piece; but it's a charming work of art; and the money would fly somehow."

The forty-one-year-old Mansfield took the bait. "I still play youths of 18. The only trouble is I look too young for the part."

So powerful were Shaw's gifts of persuasion that not only did the notoriously tightfisted Mansfield agree to option *Candida* for production, but he also engaged Janet Achurch, a little-known but superb English actress, for the title role, agreeing to pay her passage as well as a stipend far better than she ever had received in London. The role had been written for her, and for years, to Bessy's frustration, the writer refused to allow the play to be done without her. Achurch was one of a series of larger-than-life women for whom he developed platonic passions, the idea of sex generally having been far more gratifying to him than its actuality.

The actress engaged only to please Shaw cost Mansfield "hundreds without making the slightest return." When Achurch arrived, the actor was appalled by her appearance. He told Shaw, "I couldn't have made love to your Candida if I had taken ether . . . I never fall in love with fuzzy-haired persons who purr and are business-like . . . I detest an aroma of stale tobacco and gin . . . I don't like women who sit on the floor . . . comb their tawny locks with their fingers and claw their necks and scratch the air with their chins. . . ."

When Achurch confronted him about his plans for the play and her, he was more concise. "You're a new woman. You play Ibsen. I detest new women who play Ibsen."

On April 16, Mansfield complied with a cable from Shaw instructing him to return the manuscript of *Candida* to Bessy. She lost no time in circulating it and within two days had an offer for it. Mansfield heard about it almost immediately, which gave him cause to reconsider. Before she could get in touch with Shaw, the actor cabled to him: "Since you insist will produce *Candida* now cable Marbury deliver manuscript."

Bessy's cable arrived the next day requesting authorization to place the play with an extremely good actress-manager on excellent terms. As Shaw was not exactly wallowing in money or success, it must have been the speed with which she had obtained a new offer that gave his ego a sufficient boost to turn down Mansfield and reply to Bessy: "Offer declined nothing can be done at present without Achurch."

When Shaw came to see Bessy in London, on April 29, he found her "quite a foot broader than she was before." He remained adamant about Achurch and *Candida*. As a result, it was two years before it was finally performed and then on a tatty tour starring Achurch and produced by her husband. Shaw finally saw his ideal in it when she gave one performance of the play in London, in 1900. Freed of his obsession by her inadequate production, he finally allowed Bessy to arrange successful productions of the play in New York in 1903, and at the Deutsches Volktheater, in Germany, the following year. The string of productions of his works set up by Bessy's New York and Berlin offices made him rich and famous. It was only then, as word filtered in from abroad, that London began to acknowledge his genius.

Being Bessy, she never could resist advising him on how to write "box office" plays. At first, he took no umbrage. A letter he wrote to her at about that time showed that nothing could repress the antic mood inspired by his newfound financial liberation.

> Rapacious Elisabeth Marbury
>
> What do you want me to make a fortune for? Don't you know that the draft you sent me will permit me to live and preach Socialism for six months? The next time you have so large an amount to remit, please send it to me by installments, or you will put me to the inconvenience of having a bank account.

What do you mean by giving me advice about writing a play with a view to the box office receipts? I shall continue writing just as I do now for the next ten years. After that we can wallow in the gold poured at our feet by a dramatically regenerated public.

*A*t the very time when Bessy was about to begin to share a life with a person of her own sex, the trials of Oscar Wilde, based on an admittedly more erotic commitment to a person of his own sex, not only ended a brilliant career but also would hasten the end of his life. Against that background, Elsie and Bessy seem nearly heroic to have been so open about their relationship and nearly triumphant to have been so much happier, more acceptable, and more famous than many of the pious people who cast out Oscar Wilde and his ilk. It must be added, however, that whatever it was that Bessy and Elsie did, it was not sodomy and not yet a crime against man, state, or God.

But times were changing, and the world in which passionate friendships between women were unquestioned was drawing to an end. Five years later, Dr. William Lee Howard would write in the *New York Medical Journal:*

> The female possessed of masculine ideas of independence, the virago who would sit in the public highways and lift up her pseudo-virile voice, proclaiming her sole right to decide questions of war and religion, or the value of celibacy and the curse of women's impurity, and that disgusting antisocial being, the female sexual pervert, are simply different degrees of the same class—degenerates.

That same year, the renowned sexologist Henry Havelock Ellis described the female invert in terms that could serve as a portrait of Elisabeth Marbury:

> The brusque energetic movements, the attitude of the arms, the direct speech, the inflexions of the voice, the masculine straightforwardness and sense of honor, and especially the attitude towards men, free from any suggestion either of shyness or audacity, will often suggest the underlying psychic abnormality to a keen observer.

It is doubtful if Bessy was yet aware of this new and disquieting bigotry, but had she been, her shrewd political instincts might well have led her to reply, with that English turn of phrase she so liked to affect: "Pshaw, m'dear! Sex has nothing to do with it. 'Tis a question of power and those who aspire to it."

CHAPTER EIGHTEEN

That Bessy and Elsie had intended to live together, probably since Stephen de Wolfe's death, was evinced in the furniture and objets d'art they began to collect during their annual trips to Europe. They may not have been first-rate, but they surely had style. For Elsie, style would always take precedent over provenance. When Bessy took over the lease from Georgiana, the house into which they moved was furnished with a mélange of their things and those left over from the old De Wolfe house on West Thirty-fourth Street.

> It was not a pretty house. But it was good. Like many good people, it had suffered unkindnesses. Rather than protest, it had gone quietly to sleep and there it was waiting for us to wake it up. It was a bit crotchety at first, as it had so many things to be done to it. When we had thought out how to overcome one defect, it had a way of developing another. But we were patient with it. And it was not long before it gave in to us and emerged from its nap into a perfect dear of a place.

Bessy and Elsie shielded themselves from the world and possibly each other in separate bedrooms. It was not the separation that provided sanctuary; many of the heterosexual upper-class marriages of the period probably owed their longevity more to segregate chambers than to any other single factor. The appointments of their rooms were what provided the psychological armor.

Elsie's room was built around a wonderful carved walnut cupboard bed that she had purchased on one of their bicycle excursions through Brittany. Its doors could be shut to protect the occupant from assault. Mirrors were set in those doors so that should they be closed, she could be reassured by reflections of her solitary self. Her chaise longue was upholstered in the same rose-embroidered silk as the hangings suspended from her bed-posts.

Bessy's room, "while more matter of fact, had its gay moments." The white enamel furniture was enlivened by one of Elsie's first uses of chintzes, a bird of paradise design in subdued colors. Bessy's new Catholic fervor was declared on every wall in copies of cinquecento madonnas and religious scenes. An antique carved crucifix hung over her bed and a reliquary was set on a table at its foot. In all, it had that curious mix of inviolacy and elegance that must have marked the retreats of aristocratic abbesses before the French Revolution.

Years later, when Elsie was gamely playing Don Quixote into a protracted old age, at a time when lesbianism had become a part of the radical chic of the twenties and thirties, she continued vainly to tilt against what she considered a stigma as if it still mattered, just as Bessy had done by insisting that marriage and motherhood were the only rewarding roles for a woman.

> Special attention had to be given to the bedrooms, for Elisabeth and I, when starting out together, realized that if our friendship was to stand the pressure of constant companionship, we would each have to live our own lives. We certainly did not see eye to eye in many things. Our tastes lay far apart. We never liked the same men—one reason why, perhaps, we got along so well and that our friendship stood the test of time. . . . Our bedrooms . . . had to be comfortable retreats where we could spend our evenings alone when one or the other was entertaining her friends.

And so they slept apart, the one protected by doors she had converted into mirror images of herself, the other by a new religion she passionately espoused. Downstairs the party had begun, and as the renown of the couple spread, Elsie found she had at last become a star, not on the stage but in the one room she indisputably shared with Bessy—the drawing room.

Their at-homes took place every Sunday afternoon that found them in the city, at what was variously called the tea or cocktail hour in the postpuritan age that New York was entering at the end of the nineteenth century. It was not the fare that was the attraction, for it was monotonously the same and ridiculously simple for an era of gastronomic excess: sandwiches, salad, coffee, tea, and a liberally laced punch bowl. The scene was one of amiable disarray with not enough chairs to go around and people filling the Turkish corner, sitting on the floor and up the stairway in a daring new spirit of platonic intimacy.

Having no polite term for the relationship of these two women whom they took as their own, in one of its rare spasms of creativity New York society invented a designation especially for them. They were the "bachelorettes" and symbols of a new style of hospitality in which improvisation counted for more than tradition. As their friend William C. Whitney put it: "You never know whom you're going to meet at Bessy's and Elsie's, but you can always be sure that whoever they are they will be interesting and you always have a good time."

In his social history *Incredible New York,* Lloyd Morris was succinct: "They [Bessy and Elsie] were helping to create a new society in which wit, intelligence, style, creative achievement, and a lively interest in the arts took precedence over wealth and family . . . [they were] creating a vogue for the most improbable of diversions—brilliant talk."

Before they opened the doors to their salon,

> society was so snobbish and narrow and limited that artists and writers and playwrights were not sought after. Finally, it was discovered they were more amusing, so the narrow society began breaking its neck to get into what was the forerunner of cafe society. It became chic to go to . . . Bessy Marbury's . . . Elsie de Wolfe's. That made a very charming society.

Bessy loved everything about opera singers except the god-awful noise they made. Unlike opera impresarios, she adored their outpourings of temperament and suffered their fits of singing. What brought them to her table was her zest for their personalities rather than their instruments. A Sunday afternoon during the Metropolitan Opera season found the likes of Nellie Melba, Emma Calvé, and Jean de Reszke in evidence to elicit swoons from the claque clinging to their seats on the narrow stairway.

On April 6, 1895, a two-part article entitled "Interior Decoration as a Profession for Women," by Candace Wheeler, began in *Outlook,* a magazine that called itself "a family paper." Elsie may well have read it, as Bessy subscribed to every publication as part of her professional need to know what was being published where. Their friends the Hewitt sisters thought enough of the pieces for them to have been found among their papers after their deaths. Thus it is likely that the contents were discussed when the four women met, as they did regularly. The articles indicated that women were already in the field, because "there is no profession that, at first thought, seems so natural and appropriate a one for women." In quaint terms it went on to tell a woman what "*he* must have" to be a success. Wheeler's most salient points were her very early treatment of interior decoration as an art on a par with its natural mate, architecture, and her demand for the opening of schools for women that specialized in the specific studies necessary to become a competent decorator instead of merely a female with a natural flair for "interior arrangement." She was also among the first to discuss the possibility of a woman being able to have both a career and family, that the former might well enable her to cope with the vicissitudes inherent in the latter.

What Elsie made of all of this would be hard to guess. Bessy was her family, and there was never any conflict between it and her career. As with acting, she never went to school to learn how to become a decorator. When experience was added to her inordinate taste, her remarkable talent for observation, mimicry, and absorption, it proved the only education she required. All that may have lingered in that extraordinarily selective memory was that the articles suggested an alternative should the theatre ever fail her.

CHAPTER NINETEEN

During the Nineties, all of the Rutherfurds with the exception of Winty were spending most of their time in Europe. Winty divided his time between New York City and Allamuchy, New Jersey, where he continued to breed dogs. He was slowly recovering from the wounds inflicted by Alva Vanderbilt. Winty had spent several months aboard Willie K. Vanderbilt's new yacht, the *Valiant*, on a voyage that took them all the way from New York to India via the Mediterranean and the Indian Ocean and back to the South of France. Also aboard were Alva's lover, Oliver H. P. Belmont, who was also Willie's best friend, and the Vanderbilts' young and beautiful daughter, Consuelo.

By the end of the voyage, Consuelo and Winty were in love and wanted to marry. Alva could not permit this, for she had decided to leave Willie for Belmont, who himself had recently been through a messy divorce, was years younger than she, and was half Jewish. The combination was enough to ruin the social position she had labored so hard to establish. To keep it, she needed her daughter to make the kind of brilliant marriage that would force society to continue to recognize her as one of its leaders.

Alva decided upon the Duke of Marlborough, who was shopping for an heiress to help him maintain the Marlborough ancestral palace, Blenheim. She cruelly broke up her daughter's relationship with Winty and forced her into a loveless marriage with Marlborough. After her separation from Vanderbilt, Alva gave a ball in Newport for the duke, which reestablished her position.

Consuelo's father continued to be kind to Winty. There were dinners and cruises aboard the *Valiant* with another lover spurned by one of Alva's family, her jilted ex-brother-in-law Fernando Yznaga, often among the company. It was as if Willie K. Vanderbilt was declaring that all of the enemies of his former wife would be his friends.

Lewis and Anne preferred London, where those few doors not opened by their own charm and looks were unlocked by Daisy and Harry White, who continued in his post as first secretary at the American embassy. Traveling in the same aristocratic circles made it inevitable that the Rutherfurds and the Whites should become better acquainted with Winty's great and lost love, the current Duchess of Marlborough. It would not have been exceptional had the former sweethearts met, for he was often in London visiting his family and accepted because of the vaunted Rutherfurd allure in all of the circles in which she moved.

Although Consuelo never mentioned him by name in her memoirs, she did describe a weekend in the English country home of "the beautiful Daisy White," who, as she recollected, led her to a window and pointed out an older American gentleman walking across the lawn with a younger woman, also American. The occasion was one of the early meetings of Henry James and Edith Wharton, the old friend from Daisy's Newport days.

Wharton was always kind to her, but Consuelo thought she gave "the impression of disliking if not actually despising women" and that she "repelled rather than attracted sympathy," when she persisted in treating her husband more as "an equerry than an equal."

One possible source of her attitude toward Edith was that they were rivals for the memory of a lost love, having both, at different times, adored Winty Rutherfurd. Interestingly, the heroine of Wharton's last, uncompleted novel, *The Buccaneers,* was based on Consuelo.

By the standards of our times, it would seem extraordinary that these women were all present in that country house for a long English weekend—his sister, two women who had loved him, and quite probably Anne, who was his sister-in-law and who within a few years would be intimately related to Consuelo—and that they should not have spoken of him beyond, perhaps, a polite "And how is Mr. Rutherfurd?" But it would not have been impossible in that late Victorian world, in which women could be so passionate in written avowals of their feelings and so chillingly proper in the almost choreographed personal exchanges permissible within the confines of society.

If Anne was intrigued by the breed of attractive Englishmen whom she met through Daisy and Harry White, it was because they were so different from those to whom she was accustomed. These men used their wealth and connections to become the powers that ran an empire rather than, like her compatriots, merely to accumulate more money. The English exercised their power in influential positions in the government, while, for the most part, Americans used their money to acquire the whole government. It was not until Willie K. Vanderbilt came into her life that she would begin to understand the subtleties of what money could buy beyond pleasure.

When it was that Lewis and Anne discovered that he was suffering from a particularly virulent strain of tuberculosis is not known, but it was surely after the birth of their second daughter, Barbara. It was then that she also began to get unsettling messages from New York about the worsening condition of her father's health, but she could do nothing about it. It would have been impossible to return to America, leaving behind the children and a husband whose own health was rapidly degenerating. Earlier that year, Oliver Harriman's dementia had begun to advance so rapidly that the family had thought it for the best to place him in custodial care at his country home in Mount Kisco. After her husband's removal to the country and the letting of her townhouse, Laura Low Herriman moved into a suite in the recently opened, elegant Hotel Renaissance, at Forty-third Street and Fifth Avenue, with her eighty-nine-year-old father, to devote all of her energies to looking after him. The fulfillment she found in that dedication was shortlived, for James Low, Sr., died on May 17, 1898. Although he was said to have lost four million dollars in Wall Street, his remaining fortune left his daughter a wealthy woman and his granddaughter more comfortable than she hitherto had been. Death remained the likeliest way for a Victorian lady to make her fortune.

That July, Lewy and Anne journeyed down from the Palace Hotel, in St. Moritz, Switzerland, to the Château Royal d'Ardema, in Belgium. As was often the case with hotel nomads, they were a place behind in hotel stationery, and Anne wrote to Stuyvie from the Château Royal using the Palace Hotel letterhead. When Lewy felt up to it they played golf, but he became too tired to finish the game after only a few holes. They intended to leave for London soon and would be glad to get away from the snobbish Château. She ended her letter with "As Lewis says it is getting rather rich for our blood, everyday new arrivals and more toilettes and jewels—Vanderbilts, Twombleys [sic], Van Rensselaers."

$\mathscr{B}$y the turn of the century, the monolith that had been New York society was beginning to crumble. In its January 11, 1900, issue, *Town Topics* was dividing it into three parts, but it was still ruled by a small group of interrelated women. The ruling set had Mamie Fish for wit and Alva Belmont predictably for "nerve" and included Bessy Marbury's friends Sally Hewitt and Mrs. Stanford White. The second group was younger and headed by Anne's sister-in-law Mrs. Oliver Harriman, Jr., and *the* Mrs. Astor's daughter-in-law, Ava. The social rag opined that "by breeding and temper [they] do not fancy the mere superficialities of society." The third group was the old guard led by Caroline Astor; Alva's ex-sister-in-law, Alice Vanderbilt; Mrs. Whitelaw Reid; and Mrs. Levi Morton, who had given the ball at which Edith Jones Wharton had made her debut and who would soon be Winty Rutherfurd's mother-in-law. Only a few a years before, *the* Mrs. Astor had been *Town Topics'* "mystic rose." But by 1900, she was part of a group dismissed as being among those with "few personal qualifications but . . . magnificent homes and unlimited power as hostesses." The article added that "the literary school is a distinct set with Mrs. Edward (Edith) Wharton and her sister-in-law, Mrs. Cadwalader Jones, as high priestesses."

$\mathscr{O}$n June 27, 1900, Henry Adams wrote to Louisa Hooper about some of the attractions of his stay in Paris. "There are half dozen or more very pretty and very bright young married women who occasionally smile at me as they pass, because I have been accidentally near them at a restaurant:— Mrs. Lewis Rutherfurd; Mrs. Joe Stevens . . . and this kind are always coming and going."

And so Lewy and Anne were on the move again—in Paris in early summer and, by the end of the year, back in the Swiss Alps, this time at Davos Pltaz, again to seek in the high, thin, fresh air that one cleansing gasp that would make him well again.

To no avail. He died on January 5, 1901. Anne telephoned to Daisy and Harry in London. It was agreed that she would bring the body there, and they would wait there for Winty to come over. He would escort them back to Tranquility, where Lewy would be buried in the Stuyvesant-Rutherfurd family plot.

Anne was forty years old and it seemed as if her life was over. It had been a bad time when Sam died but not like this. She had still been young then, and Lewis had come into her life so quickly and so completely. And she had loved him so much more than she had Sam. It had not mattered if her formidable mother's small world had been shocked when she married him the moment the mourning period was over. She would never love like that again. Things had a way of ending badly for her, no matter how hard she tried to do the right thing. She could only wonder if she would ever live fully again, or if it was to be her lot merely to exist, to float on for the sake of the children, until the children were grown and gone. And then, what? Indeed, until then—what?

CHAPTER TWENTY ❧

It was as if the death of his father, Junius Morgan, in 1890, had liberated his son, J. P. Morgan, to fulfill the potential his father never had believed existed. By the end of the century, Pierpont would be the most powerful private banker in the world. In 1895, he used his international influence to save the United States government from financial ruin by restocking its depleted gold reserves. The alternative would have been a panic destroying international confidence in the American financial market. Similarly, he would later save New York City from bankruptcy and keep the stock exchange from having to close.

His stewardship of the railroads enabled him to stabilize the rates, thus allowing his partners the Vanderbilts to continue to live in the ostentatious manner of which he thoroughly disapproved. In a stunning series of capitalistic coups, he arranged the financing of the industrial consolidations that would form the United States Steel Corporation, General Electric, International Harvester, and the International Mercantile Marine. Between the latter company and his control of the railroads, not very much moved in the United States without Morgan sharing in the action. It was as if the industrial complex of the country was his personal fiefdom. Although he gained from everything he touched, this complex man seldom did anything only for personal gain. Amalgamation was as much his god as the One he worshiped so regularly each Sunday morning at St. George's. He genuinely believed that what was good for Morgan was ultimately good for the country, and that it would enrich the nation in far greater measure than it did him. It did not prevent him from becoming the symbol of all that was venal in Wall Street. The country carried on a love-hate relationship with him, loathing

*L*adies and Not-So-Gentle Women

what he did but admiring the fact that he *could* do it. He once complacently remarked, "America is good enough for me."

William Jennings Byran retorted, "Whenever he doesn't like it, he can give it back." As his biographer Ron Chernow, observed: "Editorial writers competed to mint Morgan titles—king of the trusts, morganizer of the world, financial titan, Napoleon of finance or, more simply, Zeus or Jupiter."

Recognizing his domain, Wall Street colleagues often placed themselves in the position of importuning courtiers, to whom he reacted with regal hauteur. After Morgan refused to grant a loan to one of them, the poor fellow followed him into the street. Morgan turned and said: "I'll walk with you as far as the Stock Exchange. After all, being seen with me might be worth more to you in the long run than the loan."

He was no less imperious with royalty. During one of his stays in London, the King of Belgium sent word that he was desperately in need of financial advice and requested that he come to Brussels. The banker replied that he had no wish to go to Belgium. If the king needed his help, the king should come to England for it, and that was what his majesty did. After an audience with Pope Pius X, his holiness's one regret was not that he had not been able to save the tycoon's soul, but that he had not asked for his financial advice.

If Morgan was a king, then his daughter Anne was surely a princess, but one with no hope of ever becoming a monarch. The best she could do was to become the consort of some young prince approved of by her father. She was perhaps a shade too tall but a handsome girl with good skin, tawny chestnut hair, and lustrous dark eyes. Like her father, she was given to putting on weight, but unlike him, she was an athlete and had the muscle tone to carry it with a certain panache. There was no dearth of eligible men, but she discouraged all of them. The truth was she wanted something more out of life without being able to define what it was.

More and more of her contemporaries were going to college. Even had she wanted to go, it would have been out of the question. Her father considered education wasted on women and with or without one, did not think females would ever be capable of handling their own finances. After his death, like her sisters, Anne would have the income from a trust managed either by her husband-to-be or a partner in the firm. In the meantime, he did trust her to have assimilated his lessons on how to be sensible about money and, instead of giving her an allowance, permitted her to draw on his personal or household accounts to cover whatever expenses she might accrue.

Anne's life had a rhythm without tempo. She was a jolly woman who excelled at sports and loved the company of women who *did* things, although she seemed not able—more likely, not allowed—to do anything beyond what was expected of her by Pierpont. She had entered society and, for her grace and breeding, been accepted by both old New York and the showy Fifth Avenue crowd. Her name appeared not only on the Four Hundred list but also on the published guest lists of all the most remarked-upon parties.

Anne Morgan was very much like any other American princess of the gilded age. Her days had the formal structure of life at the French court, where no deviation from the ordained routine was permitted. Late spring invariably found the Morgans, father and daughter, in England, where they stayed in their palatial Georgian-style townhouse overlooking Kensington Gardens. Weekends were spent at their country home, Dover House, in Roehampton. In addition to taking part in the pleasures of the social season, they enjoyed the opportunity it provided of visiting with young Jack's family as well as a score of British Harcourt relations.

They crossed the Channel in early June. In Paris they stayed in the same large, airy corner suite at the Bristol that they had occupied every year since the hotel opened. It was their Paris home, as familiar to Anne as any of the other Morgan residences. The next day, they paraded up the street to Worth's, and the shopping began in earnest. Anne could select nothing without her father's approval; more often, he did the selecting, which did not bother her. She cared little for clothes except those for sports, and, later, her uniforms, about which she was meticulous. The depth of her concern with elegant garb was measured by with whom she was emotionally involved. If it was somebody terribly clothes-conscious, then she became clothes-conscious, frequenting whichever couturiers were favored by her beloved.

After the fittings the Morgans were off to one of the fashionable spas to purge their systems and enroll in the weight reduction regimes. Anne, always fearful of the family tendency to corpulence, religiously monitored herself by making entries in her diaries of the amount she had lost on each day of the cure.

The European junket was rounded off with a cruise on the *Corsair* before returning to Paris to pick up the finished clothes and to London for a final farewell to the relatives. The crossing to the United States was made on one of the big ocean liners, on which Anne often experienced beastly seasickness. The remainder of the summer was spent with her mother at Cragston, with its views of the Hudson, and tennis, and swimming, and long-distance running: the sports she loved so well and at which she excelled.

Starting in 1898, Anne's summers were changed to make room for stays at the Adirondack camp her father purchased that year from W. W. Durant, the developers of the Adirondack camp style and life. What he had conceived was a rustic fantasy in which the super-rich could play at roughing it.

The banker and his neighboring capitalists would arrive in their private railroad cars laden with all the necessities of life in the wilderness, such as the finest bed linens, silver trays, cutlery, serving pieces, china, Champagne flutes, snifters; port, sherry, and brandy decanters; not to mention the appropriate vintage liquids with which to fill them. The servants often outnumbered the employers and their guests by 3 to 1. A Morgan or Vanderbilt would not know how to exist in a camp without the suitable staff to run it, including chambermaids, chefs, butlers, valets, grooms, laundresses, governesses if there were children in the party, and a personal taxidermist to stuff and mount the game heads that replaced the Old Masters in their New York mansions as the wall hangings of choice in the camps. It was practical for the camps to be designed as two separate villages: one for the staff and the other for the masters and their guests.

The Morgan place was Camp Uncas, which Durant had intended to be his ultimate triumph, designated for his personal use and named for the last of the Mohicans in James Fenimore Cooper's *Leatherstocking Tales*. He had started clearing and construction in 1895. It took two hundred men, working for two years, to complete the thousand-acre camp, which included all of Lake Mohican and was situated seven miles down a dirt road in the heart of a great forest. Water was piped in from the mountains on the far side of the lake via specially constructed pipes laid under it. The main house and many outbuildings were so deliberately rusticated that even the greenhouse was disguised as a log cabin. This sort of precision cost a fortune, and the builder was forced into debt. When he defaulted on a loan in 1897, Morgan took possession of the camp. That he kept it for himself was what came as a surprise. By the standards of the day, in comparison with that of men of comparable wealth, his taste in homes was almost austere: by virtue of its outrageous evocation of a rural life that existed nowhere on this earth except in the architect's imagination, Uncas was anything but austere.

If Durant's Ruritania had a rough-hewn exterior, the inside of the main house was a conceit of hand-crafted extravagance. He was such a perfectionist that he had ordered a mammoth fireplace ripped out because he noticed that one small stone had been set backward. It was the sort of compulsiveness that would have elicited an empathetic response from Morgan the collector. The enormous raw wooden ceilings of the main rooms were held up by hand-polished, peeled pine beams. After he gained possession of it, the banker was showing the Vanderbilts' attorney, Chauncey Depew, around his immense new property and remarked, "All I really need is a place to live in and a lot in the cemetery."

Almost one hundred years after her great-grandfather acquired the camp, Anne's grandniece and namesake recalled "loving it all, the whole business." During the requisite afternoon naps of her childhood, she would restlessly count "the knots in the beams over my head." Years before her visits, her athletic grandaunt found it a paradise of fishing, boating, hunting, and hiking.

If Anne's life at that time seemed to a large extent to be lived by rote, it was a pleasant exercise punctuated by the many small pleasures limitless wealth could provide. Still, she longed for another kind of activity, to be doing something more consequential, more enriching than wealth. She did not know what it could be but thought she caught glimpses of it during the autumns and winters, when she volunteered at the settlement houses in the notorious Five Points area and in the ghettos of the Lower East Side. Her father did not object to her playing Lady Bountiful. It was the sort of thing expected of young women of her class. What bothered him was the zeal he sensed in her, so different from her customary social insouciance. She would embarrass him with his guests, just as she had when a child wanting to be something more than rich, by berating them for the miserable conditions they allowed to prevail in their slum properties. He also could not overlook her interest in the women who ran these settlement houses. Many of them had elected to remain unmarried, devoting their energies to noble works and sharing their lives with companions who had made similar commitments. Whether or not she was aware of the sexual component in their relationships, they seemed to be contented in ways many of the married women of her acquaintance were not. Theirs was an increasingly attractive way of life that offered an alternative to the proscribed rigidity of the class into which she had been born.

CHAPTER TWENTY-ONE

In 1859, Peter Cooper opened Cooper Union, the school he built and endowed with his private fortune. A free school for young men and women with no bar of race, creed, or color, it was dedicated to providing a practical education in the arts, modern technology, and the sciences with the avowed end of instilling self-sufficiency and social responsibility. There was no other institution like it anywhere in the United States. When the old man included women in the student body, it had nothing to do with the nascent women's rights and suffrage movements. It was to provide them with a

Ladies and Not-So-Gentle Women

means of supporting themselves without having "to resort for a livelihood to occupations which must be revolting to the purity and sensitiveness which naturally characterize the feminine mind." He added that he also wanted "to keep them from marrying oppressive men out of desperation."

It had always been part of Cooper's plan to set aside a portion of the Union for a museum. This did not to come to pass until 1897, when his granddaughters, Bessy Marbury's good friends Sally and Nelly Hewitt, opened the Cooper Union Museum for the Arts of Decoration on the fourth floor, which they shared with the women's art school. The Hewitts found their inspiration in the Musée des Arts Décoratifs in Paris, which was originally founded by a group of artisans, craftsmen, and manufacturers dedicated to improving industrial manufacture of domestic goods by adapting the motifs and principles of the fine arts to their design. That was what the sisters hoped their museum would inspire the students at the Union to do in their future careers.

What would later become the Cooper-Hewitt was the first of several museums that would be founded by American women during the coming century, including one by Anne Morgan in France; Peggy Guggenheim's museum in Venice; Isabella Stewart Gardner's Fenway Court in Boston; and Gertrude Vanderbilt Whitney's Whitney Museum in New York. Without the participation of the Rockefeller women, the Museum of Modern Art would not have become the great institution that it is. What they all had in common, at their inception, was that they were largely concerned with those still living either as students or artists. This concern separated them from the majority of great art institutions founded by men, be they the relatively modest Frick and Morgan or the overpowering Metropolitan and National Gallery. Vanity undeniably played a part in the undertakings of both sexes, but while the establishments of the women were concerned with reaching out and giving to others, those endowed by men were initially more involved with being expressions of their powerful egos—also with intimations of the immortality of the acquisitive moguls who had gathered the great collections housed in them—than with the art itself.

On December 3, 1897, Charles Scribner's Sons published *The Decoration of Houses* by Edith Wharton and Ogden Codman. The book was Edith's first success. She later considered it the laboratory in which she experimented with and perfected the craft and style necessary to write a sustained narrative. For her collaborator, it helped to advance his career as a professional interior decorator.

The Whartons purchased a townhouse at 884 Park Avenue in 1891, which was only fifteen feet wide. A few years later, they purchased the house next door, at 882, and doubled the frontage. Edith hired Ogden to do the renovations and decor; not that she did not have and offer very pronounced opinions on both, so that whatever he did for her was, like their book, a collaboration. How far Codman and she strayed from the call to classicism in their book was made explicit in Henry James's description of the Park Avenue house: "A bonbonnière of the last daintiness." Blind as Edith might be to her own excesses, she was acute on the subject of those into which Alva had led her husband's family. "I wish the Vanderbilts didn't retard culture so thoroughly. They are entrenched in a sort of Thermopylae of bad taste from which apparently no force on earth can dislodge them."

There was no doubt that Elsie de Wolfe was profoundly affected by *The Decoration of Houses*. She recognized and would later apply to her own work the truths to be found in it, but these she attributed to Codman, who was a professional decorator whom she would seek out and cultivate. The book's cool hauteur was attributed to Edith, whom she did not like. She admitted that the woman was "a great artist" while observing "there was something sharp about her and she had a forbidding coldness of manner." When Elsie called on her at the Park Avenue house, she remarked that in an era of large formal dinner parties, there were only eight chairs in the dining room. Edith replied, "Yes, Miss de Wolfe, there are but eight in the whole of New York whom I care to have dine with me."

The ultimate put-down for Elsie was that Wharton never deigned to express publicly an opinion of either her or her work.

Ogden Codman moved from his native Boston to New York primarily to promote his career, for it was the mecca of the new rich, who were cluttering its streets with ostentatious mansions in need of a decorator of his talents. He had visions of grand dinners in Delmonico's and dancing at *the* Mrs. Astor's balls, which he never did. The city also offered the freedom to indulge his homosexual proclivities away from his family.

Characteristically, his impressions of the women he met were negative. The Hewitt sisters were "common," although they did have "interesting taste and [a] fondness for pretty things." When one considers the treasures in their new museum, that was a bit of an understatement.

Bessy Marbury was "fat and vulgar," but he had to admit enjoying her stimulating Sunday afternoons on Irving Place. Those invitations may well have been prompted by Elsie, who was obviously fascinated by his taste and studied it as one might school lessons. She would later generously assign him a place in "the brilliant coterie who gathered at our hearth."

Henry Adams, an even greater snob than Codman, described a typical Sunday afternoon at the Irving house at about the time the decorator was first invited.

I went to see the Marbury salon and found myself in a mad cy-
clone of people. Miss Marbury and Miss de Wolfe received me
with tender embraces, but I was struck blind by the brilliancy of
their world. I found Mrs. Nat Goodwin (Maxine Elliott) and Mrs.
Lawrence Hopkins (Theresa B. Dodge) that was, embracing
Harper Pennington with gout, and Marion Crawford . . . and I
don't know how many more. I had to chatter as one of the wicked
and got barely a word of business. Miss Marbury is doing well.
Miss de Wolfe is . . . in a state of anti-Semite rebellion which is the
mark of all intelligent Jews.

In 1901, when Elsie tired of the already passé Victorian clutter that characterized her first decorative scheme for the home they shared, Bessy and
she hired Ogden to redo the drawing and dining rooms. Much of what was
done in those rooms would characterize the future work of both Ogden and
Elsie. Some would later accuse her of having stolen his ideas. That was no
more true than saying Edith Wharton stole them. Both were women of excellent and definite tastes. As was always the case, when such women hired
decorators, the result was a collaboration, but, predictably, Edith and Elsie
both later had difficulty giving Ogden the proper credit for his contribution.

As was the case with many of the impecunious wellborn basically homosexual men of the age, marrying an heiress was a part of Ogden's plans for
his future. These wealthy young ladies expected little in the way of sexual
gratification from their husbands. Satisfying their modest demands and
producing a family was not difficult, if one closed one's eyes and thought of
Newport. Some did not go that far. Ward McAllister's successor as Alva's and
the Mrs. Astor's pet factotum, Harry Lehr, told his heiress wife on the first
night of their honeymoon that her body revolted him, and he had no intention of ever touching it, but he would make her fashionable and a social success. That would appear to have been sufficient. They remained married
until his death, with many of her friends who were married to heterosexuals
considering her a very lucky woman to have found a man who knew all of
the smartest people, selected her clothes, decorated their homes, gave triumphant parties, and never embarrassed her by flaunting a mistress in
public.

When Ogden met Annie Morgan, he thought he had found the girl of his
dreams. Not only was she considered among the richest heiresses in the
world, but she was also tall, handsome, magnificently dressed, and not at all
interested in men. It was perfect. Her father would surely consider a spinster
daughter on a par with a failed stock issue. She would have to marry, and

what more perfect husband than he for a girl who was not interested in men? It never occurred to him that she might be even less interested in marriage than she was in men. The only problems he could discern were her intelligence, which was greater than his, and her mother, who was "awfully like a school marm." As for the formidable Pierpont Morgan, he did not think there would be a problem. He could not suspect Ogden of merely being a fortune hunter (which he was), because he was "making so much money that no father-in-law would be worried about that. However we shall see." A good friend told him it would be a great pity for him to marry, and suggested he "might as well have dogs as children."

When Annie spurned his suit, he rationalized that it was because she considered him "too frivolous and too fond of smart people" in the wrongest sense of "smart." The only thing he could do that intrigued her was to arrange an introduction to "fat and vulgar" Bessy and Elsie. On February 7, 1901, he wrote to his mother:

> Annie Morgan came to tea yesterday at the office with Helen (Ernest) Grimmell, Lizzie Lee's daughter who is a friend of hers. I asked Miss Elsie de Wolfe, the actress who is to act in Mrs. Wharton's play which is to be acted at a matinee soon & Miss Bessie Marbury the manager to meet them as Annie Morgan wanted to meet them. I thought everyone seemed pleased and it went off well.

$\mathcal{Q}$ueen Victoria had at last died, and the coronation of Edward VII was to take place on June 26, 1902, in Westminster Abbey. By May, London was so crowded with Americans, most of whom had come over for the festivities, that one would have thought they were still subjects of the crown. Among them was Henry Adams, who described the city as "odious; cold, rainy, dirty and coronaceous." He mentioned that Bessy Marbury had preceded him over and added that he had enjoyed "a perfectly calm crossing" on the *Philadelphia,* which he had boarded on May 7. "Elsy [sic] de Wolfe and Ethel Barrymore took me between them and coddled me all the way over." They arrived on the evening of May 15. "England seemed more English than ever, but the weather was worse which may account for it." He had lunch with "Mrs. Harry" (Margaret [Daisy] Rutherfurd White) and found "the usual embassy people, and the usual infernal social jam when everybody is too busy to look at anyone else."

Adams did have one calm and pleasant interlude with Anne Rutherfurd, who had elected to live in Europe after Lewis's death. They spent an afternoon at the Royal Academy, which was having a show by the American painter John Singer Sargent. Later, he went to see Pierpont Morgan's Fragonards, which were on exhibition at the Guildhall.

On April 23 Anne and Pierpont Morgan sailed from New York on the *Cedric.* Andrew Carnegie was also on board. A year earlier, Morgan had bought out his steel company as part of a merger to form the United States Steel Corporation. Carnegie had forced Morgan to come to him and held out for almost a half-billion dollars. When the deal was completed, Morgan said, "Mr. Carnegie, I want to congratulate you on being the richest man in the world."

The latter crowed about how he had bested him. "Pierpont feels he can do anything, because he has always got the best of the Jews in Wall Street." He laughed and added, "It takes a Yankee to beat a Jew, and it takes a Scot to beat a Yankee."

In the time that had elapsed since the transaction, Carnegie had reevaluated the deal. Now, with Anne at her father's side, the two great tycoons stood in close proximity on the deck of the *Cedric,* waving farewells to their friends. They could not miss the crowd gathering around the Reverend A. E. Denning on the pier, as he thundered a denunciation of them and their kind:

> Come now, ye rich, weep and howl for your miseries that are coming upon you. Your riches are corrupted and your garments are moth eaten. Your gold and your silver are rusted; and their rust shall be a testimony against you and shall eat your flesh as fire. Ye have condemned, ye have killed the righteous One; He doth not resist you.

The words were still in Anne's head when, as if the priest's message was of no consequence, Carnegie turned to her father. "I sold out too cheap by a hundred million, didn't I?"

Morgan looked at him with cold eyes and replied flatly, "Very likely, Andrew."

*T*hat season, Morgan entertained lavishly both in London and at Dover House with Anne acting as his hostess. On the whole, he was satisfied with her. She could pour tea for a duchess with the same unaffected charm so long enjoyed by the derelicts in her Bowery soup kitchens. She was livelier than Louisa had been and could be sharply witty, although he was not amused when she got on her soapbox about the poor and slum clearance. It was enough he had to suffer through all that in Rainsford's sermons at home. What had he to do with the poor that he should be so harassed by them? He did more than his fair share for charity, and that should be an end to it.

What was most comforting about Anne was that her politics never interfered with her love for him. She knew how to rile him by equating tenement landlords and sweatshop bosses with Wall Street plungers, but she was unfailingly sympathetic during his illnesses and suffered with him when the press caricatured his nose or stigmatized him as a psalm-singing hypocrite.

Toward the end of May, Morgan and Anne, along with a party of friends and Morgan partners, left London for Paris. The traditional shopping at Worth was of uncommon importance, as Anne would need an exceptional new wardrobe not only for the coronation but also for all of the garden parties, dinners, and balls that would be given during the week preceding it. Morgan undoubtedly took charge, for Anne was the only female in his family who still allowed him to select her clothes. Louisa and Juliet were married and chose their own apparel, while Fanny had finally made it clear that she neither appreciated nor would she wear any clothing she did not select for herself.

On Sunday evening, June 22, Edward VII was stricken with acute appendicitis, which was not the simple thing then that it has since become. An emergency operation was performed the following morning. England might lose its new king three days before he was to be crowned. The country gave every appearance of having closed down, while it waited breathlessly for the latest reports. To get the news in those pre-radio days, crowds gathered outside Buckingham Palace, where bulletins of his hourly progress were posted on the gates. It was the era during which the sun never set on the British Empire, and the only significant news throughout the world was the condition of Edward on the eve of his coronation. The operation was a success, but it would take at least a month for him recuperate, and the ceremony was postponed until August.

Perhaps the English were content to sit around and wait, but not J. P. Morgan. He had a previous engagement with Edward's nephew the Kaiser of Germany, which made the emperor's British relatives very uneasy: both nations were vying for the attentions of the banker who had saved his own country from bankruptcy. Although he might have been convinced to postpone his date with the German ruler, nothing would have induced him to disappoint the woman who had just become his mistress, considered by many to be the most beautiful woman in the world.

When other actresses renowned for their beauty extolled the looks of a contemporary colleague, she must have been extraordinary. So it was with

Maxine Elliott. Ethel Barrymore exclaimed upon seeing her for the first time, "My God, it's the Venus de Milo with arms!"

Bessy and Elsie were also admirers and good friends. The latter had appeared with her in the short run of *Sister Mary,* while the former represented Clyde Fitch, who had written some of Maxine's biggest successes.

The year before, in September 1901, Maxine opened in London, in *When We Were Twenty-one,* also starring her husband, Nat Goodwin, the actor-manager who had made a star of her. By then, they were co-managers as well as co-stars, but except for their appearances onstage and in the counting-up room behind the box office, little remained of their relationship. Maxine had decided it was time to move on. Already in her early thirties, she looked into the mirror and took inventory. "Of course you're beautiful, and you know it, you're far too intelligent not to. Beauty is like talent, and you shouldn't underestimate it."

The answer to her dilemma appeared one evening at her dressing room door. In the words of Consuelo Marlborough, "the Honorable George Keppel was one of those tall and handsome Englishmen who, immaculately dressed, proclaim the perfect gentleman." She owed his appearance to a letter of introduction from a New York friend, the lawyer-financier Thomas L. Chadbourne, who would also be responsible for introducing her to Morgan. Chadbourne understood that she was in the tradition of all of the most successful courtesans and cocottes who, rightly or wrongly, considered beauty, like talent, a commodity in which one traded in the same way that bankers and brokers traded in their commodities and with a comparable degree of morality. He said, "If Maxine had been a man, Schiff would have been her secretary and Carnegie her office boy."

Keppel was a member of the king's inner circle, the Marlborough House set, as it was called after his London residence while he was still Prince of Wales. He had an arrangement with his wife, Alice, who was the king's mistress. They might each take whatever lovers they desired so long as they were discreet. Anything could be compromised except good manners and each other. There also appeared to have been a tacit agreement that should he find a creature who might amuse the king, she must be brought around, and in no time Maxine was a frequent guest in Mrs. Keppel's drawing room. That she did amuse Edward, when she met him, was apparent, but during the period in which she was under the aegis of the Keppels, Maxine set her sights on the wealthy and brilliant Earl of Rosebery, who had been the prime minister. He had been married to a Rothschild heiress who died young, and since had become a professional widower, which served to restrain women, in whom there were indications that the effete aristocrat had little interest.

That Rosebery was seen with Maxine and evidently enjoyed her company was a matter of record, but as for his unlikely proposal and her still more unlikely rejection, after her hot pursuit of him, there was only her word.

The Marquess of Queensberry had accused him of seducing his oldest son, who was Rosebery's private secretary, just as he would later accuse Oscar Wilde of seducing his youngest son, with far more disastrous results. There were those who said the criminal charges against Wilde were brought only to protect the former prime minister, whose name had surfaced in the writer's earlier civil suit.

The kaiser was not about to be outdone by his British uncle in the wooing of Morgan, and he invited him to be his guest at the festivities in honor of the presence of the German fleet in the Kiel Canal. On July 1, Morgan sailed on the *Corsair* for Germany, with a party of thirteen men and eight women. Anne was not invited; Maxine would serve as her father's unofficial hostess in her place. She was quite accustomed to seeing her father's favorites on yachting parties and even transatlantic crossings, but a modicum of discretion was always expected, which Morgan had learned could not be guaranteed with Maxine. The last time the actress and his daughter had sailed together, he had been on deck with a group of his cronies. Bored with polite conversation with Anne and the other women and needing to assert her right to be the center of male attention, Maxine had shouted to them: "Why, you men in Wall Street are like a lot of cannibals. You just devour anything that comes along—if it's edible."

While Morgan had joined the others in raucous laughter, he was not amused by such familiarity in the presence of his daughter. He must have decided at that point not to allow his new mistress another such opportunity. As for Anne, she could not have cared less. She might even have been amused, as she undoubtedly had been when her father's frequent visits to the home of the buxom musical comedy star Lillian Russell were noted, and he had excused them on the grounds that he was advising her on her Chinese porcelain collection.

It was unfortunate that Maxine's momentary lapse had led to Anne's not being allowed to become acquainted with the actress's other striking qualities until much later, through Bessy and Elsie. But at the time she had her own agenda, having already embarked on what would be her life's work, helping to improve the conditions of poor workingwomen, a category that decidedly did not include Maxine Elliott.

Morgan's relationship with Maxine lasted for a longer time than his relationships with many of his other mistresses. This was partially because of the exigencies of a career in which she was expected to tour for months on end, but that was not the full explanation. He was not the type whose heart was made fonder by absence; his appetites were too enormous for that. It was that hard, bright, logical intellect, wrapped in a beautiful package, that kept him interested. The depth of his feelings for her was evidenced by the fact that he allowed her liberties that nobody, not family or friends or even monarchs, was permitted. When the King of England once asked why a painting was hung where it was in his London mansion, Morgan stared ferociously and replied, "I like it there." Edward said no more.

Of all of his possessions, the *Corsair III* was the closest to him. He had planned every inch of his beloved yacht, and none of his children would have dared criticize any of the appointments, no matter how uncomfortable they might be. Not Maxine. She told him that the layout of the boat made no practical sense, and he listened. "He had the cabins on a lower deck where there was no light, and the dining saloon on the upper deck. I had him change the whole thing so we could dine below, where we needed no outside light, and all the sleeping cabins could have proper portholes."

In 1908, the affair was still going on. What Maxine wanted above all was her own theatre, and Maxine Elliott's Theatre was to open at the end of that year on West Thirty-ninth Street. Although there were many actresses far more gifted and better-known than Maxine, it was the first theatre in the United States named for an actress, and the second in the world, the Sarah Bernhardt having opened ten years earlier in Paris. By then, the couple was openly traveling together. They returned home from Europe a few months before the opening. When they disembarked, he was accosted by reporters asking question about his participation in the project. His reply was, "The only interest I have in Maxine Elliott's Theatre is that I'd like to get a free ticket on opening night."

The Satterlees joined Morgan and Anne in London during the summer of 1902. On August 9, the morning of the coronation, they arose early and were down at breakfast by seven to greet Anne and Morgan when they descended, resplendent in their court attire. In his knee breeches, gold-buckled shoes, and sword, he looked rather like the pirate Henry Morgan, with whom he facetiously claimed kinship, decked out in his Sunday best. The tall and poised Anne was truly magnificent in a Worth gown and cloak splashed with an array of the collective best of the family jewelry.

Ever sensitive about how his afflicted nose photographed except in formal sittings that he could control, a surprisingly nimble Morgan side-stepped a photographer waiting in the street by leaping into his brougham. The brilliant sun with which the day had begun was now shrouded, but happily no rain fell. The route to Westminster Abbey was banked with people, many of whom had spent the night there to assure their advantageous places.

By 9 A.M. the doors of the great cathedral were closed, and the brilliant assemblage was in place. After the ceremony, the Morgan brougham returned to Princes Gate at a crawl, having to take care not to hit the jubilant crowds thronging into the streets. A huge family meal awaited at home, with Anne and Morgan presiding in all their finery, as if they were the newly anointed monarchs. It was agreed that the ordeal at the abbey had been worth it, for there would never be another coronation of comparable splendor, might never be another coronation, for even then it was thought by many that the royal family was outliving its usefulness in this increasingly democratic country.

In the autumn of 1903, Anne assembled a group of friends for a hunting and camping trip along the mountain trails of Colorado. Her idea of roughing it in the wilderness included the private railroad car her father provided to carry the party, servants, guides, and gear. French personal maids were all the rage in her crowd, but Anne drew the line at permitting any of the women to bring them along. "No maid could stand such roughing it. It's all very well for a lot of New York girls to rough it, but when you ask a French maid to eat flapjacks and venison steaks, she turns up her pink little nose and inquires if Madame engaged her for that."

The Worths, selected by her father, were left at home. Her wardrobe consisted of corduroy skirts, cut very short (ankle-length); flannel shirtwaists; heavy russet-leather shoes; rubber boots; woolen cardigans and pullovers; a soft felt hat; and a big Mexican sombrero. They started into the unspoiled wilderness from Glenwood Springs and spent four weeks on bronco and in canoes, exploring 125 miles of the untamed Colorado Rockies. They climbed and camped in mountains rife with wildcats, bears, mountain lions, lynx, and coyotes. At night, their only shelter was three large tents— one for the women, another for the men, and a third for the cook and guides. At tables knocked together from whatever trees they could chop down, they ate meals made from the game they shot and the fish they caught. The prize specimen among the trophies was the head of the seven-pronged elk that Anne brought down and shipped east to hang among the other prize specimens at Camp Uncas.

Their guide, William Baxter, spoke admiringly of her. "Seems to me that the Morgans must have a shooting gallery in their house in New York. Mighty few young ladies can shoot as straight as she does. And she's the pluckiest mountain climber I ever saw. Nothing ever upset her. . . . Why, she

Elisabeth Marbury in her late teens.

Elsie de Wolfe.

Anne and Juliet Morgan, ca. 1888.

The Morgan children: *from l to r:* Jack, Annie, Louisa, and Juliet.

J. Pierpont Morgan.

Mrs. J. P. Morgan.

The Morgan mansion, 219 Madison Avenue,
New York City.

Emma Lazarus.

Caroline Astor.

Alva Vanderbilt Belmont.

Oscar Wilde.

The Irving House at the
time when Elisabeth
Marbury and Elsie de Wolfe
shared it.

George Bernard Shaw at the time he first met Elisabeth Marbury.

Elsie de Wolfe shortly after her Broadway debut.

Isabella Stewart Gardner, 1905, in a De Meyer photograph.

Elsie de Wolfe wearing the costume made for her by Paquin in *The Bauble Shop*.

Anne Morgan at the time she first met Elisabeth Marbury.

Henry Adams. Crayon sketch by John Briggs Potter, 1914.

Bernard Berenson.

Clyde Fitch.

Charles Frohman and David Belasco.

Elizabeth Robins.

The Duchess of Marlborough, née Consuelo Vanderbilt, and her son, the Marquis of Blanford, at Blenheim Castle, 1902.

Elisabeth Marbury in the costume she wore to James Hazen Hyde's ball in 1904.

Elsie de Wolfe in the costume she wore to James Hazen Hyde's ball in 1904.

Mrs. J. Borden (Daisy) Harriman.

Stanford White.

Reception room in the original Colony Club.

Original Colony Club designed by Stanford White.

Anne Harriman Vanderbilt, ca. 1905.

William Kissam Vanderbilt.

brought down her big seven-pronged buck at three hundred yards [sic] on her first shot. She caught him plumb through the heart."

Wherever she went, she made friends. The more esoteric were calling her "Diana of the peaks" and "a Nimrod in skirts." A reporter wrote:

> Colorado salutes New York. If all the daughters of "five hundred and fifty" can conquer this rough and ready state as did Miss Anna Morgan [sic] ... then admiring Colorado wants to see them all out here next summer. Women hold office in this state; if Miss Morgan cared to run now, she could have almost anything from Governor to town constable.

Anne simply laughed. She bypassed the notion of a woman going into politics and stuck to talking about her hunting.

> I didn't have any buck fever at all. I shot two deer and never missed a shot. That's nothing. It isn't anywhere near the first time I have been hunting. I am very fond of shooting, and my friends have been kind enough to say I'm a good shot, but I am sure I am no wonder. What I am proudest of in the world is my father. I would rather be known as his daughter than share the throne of any court in Europe.

CHAPTER TWENTY-TWO

During the five final years of the nineteenth century, before Ogden Codman's introduction of Bessy and Elsie to Anne Morgan, not only had the two women helped to alter the nature of New York society, but Bessy's theatrical career had also proceeded from strength to strength as she reshaped the role of the play broker, changing it from that of glorified salesperson, peddling a script, to that of an author's representative in every sense of the term. She believed that a "good agent, one who is really worthy of the name, should indeed be a guide, philosopher, and a friend."

Her aesthetic taste was often limited by a sixth sense of what was commercially viable. As a result, she preferred the farces of Georges Feydeau and Sardou's well-made plays to the more hazardous Sturm und Drang of Ibsen and Hermann Sudermann while at various times handling the works of all of them. This put her at odds with Shaw, who in his role as critic had coined the word "Sardoodledom" to describe the works of one of her most consistently lucrative clients. Nevertheless, she did have the discernment to value Shaw over another early British client, Arthur Wing Pinero, then the more profitable of the two.

Her American list was expanded by the addition of promising young women such as Rachel Crothers to her already established female writers including Frances Hodgson Burnett, Jeanette Gilder, and Edith Wharton (as a dramatist). In an observation that linked her career as an agent to her earlier entrepreneurial endeavors with chickens, it was later said: "She invented the maternal relation to the American theater and became the original incubator of dramatists."

When her virtual monopoly on quality and commercial success was finally broken, at the end of the nineteenth century, it was by a number of women who were following where she had led. Her former secretary Alice Kauser and her aforementioned old friend and client Jeanette Gilder were among those who set up shop as playwrights' representatives. Gilder freely admitted she had learned all she knew about the business by being "associated with Miss Elisabeth Marbury who is the greatest play broker in the world."

By the time Henry DeMille, a moderately successful playwright and collaborator of David Belasco, died, leaving his wife, Beatrice, with little money and three children to support, Bessy had made play brokerage a suitable profession for "ladies": the destitute Mrs. DeMille entered it. She became the first agent actually to specialize in women writers, with clients including Mary Roberts Rinehart and Zoë Akins. Her initial modest office was in the Knickerbocker Theatre Building, but it was not long before she became "the DeMille Company," with a large staff and a suite of offices in the Astor Theatre Building. Bessy would eventually buy her business, but not before Beatrice had obtained the film rights to *The Squaw Man* for her younger son: it would start Cecil B. DeMille on his incredibly long and flourishing career as a motion picture director.

In 1895, Bessy was inadvertently responsible for one of the most successful unions in the history of the American theatre. To manage her London office, she had hired Addison Bright, a young man who moved in the best theatrical and literary circles and who would give her access to the most promising new writers. His good friend James M. Barrie was hardly a new talent, having already written a few moderately successful plays and books. That season his career had taken a turn up with the publication of his first best-seller, *The Little Minister,* which Bessy thought would make a lovely play. She convinced Frohman to commission the work, offering an advance large enough to overcome any qualms Barrie might have about making the adaptation. The terms were transmitted to London. A contract was negotiated between Bessy and Barrie authorizing her to serve as his representative on *The Little Minister,* collecting royalties from Frohman and deducting 8 percent as her commission.

The Barries and their party arrived in New York on Saturday morning, October 3. They were booked into the Holland House, where the concierge informed them that Mr. Frohman had booked a box for the party that evening at his Empire Theatre. A young actress on the verge of stardom, Maude Adams, was appearing in a play called *Rosemary.* It was a pleasant piece of no great merit, but there was no denying the talent and charms of Miss Adams.

Early on Sunday, Bessy stopped by the hotel to welcome the Barries to the city, pick up the script, and undoubtedly invite them to that afternoon's at-home on Irving Place. She reassured the playwright that she would personally place the script in the producer's hands, and that he had promised to read it and give them his answer by the end of the week.

True to her word, she placed the script in the pudgy hands of the impresario early the next morning. She returned on the following Saturday morning. Frohman wasted no time in getting down to business. "The play is all right. There is nothing the matter with it; only it is no good for me. . . . It is a man's play, whereas I am looking for a play for Maude Adams. I haven't any young actor I want to star in it."

She had been so convinced of the acceptance and production of the property that she was shocked into an uncustomary silence. Frohman's grounds for rejection indicated he had not read the book before commissioning the play or he would surely have known it was the man's story. He had paid the advance only on her recommendation. Ever quick on her feet, Bessy recovered after a few moments. "How would you feel about it if Barrie would rewrite it and make Lady Babbie the leading part?"

"Oh, that would be fine: but I don't believe you can get him to do it."

Barrie was obdurate. A work entitled *The Little Minister* must be about the title character and no other. Bessy used every argument that came to mind. Her powers of persuasion were notable, and although they were not working on him, she could see they were having their effect on Mrs. Barrie. She had found an ally in a clever wife who ran the show by allowing her popinjay of a husband to have his artistic tantrums and amorous peccadilloes, neither of which threatened her, while she attended to business, where a failure would indeed have been a threat. Realizing that time, in the attractive shape of Mary Barrie, was on her side, Bessy withdrew, saying she would return on Monday for his final decision and urging him to reconsider.

By the end of the weekend, Barrie was considerably less adamant. It would take one more argument to win him over, and Bessy pointed out that Maude Adams was extremely popular. The play that made a big star of her would undoubtedly bring both fame and fortune to its writer. He was at an analogous point in his theatrical career, where one great success would bring him the renown he desired. Barrie agreed to make the changes.

The Little Minister fulfilled its promise by making both a new star and an acclaimed playwright who would later create *Peter Pan* for her. His royalties from the American productions of their play came to eighty thousand pounds, which in contemporary currency would be in the grand neighborhood of two million dollars.

*O*n June 19, 1896, Bessy celebrated her fortieth birthday with Elsie during their summer abroad. The nineties had been a period of rising successes for her with each year more triumphant than the previous one. Equally rewarding was her life with Elsie. For the latter, the years since her father's death had been marked by fluctuation rather than ascendance. Their private life was satisfying, with Bessy indulging her every whim, but her career in the theatre had been comparably dispiriting, with each forward thrust blunted by a step backward.

Elsie had minor roles in three Empire plays during the following season but Bessy was the major player, as the writers were all her clients. An apocryphal story began to be circulated that season that lasted longer than any memory of the plays in which she appeared. Henry Miller and Elsie played a Jewish sister and brother in *A Woman's Reason*. When their roles were coupled with their surnames, it started the rumor that they were Jews, which would be repeated "on good authority" for the rest of their lives.

Her disappointing year was climaxed by the news that Frohman would have nothing for her in New York during the fall season. He was placing her with a company scheduled to play in Chicago for several months. The earliest she would be able to get home or hope to appear on Broadway would be the spring of 1897. This prolonged separation would not be like the old days, when her friend would come out to be with her when she was on the road. She knew Bessy would be far too busy with her own thriving business to spare the time.

In the three plays in Frohman's Chicago schedule, her only good role would be one of the leads in Pinero's *The Benefit of the Doubt*. To underscore her importance to Frohman, she was determined to have a great success in it. Bessy prevailed upon the writer to work with Elsie.

Both women were professionals. Their vacations were devoted to their careers, as was exemplified by that summer. Bessy spent much of her time dashing from her London office to her Paris office, to her Berlin office, and back again, attending to the needs of her clients, conferring with producers, signing new writers, scouting plays. When Elsie was not diligently rehearsing with Pinero in London, she was in Paris spending numbing hours being fitted for her new clothes. More than anything else, it was undoubtedly this need for employment that would sustain them during their first long separation.

It was more difficult for Elsie than for Bessy. Exiled to Chicago and deprived of the comforts of her own home, she had little to do with her free time once the rehearsal period was over. That actors lived on the wrong side of the clock was a particular problem on the road. While others worked or attended to their families and homes during the day and were at liberty to amuse themselves during the evening, the performers' schedule was the reverse, which increased their isolation, especially during extended engagements in strange towns. That season in Chicago was not improved by a winter that roared in across the lake and had to be the worst she ever had experienced.

In such circumstances, the theatrical company becomes a family huddling together for warmth and affinity, but it often proves a dysfunctional one, replete with sordid romances, base jealousies, niggling gossip, and small cruelties. Elsie loathed its pettiness and longed for Bessy's expansiveness, but there was no escape to that haven if she wanted to pursue her career.

Elsie may not have proven her worth as an actress in the Pinero play, but Frohman continued to value her as a second woman in the Empire Stock Company, which was among the best acting companies in the country. As she later admitted, she was never among its great stars. "Whichever way I looked at it—from the point of view of talent or of recognition—my success was only mediocre. I hate mediocrity."

Frohman brought her back to New York, early in 1897, to play a supporting role in a new farce, *Never Again*, which opened a successful run at the Garrick Theatre on March 8. In a very good review for the play, Edward Dithmar said that Elsie had "scarcely anything congenial to do. . . . But her dresses are expressions of the latest fancies of folks who study how to make women look attractive at a great cost, and they are perhaps [the show's] most striking pictorial features." Another review said no more than that "Elsie de Wolfe wore some very handsome costumes."

The plays in which Elsie appeared were almost always written by Bessy's clients. As was demonstrated by Wilde's endorsement of her for the first American production of *A Woman of No Importance,* the agent did all she could to advance her prospects, which probably explains her continued engagement in the Frohman company at a salary purportedly far in excess of her worth. Frohman needed Bessy for product and wanted first refusal on the best she had to offer. Employing her chum was a logical and painless way to ingratiate himself with the increasingly powerful woman, especially since Elsie was a quick study and hard worker who was continually honing her skills.

Although the other women involved did not necessarily share a home, what Bessy was doing to promote Elsie was a part of something beginning to happen in artistic, professional, and academic circles that, for want of a better name, might be called an old girls' network. The members were all attempting to gain their economic independence, and preferred others of their own sex for intellectual, sentimental, and/or erotic arousal. They generally advanced one another's opportunities whenever possible. The paradox was that when completely heterosexual women sought careers, they were initially ungenerous to their female colleagues. It could have been that competition for the few good places available was so keen that beneficence was expendable; it could as well have been that their role models were the often combative men with whom they were emotionally involved.

Frohman showed his appreciation of Elsie's taste during the pre-production preparations for *A Marriage of Convenience* when he asked her to supervise its eighteenth-century costumes and scenery. It was her first foray into professional decoration, and during that summer in Paris she prepared for it exceedingly well. Although she was unaccredited, her success was apparent in Dithmar's review:

> The scenic setting, comprising a single interior, with painted panels, and the ornate furniture and gilding belonging to the epoch . . . could not be surpassed. The costumes are accurate and beautiful, from the cut of the brocade coats to the fashion of a snuff box or the design of the silver embroidery on the back of a glove.

From then on, Elsie had something to contribute to the look of every play in which she appeared. Other actresses allowed her to supervise their wardrobes, secure in the knowledge that she would make them look their best, and that her immaculate discretion would not permit her, in a supporting role, to outshine the star.

$\mathscr{E}$lsie could entertain at any gathering with a series of anecdotes about her life in the theatre. They were amusing stories told with good nature, and she was often the butt of them. But there was no doubt that Elsie was frustrated by the inconsequential roles, the indifferent plays, and the lack of forward direction in her career. Her dissatisfaction was no secret to Bessy, who, for all her efforts on her friend's behalf, could do nothing about it. It was only human to find Elsie an ingrate for carping in light of all she had done and continued to do for her.

Bessy was at the top of her profession, a woman of power, surrounded by adulation, and paid court to by any number of attractive, gifted men and women. It had to have been a bore to come home to Elsie's complaints, especially since there was no indication of compensatory physical intimacy. There is no proof that Bessy ever strayed, but when Elizabeth Robins appeared upon the scene she was—at the very least—tempted.

Robins, a worldly beauty of acknowledged accomplishments, was then in her late thirties. She had been a young American actress of no reputation in her own country when she decided to try her luck in London. It was not long before she was a protégée of Oscar Wilde's, amorously pursued by Herbert Beerbohm Tree, and the subject of George Bernard Shaw's more intellectual ardor. She proved more than worthy of this attention in a series of performances that established her as London's foremost interpreter of Ibsen's heroines. She had also begun to publish some very promising fiction.

At the beginning of 1898, Miss Robins decided that it was time to display her art in New York after over a decade of acclaim in London. It was logical that one of her English admirers, all of whom were represented by Bessy, should recommend the actress to the agent. In her first letter Bessy knew so little of the actress that she misspelled her name. Although she tried, it was not easy to help Elizabeth Robins, not because managements did not want her in one of their productions but because she was so single-minded in wanting to do only *Hedda Gabler,* which had featured her most admired performance in England.

The best Bessy could do was to arrange to mount two matinees of *Hedda* at the Fifth Avenue Theatre. They were much admired, but nobody was willing to put on a full-scale production with an unknown actress in an "arty" play. In the course of their negotiations, the tone of Bessy's correspondence was in turn polite, professional, and irritated. By the time the show closed, she was addressing Robins as "Dear Sympathetic Soul" and wondering,

"Shall we ever be able to draw apart *together* for a quiet hour to talk over *quiet* things?" She asked, "Why don't you put on a loose gown and come up here tomorrow and rest on my sofa with me in the big chair beside you?"

Whatever may have come of it, Robins became "Saint Elizabeth" in Bessy's letters to her over the next few months, letters largely concerned with finding ways to meet on the continent or in England. Robins later gave up the stage to concentrate on her career as a novelist. Bessy remained her close friend and agent for the rest of her life.

*I*n 1885, the Criminal Law Amendment Act had made sexual relations between consenting male adults illegal for the first time in the history of English law.

> Any male person who in public or private, commits, or is a party to the commission of, or procures or attempts to the commission by any male person of, any act of gross indecency with another male person, shall be guilty of a misdemeanor, and, being convicted thereof, shall be liable, at the discretion of the Court, to be imprisoned for any term not exceeding two years with or without hard labor.

The law would prove a bonanza for those who made their living by blackmailing homosexuals and would, a decade after its enactment, contribute to the ruin of Oscar Wilde. When one of Queen Victoria's ministers observed that there was no mention of acts of "gross indecency" between two females, the queen, true to the age she inspired, was alleged to have replied, "No woman would do that."

On February 28, 1895, Wilde arrived at his club, the Albemarle, to find a card left for him ten days earlier by the Marquess of Queensberry, the father of his lover, Lord Alfred (Bosie) Douglas. It was addressed: "To Oscar Wilde posing as a Somdomite."

He was neither amused by his accuser's manifest illiteracy nor moved to dismiss it as the poignant error of a distraught parent. Caught between a sociopathic father and a psychotic son, both eager to score points off each other at his expense, to which could be added no small measure of his own fatal self-destructiveness, Wilde was pushed into bringing up the marquess on the charge of publishing a libel against him. It was a charge that could not be sustained in the ensuing trial, for there was ample evidence that Queensberry's accusation was accurate in every sense except its spelling. On the basis of the testimony in that trial he was subsequently found guilty of violating the Criminal Acts Amendment, and on May 25, 1895, was sentenced to the maximum sentence allowed by law: two years at hard labor. It had happened swiftly, less than three months between finding the card and what would amount to the destruction of both his life and his wife's. Douglas retrieved from the tragedy a celebrity that would sustain his narcissism for years after his victims' deaths.

When all else failed Wilde, his wit defended him. While standing in a queue of convicts, on the rain-sodden railroad platform awaiting transport from one prison to another, a reporter asked how he felt being treated like a common criminal. He reply was: "If this is how Her Majesty treats her prisoners, she doesn't deserve to have any."

That spring, both Frohman brothers courageously had gone ahead with their productions of new Wilde plays despite the scandal of the Queensberry case. On April 22, 1895, Charles Frohman opened *The Importance of Being Earnest* at the Empire. On the morning of the twenty-third, while New Yorkers were reading the splendid reviews of his greatest play, an English grand jury was indicting him on criminal charges of sodomy and indecency.

What would later prove phenomenal was the inaccuracy of Bessy's autobiographical recollections of events concerning Wilde during this period. *My Crystal Ball* was filled with a combination of factual errors and maudlin sentimentalizing, but nowhere was that so extensive as in the comparatively few pages devoted to Wilde. It would seem as if she had been too traumatized by her slight personal relationship to his tragedy to look into her own business records to verify the established facts of her more profound professional connection to him.

Elsie was equally baffling. Years later, in her memoir, *After All*, she mentioned Wilde only once, in a laundry list of celebrities at Irving Place parties he could not possibly have attended as he was either in prison or dead at the time they took place. The book, principally a collection of anecdotal material about her relationships with the famous and infamous of her long day, was singular in its exclusion of Wilde, who had both helped to shape her taste as a decorator and also offered a friendly professional hand to her as an actress.

Before examining what might have motivated both women in their treatment of him, one must deal with Bessy's inaccuracies. She mentioned Daniel Frohman's New York production of *An Ideal Husband* "at the moment of Wilde's downfall" but neglected to cite his brother's presentation of the infinitely finer *The Importance of Being Earnest* at the same time. In London, Beerbohm Tree closed his production of *An Ideal Husband,* and George Alexander, his of *Earnest.* For the latter, Bessy reserved her deepest scorn. Her rebuke of the actor-manager for withdrawing this great play included an intimation of Alexander's own homosexuality. "He lacked the courage to continue, for like many others he was afraid of public opinion and dared not be classed with the few friends who stood loyally by Wilde even in his darkest moments."

As would always be the case, her moral indignation did not interfere with commerce. There was never a conflict between her private principles and the base ethics of her trade, which demanded that she get the best deal possible for her clients. Personal disapproval was not a bar to her doing business, any more than it would have been for a Morgan, Frohman, Vanderbilt, or any other male entrepreneur. At the moment when her contempt for Alexander must have been strongest, she was negotiating with him to produce *The Prisoner of Zenda*.

At the time Wilde was imprisoned, an impressive amount of royalties had accumulated for him in Bessy's accounts. She claimed to be waiting to communicate with him hoping that this sum might be saved from the wreckage for his family. Unfortunately, when interrogated by the bankruptcy court, he said his American agent undoubtedly "had funds that could be appropriated toward the liquidation of his debts." She was notified that all royalties collected for him would have to be disbursed to his creditors and confessed "to a sneaking disappointment at this turn of affairs, for sentimentally I felt the deepest sympathy for that wife and those little lads upon whom the sad fate of the husband and father had fallen."

Her compassion becomes a trifle mawkish when examined in light of the facts of which Bessy could not have been unaware. Although she was living in vastly reduced circumstances compared to those of the life she shared with her husband in Tite Street, Constance Wilde's private income was sufficient to care for her sons and herself. Indeed, after Oscar emerged from prison, his existence, threadbare as it was, depended on the allowance she set up for him that continued even after her own death the following year.

Bessy alleged that her own concern for his survival caused her to find a modest house to which he could retreat after release from prison. She placed it in the Versailles neighborhood in which Elsie and she spent their holidays. Impossible. Wilde was released in May 1897, and the women did not begin to summer in Versailles until 1898.

Perhaps her most exceptional example of the misinformation concerned the writing and American publication of *The Ballad of Reading Gaol*.

> From time to time he wrote to me from prison; then one day I received from him a roll of manuscript in his own handwriting. It was the "Ballad of Reading Gaol." He said he had scribbled it

down and wondered whether I would be his good angel and get him a few pounds for it, as he needed some personal articles which the sale of this poem might supply.

As I read it, it seemed like a voice from the dead. I remember that the tears rolled down my cheek. Then I realized that to sell it might, after all, be difficult. My fears were justified for after peddling it about unsuccessfully, I sold it to the New York World, which paid me $250.00 for it. This money I sent to Wilde, together with the manuscript which he wished returned. I have often wondered whether this original is still in existence.

Not a word of this account was true. Wilde did not write *Reading Gaol* until he was living in exile, in Dieppe, the summer after his release from prison. Within weeks of its composition, he was in touch with the publisher Leonard Smithers about bringing out an English edition the following winter on which his name would not appear. The author would be listed as "C.3.3.," his cell number at Reading Gaol. Bessy's first connection with the work did not occur until late October. At the time, Smithers was acting as Wilde's representative and attempting to arrange an American publication of the poem. His lack of success prompted a letter from Naples, where the writer had moved. "There is in New York my own agent for my plays—a woman of the highest position—agent for Sardou, and indeed all the dramatists—*Miss Marbury*. . . . She is in touch with everybody of journalistic position in New York. . . . It would be best to send Miss Marbury the manuscript and let her get terms."

Smithers had built up his hopes of a publishing coup in America. But by October 28, a disconsolate and very nearly destitute Wilde wrote to his dearest friend, Robert Ross: "I fear I have built air castles of false gold on my dreams of America. My hope now is in Miss Marbury who is on the spot."

By the end of November, Bessy still had not seen the work she claimed to have read a year earlier, for on the thirtieth of that month, Wilde again wrote to Smithers, who was apparently disinclined to allow Bessy in on the deal:

Do send a copy at once to Miss Marbury and Reynolds [a New York literary agent with whom she was associated]: they *cannot* get an offer unless the poem is read: and I don't think that a New York paper of standing would pirate, any more than a magazine. All my plays went to Miss Marbury. She is a woman of the highest position, and would not allow any nonsense. So pray let her have a copy at once.

Alfred Allan Lewis

During the first week in December, Bessy communicated directly with Smithers with suggestions for its publication despite not having yet read the work. He informed Wilde of what she said. Wilde wrote back on the sixth: "I am very glad you have heard from Miss Marbury, but do send her the poem. Her suggestion of *illustration* is of course out of the question."

By the beginning of 1898, Bessy had at last read the poem. Wilde had one final, disheartening suggestion for her:

> As regards to America, I think it would better now to publish there *without* my name. I see that it is my *name* that terrifies. I hope an edition of some kind will appear. I cannot advise what should be done, but it seems to me that the withdrawal of my name is essential in America as elsewhere, and the public likes an open secret.

Even in despair he could not resist a bon mot, and added: "Half of the success of Marie Correlli [sic] is due to the no doubt unfounded rumor that she is a woman."

On January 26, Smithers wrote to Wilde that he was "waiting for Miss Marbury's success in selling book" before setting a formal publication date, which she and he had agreed would be the same in both countries. He could not know that a letter from her was in the post written the day before from New York with disappointing news.

> Nobody here seems to feel any real interest in the poem, and this morning I received from the *Journal* their final offer which, alas, is only $100. The *World* refuses to give us anything and no syndicate will handle it. Unless you hear further from me by cable you may know that this is the best offer I can get. We shall want permission to publish it on Sunday February 13th if you accept the *Journal's* offer. Kindly cable me on receipt of this. By using my office code at 5 Henrietta St., Covent Garden, you can cable more cheaply.

During the first week in February, while awaiting the publication of *Reading Gaol*, Bessy managed to fill a week in Rose Coghlan's company with a revival of *A Woman of No Importance*. The manager of her London office, Ada Woolridge, remitted the royalty of one hundred dollars, less her commission of 8 percent, to Wilde through Smithers.

Sunday, February 13, was the day before Valentine's Day, and when Bessy opened her copy of the *New York Journal,* she raced through page after page of photographs of lovely young debutantes and brides-to-be framed in hearts as well as several sentimental ballads dedicated to the Christian Eros. But there was no sign of *The Ballad of Reading Gaol*. That Hearst intended to publish the poem was confirmed by the check for $88.59 that Bessy had sent to Smithers the preceding Friday. It represented $100 from the Hearst organization less her commission and $3.41 for a cable and wire. Bessy might have reasoned that the editors had deemed the work inappropriate to an edition consecrated to a martyred priest and illuminated with pictures of what were presumably demure young virgins. If this was actually the case, the ballad would undoubtedly appear on the following Sunday. But it was not to be.

The United States battleship *Maine* was sunk by a mine in Havana Harbor two days later, on the Tuesday after Valentine's Day. If there had been any thought of the *Journal* publishing *The Ballad of Reading Gaol* on the following Sunday, it was set aside. Hearst ordered that the edition be devoted to agitating for war against Spain on the pretext of the sinking of the battleship. It is the most frequently cited example of yellow journalism in all of American reportage. Poor Wilde. The American history of his near-masterpiece was a mirror image of his own history—scuttled first by love and then by war.

Wilde was in Paris on the thirteenth in preparation for what he hoped would be the triumphant double publication of his poem. If he was disappointed by what transpired in New York, he must have been elated by the reception in England, where it outsold any poem that had been published in recent years. The open secret of the identity of C.3.3. was finally admitted in the seventh edition, on which his name appeared as author.

During the summer of 1899, Wilde sought Bessy out in Paris. She was shocked by his appearance and circumstances: "unkempt, forlorn, and penniless." How far he had descended from the glory days in London society, where "he reigned supreme, flattered, honored, sought after and imitated—literally without a rival"! He made a gallant attempt at humor, informing her that "he had just staged a miracle play in the Latin Quarter."

What was most heartening to her was that he was apparently beginning to think creatively again and ready to start developing an idea that had come to him for a new "modern comedy drama," *Mr. and Mrs. Daventry*. The plot sounded promising, rife with possibilities for the exercise of his special blend of sentiment and epigrammatic wit. She contacted Charles Frohman, who agreed to commission the work and instructed her to draw up a preliminary agreement. Wilde desperately needed whatever money Bessy could get for him. His resources were so depleted that he was living in a depressing room at the Hôtel d'Alsace, in the rue des Beaux Arts, a picturesque street of seedy hostelries running off rue Bonaparte, on the Left Bank.

The negotiations continued through September. The original terms called for a five-hundred-dollar advance for a play to be delivered by June 1, 1900, with an additional one thousand dollars at that point, if it was acceptable. Bessy felt her writer needed more funds immediately in order to survive until he could complete the work. By the time she signed the contract for him on October 4, she had managed to reverse the terms, giving Wilde the larger sum up front. He received two hundred pounds ($978) on signing, with another one hundred pounds due upon acceptance.

This would give Wilde a smaller aggregate sum, but all that mattered to him was the initial payment, for he knew he would never be able to complete the play. The creative impetus was gone. While Bessy might take a synopsis of the plot of *Mr. and Mrs. Daventry* as proof it was still there, the sad truth was that not even the synopsis was new. It originally had been devised in 1894 as a possible vehicle for George Alexander, if that actor would agree to give up *The Importance of Being Earnest* so that it could be done by Charles Wyndham, an actor the playwright considered better suited to the leading role. When Alexander refused, the idea was shelved, not to appear again until the creatively depleted writer took it down again as a means of wresting money from Frohman. Those funds were spent by the beginning of 1900 with no work to show on the play. In February 1900, Wilde took advantage of the sad predicament of Ada Rehan, the great Irish-American star, who was being forced to find her own vehicles because of the death the year before of her mentor and producer, Augustin Daly. Unbeknownst to Marbury or Frohman, he resold it to that desperate lady, and without telling her sold it yet again to his publisher Leonard Smithers. By March, he had garnered some four hundred pounds from three concurrent options on a play he was too blocked to write. At that point Frank Harris appeared on the scene, saying, "If you can't write your play, why not let me do it for you, and we can share the royalties."

Wilde was joyously relieved to sign a collaboration agreement with Harris without telling him of the existing contracts with Frohman, Rehan, and Smithers. Liberated from the onus of having to produce *Mr. and Mrs. Daventry,* he searched for another way to make money by means of a craft he could no longer practice and found it in *L'Affranchie,* a great Paris hit by one of Bessy's successful *boulevard* writers, Maurice Donnay. Surely, she could get somebody to buy it and commission him to make an adaptation.

On April 30, Bessy had been in London for five days when she received a letter from Wilde that was a follow-up to an earlier cable to which she had not replied. Her prompt answer explained that Ada Woolridge, her London secretary, had not known the true identity of the wire's signatory, Sebastian Melmoth, a name he used to evade identification. She assured him that she would try to close on the Donnay adaptation and inform him of the terms. After asking when he was returning to Paris and "what about the other play for Mr. Frohman?" the letter closed with, "You see I am asking you a good many questions."

That last line indicated that although she might not know of his treachery to Frohman and her, she did suspect that something was amiss.

Harris secured an option for *Mr. and Mrs. Daventry* to be produced in London as a vehicle for Mrs. Patrick Campbell. Harris then signed an agreement with Wilde, who was ill in Paris, to pay him 175 pounds on signing and more if the play proved a success. According to Wilde, he received twenty-five pounds with the promise that the balance would be forthcoming within a week, but his erstwhile collaborator departed for England that evening. Wilde wrote: "It is outrageous, your leaving me as I am, ill in bed, operated on twice a day, in continuous pain, and without a penny."

Harris claimed he already had given him fifty pounds with the understanding that Wilde would provide Act One for an additional fifty pounds. That act was never forthcoming, and having been forced to write it himself, Harris asserted that he need not pay the playwright another nickel. The play opened in October to terrible reviews, but the presence of Stella Campbell, a naughty plot, and the rumor that Wilde had written it combined to make it a moderate success. Wilde cried, "You have not only stolen my play, you have spoiled it."

Needless to say, this was done without consultation with Bessy or regard for Frohman's rights until it was an accomplished deed. When Wilde demanded his royalties, Harris replied they had been used to pay off the claims of Frohman, Rehan, and Smithers. What really hurt Oscar was that the production had put an end to his scam. "Frank has deprived me of my only source of income by taking a play on which I could always have raised 100 pounds."

In 1904, Bessy got *Mr. and Mrs. Daventry* optioned for Broadway, but nothing came of it, and the play was never heard of again.

The last time Bessy saw Wilde was during the autumn of 1900, when he lay dying in a "wretched" attic room in the "squalid" Hôtel d'Alsace. He barely recognized her, and the memory of that meeting would remain a painful one for the rest of her life.

His still-bulky form was covered by "a hideous brown blanket. The furnishings were plain and ugly with hardly any creature comforts." She recalled the house in Tite Street. "The contrast was appalling."

On his deathbed, Wilde had the last witty word on his final abode on this earth. "When I first came here, I took one look at the wallpaper and knew one of us would have to go."

To understand why Bessy reinvented as much as she did about Wilde and her professed attitudes on his behavior, one must note the years of his tragedy. The end of a century often elicits fanatical efforts from the forces of reaction to dam the tide of enlightenment threatening to spill forth into the new age and engulf them. Their favored weapon is the evocation of God to cloak gaudy political ambition in what they hope will be mistaken for shining moral armor. One hundred years ago, this reaction fueled the Wilde and Dreyfus cases in Europe, and the rise of Comstockism, the Ku Klux Klan, and the anti-suffrage movement in the United States.

It was no climate in which to challenge the status quo, but that was what Bessy and Elsie were doing, and in no sedate, spinsterish way. They had set up housekeeping together during the year in which Wilde was tried and convicted. Bessy's professional life was linked to the most notorious homosexual scandal of the century at a time when homophobia was rampant on both sides of the Atlantic. In her private and public lives, she was vulnerable to attack by the same forces that helped to bring down Wilde, and yet she stood by him after many of his closer friends had fled. What it cost to become the bachelorettes during the spring of Wilde's trials could have inspired her twisting of the facts, just as it may have contributed to Elsie's omission of them.

Bessy had heard "incessant innuendoes as to the flagrant offenses" in his private life. Through Jennie Churchill, Minnie Paget, Cora Brown-Potter, and the connections of her father, who had been attorney for the British government, she and Elsie had moved in the same high social circles frequented by Wilde, and were in a good position to be privy to all of the most piquant gossip. In an oblique reference to the sexual preferences he shared with Rosebery and some members of the royal family, she indicated that his intimacy with that social set had contributed to his ruin. "Knowing as I did that he was the center of a circle which was powerful in its connections and influence, I never believed that Wilde would be the scapegoat of this band, yet such was the case. I could not reconcile myself to the fact that he alone was singled out to pay the penalty."

At length, she had to admit: "It was Wilde's egotism which eventually ruined his life," but added, "It was such a magnificent gesture that it frequently inspired one to admiration."

What had evoked Bessy's many evasions, untruths, and half-truths became substantive in her delineation of the climatic event of Wilde's life. A Catholic priest from St. Joseph's Church was present when he died, but, according to Bessy, whether or not he became a deathbed convert to the faith in which he had a "mystical belief" would remain a mystery "until the day when the secrets of all hearts shall be revealed."

It seems inconceivable that Bessy did not see the last interview Wilde ever gave. It was printed three weeks before his death in the *London Daily Chronicle*. The efficient Miss Woolridge would have posted it to her. In it he was quoted as saying: "Much of my moral obliquity is due to the fact that my father would not allow me to become a Catholic. The artistic side of the Church and the fragrance of its teachings would have cured my degeneracies. I intend to be received before long."

Wilde's literary executor and closest friend, Robert Ross, had also been his first male lover. If Bessy and Wilde's beloved "Robbie" were not already good friends in 1900, they assuredly were by the time he appointed her sole American agent for the Oscar Wilde estate in 1908. They worked closely together for several years. It seems highly unlikely that at some point she did not ask him about the last months of Wilde's life. It was Ross, a Catholic convert, who, in a paroxysm of guilt over his part in Wilde's downfall, wanted to save his former lover from perdition by having him embrace the faith in his final moments.

On that last day, numbed by the realization that the end was close, Ross had raced across the inappropriately blazing autumnal beauty of Paris, enmeshing himself in the spokes of Baron Haussmann's glorious Arc de Triomphe de l'Etoile, and continuing northeast on the avenue Hoche to the seat of the Passionist Fathers, at St. Joseph's Church. What appeared unfathomable was why he should have gone that distance when the Church of St. Germain des Prés was a short three blocks from the Hôtel d'Alsace, unless, of course, he wanted an English-speaking priest lest there be any confusion. Wilde was fluent in French, but as is often the case with people slipping in and out of consciousness in a terminal state, the second language may have been depressed.

Father Cuthbert Dunne returned with Ross to the rue des Beaux Arts. He asked Wilde if he wished to be received into the church, and the dying man held up his hand. Interpreting that signal as an affirmation, the priest administered both baptism and last rites. Ross later wrote: "He was never able to speak and we do not know whether he was altogether conscious. I did this for my own conscience and the promise I had made." That promise stemmed from Wilde's avowal that it was permissible to live as an Anglican, but "Catholicism is the only religion to die in."

The points of Bessy's sense of identification with Wilde were as clear as the points by which a fingerprint is identified. Physically, they were similarly androgynous in a large fleshy way. Both were flamboyantly witty, with theatrical personalities that did not preclude positions in society. Both found their chivalric calling in love, honorably giving more than they ever received. The qualities they shared were among those most strongly contributing to his ruin during the same period that she seemed to be admitting their sexual kinship by living with Elsie.

CHAPTER TWENTY-THREE

In the summer of 1898, during their annual hegira to Paris, Elsie and Bessy met Minna Paget, the dowager Marchioness of Anglesey, a woman who would introduce them to the place Elsie would come to love above all others. To look at her, Minnie seemed as fragile and lovely as the *blanc de Chine* flowers and figurines that she collected. At her invitation, Bessy and Elsie drove out to Versailles for her next at-home. Elsie ingratiated herself with her hostess to such an extent that Bessy and she were offered the lease on an exquisite small pavilion in the lovely garden of her estate, effective immediately. They were free to move in at their own convenience. To have their own home in a chic milieu, within easy commuting distance of Paris, was a dream come true.

She was born Mary Livingstone King, of Sandhills, Georgia, and her father had come through the Civil War with his fortune undiminished and was able to purchase for her a reputable younger son of a baron. Minnie was not in England long before discovering that younger sons were a drug on the market. When he died five years later, his handsome widow, having inherited a sizable fortune from her father, determined that her next husband would be able to give her a title of her own.

Henry Paget already had been married twice. When his childless half-brother died, he would become the forth Marquess of Anglesey. The price tag the prospective marquess placed on his impending title was $200,000. No fool, Minnie was not about to shell out until the coronet was securely on Henry's head. The third marquess died in January 1880, and the fourth marquess married Minnie at the British embassy in Paris. Anglesey preferred to live in England while his new wife adored Paris. She would cross the Channel in the spring of each year to stay with him for the London season. It was the perfect arrangement and lasted until Henry died, a few months before she met Bessy and Elsie.

The nature of her new tenants' relationship was undoubtedly a large part of what Minnie Anglesey found attractive about Bessy and Elsie—that as well as the ease with which they moved amid the wildly disparate group that surrounded her. With the Bohemians and *gens du monde* there was another set frequenting her salon. She was Aunt Minnie to an eclectic group of lesbians that included Princess Polignac, nee Winnaretta Singer, the American heiress who was a gifted musician equally renowned for the brilliant, often avant-garde concerts she gave in her home as she was for her tempestuous sapphic love affairs, one of which was with the celebrated American painter Romaine Brooks to whom she had been introduced by Minnie.

In common with many wealthy and artistic lesbians coming of age before the last quarter of the twentieth century, Polignac could find liberation to be her true self only in an arranged marriage. It was a consequence that often eluded her heterosexual contemporaries who acquired husbands for the same purpose and in the same way. Heiresses seldom married for love (a few might marry for lust, which was quite another thing). The difference was that the lesbians had no need to delude themselves into hoping that love would become a by-product. Quite the contrary. Their marriages were contracted to enable them to be themselves without the unpleasant alternative of having to rebel against their families and the mores of the class into which they had been born. The men selected to be their husbands had the same aspirations.

After Romaine was thrown over by Winnaretta, she found the great love of her life, another American heiress, Natalie Barney. The two lived together in the rue Jacob, on the Left Bank, and became one of the three sets of famous American lesbian hostesses in Paris. The other two were Gertrude Stein and Alice B. Toklas, and, of course, Bessy and Elsie, the only couple who may not have consummated their relationship, which did not make it any less homosexual. For an often overlapping group, Friday afternoons were spent at the Barney-Brooks salon, Saturday evenings at the Stein-Toklas Studio, and Sunday luncheons in the country chez Marbury/de Wolfe.

The following year, Elsie and Bessy departed for Europe in April. They intended to be gone a full six months and had brought along the children, two darling French bulldogs, Riquette and Fauvette. They were prizewinners, and Bessy had turned down an offer of two thousand dollars for one of them. Approaching the breeding of dogs with the same fervor she once had reserved for chickens, Bessy became so expert that she would be among the first women asked to judge at the very social New York Dog Show, precursor of the prestigious Westminster.

They were going home to Versailles, their first home in Europe. From the beginning, Bessy enjoyed the life they made and shared in the classical pavilion in the middle of Minnie Anglesey's charming garden. She kept a victoria and two horses that drove her to her Paris office each day. She also took quick business trips, sustained by the thought of returning to a place of their own, a home Elsie was making for her.

Versailles was an Edenic affliction from which Elsie would never recover. Bessy and she "soon became *'des ferventes de Versailles.'*" Having been trained by their mothers, both were expert housekeepers, and in Irving Place shared the chores, as each had careers that took precedence over their domestic lives. That summer, Elsie was free of professional demands, beyond ordering costumes, and relished playing the traditional role of homemaker for a working mate with control over every aspect of the ordering of a house for the first time in her life.

Versailles also provided the transcending learning experience of her life, the beginning of an education in taste that would change the way she perceived things ever after. Minnie Anglesey's house was an homage to Versailles and the styles in furnishings associated with the three Louis Bourbons who had lived there: XIV, XV, and XVI. She had a discerning eye and the purse to indulge her obsession. Every chamber, the attic, the basement, the storerooms, were filled with rare objects from the workshops of Boulle, Sèvres, the Gobelins, Cressent, Aubusson, Riesener, Delanois, and Jacob. There was such an excess, it spilled out into the pavilion, so that Elsie lived intimately with these things, caressing marquetry, letting her finger explore the boulle and inlay, the ormolu, the carved and lacquered surfaces, the petit point and silken upholstery, until she could recognize them by touch. Beautiful surfaces were what she loved more than anything or any person including Bessy. Most of what she knew about furniture she learned by imbibing it through her fingertips. Her knowledge was admittedly slight, but it was a profound part of her, having seeped into her arid depths to slake her thirst for beauty.

While visiting the royal château, she was observed by a new friend, Pierre de Nolhac, who was soon to become *conservateur* of Versailles and begin the long process of restoring the palace to its eighteenth-century glory. He remarked to her: "You are not a modern woman. You are a ghost who has come back to us from the court of Louis the Fifteenth."

Elsie did not doubt it for a moment.

Part of the rent Minnie Anglesey exacted for that lovely home in her garden was that its two new occupants play handmaidens at her many soirees. This task was no chore, for in addition to intriguing tribadies, her salon included a cross section of artistic and expatriate Paris. Minnie's faith in her new renters was rewarded many times over, when Bessy was able to add all of the most illustrious names in the French theatre to the group that now gathered in both houses on her property.

Henry Adams was among the most interesting people to join their Sunday circles that summer. Whether or not they met through Minnie or another of the many acquaintances they had in common, Bessy and Elsie became the attractions that, week after week, drew him out to Versailles from the flat he was occupying in Paris. The son of a statesman and grandson of one president and great grandson of another, he was a dapper little curmudgeon of minor literary genius and opinions so rigid they creaked if anybody tried to bend them.

Adams adored the attentions of attractive youngish women whom he called his nieces. Elsie definitely fell into this category, but Bessy insisted she was his only aunt. Others claimed she was his only nephew. His admiration of her was expressed in a letter he wrote to Elizabeth Cameron, whose apartment he was occupying in Paris.

> Miss Marbury is magnificently mistress of her society, and surveys it with a splendid air of indifferent mystery. Miss de Wolf [sic] is less majestic. Both of them are coming in to stay with me about the 10th. . . . Please spread it about that I am living with actresses in your apartment. It will give a lurid interest to my dissolute age.

A new dissatisfaction with life in America was beginning to surface in Elsie that was moving in tandem with her disillusionment with her career. Except for a short tour of *The Surprises of Love* after its disappointing New York engagement, Frohman had nothing more for her that season. She lived in anticipation of the day when Bessy would be ready to return with her to Minnie Anglesey's civilized, if somewhat quixotic, court in Versailles.

That season Bessy's largest successes came from her American clients. William Gillette was reveling in the triumph of a lifetime, starring in his own adaptation of Conan Doyle's *Sherlock Holmes*. Many of the things that have come down through the years as "Holmesian" were embellishments added by Gillette that were never in the original stories: the deerstalker hat, the pipe, the Inverness coat, the razor-sharp profile. Clyde Fitch was proving a one-man hit factory. Maxine Elliott and her husband had two big Fitch hits in their touring repertory: *Nathan Hale* and *The Cowboy and the Lady*. Fitch also gave Frohman one of his biggest successes of the season: *Barbara Frietchie*. Frohman was so fearful of the potential threat offered by Clyde's affection for Maxine Elliott that Bessy was able to negotiate a contract by which he paid the writer to have first refusal of his future work. She was looking ahead by agreeing to handle the plays of an untried playwright, Booth Tarkington, who had published two promising novels. By the time he became the most successful novelist-dramatist in America, she would be handling all of his work. If any proof was needed of her position as the leading agent in the world, it was given on the evening of April 9, when something unique occurred in the annals of the theatre. She was shuttling up and down Broadway between the New York Theatre, at Forty-fourth Street, where Stanislaus Stange's adaptation of *Quo Vadis* was opening; and the Herald Square, at Thirty-fifth Street, where Jeanette Gilder's version of the same book was opening. She did not represent the novel, as one might have expected under the circumstances; she represented the plays, with both dramatists insisting that she alone could handle their work, and neither complaining then or later that she had shown any favoritism.

*I*n the small world of old New York society, Bessy and Edith Wharton were well acquainted, possibly friends, if for no other reason than their mutual regard for Edith's sister-in-law, Minnie Cadwalader Jones, who knew everybody who was anybody in New York artistic circles. In her "charming old house" on West Eleventh Street, Minnie gave Sunday luncheons that were among Bessy's "most cherished reminiscences."

For Bessy, food had become almost as essential to a good party as the guests, and she could recall "her lobster mayonnaise and her rice pudding as symphonic poems." Many of Minnie's guests appeared later in the afternoon for tea at the Washington Irving house. One January, Henry Adams's ship arrived in New York Harbor from Europe after being delayed by a blizzard. What he minded most was what the storm had done to his social calendar. "I got ashore Sunday afternoon, missing lunch with Mrs. Fred Jones (Minnie), but just in time to catch an hour at Miss Marbury's [and] kiss all the actresses—metaphorically."

Minnie Jones undoubtedly promoted the friendship between her good friend Henry James and Edith. Initially, he was as indifferent to the woman as he was to her work, and would remain ambivalent about both throughout their long and close relationship. As Elsie put it, "There was something sharp about her and she had a forbidding coldness of manner," although, unlike James, she did admit that she was "a great artist."

Edith could never bring herself to concede what she owed to other women in her professional ascent. In her memoir, *A Backward Glance*, the only woman to whom she acknowledged any gratitude was the erudite lesbian Vernon Lee, a distant Paget cousin to Minnie Anglesey. Edith dedicated the admirable but least read of her works, *Italian Villas and Their Gardens:*

"To Vernon Lee who, better than any one else, has understood and interpreted the garden-magic of Italy."

She never mentioned Minnie in the book despite her having been at various times Edith's surrogate mother, protector, sponsor, and business representative. As for Bessy, who represented her in all of her efforts to become a dramatist and in most of the efforts of others to adapt her fiction to the stage, she was a "forgotten . . . intermediary." She also mendaciously claimed that her many theatrical forays were "thrust on me and not solicited."

In mid-April, Bessy and Elsie arrived in London at the same time as Edith and her husband. Bessy apparently had faith in Wharton's gifts as a dramatist. Her good friend Marie Tempest had deserted the musical comedy theatre and had a great success in *English Nell*. The commonness that even Henry Adams admitted to finding charming, when they met in Versailles, made her a great star in the nonmusical theatre playing courtesans and actresses.

Bessy convinced Tempest that Edith was the perfect writer to dramatize Abbé Prévost's eighteenth-century novel *Manon Lescaut* as a vehicle for her. There were already two successful operas based on the book, by Massenet and Puccini, respectively, and some doubted the world was ready for another version, but the three women plunged ahead. Edith completed a four-act work and signed a contract with Bessy for her to represent the play. For any number of reasons, which may or may not have included its lack of merit, the play proved unproducible.

Edith persevered in her dramaturgical efforts. If somebody as theatrically wise as Elisabeth Marbury continued to have faith in her, who was she to quarrel? That year she completed two acts of another play, *The Man of Genius*. Elsie performed one act of it at a charity matinee, which stimulated some interest but not enough for Edith to want to complete the work. Because of her admiration for the woman's tenacity at the beginning of what would become a dazzling career, Bessy continued to represent her.

Their third summer in the little house in Lady Anglesey's garden was, if anything, more glorious than the others. The women began to keep a guest book signed by those who came to call upon them. A small volume, a little over six inches by five inches, bound in green leather and studded with eleven moonstones, it covered the first six years of their annual summer residence in the shadow of the great château of *le roi soleil*.

A simple French verse etched in gold traced its way around the sides of the book's cover:

I love you . . .
I swear to you . . .
And I will never break
The agreement.

It was a declaration devoid of conditional, pluperfect, or subjunctive, a simple statement comprehensible to any freshman French student. A sampling of the names inscribed in the book bears witness to how public their pledge was: assorted Havemeyers, Hewitts, and Harrimans, Henry Adams, Edith Wharton, Bernard Berenson, Coquelin, Sardou, Belasco, Charles Dana Gibson, Olga Nethersole [an actress who was arrested for her shocking soul kiss in Fitch's *Sapho*], Richepin, Raoul Dufy, Otto Kahn, Stanford White, the Duchess of Marlborough, Augustus Saint Gaudens, Edith Wharton, Maxine Elliott, Maude Adams, Chester Alan Arthur (son and namesake of the American president), Emma Calvé, Oelrichses, Goelets, Armours, Canfields, Bibescos, and on and on and on. It was almost as if everybody who was anybody—the flamboyant silhouettes fluttering through the twilight of Belle Europe—had signed in.

*E*lsie's taste always had been remarkable, but under the tutelage of her landlady, she felt as if she was at school.

> Looking back at those days, I feel that Minna Anglesey influenced my outlook on life and my attitude more than any one else I have known. She was far ahead of her time in her ideas of health, hygiene, and beauty. A confirmed vegetarian, she taught me the dietary value of properly cooked and uncooked vegetables. Her impeccable taste often guided me into new areas of beauty.

Minnie had the eccentric passion of an obsessed collector. Neither utility nor beauty nor intrinsic value governed her purchases, and the storage areas of her villa overflowed in almost equal measure with invaluable antiquities and gimcrackery. Elsie consigned to the latter category Milady's purchase of the entire Art Nouveau room that the department store, Le Bon Marché, had exhibited at the Paris Exposition of 1900, which she installed in her salon. She, who was only beginning to find her way through the glories of the baroque and rococo, would never have her mentor's eye for the original, nor could she understand what Minnie found so fascinating about the first new decorative design concept since the eighteenth century. After the end of her acting career, Elsie's art would continue to be that of an interpreter, brilliantly manipulating nuances of texture and color but never daring to challenge the established line. She would always consider the style to be in "bad taste," but years of success gave her the confidence to admit that "it was *l'art nouveau* which broke the tegument binding us to a past stifling in many respects and opened up the way for much that is fine in modern art and decoration."

CHAPTER TWENTY-FOUR

The summer of 1900 slipped by quickly enough, and Bessy and Elsie sailed for home. Frohman had nothing for Elsie, who found being idle an almost impossible task.

During the 1900–1901 season, while keeping Elsie at bay, Frohman produced more plays than he had in any other season of his career. Her impatience with the lack of progress in her career steadily grew. Being an actress was not enough, just as being accepted in society previously had not been enough, and being a successful decorator later would not be enough. What was necessary for absolute realization was to become a star. Her gift for self-promotion was such that her name was better known than that of many performers who were stars, but the woman was a realist and knew that what would later be called "fifteen minutes of fame" was merely illusion. She looked good as she entered a room and better as she made an entrance onstage. Stardom remained a possibility, but time was running out. The life expectancy of the era made her middle-aged by any chronological count, even her own. Her ambition would never be realized, if it did not happen soon.

Clyde Fitch was devoted to Bessy both professionally and personally. He also admired Elsie's taste and considered her a gifted if limited actress. Aware of the latter's frustrations and probably prodded by the former to do something that would help to alleviate them, he borrowed both a title and point of view from Congreve and wrote *The Way of the World* with a starring role for Elsie that was "discreetly made not too heavy for her fair shoulders to carry."

It could not have seemed possible to them that Frohman would reject their project but that was what he did do, accepting in its stead another effort by the prolific Fitch, *Captain Jinks of the Horse Marines*. He intended to give its production the personal guidance usually reserved for a Maude

Adams vehicle: in this instance, the object was to make a star of young Ethel Barrymore, who was as stunning as she was gifted. It had to have been galling to Elsie to be supplanted by a twenty-two-year-old beauty whose New York debut, only five years earlier, had been as her understudy in *The Bauble Shop.*

Bessy sent the script of *The Way of the World* over to another established producer, George Lederer. Although it was made clear to him from the beginning that Elsie intended both to star and to have her own company, he agreed to produce and stage the play. It was rumored she had put up most of the capital, but more likely Lederer went into partnership with Elsie, because she had a great deal to offer other than financing. Getting one's hands on a play by the most successful playwright in America was an attractive proposition. What the work needed was an extremely smart look, and Elsie's uncredited work on Frohman's sets and costumes proved she could provide the ineffable quality often missing on Broadway: class.

*B*y the time Elsie and Bessy were ready to depart for their summer in France, the essential ingredients for an autumn production were in place. This would be their first season in Versailles not spent in the charming villa in Minnie Anglesey's garden. The women owned no property there but giving up the delightful Parisian suburb was out of the question. They found a lovely property to lease at 69 boulevard St. Antoine. Called Les Buissons and owned by the American widow of an English painter, it was a French house with American improvements installed by an English artist with an aesthetic appreciation of the original domain.

At the front of the villa, an iron gate in the brick wall opened to a drive leading to the entrance. Behind the house stretched an acre or more of "the loveliest garden in Versailles, a city of lovely gardens."

So it was that once they were ensconced, the pleasures of summer 1901 lay before them with a particular promise. These delights included a visit from Clyde Fitch, who was to stay with them to rehearse Elsie in her role in *The Way of the World.* He arrived in Versailles during the last week in June to spend "five very pleasant days with Bessy and Elsie." Every morning at eight, his breakfast was served on a balcony off his room overlooking "a lovely garden with millions of rose bushes and big trees," where they spent most of their time, "trotting off to bed at 9:30!" He found that Elsie rehearsed "splendidly" and was "going to be *awfully* good in the play."

After *The Way of the World* opened in New York on November 4, the headline on the *New York Times* review was, ELSIE DE WOLFE AS A "STAR." The quotation marks told the story about a review so innocuous and a critic with so little to say that he devoted a part of his space to a list of the prominent society people present and providing "a pleasant atmosphere . . . through which waves of friendly feeling undulated." The reviewer noted "an electric current of curiosity" over Elsie's first appearance as a star, although he felt impelled to add: "Of course, the appearance of a new star in the theatrical firmament is not to be taken quite so seriously now as it would have been twenty years ago."

The rest of the reviews were in the same damning-with-faint-praise vein, and *The Way of the World* closed after thirty-five performances.

Sensing Elsie's frustration, Bessy did as much as she could by encouraging Frohman to use her and by arranging her schedule to spend as much time as possible in Versailles. She stretched her time abroad to six months out of each year on the pretext of looking after the European end of her burgeoning business. Her Paris office could be attended to from Versailles, and Berlin was supervised by nipping over from France for a few days at a time. She took care of England by allowing her London manger, Addison Bright, to hire his younger brother, Reginald Golding Bright, to assist him, enabling her to expand her operations there while spending the greater part of her European sojourn across the Channel.

It must have amused her to recollect Golding's original attitude toward the word of a man he would now be representing. He was the one booing heckler in the wildly enthusiastic audience at the London premiere of *Arms and the Man*. When Shaw came forward at the end of the performance, he addressed his curtain speech to this solitary dissenter: "My dear fellow, I quite agree with you. But what are we against so many?"

*T*oward the end of 1900, Bessy's second career, as a theatrical manager, had reached its zenith when she brought over Sarah Bernhardt, Coquelin, and a company of thirty actors for a six-month tour of the United States. The divine Sarah and she had met at a dinner party given by Sardou to introduce his magnificent French star to his magnificent American money-making machine, and the two, each exceedingly important to the writer's financial well-being, struck it off immediately. Bernhardt loved to surround herself with strong women and effete men. Bessy was *"ma chère Marbury"* during an intimate friendship that lasted until the actress's death twenty-three years later.

In a world in which theatre remained the leading form of entertainment, Bessy's business had truly become global. There was an enormous market for plays in every part of the British Empire, from Canada to Egypt to what is now Israel to India to Australia, and Marbury supplied a larger portion than any other source. When touring theatrical companies ventured into the backwoods of any part of the world, they were likely remitting royalties to her office for most of their repertory.

Bessy was in London early in the spring of 1902. She could take pride in having signed a contract with one of the greatest writers of the day, Mark Twain, giving her the exclusive right to handle the dramatizations of his works. His first contract for him was what had brought her to England earlier than usual. It was with C. B. Dillingham for a dramatization of *Huckleberry Finn* to be made by a mutually agreed-upon playwright and produced later that year in London. She never made much money from Twain, but no agent could fail to be honored by having him on her list.

She was to make a packet from three scripts given to her by the Brights. They were all written by the same unknown playwright, Hubert Henry Davies, who had stopped by the office one afternoon and left them with the receptionist. Although English, he had spent some years as the drama critic for the San Francisco *Argonaut* and claimed to have learned the art of writing plays by criticizing them. The plays were written in rapid succession. After unsuccessfully trying to place them with American producers, he brought them back to England.

She took them back to her lodgings that evening and read the first, then, without stopping, "read the other two as fast as her eyes could follow the text." There were times when she claimed she had to "read a play over six times and make suggestions in one way and another until the play is in salable condition." That was not the case with Davies's work. They were ready for submission as they were, and within a few weeks had "gone off like hot cakes."

The first, *Cousin Kate,* she sold simultaneously to Frohman as a vehicle for Ethel Barrymore in New York, and to Cyril Maud for his Haymarket Theatre in London. The second, *Mrs. Goringe's Necklace,* went to Charles Wyndham, who planned to produce it at his Wyndham's Theatre, in London. The third Davies play, *Cynthia,* was brought back to New York for Elsie, who, having completed the tour of *The Way of the World,* was in need of something to do the following season.

For her production of *Cynthia,* Elsie used her manager, Nat Roth, as the nominal producer. Despite a generally favorable reception, the play only lasted for thirty-two performances with only a socialite and dressmaker following that was exhausted within a month. The character of Cynthia was a naive, somewhat addled ingenue. By Elsie's or anybody else's count, she was somewhere between thirty-eight and forty-five years old and always had succeeded best as a sophisticated woman of the world. Her special audience wanted to see its Elsie swooping about in a soignée gown as if she knew her way around a boudoir as well as she did around a ballroom. Her gloom was compounded when Frohman exercised his English option to produce *Cynthia* in London with the twenty-four-year-old Ethel Barrymore triumphing in the title role. The circle was completing itself in a most disheartening fashion. Her former understudy was displacing her as the star of a play she herself had produced.

In her memoir, Bessy never referred to Elsie as other than "Miss de Wolfe" or "Elsie de Wolfe." She implied a good deal more intimacy in her delineation of their emotions upon first viewing of what she described as "probably the most perfect small country place in the world," the house that would become Elsie's obsession for the rest of her life and which they assumed would "always remain as a monument to the artistic gifts with which Miss de Wolfe is so richly endowed."

> As we gazed at this beautiful place . . . we decided that Versailles was the one spot on earth where we desired to locate. We had lived there so long in rented houses that if we bought anywhere, it would naturally be in this paradise of our choosing.

It was in the environs of Les Buissons, down the boulevard St. Antoine, and the women passed the property during their daily constitutional. They would pause to peer through the gate at the deserted villa with shuttered windows set amid overgrown gardens, with ivy growing haphazardly up the trellises set against its crumbling walls. The place fired their romantic imaginations, which, after all, were influenced by the theatrical melodramas with which they were so often professionally involved. Elsie described the house as "a beautiful woman who had a tragic history and who had grown worn and faded before her time."

After the failure of *The Way of the World,* the dream of owning the Villa Trianon took hold. It was the only thing that alleviated Elsie's depression. Bessy would do anything to make her happy again. She was making a good deal of money and could afford to put some of it in real estate, but was this property a sound venture for her hard-earned capital?

Her good friend and client Victorien Sardou knew all about such things. He lived only four miles away, in Marly, and came almost every Sunday to dine with them. She inveigled the key out of a local estate agent and, with Elsie and Sardou, went in to investigate the place. They were enchanted by its aura.

The gardens, wilderness as they were, were fragrant with poetry. The house, unlived in as it had been for decades, spoke to us with regret and resignation of the passing of an old grandeur.

After Louis Philippe acceded to the French crown in 1830, the Villa Trianon became the property of his son, the Duc de Nemours. A source of wonderment to Bessy was how his household, numbering twenty-five, were all lodged in the sixteen-room villa with only one bathroom and toilet among them. She was reminded that at the time "[it] was doubtless regarded as the last note of modern luxury."

After the abdication of the duc's father, the place had passed through many hands and decades of neglect before disintegrating to its present state, a sorry relic owned by an absentee landlord. Sardou studied it carefully. He thumped his heavy walking stick on the stone terrace and announced: "My children, I advise you to buy this property, if you can get it for a reasonable sum. It will prove a good investment."

Further investigations uncovered the landlord's identity, a jeweler who had been ruined by bad investments. The place was so eaten up by liens that the owner was prepared to sell at almost any price, or so Bessy was told. She decided to see if any price was as reasonable as sixty thousand francs and made an offer that was spurned as *"Ridicule!"* The real estate agent intimated that if she added five thousand francs, he thought they could make a deal.

Bessy played hardball. No way! Nobody was banging down his door. Let him hang on to the property and pay all the expenses of upkeep, taxes, and mortgage. She would not budge. The following Sunday, Sardou went with them to take a last look at the property. As Elsie recalled, the rain was pouring down as she stood in the garden with tears in her eyes. The playwright, who seemed to favor the gesture, thumped his old umbrella on the ground. "If you don't buy it by tomorrow, I shall do it myself."

The next day Bessy closed the deal. It took a year of litigation in the French courts to purge the property of all claims. By the middle of the next summer, Bessy took title on the Villa Trianon and Elsie's dream came true. Bessy was able to tell her that it was hers to remake as she chose. The credit for what it became she would always generously give to her beloved friend, and Elsie de Wolfe's life's work began. Years later, she would be able to look at it "as an artist may look upon the masterpiece to which he had devoted his best efforts."

CHAPTER TWENTY-FIVE

A few years after his divorce, Willie K. Vanderbilt took an apartment in Paris, at 138 avenue des Champs Elysées. The Champs Elysées was then an avenue of splendid residences, elegant French flats, and refined hotels. Marlborough had no objection to his wife's frequent visits to her father. Consuelo always returned with funds that supported his obsession with making Blenheim still more magnificent and helped to build Sunderland House, their sumptuous new London residence in Curzon Street, which Willie wisely insisted be put in her name.

The unhappy couple, tied to each other by the morality of the times and their two young children, had other reasons for welcoming her stays in Paris. Each already had found a new love. Marlborough had become ensnared by Gladys Deacon, a beautiful young American without a fortune to call her own, let alone his.

Jacques Balsan, who had become part of Willie's inner circle, had first seen his daughter several years before, when Alva had brought her to Paris as a young debutante. He had been attracted then but stood even less chance of gaining her mother's approval than Winty Rutherfurd had. Both her parents and she were in different places in relation to each other when she had met him again in Paris. Indeed, Willie might well have felt guilty about his part in Consuelo's unhappiness and, deciding that he owed her a good romantic fling, played the beard in her affair with Balsan.

The year of 1901 began as among the worst in Anne Rutherfurd's life. It was the end of January before Lewis was finally laid to rest in New Jersey. She returned to London to place her sons in English schools. And then she took her daughters to Paris, leasing the *garçonnière* of a *hôtel particulier* on avenue du Bois de Boulogne.

On May 31, her mother died, and on December 17, her father was declared legally insane, his fortune of over fifteen million officially placed under the control of his children. Anne was a rich and lovely widow, but could not be faulted for feeling more akin to Job than Croesus.

At about the same time, Willie K. gave an interview to a reporter for a London publication, *Week's End*, which sounded a note of melancholy and dissatisfaction that would appear to motivate a desire to make changes in his life.

My life was never destined to be quite happy. It was laid on lines which I could foresee from earliest childhood. It had left me with nothing to hope for, nothing definite to see or strive for. Inherited wealth is a big handicap to happiness. It is as certain death to ambition as cocaine is to morality. If a man makes money, no matter how much, he finds certain happiness in its possession, for in the desire to increase his business, he has constant use for it. But the man who inherits it has none of this. The first satisfaction, and the greatest, that of building a fortune, is denied him. He must labor, if he does labor, simply to add to what may be an over-sufficiency.

The reporter persisted, "And you, Mr. Vanderbilt?"

Possibly thinking he sounded a bit self-pitying, Willie lightened up. "Oh, I get all the fun I can out of life, and I am quite pleased if other folks get something out of it also."

By the end of 1902, there were rumors in the American colony in Paris that Willie was seriously attached to Mrs. Lewis Morris Rutherfurd, described as a tall, blue-eyed, blond beauty. There was never any gossip that his money was the attraction, for she was wealthy in her own right. Willie's kindness, charm, and good looks were the lures. If she was beginning to love him, it was for himself, which was surely a novelty in his life.

Early on the morning of April 8, Willie secretly arrived in London and made his way to Tallant's Hotel, in North Audley Street. A modest establishment, it had few of the modern conveniences to which he was accustomed, and catering to a genteel, middle-class clientele, it was a place in which it would be most unlikely to find a Vanderbilt. During the week following his secret journey to London, one of his American attorneys petitioned the New York State Supreme Court to put aside the clause in his divorce decree that forbade him to remarry as long as Alva lived. The press got wind of it and deduced Vanderbilt was about to make a significant change in his mode of living.

All of her adult life, Anne had moved in the highest European and American social circles with an admirable circumspection that had kept her true to her mother's dictum of when a lady's name should appear in the newspapers. Suddenly she could not so much as purchase a pair of gloves without some reporter hot on her trail, speculating about whether or not she was assembling a trousseau. She had survived too many tragedies not to have become strong. The important events in her life were not about to become a public-relations circus. It was her intention to have a wedding as circumspect as possible.

*L*adies and Not-So-Gentle Women

On Monday, April 20, Justice Giegerich struck out the provision in Willie's divorce degree that prohibited him from remarrying, on the grounds that his conduct had been exemplary in the eight years since it was granted, and he presently "desires to marry again and proposes to consummate said marriage in France or England forthwith."

From then on, the front-page bulletins were printed daily. When was the marriage to take place? In which country? Who was to be present? Would it be a religious or civil ceremony? Each report brought fresh speculation. The ensuing confusion was orchestrated by Anne and Willie, with the connivance of their families and friends, to cloak their true intentions.

By Friday the twenty-fourth, the press was befuddled. They did not know Willie was back in the rooms he had retained, at Tallant's Hotel. Resisting all temptations to go to the track, the theatres, the better restaurants, his club, tailor, haberdasher, or bootmaker, he had been content to have the hotel's indifferent fare served in his chambers, occasionally sharing it with a few of his most trusted friends and business associates. Given his sybaritic nature, it was an act of abstinence that could easily be mistaken for valor.

It was also a gesture of love for Anne. Tallant's had been selected for its proximity to St. Mark's Church, which was only a few steps away. She wanted a church wedding. She always had been married in churches and saw no reason why this should not continue to be the case.

There was another reason for selecting St. Mark's. King Edward was Willie's pal from racing and yachting circles as well as a friend and admirer of Consuelo Marlborough. He was also the titular head of the Church of England, and although he might not have much influence with the Archbishop of Canterbury when it came to his opposition to the remarriage of divorced persons in the church proper, he did have quite a bit with his own honorary chaplains. Among them was the Reverend R. H. Hadden, the Vicar of St. Mark's, which may well have been why the latter agreed to marry the couple if the proper licenses could be procured.

Early on the morning of the twenty-ninth, the wedding party arrived at St. Mark's. Willie was the first to arrive, accompanied by his friend and best man, Winfield Scott Hoyt. Consuelo and Sonny, who were to serve as witnesses, came next. A few minutes later, Anne and Harry White arrived in his carriage and entered the church through the vicarage. Aside from Reverend Hadden, the only other person present was the church verger.

Harry White gave the bride away, and the simple Anglican ceremony took no more than fifteen minutes. It was not until he was sure the newlyweds had reached Calais and boarded the Paris train that White made an announcement of the marriage to the press. Most newspaper editors assumed that the couple was aboard the Vanderbilt yacht anchored in the south of

France and alerted their correspondents on the Côte d'Azur. Not James Gordon Bennett, publisher of the Paris edition of the *Herald,* who knew Willie well enough to be certain that he would not be leaving Paris during the racing season. He dispatched a reporter to cover the arrival of every boat train from England, and was vindicated when the *Herald* could crow: "There were few persons at the Gare du Nord who knew of their expected arrival as they came through the gateway unattended, and Mr. Vanderbilt handed in their tickets just as did the other passengers preceding him."

In a letter written to Elizabeth Cameron on the day after the wedding, Henry Adams noted the change in the status of their mutual friend. "The Sunday newspapers are full of portraits of Ann Rutherford [sic] today, one more unlike than another, till I wonder whether I know her or whether you do. Anyway she is no longer in existence for us, I suppose, and New York is to inherit her. She has a big load of millions to carry. Payne Whitney says it's a hundred and twenty-five." He added wryly: "So unjust is life that here are we still without even our fifty." Before the year was out, his innate bitchiness would have him referring to Anne as "Mrs. Willie K. Rutherford etc."

Any doubt that marrying Anne was Willie's good luck vanished two days after the ceremony. With her at his side, on a cloudless day at St. Cloud, he saw his entries win the two most important races of the day. Biltmore took the Prix Bataille, and Marigold the Prix Soleil.

Willie's colors grossed $125,000 that season. That probably did little more than pay for the upkeep of the horses, but men such as Vanderbilt, Belmont, and the King of England were not in the game for the profit; it was truly *pour le sport.* He rapidly became the most successful racer in France and, to Anne's delight, was seldom moved to return to America except for brief visits. Neither her old place nor his flat on the Champs Elysées proved large enough for the style in which they lived in Paris, and he bought a lovely *hôtel particulier,* at 10 rue Leroux in Passy, which was truly her home, the first she could call her own in almost twenty years, since Sam Sands and she had bought the house in Garden City.

For a combination country place and stud farm, Willie purchased a decaying château, Le Quesnay, in Normandy. It was in style not unlike the Fifth Avenue mansion Alva had commissioned for them, with the important differences that it was authentic and, instead of being squeezed into a Fifth Avenue block, was built in the country for which its proportions and design were intended. When Anne had finished supervising the interiors, the differences between Alva and her were once more apparent. The house, while comfortable and elegant, was neither pompous nor egotistical. The following year, Anne's father died. Her brothers' astute management of his estate had increased its worth to twenty million dollars, in which she shared equally with her sisters and them. She no longer had need of the additional funds, but it did mean that her four children would one day have adequate, if not great, fortunes of their own. Her expectations for them expanded. Given the age and her background, visions of brilliant marriages must have meandered through her mind. The first marriage of one of her children occurred almost exactly two years after her own to Willie, when her older son, George Winthrop Sands, married Tayo Newton, the daughter of a retired physician. It was not a "brilliant" match from the perspective of the groom's new prominence and decidedly not what his mother would have chosen for him. The wedding reception was in the home of the bride, its modesty excused on the ground of the illness of her mother. Although George's brother, Sam, acted as his best man, his mother and stepfather did not bother to return from Europe for it, and there were few members of the Harriman, Sands, Rutherfurd, or Vanderbilt families present. The whole affair had been set up in what appeared to be an unseemly haste, and it was thought Anne could not ask her husband to rearrange his schedule during the racing season, as she would see the young couple soon enough when they arrived in Europe on their honeymoon. The truth of the matter may have been that she felt advantage had been taken of her son. The feeling might have been irrational in light of the circumstances, but as his mother she would have blinded herself to his culpability.

The reason for the dispatch was that the bride was pregnant. Anne had been brought up to believe that one of the responsibilities of an unwed young lady was to say no, and she blamed the bride. She would forgive her only after George's irresponsibility became too manifest to be ignored. She would always be there for her children, forgiving them their foolish trespasses, and this was but the first of a progression in a life made weary by events beyond her control.

CHAPTER TWENTY-SIX

The genesis of the Colony Club occurred in the summer of 1902 when, as was their custom, the J. Borden Harrimans rented a cottage in Newport for the season. Daisy took advantage of their being away to have the painters and plasterers in to redecorate their townhouse, in East Thirty-sixth Street, less than a block away from the Morgan mansion in which her childhood friend Anne still resided. Being obliged to go down to New York for a few days, she said, "I can't stay in the mess. What hotel shall I go to—the Waldorf?"

"I don't approve of women going to hotels alone, especially to large ones," Bordie replied, reflecting a typical turn-of-the-century male attitude.

When Bordie Harriman "laid his disapproval down like family law," his wife exclaimed, "But, Bordie, what can women do? Of course, there ought to be a women's club, and we could go to that in the summer, and have parcels sent there and do telephoning."

Daisy Harriman was an early suffragette and as liberated as a woman of her background and times could be, but she was well aware of the fact that nobody could raise the money to erect a large clubhouse without the fiscal support of wealthy men.

The original members of the male advisory committee were Pierpont Morgan, Charles T. Barney, president of the Knickerbocker Trust, whose daughter, Helen, was a founding member of the club, and Frank Polk, an influential Wall Street attorney who also was a liberal Democrat.

Morgan took the first practical step toward making the club a reality by subscribing ten thousand dollars to the building fund on condition that nine other matching pledges be found. They were not long in coming in. E. H. Harriman agreed to contribute on the condition that an art and literature department be added. This was no sacrifice, as it was and would remain a staple of almost all women's clubs.

Daisy was not about to leave the business details of the club totally in the hands of men. She cast around for a woman who was both so successful in business she could deal with men on an equal level and was also socially acceptable to the other members. Of course, she came up with Elisabeth Marbury. Bessy would eventually enlist Maude Adams, Amy Lowell, Frances Hodgson Burnett, Emily Post, Jane Addams, and Kate Douglas Wiggin, giving rise to the erroneous comparison of the Colony to London's Lyceum Club, a women's club that demanded professional status of its women.

One of the prime requisites was that the prospective member had to be "clubbable," which, of course, meant that the blackball could and would be exactingly used as it was in men's clubs. There would be no Jews or Catholics, and members of any race other than the white would be as automatically disqualified as males. What would disappear with time was the otherwise liberal makeup and social consciences of several of the original "Colonists." Perhaps symbolizing this loss of progressive temperament was the fact that after 1924, there would never be a woman who chose to remain

Ladies and Not-So-Gentle Women

unmarried, for whatever reason, among the officers of the club. But in the beginning, when newspapers headlined articles about the Colony with "Death Knell to the Home," "Free and Easy Is Their Motto," and "Where Will This Lead?" it was a club in the thrall of feminist zest. The first treasurer was *Miss* Anne Tracy Morgan; the first and second "chair*men*" of the house committee were *Miss* Elisabeth Marbury and *Miss* Mary Parsons; the second president was *Miss* Ruth Morgan; the second first vice president was *Miss* Mary Parsons; and the fourth secretary was *Miss* Ruth Vanderbilt Twombly. By the time Ruth finished her term as fourth treasurer, in 1930, she was still unwed. Yet she was listed in the club's official book, *The History of the Colony Club,* privately printed in 1984, as *Mrs.* Ruth V. Twombly. That would indicate how far the Colony had come by then in a new prejudice—fear that any of its "girls" might be suspected of being not spinsters, but lesbians.

But at the beginning there were several gay women, and the others were happy to have them: they were the ones who fearlessly took their stand against those men who would have stifled the whole thing. As chair*man* of the house committee, Bessy came up with the club's coat of arms, "a beaver, signifying activity, and a crown, suggesting that in democratic America each woman was a queen." She undoubtedly would have preferred to substitute "industry" for "activity," but this was as far as the others were able to go. Industry was a man's thing, while equally busy women were merely engaged in activities.

For Christmas 1903, Anne Morgan's present from her brother-in-law Herbert L. Satterlee was a five-year Line-A-Day pocket diary. This was the first she ever kept, and with a ten-year gap during the twenties, she would continue to keep diaries until the end of World War II. The book was inscribed to her childhood sobriquet, "Annie." Before that first volume was filled, her life would change so radically, no intimate would think of addressing her by any name but the adult "Anne," while to those who knew her less well, she would always be "Miss Morgan."

Anne noted in her new diary the first meeting of the new "theatre club," on the twenty-fourth. Unless there was a sudden rash of new clubs, she must have been referring to the not yet officially named Colony, for those mentioned as attending were all Colonists: Daisy, Bessy, Ava Astor, Helen Hastings, and Katherine Duer.

At their last meeting during the first week in April, the women selected Stanford White to be their architect. White was the preeminent architect of private clubs in America, having already designed the Century Association as well as the Metropolitan and Players clubs. For the Colony, White eschewed the massive Italian Renaissance palazzo style of the male clubs, so symbolic of the autocratic power of their members, in favor of the orderly, pretty grace of southern antebellum Federal revival, the most feminine as well as the coolest of architectural orders. The six-story clubhouse was inspired by the Nathaniel Russell house in Charleston, South Carolina, with white limestone used as window trim and cornice. The wrought-iron balconies and porch superimposed upon the front found their inspiration in an Annapolis mansion. The whole did give the feeling of homeyness but on the grandest of scales.

With no more to do until White submitted his plans, Daisy, Bordie, and their daughter, Ethel, sailed for Europe two days after the club meeting on the same ship that carried Anne Morgan and her father. Anne methodically noted the distance they covered each day in her Line-A-Day. Bessy also departed for the continent sometime that week, carrying, one can be assured, Elsie's detailed instructions for the refurbishing of Villa Trianon. The latter had to remain behind in the still-flourishing production of *The Other Girl,* which Frohman did not intend to close until the beginning of June, when the advent of the New York summer heat made the theatres too uncomfortable to operate.

Anne came down with a case of acute conjunctivitis during the crossing. Despite the contagiousness of pink-eye, Daisy dutifully came to her cabin every afternoon to read to her. They arrived in Liverpool on the thirteenth, and proceeded directly to London, where the Morgans took up residence in their double-townhouse at Princes Gate. Anne was very eager to get to Paris, and seeing a great deal of Daisy and Bordie helped to pass the week in England.

Anne and J.P., along with the Harrimans, left for Paris at two-twenty on the twenty-first. Arriving at nine-twenty that evening, after a very good journey, they went directly to the Bristol, where the large corner suite was waiting for them. He took his daughter to Worth's first thing the next morning to begin fittings on the clothes he still selected for her. She was disappointed to learn "Miss Marbury ill bronchitis," probably the result of the terrible weather Adams had noted earlier that week. That afternoon she lunched with Daisy before setting out with the Harriman family to see the new Whistlers and Sargents at the annual salon of painters.

Anne finally "saw Miss Marbury," on Sunday afternoon, after services at the English church. The next day, morning and afternoon, was given over to fittings at Worth's and the following day to fittings for hats. Finally, on Tuesday evening, there was a "*great* dinner with Miss Marbury." Her father allowed her to have the next day off for a visit to Chantilly, but on Thursday morning the shopping resumed apace. That afternoon, her reward was lunch at Louis's and a drive in the Bois with "E.M."—politely "Miss Marbury" no more nor ever again to be. On Saturday, "E. Marbury" was at the Bristol in the P.M. There was no mention of whether or not her father was present, but that evening Bessy took her to the theatre to see Réjane and Coquelin, and there was undoubtedly a supper afterward with these two good friends. It was a new world that was being opened to Anne—not simply the glamour of the theatre, but a new vision of what a woman could accomplish.

The next day the love affair began in earnest. There was no church on that Sunday morning. "Versailles with E.M.!!" It was Anne's first sight of Villa Trianon, where Bessy was in residence. They had a lovely drive through the Great Park and a short walk on the grounds of the palace. Afterward, there was a splendid high tea at the Hôtel des Reservoirs. Anne closed her entry for Sunday, May 1, with "Heavenly drive home. Beginning of perfect."

The next morning she was back in the shops with her father but was rewarded by a "perfect afternoon with E. Talking a joy." She was leaving the next day to take the cure at Aix with her father and a party of his friends. The morning was filled with chores, but she made certain they were completed in time for an early lunch, at Laurent, with Bessy. "All happiness except that it is the end of Act I."

On each day of her stay at the spa, she methodically noted the fluctuations in her weight. Less calculatedly, she often gave a reading of her emotional fluctuations by her reactions to the mail. Although she did not mention her by name, it was quite obviously that the letters that agitated and delighted, in turn, were from Bessy.

Anne had fallen madly in love with Bessy, but what was Bessy feeling? She was obviously encouraging the infatuation, but was she reciprocating? She was a grossly overweight woman one month short of her forty-eighth birthday. It had to have been very flattering to have this tall, handsome, vital young woman—a Morgan heiress, no less—enamored of her.

When George Tyler came to call on her soon after Anne's departure, he found her in a decidedly mellow, if not romantic, mood. The season before, with his partner, Theodore Liebler, he had produced three big hits in succession, all represented by Bessy: *Mrs. Wiggs of the Cabbage Patch, Raffles,* and *Merely Mary Ann.* His one desire was to overtake Frohman as the most important producer in New York. He had come directly to Bessy after opening the London production of *Merely Mary Ann.*

On a late spring morning, as they were driving through the Bois de Boulogne, her mind was not on business as she expounded on the glories of the sunshine, the flowers, the attractive people—on "Paris at its absolute best." Tyler's response, in those "idyllic" surroundings, was a tirade against Frohman, who "was always under foot and getting in the way."

Bessy laughed and chided him for "having a one-track mind" that could not stop talking "shop" even in paradise.

The Morgan party left Aix on May 17, to go down to Cannes to board the *Corsair*, which Pierpont had brought over from the States for a ten-day Mediterranean cruise. They did not arrive at the mansion in Princes Gate until June 5. Anne managed to detach herself from hordes of family to go around to Green's Private Hotel, where Bessy was staying, to have dinner with her. The hotel, at 16 and 17 St. James's Place, was part of a row of seventeenth- and eighteenth-century townhouses that looked out over Green Park. Many of the buildings were destroyed in the air raids during World War II, but Green's, elegantly refurbished, still exists as the Stafford Hotel.

They had not seen each other for over a month, and the relationship was renewed with increased ardor. Their passion could only have been intensified by the courage it took for Bessy to have written so many compromising letters that could have fallen into the hands of Morgan, who had the power to impose any vengeance he chose on her. With little more than two weeks before Bessy was to return to Paris to meet Elsie, there was an urgency of time. They would not see each other until October, three months during which Bessy would be subjected daily to the wiles of Elsie.

CHAPTER TWENTY-SEVEN

Soon after Elsie arrived at the Villa Trianon, Bessy and she entertained their first guest, the art historian Bernard Berenson. Clyde Fitch had introduced them to BB and his wife, Mary, during their visit to New York the previous winter. Elsie invited the couple to come to see her in *The Other Girl*. Afterward, Mary observed, "She's not much of an actress, but she dances well and looks ladylike."

The winter they met Elsie, the Berensons visited a mutual friend, Henry Adams, at his Washington home. After they left, Adams ranted: "I *can't* bear it. There is in the Jew deprecation something no weary sinner ought to stand.... I did murder Berenson ... I tried to do it gently, without apparent temper or violence of manner. Alas, murder will out."

Ladies and Not-So-Gentle Women

During his stay at the Villa Trianon that first week in July 1904, Berenson had the opportunity to pursue further a friendship with Henry Adams and found him his usual "burbero" self but "as ever, dying to be approached. . . . I like him and feel drawn to him."

For intellectual stimulation, like many who were taken with Elsie's social graces, Berenson turned to Bessy. They went together to explore the museum at St. Germain-en-Laye, where they were joined by the archaeologist Henri Hubert. Later she introduced him to Sardou, who "talked charmingly of his trees and plants." The introduction was so successful she had them both to an intimate dinner at the Villa Trianon, where the playwright could dazzle with his "great gift for words" and the historian with his intellect.

With Elsie, Berenson could flirt and play a harmless game of romantic speculation. She encouraged and responded to Berenson out of a need to feel desirable. Her life appeared to be approaching a dead end, and she needed some cosseting. If Bessy could enjoy the infatuation of Anne Morgan, why should she not find a comparable pleasure in the approaches of this elegant man? She could only hope that Bessy's responses were as innocent as her own.

Elsie turned her energies to decorating the Villa. It was becoming clear to her that only in Versailles was a measure of happiness to be experienced and only in the making of the house, fulfillment. Bessy was wonderful about allowing her to spend whatever was necessary to bring their future home up to her standards. The house itself was so solid that with the roof restored, and the rooms cleaned and painted, they were able to start to move in by the end of that summer. Under her exacting stewardship, the refinements of landscape and decor would take another two to three years to complete.

On the ground floor there were two spacious salons and a more than ample dining room. The upstairs bedrooms were large and airy. In pursuit of her vision, Elsie kept letting in more and more air and light. It was all so completely different from the claustrophobic New York style, and that was as she intended it to be. Her first large renovation was viewed by the natives as almost as revolutionary as the destruction of the monarchy that built Versailles.

There was but one bathtub in a villa of sixteen rooms, while the more intimate bodily functions were taken care of in an outhouse. After all, this was an improvement on the great days of Versailles, when it was *comme il faut* to relieve oneself in André Le Nôtre's magnificent gardens as well as on the palace's terraces and stairways. This was the land of magnificent perfumes and *la douche française,* in which the aforementioned product served to hide a multitude of more offensive aromas.

As far as Elsie was concerned, the only permissible outhouses were music pavilions and potting sheds: to the locals, her demands were stupefying. She insisted upon installing a private bathroom for every bedroom. A dowager marquise, a member of the *ancienne noblesse,* lived in a neighboring château, a veritable museum of priceless antiques, perfect in every detail except that it had no bath. After Sunday mass, it was her custom to go with her maid to the public baths for their weekly ablutions. When told the crazy American ladies were putting six bathrooms in the Villa Trianon, she exclaimed, "*Formidable!* No fortune, however great, can resist such unparalleled expenditure."

It was thanks to Minna Anglesey's purchase of that Art Nouveau room, which Elsie had so loathed, that the Villa acquired the things that determined the color motif for the reception rooms on the ground floor. A boiserie, coated in thick whitewash, was among the objects Minna displaced to create a space for her new room. Elsie suspected that there was something marvelous beneath it, and Bessy purchased it for her for a pittance. With careful chipping away of the surface paint, there emerged a stunning carved blue-and-white paneling. It was set off in the dining room by blue walls with white molding and in the salons by white walls with blue moldings. It would take years for Elsie to assemble the magnificent things that eventually furnished the Villa Trianon, but she had made a good start. On September 28, 1904, Adams wrote to his intimate friend John Hay, who was the secretary of state. Two months earlier, Hay had been given the Grand Cross of the Legion of Honor, the highest honor the French government could confer.

> I want the Legion of Honor for Bessie [sic] Marbury. Sardou is superintending, and all the French literarers are in it, writing letters for her. Please write somebody a letter saying how glad you would be to have her under your command. You being an officer have a word to say. I will get La Farge to march in your regiment, too, and Falstaff never had two funnier recruits than La Farge and Bessy Marbury.

Adams stressed that Bessy had done more for French interests in America than all of the other honorees put together. "She has the whole French literary, theatrical class in her pocket." He went on to chide Hay for having given the French forty million dollars for their rights to build a canal in Panama. He got them out of a big hole, but the French being what they were, "they will always believe that you cheated them; whereas Miss Marbury has stuffed their pockets with thousand-franc notes, all pure gain. They are grateful to her. I don't believe they are grateful to you. Anyway, in my capacity of winning France over to our interests, I want the Legion for her."

Her childhood friend Theodore Roosevelt was president of the United States, and added his endorsement to that of Hay; Jean Jusserand, the French ambassador to the United States; Robert McCormick, the American ambassador to France; and the entire French literary establishment. Despite these eminent supporters, the decoration was not bestowed upon her. The reason for the denial was not specified.

Sardou made another petition on Bessy's behalf just before he died, in 1908. A third attempt was made in 1912. The letters of commendation were still more impressive. In addition to those from a Who's Who of the French theatre, there were letters from two American presidents, Roosevelt and William H. Taft, the ever-present Jusserand, and three of the four American ambassadors in the years since 1904: McCormick, Harry White, and the man then serving, Myron T. Herrick. The only ambassadorial absence was Morgan's beloved and beautiful former partner Robert Bacon, who had served in the Paris embassy from 1910 to the beginning of 1912.

Some pages found among the James Hazen Hyde papers, in the New-York Historical Society, offer a clue to the business. On April 7, 1920, Bessy wrote to Hyde, in Paris, saying that if he could offer "a good word on my behalf," she would be "duly appreciative." According to some addenda attached to her letter, he went to see his good friend former Ambassador Bacon, to ask him to do something to help. Hyde was given some information that would seem to explain why Bacon was the only American envoy to France not to have contributed an accolade to the 1912 dossier. Morgan made only one request when his former favorite took up his assignment in Paris, and that was to prevent Bessy from getting the award. The banker reputedly said that his motivation was that she not only had stolen his daughter away from him but had also turned her against him by accusing him of having "compromised her by using her as a chaperon when he travelled with his mistress, Mrs. [Adelaide] Douglas."

This was a total fabrication. It does not explain why she was rejected in 1904 and 1908. By April 1920, when this meeting between Hyde and Bacon was alleged to have taken place, the latter was no longer alive, having died on May 29, 1919. Moreover, Anne had a good relationship with Mrs. Douglas. She even introduced Bessy to her. Adelaide Douglas was a Townsend and possibly Bessy's distant cousin. By the time Bessy became important in Anne's life, the latter was certainly aware of Adelaide's position vis-à-vis her father.

The reason Bessy Marbury was never honored for her many services to

France must remain a mystery. It could have been related to why Gertrude Stein was also overlooked: in their time, they were too threatening to the masculine establishment. It was not that they were lesbians—many lesbians were honored; it was that they were mannish in their miens and attire (*le smoking* not having become the rage until well after their deaths). The French of their period could forgive a woman almost anything so long as she looked smartly feminine while doing it. Colette wrote gloriously of her lesbian love affairs in a series of books that made her among the most acclaimed writers in France, but often was photographed in clothes so *faire frou-frou feminin* they approached caricature—perhaps, that was the point.

*W*hen Bessy did arrive home toward the end of September, Anne and she slipped back into their intimacy with apparent ease. Anne's life seemed to divide into two equal parts: "glorious" and "heavenly" afternoons and evenings with Bessy and dutiful ones with her mother. The century had turned. Victoria was gone, and in the permissive age of Edward VII, many things hitherto considered impossible could come to pass, and it is quite possible Anne was Bessy's first and only sexual partner. If such was the case, how stunning it must have been to this obese woman almost old enough to be her mother!

And where was Elsie while this was happening? She was right there, in residence at Irving Place. The census taken that year listed Bessy as "the head of the household" at 122 East Seventeenth Street, and Elsie as her "partner." Both had begun to lie about their ages, with Bessy claiming to be forty-two when she was forty-nine, and Elsie giving thirty-five when she was "somewhere between 40 and death."

At first, Anne tried to ignore Elsie's existence. The latter was not working in a play, but there was no mention of her being present in her own home during the many evenings Anne spent there, nor was she mentioned as being present on November 10, when Anne had tea with Réjane at the Irving house. Her first mention was as being part of an outing in the country with Bessy on November 12. Anne had Thanksgiving dinner in their home without mentioning the second of her two hostesses. On the next afternoon, however, she asked Bessy to bring Jeanette Gilder and "Miss de W." to lunch at the Morgan mansion. It was Bessy's first visit to the house and Elsie's second mention in the diary. Her name did not appear again for another year, although Anne was spending an average of three evenings a week on "E. 17 St.," as she called it, and stayed at the Villa Trianon for half of the following summer.

Early in the week of December 11, Bessy and Anne were part of a party of New Yorkers filling two railroad cars that Isabella Gardner brought up to

Boston for a week of festivities, culminating in a dance she was giving in honor of the debut of her niece, Catherine, on December 16, at Fenway Court. This remarkable mansion filled with treasures—some selected in accord with her own occasionally eccentric, always eclectic taste, others with the help of her protégé, Berenson—was already destined by her to become one of the country's most idiosyncratic museums. Preceding the Phillips Collection in Washington, D.C., Anne's father's decision to make his library a public institution, and the building of Frick's mansion, Isabella Gardner became the first American to propose turning a part of her private residence into a public institution to display her own art collection. She joined the Hewitt sisters among the group of women who were beginning to make distinct contributions to the nation's cultural life through the museums they established and to a large degree funded.

Anne left for Cragston on January 4, and Bessy came up to spend a "heavenly evening" on the following day. Both were in town to attend the Colony Club luncheon on Monday the ninth, where there was a discussion of the interior decoration of the clubhouse. In accord with the custom of the day, many assumed White would select the furnishings as part of his job as architect. Others felt the club should have a uniquely feminine look, and that a committee of members should be formed to work along with him. Bessy knew her friend well enough to be certain that one thing Stanny White would not do was work with a committee of women. She was beginning to formulate a solution to the problem of Elsie's future as early as that meeting.

During the previous autumn, while Bessy and Anne were consumed with each other, Elsie was cast in Arthur Wing Pinero's *The Wife without a Smile*. Frohman had purchased it for America after its success in London, but Elsie was convinced that its success would not be repeated. She wrote to Berenson: "Though I know the play is a foreordained failure, *enfin*—it will give me some money which I need and let me go to Italy which I long for."

Money was important. She no longer felt she could be dependent upon Bessy, whose affections she retained but not exclusively. Her salary was four hundred dollars a week, a considerable sum, but paid only during the actual run of the play. It was considerably less for the rehearsal period and stopped completely when she was not playing.

Elsie had no intention of going to I Tatti, Berenson's house, with Bessy. She longed for Italy rather than Versailles, because Italy represented Berenson, and Versailles was Bessy. The innocent, flirtatious flattery of this erudite *élégant* was what she craved at that time, when both her professional and private lives had reached their nadir. Never had Elsie's desperation been more manifest than when she lamented: "The life here grows more and more impossible, and I grow more and more unfitted for it."

When Elsie finally did arrive at I Tatti, on June 1, 1905, she was traveling alone. By then, her life had changed completely.

*T*he *Wife without a Smile* opened to a hostile reception. As Elsie made her final exit with the line "It can go to the pigs," she thought she heard somebody in the second balcony say, "Those are the last words you will ever speak in the theatre." Elsie claimed: "It was my own inner self speaking aloud to me." Her less charitable colleagues insisted that it was Charles Frohman.

When the play closed on New Year's Eve, after only sixteen performances, Bessy was out of town for the holiday weekend. Elsie was alone to face the cheerless start of the new year. Overwhelmed both by her failure as an actress and by the consequences of Anne Morgan's appearance in Bessy's life, she was entering the darkest period of her life. "I could not but feel that the mediocrity of which I have always had a horror was closing in on me."

Bessy had never thought very highly of Elsie as an actress. Before any decisions about the future could be made, a profession that would utilize Elsie's assets had to be found. Foremost among these was an almost visceral feeling for decor. Her perfect sense of color and proportion, the delicacy with which she arranged objects and flowers—Bessy was certain there was something in these uncommon gifts that could be exploited.

She recruited Sally Hewitt, and they sounded her out on the subject. Elsie grew expansive and, as always, revealed more of her innermost feelings through a discussion of interior decoration than she ever did when speaking of herself. She told Bessy how their home had sustained her during this difficult period in their relationship. To live in an ugly place was depressing. Only beauty and order could "lift one beyond the nagging details of life, giving a sense of security and peace."

Elsie's future suddenly became clear. Seconded by Sally, Bessy cried, "Elsie, that is just your *métier!* . . . Why not go ahead and be America's first woman decorator?"

What she had in mind was not what Elsie ultimately made of interior decoration but what it actually was at the turn of the century. Furniture marts and decorator centers, which now exist in most large cities, were unheard of. She envisioned for Elsie an establishment where a customer could come to see some samples of fabrics and furniture—perhaps a near antique—of carpets and rugs, and get some advice on color and placement. It might be an office with a small warehouse or what was later known as a decorator's shop. There was no innovation in this idea: such enterprises already existed but were managed by men, who might do as little as making new curtains or as much as decorating the whole room from chandelier to carpet.

A woman dealing with women, on the intimacies of one of the few "female" domains, the home, was a grand if not new concept. It never occurred to either Elsie or Bessy that her lack of education could be considered a hindrance. She was a quick study and had mastered the only periods of lasting importance to her, the Louis' XIV through XVI. She never did bother to learn how to draw and valued suitability above authenticity in all things. Her example would be followed by those who came after her. Few would know how to draw. Fewer still would have any knowledge of the provenance of a piece unless a reputable dealer put it in writing. As for period, most would recognize a Louis only by its legs and be befuddled by the subtle differences between Empire and Regency.

In *Good-bye, Mr. Chippendale*, T. H. Robsjohn-Gibbings, a well-known furniture designer, summed up Elsie's contribution with an asperity that was nonetheless accurate:

> The period furniture of France inspired *her first and last love* [italics mine] and . . . when she opened shop, they were the stuff that the dreams of her clients were also made on. Nothing, it seemed to her and to them, could be more appropriate than to house the industrial kings of America in the antiquated surroundings of the Bourbons. And this Elsie de Wolfe did superbly.

Elsie sent out engraved cards announcing that she was going into the interior decorating business. Still, she was not yet ready to make any permanent commitment to a new career. When questioned about it by *Vanity Fair,* she replied that she was leaving the stage for a short time

> but not forever. I am going in now for interior decoration. By that I mean supplying objets d'art and giving advice regarding decoration to wealthy persons who have not the time, inclination, nor culture to do such work for themselves. It is nothing new. Women have done the same thing before.

Her description of this period in her memoir includes the only intimations of intimacy in the book and, of course, they refer to Bessy. With the traumas in their relationship caused by Anne Morgan, as well as her own fading theatrical career, she suddenly became sensitive to "my long suffering Elisabeth who always had such infinite patience with my many vagaries."

In recounting an uncommon scene of domesticity, she casts herself in the role of the little woman sallying forth on a career. Bessy is cast as her long-suffering spouse who, upon returning home from a hard day at the office, finds his way blocked by pieces of furniture and objets d'art filling the narrow hallway. In the drawing room, the little woman is measuring off chintz, and Bessy gives her "a look of utter dismay."

"Listen, Honey," she says. "We can't go on like this. First thing you know we will all be sleeping on the sidewalk." She continues in the tone of the expansive, patronizing husband. "No doubt you are going to be a great success, and you simply will have to have an office."

The time had come to decide whether or not she was going to persist in this new profession. Bessy swung into action. The decoration of the new clubhouse was on the agenda of the February meeting of the Colony Club board of governors. It was assumed that Stanford would do it as part of his design for the building. Bessy had another idea and called upon Anne Morgan and Daisy Harriman to second her suggestion that they commission Elsie to do the interiors. One of the female governors asked imperiously, "Are you all out of your heads, giving an important job like this to a woman who has had no experience?"

Bessy already had primed White on her proposal, which would relieve him of having to work with a committee of twelve women all of whom were convinced they had excellent taste.

When he was sent for, he said firmly, "Give it to Elsie, and LET THE GIRL ALONE. She knows more than any of us."

On March 1, Anne and her father sailed for Europe aboard the *Baltic*. With her out of the way, Elsie and Bessy could take the time to examine their situation and arrive at a *modus vivendi*. Bessy did not want to live with anybody but Elsie. They had been together for almost twenty years and were used to each other's ways. The original terms of their love had not changed nor had their affections lessened. That did not preclude sharing that part of herself that lay beyond them with somebody else. It was in the grand tradition of wife and mistress, except, in line with her closer kinship to Edward than Victoria, Bessy insisted that her relationship with Anne not be some sort of backstreet affair, that room be made in their lives for her.

On May 1, Elsie announced that she was leaving the theatre for good, and "sailed for England with my head in the air and a retainer of five thousand dollars in the bank. An enormous sum to me then—I had been poor for so long." What she meant was she had been dependent upon Bessy for so long. She was about to claim her independence although, once again, her beloved companion had provided the direction and opened the door. As Elsie entered a new professional door that year, so Bessy passed through a new emotional one. Once on the other side, they found that they were still together but in a different place.

Elsie spent May in England, where she "lived in ecstasy" going among the antique dealers "selecting beautiful stuffs, furniture, mantels, etc." Across the Channel, Anne and Bessy had fallen into a happy routine. The former's dreary daily fittings at Worth were often rewarded with "heavenly" or "perfect" evenings at Villa Trianon. When her father was out of the city, they would spend the night in Paris.

On June 1, the day Elsie arrived at I Tatti to visit Berenson, Bessy was in Paris seeing Anne off for her annual stay at Aix for the cure. Anne arrived back in Paris on the twelfth and, except for a brief visit to London, remained at the Villa Trianon for all of July.

When Bessy had a severe earache on July 4, she took her into Paris to see a doctor. The ear needed to be lanced for an abscess, and she was alarmingly ill for a week, suffering from a contraction on her right side that drew "her eye, mouth, and the whole side of her face awry." Anne never left her bedside. Deeply concerned about Bessy, Henry Adams came out to Versailles almost daily. By the twenty-fourth, the prognosis was still not good. The discomfort of the paralysis was aggravated by the pain from a revolutionary new electrolysis treatment prescribed to cure it. She had been ordered to drop everything for two months and keep her mind completely at rest. For Bessy, that sounded like a death sentence.

With Elsie's professional chores forcibly suspended by the annual *août vacances,* Anne was able to leave Bessy in her charge and spend the rest of the summer with her mother, at Cragston. Fortunately, the electrolysis was successful. By the time Berenson came to dinner a few weeks later, Bessy's condition must have been vastly improved, for he made no mention of it, and the social life at the Villa Trianon was proceeding at its usual jolly clip.

She was totally recovered by the time she returned to New York in the autumn, and her daily rendezvous with Anne resumed. On Wednesday, November 1, they went to Ringwood for an extended, if lopsided, weekend with the Hewitt sisters. They had to return to the city on Saturday evening for Bessy to attend the Sunday final dress rehearsal of Frohman's production of Barrie's *Peter Pan,* with Maude Adams. She was the producer's guest at the triumphant opening the next evening and sent Anne, along with Elsie, to see it on the seventeenth. It was the first mention of Elsie in Anne's diary in almost a year despite their shared concern that summer over Bessy's illness. For the next twenty years, their enforced intimacy would be closer to détente than entente.

On the day after Christmas, Anne and Bessy went up to Cragston for the rest of the holiday week. Although Morgan would never set foot across

Bessy's threshold, he would no longer offer any resistance to her crossing his. It was of slight importance whether he was there on that occasion; Bessy and he were working together on the baptism of the Colony Club. She did not approve of the unyielding capitalism he represented, but she did respect his power; and, no matter how grudgingly, he was forced to acknowledge her business acumen. They probably got along superficially, linked by their love for Anne and a common desire to make her life as happy as possible. These were two larger-than-life characters who shared an almost gluttonous appetite for food, drink, and tobacco; an appreciation of physically beautiful members of both sexes to the point at which the physiognomy of each was undoubtedly distasteful to the other; a certainty that, when expressed by them, any matter of opinion was perforce a matter of fact. By the time they completed the job of shaping Anne, she would be made more in their joint image than in that of Pierpont and Fanny.

The new year of 1906 had barely begun when, on January 4, there was a long club meeting. The construction of the clubhouse was going so well that Daisy could anticipate an autumn opening. No longer awed by her advance of five thousand dollars, Elsie had spent almost ten times that on the purchase of the major pieces of furniture and fabrics, which were either soon to be delivered or already stored in warehouses. Stanny White and she had worked with sketchers on a series of renderings of the major rooms complete with swatches of the fabrics to be used in them and samples of the colors she had chosen for walls and woodwork. It was from the illustrations that Elsie's problems emanated. The decorating committee felt it had the right to question any and all of her decisions. Did they not have more experience than she in decorating great establishments? Was not their taste the equal of hers? Dealing with that committee of twelve women prepared her for all of the difficulties she would encounter with clients throughout her career. "They all had different ideas and different tastes—tastes, I must say, which in some instances were none too good."

One was aghast at the thought of using chintz in their drawing rooms. Elsie prevailed, and the era of chintz for city houses was born, as was her sobriquet: "the Chintz lady." The closer she came to completing the job, the more irritating the interference of committee members became. Elsie would leave the premises late in the evening, exhausted after spending tedious hours carefully and slowly placing the furniture, room by room. The next morning she would return to find all of her hard work undone by some tasteless gremlins who had rearranged everything. Weary and disheartened, wondering if the job would ever be completed to her satisfaction, support came from the unlikely source of Anne Morgan.

That winter, Anne was seeing a great deal of Sir Purdon Clark, her father's choice for director of the Metropolitan Museum of Art. He was teaching her how to look at paintings. She dined with Bessy almost every night and often went to the theatre, where, in a sense, she was being instructed in dramaturgy. At that time she was consumed by self-improvement. Not only had she started taking classes at Cooper Union, she was also continuing her sewing lessons, had added Italian, and was learning how to play squash. When her father left for Europe, on February 17, it was the first time in many years that she did not accompany him; nor did she go with Bessy, when she sailed on the *St. Paul* on April 21. Until Bessy's departure, Elsie was mostly mentioned in absentia in the Line-A-Day, as on April 13: "Dinner 17th St. Elsie in Washington."

Throughout the rest of April and into May, she began to see Elsie for lunch, where the latter's problems with the committee were discussed. Anne's backing helped to give her the courage to summon a meeting of the full committee on decorating. They were a dozen formidable ladies representing the best in New York society, a group before which she once had felt obliged to grovel. She was beyond that period in her life, but knowing that her future depended on the critical reception to the decor of the Colony Club, she was not without trepidation as she rose to address them.

> Ladies, in common fairness I must ask you not to touch anything in any room until I have finished. I can't carry out my plans if every time I return the following day I find it in disorder, after having been taken apart and put together again according to the ideas of a dozen minds. Once the club is open you are free to change everything. In asking this I hope you will agree that I stand to win or lose more than anyone by it.

Decency prevailed and "from that time on nobody moved as much as a pin-cushion." With a great sense of relief, Elsie left for Europe toward the end of May, looking forward to the opening of the club in the autumn.

Anne did not depart for France until June 20. Bessy and Elsie were both in Versailles, and she was still at sea, when a stunning event delayed the fulfillment of Elsie's dreams for almost a year.

On the evening of June 25, the premiere of *Mamzelle Champagne* took place at Stanford White's Madison Square Roof Garden. It attracted a raffish crowd of gentleman on the loose, their wives safely out of the city for the summer. Even were they in town, it was not the sort of place to which a gentleman took his wife, unless, of course, the gentleman was Harry Thaw and the wife, Evelyn Nesbit, who, before marrying him, had been White's mistress. She could easily have passed for one of the group who formed the bulk of the females in attendance: the young and flamboyantly pretty girls of the summer evening, clad, like her, in filmy white gowns and large picture hats. To emphasize the point Thaw was apparently making, namely, he had married a tramp, Thaw's guests were two young men. No lady would ever appear in public as the sole female in a party of three men.

The roof was the architect's toy, where he played at being the impresario of the ribald revues that were its warm-weather fare. His wife was not present at openings of his spectacles nor would she attend any of their subsequent performances. Even his son, a Harvard sophomore with whom he had dined on that evening, was sent to see the "respectable" George M. Cohan musical rather than be allowed to accompany his father to the roof.

If there was anybody in that audience who was shockable, they would have been shocked when Thaw left his wife alone at the table with two young bachelors while he prowled the premises. Sooner or later, he knew the architect would have to put in an appearance. If Evelyn was a whore, then White was her whoremaster, and the only way to redeem her was to eliminate him.

White did not arrive until late in the performance. He was alone and made his way to his ringside table, greeting friends along the way. Surrounded by twenty beautiful young women all personally selected by White, the comedian was in the middle of a number called "I Could Love a Thousand Girls." It took a while before Thaw was able to edge his way to the table. He withdrew a revolver from his coat pocket and, as White turned to face him, fired three shots, killing him instantly.

*A*nne Morgan received the news via the ship's wireless. The other members of the Colony Club were either in their summer homes or abroad when word reached them. Elsie and Bessy were in Versailles. It was only two years earlier that Minnie Paget had brought Thaw and Nesbit out to see them in the hope that Bessy would be able to do something to further the girl's career. *Whimsical* would have been the kindest word for his behavior on that occasion. This was a young man who clearly should never have contemplated marriage, least of all to a flibbertigibbet incapable of fidelity. From the beginning, the recipe for a *crime passionnel* had been there for anybody to read, but even with her taste for melodrama in theatre, it had never occurred to Bessy that her friend Stanny White was in danger. That sort of thing did not happen to anybody one knew, certainly not to a man so high-spirited and generous, so capable of handling himself in any situation.

In a stunning example of what Thaw millions could do to purchase a defense, the case was the first in this century to practice what has since become a common legal ploy. The press and jury were manipulated so that by the end of the trial the victims, White and Nesbit, were found guilty, and Thaw, the killer, was not guilty by reason of the insanity to which their actions purportedly had driven him.

There was a postscript. Not long after Thaw's release, he picked up a nineteen-year-old young man, Frederick Gump, Jr., in an ice cream parlor in Long Beach, California, whom he paid to come to a hotel with him. The boy was found flogged into unconsciousness but was later paid off not to press charges.

*C*ompleting the final details on the Colony clubhouse was not the first order of business for White's partners, Charles Follen McKim and William Rutherford Mead. As far as the members were concerned, it was probably for the best. The last thing anybody wanted was to open a women's club designed by White in the glare of daily headlines about his reputation as a womanizer. With any luck, they would be able to open after the trial and avoid any association with the unfortunate business.

Elsie was probably more disappointed than the others. The opening was to signal the start of a new life. It was a setback, but she was a pragmatist and would survive it, as she had the end of her career in the theatre and the recent change in her relationship with Bessy. Elsie measured her life from where she began and not where she ended, so that at any given point she could think of herself as on her way up rather than on her way down. Once the autumn came, she would complete her work at the clubhouse. Until then, there were the pleasures of another summer in Versailles. Anne and she had reached an accommodation and, though they would never be best of friends, found that they could remain amiable with each other while sharing their life with Bessy. The third part of the new Versailles triumvirate agreed to pay her share of the expenses of running Villa Trianon. The extra revenue enabled them to buy a parcel of land adjoining their property. Elsie, with Nolhac's advice, began laying out a formal garden along the lines conceived for the grounds of the grand château by Le Nôtre, Louis XIV's landscape artist.

*T*he Colony Club announced that its opening would finally take place on March 12, 1907. The anxiety with which the members approached it is shown in a letter Henry Adams received from one of them, saying that "the new Club has upset Miss Marbury and all the other women to the point of nervous prostration, shown by volubility beyond control."

*A*lfred Allan Lewis   ✧ 225

Such a singular event could not pass without publicity, but during the press previews of the new clubhouse, a great effort was made to mute the architect's contribution and concentrate on the interior decorator. In a long piece on the club in *Putnam's Monthly,* White was mentioned once in passing. In a new *Harper's Bazaar* piece, he was not mentioned at all, while Elsie was credited for all that was choice in the building:

> For it is in a fine appreciation of detail that Miss Elsie de Wolfe has preeminently distinguished herself, winning at one stroke, as it were, a recognized place among the decorators of the country.

White's tragedy became her triumph. She was even credited with what was surely his contribution. White had designed pools for some of the other clubs he had built, but none was more striking than the one in the Colony Club. The pool was sunk in white marble and reflected on three sides in Venetian mirrors extending from marble coping to ceiling. The illumination was a soft yellow light through a translucent ceiling hung with grape clusters and vines. The wall glass sconces were in the form of bunches of green and white grapes. With its subtle pagan eroticism, the pool room jolted the senses after the staid colonial elegance of the other rooms.

Harper's Bazaar likened it to "some enchanted cavern of fabled times." Nothing Elsie ever did then or after resembled this setting. After outhouses came indoors, she gained a certain notoriety for decorating bathrooms, but her efforts were designed to disguise the bodily rites performed in those rooms, while the Colony pool was a Dionysian celebration of them. The concept was entirely in keeping with the subtle amalgam of sensuality and classicism that characterized White's best work. How he must have relished the private joke of designing an orgiastic plunge for the ladylike dips of the members of the Colony Club! The women would become the butt of a hideous public joke if it were to get out that a man being castigated for his indulgences with nymphets had designed a pool "to tempt nymphs" for them. It was far better to attribute it to Elsie, who already had a reputation for the genteel good taste that would become fundamental to her work as a decorator.

The pool room aside, the Colony Club was Elsie's triumph from basement to roof. She had let the light flood in through White's tall, ample windows to illuminate the standard she had set for refined post-Victorian taste. It would prevail for almost one hundred years.

Daisy Harriman counted the club a success from the time she met a member going into the dining room who was herself the wife and mother of club presidents and governors. "That valiant spirit was beaming. 'I've waited for this evening all my life. I have just called home and told them not to wait dinner for me. I was having it at my club. My dear, I've been getting that message for years—now I'm giving it.'"

CHAPTER TWENTY-EIGHT ॐ

The murder of Stanford White was undoubtedly the largest society scandal of 1906. But the year had opened with another that involved a still grander list of big names and which, though lacking in tragedy, more than compensated with the titillating spectacle of a parade of some of the most important men in the country, whose egotistical duplicity had made them the quarry of a master blackmailer.

Justice Joseph H. Deuel, of the special sessions court, started his association with Colonel William D'Alton Mann by serving as his legal adviser, particularly on the libel laws. He would go over every line of copy in Mann's society rag, *Town Topics,* to make certain that nothing gave grounds for suit. He helped the publisher invent the blind item, which ever after would be a favorite dodge of gossip columnists: "What playboy was seen, at 3 A.M., stealing out of the Newport cottage of which prominent social leader, while her husband was in New York?" This would be followed by a harmless paragraph that gave the key to their identities. "Mrs. John Jacob Astor entertained at a small dinner party at Beechwood. Prominent among the guests was one of the resort's favorite bachelors, Mr. Creighton Webb."

Mann thought so highly of Deuel that he allowed him to buy stock and become a partner in *Town Topics.* Peter F. Collier, publisher of *Collier's Weekly,* was one of their favorite objects of derision. They castigated him as "a Bible peddler who had ridden into society behind a pack of hounds." This gained the enmity of the man's son, Robert, who had taken over the modest family magazine and, with the help of two brilliant associates, turned it into one of the most popular periodicals in the country. His business manager, Condé Nast, would soon start his own publishing empire and teach the world how to write about American society with such style he would actually make it seem clever as well as respectable. His editor-in-chief was a muck-raking crusader named Norman Hapgood. The three young men bided their time waiting for the appropriate moment to use their larger circulation to deal a mortal wound to *Town Topics.* It came when Mann printed an article implying President Theodore Roosevelt's daughter was drinking to excess during her visit to Newport. In that more innocent age, this was considered an insult to the presidency delivered in outrageously bad taste. Hapgood delivered a beautiful written and stinging rebuke. Of Justice Deuel, he said: "He is part owner and one of the editors of a paper of which the occupation is printing scandal about people who are not cowardly enough to pay for silence."

The piece appeared in the August 5 issue of *Collier's,* and Justice Deuel brought charges of criminal libel against Hapgood. If his case was successful, Mann intended to bring a civil suit against *Collier's* demanding a great deal of money for their slander of a publication he considered so finely written that it could be used as a text in English composition courses.

As was often the case in the pursuit of justice, the innocent were among the greatest victims. Mann was never convicted of any crime and died peacefully, leaving an estate in excess of one million dollars. *Town Topics* continued to be published until the early Thirties, although it was never taken seriously after the trial. It had come out during the proceedings that the periodical had a list of "immunes," gentlemen about whom it would never print anything that was not flattering. To get on it cost money. Mann admitted on the witness stand that he had borrowed $184,500 from some of the greatest financiers in the country. He was proud to add that they valued his friendship so highly, none of them ever had pressed him to return any portion of his debt, although in cross-examination he had to admit he had met some of them only once or twice. Judge Deuel proved more colloquially colorful when he compared their prey to "Davy Crockett's coon," adding, "All you need to do is to point your gun and every high-tone, desirable citizen of Palm Beach may tumble in your basket."

Some of the men were embarrassed by being on the list, others proud to find themselves in such lofty company, but the innocent victims were the wives and daughters who were publicly humiliated. They had to ask themselves whether their personal superiority or bribing Mann was responsible for the press that made the world view them as leaders of society. As bad or worse, they knew their husbands had been paying to conceal degrading infidelities. No matter how it was viewed, the ladies were the real losers.

Pierpont Morgan had only "lent" $2,500 to join the list of "immunes," but the loan of any money was something he took far less lightly than many of the others. It could have been no accident that a short while after his exposure as one whose life made him vulnerable to blackmail, his daughter Anne openly defied him for the first time by joining the National Civic Federation, an organization of which he disapproved, and allowing her name to be used as one of its sponsors.

In the years between his divorce from Alva and his remarriage, Willie K. Vanderbilt had lent $25,000 to Mann and was too much of a realist not to know what he was paying for. Not only had he not expected to see the money again, but he also returned the stock in *Town Topics* that had been put up as collateral. Mann approached him for another "loan" after Anne became his wife, and was turned down. Willie no longer had any need to fear what might be written about him. Although grateful for that, Anne was distressed to find her brother Oliver among the "immunes." It appeared that all of the men she esteemed most were in thrall to this dreadful blackmailer.

There was a more pressing reason for the Vanderbilts to remain abroad. It concerned a scandal that, had *Town Topics* discovered it, would have filled its pages for weeks. Toward the end of October 1905, Consuelo Marlborough told her husband she would be going to Paris to order her winter clothes and visit her father. His response was to tell her to go and stay. He was going about London accusing her of having three—some said six— lovers, although none of the private detectives he hired ever came up with any evidence. His own mother found his claims so vile that she henceforth took her daughter-in-law's side in all of their disputes. The truth was, as Consuelo knew and was too proud to mention publicly, it was a matter of his adultery and not hers: he already had begun his affair with her former good friend Gladys Deacon, and wanted a divorce. Her only possible adultery was with Balsan, a relationship which began after her husband's public humiliation.

Alice Vanderbilt was in Paris and pressed Anne for details on the state of her niece's marriage. Her ever discreet sister-in-law would make no specific charges against Marlborough but had to admit he was impossible and had insulted Consuelo in every conceivable way. Although bound to her mother by a psychic tie stronger than any umbilical cord, Consuelo adored her stepmother and must have confided in her, for Anne knew the unendurable problems in the marriage started two years before when Marlborough began his affair with Gladys.

Willie's aversion to scandal was so palpable he not only had allowed Mann to blackmail him but also had given in to all of Alva's demands despite having evidence on her that would have ruined her both socially and financially. He would not hear of Consuelo getting a divorce, which Alice found "queer . . . after his own experience!" Instead, he went to London to negotiate with Marlborough, whose love for Gladys Deacon was not as strong as his love for Vanderbilt gold. They negotiated a sum for which Marlborough agreed to a legal separation rather than a divorce and gave Consuelo joint custody of the children. She would live in Sunderland House, the London mansion Willie had built for them and wisely put in her name. Once he saw his daughter settled in England, he rushed back to France to be with his horses. Consuelo once again had allowed the wishes of a parent—this time her father—to supersede her own desires.

*T*hree months before the *Town Topics* trial opened, *The House of Mirth* was published and immediately proved itself that headiest of literary couplings: a critical success that was also a best-seller. The world at last acknowledged what Edith Wharton always had known about herself. She was walking in the company of Henry James both literally and literarily, and what was more, she was outselling him.

In Lily Bart, Edith created an archetype for a generation of young ladies. Until the start of World War I, whenever it was said that Miss So-And-So was a Lily Bart, the listener knew immediately what was intended. The character's theatrical potential was not lost on playwrights and producers, who began to besiege the writer with requests for the dramatic rights.

On November 12, she took the train down to New York from Lenox, Massachusetts, where, in her final, often acrimonious collaboration with Ogden Codman, she had built her palatial country home, The Mount. She proceeded from Grand Central Station to Bessy's office in the Empire Theatre building, where she had an appointment to discuss the dramatization. Bessy had been her supportive play agent during her many unsuccessful attempts to establish herself as a playwright, and it was she to whom the author turned for advice on *The House of Mirth*.

Edith was fearful of attempting the dramatization herself but knew little about the capacities of those who were asking for the rights. Bessy heard her out, shrewdly realizing she really did want one last fling at the theatre. An agent's success often depended on her talents as a matchmaker, and she was among the wisest of them. She put the best together with the best by letting Edith believe that Clyde Fitch was interested but only if he could collaborate with her. He was the most successful playwright in the country, if not the world, and she was flattered that he should want to work with her. Although no great admirer of his work, as one skilled craftsman appraising another, she did appreciate his grasp of dramatic structure. Bessy suggested that she set up an appointment for the following month, when Mrs. Wharton would have returned to the city to take up winter residence in her Park Avenue townhouse.

Edith was put off by her first sight of Fitch: not her type at all—a plump, flamboyantly dressed little dandy with an olive complexion and far too many rings and fobs. It was a closer look into "his beautiful Oriental eyes full of wit and understanding" that won her over. From the beginning, they were matey, filled with anecdotal revelations and delicious gossip about mutual friends. She found in him a "sense of the irony of life" that complemented her own. Then, of course, they were drawn together by their shared fascination with interior decoration. Her good furniture and frilly *bonbonnière* of a house was precisely to his taste.

He suggested that he would write a detailed scenario supplying the structure and movement of the play, and that she would then fill in all of the dialogue. It would prove precisely the wrong approach, for it had him writing prose, which was her métier, while she wrote dialogue, which was his.

Bessy had no difficulty in selling the project to Charles Frohman, and by the end of February they were hard at work. On March 10, the Whartons sailed for Europe, and Fitch joined them in Paris. The play was completed in May, in Versailles, where Clyde was staying at the Villa Trianon. With Anne Morgan and Elsie not yet in residence and Bessy away much of the time, the collaborators had the opportunity to work there without interruption. Frohman accepted the script but felt a great deal of fine-tuning had yet to be done before it was ready for production, and August found Clyde and Edith back at work at The Mount. Dialogue can only be fine-tuned up to a point: go beyond that point, and it becomes stale. One day Edith cried out in despair, "I can't see how you ever thought there was a play in this book."

"But I never did!" He had been told that she had wanted him to dramatize the book and had refused to have anybody else in the hope of inducing him to do it. She had been told he was so eager to do it that he was willing to agree to a collaboration, something he never before had contemplated. They stared at each other, realizing that they had been tricked into it "by an unscrupulous intermediary" who, of course, was the estimable Miss Marbury. They burst out laughing, realizing she had them and it was too late to withdraw.

Edith gasped, "I was so flattered."

He nodded. "So was I."

$\mathcal{E}$dith later rationalized the failure of *The House of Mirth* by claiming that an American audience could never accept an unhappy ending and a negative hero. She took refuge in words William Dean Howells allegedly spoke to her as they left the theatre after the New York first night. "What the American public always wants is a tragedy with a happy ending."

The real reason for the failure was that Wharton and Fitch had enjoyed themselves too much. These two supreme craftsmen had pussyfooted around, one never challenging the other, too intent upon becoming friends to take the adversarial positions necessary for a successful collaboration. He was all too aware that not only in America but also in Europe, where he enjoyed comparable success, audiences wanted tragedies with happy endings. The greatest fault with many of his better plays was that he compromised their brilliant construction, wit, and characterization by providing them with an audience-pleasing climax. Despite knowing it quite possibly would have assured success, as an artist he had too much respect for the book to suggest Edith compromise her work by allowing Lily to live. That was what he had meant when he admitted never believing there was a play in *The House of Mirth,* at least not his kind of play. He may also have learned enough about his new friend to realize Lily was that part of Edith who had failed in New York society and had to die to allow the artist to rise phoenix-like from her ashes.

Edith could forgive everybody connected with the production except possibly Bessy. Although they sporadically continued to do business, and her respect for the agent's professional acumen remained undiminished, their social contacts began waning at that point.

Wharton may have been unforgiving, but Fitch's faith in his representative was unabated, and for Frohman, despite the loss of a great deal of money, it was business as usual. They understood that Bessy believed she was putting together a package bound to succeed. No agent of her caliber did that much work in the expectation of earning no more than the commission on advances.

Bessy's attitude toward Wharton can be surmised from her memoir. That book was published at a time when Wharton was among the most famous American writers in the world, and yet, in all of its name-dropping pages, Bessy mentioned her only once, and that was parenthetically, as Mary Cadwalader Jones's sister-in-law.

CHAPTER TWENTY-NINE

Before the summer was out, Elsie's career was launched with an impetus that propelled her to the top of her profession. Not only did commissions come from the members of the Colony Club but also from those wealthy women she had cultivated during her forays into society and from the stars she had supported during her career in the theatre. Business was so good, she moved into a showroom and office on Fifth Avenue. Her name at last adorned the *New York City Directory* at that address to which she so fervently, and for so long, had aspired.

At the same time Elsie was emerging as a spectacularly successful interior decorator, Bessy was consolidating her position as the most powerful playwrights' representative in the world. She was more circumspectly initiating an equivalent of the old boys' network for the women and gay men among her clients. This network already had paid off admirably in the case of Clyde Fitch. Few of her clients of any sexual persuasion could fault her for lacking an encouraging amalgam of nurturing and professionalism. No matter how long it took for some financial return on her investment of time, Bessy never gave up, especially not on the gifted young women who came to her with their work. Such was the case with Rachel Crothers, a young actress and would-be writer who was touring in E. H. Sothern's company. Just as she had once convinced Daniel Frohman to stage her own one-acters at special matinees, she convinced him to do those of Crothers at the Lyceum and Madison Square. Bessy subtly guided her work through the early years of the century until 1906, when she wrote her first Broadway hit, *The Three of Us*. In 1908, Maxine Elliott contracted to produce and star in *Myself Bettina* and insisted that the writer serve as her director. Crothers continued to act in that capacity for the thirty plays she wrote over the next thirty years, which could well serve as an archive of the changing attitudes of women toward society, and society toward women, during those three decades. It is conceivable that today's innovative directors, working with gifted actresses, could stage successful revivals of the best of her work: *Mary the Third, Let Us Be Gay, As Husbands Go, When Ladies Meet,* and *Susan and God.*

*S*hortly after the turn of the century, the Bright brothers suggested that Bessy take as a client a young English novelist who was determined to make his mark as a playwright. W. Somerset Maugham—Willie—had written one promising novel, *Liza of Lambeth,* after which he persisted in grinding out a series of meretricious efforts with a deadening regularity. What captivated her were the unproduced plays, which revealed a gift for precise, witty dialogue as well as a flair for improvisation within conventional dramatic structure. There was much that was reminiscent of Wilde except for an unmistakable paucity of genius, which fortunately was not necessary for commercial success in the theatre. Indeed, it often proved a detriment to it. Bessy had to have taken Maugham as a client by 1901. It was in that year that his friend Chavalita Dunne, a feminist writer, married Golding Bright, and Willie wrote a teasing note of congratulations:

Of course no nice minded person can fail to see that you took an unfair advantage over me in marrying your dramatic agent. I see the only thing for me to do is marry Miss Marbury, and I am starting for Paris at once.

Willie was a wellborn, compact Edwardian dandy who was both more talented and less flamboyant than Fitch. Haunted by Wilde's tragedy, he was a closeted homosexual who by his own reckoning had several heterosexual affairs, culminating in a calamitous marriage that led to a scandal akin to Wilde's and every bit as public. The difference was the times. In the post-Victorian era, homosexuality continued to be a legal crime and a religious sin, but neither Maugham's career nor his social position was in any form diminished by the revelation of his gaydom.

$\mathcal{B}$essy Marbury may have inspired Anne Morgan to do something with her life, beyond the Lady Bountiful philanthropies to which a young woman of her wealth and position was expected to devote a few hours of her time. But she could not direct Anne on what course to follow. It was not as simple as it had been with Elsie, setting her up in one profession after another until she found the one for which she had a real talent. For one thing, there was no question of a daughter of Pierpont Morgan taking a job for which she would be paid. She was considered one of the wealthiest heiresses in the world and, in addition to her father's disapproval, would face public vilification were she to take employment away from "a girl" who needed the wages.

Bessy motivated her, but it was her old pal Daisy Harriman who started her off in the direction she would follow for the rest of her life. Daisy was extraordinary. She was raising a splendid daughter, and running two houses, on far less money than many of her closest friends spent on one. There was not a movement for social reform with which she was not as familiar as she was with the bloodlines of those families whose names shared space with hers in the *Social Register.* In her own words, "As soon as I had thought about it, I had been for suffrage."

A debate on the subject had begun at the club. On one particularly dramatic winter afternoon, the socially impeccable and beautiful Katherine Duer Mackay came bursting into the reading room, where she was to lead the "anti's" in a discussion of the issue. Her arms were filled with books and papers, and she was followed by a footman carrying still more. They were dumped down on the library table in the center of the room. "I've read them all in a week," she said, "and I am converted."

The debate was ruined when she turned to the "pros," opened her arms, and cried, "Comrades!"

In Mrs. Mackay the suffragettes gained an invaluable patron. She would later introduce Alva Belmont into their ranks, who in turn would not only convert her pliant daughter, Consuelo Marlborough, to the cause but would also outdo all of them in her devotion to it.

Daisy's was a unique gift for merging the two halves of her life, so that her position in the small world of New York high society often worked in tandem with her zeal for improving the lot of those forced to be a part of that larger, downtrodden society that existed around it in the same city. At a fashionable wedding she ran into August Belmont, who asked her to invite Gertrude Beeks to be a guest speaker at one of the Tuesday afternoon lectures that she had initiated at the Colony. Miss Beeks recently had returned from investigating the condition of American laborers in the Panama Canal Zone and had an interesting story to tell about the government's failure to ensure their well-being. Daisy was so moved by what Beeks had to say that she organized Anne Morgan and a group of other like-minded members into a women's department of the National Civic Federation, which Belmont had organized to improve working condition for government employees. They expanded their operations to include female workers so often underpaid and abused by their male bosses. Their investigation of the working conditions of women holding menial jobs at department stores, factories, restaurants, and hotels brought them into contact with the leaders of labor unions who were often just as remiss as the most repressive capitalists in their attitudes toward women workers. Anne Morgan was in daily communication with those elements of the workforce who were considered natural enemies by her father. To his credit, he disapproved but never did anything to prevent her from fulfilling her commitment to the victims of their world. For her part, no matter how justified she might secretly have found the criticisms leveled at Morgan by her new associates, never did she utter a single public word against him.

*J*ournalism was one of the fields that had opened to women during the previous century. They were generally employed as reporters on subjects considered of greater interest to women than to men—the arts, fashion, society, gossip, homemaking—but there had been a handful of women who covered "hard news." With her letters from Europe to the *New York Tribune,* in the 1850s, Margaret Fuller became the first woman foreign correspondent. One of the most famous reporters of the last quarter of the nineteenth century was a woman, Elizabeth Cochrane, who wrote under the name of Nellie Bly.

Bly made her reputation on stories about workingwomen and slum life for the Pittsburgh *Dispatch*. She was expelled from Mexico for doing a series on government corruption and the dismal condition of the peon in that country. Joseph Pulitzer was sufficiently impressed to bring her to New York to work for the *World*. She had herself committed to the insane asylum on Blackwell's (now Roosevelt) Island to do an exposé on the treatment of inmates, which led to improvement in patient care. There were other headline-grabbing exposés of sweatshops, prisons, and bribery by lobbyists in the state legislature. By far her most famous exploit took place at the end of 1889, when she traveled around the world alone. The purpose was to better the eighty-day time of Jules Verne's fictional Phineas Fogg, which she did by eighteen days.

Beginning with Nellie Bly, women journalists began to win an audience for their stories, many of which dealt with social injustice and the plight of the disenfranchised, particularly disenfranchised women. Their male colleagues took them seriously enough to feel threatened and felt obliged to invent a belittling label that would hold them up to ridicule, and "sob sister" entered the lexicon. What was not often remarked upon was how often the sob sister displayed the talent for muckraking of a committed social reformer. Through much of her career, Ida Tarbell was demonstrably in this tradition. Her prim, ladylike demeanor masked a commitment to change that amounted to passion.

When Anne Morgan met her, Tarbell was approaching fifty and at the height of a career that included well-regarded biographies of Napoleon Bonaparte, Madame Roland, and Abraham Lincoln in addition to her muckraking magazine pieces. The best-known of the latter were the nineteen articles published in *McClure's Magazine* on Rockefeller and the growth of Standard Oil, which were collected and published in two volumes in 1904 as *The History of the Standard Oil Company*. Her interest in Rockefeller was not entirely objective: years earlier, he indirectly had ruined her father, an independent oilman, who had held out against his formation of the trust. In her duel with Rockefeller, she satisfied her father's honor, for her work aroused public opinion to such an extent that a federal investigation was called for that eventually led to the dissolution of Standard Oil of New Jersey. An unintended result was the displacement of Morgan by Rockefeller as the name most symbolic of the iniquities of capitalism.

In 1906, she purchased the *American Magazine* conjointly with her fellow journalist Lincoln Steffens; William Allen White, whose Emporia *Gazette* had made him the country's exemplar small-town editor; the satirist Finley

Peter Dunne; and Ray Stannard Baker, author of one of the earliest exposés of the heinous condition of the American black, *Following the Color Line,* and later official biographer of Woodrow Wilson. Through Tarbell, Anne became lifelong friends with all of her colleagues, including Baker, who had written an article, "What United States Steel Really Is," in which he described her father's company as "a government unto itself."

The unlikely relationship between the heiress of Morgan and the priestess of muck began when Bessy Marbury introduced them. Tarbell and Bessy were already intimate through the many friends they had in common, particularly Jeanette Gilder, who had a weekend country home close to the one Ida shared with her mother, in Redding, Connecticut.

The friendship of Tarbell and Morgan was so enduring and of such intimacy that it was later suspected they had been lovers. What was perversely judged to give evidence of this was the fact that Anne was not mentioned in Tarbell's autobiography, *All in the Day's Work,* nor was Bessy, nor were any of the other women with whom she was known to have shared intense friendships. One of the few exceptions was her colleague on *McClure's,* Viola Roseboro, and most of the references to her were professional. In her book *Ida,* a single woman, seemed to live in a world devoid of other single women. She was forty-five years old when Victoria died, and her sexual attitudes remained those of the late nineteenth century, during which women could openly express intense feelings for each other without fear of libidinous interpretation. But by the time she put her story down on paper, in 1939, any written expression of same-sex emotional commitment implied, at the very least, latent homosexuality. It was an implication with which she preferred not to deal.

Like Anne Morgan, Ida Tarbell was a liberal Republican for most of her life, having reached middle age in that era, bracketed by Lincoln and Teddy Roosevelt, when the progressive wing of the Republican party was far more enlightened than its counterpart in the Democratic party. The two major demands of the women's political movement were suffrage and prohibition. Although neither Anne nor Ida were pro-suffrage, they would later enjoy pointing out to the more radical feminists that the two amendments guaranteeing them were passed by a Republican administration. Bessy, the liberal Democrat, was against both. She thought the vote by itself would do nothing to improve the lot of women. As for prohibition, there was no such thing as laws that could successfully stand between people and their private vices— be they alcohol, tobacco, narcotics, prostitution, or pornography. All they succeeded in doing was turning thugs into overnight, tax-free millionaires.

A witty and perceptive sketch of the three women was given in a hasty diary entry made by the English writer Arnold Bennett after lunching with them in New York. He described Bessy as "a very business-like woman. Fat. Human. Kindly. Shrewd. Very shrewd and downright in her remarks." Anne was "beautiful but waning. . . . Apparently doing nothing but interested in everything. . . . Evidently an energetic woman with no outlet. . . . Good judge of human qualities and wide in interests." He found Ida to be "the most wistful and inviting of these 3 spinsters."

What impressed him most was that they were "all extremely interesting, all different, yet intimate, putting arms around necks and calling each other by Xtian [sic] names, coming together on a purely personal basis, just like men." When Ida was invited to come down to Washington with Anne and Bessy, she replied, "I've only just got back. I haven't been at my desk for four or five days."

Bennett reiterated, "Just like a man."

No matter how filled with activity Bessy's business, Elsie's new career, and the awakening of Anne's social conscience had made that autumn, winter, and spring in New York, the joys of the summer of 1907 in Versailles were sacrosanct, as they had been in the preceding years and would be in the years that followed until World War I. On June 5, Anne sailed on the *Oceanic,* arriving in Cherbourg on the thirteenth and proceeding directly to Versailles. That Sunday, loads of people descended for tea, including Minnie Anglesey, Henry Adams, the well-known couturière Mme Lucille, and her husband, Sir Cosmo Duff Gordon.

When Berenson arrived for his annual stay, on September 21, the talk among the half-dozen guests already assembled was, as usual, "very brilliant, very gossipy, and nearly witty." Bessy's weight was approaching the two-hundred-pound mark, which made her "more formless than ever." It mattered as little to her as it did to those upon whom she chose to turn the full strength of her personality. They found in it an intelligence and effervescence far more seductive than the curve of a slender waist.

But the surprise was Elsie, who had shown signs of being so disheartened during her visit to I Tatti. Totally restored was the élan, the chic, the vivaciousness that had enchanted him from their first meeting. That evening, he swept his three hostesses off to dinner at a fashionable restaurant, where their diverse charms could not help but be remarked upon. For the ambiguity of their relationship and the allure of their hospitality, they had been christened "the nymphets" by the wealthy expatriate painter Ralph Curtis, of whom Berenson once had observed: "He grows more charming but not more interesting."

∞

*I*n October, Bessy and Elsie sailed on the *St. Paul*. They went directly to the Colony Club, where they would stay until the completion of Elsie's latest renovations on the Irving Place house. As was its custom, *The New York Times* sent a reporter to interview them. The corpulent Bessy boasted: "I never felt better in my life. I am full of enthusiasm—and good news."

She went through an exhaustive list of all of the projects she had initiated and the plays she was bringing back for American production. Of the more than five months she had spent in Europe, she said: "I had one month's vacation . . . and I spent it in an automobile. I never left my seat and have returned automobile mad. I went 2,000 miles in my car through Germany, up the Rhine, and in the Black Forest, and broke the record for tires. Only one air chamber blew out and not a tire was injured."

Elsie had spent her time "buying furniture, hangings, and objets d'art. I filled my eye with beauty and color, and planned how I could transfer some of the wonderful ideas to New York."

She had contracts to do houses in the city, but she also had to put the finishing touch on the Colony Club—a winter garden on the roof. "Its success will depend chiefly on the heating which will not be furnished by the sun . . . [but] by earthenware stoves, according to the Italian style. In fact, the decorations, or those which I will install, are modeled after the style of Luca della Robbia. . . . With these Italian stoves, which are ornamental as well as useful, the greatest charm is the even heat they throw out."

The roof garden was to open in December, and she predicted that it would revolutionize heating in New York as "there will be no uncertainty about regulating the temperature."

Next to her professional plans, the most exciting news was of the picture, by Charles Le Brun, she was bringing home.

> Miss Marbury and I came across this treasure quite by accident. We love to look into all sorts of funny little shops, for one never knows when something of artistic value will come to light. In the rear of an old shop in Paris, we found this painting, which is four yards long by three high, and a splendid mural decoration. It was covered with dirt, but one place showed a boy carrying a tankard. I saw at once it was something fine. We had it cleaned and were rewarded by discovering its history.

Undoubtedly having both Berenson and Pierre de Nolhac at hand helped them immeasurably to identify and authenticate their find.

*A*lfred Allan Lewis

In the interview the discretion of the two women was admirable. It was as if Anne Morgan had not become a part of their lives in Europe. Elsie's story of the discovery of the Le Brun implied they were, as always, intimately attached only to each other, and Bessy did not indicate that Anne had been her companion on those motoring jaunts.

For the rest of the year in New York, Bessy and Anne were constantly together at luncheon and meetings of the Colony board of governors. Several times each month, they went to the theatre together to endure plays by Bessy's clients that Anne usually dismissed as "miserable." Their time apart was filled with their various activities. Bessy had her business, and in addition to her new involvement in liberal causes, Anne was teaching the Colony Club members how to play basketball.

The time had come to test the nature of Elsie's continuing relationship with the other two women. Not only was she at last financially independent, but had she chosen, she also could have bought Bessy out and gained complete control of her beloved Villa Trianon. Instead, she chose to buy only a share of it, thus remaining partially in thrall to her old love, the only true friend she ever had, and making a permanent accommodation with Anne Morgan, who had become a part of their lives.

CHAPTER THIRTY

In 1907, Anne Vanderbilt celebrated her forty-eighth birthday. She had known her share of ecstasy and tragedy, of the best and the worst the world had to offer, and after close to a half-century her life at last had settled down to a pleasant, tranquil gait that no longer raced between extremes. The only excess was of wealth. Not even Morgan or Rockefeller kept an oceangoing yacht plus four residences: the Paris *hôtel particulier* that Willie had bought for Anne shortly after their wedding, the château at St. Louis de Poissy, the Long Island estate Idle Hours, and the Fifth Avenue mansion. Anne still thought of this last as Alva's house, and liked it least of all, but her husband would not relinquish it because of all it represented, good and bad, to him. Each residence had its own staff except for secretaries, personal maids, and valets, who traveled with them from place to place. All that need be done was to telegraph ahead for a house or the yacht to be ready to receive them. And there were Anne's private indulgences—no small matter—the furs, and jewels, and frocks. At last, her quiet, exquisite, and very expensive tastes could be gratified to the boundless limits of honeyed prodigality.

After the birth of her first grandchild, a girl named for her, Anne had made her peace with her son George and his wife, Tayo, whom she always had liked and with whom she currently shared the common frustration of George's inability to get his life together. He had squandered his Sands inheritance to buy a seat on the New York Stock Exchange and had ended up selling American automobiles in Paris.

Despite their mother's fulminations, Willie's children were not displeased with their stepmother. She made no attempt to place a bar between their father and what they considered their rightful share of his worldly goods. A very good settlement, estimated at between five and ten million dollars, already had been made on Anne. There were no further demands. What need had she of making any demands, when her slightest wish was granted as it was forming on her lips? As Anne had a gift for matrimony, so Willie had a gift for indulgence. It certainly gave every sign of being a perfect union as they boarded the *Valiant* for a two-month cruise of the Mediterranean at the beginning of 1907, a trip designed, in part, as a public display of the reconciliation of George and Tayo, who had wanted to leave him.

The guests included Anne's other children, the latter couple, and Consuelo Marlborough, who, by the terms of her recent separation agreement, could not take her two sons out of England and came away alone. Her father reveled in the familial atmosphere, an atmosphere her own mother never had been able to create during the years in which Consuelo was growing up.

Willie and Anne were back in Paris that spring when he received word that Oliver Belmont had died of peritonitis after an operation to remove his appendix. Consuelo Marlborough was sailing for America to fetch his bereaved widow and bring her over to stay with her in London.

The Belmonts had been an arrogant, disliked couple. Ollie had spent two undistinguished years in the United States Congress, during which his chief objective seemed to have been to irritate his highly regarded family and their friends. Edith Wharton would never forgive his cruelty to his first wife, Sally Whitney Rives, who had been her good friend, nor could she countenance his lack of interest in the daughter of that first marriage, Natica, who herself had died earlier that year, of carbon monoxide poisoning when the gas lamp at her bedside blew out during the night.

∞

*O*n June 14, Willie and Anne Vanderbilt were in their box at the Long-champ racing course, in the Bois de Boulogne. She was dressed magnificently, as were all of the women in the boxes that stretched out on either side of them, for not only *tout* Paris but many of the figures familiar from the rotogravures in the London and New York newspapers were there to witness the running of the Grand Prix in the presence of M. Fallières, the president of France. From the starting post on, there was little doubt that Willie's Northeast would win, and when she streaked under the closing wire, all of their friends gathered around the Vanderbilts, almost bearing them triumphantly down to the winner's circle, falling away only when President Fallières made his way through the crowd to congratulate them.

At the next big race of the season, the President of the Republic stakes, Vanderbilt's beautifully formed bay colt Seasick II led the pack from the start of the mile, four and a half furlongs race. Willie was at the top of European racing. His Maintenon already had earned over a million francs in a spectacular career. By the end of 1909, the Vanderbilt colors would rank first among all of the French entrants, garnering $246,000 in stakes. With the lovely and gentle Anne at his side, it was surely among the happiest years of his life.

*A*nne Morgan had arrived two days before and gone directly to Versailles. In two weeks, she would be sailing high above Versailles, Rambouillet, and Chartres in a gas balloon, an experience she would later describe as "Beyond perfect!"

In July, Bessy and Anne embarked on an automobile journey that should have been another "beyond perfect" experience. Bessy kept an office in Berlin from which she had helped to launch Maugham's and Shaw's theatrical careers, and the world of the arts and theatre would be open to them. Pierpont Morgan was one of Kaiser Wilhelm's financial advisers, and his daughter and her friend would also be made welcome in the most aristocratic circles.

Less than twenty years earlier, Bismarck had established the world's first social security system in Germany, and with her newly born social conscience, Anne was interested in how it functioned as well as in the plight of the German workers. She sent ahead a request to view the working and living conditions of the proletariat, which, coming from a Morgan heiress, must have stunned German officialdom.

The Berlin in which Bessy and she arrived on July 12 was a city to rival Paris in the grandeur of its boulevards and official architecture, in the extravagant lifestyle of its upper classes, and in the adventurous nature of its artists, and to surpass the French capital in the quality of its music and theatre. Indeed, despite its despotic emperor, it was a city of such remarkable tolerance that a Dreyfus or Wilde case would have been unthinkable.

The next morning, a delegation from the city council arrived to escort Anne on a tour of the Municipal Labor Housing Development, model workmen's dwellings provided for the city's workers by its government. The flats were immaculate and the sanitation facilities faultless. Nothing like it existed in the United States, where the British and American Astors were still raking in fortunes from their tenements. Her special interest was the living standards of American workingwomen, which were universally wretched. Her investigation of this exemplary project started her thinking of ways to improve their fortune.

The next morning, the newspapers carried accounts of her arrival at the Adlon, adding that she was soon to come into a fortune of between $50,000,000 and $62,500,000. It was extraordinary how they had discovered those figures when she had no knowledge of them. She was both touched and amused by the first requests for aid from the city's charitable organizations. But that soon turned to irritation, when Bessy and she were besieged by telephone calls, telegrams, and express letters from representatives of hospitals, orphan asylums, institutions for the blind and disabled, churches, crank religions, and every form of beggar and begging institution in the country. The topper came when an assortment of aristocratic but indigent gentlemen encamped in the lobby with the sole objective of doing her the honor of offering their hands and titles in matrimony.

Peace and pleasure were at an end. They had planned to spend the better part of a week touring the city's theatres, galleries, and museums, but that was clearly impossible. They ordered the maids to pack their trunks and asked the chauffeur to see that they were placed in their large touring car. By mid-afternoon, they were on their way to Wiesbaden for the purgative waters that Anne's Berlin experience had made more necessary than ever.

*O*n July 27, Willie and Anne Vanderbilt, along with her two daughters and her younger son, Sam, took up residence at St. Louis de Poissy. Tayo Sands had preceded them to Normandy along with little Annie and her new six-week-old baby.

The next morning, George Sands was motoring down from Deauville to join them. The reckless young man took the wheel, not trusting his chauffeur to drive fast enough. Along roads never intended for automobiles—let alone speeding automobiles—he was barreling along at "the frightful speed of seventy-five miles an hour." He was crossing a small bridge just outside his stepfather's property when suddenly a tire burst. The car swerved off the road, hitting a tree and overturning into a ditch.

He died at nine the following morning. It was left to Anne to inform her daughter-in-law of the death. She could not help thinking of the death of the boy's father in another horrible accident, when his horse rolled over on him. It was so tragically ironic that after she had done all she could do to keep her sons from becoming horsemen, one of them should die behind the wheel of an automobile.

Henry Adams was particularly upset by the accident. George Winthrop and Tayo were attractive, pleasant enough young neighbors whose second child had been born in the flat below his only weeks before. His choler over the senselessness of the accident was not improved by receiving a telegram from Harry and Margaret White, on Friday, the thirty-first, reminding him that he was invited to come down that day to spend the weekend at Meridon, their country place. The funeral was scheduled for Saturday, and he thought it inconceivably insensitive of them to continue with their festivities. They had known the dead man since he was a child, even before his mother had married Margaret's brother, and he had grown up treated as a near relation of their own family.

He wired back that in view of the funeral, he took it for granted they were canceling their plans. Another wire came from the Whites that he was to come all the same. His final reply was he would rather not come until after the services. To Anne Vanderbilt's good friend Elizabeth Cameron he commented tartly: "It is a strong hint to an ambassadress, but I am old enough now to have my way, and I don't care to be left all day at Meridon while they come up to the funeral, nor do I want Mrs. Vanderbilt to think me a brute or White a block." At the end of his letter he turned the calamity into an extension of himself. "To me, everything seems lurid, as though I were poor young Sands, burning up under my buckled automobile, with my limbs torn off. Ugh! It makes me sick."

The unsentimental Mrs. Cameron had her own opinion of the calamity. "Aside from the shock and the horror of it, his death is really a benefit all around . . . he was a poor creature only, with much charm." She was sorry for his wife but her small stock of feeling was reserved for his mother. "Poor Anne! I think her life has had too many tragedies in it."

*A*t the beginning of 1908, Anne and Bessy, along with Daisy Harriman, boarded the *Congressional* on Monday morning. They were to have lunch at the White House on that day. It was Anne's second visit in less than a year and an indication of how far she had progressed in gaining an identity of her own, separate from that of being her father's daughter, in the vanguard of causes with which he had no sympathy. Indeed, it was an array of those causes that was bringing the women to the capital. They had been invited because President Theodore Roosevelt had expressed an interest in learning more about the Colony Club's involvement in social reform, which, knowing the families of its members, must have come as a surprise to him.

Daisy was seated at the president's right. The guest at his left talked about nothing but big-game hunting in Africa, while Daisy tried to steer the conversation around to the club's activities. No matter who was saying what, the president interrupted to tell what a terrible amount of wife-beating went on in America. At her expression of incredulity, he became emphatic: "It goes on in England, it goes on here. I tell you I would rather my sons did anything else in the world than beat their wives."

Although probably not below the salt, Bessy was seated at an unremarkable part of the table. She could not have been blamed for looking down the table at Teddy and regretting that she had not been more attentive instead of nodding off while he practiced his political speeches on her all those years before, when they were both young in Oyster Bay.

Anne Morgan was seated next to the president's military aide, Colonel Archie Butt, who did not know her identity, the name Morgan on a place card being such an anonymous one. She struck him as "a most marvelous person . . . a woman with a wonderful mind." He later asked the First Lady who she was. Edith Roosevelt laughed. "You don't know you took in the daughter of Mr. J. Pierpont Morgan?"

Of the thousand and one useful things in which she seemed to participate, there was one Anne singled out to describe. It was a program in which the Colony women were interested that would help poor white people in the rural South to get industrial educations. She was eager to interest Congress in the work. Butt pointed out that, more than legislators, it was money for such projects that was necessary. Anne was very much her rich father's daughter. She cut in: "Money is the least thing. We will raise the money if we can get help in other ways."

What impressed Butt most about her was the way "she simply blue pencilled conversation." She drew him out about his job at the White House and his interests, but if he said one word too many or got on a subject she did not wish to discuss, "she would promptly run her blue pencil through it" and bring him back to something of concern to her. Compelling even before he discovered who she was, this woman had taken an astonishing grip on his focus.

It was the first luncheon at the White House that I ever remember feeling indifferent to what the President might be saying to the others in general conversation. And there were a lot of interesting people there, too.

CHAPTER THIRTY-ONE

The five-year Line-A-Day diary given to Anne Morgan by her brother-in-law Herbert Satterlee for Christmas 1903 had run its course. The most momentous event recorded in it, albeit with great discretion, had been her falling in love with Elisabeth Marbury. It was fitting that her second diary should be a present from the co-star of the first.

> To Anne—
> Write deserve [sic] of thoughts on every page.
> > Elisabeth
> Jan., 1909

For all of the independence of her new Bessy Marbury–imbued spirit, Anne Morgan continued to live at home out of both love for her father and a desire to give her mother the semblance of domestic support. That she remained on her own terms rather than Pierpont's was made manifest when, on January 27, 1909, she held a meeting in his precious library with Samuel Price, delegate of the Cigar Packers Union, regarding labor conditions in the cigar factories. As a member of the women's division of the National Civic Federation, she needed to examine the sanitary conditions in the factories. The press was called in, and Price announced he was going to take Miss Morgan on a tour of the unhygienic factories.

Less than two months later, Anne was in Washington with Bessy, hosting a reception for female government employees, in conjunction with the New York and Washington women's sections of the NCF. It had been anticipated that she would give a speech, but at the last minute she demurred, contenting herself with personally meeting as many of the workers as she could. Although she would later do a great deal of public speaking, it was a trial for her at that point. Bessy had no such reticence and made a speech urging the women to be self-reliant and earn their own livelihood whether or not they were married. She would always avow marriage was the best state for a woman but did not believe economic dependence on a husband was the best condition in which to live in that state.

The women's division of the National Civic Federation made Anne Morgan the chairman of its investigation of the workplace conditions of government employees. She was shocked to discover that in most locations there were no cafeterias set up to offer cheap, good food to the workers. Instead, they had to leave their places of employment to buy inferior meals at high prices and often opted for stopping at a local saloon to drink their lunches. The practice was proving deleterious to both their health and finances, while the sloppy work done when they returned to the job was demonstrably wasteful for the government. Anne got the NCF's okay to open a pilot restaurant to prove to Washington the soundness of the idea of correcting the situation by providing hearty, inexpensive fare in on-site, attractive surroundings.

For a variety of reasons, the Brooklyn Navy Yard seemed an ideal venue for the project. An investigation of the yard had turned up a large, empty warehouse that would make an ideal restaurant. By the middle of March 1909, she was ready to announce the project to the press.

> Charity is not the object. The restaurant is only one of many things that should be introduced to improve the conditions surrounding government employees, but it is especially needed there at this time. What we hope to do by providing the restaurant in one of the buildings right in the yard is to prove to the government authorities that such a plan can be carried out on a self-paying basis. It will then be up to the government to take it off our hands and start branches in other departments of the service. The main thing is to show to the government that this whole thing is a business proposition; that it works out as such; that the men can do better work being better fed; that the whole proposition is practical "good business" and need not be approached in any emotional way whatsoever.

Although it would not open for business until noon on June 7, the Navy Yard Restaurant had an official dedication on the evening of June 3. An evening had been selected to allow the workmen to bring their wives and girlfriends to preview the handsome new lunchroom, complete with red-checked tablecloths. A crowd of six thousand workers and their women appeared to see this thing they had been hearing about, which was being promoted as *their* thing. They arrived early to find all of the best seats had been reserved for the society women on the committee, while they had to be contented with fanning out around the rear and sides of the room or standing in the window to look in from outside. The crowd grew restive, especially the women, who were beginning to feel that, as usual, their men were being had by a system that only wanted another excuse to pat its own back.

Their suspicions were borne out by the first speakers, Captain J. B. Murdock, commandant of the Navy Yard, and his superior, Rear Admiral Goodrich, who, in the tone of a benevolent despot, spoke of what a fine thing the navy was permitting these good ladies to do for their civilian employees. By the time Murdock introduced Chairwoman Alexander, of the women's division of the NCF, the speakers could not be heard above the jeers, and hisses, and rude retorts coming from what had become an unruly mob.

Sitting in the front row, Anne Morgan felt the project sliding toward failure. The press was there, and the newspaper accounts of the evening would be disastrous. Something had to be done. She quietly signaled to Mrs. Alexander to introduce her as a last, desperate effort to save the evening.

There was a silence as curiosity about Pierpont's daughter momentarily overtook hostility. They saw a tall, handsome, husky woman, more athletic than fat, wearing a simple russet dress and becoming flower-trimmed hat. She strode with seeming confidence to the center of the speaker's platform and turned to face her audience. There were whistles and catcalls from outside the windows, and a great buzz of conversation from those standing in the back of the room. It was an era before amplification, and conquering her fear of public speaking, she began "in a loud, clear, determined voice" that rose above the din and "could be heard everywhere in the hall."

Her opening remarks were not patronizing nor were they angry. There was only authority as she spoke of the volunteers who had worked so hard to make a reality of the restaurant. "I want to say a few words for these women."

The jeers gave way to a murmur that softened to a whisper before dying, as she continued in silence. She explained that the navy was in no way responsible for the running of the restaurant. It had been taken up by the committee women "independently and enthusiastically because of the feeling that it would fill a great need."

She spoke to them as equals, laying out the situation as she might were she explaining it to a powerful board of directors.

> If we bring out the best, each is sure to take away a better understanding of the other's point of view, and that means brother-

*L*adies and Not-So-Gentle Women

hood. We must make it a central interest. We must prove to Washington that it can succeed on these lines. Then other restaurants and like improvements will follow, not in navy yards only, but wherever the government is a large employer.

From this beginning, better conditions now obtain for your children and for those who follow. Finally from this beginning, it may come about and it should—we all live and believe in our government, and some don't require suffrage to make us proud to be American citizens—that the government takes the place of the model employer to the country at large.

A call for big government from the daughter of J. Pierpont Morgan! She concluded, and then she smiled at the audience. *The New York Times* reported that as she left the stage, "the storm—a roar of cheers from without and within—began. It continued until she had taken her seat. . . . She had completely turned the audience."

*A*ll three nymphets were in Versailles, on the evening of July 18, to give the grandest party of their careers as hostesses. The guest of honor was the Duke of Sparta, the future King Constantine I of Greece. Elsie recalled "'Tino,' as we who loved him always called him." Tino had good reason to be out of Greece that summer. After having failed in a disastrous attempt to wrest Crete from the Turks, he was extremely unpopular at home, and the fawning of Paris society must have been tonic to him.

All of the arrangements for the party were made by Count Boni de Castellane, who proved "a perfect *metteur en scène*." Boni was very much in evidence that summer and the next. After the former Anna Gould divorced him to marry his cousin the Duke of Talleyrand, he desperately needed a new heiress to replace the one he lost and had begun again to court Anne Morgan.

The hostesses viewed his handiwork before the guests arrived. "It was a perfect night with a golden moon and a singing silence in the air." Boni had created the illusion of a garden in fragrant bloom with thick ropes of enormous cabbage roses looping from tree to tree. Small tables were set on the lawn for dinner, each placed on its own square of rose-colored carpet.

Once the guests arrived, the perfect silence was pierced by hunting calls played by the Corps de Chasse, which had been placed unseen, like ghosts from some bygone day, in the forest of Versailles by special permission from their friend Pierre de Nolhac, who had been made curator of the great château. The "Prince of Aesthetes," Robert de Montesquiou, and Marcel

Proust were among the select group in attendance. It was at such fetes, on such evenings—so magical one could sense decadence in the heart of their perfection—that Proust secretly observed Robert as if posed in an ideal setting for his portrait of him, as Baron de Charlus in *Remembrance of Things Past*. As he was departing at the end of the festivities, dear Tino gushed: "I have spent an evening in fairyland."

Boni was the most persistent of the "pretenders" to Anne Morgan's hand, but he was far from the only one. At the party she had been besieged by "a regiment of suitors." Even in the relative seclusion of Versailles, it was not unlike what had occurred at the Hotel Adlon. The moment the news was out that she was "in residence," every broke and broken-down nobleman who could make his way to Paris by any means was there exhausting all their mutual friends with efforts to secure an invitation to Villa Trianon.

On one occasion, Boni's ex-niece Marjorie Gould was staying with them in Versailles. The word that Morgan and Gould heiresses were both under one roof quite overcame the Duc de Leuchtenburg and his son, Grand Duc Alexandre. While his father pursued Anne, Alex went after Marjorie. Anne laughed at their ardent antics. "If my engagement to 'Papa' were to be announced, and Marjorie's to 'Sonny' . . . I can visualize the headlines now—'Two great American fortunes united by marriage!'"

At the beginning of August, Edgar de Wolfe sent word to Elsie from San Franciso that their mother had died. There was no way she could get from Paris to California in time for the funeral and, for her, really no point in going at all. There was no estate to be settled: her brother and she had been supporting Georgiana for years. If there was any remorse, she would find what cosseting she needed in the ample bosom of her real family, Bessy, and was better off where she was. All knowledge of the true facts of her past were in the grave with her mother, and she was at last free to recreate herself completely, with no fear of contradiction, in the image she had been cultivating since she first saw the Villa Trianon.

Elsie always became the places in which she lived. In the Irving Place house she tried to transform herself into a nineteenth-century belle of old New York. In the Villa Trianon her aim was to be a part of the Bourbon court. How well she succeeded, as well as a sense of sweet melancholy induced by her mother's death, was projected in a letter Berenson wrote to Isabella Gardner after a stay in the latter part of August.

> Did I write you from Versailles? I must have. I went there for a
> quiet ten days with Elsie and Bessie, and the death of Elsie's

mother turned it into a charming solitude. I strolled about a great deal under the elms in the park, read, dozed and really rested. We talked of you often and often Elsie and I [sic]. She is such a perfect reincarnation of the early 18th century that to one, who like me, revels in completeness of character, she is a constant joy.

When Berenson left Versailles, Bessy and Anne also departed for the drive down to what was to become their favorite spa, Brides-les-Bains, in Savoie, not too far from where the borders of France, Italy, and Switzerland come together. Shortly after they arrived, Bessy received a telegram from Eugène Gauthier, a young Frenchman who had been spending the summer motoring around Europe with Clyde Fitch. It was a terse message relating that Clyde was at the Hôtel de la Haute Mère de Dieu, in Châlons-sur-Marne, where it was recommended that he undergo an immediate appendectomy. The pain must have been unbearable, if he could not hold out three hours longer to get to Paris and was submitting to treatment at a provincial French hospital. Telegrams were exchanged daily until a final one a week later informed her of his death. When she arrived in Chalons on Sunday morning, Gauthier filled in the details.

Whatever the true nature of her Catholicism, it asserted itself in times of pain. Bessy was consoled that he was nursed by the Sisters of the Order of St. Joseph. In lieu of his mother, who would not be able to get there for another week, she took charge of the remains of her Protestant client. The little Catholic mortuary chapel adjoining the hospital was completely lined with flowers with Clyde's bier in the center illuminated, night and day, by candles. Bessy was quite overcome by her stage management of the period before Mrs. Fitch arrived to claim her son's body and take it back home for burial.

> The sisters with gentle voices sat one on either side of the body reciting the prayers for the dead. I could not but feel that this atmosphere of beauty and of peace would have been Fitch's own selection.

On October 13, Bessy and Anne sailed for home aboard the *Kaiser Wilhelm II*. Anne was not a good sailor, and it was an exceedingly rough crossing with gale-force winds and high swells all the way to New York. It was prophetic of the political and social storms into which she would sail before the year was out.

CHAPTER THIRTY-TWO ᴈᴑ

On November 24, 1909, two days before Thanksgiving, twenty thousand workers walked off their jobs in the city's shirtwaist factories. What set this apart from other strikes was that, with no more than five hundred men involved, the vast majority of the workers were Jewish women and girls, between the ages of fifteen and twenty-five, who were either immigrants or the daughters of immigrants; the rest were Italian females of similar age and backgrounds. In this land to which they all had come, dreaming of Goshen only to awaken in a purgatory, to starve in squalid, overcrowded tenements, to be abused and badly paid for long hours of back-breaking labor, the holiday had as little meaning as it did to the daughters of Massasoit. It was a feast day of the *goyim:* the Astors, the Stuyvesants, the Goelets who owned the unspeakable hovels in which these women and their families froze in winter and roasted in summer.

The emergence of the great department stores, at the end of the nineteenth century, created a vast market for ready-made clothes. With its great port bringing in fabrics from Europe and its vast railroad hubs carrying manufactured goods to every part of the nation, New York City was the heart of that market. This, plus the large pool of cheap labor in its immigrant class, made it plausible that the "rag trade" should be centered there. By the time of the strike, it had become a fractious family business. The owners of the factories and sweatshops were the conservative, established elders of the patriarchal Hebrew faith, while its labor force was composed of its rebellious sons and daughters, the socialists, often also Zionists, who gave birth to the first organized American Jewish labor force, the International Ladies Garment Workers Union (ILGWU).

Most New Yorkers knew little and cared less about the internecine fracas between the garment manufacturers and the young union. If heads were being bashed, they were Jewish heads and of no consequence. So it probably would have remained had Local 25, of the ILGWU, not come into existence, and that would not have happened were it not for the modest shirtwaist.

Starting in the Nineties, when tucked into a nondescript dark skirt, the shirtwaist served as the uniform of the New Woman, worn by all of the women who had entered the workforce with the exception of the poor wretches who made it. It was also worn by both faculty and students in the proliferating women's colleges as well as by the young female athletes in their sporting endeavors—golfing, archery, sailing, or tennis (table or court). With or without a fetching straw boater, it was often the garb of the idealized young American beauty, the Gibson Girl, as conceived in pen and ink by Charles Dana Gibson for the pages of the nation's most popular weeklies. The unperceived paradox was that the manufacture of this symbol of the recently emancipated middle-class American girl became the instrument of the near enslavement of the poverty-level American girl, "new" only in the sense of the length of time she had been in this country.

A work week of sixty hours was not exceptional for these immigrants often still in their adolescence. Even when things were slow, they were at their machines from 6 A.M. to 6 P.M. daily and half-days on Saturdays. The bosses also charged the women for the use of the machines, chairs, needles, thread, and even the lockers in which they stored their meager belongings.

The abuses were so flagrant that by 1906, they could no longer be endured, and thirteen shirtwaist workers, seven female and six male, formed Local 25, the Ladies Waistmakers Union, of the ILGWU. Three years later, there were only one hundred members in the local, which had four dollars in its treasury. There were many reasons for this lack of response in the face of such exploitation. Primarily, it was a small industry whose workers were overwhelmingly female, and union leaders, as chauvinistic as the bosses, did not take women seriously. They did not believe they belonged in factories, let alone unions, except on picket lines, where they could be used to garner public sympathy while simultaneously shielding the men and taking the brunt of the blows from billy clubs wielded by industry thugs and police alike.

The shirtwaist manufacturers were among those most severely hit by the recession of 1908–1909. They were forced to let go many of their workers, while those they kept had their wages drastically reduced and were expected to work longer and harder than ever before. Protests, in the form of scattered walkouts and picketing of individual companies, continued through the autumn of 1909. The unrest, spreading through the industry, brought thousands of new recruits to Local 25. Supporting as well as contributing funds to the unionizing effort was the Women's Trade Union League, which had been founded by a combination of upper-class bluestockings, led by Jane Addams, and a group of the first of the women labor organizers, led by Rose Schneiderman. Its purpose was to encourage women workers to join unions and male union leaders to organize them. To this end, it enlisted in its ranks the few recognized women labor leaders in the country, among them Schneiderman, a Russian-Jewish immigrant and organizer for the ILGWU, who would sardonically refer to her new associates as "the mink brigade."

If one single incident can be said to have led to the general strike, it was what occurred at the Triangle Shirtwaist Company. The membership of Local 25 grew impressively when workers joined out of indignation at the treatment of some of the girls who already had gone on strike at some of the individual companies. The Triangle management learned that 150 of its workers were union members. They were singled out and told there was no more work for them. According to Alice Henry of the WTUL: "The girls took their discharge without suspicion, but next morning they saw, in the newspapers, advertisements of the company asking for shirt-waist operators at once. Their eyes opened by this, the girls picketed the shop."

What happened next was uniformly the same at every strike site. The companies employed local gorillas to rough up the strikers and clear paths for the scabs to enter the factory. Local prostitutes were then called in to provoke the picketers. These were women of the same class as the workers who seemed to resent them for being able to earn their livelihoods in ways other than their own. When a sufficiently large disturbance was created, the police appeared out of nowhere to haul the picketers off to magistrate's court, where they were charged with disturbing the peace and disorderly conduct. The workers at the Triangle were enraged and 500 shirtwaist strikers came to picket with them. At the nearby Leiserson factory 98 women picketers were arrested and fined. These two companies were located in buildings adjacent to the graduate school of New York University on the east side of Washington Square.

Disturbances at factories farther east and south were easier to ignore than one in Greenwich Village, a neighborhood in flux. In the Village, in a way unique to Manhattan, out of all the world's major metropolitan areas, groups of great cultural diversity tumbled over one another. There was so little space that neighborhoods were constantly fought over and recycled. Socially enlightened graduate students were the workers' immediate neighbors. Stanford White's Washington Square Memorial Arch was one of the city's big tourist attractions. Many members of pre-Vanderbilt old New York society still lived in their handsome Greek Revival townhouses along the north side of the Square and up lower Fifth Avenue. Artists and radicals were moving into the low-rent picturesque older buildings in the West Village. Any number of members of these groups would pass the shirtwaist factories at least once a day on their way to the new Interboro Rapid Transit subway station, or to worship at the elegant Grace Church, or to shop at Wanamaker's department store, which had taken over Stewart's store stretching along Broadway from Ninth to Tenth Street.

The neighborhood was a vibrant one. Thugs and policemen, mauling helpless young women picketers, would not go unnoticed or unprotested by its inhabitants with their connections both to the media and to the city's powerbrokers. It was the situation for which the Women's Trade Union League had been searching, one into which it could insert itself and make a difference. Once the women of Local 25 started picketing in the early autumn, a group of WTUL volunteers came downtown to bear witness, hoping their august presence would deter violence. Instead, they contributed to it by being unable to resist the thrill of hurling their well-upholstered selves into the front line of pickets. The "mink brigade" was thrilled when two of their number were arrested and made the front pages, for the incident fulfilled the goal of creating a sympathetic press. When challenged by members of their own class to explain why they were bothering with these disorderly wretches, the explanations of the well-shod bluestocking executives of the WTUL were sincere, indeed heartfelt, but they had no idea of the Lady Bountiful condescension implicit in them. Joining a union, they averred, would lead to the "Americanization" of these girls. In union they would have power and soon become "assimilated citizens." For their part, the exploited young workingwomen only wanted economic parity—an honest day's pay for an honest day's work in conditions that allowed them some dignity.

The headlines made by their wealthy supporters were necessary if the strike was to be a success, but the real heroines were the young women of Local 25—adolescents such as Clara Lemlich, who at sixteen was a skilled veteran of the sewing machine earning $15 a week, and willing to risk losing everything because her wages were blood money so long as so many of her sisters were only earning $3 or $4 a week.

When things became intolerable for its members, and Local 25 had to ponder the perilous option of calling a general strike, more than publicity or a superficial feeling of oneness, the most important thing the mink brigade had to offer was money. With funds provided by the brigade, the local was able to call a meeting of workers at Cooper Union on November 22. Thousands came spilling out of the auditorium into all of the rooms adjacent to it. The distinguished speakers followed one upon the other: Samuel Gompers, head of the American Federation of Labor; Mary Dreier, president of the WTUL; Meyer London and Jacob Panken, the leading Jewish socialists of the day; representatives of the ILGWU and Local 25. They backpedaled, procrastinated, vacillated, hemmed and hawed, without actually saying anything until, from out of the heart of the throng, young Clara Lemlich raced up to the platform. In a deceptively girlish voice, she loosed a stream of molten Yiddish.

I am a working girl, one of those striking against intolerable conditions. I am tired of listening to speakers who talk in generalities.

What we are here for is to decide whether or not to strike. I offer a resolution that a general strike be declared—now!

The hall ignited in the thunder of stamping feet, an unfurled flash of red handkerchiefs, a searing affirmation that must have shot up to engulf the quiet, sedate exhibition halls in the Hewitt sisters' museum at the top of Cooper Union.

On the day the strike was called, November 24, instead of the five thousand strikers anticipated by Local 25, there were twenty thousand. By the Monday after Thanksgiving Day, that number had increased to thirty thousand. Seldom had the city seen a strike of this magnitude and never before one carried out almost exclusively by women.

Women had taken their protests to the streets in the past—suffragettes, prohibitionists, abolitionists—but a majority of these had returned at the end of a day of marching to comfortable homes, hot meals, warm beds, and servants to lay out fresh clothes for the next day. They might lose their battles and wound their pride but none would have to give up their accustomed prerogatives. Clara, and the other women of Local 25, could lose everything—the jobs and meager salaries that helped to feed their families, the rent money for the miserable roofs over their heads, new warm clothes for the coming winter, kerosene for the lamps that held back the darkness, wood for the stoves on which they cooked and from which they derived insufficient heat. Every slight material comfort and—if things got uglier— their lives. Certainly, physical violation was a daily possibility. Never before and seldom since had women voluntarily given so much for a cause.

The WTUL was swift in enlisting personal friends in the upper reaches of American society. Anne Morgan, Bessy Marbury, and Alva Belmont were among those who joined with the workers almost immediately. The presence on the WTUL board of the daughter of the world's most powerful banker, and a woman who figuratively and literally married the Belmont and Vanderbilt fortunes, proved too much for the manufacturers, who cursed them as "uptown scum." From their point of view, of course, they were right to castigate these new enemies who were serving their public-relations purpose only too well. The press was impressed, indeed astonished, by this new sisterhood that crossed economic lines, and could not help contrasting it with "the aloofness of men of wealth when there is a strike in which only men are involved."

However, uptown ladies and downtown women were treated differently by those in authority. No gorillas ever mauled any of the socialites on the picket lines nor did the police dare to manhandle them. Once they were brought before the court, the magistrate would reprimand but never harshly. One was told, "It is women of your class, not the actual strikers, who have stirred up all this strife." With no more punishment than this rebuke, she was released.

Contrast that with the patriarchal tirade unleashed at one of the shirtwaist workers by Magistrate Olmstead: "You are on strike against God and Nature whose prime law it is that man shall earn his bread in the sweat of his brow." He then sentenced her to the notorious women's prison on Blackwell's Island.

Olmstead's statement actually worked in the strikers' favor when Bessy got to her client George Bernard Shaw for a comment. His response, so witty and eternally true, made newspapers all over the world then and merits repetition now: "Delightful. Medieval America always in the intimate personal confidence of the Almighty."

Anne Morgan was not interested in spreading the word about the strike among those already on the side of the strikers. As Bessy had carefully taught her: if you want to effect change, the important thing is to know where the power was and go to it. The women of the Colony Club were linked by family and intimate friendship to the most influential people in America. In this instance, their aggregate wealth was equally important. The expenses of bail, lawyers, some form of minimal aid for the strikers' families, made starting a strike almost as expensive as starting a small business. The club members were among the wealthiest women in the country, and if they could be convinced the cause was a just one, they would be very generous.

Together with Bessy and Mrs. Egerton L. Winthrop, Jr., Anne issued an invitation to the membership to be their guests on Wednesday afternoon, December 15, to hear representatives of the WTUL and the shirtwaist makers explain their side of the controversial strike. They selected the gymnasium for the meeting, which would be chaired by Mary Dreier, of the WTUL. To pass the plate, Anne enlisted Elsie, whose gift for separating money from the very rich was becoming legendary, and Rita Lydig, whose looks were so appealing that even women had trouble denying her anything. When John Singer Sargent painted her portrait, the artist described her as "art in its living form."

Daisy Harriman opened the meeting. She was careful to underscore that the club was a social organization and not taking sides in the strike, although many of the members did sympathize with the shirtwaist makers. She turned the meeting over to Mary Dreier, perhaps surprised to see the excellent turnout considering the conservative politics of the majority of the husbands and fathers of the members. The gym was packed with 150 of the most fashionable women in New York. Their first impression must have been of how young these working girls were—as young as their daughters, in some instances their granddaughters. They made shirtwaists, skirts, dresses for a living but were themselves threadbare even when dressed in their best, as they were on this occasion. But when they began to speak, the small, sheltered world of the uptown women opened to encompass vistas of the unimaginable. One after another, they rose and described conditions that were Dickensian, only they were not happening to stalwart Nicholas Nickleby, or Pip, or Oliver Twist, or David Copperfield, but to undernourished girls, little more than wraiths. And this was not in Victorian England but daily occurrences in their modern, smug New York City, in some cases only a mile away from where they were seated.

Rose Schneiderman rose to speak. Her hair pulled back in a severe bun, neatly attired in one of the shirtwaists that had started the controversy, she had risen in the ranks from factory worker to WTUL union organizer and considered herself the equal of any of the women in her audience. She had been investigating many of the shops and told the audience that if they saw where some of the wedding dresses in the smart stores were made, they would not want their daughters to wear them.

> In many places, the girls are known by numbers. Two girls will work side by side for weeks without knowing each other's names. Italians will be placed by the side of Jews, and race antagonism worked on to keep the girls at daggers' points, so that there will be created a distinct feeling against any sort of organization and fellow-feeling. A good many girls in this fight have come to know each other's names and to know a sisterly feeling for the first time in their lives.

Moved by her own feeling of sisterhood, Mrs. Archibald Alexander rose and asked Mary Dreier what was most needed.

The reply was, "Money to fight with."

Mrs. Alexander nodded. "I hope I may have the honor of beginning the collection." Elsie and Rita passed the hat. The sum collected amounted to a little more than $1,300, which was less than $100 a head. It was paltry when compared to the aggregate wealth of the ladies assembled. A point may be made for the Colony women vis-à-vis the size of their contributions. Most did not have personal checking accounts. The paying of bills and charitable contributions, even to their own pet causes, was generally made by their husbands and fathers, and helping unionism was not something for which they were likely to open their wallets. Even the widows and great heiresses had trustees, banks, or lawyers to write their checks. Such matters were considered too sordid for ladies to handle. What they gave was what was in their reticules at that moment. Many made larger donations later on.

The blue laws of New York City being what they were, the only places of entertainment permitted to have Sunday performances were the Yiddish theatres in the Lower East Side. Carnegie Hall would perforce be dark on the first Sunday of the new year, January 2, 1910. As a union rally would not constitute entertainment and would be exempt from the law, the Women's Trade Union League persuaded the Hall's management to donate the premises to the cause of the shirtwaist strikers.

One of the first things Anne, Bessy, and Elsie saw upon entering the hall was a large sign tacked to the speaker's platform: "The workhouse is no answer to the demand for justice." Another placard proclaimed: "Peaceful picketing is the right of every worker." It was a protest against the harsh, allegedly illegal treatment of the striking women by the city's law-and-order establishment. One box in the first tier was significantly unadorned by the bunting and banners that festooned the Hall. It was reserved for the magistrates who had been meting out such cruel punishments, and who had been invited to participate. The box would remain empty for the entire evening.

The audience that filled the Hall was predominantly female and was enthusiastically described as "an uprising of women." They came from almost every stratum of society in which females played, or were beginning to play, significant roles: Fifth Avenue matrons, office workers, professional women, artists, teachers, and college students, as well as the shirtwaist girls. The WTUL's Leonora O'Reilly declared that the strike had done more to make people of all classes recognize their kinship than the preaching of all the churches and ethical schools had done in years.

That night a number of reputable citizens made stirring, often eloquent speeches condemning police brutality, the harsh and unjustified sentences imposed by the magistrates, and the illegal actions of the members of the law-and-order establishment. But ultimately the strikers said all that need be said without uttering a word. The stage was massed to overfilling with almost four hundred very young, often wraithlike, shabbily dressed women. Their blazing eyes branded the city and nation beyond with their moral judgment. They wore banners across their breasts in the frivolous manner of girls entered in beauty contests, but printed on them were the one-word recriminations hurled at those who had assaulted them in the name of justice. ARRESTED, printed in large black letters, was on a majority of them, while twenty in the front row wore the word WORKHOUSE. Those youthful faces, bearing witness in those words, eloquently delivered the message, but it did not silence those who would use their strike as a vehicle for other agendas.

Although Anne Morgan concurred with the moral indignation of the more humane orators and was tremendously moved by the girls, when the socialists got up to use the strike as an excuse to call for the dissolution of the entire American system, she became more than a little piqued. *The New York Times* called the next day to ask her opinion of the meeting, and she was her usual forthright self.

> I am heartily in favor of the strikers and think they have been very badly treated by the courts. . . . It is necessary to appeal to reason and sound judgment, but it was dangerous to allow the socialistic appeal to emotionalism, and it is reprehensible for the socialists to take advantage of this time to preach their fanatical doctrines.

Delighted to have incensed J. P. Morgan's daughter, the Socialist party responded that far from having gone too far, the meeting had not gone far enough. The WTUL had larger problems than Anne Morgan's peeve. There were signs the strikers were beginning to lose the moral high ground. By the beginning of the new year, the ILGWU had come to an agreement with the manufacturers in which they agreed to reduce the workweek to fifty-two hours, provide the needles, thread, and sewing machines, hire back the strikers, institute a few paid holidays, not discriminate against union members, and arbitrate any differences but only with the workers they employed. The girls turned down the terms the union had accepted, claiming that without outside arbitration and a union shop, there would be no way to enforce the concessions, and it would not be long before they were back where they started from. All their sacrifices would have been for nothing. Public sympathy began to turn against them. The subtleties of union or nonunion shop were lost on most people. Who did these immigrant kikes and dagos think they were? Immigrants with no right to be complaining about American justice, who should be grateful to have been taken in by this great country—that was who they were. Besides, weren't they just girls only working until they could find husbands to take care of them? If they were starving, and their bosses offered half a loaf, they should take it and be done with it.

There were also signs that women of Anne and Alva's class were beginning to be a public-relations liability to the WTUL cause. *The New York Times* printed a letter to the editor dated the day of the rally. The writer

*L*adies and Not-So-Gentle Women

mentioned having seen Miss Morgan quoted as saying the shirtwaist strike was the beginning of the struggle workingwomen would have to endure "to put unionism on firm ground."

> I would like to know if either Miss Morgan or Mrs. Belmont would take such an interest in . . . a strike of the female domestics they employ. . . . As charity begins at home, a good New Year's resolution would be to see if the girls who work for the rich . . . had as good times, wages, and conditions, as the strikers whom the society dames are putting up funds for. Of course, we should not see such big headlines in the papers if it was only "Mrs. ———— raises her domestic help's wages $5 a month: they are now getting six cents an hour" or "Mrs. ———— has given her girls in the house a whole day to themselves every month." But their help would work for them much more cheerfully.

The letter was signed A WORKINGMAN, but judging by the syntax and glossing-over of the strikers' conditions and demands, it was undoubtedly written by a representative of the manufacturers who wanted to reflect unfavorably on the enemy. Nevertheless, there was enough truth in what was described in it to make several of the "society dames" feel a bit uncomfortable in the role of strike enthusiasts.

A second letter to the editor followed within two days that painted a still more devastating portrait of the life of a servant in a great house. It included allusions to women who kept their help in bondage merely by refusing to write the necessary letters of recommendation should they want to leave before their employers were finished with them. The letter ended:

> I have had nine years experience as a private servant and am now out of service, thank goodness, and as long as I can earn enough to keep myself respectable, I will stay out of it. If some of those who are doing good work in public would try to help their own servants by a little appreciation and a kind word, it would be well repaid.

It was signed BELOW STAIRS and had a much truer ring to it than the first letter.

As the month wore on, more and more of the shirtwaist strikers were being forced to settle with the bosses for what little they could get. They had families to think of and could not continue to live on charity indefinitely. It was more important than ever that the role of women in the union movement seem as viable as it ever had been. When the WTUL lost Alva and several of the other society glory-seekers, it was essential to Anne that there be no confusion about her fidelity to the cause and the organization. She issued a statement to the press that her remarks on the behavior of the socialists at the Carnegie Hall rally in no way implied that she did not continue to endorse the methods of the WTUL. Not only did she fully approve of them, but she proposed the start of a campaign to unionize all women workers. She reiterated: "I am a member in good standing of the Women's Trade Union League."

The winter cold turned picket lines into physically numbing experiences. The strike gradually came to an end, with settlements reached with company after company, including the worst offenders. There were improvements in conditions and wages, but there was no guarantee that these changes would be permanent. Because they had not achieved their most important objectives—the union shop and the right to outside arbitration—it was said they had achieved nothing: the bosses were still in control. This was not true in either the more restricted or the broader sense. When the ILGWU went on strike the following year, they obtained both of those objectives. Some claimed that they won because this was a male-dominated strike, but that lost sight of what the women had accomplished. The losses their strike inflicted on the shirtwaist manufacturers had been so noteworthy that it was impossible to deny that many of the garment manufacturers settled rather than duplicate the experience.

On a much larger level, the women had proven themselves a force to be recognized. They could no longer be dismissed as temporary workers who labored in the factories as if at some waiting station between adolescence and marriage. The unions might try but would never again succeed in condescending to their female members, nor would the bosses carelessly be able to assume that they could be bullied into submission.

*I*t was not until almost fourteen months after the shirtwaist action was settled that its true culmination occurred with the inferno that was remembered long after the strike that preceded it was forgotten. Ironically, that climax transpired in the same place where the strike began: the Triangle Shirtwaist Company.

On Saturday, March 25, 1911, the clock struck 4 P.M., ending the workday at the Triangle. Nineteen-year-old Pauline Couio was still sitting at her machine. There was no rush. The door was still locked and would not be unlocked until they were all searched to make certain they had stolen nothing. While she fixed her hair, as was their custom at the end of the day, the male cutters started smoking. One of them carelessly tossed a lit match into a straw basket of scraps, and it instantly caught fire. Pauline saw the flames and raced for the door. There were over one hundred people screaming, and shouting, and banging at the metal door that would not give way even to the pressure of this mob.

> What the hell did they close the door for? What did they think we're going out with? What are we gonna do, steal a shirtwaist? Who the heck wanted a shirtwaist?

Of the 500 Triangle shirtwaist workers locked in the factory at the time the fire broke out, 147 women and girls perished. The Triangle tragedy elicited the sympathies of the entire city. Three days after the fire, the WTUL held a funeral procession for the seven victims who remained unidentified. One hundred thousand factory workers and professionals from all fields of endeavor walked in cadenced unison, while another 400,000 lined the streets. There were no hosannahs, no speeches, no marching bands, no banners—only the awful sound of those marching feet hitting the wet pavement.

At last there was a rallying point for those who had been struggling against great odds to get amendments to the labor laws and to those governing the safety conditions in factories. A committee on safety was formed with Henry L. Stimson, who was later secretary of war for both the Republican William Howard Taft and the Democratic Franklin Delano Roosevelt, as its president and an executive committee that included Henry Morgenthau, Sr., Mary Dreier, Bayard Cutting, Henry Moskowitz, and Anne Morgan. It recommended that the state appoint a commission to investigate the urgent need for more stringent fire prevention laws. In a more general sense, it sought ways to improve labor-management relations that would lead to a less fractious operation of the state's manufacturing base.

On Sunday afternoon, April 2, Anne Morgan rented the Metropolitan Opera House for a memorial for the slain that reflected her own brand of humanism. It was her conviction that true progress and healing would come out of a coming-together for an exchange of ideas by all the sympathetic members of all of the economic classes in the city.

The workers and their families up from the Lower East Side, many in mourning, began to file into the three balconies well before the appointed hour. For the uppermost gallery, they had to use a modest entrance on Fortieth Street and climb up five unadorned flights of iron stairs, but nevertheless the opera house's upper circles were filled by the time the well-dressed members of the power establishment took their places, some in their traditional Monday-night boxes in the diamond horseshoe, others in the second tier of boxes and on the orchestra floor. With the upper classes using the carriage entrance, on Thirty-ninth Street, the lower classes going in the gallery entrance, and those between probably using the main entrance on Broadway, at first glance it looked as if Anne's dream would be as difficult to achieve as integrated seating. But when the great red curtain swept open, the rows of chairs on the stage were filled with a mix of labor, business, social, and religious leaders.

The meeting did not coalesce until it was Rose Schneiderman's turn to speak. This slight, deceptively frail-looking creature, her hair neatly plaited and coiled into a large bun under her hat, tested the excellent acoustics of the opera house by speaking in a voice barely above a whisper. The audience, transfixed, strained forward not to miss a word.

> I would be a traitor to those burned bodies, if I were to come here to talk good fellowship. We have tried you good people of the public—and we have found you wanting.
>
> The old Inquisition had its rack, and its thumbscrews, and its instruments of torture with iron teeth. We know what these things are today: the iron teeth are our necessities, the thumbscrews are the high-powered and swift machinery close to which we must work, and the rack is here in the firetrap structures that will destroy us the minute they catch fire.
>
> This is not the first time girls have burned alive in this city. Every week, I must learn of the untimely death of one of my sister workers. Every year, thousands of us are maimed. The life of men and women is so cheap, and property is so sacred! There are so many of us for one job, it matters little if one hundred forty-odd are burned to death. . . .
>
> I can't talk fellowship to you who are gathered here. Too much blood has been spilled. I know from experience it is up to the working people to save themselves. And the only way is through a strong working class movement.

No applause broke her speech nor did any follow it. In a silence almost as moving as her words, Anne watched her—a small figure of incalculable stature—return to her seat near her own in the front stage row. She had welded all of her diverse listeners into one, and the purpose of the meeting was achieved. There were even resolutions passed to ringing endorsement from all parts of the auditorium.

When first asked to join the board of the WTUL, Anne had been extremely attracted to this woman with her unassailable belief in what she considered justice no matter how radical it might seem to others, and it was not long before she was referring to her as "my friend." Her scorching words that evening doubtless revealed that any deep relationship was impossible. Too much history, like a wild unfordable river, had coursed through both of their lives; and they stood, for all of their high regard for each other, on opposite shores.

CHAPTER THIRTY-THREE

By 1910, Elsie had accumulated enough capital and reputation as a decorator to experiment with earning profits by investment in herself. The despised rows of high-stooped brownstones, monotonously filling street after street of Manhattan, did offer the amenities of middle-class living while simultaneously solving the problem of providing a maximum number of private residences in a burgeoning island metropolis desperately short of space on which they could be erected. If only something could be done to make them more attractive! That would be her experiment. To conduct it, she purchased a narrow brownstone at 131 East Seventy-first Street and for the architectural renovations relied on Ogden Codman. As she put it: "Ogden . . . and I waved the divining-rod which brought its latent graces to the surface."

The primary exterior architectural change was to remove the ugly high stoop, replace its parlor-floor doors with a window, and move the front door to the center of the basement level, an innovation that Stanford White had been the first to dream up for his conversion of the Hewitt mansion almost a quarter-century earlier. What was new and attractive was Codman's creation of a courtyard in the front of the house in the space that had been occupied by the stoop and an adjacent tatty little garden.

It enabled him to open a gracious foyer in place of the narrow corridor through which one normally entered the living quarters of a brownstone. In place of steep stairways clinging to exterior walls, a spiral stairway in the center of the house wound its way from the basement floor to the attic. "With a very narrow balustrade, it was light and gay." The landings on each floor led into rooms front and rear and allowed them to take full advantage of its slight eighteen-foot width. The decorating would come later, after Ogden and Elsie had shopped the Paris markets for the furnishings and fabrics. Whenever they worked together, he would do the architectural designs, incorporating her suggestions, and then they would collaborate on the decor.

*I*t had become increasingly clear to Bessy and Elsie that they would have to move the following year, when the lease came up for renewal on the Irving Place house. It was no longer suitable to their new and elevated positions in the world. Where the neighborhood between Union Square and Gramercy Park had not become commercial, it had become a mix of dowdy and raffish.

The two women, both very shrewd about money, set out to find a house that was in the right neighborhood for the right price and on which the plans Codman already had drawn for Seventy-first Street could be superimposed at a great saving. They eventually found "a grimy, four-story high-stooped brownstone front" at 123 East Fifty-fifth Street. There was no rush on the new house. The lease would not begin until late autumn, and in the meantime Codman and Elsie could complete Seventy-first Street as well as start to work on a project still dearer to her heart.

Ever since Anne Morgan bought the property adjacent to the Villa Trianon, she had been postponing her dream of building a music pavilion on it. How perfect it would have been for the concert and dancing on the evening of their great party the previous summer! Codman agreed to help her with it during the coming season. It had to be classic eighteenth-century, and it had to be perfect, a far more perfect architectural example of the period than the château itself.

*I*nterviewers were beginning to describe fifty-four-year-old Bessy Marbury's age as "about the usual one of a successful young business woman." She was often depicted as "young" at an age when most of her contemporaries were grandmothers. In the private life shared with Elsie de Wolfe and Anne Morgan, she had become quite content to follow where once she led. It was only in her career that she insisted on dominating and remained peerless. David Gray summed up her position in the theatre in an article he wrote for the *Metropolitan* magazine:

> The three estates of the dramatic world are playwright, actor, and manager. The fourth is Miss Elizabeth [sic] Marbury. She is an institution without precedent, without a possible successor, self evolved, autogenerated. . . . She was the first American play broker, but that term falls conspicuously short of describing either

her or her usefulness. Her business is as broad as her sympathies, as far reaching as her interests, and as deep as her personality. She invented the maternal relation to the theater, and became the original incubator and breeder of dramatists.

On June 17, Anne arrived in Versailles, where Bessy was waiting, and, on the nineteenth, they celebrated Bessy's birthday. Berenson was sufficiently recovered to appear that week and maneuvered to have a dinner tête-à-tête with Anne, in Paris, on the evening of the twenty-sixth. Of great interest to him and the art world was her father's decision to remove to the United States the significant works of art that until then had been kept in his Princes Gate mansion, because the American government had decided to revoke its import duty of 20 percent of their declared value on all pieces of art over twenty years old. Britain's chancellor of the exchequer, David Lloyd George, simultaneously imposed a 10 percent death duty on all works of art housed in England at the time of the demise of the owner no matter what his nationality. The two changes in law made it a propitious time for Morgan to move his London collection, valued at over fifty million dollars, to New York.

Bessy and Anne were booked to return to New York on the *Oceanic,* one of the world's great passenger liners. Traveling aboard any White Star ship always offered the women an extra measure of attentiveness: the line was owned by Anne's father. He recently had announced plans to build the *Titanic* as a grander sister ship to the *Oceanic.* The design called for one hundred additional first-class cabins and unique athletic facilities, which might well have been suggested by his daughter. It was to have the first swimming pool ever placed on a ship as well as a gymnasium, a squash court, and a Turkish bath for the use of the first-class passengers. Anne's egalitarianism did not extend to her private pleasures, and though it began to sound as if the *Titanic* would be a seaworthy Colony Club, her father's underlying scheme was to offer any attractions that would make these two great liners so irresistible they would help him to crush Cunard's domination of the transatlantic passenger trade.

When they docked in New York, Anne became the first Morgan to test the new tariff laws. She had brought back a medieval cross she had purchased during a trip to Oberammergau that summer and listed it as a duty-free antique in her customs declaration. When she showed it to the customs inspector, he asked what made her think it was an antique. "Because it was made in the thirteenth century," she replied, with an hauteur that marked her as her father's daughter.

He persisted, "How do you know?"

"Well, I wasn't there, but I know it is an antique."

He would not relent and asked if she wanted to pay the duty or have it sent to the government appraiser. She dismissed him with a wave of her hand. "Do as you please."

The crucifix was confiscated for appraisal. It was the end of an increasingly irritating afternoon. While waiting for her luggage to come down, she had been assailed by a group of reporters who had received a wire service report that she was engaged to marry the Spanish pretender, Don Jaime de Bourbon. Elsie, Bessy, and she had met him through mutual friends in Paris. He invited them to visit Spain, but the plans for the trip to Oberammergau were already made. Anne had said she would be happy to consider a visit for the following summer. This was the extent of her intimacy with Don Jaime. These unending reports of imminent marriages were extremely irritating. She exclaimed: "What nonsense! It is absolutely hopeless for the newspapers to keep up this sort of thing. I am not engaged, and I don't intend to be. That ought to settle it."

*F*ew would contest the assertion that Bessy remained the most powerful woman in the American theatre. Her business was getting so large that she decided to take in some partners and expand the services she offered in another direction. The original American Play Company was formed with herself as president, her protégé Roi Cooper Megrue as secretary, and two bright young play brokers, Edgar and Archie Selwyn, as vice president and treasurer respectively.

She had known Edgar, the older and handsomer of the brothers, since he made his debut as an actor in William Gillette's *Secret Service,* and had handled his work when he turned to playwriting. A few years earlier, she had staked the younger Arch and Roi Cooper Megrue when they needed three hundred dollars to buy a concession at Coney Island's Dreamland amusement park, which, alas, did not make their fortunes. The boys would fare better in the future. By the time Bessy joined forces with the Selwyns, Megrue had been promoted from indispensable assistant to associate in the business with a position on her letterhead similar to Bright's on her London stationery, while Arch and Edgar were making a good thing of their play brokerage business. By combining the stock rights to the works of Bessy's writers with those controlled by the Selwyns, the American Play Company became the largest source of dramatic material in the country.

Her sharp business practices occasionally conflicted with her ideals, and when that happened business usually won, as in the case of writers selling their rights for a lump sum versus continuing to collect royalties on every production. Bessy had started her business on the lofty premise that writers must always own their work and collect their fair share on every single performance, but when Bessy became the buyer, she apparently had no problem with outright sales. She bought all the rights to a number of plays that had failed on Broadway, gambling on the possibility of a future life in stock and amateur productions. As a result, the American Play Company owned many of the plays it controlled. Film studios later would gobble up the motion picture rights to almost anything that ever had been staged, including an inordinate number of these flops. The motion picture sales made a small fortune for Bessy in which the writers did not participate. It was not one of her shining moments, but she could rationalize that she had risked her own money to provide a windfall for a number of writers who had dismissed their plays as having no future lives.

Before the year was out, Bessy arranged to move her headquarters out of Frohman's Empire Theatre Building. The American Play Company would be located two blocks up Broadway, in the Knickerbocker Theatre Building, and the Elisabeth Marbury Company would move around the corner, to 105 West Fortieth Street. The move was motivated by a combination of a need for more space for her expanding activities and a desire to put some distance between her first great patron and herself. Frohman continued to be one of the most active and powerful theatrical managements in the world, producing during 1910 alone nineteen plays on Broadway as well as a repertory of twelve new plays in London's Duke of York's Theatre, four more in other West End theatres, and numerous road companies on both sides of the Atlantic. As a preponderance of these plays were written by Bessy's clients, he remained her most lucrative customer. However, it was growing increasingly clear he would not remain the greatest power in the American theatre for much longer, thus it was incumbent upon her to dispel the notion that her first allegiance was to her old friend and benefactor by putting some distance between them.

The Shuberts were the future and a problem for Frohman. It was assumed along Broadway that Lee and J.J. would inherit Charles Frohman's position as the paramount theatre operator and producing entity in the country. For the brothers to topple the monarch of the Empire Theatre, they needed access to Bessy's goodwill, which would get them a crack at plays of a quality equal to those she sold to him. They were accordingly so sympathetic to projects she brought to them that they indicated that they might not be averse to partnership with her in their production. So congenial did Lee in particular seem that Bessy could be forgiven for naively speculating on the possibility of her replacing the deceased Sam, who had founded the business, as the third Shubert brother. The truth was that Lee was using her.

He did not even want J.J. to replace Sam, let alone Bessy. As far as he was concerned, there was only one Shubert brother: in the past, it was Sam, in the future, it would be Lee.

The Shuberts had gained control of seventy theatres in major cities across the country, including thirteen in New York City, and by the end of 1910, their appetite for material was so voracious that they were holding thirty-one manuscripts from Bessy's office for reading or consideration. Copies were rare and expensive items in those days before mechanical duplication, and Megrue spent much of his time trying to get them returned. On December 15, he wrote to the Shubert office manager listing ten manuscripts he wanted sent back and to Lee personally asking for two more.

*E*lsie and Codman finished the Seventy-first Street house on time. They were both such social gadflies that between them they knew everybody worth knowing and gave a reception on the premises for *tout* New York and, of course, the press. So successful was the completed work that without exception the guests at the reception "went away applauding," and the house was soon sold at "an encouraging profit."

Paul Chalfin, who worked on the house, had been one of Elsie's assistants for almost a year. An elegant dandy of exquisite temperament that fortunately was matched by his taste, he started his career in the arts impressively with an appointment to the post of curator of Chinese and Japanese art at the Boston Museum of Fine Arts while he was still in his twenties. Painting was his true love, and he left the museum after receiving a scholarship to study mural painting at the American Academy in Rome. When he found his work did not excite the interest he felt it merited, he claimed to have developed an allergy to oil paint and retired from the field. It was at that point he entered Elsie's employ, probably via a recommendation from Isabella Stewart Gardner. One of her early assignments for him, during the 1909–1910 winter, was to organize a series of lectures on art, decoration, and architecture for the ladies of the Colony Club.

*J*ames Deering had been vice president of the Deering Harvester Company, a company founded by his father. In August 1902, Pierpont Morgan had merged Deering with the McCormick Harvesting Machine Company to form the International Harvester Company and three smaller companies. The move rendered Deering both absurdly wealthy and ultimately unemployed, a combination that allowed him to keep homes in

Chicago, New York, and Paris, traveling among them with a personal complement of male servants including a valet, chief, butler, and chauffeur.

When Morgan finally succeeded in ousting the last of the Deerings and McCormicks from International Harvester, in 1910, James decided to build a winter home, Vizcaya, in the jungle bordering Biscayne Bay, in the Coconut Grove district of Miami. It would have to be comfortable—he was used to comfort—and unpretentious, for he was that anomaly: a man of punctilious tastes and few pretensions. Elsie had done work for him in both his Chicago and New York houses and had entertained him at the Villa Trianon. It was natural that he should turn to her for help on the contemplated new house. Elsie was not interested in working in some jungle for this overly fastidious old maid of a man and turned him over to Chalfin. This would prove one of her biggest errors.

The discreet Deering and the flamboyant Chalfin were a case of opposites attracting. That they became lovers was doubtful. There was never a doubt of Chalfin's homosexuality, but no evidence existed of either Deering's hetero- or homosexuality, with most of his friends and acquaintances tending to think of him as neuter.

The house became their child, and the child grew increasingly splendid as they spent years raiding Europe of furniture, artwork, and architectural set pieces. Much of what could not be spoken ran as an undercurrent through a letter Deering wrote to his decorator before Vizcaya was finished, in which he wondered at the fact that it had been five years since they first "hitched our horses together." He was grateful that "except for food, water and flirtation," Chalfin had given all of his "time and thought" to him.

Miamians like to describe Vizcaya as "a mini San Simeon," which is inaccurate. It is an estate on a much smaller scale but is of a gemlike perfection unequaled in Hearst's domain. Now a Miami–Dade County museum and one of the largest tourist attractions in the area, Vizcaya, with Chalfin's décor, so obviously influenced by Elsie's work, remains much as it was the day he set the last piece of furniture in place. It is a source of delight to the scores of people who visit each year. It is a monument to Chalfin's taste, but had Elsie so chosen, it could have been her enduring triumph.

CHAPTER THIRTY-FOUR

What was astonishing to all who, like Anne Vanderbilt, profited from its beneficence was how endless the Vanderbilt money seemed at the time, especially since nobody appeared to do anything to generate it. The family did little with this great fortune beyond gratifying their every whim. Old Commodore Vanderbilt had been talked into donating one million dollars to the founding of the Central University of Nashville, immediately renamed Vanderbilt University in the hope of eliciting more contributions from the family. His son, Anne's father-in-law, left $200,000 to the school, and that was it, until Anne convinced Willie to make a sizable donation.

Anne felt that it was also essential that something be done for a school in the city in which the fortune was made, and thought immediately of Columbia University, with which she had familial ties. Her cousin twice removed, Seth Low, had been its president, and her late father-in-law Lewis Morris Rutherfurd had been a trustee and the founder of the department of geodesy and practical astronomy. The acquiescent Willie was again generous. From the moment Anne married him, it had seemed to her that the family name should grace something at once more meaningful and less ostentatious than Fifth Avenue's Vanderbilt row, and she talked him into endowing the Vanderbilt Clinic, at Presbyterian Hospital, for the treatment of tuberculosis. It was named in honor of one husband but privately dedicated to the alleviation of the suffering endured by another, Lewis Rutherfurd, the great lost love of her life.

When the Vanderbilts returned to New York City in the autumn of 1908, Anne met with Dr. Henry L. Shively, the tuberculosis specialist at the clinic, to ask about the more pressing concerns of the needier of his clinic patients. Proper housing was near the top of the list. These poor people could not afford the sanitariums such as those in Switzerland that had made Lewy's ordeal so much easier for both of them to endure. The dark and dirty tenements, in which the city's poor were forced to live, contributed to the spread of the infection as well as hastening the death of those already afflicted.

Anne and Dr. Shively developed a plan that called for her to contribute one million dollars to acquire land on which to build a complex of four tenements, each six stories high, that would provide flats for impoverished families with one or more tubercular members. These tenements would be designed to bring as much light and air as possible into the lives of the ten-

Ladies and Not-So-Gentle-Women

ants. Anne announced that an auxiliary aim of the project was to demonstrate how civilized housing could be built for the poor and be profitable to the landlord. The editorial page of *The New York Times*, on February 26, observed that none could help but "approve of Mrs. Vanderbilt's undertaking as providing examples worthy of imitation when the good time comes for making every tenement house fit for human occupancy."

A site for the project was found, running from East Seventy-seventh Street to East Seventy-eighth, between Avenue A (now York Avenue) and Avenue B (the start of East End Avenue).

She selected Henry Atterbury Smith as architect for the project. He was a young man who thought of himself as a social engineer rather than an architect. The four buildings in the Shively Sanitary Tenements project (or East River Houses, as they were sometimes called) provided housing for 384 families in flats ranging from two to five rooms plus bath. The buildings were constructed around courtyards that provided every apartment with cross-ventilation. Decorative details and intricate ironwork related the buildings much more closely to middle-class housing than to tenements.

All of Smith's innovations were created in collusion with Shively and Anne and sprang from the specific needs of those afflicted with tuberculosis. Wrought-iron balconies ringing the buildings were designed to allow the tenant-patients to sleep outdoors in good weather, as they did in the sanitariums Anne knew so well from Lewy Rutherfurd's stays in them. The windows were triple-hung and allowed for more air and light than many of those in the far grander apartment houses of the era. It was observed that "the delicate handling of the forms made the complex a very special oasis in the city."

So felicitous was the design that the complex exists to this day, looking much as it did when it was first erected. Called the Cherokee Flats, in honor of Cherokee Place, the street that was cut through John Jay Park to give access to the very fashionable East End Avenue, the buildings function as a middle-class condominium in what has become an upscale neighborhood.

*D*espite Anne Vanderbilt's zeal to spend all of her time doing some good in the world, everything in her background kept her anchored to the role for which her world and class had started to prepare her on the day of her birth almost half a century earlier. She was an acknowledged, if reluctant, leader of society, crammed into Alva's shoes like some miscast, middle-aged Cinderella. At the same time, she was trying to be a responsible mother, but who, for all of her efforts to provide the best *for* her children, consistently failed to bring out whatever was the best *in* her children.

Anne Vanderbilt and her daughters had returned to New York on October 11, 1910, aboard the *Kronprintzen*. She could anticipate a schedule that included marrying off her remaining Sands son and arranging for the debut of her older Rutherfurd daughter as well as fulfilling the myriad obligations to New York society that came with being Mrs. William Kissam Vanderbilt. Clothes were her great weakness. She enjoyed ordering them in Paris every bit as much as Elsie had when she was the acknowledged clotheshorse of Broadway. Because of the exquisite taste that made her stand out as one of the best-dressed women in any room, Anne's attention to clothes did not go unnoticed and, in the eyes of some observers, seriously compromised her sincere dedication to helping others.

When the liner pulled into its New York berth on that afternoon, it took a customs inspector and appraiser five hours to examine the forty-five trunks that comprised her luggage. A duty of $11,000 was assessed on the gowns and hats that had been purchased that season. She was also carrying $200,000 worth of jewels but paid no duty on them, as they either had been purchased in the United States or on previous trips abroad. The apparel and adornments incurred criticism during a period when factory girls considered themselves fortunate to be earning $30 a month. What went unnoted by her critics was that within herself, she never confused her roles. The dazzling wardrobe was for society, but when she was at work with those in need of her help, her garb was so modest she often passed unrecognized.

Exactly a week later, on the afternoon of October 18, Anne was present at the marriage of her son, Samuel Stevens Sands, to Gertrude Sheldon in a quiet ceremony at the home of the bride. The bride was everything Anne Vanderbilt could have desired and, with objective appraisal, probably a good deal more than her son deserved. She made her approval known by her extravagant gifts to the girl, which included "some exceedingly fine diamonds."

Her son's best man was Ogden Livingston Mills, and during the reception Anne must have noticed how attracted he was to the lovely Margaret. She could only hope his interest would be sustained through her daughter's debut that winter and her subsequent "season." Not only was he a promising lawyer with political ambitions, whose grandfather Darius had made a great enough fortune in California banking to sustain those ambitions, but he came with truly breathtaking lineage. His mother was a Livingston, which was as good a name as old New York society could offer. Among his uncles were Henry Carnegie Phipps and Anne's old friend Ambassador Whitelaw Reid. Suddenly, the future of Anne's daughter was leaping much further forward than warranted by her intelligence.

Alva would undoubtedly have thought the coming-out party the second

Mrs. Vanderbilt gave for her daughter was chintzy by the standards she had set for the Fifth Avenue mansion she had built. Others had been thinking for some time that Anne's entertainment brought a measure of sane and discreet good taste to Alva's marble white elephant. For Margaret Rutherfurd's debut, the ornate dining and reception rooms were dressed in quiet Christmas green demurely festooned with holly berries. The enormous expanse had often accommodated more than triple the 160 guests Anne had invited. It was very much a family affair, which meant that it was as patrician an assemblage as could be gathered in New York, including all of the young Vanderbilts, Harrimans, Sandses, and Rutherfurds. Anne was pleased to note that Ogden Mills was still rushing Margaret, for when added to Sam's recent suitable marriage, it augured that things were beginning to progress in accord with her own ambitions for her children.

*A*nne Vanderbilt was far too retiring by nature to enjoy playing the role of great society hostess. She had to do her share of entertaining either because Willie expected it or to help to launch her children in society, but it was always in her own style, closer to the European way she had observed during her long residences in Paris and London than to the ormolu New York fashion of *the* Mrs. Astor and Alva after her.

In unparalleled programming, the Met was offering its audiences world premieres of operas by two major composers within a month of each other. Both men were in New York to supervise rehearsals and attend the openings of their works. Engelbert Humperdinck was there for *Königskinder,* and Giacomo Puccini for *The Girl of the Golden West,* based on a David Belasco play, adapted from a Bret Harte story, and starring Emmy Destinn and Enrico Caruso.

It provided Anne an opportunity to offer her preferred style of entertaining. She gave a dinner party in honor of Puccini and Humperdinck. Eleanor Robson Belmont (Mrs. August) was there and would for years after recall the special allure created by "an exceptional hostess." Among the other guests were Arturo Toscanini and Josef Hofmann, one of the greatest pianists of the day. Late in the evening, after most of the guests had departed, Eleanor recalled Hofmann going to the piano and playing, while Puccini and Humperdinck draped themselves over the instrument on either side of him.

> Like children entranced with a fairy story, the visiting composers begged for more and more, and we, the happy few, stayed on in a magic circle of enchantment far into the night.

*A*lfred Allan Lewis

The crying infant, swathed in tatters, had been left unattended at the top of the flight of stairs leading to the children's court in lower Manhattan. A decorously dressed lady passing by stopped to pick it up and, cooing gently to it, brought it into the courtroom to turn it over to the authorities who would know where and to whom it belonged. This same lady had been coming to the court regularly for several weeks, sometimes accompanied by other ladies of similarly inconspicuous mien. Her particular interest was in the cases of the girl prisoners, who frequently had been abused and often owed their arrest to the lack of proper guardianship and the unwholesome environment of the places in which they were forced to work. In contrast to Alva's well-publicized and overdressed appearances in court for her causes, Anne Vanderbilt typically turned up in this unpretentious guise, her identity known to only a few officials.

What especially appalled her was that while the boy prisoners could seek help from the Big Brothers organization, and there were Jewish and Catholic organizations looking into the cases of the girls of those faiths, there was no help offered to Protestant girls by any of the wealthy Episcopal, Presbyterian, or Baptist congregations. She made it her personal mission to find suitable employment for the older girls who had been working in degrading situations, and foster homes for the younger ones being reared by families unfit to care for them.

In its articles of incorporation, the stated objective of Big Sisters was

> to organize and direct a body of women of good will whose purpose shall be to interest themselves in the welfare and improvement of children, especially girls, brought before the children's courts of New York City and similar courts throughout the country, especially girls whose physical, mental, and moral development has been hindered and endangered because of bad environment and other societal conditions. Individually to take, and to secure others to take, individual friendly interest in such children and to provide methods and means whereby their physical, mental, and moral welfare shall be promoted and thus aid them in becoming good citizens.

It was the end of June, and Anne was back in Paris before the approved articles of incorporation were finally forwarded for her signature. After signing and returning them, she turned to the joyous business at hand—the announcement of the engagement of Margaret and Ogden. The story of the coming union of two young people of such social standing was, of course, picked up all over the United States and, with the Marlborough and Reid connections, across the British Isles.

Anne made a French country wedding for the young couple. It was on the cusp of autumn, September 29, 1911, at the Vanderbilt country estate in Normandy. At the end of the afternoon Anne was being congratulated on having given one of her most exquisite parties.

For her the social coup already had ceased to matter as much as it still did to the family and to many of her friends. There would soon be new friends, and the old ones she retained would be transformed. That September was the beginning of the real (versus chronological) end of the long, splendid nineteenth-century summer during which the marrying-off of offspring was among the most important events in the lives of women of her class.

CHAPTER THIRTY-FIVE

Anne Morgan's belief in a limitless world for women would never convert her to militant feminism, and some of her choices seemed, to put it kindly, capricious to those who espoused that cause. The Morgans, father and daughter, were far too complex for glib labeling by the politically correct. They considered their private behavior to be their business and would not condescend to explain themselves or each other to the press or public.

Eleanor Robson Belmont had known Anne Morgan for years, but it was their work in the NCF and shared interest in the plight of disadvantaged young women that made them friends. It was a measure of how sheltered they were that they could be shocked to discover how many of these women had never been out of the city—never had had a vacation. Their naive initial conclusion was it might have been logistics. Everything beyond the city limits was alien and frightening—a foreign country in which the women would again be greenhorns at the mercy of unscrupulous marauders. They did not know where to go or how to get there.

A committee was assembled to do the difficult legwork necessary to uncover boardinghouses in rural areas where the air was clean and there was room to stretch, respectable places run by respectable people who would provide clean accommodations and three square meals a day for a nominal price. After compiling a list, the real problem finally surfaced. "A . . . list of boarding houses was obviously of little use to the working girl without means with which to pay her railroad fare into the country or to pay board when she had reached there."

Morgan and Belmont conferred with their committee, together with a delegation of workingwomen, and came up with the idea of the Vacation Savings Fund. As had been the case with the Colony Club, Anne was elected treasurer. The mystique surrounding the Morgan name made it a position for which she was automatically assumed to be qualified, and it was given to her in a great many of her fund-raising endeavors.

The idea was a simple one. The workers would agree to put aside a small portion of their earnings each week. This would be deposited at stations near their jobs that would be opened by the fund and would offer interest on the deposits, functioning in the same way that banks did. Indeed, these would be the first banks or savings associations in history that were operated by and for women. It would take almost three quarters of a century before similar institutions were organized.

Programs were organized to help the women along. Among the first were "vacation evenings," get-togethers of the workers with the leisured women who wanted to help enable them to have their holidays. Each was pleasantly surprised by the intelligence of the other and by how much they had in common simply by being female. One unconscious note of chauvinism did surface. The workers were consistently termed "girls," while the members of the committee were invariably "women."

Though many of the workingwomen were trying to put money aside, their incomes were too low and the familial demands too great for them to succeed. During the evening parties, it was agreed a high priority had to be given to raising money that could be added to the fund to help them achieve their goals. It was an era of private dances given in the ballrooms of the great mansions that lined Fifth Avenue and of charity balls like the Christmas cotillions that introduced each year's crop of debutantes in the ornate ballroom of the new Ritz Carlton Hotel. The girls had never been to a ball and were wild about Anne's suggestion that they raise money by having one of their own.

Hiring the ballroom of the Ritz Carlton was, of course, a mad idea well beyond their means, but there was a large space available two blocks east of the Ritz, the Grand Central Palace, which was designed by the same architects, Warren and Wetmore. The general admission was fixed at twenty-five cents to keep it within the range of any girl and her escort who might want to attend. The ball was "a revelation" to Anne. The workingwomen took over most of the work, displaying "the truest qualities of leadership." A trace of maternalistic condescension occasionally crept into Anne's attitude, but it was balanced by her feeling that she, as a do-gooder, was equally rewarded.

> Personality of the most admirable sort continually crops up: the movement gives it outlet and educates the girls and those who would be helpful to them in like measure.

Bessy sailed for France at the end of April, and Anne followed as soon as her many projects allowed her to get away. Pierpont Morgan still resolutely refused to visit the Villa Trianon. As Bessy observed: "To acknowledge defeat was foreign to his temperament. He was always loyal to his mistakes."

During that summer of 1911, he was in Belfast to inspect progress on the construction of the *Titanic*. While there, he had approved the decor of his own suite, on deck B, which he intended to occupy during the ship's maiden voyage the following April.

On October 3, three weeks before she was to sail for home, Pierpont took Anne to lunch at the rue Lafitte flat of Sir John Murray Scott. Morgan inspected the sumptuous antique furnishings and artwork with open covetousness. What he saw was comparable to what was on exhibit in London's magnificent Wallace collection, for the same man had assembled both.

Those gathered around the table that afternoon quite literally provided an illustration of the moral hypocrisy of a man who would not visit Villa Trianon because Bessy Marbury allegedly had told his daughter about one of his mistresses. Playing hostess for Sir John was Lady Victoria Sackville and among the guests were her husband, Lionel, and her nineteen-year-old daughter, Vita. Victoria was Murray Scott's mistress, a privilege Morgan hoped soon to share with him. He was ardently courting her at the time he brought his daughter to meet her. Their relationship had begun earlier that year, after he bought Gainsborough's *Mrs. Linley and Her Brother* from Victoria's husband. Despite his obesity and age, Morgan remained a fascinating figure to women. Lady Sackville West was soon confiding to her diary that she was apprehensive about "what may follow from this great friendship." She admitted she could think of nothing else. "That man has such a marvelous personality and attraction for me."

Of the group, Anne was probably most fascinated by the beautiful Vita. The girl already had met Harold Nicolson, to whom she would be married within two years, but was, at that moment, the lover of Rosamond Grosvenor and would later have famous liaisons with Virginia Woolf and Violet Keppel Trefusis. The latter was the daughter of Edward VII's last mistress, the same Mrs. Keppel who once tried to set up the king with one of Morgan's mistresses, Maxine Elliott, and often came to visit at Villa Trianon. (She was also the great-aunt of the current heir to the throne's mistress, Camilla Parker-Bowles.) Virginia would immortalize Vita in what has been called literature's longest love letter, *Orlando*. All told, it was a luncheon worthy of note in Anne's Line-A-day.

Fanny's First Play opened in London on April 19, 1911, and provided Shaw with his first British commercial hit. Until then, it was the successful productions in the United States and Germany, set up by "rapacious Elisabeth Marbury," that furnished the income that allowed him to devote all of his time to writing plays. Bessy optioned it to Lee Shubert during his July visit to Paris for an advance of $1,500 against a straight 10 percent royalty. Shaw insisted that Harley Granville Barker, who had staged the British production, be hired as director. There was nothing Barker wanted to which Shaw would not have yielded. The writer lived on terms of a respectful but platonic affection with his wife and enjoyed epistolary head trips with several well-known actresses that rarely ventured below their waists, but the beautiful Harley Granville Barker was probably one of the great loves of his life but lacking Wilde's reckless courage and passion, he appeared to have done nothing about it.

Fanny's First Play was almost as great a hit in New York as it had been in London. It was as if this transatlantic success liberated Shaw from any obligation or loyalty he owed to Bessy for her past services. The first thing he did was transfer the collection of his British amateur fees to the Society of Authors on the pretext of setting an example for other dramatists. To his credit, he did attempt to get the Society to deal with her agency in the manner of her previous arrangement with the society of French writers. He told Golding Bright for transmission to her: "I am not taking this step because I am dissatisfied with Miss Marbury's services. . . . On the contrary, I think it highly probable for a year or so at any rate, the arrangement will be to my own disadvantage."

So long as she could keep him as a client for his new plays in England as well as all of his work in America and Europe, Bessy was not averse to giving up the British amateur rights, which, given Shaw's disposition, were probably more trouble than they were worth. It was his dismissal, some months later, of her services on the English productions of his new work that really must have rankled. He wrote: "If the manager does not wish to deal with me directly and approaches me through you, it must be understood that you are acting as his [representative] and not as mine. As I shall have to do all the work, it is only fair that he should pay all the commission. Anyhow I won't pay any."

Bessy remained his American agent, a position she held until after World War I when, repeating his earlier behavior in England, he felt that he was sufficiently well known in America to do his own negotiating although, knowing how thorough she was in such matters, he did allow her to retain control of the stock and amateur rights until 1925, when her company was unintentionally late in the remission of some fees that caused a problem with the IRS.

Miss Marbury remained the perfect lady even after his departure from her management. She would say no more than that there were those who could not tell "whether Shaw was being funny to please himself or funny to confuse others." Those who knew the truth of their relation heard the unspoken rebuke in her afterthought.

> However, this very query proved a good box office asset, so that there is always to be found an eager public for any play Bernard Shaw writes, no matter what he writes or how he writes it, and the early habit he acquired of indulging in a bank account has become chronic. He could not avoid his fate.

When Bessy and Elsie arrived in New York, they went directly to East Seventeenth Street to supervise the packing of their possessions in preparation for their departure from the house they had shared for twenty years.

> One morning we watched the furniture vans move off towards our new home on East Fifty-fifth Street. Turning the key in the lock, we turned our backs on what had been a tried and worthy friend.

By November 25, 1916, Elsie had finished refurbishing 123 East Fifty-fifth Street, and Anne was the first guest for dinner. The deliberate and formal opulence of the new residence—nouveau riche in good taste—contrasted sharply with the somewhat ramshackle warmth of Irving Place, which had always looked improvised despite Elsie's control of the placement of things. It dictated the style in which they lived there during those few years before the war changed everything. Gone were the informal Sunday afternoon parties with the invited guests augmented by the most unexpected people dropping in for no better reason than that it was the bachelorettes at home, which meant everybody would be having a wonderful time meeting people they never would have met anywhere else. Henceforth, it would be Elsie's formal lunches with place cards and everybody there having been expected, saying things that were equally expected. Bessy would sneak a few cronies off into the library for cigarettes and coffee, and conversation that was more substance than form though not undiluted by a little breezy repartee. On one occasion, her old friend Nellie Melba remarked it was one of the few households in which she was never asked to sing for them. Bessy, who loathed the opera, replied: "Nellie, we love you not because you are a prima donna but in spite of it."

The house at 123 East Fifty-fifth Street was torn down years ago and is often forgotten even by those who are aware of the special quality Elisabeth Marbury and Elsie de Wolfe brought to life in New York City. When they are remembered as a couple in articles and books, it is as they were during the years they spent in the misnomered Washington Irving house, which, except for a restaurant that has been installed in the basement, still stands, looking from the street much as it did when they were in residence.

CHAPTER THIRTY-SIX

The work of Elsie de Wolfe was largely responsible for interior decoration (she would have shuddered at the impertinence of the word *design*) having become a field liberated from categorization as an adjunct of architecture or antique and furniture dealing. What started with Elsie in America quickly spread to Europe, but her single greatest accomplishment was making interiors the first relatively big business dominated by women, one in which men other than architects did not play significant roles until after World War I.

It was only a matter of time before it occurred to somebody that the most famous decorator in the world should put her ideas down on paper. There had not been a successful book on decorating since the publication of the Edith Wharton and Ogden Codman collaboration, *The Decoration of Houses,* in 1897, and the possibility of besting Edith, whom she never had liked, was irresistible. Elsie signed a contract with the Century Company to produce a book to be entitled *The House in Good Taste,* with publication preceded by serialization in *Delineator,* a popular women's magazine of the period that from a literary perspective was a cut above its rivals. At one point it was edited by Theodore Dreiser, who published such unlikely "women's writers" as H. L. Mencken and Walter Lippmann, but put the monthly decorating features in the hands of a woman. They appeared with an accompanying box that read: "This department is conducted by Mrs. Ruby Ross Goodnow, who will gladly help you with your homemaking problems if you will make your questions very definite and enclose a self-addressed stamped envelope with your letter." Having neither the time nor talent to write the book, Elsie needed a ghost, and Mrs. Goodnow got the job. Her magazine series was printed under the arch title "Our Lady of the Decorations."

What Elsie definitely contributed was parts of a memoir as viewed from the vantage of the houses in which she lived. One of its earliest chapters was "The Old Washington Irving house," and one of its last, "Villa Trianon," with a stop along the way at "The Little House of Many Mirrors." The illustrations, all her work, indicated the decorative concepts also came from her; but, as is often the case in this sort of collaboration, the philosophy, structure, and point of view were the contribution of the ghostwriter. It was equally true that Ruby made a good thing of the connection as it was that Elsie was pleased with her work. Under her own name, she was encouraged to do "The Story of Elsie de Wolfe," for *Good Housekeeping,* and "The Villa Trianon," an illustrated two-part piece published in *Vogue,* in which once again the fact that she owned the place with Bessy, and they shared it with Anne, was treated unexceptionally. Ruby neither winked nor blinked at the precise nature of their relationship: it simply did not pertain.

*E*lsie's unspoken message was that while men still shaped the world in which we lived, it was women who shaped the style in which we lived in it. However, it was increasingly apparent this was not sufficient for many women, including Elsie herself, whose growing enthusiasm for the suffrage movement led to her announcement that she would participate in the movement's parade on May 4, 1912.

The parades had been annual late-spring events over the previous forty-three years, but this promised to be the mother of all suffrage parades, for who was better at creating a great public spectacle than the redoubtable Alva Belmont, who had become one of its sponsors? That Elsie chose that moment to go public with her advocacy of the cause was not disassociated with the exalted social positions of so many of the new suffragettes, including

Alva, Rita Lydig, Katherine Duer Mackay, and Daisy Harriman, but there was more to it than that. Better than any of them, Elsie knew of the discrimination that businesswomen faced in the areas of pay and promotion and the narrow scope of positions they were allowed to fill. It was a mystery to her why women like Anne Morgan, so committed to bettering the lot of women workers, could not see how helpful the vote would be to their cause.

The anomaly was that although Bessy and Anne were not pro-suffrage, they were deeply involved in the political side of government and had a far more practical view of how it might be manipulated to achieve their ends than either Elsie or Alva. Along with Ida Tarbell, who was also anti-suffrage, they were not so much averse to the vote as irritated by this essentially middle-class movement for insisting its personal agenda take precedence over the more pressing feminist issues of workplace safety and hygiene, equal pay for equal work, sexual battery, family support, child labor, and, above all, the needs of women of the helpless underclass, whose despair was such they would seldom exercise the franchise even if it was extended to them.

Anne defined her position on the subject.

> But I'm not an anti-suffragist. I'm not anything so foolish, so illogical. . . . I am simply not interested in suffrage. I believe there are many things more immediately necessary for women. You and I know that suffrage for women is as certain to come as that you and I are sitting here in this room. But I am more interested in making an effort to prepare women so that they may be able to use the suffrage properly when it comes. . . . Is it absolutely necessary that I should utter a lot of bromides? Of course, we all know that no woman is happy who does not work. Work is the greatest of human privileges.

To make her views palatable, she felt forced to retreat to the banal bromide Bessy so often used. Observing a woman's nature was essentially creative, she added a woman was happiest when that creative force was engaged in "a happy marriage, the making of a home, and the rearing of children." Then her life was "the fullest, the most splendid." When denied this "happiness," women must "express their creative powers in their work." And she reiterated what she believed was the fundamental truth for women: "The greatest happiness of life comes from work . . . from usefulness . . . from service."

May 4 was a glorious, unforgettable afternoon. Mostly clad in white festooned with yellow suffrage ribbons, ten thousand suffragettes marched up Fifth Avenue, thronged with both pro and con spectators, from Washington

Square to Fifty-seventh Street and then over to Carnegie Hall for a giant rally. Their ranks included a large male contingent—religious leaders like Rabbi Stephen Wise, socialites like Oswald G. Villard, and students from all of the Ivy League colleges.

In her memoir, written three decades later, Elsie described how her two friends and she had "any number of high arguments" over the advisability of her taking part in the suffrage parade, but "in spite of Elisabeth's protests," May 4 found her marching up Fifth Avenue side by side with Rita Lydig, carrying a "Votes For Women" banner. Elsie would naturally choose as her partner one of the most beautiful and fashionable women in New York society.

It made a grand tale she often told, but whether or not Rita was marching, *Elsie definitely was not!* She was on the high seas, having sailed two days earlier aboard the *France*. Her name was on the list of passengers provided by the Compagnie Genérale Transatlantique along with those of Anne and Bessy, Anne's mother, Mrs. J. P. Morgan, and her sister and brother-in-law, Mr. and Mrs. Herbert L. Satterlee. That she did not cancel at the last minute was verified by Anne's diary and a story that appeared in *The New York Times* on the day after the sailing. The reporter mentioned Anne, Elsie, and Bessy as being among the most prominent of the passengers aboard the ship.

The thrust of the *Times* story was on Anne, who, at that time of the great march, was the one dedicated feminist among them, no matter what her stand on suffrage. She promised to return to the States to fight hard for the minimum wage as the proper legislative cure for the practice of paying girls and women far less than men and boys were offered for the same work. She went on to condemn the terrible conditions in factories and workshops, which also had to be regulated by law so that the health and morality of the workers might be conserved.

The *France*'s May 2 sailing was the return crossing of its maiden voyage to New York. That April, another liner had been launched on its premiere transatlantic crossings, and the *France* had been overshadowed by the debut of its competitor, the *Titanic*, which had sailed within days of it. Owned by Pierpont Morgan's White Star Line, the *Titanic* was the world's largest and most luxurious ship. Elsie, Bessy, and the Morgan party were originally scheduled to sail on its maiden return two weeks earlier, on April 20. They considered themselves fortunate to secure space on the French ship, which had been booked out almost immediately after news was released that the *Titanic* had hit an iceberg and sunk only days after its much-heralded initial sailing from Southampton. What remains a mystery is why they did not book on Pierpont's other great liner, the *Olympic,* a sister ship of the *Titanic,* which was only a year older and due to sail from New York two days later, on the afternoon of the parade. It would have been a big vote of confidence to have the Morgan family aboard a White Star vessel so soon after the disaster and undoubtedly would have been picked up by the press. However, Anne had joined the *Titanic* Relief Committee and had been on the pier to meet the survivors when they arrived in New York.

Were it not for that rare combination of self-indulgence and an abhorrence of the hoi polloi that characterized Pierpont Morgan, the tragedy for his family might have been far greater than the loss of a heavily insured ship, matching that of the families of the 1,513 passengers who lost their lives in the disaster. When word got out that the financier would be on the maiden voyage of his great new liner, White Star was besieged by requests from an array of con men and Wall Street speculators, all wanting to book staterooms on the *Titanic* in the hope of cornering him at sea, where he had no escape, to badger him into financing their sure-to-make-millions schemes. He canceled his own booking, announcing he had no plans to return to the States until summer. At the same time, he fortuitously gave orders that his art collection, which was being shipped to New York, not be placed aboard.

He had another reason for not rushing home. Frustrated in his pursuit of Lady Sackville-West, the apparently insatiable old tycoon had found a new French mistress who was making him feel younger than the springtime of their dalliance. Word of the catastrophe reached him in Aix-les-Bains, where he was taking the waters in the company of that charming lady with whom he planned to celebrate his seventy-fifth birthday only two days later.

Bessy and Anne arrived at the Villa Trianon on May 9 and stayed only long enough to load up their limousine in preparation for departure the following day for a three-week tour of Spain. It was not until her return that Anne had an opportunity to see her father. He was deeply depressed by the sinking of the *Titanic,* as much because it was the end of his dream of a fleet of transatlantic liners that would rival Cunard as for the loss of life.

*O*ne of the great sadnesses of that summer was not having their good friend Henry Adams among the guests at the Villa Trianon. That spring, he had suffered a stroke while dining alone in his Washington home. They all had been looking forward to sailing together on the *Titanic,* and when it went down, Adams had been deeply saddened to find two friends among the passengers who had not survived: the painter Francis Millet, and Archie Butt, Roosevelt's aide who had been so impressed by Anne Morgan when Bessy and she lunched at the White House. The greatest maritime disaster of the century became entwined in Adams's mind with the moral and political disasters he saw all around him. He wrote to a friend:

The foundering of the Titanic . . . strikes at confidence in our mechanical success. By my blessed Virgin, it is awful! This Titanic blow shatters one's nerves. We can't grapple it. . . . No ship seems safe, and if I am wrecked I might as well go under.

On September 11, 1912, the American Play Company, in association with Al Woods, presented its first Broadway production when *Within the Law* inaugurated Woods's new theatre, the Eltinge, named for the most renowned transvestite in theatrical history. Julian Eltinge was then at the height of his career as a Broadway and vaudeville star. The secret of his unique success was that there was no camp in his performances. Always tastefully dressed and made-up, Mr. Eltinge was utterly convincing in his portrayals of beautiful young ladies.

Within the Law ran an astonishing 541 performances. Not only was the writer, Bayard Veiller, Bessy's client, but, recently having decided to manage actors and dancers, she also represented Jane Cowl, who became a star in the play. It was not unusual for Bessy to miss the opening night of a client whose work opened either late in the spring or early in the autumn, but that she missed her own opening, the fulfillment of one of her great ambitions, seems incomprehensible. At last, she was the producer of a Broadway play and, to top that, a great hit. After having contributed her experience to the shaping of the script, she did not find it illogical to go abroad and trust the preproduction details to her partners, all of whom were highly experienced men. What can only be credited to the depth of her feelings for Anne Morgan is her decision to go to a spa with her instead of going home to take her share of the bows on that brilliant first night.

Bessy and Anne did not sail for home until October 19, on the *France.* They docked in New York on the twenty-fifth, at 4 P.M. Morgan was waiting to welcome Anne and whisk her off to the mansion at 219 Madison Avenue. Fanny, the Hamiltons, the Satterlees, his son, Jack, and his family were all present at the dinner party he gave that evening ostensibly in Anne's honor. In hindsight, it appears he was beginning to feel his mortality and wanted his family around him.

Anne and Bessy both had extremely cluttered calendars the following week and did not see each other, although Bessy assuredly saw *Within the Law* before they reconvened to spend the night of November 2 at Ringwood, with the Hewitt sisters. That Monday evening, the two of them attended *Within the Law,* and Anne, who hated almost everything she saw with Bessy, thought it was "wonderful" and that Jane Cowl was "splendid."

They went again two Saturdays later and had Miss Cowl to supper, on East Fifty-fifth Street, on the Sunday before Christmas.

Shortly after she had got back to New York, Bessy had learned the Shuberts were building a new small theatre with a capacity of only three hundred seats. On November 7, she wrote to Lee, asking for the location of the theatre and when it would be finished. She said, "I believe I could utilize such a theatre and manage it successfully."

He replied that it would be located on Thirty-ninth Street opposite the Maxine Elliott and be called the Princess. It was being built in partnership with a young producer yet to have much success, F. Ray Comstock, and Holbrook Blinn, who had gained his reputation as Mrs. Fiske's leading man. The plan was to do a series of Grand Guignol plays with Comstock as producer-manager and Blinn as director-star. That left Bessy out for the moment, but it would not be the end of her association with Comstock and the princess. A future collaboration would help to make theatrical history.

*O*n January 7, 1913, Anne Morgan accompanied the rest of the family to see her father and sister, Louisa, off on the *Adriatic.* They were headed for Egypt and a trip up the Nile to Sudan aboard one of the luxurious houseboats that plied the river. Morgan had made this voyage many times over the years whenever his nerves were so shattered that he felt he could not go on. Each time, it had helped to make him whole again.

On February 14, the firm received a coded cable from Luxor that Morgan had been too ill to accompany the shore party for a tour of the Valley of the Kings. His son wanted to leave for Egypt immediately, but, through Louisa, who had accompanied him to Luxor, Morgan vetoed that idea. She wired her brother that it was their father's wish that he stay at the bank to look after their interests, for any word of Pierpont's illness could cause the market to panic.

Back home, the Morgan family gathered at the Satterlee townhouse just east of the library to settle on a course of action. It was decided that the devoted Herbert Satterlee leave immediately for Egypt and take with him Morgan's personal physician, Dr. George Dixon. Soon after they arrived, they agreed that Rome would be more salubrious than Cairo. The Morgan party crossed to Italy and moved into a large suite at the Grand Hotel.

Louise, determined that her father's last words would be to and for her alone, refused to leave his side. Poor Satterlee watched dolefully as his beloved idol slowly passed away. Intent that the Satterlees not be alone in representing the family should anything concerning their collective interests transpire, a Morgan grandson was dispatched to stand in for his father and a Hamilton granddaughter for her mother. Only Anne was not represented, which was not remarkable, for there was nothing she could do for her father in Rome, and should it be necessary, she could be of service to her mother in New York. Less than three weeks short of his seventy-sixth birthday, Morgan's last words were not for Louisa but for the long-gone boys in some delirium of his prep school days, in Switzerland. "I've got to go up the hill."

*A*nne Morgan was left a trust fund of $3,000,000, which is the equivalent of between $35,000,000 and $40,000,000 in modern currency. Soon after coming into her money, Anne instructed Elsie to build and decorate an addition to the Villa Trianon that would contain a private suite for her own use. Elsie was delighted, as she was about anything that might enhance the value of her beloved villa, and she playfully suggested it be known as "the Morgan wing."

Anne Tracy Morgan would celebrate her fortieth birthday that year and was at last free of the one person for whom she ever felt constrained to modulate her opinions or way of life. Whatever her private grief over Pierpont's death, it did not interfere with her commitments, and less than a week after his funeral, she wrote a letter to the governor of New York, asking that $300,000 be reinstated in the state budget to be designated for the use of the Bedford Reformatory for Women, a model facility of its kind.

At that time, at Daisy Harriman's behest, she became involved in the Big Sisters movement started by Daisy's sister-in-law Anne Vanderbilt. The following month, Vanderbilt opened Locust Farm, a country estate she had leased in White Plains for the use of the "little sisters," those young girls brought into court for minor infractions of the law, mostly misdemeanors, and placed in the custody of the Big Sisters for their rehabilitation. The farm was to be an experiment to see how much they could improve the morals and characters of the girls by having them instructed in the sewing and housekeeping skills that could help them to earn a living. It was a lovely May, and as women of their class and experience, the Big Sisters could think of no better way of inaugurating the project than by bringing some of the girls up to the estate for an apple blossom tea party. Misguided and naive though their aspirations may seem with hindsight, the alternative was to place the little sisters in penal institutions, where they would learn the skills of the petty thief or prostitute and remain forever entrapped in the cycle of release and incarceration. The Big Sisters thought in terms of domestic skills, for their own educations had equipped them for little more, albeit on a grander scale.

CHAPTER THIRTY-SEVEN ❧

The high spirits that traditionally prevailed at the July 4 parties given by members of the American colony in Paris and Versailles were lowered that year by the news of the tragic death of Samuel Stevens Sands, the second son of one of its most popular members, Anne Vanderbilt. The extraordinary coincidence of the sad affair was that he was killed exactly as his brother had been six years earlier, in an automobile accident, while racing home to his wife and baby who were expecting him at their summer cottage in Southampton, Long Island. How many losses, her friends could not help wondering, could this admirable woman be expected to endure before the relentless God in whom she placed her faith yielded and indicated she had suffered enough?

The women residing at the Villa Trianon gave one enormous gala each season, in addition to their traditional Sunday afternoons and intimate luncheon and dinner parties. In 1913, this fete was of such rare beauty and originality that many recalled it as the last great party before the beginning of the end of the world as they knew it. Bessy credited its success to the effective combination of Elsie's "cultivated taste and imagination" with Anne's "sympathetic enthusiasm."

The flower beds were outlined by tiny lights, while garlands of electric bulbs hung from the trees, and cascading fountains were highlighted by colored lights. Under a sky brilliant with stars and moon, on a late June evening cooled by a gentle summer breeze, forty guests dined at small tables set up on the lawn, serenaded by the best orchestra Paris could provide, which was separated from the company by the formal rose garden. Bessy recalled that on that evening, "the lions and the lambs were to eat together," for the group included not only the American ambassador, Myron T. Herrick, but the official representatives of England, Germany, Belgium, Greece, Italy, Spain, Austria, Turkey, and Russia, all subtly spiced by *tout* Paris. Forty more guests—owners of neighboring châteaux and American friends over for the season—came in after dinner for a concert of eighteenth-century chansons interpreted by members of the Paris Opera. With perfect 20-20 hindsight, Bessy saw "creeping across the corner a dark shadow which slowly but surely was to almost efface this memory of wit, gaiety and laughter, for even then there was a strange and sinister vibration in the air which made conversation pause and which forced optimism to hesitate."

That summer was indeed the most brilliant of any they had spent abroad. The eternally beautiful Comtesse Greffuhle (the model for a heroine of *Remembrance of Things Past*) gave brilliant receptions at which all those who could change Europe's destiny met with elegant politesse. "It was kaleidoscopic and thrilling" to be "swept along, afraid to think and dreading to prophesy." Proust's world lay dying, "while debauchery and sensuous indulgence were the order of the day and night."

There were so many parties, and the women had been entertained with such dizzying excess, that an unprecedented second grand party was mandated. They opted for a large sit-down luncheon served at little tables set up around the pool in front of the music pavilion. The date, July 31, was determined by Elsie's insistence that they hire the Castles to give a dance recital in the pavilion, and that Thursday afternoon was their last opportunity to have them. The English Vernon and his American wife, Irene, had become the dancing darlings of Paris during their appearances at the intimate Café de Paris the summer before. They were closing their second sold-out engagement on that evening and leaving the next day to open the season at the casino in Deauville.

The Castles lingered in Bessy's mind during that autumn. If she were to sign them, she wondered how she could use them. It was not that they were the best dancers around, but that they were different. Vernon and Irene's uniqueness lay in an antic, high-spirited energy. They were so clean, so accessible, so—despite his being British—American. Their sexuality came from an appreciation of each other rather than a seduction of the audience.

According to Bessy, she happened to be lunching at the Ritz Carlton when she glanced across the street at the double townhouse once occupied by a fashionable dressmaker, and had the idea of turning it into "a smart dancing centre" that would capitalize on the personalities of Vernon and Irene. She even visualized its trademark and name: "Castle House."

After she signed them to a management contract, one obstacle had to be overcome. Vernon and Irene were performers, and it would take more than an interest in a dance school to lure them away from their lucrative engagements dancing in supper clubs. Charles Frohman was producing the American production of an English musical hit she represented, *The Sunshine Girl.* To solve her problem, she sold him on casting Vernon opposite Julia Sanderson, the biggest musical star of the day. He had been featured in several shows, but this would be his first leading role. That left Irene with nothing to do, and Bessy convinced Frohman to give her a featured spot in one dance routine with her husband.

The show was a big success, although the most memorable dance turn in it was not the one Vernon did with his wife, but the tango he danced with Julia Sanderson. It did not matter to Irene, for by opening night Bessy was well on the way to making her the most imitated woman in the United States and, incidentally, helping to invent the business of licensing a name as if it were by itself a piece of merchandise.

To turn Irene into the best-known unknown in New York, Bessy repeated what had worked so well for Elsie: Irene, who had wonderful taste, became famous for it. That she was so good-looking and wore clothes so well proved a great advantage in lining up the best photographers to take pictures of her. Bessy bombarded editors with these photographs and made picture cards to be sold to fans at newsstands. In assembling a newsworthy wardrobe, the women were fortunate. Elsie's good friend Mme Lucille (Lady Duff Gordon) had opened salons in London, New York and Paris, and become the first international English fashion designer since Charles Frederick Worth. Bessy persuaded her to design a few dresses for the dancer. The result is described by Caroline Rennolds Milbank in her encyclopedic book, *Couture:* "The combination of Lucille's airy dance frocks and Irene's lithe body and charismatic beauty exerted tremendous fashion influence on both sides of the Atlantic."

Bessy followed the dresses by leasing Irene's name to a long series of products ranging from cigarettes to automobiles. Irene became such a trendsetter that when she bobbed her hair, girls all over America followed suit and cut off what had previously been known as their crowning glory. She made her client the most famous dancer in America before anybody knew whether she could do more than follow her husband in an unmemorable number inserted into a show starring somebody else.

The essential thing was to have the Castle House in operation in advance of the Christmas balls and cotillions, so that all the young debs would be able to enroll for dance lessons before attending them. Bessy devised a schedule for the club. Mornings were given over to dance lessons, for which she personally selected the instructors and assistants. In addition to being able to dance all of the latest steps, they had to be clean-cut, personable, well dressed, and with good enough manners to pass for ladies and gentlemen. In the afternoons tea was served—and here was Bessy's moneymaking *coup de foudre.* It was poured by her very social friends Mrs. Stuyvesant Fish, Mrs. William Rockefeller, Mrs. Oakley Rhinelander, and their ilk, who had become as dance-crazy as their daughters. On every afternoon except matinee days, the Castles gave an exhibition of some of Vernon's innovations such as the Castle walk and the Maxixe. On occasion he would also give lessons, something Irene admitted she had neither the inclination nor the talent to do.

From its opening day, Castle House was a sensation. The place was so jammed that the floor space often proved inadequate. Where else could a modest two or three dollars buy a dance performance by the Castles (with luck, a dance *with* Vernon) and a cup of tea poured by a queen of society fit for a real castle?

Aware that many of the new dance steps were coming out of the black ghettos, Bessy hired the New Orleans black conductor Jim Europe and his orchestra to provide the music. To have black artists play for young socialites, some not yet formally out, was a courageous thing to do in 1913, but Bessy was as much an anomaly in her attitudes toward race as she was in those toward religion. She had all of the traditional prejudices of her class and era but too much respect for accomplishment to allow those prejudices to influence her professional or social relationships. Soon after hiring him, she augmented his income by placing one of Europe's dance compositions, "Ballin' the Jack," in a Frohman production. It became a pop classic that is still being played by dance orchestras all over the world.

Anne Morgan's efforts with both the Navy Yard Restaurant and the Vacation Savings Fund had succeeded beyond all expectations. The latter had grown to fourteen thousand depositors in two years with $100,000 to their credit, which was exceptional for a group of young women earning an average of between ten and fifteen dollars a week. A new cause came into focus to which she would devote a large part of her life. Adequate housing at a price she could afford was desperately needed by the working-woman if she was to become productive, ambitious, and virtuous. Anne's first major project after her father's death was to provide this necessary housing under the auspices of the Vacation Savings Fund.

A brownstone was leased on West Thirty-ninth Street, and two more directly behind it, on Thirty-eighth Street. Every aspect of the project proceeded after consultation with working-class representatives of the savings fund depositors. The latter's active contributions to management were especially important to Anne, for she would not countenance her projects being thought of as philanthropy. "If I understand philanthropy, it's working *for* people. We are working *with* people. There's all the difference in the world between *for* and *with*."

With a prescience that made the observation valid almost eighty years later, she added: "I don't believe there are any [words] which have been more abused than *charity* and *welfare.* They have simply been murdered. One can't use them anymore for their old significance has been killed."

The three buildings would constitute both residence and clubhouse. Anne convinced Elsie to supervise the renovation and decor of the new center. Eleanor Belmont and she were underwriting the cost. The budget was necessarily modest, for there was a limit to how much of their own incomes they could devote to the project. Elsie displayed an ability to execute extremely attractive premises for very little money although once it was demonstrated, she never cared to exhibit it again.

Coming from such a different background, it was remarkable how sensitive Anne was to the needs of these young women. Many of them lived so far from their jobs there was rarely time to go home to freshen up nor were there facilities where they worked. They needed their own space, a place to be private. Elsie solved these problems with a combination of improvisational common sense and a revamping of some of the features of the Colony Club.

The Thirty-ninth Street house was the headquarters and recreational center for the Vacation Fund. The third floor was the Colony in miniature, giving the members all of the privileges they would have enjoyed in a women's club. There was a small writing room and a large bright lounge in which they could read, visit, or simply relax in solitude. This was separated by the ladies' cloakroom from what was described as "one of the best features of the house: a large dressing room complete with dressing tables, cubicles for changing clothes, and private bathrooms in which the girls could soak in warm, relaxing tubs before preparing for the evening."

On the parlor floor, a reception room was set aside in which a girl could meet her young man in attractive surroundings and in an atmosphere that enhanced "her own self respect and the respect of her man friend." Elsie thought of everything. She even installed a "men's cloak room," a euphemism for a *toilet* as well as a place to hang his hat.

The Thirty-eighth Street houses had twenty-four single bedrooms and six large doubles. Elsie's influence was seen in the attractive lounge reserved for the exclusive use of the residents, in the bedrooms that were far more attractively furnished than those in the average boardinghouse, in details such as a private closet for each person—something most residents had never before possessed—and in getting as many bathrooms as the budget would allow, five in this case. The weekly rent was five dollars, which was very high when many young women earned only between five and ten dollars a week.

It was in rationalizing the cost that elitism surfaced. It was impossible to offer the amenities available at the clubhouse for less. Economics forced them to divide working girls into three categories: (1) the majority who earned between five and twelve dollars; (2) those in the twelve to twenty category: (3) the few whose wages exceeded twenty dollars a week and who could afford to live "properly" in the best kind of boardinghouse. The lowest category lived at home except for a fortunate few able to find affordable room and board in charitable institutions such as the Y.W.C.A. They were aiming for the middle category girl—middle-class "from the point of view of income"—who could not afford the best boardinghouses and who were too well-off for charity. Her higher wages indicated that as a rule, she was better educated and more intelligent than the majority. This demographic girl came from a good family and was brought up in an atmosphere of refinement and comfort, but through some reversal of fortune was forced to earn her own living.

It was in opting for this group that they were open to criticism from the more liberal elements of the reform movement. Why not reduce the number of polite niceties and bring the rent down to a level those most in need could afford? Everything in their backgrounds conspired against making these concessions. Anne refused to countenance anything her critics said. All she was doing was providing the means of future growth for all working girls, for she considered herself one of them. She did not want to be paid for her efforts, because she did not have to be paid for them. It was simply her good fortune that she could work without being dependent on salary. "I am with a certain position and influence, due to no efforts or merits of my own. I have . . . had an immense amount of ground cleared for me, and I can take advantage of that fact to help those who have not enjoyed as many favorable opportunities as I have."

*W*illie K. Vanderbilt had never known a moment's tragedy in the entire sixty-five years of his charmed life. With what helplessness he viewed the progression of tragedies in his second wife's life. He did what he could, but her desires were slight. Where his first wife had demanded palaces, Anne was grateful for a mausoleum on the grounds of Idle Hours in which her sons could be together in death. She devoted her mourning spirit to helping those trapped in a despair with which she could empathize.

During her visits to the courts while working with Big Sisters, Anne Vanderbilt was struck by the number of young people whose lives were being ruined by drugs. Her investigation of the problem turned up some remarkably familiar statistics: one-third of the crimes committed in New York City were attributable to cocaine and morphine addicts, 40 percent of those confined on the city prison were addicts, only one-third of those arrested for selling drugs were held overnight and only half of those were convicted.

Alfred Allan Lewis

Certainly, the laws for the punishment of traffickers had to be stiffened to prevent them from escaping punishment, but it was the rehabilitation of the addicts that was her primary concern. From the beginning, she believed the few existing laws did not address the problem, and that the solution for the victims was in treatment rather than incarceration.

Early in January 1914, Anne set up a meeting with all of the most prominent officials directly concerned with the drug problem. On the agenda was the need for legislation to ban the sale of heroin, which was still legal. Much cheaper than cocaine, it was in greater use in the slums and a source of the criminalization of many of its young people. The point was brought home to Anne a short time later when a probation officer interested her in the case of Marian Young, a young woman charged with possession of cocaine. She sat in at Young's arraignment in Special Sessions Court with the hope of getting her released on condition that she enter treatment for her addiction. It was found that it was heroin, not cocaine, that she was carrying. With no law against the use of the substance, the charges were dismissed, and the girl was free to return to the streets that had fed her addiction without any proviso that she must seek help.

A strong anti-drug bill was drafted by one delegate to Anne's conference, Charles Towns, a police official who had long been an anti-drug crusader. It was approved and given to state senator John Boylan, who brought it up before the New York legislature. Anne used all of her considerable influence to counteract the powerful drug lobby and see that it was passed immediately. While this was happening in Albany, she made a visit to the Tombs, in New York City, to see for herself the number of addicts confined there, the awful waste of potential and young lives, the dreadful cost to their families and to the state of keeping them there. On April 16, Governor Flynn signed the anti-drug act into law.

The bill accomplished her primary goal of providing treatment, but the next step would have to be couched in terms of fiscal prudence. As things stood at that moment, New York State had a very strong law, but in New Jersey there was no restriction on the sale of habit-forming drugs. All the pusher need do was to take his chances with the New York police and cross the river to purchase legally all he needed to satisfy his customers. The New York law could only be made effective if there was a national law. The federal lawmakers would only be interested in a New York problem if it seemed to be in the country's economic interest. That would take a great deal of time and effort. Before she could become immersed in a national anti-drug campaign, events that transpired in Europe during that summer would deflect her attentions to what appeared to be the larger problem of a world war.

∞

*A*t the beginning of May, Bessy sailed for Europe, taking along one grandson of her late brother Francis, her twelve-year-old great-nephew Ross Marbury, whose education, along with that of his older brother, John, she was already underwriting. "He is a dear kid and really it has been a pleasure having him as a companion. . . . He is certainly a credit to his mother."

Ross and she were studying French history together, and she also arranged for him to have riding lessons. Her reports to his parents were meticulous, covering everything the boy did from the moment he got up until bed-time, including his toilet habits. "He goes *twice* (morning and night) to do *'serieux'* and has never missed since we left." Perhaps that was the reason his cheeks were "bright pink all the while."

*F*or Elsie de Wolfe, that spring was crowned when Henry Clay Frick decided to hire her to decorate the second-floor private family rooms in what was surely the most eagerly awaited Fifth Avenue mansion since the 1880s, when Alva and Alice Vanderbilt battled it out for who would be chatelaine of the most ostentatious residence on what was surely the most ostentatious avenue in any city in the world. The assignment was so prestigious that she agreed to accept a 10 percent commission on the pur-chases she made rather than her usual 30 to 40 percent. She had been brought in just as Carriere and Hastings, the architectural firm, was com-pleting the two-year construction of "the largest and most elaborate Mod-ern Renaissance mansion in New York," stretching the full block from Seventieth to Seventy-first Street.

Possibly because she did not do as well financially as she would have liked, Elsie created a legend about the job that cast Frick in the role of a fool in need of her guidance, which was surely far from the truth. Frick's biogra-pher, George Harvey, added to future confusion by remarking that the in-dustrialist did not take his annual trip to Europe in 1914 because of the approaching war, which made it seem logical that Elsie and he had gone abroad on their buying trip the previous year. As will soon be seen, it would have been impossible for them to have acquired the furniture they did buy, where they did and from whom they did, at any time other than in the late spring of 1914.

These pieces were among furnishings that had impressed the Morgans when Pierpont took Anne to lunch at the rue Laffitte apartment of Sir John Murray Scott, on October 3, 1911. A little more than three months later, on

January 17, 1912, Scott died. In his will, Lady Victoria Sackville was left 150,000 pounds, a Houdin bust, some important jewelry, and the contents of the apartment at 2 rue Laffitte, which, it was estimated, would add 350,000 pounds to her bequest. Scott's siblings sued, charging that she had used "undue influence" on their brother.

It was at this point that Elsie's fabulation began to run counter to the truth. According to her, the antique dealer Jacques Seligman had told Lady Sackville: "I will finance your lawsuit with the understanding that if we win, I will have the sole right to sell your collection. No other dealer must come into it."

Her attorney, Sir Edward Carson, the man whose defense of Queensberry ultimately had led to Oscar Wilde's incarceration, was among the most expensive in the world. Under no circumstances would an antiquarian known as the "fox of the world" have paid his fees on a case of undetermined duration for the chance to buy a collection he later admitted he had not seen and which might not be hers to sell. Although Victoria Sackville-West would have to conserve her good name and stood to lose a great deal should the verdict be for the Scott family, she was neither plaintiff nor defendant in the case. It was F. W. Capron, the solicitor-executor for the Scott estate, who was instituting the suit on its behalf, and it was the estate that would pay for Carson.

The trial opened on June 24, 1913, and ended two weeks later with Lady Victoria's complete vindication. Up to that point, there was no mention in her diary of Frick, Elsie, or Jacques Seligman. It was not until late in July that Seligman made inquiries about the disposition of the contents of the apartment. By then, Lady Sackville knew she was liable for 38,000 pounds in English death duties and an additional 42,000 in French duties on the furniture. The latter assessment could not have been made without a detailed inventory of everything in the apartment and its value, which in total came to 350,000 pounds. She was so desperate for money to pay the taxes that she accepted Seligman's offer of 250,000 pounds, made on the basis of "inventories done by 5 experts."

That was not the end of it. When he did finally see the furniture in September, he was "upset" and "making himself a nuisance by appearing to be dissatisfied with the Paris furniture." They continued to haggle until May 22, 1914, when she heard in Rome, where she had gone for a visit, that Seligman had given in and would pay the 250,000 pounds on condition that she empty the apartment of her possessions by the evening of June 8, when the furniture was to be transferred to his gallery for exhibition.

Seligman's son alleged that Frick and Elsie came to see the furniture just as few days before it was moved, which would place their visit during the first week of June 1914. There is no reason to dispute that. The "fox of the world" was not likely to have shown Elsie anything he did not already own, for he had to have known that she was sufficiently vulpine to go behind his back directly to Lady Sackville, with whom she had many friends in common, to make a better deal.

Elsie's description of the events leading up to the Frick purchases was pure comic melodrama out of one of the plays in which she had not succeeded in becoming a star. According to her, the rue Laffitte house was sealed by order of the French courts and only Seligman was permitted entry. But the house was never sealed. There were tenants living in it. Only Scott's apartment was sealed, and that seal had been removed almost a year earlier. Until it was removed, not even Lady Sackville had been permitted entry, let alone Seligman.

According to Elsie, Frick did not want to be bothered with the dealer, and she had to view the collection before involving him. The only way she could get by the caretakers to do this was to dress in black, carry a notebook, and pretend to be Seligmann's secretary. The collection was staggering, and a date was set for her to bring Frick to view it. She claimed Frick wanted to cancel because he had a golf date, and she had to plead with him to give her a half-hour before proceeding to the links. How she allegedly got this gentleman in plus fours past the caretakers, when she had to go in disguise, was never explained. Elsie continually embroidered on her tale of what was supposed to have happened once she had Frick on the premises, pointed out a few choice pieces, and assured him they were all beyond value.

> He went through the house like a streak, while I followed at his heels, aghast, as his purchases mounted up into millions of francs, and I realized that in one short half-hour I had become what was tantamount to a rich woman. I was also astounded at the revelation that a business man, so astute and even cold as Mr. Frick was known to be, could spend a fortune with such nonchalance in order to keep a golf appointment.

It was Elsie's portrait of Henry Clay Frick that made the least sense in her droll tale. He would never have exhibited this attitude of mindless disregard toward viewing a collection that was an extension of the Wallace collection, of comparable quality and amassed by the same men. According to the introduction to the Frick collection catalogue written by the celebrated aesthetician Sir Osbert Sitwell, it was that collection that had inspired him to build his own:

It appeared to have been after his first visit to the Wallace collection in Hereford House . . . that Mr. Frick first realized the value of a museum of other works of art as accessories to the pictures, comprehended that it was more easy to appreciate paintings when the atmosphere of a private house continued. . . . To the task he set himself, that of forming a collection in a private house, he brought, not only as we have seen, a well-formed taste, but that same quality to decide quickly that had made him a force.

Sir Osbert and Elsie did apparently agree on one thing: the speed with which that intelligence made its decisions. In view of Frick's collection, Sir Osbert felt, not only did the financier's taste and discernment far exceed Elsie's, but it was also greater than Scott's and Sir Richard Wallace's taken individually.

All these treasures were chosen by one man . . . even the Wallace collection was the result of three celebrated connoisseurs in succession [the third and fourth Marquesses of Hertford and Sir Richard Wallace]. . . . The Frick collection, however, can bear comparison with any assemblage of pictures and works of art in the world, and stands as an undying monument to the man who made it.

*D*uring the last few years, a gradual fissure had been opening between Bessy and Elsie. It was more than Bessy's relationship with Anne that lay at its heart. Theirs had been a game played with artists, celebrities, minor nobility, and expatriates—an amusing charade to pass the idle summer days in Versailles. To Bessy's dismay, Elsie was beginning to mistake the game for real life, to believe a famous or notorious name automatically conferred worth as a human being. She was drawing closer to the people Anne and Bessy were beginning to shun. Nevertheless, to outward appearances they remained an intriguing *ménage à trois,* and that June, Elsie cheerfully completed another decorating chore: a new bedroom for young Ross Marbury about which Bessy reported to his older brother, John: "It is very pretty and the furniture is white and looks so spotless and clean. I tucked him in his bed and said good-night and wished him very happy dreams. He said this morning that the new bed was fine!"

The letter to John Marbury indicated how seriously she took her responsibilities to a child placed in her charge.

You see I plan each day out for Ross so that he has a variety of enjoyments as well as occupations. He studies hard from 9 to 11 each morning. Then play until lunchtime. In the afternoon, he rows, or rides on his pony, or his bicycle, or walks, or goes to the pictures. Then each week, he spends two afternoons sight-seeing. Yesterday, as it was warm enough, he and Miss Francis had a nice lunch put up. . . . They took the basket out in the Park under the great shady trees and there they had a real picnic.

The second Sunday after Bessy's birthday was a day climaxed by the news that Archduke Francis Ferdinand, heir apparent to the Austrian throne, and his wife had been assassinated in Sarajevo. The nymphets appear to have paid so little attention to the tragedy that it was not so much as noted in Anne Morgan's Line-A-Day. In the middle of July, Elsie left for her cure at Baden-Baden. Only ten miles over the border from France, she found German soldiers drilling in the lovely squares, while zeppelins flew overhead day and night. Wherever people gathered, there was talk of the coming conflict, but it did not penetrate Elsie.

Bessy and Anne were no less sanguine as they went about making preparations for their sojourn at Brides. They arrived there during the last week in July, accompanied by Ross and his governess, Miss Francis.

During the drive down, Ross was more curious than the adults about the troops of the French Alpine regiments marching along the road that occasionally delayed their vehicle. When they arrived in Brides, Anne left her maid to do the unpacking and lost no time in getting down to the baths to begin her cure, weighing in at 78.6 kilos. Three days later, a wire from Elsie informed them that she was leaving Baden-Baden for Spain that morning and would be stopping the night in Chambéry, only some thirty-five miles from them. Wouldn't it be great fun if they came over to dine with her? Amazingly, the three women still had no idea that war was imminent. After a good meal, Anne and Bessy wished Elsie a good journey and returned to the spa.

Full mobilization was declared that Sunday, August 2. The chauffeur had to leave for the army. He took the precaution of removing key parts from the engine of the limousine and giving them to Bessy for safekeeping before locking the car up in a garage—just in case, he explained, somebody attempted to "requisition" it. His departure was a nuisance to Anne that was countervailed by the happy news that she had lost four pounds in the four days since arriving.

CHAPTER THIRTY-EIGHT

On August 3, Bessy and Anne were having coffee on the *terrasse* in front of their small hotel when, from the street above, they heard the town crier, who was rushing from village to village broadcasting the news that war had been declared. They dared not look at each other or speak until their silence was broken by the tolling of the village church bells. It was the ancient cry to arms that had not been sounded in forty-four years. The old people remembered, as the past returned to become the present, for in 1870 it had been another war with Germany.

Bessy's thoughts were of Elsie's progress. How far could she have gotten along the way with a maid, two poodles, and a French chauffeur whose military papers were in his pocket? Feeling a bit superfluous and not knowing what else to do, Anne returned to the spa, where she found her weight was down three-tenths of a kilo since the day before. She noted helplessly: "No definite news terrible sorrow in village."

The fourth was a depressing rainy day with the weather ruling out a walk. There was no news of Elsie and very little of any other kind beyond rumors. It was not until Friday, August 7, that Bessy received a telegram from a Perpignan hotelier saying that Elsie had passed through on her way to Spain "and that all seemed well with her." A letter also arrived that day from their good friend, the art editor Augusto Jaccaci, who also lived in Versailles and who informed them the town had been taken over by the army as one of its centers of regional command. The needs of the military superseded the rights of the owners of private properties. He had looked in on the Villa Trianon, and thus far all was well.

The next day, they received an unofficial report that the Germans were already at Compiègne, and the day after, a calamitous wire from their *gardien,* or caretaker, at the Villa Trianon, saying that he had been informed that should the German advance approach Versailles, the French army would have to raze the house in order to defend the palace. With no chance of going home—possibly, no home to go to—no news of Elsie, and their money running out, Bessy felt for the first time in her life no longer in control of her destiny. She wrote to Ross's mother, Julia, that events had rushed ahead and "made us only children of fate to a most tragic degree."

On Saturday, a letter arrived from Elsie in Barcelona, but the next few days were awful. The passenger trains had been stopped, and supplies in the hotel were running low. As reserves of meat and bread began to run out, the local vegetables, salad, and potatoes became their daily diet, which actually suited Anne, who complained of nothing but the heat and lack of news. She spent her time jogging and getting Bessy, Miss Francis, and Ross out on long healthy walks. That week, she wired her brother, Jack, that she was well and found the "atmosphere most thrilling." The more important part of her message was that she was running out of money as it was impossible to get so much as a few hundred francs wired from the Paris branch of the bank, which, as Bessy observed, was "a sad predicament for a daughter of the house of Morgan!"

Within a few days, Jack Morgan managed to come through with American letters of credit, and they were once again solvent. Word also arrived to meet Elsie in Biarritz. It had been prescient of Bessy's chauffeur to have removed key parts of her car's engine and deposited them with her. The authorities were requisitioning every motor vehicle in sight and, when they came upon hers, gave it up as worthless. Bessy telegraphed Henri, a chauffeur she had once employed in Paris who was too old for military service, and offered him a job. It took five days for him to make the journey from Paris to Brides, which normally took twelve hours.

On the morning they were to depart, Bessy took the time to write another lengthy letter to Julia Marbury explaining their situation. She began by being totally reassuring that the best was being done for her son. Miss Francis was keeping up with his lessons and the regimen at the spa had done the boy a world of good. As for their immediate plans, Biarritz would provide the best destination as it was "as far removed as possible from the lines of battle . . . very near the Spanish frontier." She could not decide if it would be less fatiguing for Ross to make a long motor trip, which he detested, or to put Miss Francis and him on a train when they reached a functioning rail center. "In any event," she said, "rest assured I am looking after his welfare even more than my own—Do not worry about Ross in any way."

During the drive to Chambéry, they were stopped eleven times at barricades of armed sentries asking to see their papers, for at the beginning of the war, every stranger was a suspect until his or her identity was verified. The number of times they were stopped replaced her weight as Anne's daily preoccupation. It was a joy to find that the Chambéry prefect of police was "most courteous" about arranging for the proper documents for their journey. Nobody ever explained how or why it came about, but in Chambéry they apparently took charge of the two children of American friends, the Stewarts. With trunks strapped to the roof and valises to its side, their Peugeot was crammed with Bessy, Anne, their personal maids, Miss Francis, three children, and chauffeur when it started for Lyons early the next morning. Only a bit more than fifty miles away, Lyons was a rail center, and the

United States consul arranged to send the luggage ahead in the charge of their maids.

At length they reached Biarritz for a reunion with Elsie, which, as Anne put it, was "all enchanted together again." She did not neglect her arithmetic and noted that they had been stopped forty-one times since leaving Brides.

Once the enchantment wore off, Elsie counted Ross, Miss Francis, and the two Stewart children, plus their nurses and governess, who also had arrived on the scene. What was Bessy thinking of, traveling clear across a country at war like some sort of Pied Piper? The children and their entourage must be packed off on the first train to Paris, where they would be much better off than tagging along with them in these uncertain times. Bessy would agree to send only the Stewart party to Paris and insisted that Ross remain with them. Within a matter of days the Stewart children and their nannies were returned to them.

Initially, there was a definite holiday atmosphere in Biarritz. The town was crowded with old friends who had fled the war in the north. There were dinner parties and card games and automobile excursions. Anne could have her daily swims in the sea and had begun to take golf lessons, a sport that would become one of the great joys of her life. Bessy wrote to Frank Marbury that Ross was *"thriving"* in Biarritz and "seems to like this place better than anywhere he has been—and no wonder!" Their rooms in the Hôtel du Palais were "beautiful and tasteful!" with an "ideal sea" as part of the view from Bessy's window. Instead of hideous boardwalks, there was a paved, terraced ocean walk and drive "with lovely stone balustrades and green lawns and gardens running to the sea." Bessy was painting an Eden for the frantic father, trying to assure him it truly existed in the chaos of a country at war.

The plan was to sail for home aboard the *France* on September 26. The next day, two letters arrived from the boy's overwrought parents, to which she replied after her rational fashion. "I fancy that the American press is doing its best to keep you all stirred up and anxious." She reassured them that she considered Ross a "very *precious* responsibility."

Life for the women resumed in earnest with the arrival of a wire from Jaccaci on the first of September. While awaiting a decision from the army on what they intended to do with it, the Villa Trianon was to be closed and all of their things stored in the cellar. One day there was word that the Germans were on their way, and the next that all was well, but they had no further news about the villa until Jaccaci himself arrived on the sixth. The bad news he brought was for Anne alone. The army had requisitioned Imperial, the great thoroughbred her father had given to her. She took it well in a fatalistic *c'est la guerre* fashion. It had cost ten thousand francs: eventually the army would pay a reparation of five hundred francs.

His good news was Villa Trianon would be safe for the moment, although they would not be permitted to live in it until further notice. The army's most recent plan was to use it as a storehouse. But it was in future danger, and that danger came from the French rather than the Germans. How much more ghastly it was for Elsie than the others, who did not have her sense of intense, personal identification with the house. *Her* beautiful Villa Trianon was being treated in this contemptible manner—as if they thought it was the same as any other place that might be in their way.

Anne again proved she was that rare combination of pragmatism and compassion. When she heard their American neighbor in Versailles Mrs. Paul Morton wanted to turn her house into a convalescence home for the wounded, with Bessy's approval she offered the house Bessy rented next to their villa to be used as part of it. On a practical level, she also offered the villa itself, should its only salvation lie in finding a military purpose for it. Jaccaci was asked to look into the possibility and told that if it was a question of money to equip it, that could be arranged.

Biarritz was stultifying, and they wanted to get out as soon as possible. They were prevented from acting immediately by a storm the next day so fierce it knocked out the telegraph and telephone wires. Two pieces of good news got through before the wires went down. The first was that the Germans were encountering unforeseen resistance at the Marne River. The second was that the French minister of war agreed to allow an *ambulance,* or French military hospital, to be established at the Villa Trianon. As soon as the wires were repaired and full service restored, they made arrangements to put the children, their nannies, and the maids on the train to Bordeaux, while they drove up in the car to meet them. The sole exception was Anne's personal maid, Alice, whom they agreed to share, for it was unthinkable for them to travel for even so short a distance without any servant.

Once in Bordeaux, they found the entire French government had moved there along with most of the foreign ambassadors. It did not indicate any great faith in the French army's ability to keep the Germans from invading Paris.

They picked up their brood of servants and children and set about finding accommodations, which was nearly impossible in the overcrowded city. Elsie later claimed they found "an unspeakably filthy house" for the children, while Bessy, Anne, and she were forced to share one hotel room. Anne Morgan, a great deal more accurate if a bit less dramatic and writing at the time of the events, observed they found an adequate house in which there was room for all of them, at 60 rue de Vannes.

When it was taken at the elegant Chapon Fin, dinner was not only excellent but theatre worthy of the Comédie Française, which had also removed to Bordeaux. Each of the government bureaus had its own table as did the stars of the Comédie and the foreign delegations. Elsie was proud to note that the American ambassador, Myron Herrick, was one of only two (Spain was the other) who had not deserted his Paris post. Of course, as neither Spain nor the United States was at war with Germany, they had little fear should that country occupy Paris.

Saturday dawned with the splendid news of a French victory at the Marne, which removed the threat of occupation of Versailles. As it unfolded, the heroic saga of the battle was thrilling, until one heard the appalling cost in lives. Paris was saved, but at the cost of losses to each side that approached 500,000. The slaughter of almost one million men in six days made valor synonymous with insanity. It was as if that one battle, with its devastating losses, sapped the energy from both sides. From then on, most of the war in France would be fought in a comparatively small crisscross of trenches on and near the Aisne River, a region Anne Morgan would know intimately before its end.

*T*hey left Bordeaux and reached Le Havre nine days before their ship was to sail, more than enough time for them drive to Paris and, if possible, Versailles. As it was unthinkable that Bessy not remain with Ross, Elsie and Anne decided they would go south alone.

They left the next morning, following a route that would keep them well to the north and west of Paris and away from the front, which was to the east. In Anne's words, it was a "terrible day" made interminable by the endless roadblocks at which their papers were examined. In Elsie's dramatic account, "When dark came down there was not a light to be seen on the road or in the distance. It was just like passing through a world hushed in death."

The day after they arrived in Paris, where they were staying, as her family always did, at the Bristol, Anne went to see the gallant Ambassador Herrick. He impressed her as being "very tired but most interesting." He told her he had ordered an American flag hoisted in front of the Villa Trianon, which would protect it from being destroyed. He also invited her to lunch the next day with her old friends Whitney Warren and Robert Bacon.

Bacon had returned to France as soon as war was declared, determined to do all he could to help. One of his first efforts was to associate himself with Anne Vanderbilt on the expansion of the *ambulance* section of the American Hospital in Neuilly. The French government had contributed the Lycée Pasteur for that purpose, and Willie Vanderbilt had given forty thousand dollars to equip it. Mrs. Vanderbilt had not deserted the hospital during that most dangerous period, when the government and so many of her Parisian friends had fled for fear of occupation. She had remained behind to supervise its reorganization into a military facility.

The hospital and its *ambulance* were her projects, but Anne Vanderbilt was wise enough to know that during the war, a man who had important contacts in Washington should head an American military installation in France, and she supported Bacon's nomination as president of the American Hospital. She also knew not even Vanderbilts had enough money to finance the project independently, and enthusiastically endorsed the suggestion that Bacon's wife, Martha, take charge of raising funds in the United States.

Probably at Anne's suggestion, Bacon convinced her niece Gertrude Vanderbilt Whitney to finance another American *ambulance* closer to the front lines. Bacons and Vanderbilts were not unique among Americans, especially American women, in giving invaluable support to a France at war long before their government declared itself. Before Edith Wharton left for England, where she remained during the period when Paris was most in danger of being besieged, she had started an *ouvroir,* a workroom employing out-of-work seamstresses to make garments for the army. She returned to France late in September to establish the American Hostel for Refugees to tend to the needs of homeless victims of German aggression in Belgium and France who were beginning to stream into the city. She would generously continue "Mrs. Wharton's charities" until the end of the war at the expense of her work, her finances, her health, and alas—Edith being Edith—the feelings of many of her colleagues.

*F*or many Americans, it was not the right or wrong of the German cause that turned them against the kaiser, it was the barbarity with which his army pursued it. The mindless devastation was impressed upon Anne Morgan at that early stage when they passed through what remained of the village of Courtaçon, which had practically been destroyed for no better reason than that it was there.

Morgan's daily notes were majorly devoted to her activities in Versailles during that September. She went out there to see Jaccaci, who had just returned from the south. Back in Paris the next day, she lunched with Herrick to discuss the plans Mrs. Morton and she had formulated for the convalescence hospital.

Time was growing short: they were to sail on the twenty-sixth, and on the twenty-third, Anne was back in Versailles to see the first twenty patients installed. On the twenty-fourth, she concluded her business in Versailles by arranging for the Sisters of Notre-Dame de la Capucine to take over the supervision of her hospital, and started back to Le Havre. Presumably, Elsie was with her all of the time, although neither ever made any mention of her presence.

While her friends were away, Bessy volunteered to work as a nurse's aide in the Le Havre casino, which had been converted into an *ambulance* for the first of the wounded who were already being sent back from the front. Conditions were primitive and unhygienic. Bessy was not surprised to learn that 80 percent of the earliest wounded died of gangrene rather than their wounds. "No modern equipment of any kind. The generals were old, the surgeons were old, the nurses were old, the materials were old."

What was impressed upon her, and would later cause conflict with Elsie, was that war was a young people's game. She was unskilled and as old as the rest of the staff. Her most important skill was being able to scour floors and walls with the best of them: the wife of the mayor of Le Havre, in charge of volunteers, had gratefully accepted her help.

Elsie and Anne became enamored of the French for their courage and dignity under fire. Bessy had fewer illusions. When her friends spoke of France's pride in never having asked for charity, she agreed the statement was irrefutable but added that, fortunately for France, her friends "did the asking [for her] while she was worshipped for her grace in receiving."

As they sailed for home, they agreed the great, good times in France were over, at least for the duration. What they did not discuss was what the war also had sundered: their years as the nymphets were ended forever.

CHAPTER THIRTY-NINE ❧

Of a far more liberal turn of mind than her close friends, Bessy Marbury saw war for what it was—in the vernacular of her beloved Broadway, a chump's game. She loved France and many of the French people, but did not hold them in the same high esteem as a people that Anne Morgan did.

In a sense, France was Anne's second native land, the place where she had been reborn during that summer a decade earlier in which they first became intimate, enabling her to become the person she hitherto had not been: the formidable and compassionate woman now resolved to rouse her first country to step in to save her second country.

As for Elsie, she would later claim it was Bessy who had prevented her from turning right around and going back to Europe to give her all for the cause. But the reason Elsie stayed home was because of the extreme indifference to the war among the women she most admired and wanted to emulate. When that situation changed a year and a half later, and war became fashionable, she returned to Europe.

Bessy wanted nothing so much as for things to stay as they were before the war. That so plump a person had such interminable energy—which showed no signs of abating even in advanced middle age—was one of the wonders of the theatrical world. One way of finding the time for all of her activities was seldom sleeping more than five or six hours. Another stemmed from an objective assessment of her own appearance. Realizing neat dignity was the most she could expect of clothes and cosmetics, she wasted little or no time shopping. If it could not be found in the Sears Roebuck or Montgomery Ward catalogs, it was not for her. She was a mail order devotee long before a generation of career women made it a trendy way to shop.

Her agency business, split neatly between the American Play Company and the Elisabeth Marbury Company, continued to prosper. She doubtless would have done nothing to change it had her associates remained content with the arrangement, but they were ready to start off in new directions. That August, while Bessy was caught in the war, Edgar and Arch Selwyn had produced a play written by Megrue, *Under Cover.* When it was an immediate hit, the brothers decided to leave agentry to pursue careers as producers, and Megrue resigned to become a full-time writer. Arch and Edgar asked Bessy to buy them out of both the American Play Company and their own agency. It was something she could easily have afforded to do, but without Megrue she was loath to take on greater professional obligations at a time when she, too, had begun to think of changing direction. Fortunately, John Rumsey happened along at that moment.

Born in London, Rumsey had worked as a Pinkerton detective before emigrating to the United States and embarking upon a career in the theatre. It was when he was employed as house manager of Daniel Frohman's Lyceum Theatre that Bessy first met him and became impressed by both his business acumen and his gentlemanly ways. He was twenty-two years younger than she, and there was something about him that would remain the perennial bachelor English clubman. Rumsey had become a play agent in 1912, and the following year bought Beatrice DeMille's agency, when that lady decided to follow her sons, Cecil and William, to Hollywood. Bessy was thinking of reorganization, and he was thinking of expansion: it was natural to get together. The new partners bought out the Selwyns and merged their own businesses. In October 1914, they reorganized as the American Play Company, Inc., and became the first global super-talent agency, representing some 80 percent of all the plays produced anywhere in the United States, Great Britain, Europe, and the colonies of the American, British, and European nations. The new company also represented the literary works of many of its playwrights and was the first play agency to have a special department devoted exclusively to motion picture sales. Again deferring to a man, Bessy allowed Rumsey to act as president and general manager, while she assumed the title of vice president. She would remain responsible for the European writers as well as those Americans she already handled.

Rumsey's taste ran to light American fare, making him the perfect counterbalance to Bessy. Jack, as he was called by one and all, once said: "I have always favored comedy and farce. The lurid plays that depict the loathsomeness of life are, I think, totally unnecessary."

In filling their large staff, Rumsey and Marbury took in Richard J. Madden, a company manager for George M. Cohan, as head of the new play department. It was fortunate for his associates that he shared neither Bessy's taste for the Europeans nor Rumsey's for comedy but remained centered on those "lurid" plays that honestly depicted the human condition. Two years later, Dick Madden became enamored of the work of a young playwright whom he saw at the Provincetown Playhouse and offered to add him to the roster of the American Play Company, an offer Eugene O'Neill eagerly accepted.

*V*ia her other office, the Elisabeth Marbury Company, Bessy not only reopened the Castle House but took over the enclosed roof garden on top of the Shuberts' 44th Street Theatre and opened the more sophisticated nightspot Castles in the Air, where the popular couple could be seen dancing nightly after the show. She negotiated with Charles Dillingham for the Castles to star in *Watch Your Step*. At its Broadway opening Bessy saw something that started her thinking about a new direction for the American musical comedy. The sets and Mme Lucille's clothes had a breezy and contemporary lightness of touch. Irving Berlin's score was totally American, owing nothing to *mittel-Europa*. Bessy adored it. Song and dance were of equal importance. The one defect in this otherwise flawless musical was that what plot there was functioned as no more than an excuse to tie the musical numbers together. Bessy began to think about a musical that could be done at the tiny Princess Theatre. If she could integrate the innovative parts of *Watch Your Step* into a book that was both lighthearted and contemporary, she might realize the show that had been dancing around in the back of her head.

∞

$\mathcal{A}$nne Morgan's dedication to helping those victimized by the war in Europe was not muted by American determination not to become involved in it. Her activities were so varied during that first autumn of the war, the results might have been scattershot had it not been for the entrance into her life of the woman who would remain her devoted secretary and friend for almost thirty years. Daisy Rogers came of a good family and was possessed of impressive references. She was originally employed as Fanny Morgan's social secretary, but with that lady's withdrawal from any society other than her immediate family, there was little for her efficient employee to do. When it seemed as if her daughter would wear herself out with her projects, she suggested that Anne employ Daisy. Her new secretary proved a blessing. Anne was a model of efficiency in organizing great undertakings, but Daisy could organize her so that her energies were most expeditiously channeled.

That October, *Woman's Home Companion* magazine announced a four-part series of "talks" by Anne Morgan entitled "The American Girl," which would begin running the following month. Undoubtedly, Bessy negotiated the contract, which included a publication of the pieces in book form to be released the following spring by Harper & Brothers. What she wrote often related directly to the situation being faced by the depositors in the Vacation Savings Fund.

> That modern trade unionism is developing a mistaken attitude of class warfare and class consciousness in no sense does away with the fundamental truths of . . . collective bargaining and organized effort. . . . Class barriers and group distinctions are as dangerous in trade unions as in college clubs. . . . We have reached the day when the community can no longer afford an industry that cannot pay a living wage.

Because markets were closing in Europe, factories that exported their product were closing in the United States. Many VSF depositors were out of work. Anne organized a free employment bureau to find them regular work at regular wages. Until that was accomplished, she set up a factory similar to Edith Wharton's *ouvroirs* in which her unemployed depositors were paid a minimal sum to make bandages, nightshirts, socks, scarves, and whatever else was deemed necessary to make life a little easier for the allied troops on the front lines. The wages were underwritten by donations from their sister workers who contributed the pittances that would ordinarily have gone toward their summer's vacations.

Bessy talked the Shuberts into allowing Anne to have the 44th Street Theatre, on December 11, for a matinee amateur performance to benefit the unemployed women of New York. The theatre's operating costs were to be paid for by 5 percent of the gross. The afternoon had to have been a failure, because all the Shuberts were paid was $34.34, which Bessy convinced them to contribute to a fund for unemployed actors.

This was the first of many requests she would make of the Shuberts throughout the war for the donation of a theatre for one benefit or another. They never turned her down. Four months after the 44th Street benefit, they lent the Maxine Elliott to Bessy, Elsie, and Anne for a benefit for the hospital in Versailles. Time after time, Bessy talked the brothers into lending Anne costumes for her extravaganzas for the Vacation Savings Fund, which had been renamed for the duration the Vacation War Relief Society. The only time the Shuberts turned Anne down was when she asked for a reduction in the price of blocks of balcony and gallery seats for her Workers' Amusement Club. Lee replied they were already cheap enough, but he would be happy to see that she got the best locations.

*B*y November 1914, Willie K. and Anne Vanderbilt were back in residence in their Fifth Avenue mansion. War or no war, her second daughter, Barbara Rutherfurd, was nineteen and had to take her place in society's mating derby. Perhaps a suitable marriage would help the girl come into her own. She had always dwelled too much in her own world of shadows, feeling ill-used and suspecting she was only a distant second to her beautiful sister.

Anne had done all of what were considered the right things for her children, just as she had for her husbands and parents, but by this point had to be feeling it was something beyond bad luck that they all turned out such disappointments—parents, husbands, children, the lot. More and more, it seemed, her only gratification came from what she could do for people more desperately in need of what she could give than her family was, people to whom she felt no emotional tie. Her devotion to such causes as the Big Sisters and those afflicted with tuberculosis continued, as did her prodding of Willie K. into uncharacteristic acts of charity.

The war crowned her causes with a new dedication of a more intimate nature, one that put faces to the faceless needy and names to the unnamed victims—the wounded whom she had been professionally trained to nurse.

Willie's Christmas gift to her that year was a check for $25,000, to be donated to the *ambulance* she had established at the American Hospital. The largest individual gift made by a New Yorker up to that date for the relief of suffering in Europe, it would be applied to the separate American Ambulance Fund she had set up to equip and run one hundred American-built motor ambulances. A letter from Whitney Warren indicated her presence was possibly more important than her generosity.

> I wish for everybody's sake you could get back. It would mean so much to France. . . . While material aid is necessary and deeply appreciated, what is really wanted is the moral sympathy and sacrifice—that which goes to the heart, not to the stomach.

On January 15, 1915, at a meeting at the Hotel Astor, the National Institute of Social Sciences presented one of its annual medals to Anne Morgan. The president of the institute described her as a woman who had made the public welfare her private work and responsibility. Anne responded that the award was really intended for the group of women with whom she was associated.

> We have no new message. We are neither discoverers nor teachers—we are simply women and we believe that every woman in the community must of necessity be a worker, too. Only in this way can we carry on the message of an ideal where individual effort expresses itself in group responsibility. . . . Every woman under whatever conditions she may work and live, must come to realize that the problem of society is hers to solve—she with her neighbor is also responsible for whatever wrong there is.

On the same day Anne Morgan was awarded her medal, Anne Vanderbilt donated $44,500 to the National Committee for Mental Health. The medical director of the organization, Dr. Thomas W. Salmon, declared that she was in descent from Dorothea Dix, who in 1840 had inaugurated the first reforms in treatment of the mentally ill.

It was quite possible her interest was prompted by concern for Barbara, who was known to be delicate, difficult, or disturbed, depending on who was describing her behavior. What her mother might already have known was that the girl was clinically schizophrenic. She would have a history of breakdowns and institutionalization, which may well already have begun.

She tried never to let Barbara out of her sight and, despite its being the year of her debut and the height of the season, took her along when she left a short time later for a two-month tour of the American relief services at the front-line hospitals in France.

Barbara and she were booked to return home in April on the *Transylvania*. Before leaving Europe, Anne held a press conference. "If Americans knew the imperative of aiding the wounded soldiers of France, they would pour money into the country. I am going home to try and wake America up."

She illustrated her remarks with photographs of mutilated soldiers being saved from permanent disfigurement by volunteer doctors working in her *ambulance*. "They speak eloquently . . . I want them thrown on a screen in New York." As would become customary with many of the women trying to raise money for worthy causes, she applied to Bessy Marbury to use her influence to get a theatre donated for the purpose.

*M*ore and more, Anne Morgan was finding herself in the eccentric position of having to defend her position as a member of the upper class while at the same time declaring her oneness with the lower class. She equivocated: "There is only one class, and it consists of the folk who work and achieve. . . . Every cent of money a person has must be earned either by himself or herself"—and, remembering who she was, she added, "or their relatives."

Her praise was too often reserved for women like herself and thus sounded suspiciously close to a need to justify her own life.

> I can give you the names of scores of society women who devote many hours a week to working for the various interests that tend to uplift and better the conditions of our citizens. They do not make it a fad, but really toil, and the spirit of self-sacrifice is in their labor.

The curse of Anne Morgan's wealth, class, and sex was how often it hobbled her with the need to justify herself. Pride enabled her to rise above apology, while a blend of humility and arrogance provided the combustible fuel that continued to drive her toward her goals. To say nothing of her passion. Anne Morgan, like her father, was a person of great passion.

CHAPTER FORTY

After two years of continual failure as manager of the intimate Princess Theatre, Ray Comstock was receptive to Bessy's idea of presenting a new kind of musical. She told him that some of her French clients had been successfully adding popular music to traditional farces, creating plays with music, small casts, and limited sets, and which could profitably be staged in a small venue.

He saw possibilities immediately, and the two formed the Marbury-Comstock Company with the aim of producing a new style of musicals at the Princess Theatre. A decade earlier, Bessy's English client Paul Rubens had written exactly the kind of show she had in mind, *Mr. Popple of Ippleton*, which had been very successful in London. The overall structure was sound, but it had to be adapted to an American locale. There were also problems with the score and, of course, the title. The latter was easily taken care of by changing the name to *Nobody Home*. For the new songs, Bessy insisted on Jerome Kern, a young client for whom she had gotten the commission to provide additional songs for a big hit, *The Girl from Utah*. They included what many consider one of the best songs ever to come out of the American musical theater, "They Didn't Believe Me."

With few dissenters, it is the opinion of theatrical historians that the modern American musical began with the Princess shows. It had predecessors that were perhaps more innovative in one or another aspect but the Princess shows were the first to bring all of the innovations together in one cohesive entity. Although Bessy was associated with only the first two, the tone, form, and style of all five were set in the first, *Nobody Home,* and everything about them bore her imprimatur. It was the sum of her experience, both in the theatre and out of it, that created these shows. P. G. Wodehouse had it right. "It was Elisabeth Marbury, dear, kindly, voluminous Bessy Marbury who first thought of musical comedy on a miniature scale. . . . It was one of those inspired ideas that used to come to her every hour on the hour."

With a little hyperbole, Bessy would later boast that *Nobody Home* had been "produced, costumed, staged, and press-agented by women." Her female press agent was Dorothy Richardson, her advance road woman, May Dowling, and of course, Elsie designed the show.

Some of the backstage reforms Bessy instituted were primarily designed to improve conditions for the underpaid and often sexually harassed chorus girls, but they improved the situation of all players. She did not wait for Actor's Equity to grow teeth before making it policy that her companies were paid fair salaries and compensated for rehearsal time, something few managements of the day deemed necessary. As the production of *Nobody Home* approached its opening night, rehearsals grew longer and more exhausting. It was not unusual to work through the night, and Bessy saw to it that there was a spread of sandwiches, hot soup, and coffee available for the stagehands, actors, and staff for these calls, which often lasted from 7 P.M. until 8 A.M.

Long after the theatre ceased to be her major interest, she continued to campaign for a change in the building codes for the construction of theatres. Before *Nobody Home* could open at the tiny Princess, additional dressing rooms had to be constructed for a company of thirty-two, which was much larger than the theatre had been designed to accommodate. What was considered adequate by the owners shocked Bessy. They wanted to squeeze too many people into tiny boxlike rooms with no proper ventilation, no sinks, inadequate toilets, and certainly no showers in which dancers could wash off the perspiration produced by particularly strenuous performances. With no elevators to carry the girls up to the dressing rooms that had been built in the flies, they had to clatter up and down the long flights of stairs for their quick changes and still make entrances looking fresh and filled with energy. The stage-level accommodations for the stars were only slightly better. Bessy railed: "I have never had any ambition to build a theatre for the sake of art, but I have been sorely tempted to do so in the name of health. . . . We have had enough theaters financed by impersonal millionaires."

She fulminated that all a member of an audience really needed was a comfortable seat, good sight lines, and clean, cheerful premises. The money poured into gilt, crystal, marble, and similar paraphernalia would be better spent providing a backstage ambience that promoted the best from those paid to entertain.

During the first week in April, a society preview was scheduled, to be followed by an invitational press preview before the official opening of *Nobody Home*. As the cruelest month approached, it was obvious that the show lacked the one ingredient Bessy demanded of it: charm. At Kern's suggestion, Bessy brought in Guy Bolton to work on the book. His theatrical track record left much to be desired. She was skeptical about him, had liked some of his stories for *Smart Set*, but felt his plays missed. The most she could say was "He shows promise."

"And now," Kern remarked archly, "you're going to promise him shows." As the rewrites progressed, she tended to agree with him and signed Bolton as a client for the American Play Company.

Nobody Home opened on April 20, 1915, introducing the lighthearted format that would serve as a model for musical comedies until well after World War II. It was a success on Broadway and, with its three road companies, would eventually earn its producers a $100,000 profit, which was not bad on a $7,500 investment. A week after the opening, on April 27, Bessy, Anne Morgan, two women friends, and their personal maids left Grand Central Station aboard the *Twentieth Century* on the first leg of a vacation in California. Their ultimate destination was the International Exposition in San Francisco, which was going on as scheduled despite the war in Europe.

They were in Pasadena on May 7 when they heard that the *Lusitania* had been torpedoed by a German submarine off the coast of Ireland. The Cunard liner was carrying a load of munitions and had gone down so quickly there had been no chance fully to load the lifeboats: 1,198 of the 1,959 passengers and crew had perished. Charles Frohman was among them. With what sorrow Bessy received that news can only be imagined. Although they were not as close as they once had been, he had been a loyal friend and the man most responsible for the start of her brilliant career. Equally upsetting was the lack of any word about whether Jerome Kern was with him. The composer had been scheduled to sail, Frohman having convinced him to come along so they could play golf at St. Andrews. She had to get through to her New York home to learn that Jerry had missed the boat. He had been out at an all-night poker game and overslept.

*W*hen and where Bessy met Cole Porter is not known, but it cannot be refuted that he was her discovery. That year, she placed four of his songs in a new Shubert musical, *Hands Up.* At the out-of-town opening, she told the New Haven *Evening Register* she considered Cole Porter "the most promising composer of light opera" she had ever encountered and advised the reporter to "watch him."

The Shuberts did not share Bessy's enthusiasm for Porter, and by the time the show got to New York, he had only one song in it. Bessy did not lose her faith in the young composer and, within three months, sold a second Porter song "Two Big Eyes," to be interpolated in a score Kern wrote for *Miss Information,* a flop produced between the first two Princess shows.

*I*n September, Bessy, Elsie, and Anne Morgan arrived at White Sulphur Springs, West Virginia, having decided to use an American spa, instead of Brides or Baden-Baden, for their annual pilgrimage to take the cure. Earlier that summer, Elsie had been at another American spa, Colorado Springs, where she met the very beautiful, very rich divorcée Linda Thomas, who was to marry Cole Porter right after the war. Although she was years older than he, and there is little doubt it was another of those sexless unions, it was a successful marriage lasting until her death, thirty-five years later.

The week after the women checked into White Sulphur Springs, Willie K. and Anne Vanderbilt arrived and were put into the suite opposite the one they were sharing. The Harry Lehrs were also among the spa's guests. Mrs. Lehr had been embittered by her sexless marriage to the socialite and could not later resist a bitchy description of Anne on duty at the *ambulance,* in Neuilly. It dangled haplessly between grudging admiration and a sneer.

> Mrs. W. K. Vanderbilt would glide sinuously down from the wards to join us, picturesquely attired in the white pique uniform Worth had made for her with an impressive cap like a Russian headdress, and an enormous cross as her only adornment. She was quite the most zealous person in the whole hospital.

That zeal took the form of working from twelve to sixteen hours a day with the wounded. When Mrs. Whitelaw Reid visited the hospital, she watched Anne walk up and down the stairs at least a dozen times in the pursuance of her duties. She asked: "Are there no lifts, Mrs. Vanderbilt?"

"The lifts are for the wounded," Anne replied. Mrs. Reid was moved to present the hospital with two additional elevators—one for the patients and the other for the staff.

A month before the Vanderbilts arrived in White Sulphur Springs, a telegram had arrived at the French consulate in New York City.

> I beg you to announce to Mrs. William K. Vanderbilt the French Minister of War has addressed to her a letter of gratitude for the work of the American Committee of the Vestiare des Blesses and that she is proposed for the Gold Medal of the Ministry of Foreign Affairs in order to offer to her the highest testimony of the French government for her active and useful sympathy towards the French cause.

It was the first time an American woman had been awarded the medal. A short while later, her niece Gertrude Whitney became the second American woman to receive it in recognition of the *ambulance* Robert Bacon had persuaded her to fund.

Bessy and Elsie left White Sulphur Springs on September 19. Until their

*L*adies and Not-So-Gentle Women

departure, it had seemed to Anne Morgan that every day was "about the same" but after, the days became decidedly different. Willie K. had also disappeared from the scene. Anne M. began devoting more time and attention to Anne V. than ever before. Both had been honored that year for selfless dedication to helping others, and both were capable of small pleasures they enjoyed taking together. They played golf together and went for carriage rides through the lovely autumnal countryside of Greenbrier County. It occurred to Anne M. that Anne V. also was "very lovely." On Anne M.'s last evening, they had dinner tête-à-tête in Vanderbilt's rooms. They saw each other again the next week in New York, and regularly from then on whenever they were in the same place at the same time. If there was the possibility of a more intimate bond, it was put on hold until after the war.

While the second Princess show, *Very Good Eddie,* was on the road, Bessy found a musical that she intended to mount without any co-producers. The new show, *See America First,* had a score by her young protégé Cole Porter, but the book by Porter's Yale roommate and probable lover, T. Lawrason Riggs, though not without promise, smacked too much of the kind of spoof smart young college men found deadly droll. Guy Bolton, Bessy's first choice of a book doctor, backed out when Riggs, seconded by Porter, demanded the final say on all changes. Her second choice was the still more gifted P. G. Wodehouse. That got as far as a contract in which he agreed to help Riggs "by collaborating on the text . . . and situations . . . by giving it his best attention and endeavor." Riggs insisted he could do whatever needed to be done without any outside help. Cole and he already had written some Yale shows that he was positive were far superior to anything on Broadway, including the Princess shows. When the composer again supported him on this point, Bessy backed down. She gave Porter and Riggs her notes on what she considered absolutely necessary rewrites and sent them off, hoping they were capable of coming through for her.

Very Good Eddie opened on December 23 and was a bigger hit than the first Princess show, but, within days of its opening, it seemed as if none would follow that utilized the original creative staff. Comstock was adamant about doing a musical version of an 1894 farce, *A Milk White Flag.* Bessy thought it was a dreadful idea and refused to have anything to do with it. Kern and Bolton agreed with her, and she signed them to develop a musical comedy, *Have a Heart,* which she intended to produce the following season. In the meantime, she was free to concentrate on turning *See America First* into a hit.

*O*orothie Bigelow had a promising enough voice to have been taken as a student by the great Metropolitan Opera star Jean de Reszke, but had never appeared in anything approaching a professional production. To everybody's amazement, Bessy gave her the lead in *See America First,* rather than putting her in the chorus, where she undoubtedly belonged. One of her failings as a producer was this passion for discovering unknowns. It had served her well with several of the principals in the Princess shows, and she obviously saw no reason for it to fail her in this case. Bigelow would later blame Riggs's inexperience for the show's failure, while he conversely placed the blame with her. They were both right in regard to their own limitations and wrong in the sense that the ultimate responsibility rested with Bessy, who, after all, was the one professional involved with the enterprise.

After the out-of-town opening, Porter wired his mother that the show had been "enthusiastically received" and that they had "high hopes for brilliant opening in New York." Contrary to his later condemnation of the star, he said: "Bigelow scores tremendous hit."

The writers were convinced they had a success. What rewrites Bessy managed to get from them were clumsily executed. Nevertheless, she refused to give up, and for one performance it seemed as if her efforts would be rewarded. On the night before the New York opening, Bessy's society preview of *See America First* was triumphant. There were cheers for all concerned. It was a different story the next night, when the critics came. The disastrous reviews forced Bessy to post the closing notice.

On the Friday after *See America First* closed, Bessy went over to Jerry Kern's house to hear him play the score for the almost completed *Have a Heart,* which she held under option. Wodehouse, who was doing the lyrics, lagged behind because Kern, with rare exceptions, insisted on writing the melodies first and then having the words set to them. She was pleased with what she had heard of Kern's music. Lee Shubert's faith in her as a producer had not been dampened by her recent failure, and she was certain that he would support her production of the piece.

For a woman who had just had a big flop, she left the next morning to spend the weekend with Anne Morgan, at Cragston, with a light heart and the feeling that she was on top of everything. Anne was also in a celebratory mood. Although it smacked of the reactionary notion that women of achievement had to be linked to an influential man, it was flattering that April's issue of *Woman's Home Companion* was running a pictorial essay, "She Takes After Her Father," in which she was featured along with Alice Roosevelt Longworth; Commander Evangeline Booth, the head of the Salvation

Army and its founder's daughter; and Virginia Gildersleeve, the dean of Barnard and daughter of Judge Henry Alger Gildersleeve. Of Anne, it was observed that her "inherited executive ability is responsible for many helpful enterprises mostly for working girls."

Anne had been traveling across the country proselytizing for a variety of causes. Although her priorities remained the girls' Vacation Fund and relief for the war victims of France, at a St. Louis women's club she broached equal rights for women from her own perspective.

> It is up to the women to force on the nation a realization that universal military service is the cornerstone of the nation's existence. Women demand equality—then they must share an equal part when the demand on them comes in a crisis.

Anne, Bessy, Elsie, and the Vanderbilts were booked to sail on the *Lafayette,* on June 24. The days before the sailing were particularly busy for Anne Vanderbilt. On June 20, Willie K. and she joined 431 other guests journeying out to Westbury, Long Island, for a party in Gertrude Vanderbilt Whitney's studio on the vast Whitney estate. Among them were Anne Morgan, Bessy Marbury, the Hewitt sisters, Robert Bacon, and 250 "representatives of the art world, an impressive group of painters, sculptors, illustrators, publishers, architects, dealers, collectors, and painters." It was at this party that Anne Morgan met the handsome and celebrated sculptor Malvina Hoffman, who would later play a significant role in her life.

Not too many years before, Gertrude's mother, Alice Vanderbilt, would not have permitted many of these people on her premises, and now her daughter not only played hostess to them but also had enlisted in their ranks by becoming a professional sculptor—and a good one. She had also opened a gallery on Eighth Street, in Greenwich Village, devoted to the exhibition and promotion of contemporary American artists. She would live to oversee its expansion into the Whitney Museum, thus joining Bessy Marbury's other friends the Hewitt sisters and Isabella Stewart Gardner in being the first American women to establish institutions of international reputation dedicated to their individual tastes as collectors.

Back in January 1916, Anne Vanderbilt had announced the engagement of her younger daughter, Barbara Rutherfurd, to Cyril Hatch. This match was far more unsuitable than Winthrop Rutherfurd's would have been with Consuelo Vanderbilt and proved another contrast between Willie K.'s two wives. While Alva had destroyed her daughter's chance for happiness by crushing the match, Anne allowed it, though she disapproved strongly. Cyril was eighteen years older than Barbara, of modest fortune and looks, and of no discernible occupation beyond belonging to many of the snob clubs, but the delicate girl insisted that she was in love, and her mother could only pray that she would find sufficient happiness to bring her stability at last.

On Saturday, June 24, the group boarded the *Lafayette.* For reasons of wartime safety, the French liner would be diverted to Bordeaux instead of landing in Le Havre or Cherbourg. The two Annes already had duties they were looking forward to performing in their respective relief installations. Elsie was certain that there was something she could do that would make her feel part of the great struggle—something heroic and inspiring. Though she did not yet know what it would be, she knew she would not be returning to New York at the end of the summer with Bessy, who was anxious to return even before they left. The latter had celebrated her sixtieth birthday that week, and a whole new career was stretching before her just as if she was young and just starting out.

CHAPTER FORTY-ONE ॐ

After the sinking of the *Lusitania,* no luxury liner making the transatlantic crossing could ignore the possibility of attack by German submarines. To cross on a ship owned by one of the belligerents was considered, to say the least, foolhardy, but that did not deter many of the best-known women in America, who were as anxious to get into the fray as President Wilson was to stay out of it. This was evidenced by the distinguished group sailing aboard the French Line's *Lafayette.* In an effort to avoid possible attacks, the ship was blacked out and followed a quixotic path across the ocean, but life in the soigné first-class salons retained its accustomed luxury.

The voyage was the start of Anne Vanderbilt's fifth wartime tour of duty at the American Hospital, soon to be renamed American Military Hospital #1. Not for her were the uniforms that announced service in the war on many of the other female passengers. Hers were reserved for the long hours of duty tending to the wounded. Tall and slender, arrayed in impeccable jewels and couture clothes, she turned heads as she made her way across the dining room to the captain's table, at which the Vanderbilts, Anne Morgan, Bessy, and Elsie had been invited to take their meals. Given the situation, there was no way the table talk could not concern the war.

Mrs. Vanderbilt already had given an interview to the Sunday *New York*

*L*adies and Not-So-Gentle Women

Times magazine that some of her friends had considered in execrable taste, because she had graphically described the mutilated faces of men she nursed daily when on duty in Neuilly. It had been a conscious effort to awaken her countrymen to the extreme suffering of soldiers, often little more than boys, to shock them into doing more to help. She again recounted her experiences, inspiring the others with her courage and fortitude.

Anne Morgan was the only person at the table to approach Anne Vanderbilt in wartime experience. In addition to dispatching much-needed cotton to France and organizing members of the working girls' Vacation Society as an *ouvroir,* she had founded the American Fund for French Wounded (AFFW) with Bessy and Myron Herrick as members of the board of directors. Its purpose was to raise money for the purchase of supplies and motor vehicles for military hospitals and to establish emergency front-line medical stations. Morgan had been to Europe twice since the start of the war to set up the organization and to institute its day-to-day operations.

Elsie listened avidly and felt like the person most out of it in the world. Hordes of previously self-indulgent, sometimes vain and frivolous women were flocking to the cause, as could be seen by the unprecedented number of tables in first class occupied solely by women in an array of custom-made uniforms. Unsung and often less eager to be aboard the ship were an equal number of women in the third-class dining room. They had been drafted into service, and their uniforms were of a familiar domestic design. These were the personal maids without whom none of the ladies in first class would have dreamed of going to war. They were the female equivalent of the equerries of officers and gentlemen in the old guard European regiments.

Along with the suffrage movement, this race to expose themselves to the dangers of the front lines was symptomatic of a deeper malaise, of an often unspoken rebellion against traditional roles. For many, the effort would end with the war and the vote. They would return to hearth and home, but even for them it would never be quite as it was. It might take another war and another women's rebellion before men would admit that it had happened, but the inevitable changes in women's roles in society began during World War I.

At the beginning of the war, Baron Henri de Rothschild and his wife, Mathilde, had opened a military hospital in Issy-les-Moulineaux, an industrial suburb south of Paris and some twelve miles east of Versailles, which Mathilde continued to run. Elsie was invited there to witness the new ambrine treatment for burns sustained in battle that had been developed by Dr. Barthe de Sandfort and was being administered at the Rothschild *ambulance*. Ambrine was a liquid waxy substance applied to burned skin that ameliorated the healing process. Although deemed most advanced in its day, it has long since been superseded by more efficacious treatments.

The moment Elsie saw the remarkable results of Dr. de Sandfort's treatment, she knew that she had found her cause and applied to Mathilde de Rothschild for a place in her hospital. She agreed to give Elsie a chance on condition that she develop a habit with which not even the totally addicted Bessy and Anne had been able to tempt her.

> I was told that I could not stand it unless I learned to smoke, as the odor of burned flesh would make me violently ill. I have never liked to smoke but, so eager was I to help, I was perfectly willing to smoke if need be.

Her devotion to the work of the Mission Ambrine, as it was called, did not subside until the war ended, over two years later. In the sphere of humanity, it was her finest hour.

*B*essy spent that summer assisting Anne Morgan with the work of the American Fund for the French Wounded. They sorted through the necessities and small luxuries sent by the organization and then delivered them directly to the patients in the hospitals. They visited *ambulance* installations just inside the front lines, where Anne found "every moment beyond words"; and Bessy, no Francophile, was most moved by the uncomplaining courage of the British "Tommy." She was delighted when the black soldiers from the French African colonies found her plumpness far more attractive and womanly than the fashionably slim nurses.

As they went about their work, Bessy was particularly impressed by the dedication and efficiency of two old friends. There were several ambulance services, but in Bessy's mind none were run with the efficiency of Piatt Andrew's American Field Service, which ferried the wounded from Gare La Chapelle, where they were brought up from the front, to the American Hospital to be delivered into the charge of Anne Vanderbilt, whose generosity largely endowed the Field Service. Bessy had known Mrs. Vanderbilt for years but never before had she been so impressed with the quality of the woman.

In August, Anne Vanderbilt was given permission to accompany Piatt Andrew on an inspection tour of the front line. She did not know what to expect, but as they approached their destination, she was most struck by its ordinariness. There were soldiers and other suggestions of war in the background, but over the previous two years this was to be found all over France. The road they traversed was only fourteen hundred yards from the German trenches. Not knowing exactly what she had expected of the front, she said to Andrew: "I am going to lie like a trooper when I get back to Paris. You will never catch me admitting that I did not hear a gun."

As if on cue, a battery of allied guns concealed in the foliage at the side of the road opened ear-splitting fire and almost simultaneously were answered by a German shell whistling over their head and spattering dirt over them as it landed in a neighboring field. There seemed no justification for the murderous dialogue other than the ennui of the soldiers after so many silent hours in their bunkers. On both sides, they were little more than bored, when not boisterous, teenagers with time on their hands and lethal weapons in them.

Their destination that day was a front-line dressing station. The wounded were carried in directly from skirmishes, given emergency treatment, and loaded into ambulances to be taken to hospitals by Andrew's Field Service, often dodging enemy fire with all the agility their awkward vehicles could muster.

Anne was taken a short distance into the communication trench, and this woman—nurtured in the nineteenth century—had her first vision of what the twentieth century would be when she beheld the amazingly complex telephone system connecting front-line observation posts with gun batteries miles in the rear. Neither life nor war had ever before been conducted on this level. She found a measure of comfort in turning from this fearsome apparatus to catch sight of "trailing vines and . . . wild flowers that covered these descents into hell as if they had been peaceful garden walks."

What was constantly heartening was the gallantry, the élan, of the American nurses and these young ambulance drivers who had not been conscripted, were not being paid, were not there in defense of their own country. The foolhardiness of it all, the vainglory of war, was never uppermost in the minds of Anne Vanderbilt, Anne Morgan, or Elsie as it was with Bessy Marbury. These women were being given their first chance to pursue glory by the time-honored means of men and had become like men in seeking virtue in war's destructiveness.

The sad part was that this war had nothing to do with freedom or equality. Had they wanted to fight for those things, they would have done better to stay home and march with the suffragettes.

Outside Verdun-sur-Meuse, they visited a château that had been converted into a hospital for those cases so bad they could not be moved by train or ambulance. Most of the wounded were brought there to die. Anne had never before been in a hospital where no women nurses were allowed and found the experience the most unpleasant of the trip.

> There are many things that only a woman is able to do, and if ever a woman was needed anywhere it was there in that hospital, looking after and comforting, as only a woman can, the recovery or the death of those desperately wounded men. I still feel too deeply to bring myself to talk about this. I am told it is one of the inevitable horrors of war, and it is useless to dwell upon what cannot be remedied.

Many buildings were in ruins but no more so than many of the other places through which they had passed, and, as in those places, the normal commerce of the lives of the inhabitants continued. And then she again realized how different this war was from all those that had preceded it. The Battle of Verdun had not been conducted with siege and bombardment, as would have been the case in an earlier time, and had not been waged only for Verdun but for the whole area through which they had been traveling for the past two days—the airplanes, the massive communications center she had seen the night before, the batteries of guns so distant from their targets. They wanted to stay and explore but remained in their car, feeling that their presence helped in no way. Remebering all those who died for it, "the place was too sacred for sight-seeing."

The next day, they reached Reims. Anne was again profoundly moved by what she saw.

> The cathedral, our destination, of course, may be said to stand in a sea of ruins, except for the unscathed statue of Jeanne d'Arc. The archbishop's palace gives the impression of an abandoned wreck thrown up on the shore. . . . The ruin, one felt, was final, unredeemed, and I was prepared for the same emotions when I stood by the cathedral.

The great edifice was shattered, but its outline remained, and in it she found a "new nobility, because the scars tell and will tell forever of the great tragedy through which France is passing."

*H*arry Lehr reputedly kept a diary containing observations he did not want his wife or anybody else to read. His first mention of F. D., or Francis Dike, was made shortly after the latter arrived from New York with his new wife. It was later bruited about that the Scottish Anne Murray had only married him to become an American citizen, although Lehr observed: "She is awfully pretty and amusing. They seem very much in love."

Lehr introduced Anne Murray Dike to Anne Morgan, who "at once struck up a great friendship with Mrs. D. She wants her to join her at her hospital." Anne Morgan suggested that Anne Dike could live in "her house . . . so she will be well looked after." That would certainly have meant her house in Versailles and the hospital Bessy, Elsie, and she had established next door.

The relationship between the two women grew in intensity. Morgan noted in her diary that September 3 was "not a good day" despite Anne Dike's having come out to Versailles for Sunday lunch and to stay the night. That sort of occasion usually elicited a "great" from Morgan.

What soured it was made clear by an entry in Lehr's diary two days later. He had lunched at home before retiring to take his afternoon nap. "Then there was an awful row, really it was too dreadful for words."

Francis Dike burst in upon Lehr, calling him every foul name under the sun for having introduced his wife to Anne Morgan. Mrs. Dike had joined the staff of the hospital at Villa Trianon and was living there in Morgan's new quarters. When he went out to Versailles to see her, she had made him "furiously jealous" with a story of an intimacy shared with Morgan. He intended to have it out with Morgan and was not going to permit his wife to stay one day longer. Lehr declared: "I never felt more nervous or uncomfortable in my life."

During the next few days, the rumors were flying. It was said Anne Morgan and Francis Dike had had "a frightful row" in public. Now he was running around Paris telling everybody he met that Morgan was trying to ruin his marriage.

By the middle of the next week, the situation was beginning to wear Morgan down sufficiently for her to want to get out of Paris. She left with Elsie for still another tour of the front line, although she had returned from one only two weeks earlier. Elsie was tonic, and on September 15 she noted, "Great eve Elsie," the only time, in all of the volumes of her diaries, her supreme accolade of "great" was applied to anything associated with Miss de Wolfe.

Morgan was back in Paris the following week to "lunch with Miss Dike." Bessy and she sailed two weeks later, aboard the *Lafayette*. Extremely upset that the situation with Dike was not yet resolved, she felt the need to be very near to her dearest friend and lamented, "The rooms very comfortable but Bessy quite far away in 135. I am 110."

Anne Dike returned to New York in the early part of the new year and went up to Cragston for the Lincoln Birthday weekend. On the Monday, Morgan felt "seedy & in bed all A.M." Dike came in for a talk that was significant enough for her to make note of it. They returned to the city that evening. Morgan was feeling rotten enough to spend the next day in bed but was cheered by the arrival of a letter from Dike. Morgan was back at work on Wednesday, but two more letters arrived, on Thursday and Saturday. The two women met again on Sunday for "a talk that meant much."

It was decided. Anne Dike would have her marriage annulled. From then on, Anne Morgan and she would be comrades in love and war.

CHAPTER FORTY-TWO ॐ

Bessy Marbury, Elsie de Wolfe, and Anne Morgan were back in the United States in time to witness the 1916 presidential election. Charles Evans Hughes had resigned from the Supreme Court to run on the Republican-Progressive ticket against Woodrow Wilson. With Wilson, never a man of great popularity, running on a "He kept us out of war" slogan, the incumbent was not considered the odds-on favorite, especially with the pro-war group. Anne Morgan's passionate commitment to France would have made her appreciate a franchise enabling her to vote for Hughes, who lost by less than 600,000 in the popular vote and 23 electoral votes in a race so close it took three days to determine the outcome.

Wilson's coattails were long enough for the Democrats to gain control of both Houses of Congress, making it a sad day for both armies of female militants—those marching to Europe and those marching in the suffrage parades. The latter were soon to be placated. Although the Democrats had no suffrage plank, Wilson came out in favor of it, enabling the Democratic Senate of the state of New York to amend its constitution. In November 1917, New York women were given the right to vote. While women had the franchise in several smaller states, New York was then the most powerful state in the union. Its action indicated an amendment to the United States Constitution would soon be enacted with relatively little obstruction.

Although attacks by German-made dirigibles, perfected by Graf Von Zeppelin, posed a steady threat to London, they were rarely launched against Paris, but one such raid did occur in the early hours of March 18, 1917. Bombs fell uncomfortably close to the hospital in Neuilly, and Anne

Vanderbilt wondered if the Germans had become so incensed by American efforts to help the allied wounded that they had tried to destroy the facility.

As strongly as Anne suspected the Germans might seek revenge on a still neutral America by destroying a military hospital, she also felt that French indignation at American neutrality was held in check only by the work of American volunteers in the hospitals and field stations. More money had to be raised to continue this work. It was a part of her reason for returning to New York two weeks hence. She intended to awaken the United States to the role it must assume in the war. What greater proof of the need for action was there than that on the same day as the zeppelin raid on Paris, German submarines also had torpedoed three U.S. ships, resulting in the loss of many American lives?

Anne Vanderbilt's wake-up call was not required. While she was on her way home, Wilson went before a joint session of Congress to ask for a declaration of war against Germany, declaring: "The world must be made safe for democracy." The resolution was passed by overwhelming majorities in both Houses.

During that first spring of American entry into the war, Mrs. Vanderbilt accepted a Red Cross commission to take charge of all of the canteens being set up in France for the American troops. The new responsibility was undertaken with the understanding that it would not interfere with her work at the hospital.

A week after the declaration of war, Anne Morgan commissioned Theodore Spicer Simpson to design a commemorative medal for the American Fund for the French Wounded. The first three were struck in gold and would be taken to France by the two Annes—Dike and Morgan—for presentation to Marshal Joffre, Premier Viviani, and President Poincaré. Reproductions would be sold to raise money to aid displaced civilians in the devastated areas of France. Morgan was treasurer of the effort, and Dike and Marbury among those on the committee. In July, Bessy would recommend that one of the gold medals be given to her old friend Sarah Bernhardt.

Even before new American recruits could be embarked on troopships, American women veterans of the war were on their way back to France. On May 26, Elsie de Wolfe, Anne Morgan, and Anne Dike sailed for Europe. Elsie was returning to serve in the ambrine facility for the duration. Dike and Morgan were going to take charge of ten women who called themselves the American Volunteers. They intended to establish headquarters in an unused army barracks in Aisne Département, which was among the most war-buffeted areas of France. Their first task would be to build sheds to serve as primitive hospitals, dispensaries, warehouses, and canteens.

The American Volunteers would eventually work under the auspices of the Committee for a Devastated France, which would be set up by Morgan as a semi-independent organization within the American Fund for the French Wounded. From the beginning, she treated it as her personal fiefdom, but after appointing Anne Murray Dike to the chairmanship, she modestly assumed the office of second in command. It was her custom to refuse titular leadership of the organizations she sponsored. In this instance, it also served to draw the women closer together in a relationship in which they would function as one both emotionally and professionally. Whether the affair was consummated sexually remained a matter of speculation for the rest of their lives.

*I*n her sixtieth year, an old woman by the statistics on longevity of the day, Bessy Marbury had no intention of retiring in the foreseeable future. Her ability to walk was seriously impaired by the combination of arthritis and her weight, but there was no decline in her mobility. She usually achieved what she went after with an inexorable single-mindedness that was the envy of her business associates. But she made several significant errors that year. Her decision to concentrate all of her efforts upon becoming a powerful producer was one of the largest mistakes of her career. By resigning from the American Play Company, she divested herself of her major source of power.

With the women she loved most both overseas, Bessy turned to Mercedes de Acosta, the sister of Rita Lydig and as handsome in a masculine way as Rita was beautiful in a feminine way. Bessy had been captivated by this young "boy" from the moment Rita introduced them. It was not long before she began to refer to herself as Mercedes's grandmother. Mercedes later recalled her adolescent audacity: "I made her laugh by saying she seemed such a man to me that I felt she was more like my grandfather." Bessy was so amused, she began to sign her letters to the girl "Granny Pa," and Granny Pa, or Granny Pop, she would remain until the day she died.

Although Mercedes was actually born during the last decade of the nineteenth century, she was the first truly twentieth-century person with whom Bessy became involved. She was openly lesbian from adolescence on and did little to hide her sexual proclivities, except from her beloved, devoutly Catholic mother. It was for her sake that, like many of her homosexual women friends of her generation, she got married, but it was to a much older man so acquiescent he allowed her to do the almost unprecedented thing of retaining her maiden name, promising never to refer to her by his name no matter what the circumstances. There was no attempt to discourage or interfere with her many lesbian affairs during the fifteen years they remained married.

Bessy sent Mercedes to see Nazimova in *War Brides,* a propaganda one-acter she was doing with great success in vaudeville at the Palace. After the performance, Mercedes was convinced that "she was a great soul as well as a great artist." She could dream of "nothing but meeting her" and badgered Bessy for an introduction. When they did meet, she averred that "fate brought Alla Nazimova into my life." There was no doubt they would not part that night. "We walked home together feeling the sympathy of old friends, but with that underlying excitement of having found a new one."

It was the beginning of a sexual career for Mercedes de Acosta in the course of which she would become the most legendary lesbian seducer of her era, with a list of conquests that included Pola Negri, Eva LeGallienne, Marlene Dietrich, Isadora Duncan, and Greta Garbo.

*O*n April 24, 1917, Congress passed the Liberty Loan Act, allowing the country to raise money for the war effort by the sale of Liberty Bonds. It was not long before every town gathering, every street corner, blossomed with celebrities from the worlds of politics, business, theatre, and films, all exhorting their listeners to "Give until it hurts."

Bessy always had been articulate to a fault. The ability to express herself in a warm, maternal contralto, burnished by far too many cigarettes inhaled over far too many years, was married to a talent for making a pitch, which was at the heart of her professional success. The union made her a natural tourer for Liberty Bonds. She threw herself into the work with the same zeal with which she approached any task that awakened her enthusiasm. "I will work night and day and 16 hours a day, for anything I believe in and for anything which appeals to me as my job of the moment."

Her greatest moment came down in Wall Street. On the steps of the Sub-treasury Building that faced "the Appian Way of high finance," a friend and she did "such heavyweight team work that we separated ten millions in ten minutes from the pocket of bankers."

The tandem occurrence of America's entry into the war and the inevitability of suffrage elicited from Bessy Marbury a less covert avowal of her professed Catholicism, which hitherto had been a more or less private contract between God and her. Much of her war work was done via the National Catholic Diocesan War Council, the League of Catholic Women, and especially the Knights of Columbus, a fraternal organization with which she felt a much stronger affinity than with any group of do-good females. She became the K.C.'s first female secretary and, in a manner of speaking, its apostle to women.

The first that many of her friends and acquaintances knew of her new attitude was the announcement that she was translating Maurice Barrès's book *Les Diverses Familles spirituelles de la France* (English title, *The Faith of France)* for Houghton Mifflin. Her sympathy for France was renewed by a combination of its suffering during the war and her new public espousal of religious affiliation. What appealed to her in the book was the writer's belief that the spirits of France and Catholicism were so integrated they could not be separated. It called for a spiritual rebirth of France as it emerged from the war, in which all of the faiths would remain as united as they had been while fighting a common enemy.

The inevitability of suffrage reawakened Bessy's keen interest in politics, which had been quiescent since the death of Francis Marbury. She had no personal problem with some of the questionable practices of Tammany Hall. They were pros as well as pols: she admired a professional's ability to get things done. As for corruption, she had lived too long and too intimately with the world not to know that it was often endemic to the democratic system. The least corrupt governments were generally totalitarian.

In 1913, there had appeared on the New York political scene the first of the three captivating Irish politicos who would win her heart so completely that she could overlook deficiencies in polish, manner, and, in one case, honesty. The other two Gaelic charmers were Alfred E. Smith and James J. Walker.

John Purroy Mitchell was Bessy's type down to the final *l* of his name—a tall, good-looking, well-educated, young, dark-eyed Irishman with a wicked and witty tongue so fast on the draw his mind occasionally could not keep up with it, a shortcoming that would eventually end his promising career. A thirty-four-year-old Democrat but no Tammany minion, he was nominated on a progressive, new Republican-Fusion ticket and in 1913 was elected the youngest mayor in the city's history. Theodore Roosevelt pronounced Mitchell's administration as "nearly ideal" as he had seen in his lifetime. But by the time he came up for reelection, in 1917, his brutal honesty had alienated the Republicans as well as both Tammany and his own Irish constituency, who were soured by his insistence that the city had the right to investigate the books of those Catholic charities it subsidized. His sole appearance on the ballot was as the candidate of the reformist Fusion party.

Bessy's first foray into politics was as a member of the Women's Committee to Reelect Mayor Mitchell, in which she was joined by the liberal Democrats Daisy Harriman and Lillian Wald, and the liberal Republicans Maud

*L*adies and Not-So-Gentle Women

Wetmore and Mrs. Charles Evans Hughes. For all their efforts, a Tammany hack, John Hylan, beat their candidate in a Democratic sweep that prompted the patrician President Wilson to ask of his own party's victor in New York City: "How is it possible for the greatest city in the world to place such a man in high office?"

Another Democratic victor that autumn was the Irish Catholic sheriff of New York County, Alfred E. Smith, who, when asked his opinion of suffrage, shot a stream of tobacco juice into a spittoon and said he thought a woman's place was in the home. It would not be long before a group of women including Bessy and Belle Moskowitz taught him better manners and helped to turn him into a politician to reckon with on the national scene.

Bessy was hooked. Politics were better, more exciting theatre than anything she was producing with the Shubert brothers. She decided to end her business relationship with the boys right after the musical they were doing, *Girl O' Mine,* opened in January. Once the war was over, she would arrange to return to the American Play Company to handle only those projects that interested her and those clients, such as Maugham, who were clamoring for the resumption of her services. That would leave her free to devote the larger part of her energies to coming up with schemes to help the Democrats gather the votes she so recently had spurned as an anti-suffragist.

CHAPTER FORTY-THREE

From the moment they arrived back in France, Morgan and Dike had been badgering the authorities to be assigned a zone in which to set up relief and rehabilitation facilities for the civilian victims of the war. This would be the major concern of their American Committee for a Devastated France for the duration of the war and beyond. The authorities eventually assigned them a rectangle roughly measuring thirty square miles in the Aisne district that extended west along the Aisne river from the ancient French capital of Soissons to medieval Compiègne, north along the Oise River to Chauny, across to Laon, the capital of Aisne Département, and back to Soissons. Blérancourt served as headquarters. They had twenty-five villages in varying degrees of despoliation with 850 families in need of everything from houses, to nursing, to food, to clothes—families that had been ruined by the war. To meet no more than this group's basic requirements took ten thousand dollars a month, [over fifty thousand dollars in today's currency].

The Morgan-Dike bivouacs were hastily constructed wooden shacks for which the military provided electricity. The women were up by seven and drove themselves until late into the night. What they accomplished in the first four months was remarkable. They were the first of the relief groups to establish agricultural collectives in each of their communes, which meant gathering farm tools, livestock, seeds, and young fruit trees. It was a monumental accomplishment but essential to survival. The minister of agriculture bestowed Le Mérite Agricole on Dike and Morgan, the first of their impressive series of awards.

There was an unending need for supplies. Dike wrote to the New York headquarters of the American Fund for the French Wounded explaining what was needed to a group of home-front ladies who previously had thought baby clothes headed the list:

> We need soap, blankets, warm underwear, and stockings, and we need money to buy beds, mattresses, stoves, trees and livestock. We have groaned at times under the number of babies' garments and infant dresses—babies and children are so few and far between! . . . We must have 200 stoves this winter for the people returning to their homes—each stove costs twenty dollars—not including the stove pipe. This is an expensive item in our work.

The year they arrived, Anne Morgan purchased the *domaine* of Blérancourt with its ghostly ruin of a grand château. The acreage would serve for planting crops and would provide a pasture for the herd of cows she had purchased to provide milk for the children and old people. Both Annes were extraordinarily capable executives, but from the beginning there had been vast differences in their approaches to those they were dedicated to helping and, by extension, to each other. Dike was without sentimentality—a nononsense woman counting the number of nuts and bolts to get the job done properly. The enterprise was the object. Get it done right, and everything else would fall into place. For Morgan, it was always the suffering of the people, particularly the women, that spurred her to action, as had been true of most of her crusades since the shirtwaist strike.

> Try as much as we will much of the suffering must continue to the end, but there is an indefinite amount that can be done to ease the burden and lighten the load. When we find three old people . . .

sleeping on the floor of a hovel without blankets and without a stove, you can imagine what it means to the brave woman . . . looking after them to know that we are there [with] warm clothes . . . food-stuff . . . tools to work in her garden so that they may have vegetables all winter long.

When Baronne de Rothschild moved her Mission Ambrine to Compiègne so they would be closer to the battlefields, Elsie went with them, which brought her less than twenty miles from Morgan at Blérancourt. Anne respected the person Elsie had become. The war had enabled her to retrieve what was finest in her character. It was as if Elsie had reached deep inside of herself to bring forth the long-buried qualities of courage, compassion, and wit that had enabled her to cope with all of her early tribulations. Her patients were almost always *poilus,* the unranked French conscripts, and she was marvelous with them. Often, when first brought in, their burns were so agonizing they could not bear to be touched, but she would patiently overcome their qualms, promising that their suffering would soon end. They were skeptical, but after five minutes of treatment she would hear a deep sigh accompanied by a look of infinite gratitude. Many would murmur much the same words: "*Merci, ma bonne dame! Ça soulage! Ça soulage!*"

For Elsie, it was "a reward so infinitely touching . . . that I felt as if I could go on forever."

Once the United States entered the war, the number of uniformed American women crossing the Atlantic swelled beyond all expectation despite the catapulting danger from German submarine warfare. During the month in which Congress declared war, the U-boats sank close to one million tons of shipping. The women were undaunted. The Red Cross was the largest relief organization providing volunteer female personnel in Europe, but there were literally hundreds of others contributing to this unofficial army. They paid for their uniforms, passage, and expenses once in France. They were perforce largely a middle- and upper-class group, as were the suffragettes who, though officially opposed to war, were beginning to join them now that their sons, husbands, and brothers were being conscripted and sent into battle.

The majority of the women were earnest, dedicated people risking their lives and intent upon doing the best possible job, but inevitably there were those for whom things were deemed necessities that were, in truth, privileges. World War I was the last class-conscious war, the last manifestation of that European world in which one's rank was largely determined at one's birth. These women were analogous to the British officers and gentlemen who did not go off to the war without their personal servants and Savile Row uniforms. It was not a lack of seriousness of intent: it was a recognition of war as an intermission in a way of life that in no way dispensed with that way of life.

Good work was being done. The women operating the canteens, hospitals, hospices, and relief shelters were totally dedicated and often in grave physical danger. What they did was vital to the war effort and would have gone undone, weakening that effort, if it meant soldiers had to be pulled out of the front lines to replace them. The women on the endless tours of inspection were likewise indispensable. They were the conduits to organizations on the home front and arranged for what was needed to get to where it was most needed—to make certain that what was wasteful was eliminated.

It was inevitable that in this crisscrossing of the ludicrously named no-man's-land, they would run into old friends. Edith Wharton was giving Berenson a tour of the devastated areas, and they dropped in on Elsie, in Compiègne. She described administering the ambrine to a miserable soul whose face had been burned away. He had murmured to her, *"Je voudrais vous donnez un sourire pour vous remercier."* ("I wish I could give you a smile to thank you.")

Daisy Harriman and Ruth Morgan stopped to see Anne Morgan at Blérancourt, an odd place for a reunion of the Morgan mansion schoolroom chums. The shell of the old château was an attractive place, and Daisy found the work well organized, but as they "lunched to the accompaniment of the cannon," she wondered if "they are not a little too dangerously near the front."

The strains of war were often unbearable. Those who experienced them needed someplace to which they could retreat. For Elsie, it was a leave every third weekend at the Villa Trianon. Occasionally, Dike and Morgan would be with her or go on their own. The weekends were as they had been before, except the old friends from American and French theatre and society would be mixed with ranking officials of the allied governments and dashing warrior generals. Berenson echoed the thoughts of many of the others when he said that only at Villa Trianon did he feel his "real self . . . in the midst of visual values that call back all I have striven and lived for."

*E*leanor Robson Belmont was on assignment from the Red Cross to see what could be done to improve the accomplishment of its objectives. It was by far the largest of the relief organizations but was being frustrated at every point by the military. Eleanor found a dearth of medical supplies at many front-line hospitals and emergency stations. The Red Cross had warehouses bursting with these necessities, but she was told the army refused to requisition them on the grounds that the military could take care of its own. The suffering of the wounded was intensified by a lack of simple creature comforts. When she again pointed out that the Red Cross was ready at that very moment to supply robes, slippers, toiletry kits, cigarettes, books, and comforters, the army response was, "This is war. Men at war cannot be pampered."

Eleanor returned to Paris burning to do something about these gross military errors in judgment relating to the treatment of the wounded. If there had been a commanding general of the army of women volunteers, it would surely have been Anne Vanderbilt. She was the one person Eleanor knew who might be able to cut through the red tape to reach the right people. She was not disappointed. Anne arranged a quiet dinner in her home with Surgeon General Bradley. His first reaction was to make light of Eleanor's list of regulations that should be amended, but after Mrs. Vanderbilt "gently but firmly supported every recommendation," he reconsidered. Changes were soon instituted in all of the army rules that related to these matters.

By the beginning of January 1918, the Annes, Morgan and Dike, had made Blérancourt the center of a large aid program embracing most of the Aisne district. Morgan began to think that one of the Renaissance pavilions might be renovated and serve as a private residence. Any decision would have to be postponed until after the war.

That month, Anne Dike dispatched a year-end report to the executive committee of the American Fund for the French Wounded that was an amalgam of optimism and desperation. They needed stoves but had no use for additional motor kitchens. Of the five already sent, they had need of only two but were buying enormous goodwill from the French army by lending the other three to them for the soldiers' *popote* (mess). Anne wished the committee to express their gratitude to the Edison employees for their gift of a phonograph. "The gay American music will honestly bring a great deal of joy and help . . . through the long, wearisome, wintry days."

The objects of bulk they needed were incubators, updated versions of the one with which Bessy Marbury had started her first commercial enterprise. Dike explained that the value to the country was so unquestionable, she would rather have them and fewer clothes and furniture to distribute. The thing they needed most desperately was money to keep up the programs they already had initiated. These could help make France agriculturally self-sufficient and free America from having to use tons of valuable cargo space for food to feed the country, space better devoted to those supplies necessary to win the war. Despite the amount of land in German hands, there were acres still not being cultivated because all of the men between eighteen and forty-seven were in the armed forces. This land could be used for grazing, if they could only afford to buy sheep and cattle. Dike and Morgan would also have the million vegetable seedlings that the army was cultivating for them in its gardens ready for distribution to the cooperative farms they had organized, but each hectare (two and one-half acres) required almost six hundred dollars to plant, cultivate, and harvest. Each cooperative farmer and his family had to live, and who was to pay for the twelve hours a day of hard labor they would have to devote to land belonging not to them but to men away fighting or captured by the Germans? It was beyond their resources. Dike lamented: "This is a moment of great discouragement to us, because cooperative work without funds, no matter how much good will there is, can accomplish nothing."

*A*nne Morgan's life had changed in a way that signaled the end of her relationship with Bessy as it had been. The latter's infirmity and new fascination with American politics made it unlikely she would participate in the Versailles summers as she had before the war. When Anne returned to New York to raise funds, the two met with the amalgam of pain and pleasure that limned nostalgia, but both relieved to find they were the same bully girls they always had been, still able to whip up a fine froth of enthusiasm for whatever new projects ensnared them.

Bessy's were the recreational facilities being set up by the Knights of Columbus for servicemen. These "huts" were temporary buildings originally created as small chapels but swiftly outgrowing that purpose to become "r and r" centers for boys on leave in strange cities. When the Knights were preparing to open a hut in New York, Bessy was put in charge of the operation, the first time a woman was so honored. She made the Longacre Hut the most celebrated of all, a World War I precursor of World War II's legendary Stage Door Canteen. Later, Bessy was honored by a greater responsibility when she became the first female secretary of the conservative K. of C.

In its way, the Longacre Hut was the last of her Broadway productions, an apogee in her long love affair with the theatre. The hut, with its peaked roof, dormer and bay windows, and yew-planted window boxes, resembled a Bavarian country cottage that somehow got misplaced on the island stretching from Forty-sixth to Forty-seventh streets, where Broadway and Seventh

Avenue diverge. Bessy made the place hum. She went into competition with the neighboring theatres by nightly offerings of the latest movies and of all the big stars on Broadway doing their turns, while pretty ingenues doled out cigarettes, donuts, tea, and sympathy—and all of it free of charge.

Anne Morgan had three goals in New York: to change the American concept of relief materials; to try to raise a small army of women; to reorganize priorities at the AFFW or, should that prove impossible, to withdraw her section and form an independent organization.

At a meeting of the executive committee of the American Fund for the French Wounded, on March 18, it became apparent to Morgan she would never be able to convince the AFFW to change its major thrust from wounded soldiers to the innocent civilian victims of the war. It was then that she split from it to form the American Committee for a Devastated France, with the announced objective of "keeping up the morale of the soldiers by helping their women and children to survive." She persuaded her old friend Ambassador Myron Herrick to act as president, and she set up temporary headquarters, at 4 West Fortieth Street, for the new relief group, which would form the nucleus of all of her future relief work during and after the war.

The Germans started a big push toward Paris, intending to achieve some stunning victories before the full force of the American army was in place. Morgan had no doubt the enemy was planning to sweep through the Aisne district, threatening her mission and the lives of Dike and the other women in her group. She made plans to return to France immediately. One of her last speaking engagements before departing was at the American Women's Hospital, where she called for the immediate establishment of a women's hospital in northern France to alleviate the suffering that would be caused by the latest German offensive. She emphasized the importance of the reconstruction of the area and reiterated: "You cannot separate the welfare of the soldiers from that of their women and children."

The areas previously occupied by their units had been evacuated but were not yet in German hands, and she hoped they never would be. She affirmed: "However, if everything should be wiped out entirely, it would have been worth doing and must be done again, and better than before."

Bessy was as worried about Elsie as Anne Morgan was about Dike: in Compiègne she was in equivalent danger, but little would be served by Bessy accompanying Anne to France. She was increasingly disabled by her obesity and the arthritis attacking her joints but compensatorily vivacious in the demands she made upon herself. The requisites of her profession, the bond selling, and the Hut would have sufficed for most people of her age and condition, but she kept adding new activities such as the Stage Women's War Relief, founded by Jane Cowl and Rachel Crothers, two women who in no small part owed their successful careers to her astute management. The organization was dedicated to helping actresses and other women of the theatre to find ways to assist in the war effort.

Bessy's political position during the 1918 electoral campaign was to head the women's committee for the election of Robert L. Moran for aldermanic president, the office Alfred E. Smith was vacating to run for governor. She did her best, but Moran was a political hack too ill to campaign. Realizing he was a lost cause, Bessy spent as much time as she could spare with the Smith campaign. Pragmatism was a quality Smith shared with her. When Smith was elected by a narrow margin, Bessy, the anti-suffragette, was guaranteed a higher position in the Democratic party than many of the women who had dedicated their lives and fortunes to securing the vote. This would soon become a source of factionalism.

The manner in which Marbury had finessed her play between the losing Moran and winning Smith was not lost on Tammany Hall boss Charles F. Murphy. Despite her liberal attitudes, he marked her out as Tammany's woman in the coming days, when the good ole boys would be in need of a good ole girl.

That winter was not all politicking, business, and war. Bessy found a companion in her old friend Sarah Bernhardt, who had come over for one of her almost annual "farewell" tours and remained for a serious kidney operation. They spent quiet evenings of reminiscences of the old days in Paris, so many mutual friends, many of whom had passed away. The soft focus of nostalgia made the past brighter and better than it ever had been when it was new. The divine Sarah threw an arm affectionately across Bessy's shoulder. "Marbury, I will show you my secret garden, my treasure-house which I never expose to anybody."

A maid was dispatched to fetch a square black lacquered box, which was set before her. She unlocked it with a small gilt key and removed, one by one, small and faded bits of her life: leaves of laurel from her crown at the Conservatory, yellowing pages of verse written to her by some long-dead poet, a pair of baby shoes belonging to the adored son who had continually disappointed her, a faded photograph of the boy in Scotch kilts. "Ah, how handsome he looked, my Maurice, dressed *en écossais*."

The tears rolled down her cheeks. It was as if the triumphs and tragedies of a long and turbulent life had come down to these sad mementos. The actress returned to France that summer after what at last actually was her farewell tour of America. Five years later, she died in her son's arms.

After weeks of having heard nothing, on April 12, Bessy received a letter from Elsie written some two weeks earlier, just before her enforced evacuation from Compiègne. It was in no way reassuring.

> Everyone is flying, the refugees are walking on and on with all their pitiful household goods. Bombardment for three days and nights. The General Headquarters have left bag and baggage 48 hours ago, in the night. The streets are full of struggling English Tommies, all badly wounded but still able to crawl. One man with the blood pouring out of a shattered knee, I did up in the street as best I could.
>
> I don't want to leave, but we have received marching orders and must obey. The cellar of this house is full of women and children; a woman old and trembling is at the door imploring me to take her husband who is bedridden away "before they come," she cries. Alas, I can do nothing. All of our seventeen ambulances are full to overflowing with our hospital equipment and our wounded.

Elsie refused to abandon her post until Mme de Rothschild received word they must evacuate by 7 A.M. the next day. The constant bombardments made it impossible to load their eighty patients and get off before 2 P.M. They made a glorious spectacle leaving the city "in perfect order." The blast of bombs followed them all along the way. Three evenings later, Elsie could jot down in her diary: "Eight o'clock—Paris and the Ritz. . . . Very glad to get out of the sounds of the guns."

André Tardieu's first recorded appearance in the life of Anne Dike was in a letter he wrote to Myron Herrick expressing the "entire confidence" of the French government in the work being done in the Aisne. Tardieu was a protégé of Premier Georges Clemenceau and at the beginning of a political career that would carry him to the premiership not once but three times. Unrecorded is precisely when he became Anne Dike's lover. The affair probably began some time in 1918 or at the latest 1919, and lasted for the rest of her life.

In early April, Anne Morgan was held up in the States trying to raise money to support Dike's heroic work and in organizing the new American Committee for a Devastated France. She was working very closely with Herrick, which gave rise to rumors of romance between the middle-aged heiress and the distinguished diplomat who was newly widowed. Dike was possibly already Tardieu's mistress, but there was little likelihood of Morgan knowing anything about it and no foundation to the stories of her romance with Herrick. At that time, the most important thing in the lives of both women was the effort they were making to save the people of the Aisne.

The French government recognized their work. On September 5, General Degoutte, of the French 6th Army, cited Morgan and Dike for their work helping to rehabilitate the devastated areas during the previous year and for not deserting their villages until ordered out during the spring German offensives. Two days later, in Paris, each was awarded the Croix de Guerre avec Palme.

It was little more than two months later that the bells rang out in Blérancourt and all over France. The war was over. The armistice was signed quite nearby, in a railroad car in Compiègne. By then, Morgan, Dike, and their organization had reclaimed and replanted 7,500 acres of once occupied land as well as reconstructing more than eight hundred houses that had been partially destroyed in battle.

Lovers no more if indeed they ever had been, the women continued to share a common interest in France's recovery. It was to take six more years before they felt that their work in the Aisne was satisfactorily completed. Morgan's interest in the Aisne would never flag, but as Dike's involvement with Tardieu deepened, her social life did revert to the pleasures of Versailles, where Elsie had been in residence much of the time since early summer.

CHAPTER FORTY-FOUR ॐ

In January 1918, the House of Representatives passed what many hoped would become the Eighteenth Amendment to the Constitution, granting women the right to vote. On October 1, it passed the Senate by a vote of 62 to 34, which fell 2 votes short of the two-thirds necessary to pass a constitutional amendment. The suffragettes were again denied despite a national consensus in their favor. As the country edged toward a peace Americans knew would be very different from the pre-war peace, there was a predictable anxiety. The November 5 elections gave the Republicans control of both Houses of Congress. Less than a week later, on the legendary eleventh day of the eleventh month, an armistice was signed with Germany. People took to the streets in raucous celebration after having denied President Wilson the congressional strength to join with the Allies in empowering the League of Nations treaty which was largely his inspiration.

On January 29, 1919, an Eighteenth Amendment was ratified, but it was for prohibition rather than woman's suffrage. Many feminists took some solace in the new amendment, as they were as obdurately dry as they were voteless. It would not be until August 21, 1920, that the Nineteenth Amendment gave them the vote. By then, their lives already had begun to change in ways unimaginable only six years earlier.

*E*lsie returned to New York aboard the *Lorraine,* on January 29, 1919. Less than a week later, she received a cable from the French government informing her that she had been awarded the Croix de Guerre with bronze star for her bravery under fire. It was specifically given for her assistance in evacuating the patients from the ambrine installation to a place of safety during the week of March 21, as the Germans were advancing on Compiègne.

The more Elsie saw of post-war New York, the more convinced she became that it was impossible for her to live there. France was the only place for her. It would be possible to run her business from Europe by leaving the nitty-gritty details to her brother Edgar, who was divorced and living in New York.

That left the problem of what to do about Bessy. She did not really want her in Europe. It was Elsie's turn to get solo star billing. This desire for independence did not mean she cared for her "beloved Elisabeth" any less; she loved her as much as she was capable of loving but simply could no longer live with her. There was a temporary reprieve in postponement. That June, the peace treaty was to be signed in Versailles. The eyes of the world would be on the royal town, and to Elsie that meant their home even more than the palace that had housed kings. There was so much for her to do. She fled New York to take up the job of making certain the house was at its shimmering, dazzling best. And to restore herself as well. The aging process had been cruel. Skin the shade of ivory, which once had stretched across her good bones, was puffy and discolored. What once had been her stately gait was deformed by arthritis that had been intensified by the years of damp billets, cellar shelters, and trenches.

In treating the frailty of female beauty, there was no sanitarium to compare with Paris, and Elsie used it to the fullest. To restore the glow and texture of the complexion, a new treatment had been developed not unrelated to ambrine and almost as painful. No less courageous than the bravest of her soldier-patients, Elsie underwent a torturous skin peel in which her old skin was burned off to reveal the fresh, new underlayer. Too proud to become another superannuated, banal blonde, she stopped at having her white hair stylishly waved and highlighted with silver. For the bones and joints, a gymnast taught her a system of calisthenics that would keep her limber for years to come. Anne Vanderbilt's daughter Margaret would later introduce her to yoga, to which she became devoted.

By the time the first of the dignitaries arrived in Versailles for the signing of the peace treaty, a glowing Elsie, garbed once again in the smartest couture, was ready to greet them. She might have looked more like a painted doll than an ingenue, but nobody could deny her *joie de vivre.*

*J*t was not long after Elsie's departure for Europe that Bessy was given an assignment that would allow her to follow and share in the festivities at Versailles. The wartime policy of the Knights of Columbus had been to bar females from serving in their overseas facilities for fear of tempting the boys from the, if not straight, at least narrow path. Not until they were about to close the facilities did they ask a woman, Bessy, to make a tour of their European centers. As she put it: "They suddenly decided . . . that, as I was neither young nor beautiful, they could safely ask me to go over in their interests."

*O*n June 19, Anne Morgan came up to Paris to celebrate Bessy's sixty-third birthday with her. It must have been a disappointment that Elsie could not spare the time to make the twenty-mile journey from Versailles for the occasion, which would also have marked their first reunion in several months.

Bessy was not in Paris merely to celebrate her birthday. On the following day, she was scheduled to address an estimated three thousand soldiers in a stadium just outside the city. It was the climax of her first two weeks on the road, which had begun in Le Mans, on the morning after she landed, where she had addressed two hundred boys in the Knights of Columbus clubhouse. Wearing the group's uniform, with its K. of C. shield on the arm, was another of the job's perks that she thoroughly enjoyed. Because of that insignia, the volunteers were called "Caseys."

After that first appearance, word went out that no matter what she was hawking, that old mama was putting on a better show than most of the entertainers who passed through. From then on, and for the rest of her tour of duty, Bessy was Mother Casey, and news of her appearances went ahead, filling to capacity whatever hall in which she might be speaking. She might not be quite as popular as her young friend Elsie Janis, "the sweetheart of the A.E.F.," but Mother Casey was more than holding her own.

On the morning of her birthday, before meeting Anne, she had been summoned for her first meeting with General Pershing. The legendary commander of the American army studied the fat old lady with some incredulity. Having heard from his officers that she was playing to full houses, he was forced to ask what hypnotic influence she was using. Bessy laughed. "For thirty years, General, I've been learning the secret."

He told her henceforth his office would be mapping out her itinerary. Her first assignment was the speech to be delivered at the stadium on the following day. When she arrived at the arena the following day, the crowd of soldiers had swollen to four thousand. She looked up at the tier upon tier of young men and, doubting she could make herself heard, bellowed to the uppermost row, "Say, fellows, can you hear me up there?"

A voice bellowed right back, "Sure we can hear you, you're all right, go to the mat!"

That summer, she traveled north and south along the old battle lines of France, speaking wherever there was an American base. She found the troops "restless and disgruntled," resentful of the delays that kept them in France. She went among them spreading as much good cheer as possible.

Viewed from a revisionist's point of view, Bessy's prejudices were horrifying, but she made no secret of them in her own times and was considered by her contemporaries to be a person of liberal sensibilities. In their segregated barracks, she saw no reason that black soldiers should complain about being fed the same grub as the German prisoners rather than what was served to their white fellow Americans. It was all good, substantial food, probably better than most of them got at home. As for intermarriage with French women, the idea was appalling to her. The saving grace of a naive sense of fairness would occasionally emerge. She never forgot visits Anne Morgan and she had made to front-line hospitals in 1916, where she had seen "our negroes staggering back from the front literally shot to pieces," and realized "their blood which had flowed was the same color as that of their white brothers and that the women who wept for them shed tears which were identical." But that sentimental recollection was as far as she went. She was incapable of digging deeply enough to uncover a larger sense of justice.

One of the indelible memories of her tour was the segregation (different from segregated) camp in Brest. It was in an outlying area away from the rest of the military installation and numbered some five thousand patients and prisoners, the majority of whom had contracted venereal diseases, which in those days could be cured only by long and painful treatments. No visitors were allowed and certainly no contact with females: their principal care was left to male nurses. Bessy's first impression was of the "utter dreadful dreariness" of the camp. One can imagine her surprise when its commanding officer requested an interview and asked if she would be willing to give her talks in the camp. He could not order her to do so, but it would be an act of mercy were she to volunteer. Her Yes was given without hesitation, almost cheerfully.

For the boys, she truly was their Mother Casey, the one person to come to see them, to give them hope, to remind them they would soon be home and would have many years in which to forget the pain of this moment. For Bessy, it was a period of spiritual illumination, one in which she was humbled by the religion she chose to call her own.

> From them I drew a deeper inspiration than it was possible for me to give, and when finally my work among them was over, I seemed to have learned more of God's tenderness when dealing with his little children than I had ever known before.

After Bessy's birthday celebration, Anne Morgan returned to the Villa Trianon, where, a little more than a week later, she awakened to one of those glorious summer days. The garden, viewed from her bedroom window in the Morgan wing, was ablaze with glorious color rescued from vulgar excess by the dappled sun filtering through the lush green foliage of ancient trees. Versailles on that day was all that Louis XIV had designed it to be: handsome gallants in an array of splendidly tailored uniforms, beautiful women dazzling in the sort of finery only Paris could provide, and the town, on that glorious morning of June 28, itself gorgeously arrayed in the multicolored flags of all of the victorious nations gathered to sign the peace treaty.

She arose and dressed quickly in one of her own splendid uniforms. Throughout the conference, the villa had been a command post with all of the great political leaders stopping by with word of what was transpiring at the meetings, and on that day they were having open house, with the first guests arriving for a late breakfast that would stretch into lunch. Afterward, the more significant players returned to the great Hall of Mirrors at the palace. The reflection of the signing of the treaty would be repeated unto infinity, thus lending eternal significance to an event that would prove as ephemeral as the fashionable frocks being readied in the Paris couture ateliers in time for the wives of the American delegation to take home.

The dandified former prime minister of England Arthur Balfour was among the first to turn up at the Villa Trianon for tea. As he entered the door, he said, "Well! We have signed the treaty of peace, and there are twenty-two nations still at war."

When it was all over, they went out to watch President Wilson drive through the château gates. Crowds lined the route all the way into Paris, cheering: "*Vive President Wilson!*" "*Vive l'Amérique!*"

Unlike Anne, Elsie was still under the influence of Bessy's liberal politics and thought, "It was one of the greatest days of my life." That both her politics and her life were about to change were exemplified by the guests at her dinner party that evening, for which Arthur Balfour returned. Amid a small galaxy of French socialites, British generals, and titles, including Consuelo Marlborough and her lover, Jacques Balsan, there was to be found Sir Oswald "Tom" Mosley and Elsa Maxwell.

Only twenty-three, Mosley had been elected to Parliament the year before and would remain in office for another twelve years, serving successively as a Conservative, an Independent, and a member of the Labour party. Before the war, he had been a leader of a coterie of the cleverest and most beautiful upper-class homosexuals in England, but that part of his life was coming to an end, at least on an overt level. The war had been the most traumatic event of his life. His feelings about the other guests that evening can be gleaned from the observations about Armistice Day found in his diary:

> Smooth, smug people, who had never fought or suffered, seemed to the eyes of youth—at that moment age-old with sadness, weariness, and bitterness—to be eating, drinking, laughing on the graves of our companions.

In 1920, Mosley would marry Cynthia Curzon, the daughter of Lord Curzon and the American heiress Mary Leiter. Like her mother, Cynthia would die young. In 1932, the year after being defeated for reelection, Oswald would found the British Union of Fascists and later marry a beautiful convert to his cause, Diana Mitford Guinness, one of the eccentric right-wing Baron Redesdale's six daughters, only one of whom, Pamela Mitford, was unremarkable. The others were the brilliant novelist Nancy Mitford; the equally brilliant left-wing writer Jessica Mitford; the alleged mistress of Hitler, Unity Mitford; and Debo, who did the family proud when a bit of primogenital good fortune conferred the title of Duke of Devonshire upon her unlikely husband.

Throughout this period and until his internment during World War II,

Elsie and Mosley would be a part of the same increasingly right-wing circle of what were considered by gossipmongers "the best people." When his friends contrived to have Mosley released from detention before World War II was over, the American-born Henry "Chips" Channon, considered the greatest snob in England, indicated he and most of the better types were all for it, and that only Jews and Communists were really against it. Chips and Tom were the solipsistic exemplars of the crowd and world Elsie was beginning to find so much more attractive than Bessy and America.

Elsa Maxwell earned her living as the singer of clever, naughty songs and was much sought after as an entertainer at private parties. She won the enduring and invaluable friendship of Cole Porter by performing his songs at a time when he was still unknown. She was as short and plump as Bessy, though not as pretty. When Elsie took her up, some suspected she was replacing her old lover with a reasonable facsimile. That was not the case. Maxwell lived her openly lesbian life with only one partner, Dorothy "Dickie" Fellowes-Gordon. She was merely among the first of Elsie's new playmates—a group of bright and talented either gay or bisexual people, all years younger. Life without Bessy was going to be younger, quicker, wilder as well as decidedly more right-wing.

Anne Morgan retained her interest in the Villa Trianon and continued to return to this world so alien to her own values. Having been displaced with Anne Dike by Tardieu, she understood the life once shared by the two women was no longer hers. Versailles and home were her two alternatives. There remained too much to be done in France to go home. Versailles was what remained.

When her brother, Jack, and his wife visited Paris that autumn, their old rivalry was rekindled. Jack represented the family's massive banking interests and had no patience with his sister's efforts. From the perspective of the House of Morgan, the time had come for healing, for forgetting old animosities, and getting on with the business of doing business with Germany. Anne loathed the Germans for what they had done and was in no mood to forgive them. On October 19, Jack wrote to their mother that Anne and he had "little in common," and that her nervous energy and rapid pace were getting tiring. In regard to her return to the house on Thirty-seventh Street, he warned: "Be sure you don't let yourself be put out of your way by her—it won't do for you, and you must not risk it."

Anne arrived home at the beginning of November. She found a growing isolationism that prompted her to make her plea for aid to France:

Edith Wharton, 1907.

Anne and Willie K. Vanderbilt with a friend at the races at Longchamp.

House, on East 71st St., New York City, converted from brownstone by Elsie de Wolfe and Ogden Codman; their approach revolutionized architectural renovation.

Morgan wing of Villa Trianon.

Anne Vanderbilt in mourning, 1908.

Vernon and Irene Castle.

Elisabeth Marbury and Elsie de Wolfe in their home on East 55th St., 1913.

Anne Vanderbilt, Herbert Satterlee, and Anne Morgan.

Elsie de Wolfe, 1915.

Anne Morgan at Blérancourt during World War I.

Anne Morgan and Anne Dike, 1917.

Elisabeth Marbury in her Knights of Columbus uniform in 1918.

Elsie de Wolfe and Anne Morgan at World War I garden party at Villa Tranon.

Anne Morgan and her nurses at Blérancourt shortly after World War I.

Ambassador Myron Herrick and Anne Morgan.

Portrait of Elsie de Wolfe to Sir Charles Mendl on March 10, 1926.

Sutton Place at 57th St.,
1920.

Sutton Place with
Vanderbilt and Morgan
houses in the foreground.

Elisabeth Marbury's library,
Sutton Place.

Elisabeth Marbury's house at
13 Sutton Place.

Wedding of Elsie de Wolfe to Sir Charles Mendl on March 10, 1926. *Left to right:* Sir Sidney Clive, the British Ambassador to France, Lord Crewe, Elsie de Wolfe, Mendl, Anne Vanderbilt, Myron Herrick, the American Ambassador, and Vice Admiral Sir Edward Heaton-Ellis.

Watercolor of Elisabeth Marbury by William B. E. Rankin in the library of her Sutton Place home.

Elsie de Wolfe in front of the Boldoni head of her, that she cut down from a full-length portrait.

Eleanor Roosevelt, 1933. Inscribed to her beloved friend, Lorena (Hick) Hickok.

Anne Morgan by Malvina Hoffman, executed in 1937.

Anne Vanderbilt in her Sutton Place home.

Anne Morgan with General Charles De Gaulle
during his visit to the United States soon after
World War II ended.

Lady Wallace's private guest book for 1898 before the Wallace Collection was open to the public. Elsie visited on June 11 (fourth signature from the bottom) and again on June 18 with Elisabeth Marbury and Isabella Stewart Gardner (first three signatures).

All Europe needs help. The only country that doesn't need it is America. The favorite expression of Americans in France now is: "It's time to leave France to her own salvation." That isn't right. France needs us now. Although some Americans may have misunderstood the French and some French may have misunderstood the Americans, basically, a strong entente exists between the two countries. And we want to keep it.

However much the relationship between the two countries may have deteriorated, France's appreciation of Morgan and Dike was undiminished. The two women were awarded Crosses of the Chevalier of the Legion of Honor. The decorations were military rather than civilian and bestowed for great service to the French government in the realm of the army.

*B*y the beginning of 1919, it must have seemed to Anne Vanderbilt that only in public service were her good intentions rewarded, as when, in the last days of the war, she was made a Chevalier of the legion of Honor. The darkness that had suffused so much of her private life was again descending upon her. The marriages of both of her daughters were headed for the divorce courts. To make matters worse, the fragile Barbara Rutherfurd Hatch had an infant son by a husband who was experiencing financial reverses and could not afford to support his family. Fortunately, Willie K. was generous to her children, but his health was becoming another source of anxiety.

Vanderbilt was nearing his seventieth birthday, and the bill was coming due for an extravagantly self-indulgent life. He had been suffering from angina for two years but had remained in France, where he felt the medical treatment was as good as he could get anywhere.

In mid-November, as they were finally boarding the ship to return to America, Willie had a heart attack but insisted on continuing the voyage. He spent the voyage in his berth with Anne playing her now familiar role of nurse. When they arrived in New York, he was well enough to go home rather than to a hospital. There was no doubt that he was fragile and might not have much longer to live.

*O*n December 20, Elsie invited eighty of her most intimate friends to a birthday party she was giving for herself in her new showroom at 677 Fifth Avenue. Many claimed it was a celebration of her sixtieth birthday, though officially declared her fifty-fourth. As far as her future was concerned, the most significant guest was Johnnie McMullin, who lent her his valet-cook to do the catering and bartending, which had become a very important function at every party, since Prohibition was making hard liquor more popular with more people than ever before.

John McMullin was a writer for Condé Nast's *Vanity Fair* and *Vogue*. Perhaps the best physical description of "our Johnnie" was given by his boss, Edna Woolman Chase, the first editor of *Vogue:*

> He was a sprite who had been hatched in California. He was small and slight in stature, flawlessly dressed, more a mannikin than a man, with bright brown eyes, a nose somewhat aquiline, pointed at the end, a sharp tongue, and a fund of human understanding. He was a tremendously entertaining companion and a hard worker.

Johnnie was in a line of direct descent from Ward McAllister and Harry Lehr, a small-town boy of no particular antecedents who came to New York and fell hopelessly in love with society and the women who made it. He was also openly homosexual. None of his closets could contain him, for they were too crowded with clothes. Some said he made homosexuality fashionable in New York, just as it had been said Elsie and Bessy made lesbianism fashionable. If the allegations were true, it was a listless sexuality. Both Johnnie and Elsie were much too concerned with surfaces to be truly erotic. His great passion was for clothes. He once flew into the office of British *Vogue* and breathlessly ordered his secretary: "Cancel all my appointments; I have just heard of a white dress waistcoat with *one* button in a shop in Jermyn Street. I must fly!"

McMullin was often viewed as Elsie's gofer, majordomo, walker, factotum. To a degree, he was all of those things, but only to the same degree, as Bessy had been: in truth, Johnnie was about to become her new Bessy. As she once had eased the way for Elsie, introducing her to the right people, to the world of celebrity, making her first a professional actress and then a decorator, now it was Johnnie McMullin who would be her Virgil, leading her through the successive circles of the bright and bleak post-war world.

Johnnie knew who and what was going to be "in" and was waiting just ahead for everybody else to catch up. He could lead the way for her, if he only would, but what did she have for him? To a large part, it was simply being Elsie de Wolfe. More than a celebrity, she was a legend who had known everybody who counted over the past forty years. Elsie knew how to play Scheherazade, to captivate and ensnare that part of Johnnie's nature in thrall to what was often a seminal homosexual quest, *à la recherche du temps perdu,* with the inside stories of the great old scandals, of who was where and why, and what they were wearing, and what the houses looked like. She could tell all these sumptuous tales with just the right edge of the witty bitchiness of one who had not always been accepted. In turn, Johnnie could keep her informed on the latest—the pun intended—vogue, lead her forward into the post-war era so radically different from the pre-war world in which she had made so estimable a place, introduce her to all the latest places and latest people, throw open the doors and cry, "She's not just some *démodée* old bag! She's fabulous!"

CHAPTER FORTY-FIVE

Bessy Marbury's overseas commission had been a well-publicized success. When this was coupled with her work on the Smith campaign, the Democratic party began to think of her as a comer. Suffrage would be enacted before the next election, and the party needed women politicians who understood how to manipulate the system to the benefit of the party. The leaders placed her on the party's executive committee and sent out the word that she would also be one of the delegates to the Democratic National Convention. She proved worthy of their faith by including a strong endorsement of the League of Nations in her comments to the press on what she had observed during her stay in Europe.

As the year drew to a close, other honors began to accrue. The Knights of Columbus showed its gratitude for a job well done by making Bessy its only female secretary and bestowing upon her the organization's gold service medal. In a ceremony in Times Square, she was made an honorary member of the Veterans of Foreign Wars. The Belgian government bestowed the Medal of Queen Elizabeth for her service during the war to that country. The honor that continued to elude her was the one she wanted most of all: recognition from the French government of her cultural and wartime services to that country. Those who had done far less had been honored. She made one last futile attempt to get the Légion d'Honneur before putting it out of her mind. If the story was true that Pierpont Morgan had applied pressure on the French government not to honor her over a decade earlier, that proscription outlived him.

It was not long before there were two strong indications that the French did feel it reprehensible not to have honored her for the years of service she had given to the country. The Légion remained beyond her reach, but she was awarded the great silver medal of the municipality of Paris. The French governor-general of Morocco and North Africa, Louis-Hubert-Gonzalve Lyautey, also sent notification she was to receive the highest military decoration he was empowered to bestow, the Cross of the Knight of the Ouisam Alacuite. The archetypically French need to make the *beau geste* simply exacerbated her disenchantment with the country.

*B*y the beginning of 1920, it was definite that Elsie and Bessy would not renew the lease on the house on East Fifty-fifth Street, nor would they lease and share another house. Elsie took what few things she wanted from the house, mostly pictures; and Bessy kept the Catholic iconostasis and Gothic Revival antiques that were hers. The bulk—mostly nineteenth-century French copies of Louis XIV–XVI—was sent to auction. The sale was spread over several days, and Elsie positioned her pal Elsa Maxwell strategically to act as unofficial shill. It was a highly lucrative transaction on which Maxwell undoubtedly earned a commission on those of her friends she induced to buy. Elsie did a bit of personal shilling, too. On her advice, her own customers entered the highest bids, which enabled her to profit in two ways: on commissions as their decorator and as the seller of the merchandise.

*T*he boss of Tammany Hall, Charles Murphy, was watching Bessy's progress in the party. That year, the New York State Democratic party had announced that one of its four delegates at large to the Democratic National Convention, to be held that summer in San Francisco, would be a woman. Murphy saw to it that Elisabeth Marbury was chosen to be that woman. She seemed a natural for the job. She was both a good campaigner and a nationally known figure with a quick, quotable wit. To Murphy's surprise, women's groups all over the state began to challenge her selection on the ground that it had been made by men. They wanted the right to select their own representative.

Behind this initial dispute was the much older conflict for political power between the downstate New York City machine and the upstate rural machine, which suspected Bessy of being a tool of Tammany Hall. They were not wrong. She believed that the Tammany machine was a necessary evil if the party was to retain sufficient power to push its more noble objectives through the state and national legislatures. Reformers came and went, but the political apparatus went on forever. Neither the moderates nor the progressives had any love for Tammany Hall. Denounce it though they might, there was no winning without it.

The situation was threatening to get out of control. Murphy finessed the matter by allowing two of the four delegates at large to be women: Bessy and the women's choice, Harriet May Mills, of Syracuse.

This settled things so far as the upstate Democrats were concerned, but another challenge came from an independent Democratic women's group in the city. It opposed Bessy on the solid grounds of her lack of any credentials as a suffragette. She wisely held her tongue on that issue, allowing the New York State party to declare that the group was not recognized by it, and that the national party had a strong suffrage plank enthusiastically supported by all of its delegates including Miss Marbury.

Along with Bessy, Franklin Delano Roosevelt was in the New York delegation going out to San Francisco. Eleanor was not with him: in those days, it was not considered seemly for the wives of politicians to make appearances at the often rowdy conventions. Roosevelt's specific objective was to second the nomination of Al Smith. Although Bessy was uninstructed, Smith was also first among the potential candidates in her mind. She was not well acquainted with the young assistant secretary of the navy, but being an extremely appealing mix of good looks, breeding, and wit, it did not take Franklin long to win her over. As a result, "nothing could be more delightful [to her] than the journey across the continent."

Bessy's reactions to her first convention were positive, until it evolved into one of the more tedious sessions in history. The Democrats were in disarray and divided on every issue including a candidate. Never before had she realized how many men longed to offer themselves for the presidency. As they droned on for forty-three abusive ballots, she concluded sardonically that "the Democratic party had *too* many men of noble achievement and of Christian character." It was an embarrassment of riches, but if they really wanted a national hero, she tucked her tongue into her cheek and suggested they not overlook Babe Ruth, who had broken the home run record the year before and looked fair to repeat the feat that year (he would and also the year after).

The proceedings were proving so lackluster, many of the delegates felt it necessary to break the Eighteenth Amendment, but "the drink seemed to induce melancholia rather than cheerfulness." Bessy's pity for her chums among the journalists led her to assume the function of "giving copy to the press." A good example occurred after one prohibitionist lady delegate loudly denounced it as "a disgrace to American manhood" that every man she met at the convention "reeked with the smell of whiskey."

Bessy was pressed for a comment and replied she had none. She had never smelled the men's breaths. "For a very simple reason. I am either too modest or too fat."

Her observations were all printed by a press starved for some respite from the tedium of the events. It gave her the reputation of being "the Court Jester of the Convention."

An exhausted convention, eager to have it over and done with, nominated the nationally unknown governor of Ohio, James M. Cox, on its forty-fourth try. Their new hopeful had not even been a dark horse. Although Tammany Hall had little enthusiasm for this particular New York Democrat, Bessy was delighted when Cox chose Franklin Roosevelt as his running mate. Men in smoke-filled back rooms being the gossips they were, she surely had been made aware of the love affair that almost broke up his marriage two years earlier. He was probably among those she had in mind when, after listening to candidate after candidate being offered as "men whose private lives were pure and spotless," she observed that "there was a rich field for blackmailers to be spied in the offing."

Bessy never repeated the Roosevelt story, which concerned Lucy Mercer, an accomplished, beautiful young southern belle, whose family had come upon such hard times that she was forced to take a position as Eleanor Roosevelt's social secretary. It was not long before Franklin and she began an affair that, with the connivance of Eleanor's cousin and archenemy Alice Roosevelt Longworth, became sufficiently flagrant to humiliate his wife. Eleanor offered her husband his freedom. Whether it was because he genuinely valued her or because he knew his political career would be over should there be a divorce, he chose to remain in the marriage, but he never forgot Lucy Mercer. Many assumed that Eleanor never again shared his bed.

Eleanor had been a good friend of Alice Morton Rutherfurd, who had died the year before, leaving her husband with six children to rear. She may have been instrumental in getting Mercer a job as their governess. Although twice her age, Lucy's new employer was still handsome enough to be sexually attractive to women, rich, socially registered, and now available. What impoverished southern belle could resist? Four months before the convention, Lucy had become what Alva Belmont had prevented Consuelo Vanderbilt Marlborough from becoming: Anne Vanderbilt's sister-in-law Mrs. Winthrop Rutherfurd.

*I*n her circle of intimates, Bessy was alone in her allegiance to the Democrats. She viewed her new friendship with Franklin Delano Roosevelt as one of the good things to come out of the disastrous campaign.

On the eve of the election, she sent a telegram to him: "No one in the state is praying more for you than your sincere friend."

He wired back, thanking her for her "awfully nice telegram" and observing the size of the defeat was not entirely negative, for it would spur them on. "This is the time to get things started for the next campaign, and I want to have a talk with you about this some day after I get back to New York."

Her reply indicated that no matter what strides her sex had made, she still wanted to be one of the boys when it came to playing power games. "I feel absolutely as you do, and whenever you men want to see me in conference, let me know."

Zona Gale's *Miss Lulu Bett,* Sinclair Lewis's *Main Street,* and Edith Wharton's *The Age of Innocence* were the three most critically acclaimed American novels of 1920 and, quite extraordinarily, also among the most commercially successful. Bessy always had been of a mind that good novels could be adapted for the stage, and she petitioned for the right to represent all three for theatre and screen. Miss Gale insisted upon dramatizing her own work with no assistance from a professional playwright, which Bessy thought was generally a bad idea. In this instance, she was wrong. The writer was vindicated for her faith in herself by winning the Pulitzer Prize for drama.

The moment she read *Main Street,* Bessy saw its theatrical potential and contacted the publisher, Alfred Harcourt, offering to handle the dramatic rights. He was cognizant of the power of the American Play Company "and told them to go to it and see what they could do," despite the fact that Lewis's literary agent already had entered negotiations with a producer. By the beginning of the new year, Bessy had a production commitment from Lee Shubert. Lewis elected to go with her rather than his agent. It meant he had to tie the film rights to the play production, the only terms under which Bessy would represent an adaptation, but she assured him they would be much more valuable after a Broadway production.

The play opened the following autumn to a respectful reception but managed a run of only eighty-six performances. Bessy did sell the film rights for forty thousand dollars, a handsome price at the time, especially for a novel that had been denounced in small-town meetings clear across the country. Lewis's comment, in a letter to Harcourt, was: "Rem. Amer. Play Co. get 10% on all—drat 'em."

*T*he Age of Innocence was a *roman à clef* with which Bessy could easily identify. The major action took place at a time when Edith and she were both young women "out" in New York society. She could recognize the real people upon whom the characters were based, for they were friends and acquaintances of the Marbury family. J. W. Hiltman, president of Appleton & Co., gave Bessy the exclusive rights to deal for the piece, but he insisted upon terms for the film rights to which no producer would agree. Bessy decided to apply directly to Edith. Although she addressed her letter to "Mrs. Wharton," the opening was chatty, as if written to a friend. It passed over the occasional acrimony that previously had marked their relationship.

> It seems a very long time since I had either the pleasure of seeing you, or of coming into any kind of association with you. However, time is not of as much importance after all, as years of pleasant memories.

After confiding that Doris Keane (one of the biggest stars of the day) was "enchanted with the opportunity to create the part," and that Zoë Akins, who "has only been associated with success," was willing "to put aside all her work" and concentrate on doing the adaptation (the season before, she had written a society drama, *Déclassée,* in which Ethel Barrymore had a great success), Bessy went on for several pages giving point by point reasons why Hiltman's terms would probably prove unacceptable. She concluded: "I put this matter squarely before you, and I assure you that I am giving you the benefit of my very best judgment and experience."

She did promise to try to meet Hiltman's objections but would appreciate a cable from Edith giving her the authority to act on the stage and screen rights. She suggested a second cable be sent to Hiltman informing him of her decision.

After months of negotiations, the project came to nothing as a result of Shubert procrastination and double-dealing with Akins and Keane. Bessy did sell the film rights shortly after to the fledgling Warner Brothers Company for a handsome thirty thousand dollars, half of which went to Wharton. A successful dramatization had to wait until 1928. Akins continued her admiration of Wharton and worked on and off trying to make a play based on her *The Old Maid.* Bessy had secured the rights for her. It was not produced until over two years after Bessy's death. It won the Pulitzer Prize and earned for the aging Wharton, who was to die two years later, more money than she had made from her writing in years.

As a bit of incidental intelligence, when Akins won the Pulitzer Prize for the play, in 1935, the New York drama critics were so incensed that they decided to give their own awards, the New York Drama Critics Circle awards. That year, they gave their first award to a turgid piece of bad blank verse, Maxwell Anderson's *Winterset,* which dealt with the Sacco-Vanzetti case in florid and melodramatic terms. Unlike Akins's spare, still sound dramatization of the Wharton story, the play has dated badly. It must be noted that not one New York newspaper had a woman drama critic at the time.

*D*uring the first half of the year of the election, Anne Vanderbilt did not dwell on her new enfranchisement. Her attention was focused on Willie K. Vanderbilt, who had never fully recovered from his first heart attack and was left totally incapacitated by a second, far more serious attack sustained while attending the races at Auteuil. Even after being consigned to the American Hospital, he boasted that his stable had two winners that afternoon. The hospital did all it could for him and discharged him to Anne's care. She nursed him at home for over three months.

When death did come, in the early evening of July 22, 1920, his sons and daughter were with their stepmother at his bedside. There was a quiet funeral service at the American Cathedral. His body was brought home and taken to New Dorp, Staten Island, for interment in the family mausoleum, designed by Richard Morris Hunt for the purpose of making the Vanderbilts in death social peers of all the dead and mostly forgotten monarchs of the world.

Willie K.'s estate was probated in Suffolk County and valued at $54,530,966.59, which did not include the gift of $15,000,000 he had given to his daughter shortly before his death and the trust of $8,250,000 he had set up for his widow. Anne also received $109,196 from the estate as well as a share in the Fifth Avenue mansion and all of the real estate he owned in France. The American property left outright to her was Stepping Stones, a 125-acre summer home in the Wheatley Hills section of Jericho, Long Island. It was the only Vanderbilt estate or house that Willie K. had personally supervised from the original architectural renderings to the raising of the roof. It had been designed as a tribute to the wife who had made him happy. The one who had made him miserable had never allowed him to participate in the design of the palaces she decreed, but from those that were in his possession at the time of his death, Alva received just short of $300,000 in dower rights. She spent it on erecting the Alva Belmont Building, in Washington, D.C., which served as the headquarters for her National Woman's Party.

When the smoke of accountants and auditors cleared, the inheritance tax of almost two million dollars was the highest ever paid in Suffolk County history. Within the next two generations, the majority of Vanderbilts were to go from being the richest family in the world to being among those who were no more than well off by the standards of a later time—and some, not even that.

*A*lfred Allan Lewis

*I*n the years immediately after the end of the war, the rehabilitation of northeast France remained one of Anne Morgan's most pressing concerns. Her problem was attempting to convince the American public of the continuing need for funding and volunteers. After the armistice was signed, a displaced civilian population did not live happily ever after. Devastated farms and homes were not miraculously restored. Disease and malnutrition were not cured by the signing of a paper. What occurred at Madison Square Garden on the evening of January 14, 1921, at the height of the New York social season, was an example of how inventive Anne could get in her efforts to raise funds for the American Committee for a Devastated France.

During her stays abroad, she had taken note of—if not actually partaken in—the latest post-war fad among London and Paris society women. They would don their gorgeous gowns and dazzling jewels, as if planning to attend the opera, but proceed instead to Albert Hall and the Cercle de Paris for the prizefights, shouting themselves hoarse once there to encourage still gorier heights in the spectacle. Where Paris and London fashion led, New York was sure to follow. Anne decided on a preemptive strike as a benefit for her committee.

With powerful forces in the state aligned against the brutality of the sport, the Boxing Commission decided it would be great propaganda to show what pantywaists the reformers were by filling the Garden with cheering ladies, to say nothing of the goodwill generated by helping a good cause with a Morgan fronting for it. The popular lightweight champion of the world, Benny Leonard, was scheduled to defend his title against Richie Mitchell. Lightweight fights usually did not get as gory as heavyweight bouts. It was a perfect choice for the ladies—a pair of popular and good-looking young palookas who would not spill too much blood on the pretty dresses of the ringsiders.

It might have been the rainy night or simply that fashionable New Yorkers had a better sense of appropriate garb than their European counterparts; the ladies filing into Madison Square Garden on Friday evening, January 14, were appareled in tailored suits and dresses. Only the pretty debutantes, who were selling programs for the charity, were dressed in glamorous evening gowns, providing a mightily appetizing sight for the ogling eyes of the regular fight fans.

Anne Morgan and her party, which included Bessy and Al Smith, were among the last to arrive. Their appearance was the signal for the action to begin. The Garden dimmed except for the blast of cold white light concentrated on the ring, and the preliminary bouts began. By the time the

Leonard-Mitchell match began, the ladies had become inured to the sound of fists hitting bare flesh, to the bruises and scrapes, but the main event turned out to be a particularly bloody one, causing many to purse their paled lips and wince.

Anne raised eighty thousand dollars for the committee but let herself in for some criticism from the clergy. A Methodist minister called the fight a "revolting and disgusting . . . national degradation" and described Anne as "a big, coarse, mannish woman possessed of a lot of money." A group of Baptist ministers insisted that "boxing is not to be condemned" but wondered "what the women leaders of society, who did good work during the war, are coming to." After avowing they were only trying to keep the word *Christ* in *Christian,* the Baptists concluded: "Every one regards Miss Morgan as a Christian woman. To be present upon such an occasion and to promote such an event is a falling away from grace."

CHAPTER FORTY-SIX

On July 26, 1871, the diarist George Templeton Strong described a stroll he had taken on that summer's day.

> Beekman Place on the East River from 49th to 51st Street is unlike any other part of the city and dimly suggests Brooklyn Heights. Its brownstone houses look very reputable but are separated from civilization by a vast tract of tenement rookeries and whiskey mills, and streets that absolutely crawl with poor little slatternly pretty children. The outlook over the East River is nice and includes a clear view of the penitentiary, the smallpox hospital and other places on Blackwell's Island.

What Strong had observed of Beekman Place and its neighborhood in 1871 was equally true of the extension of Avenue A, named Sutton Place, which was located along the river a scant quarter-mile farther north. Effingham Sutton had lost a fortune vainly attempting to turn it into an upper middle-class neighborhood. By the end of World War I, it had become the haven of Bohemians, artists, writers, and photographers beguiled by its views, its relative remoteness, and, of course, its low rents. What had been true of Newport, Cape Cod, and the eastern end of Long Island, among so many other creative retreats, would be true of Sutton Place. Where the artists made their Eden, the serpent of society was quick to follow. In 1920, Eliot Cross, of the architectural firm of Cross & Cross, took an option on the square block from Fifty-seventh to Fifty-eighth streets between Sutton Place and the river. He drew up plans for developing the seventeen brownstones into a private square, offering them a common garden ambling out and down a sharp decline to the river's edge. In a brick wall on Fifty-eighth Street, a house's length to the east of Sutton Place, Cross set a tablet: "Sutton Square. 1920." Cross & Cross lost interest in the project and, after laying out the garden, sold off the houses individually instead of creating a unified whole of them.

Bessy Marbury was still looking for a place to live when she heard about what was happening on Sutton Place. She walked out into the garden and looked over to a portion of the riverbank not far from where, as a little girl, she had sat impatiently waiting for a bite almost sixty years before. It was as if what she had often said in jest had come to pass—a place to fish fifteen minutes from Times Square.

After consulting with Elsie, she purchased a small three-story brownstone at 13 Sutton Place, which stood on a plot measuring only 16 feet by 45 feet. For Elsie, the first things that had to go were the stoop and brownstone facade. There was so much that had to be done that they decided it would be wise to hire an architect. Mott Schmidt was a promising young architect just getting started in his career. He was good, and he was cheap: a winning combination with Elsie and Bessy, who decided to give him the job with a budget of twenty thousand dollars. After removing the stoop, he covered the brownstone with a creamy yellow stucco and converted the floor-through flats into a single residence. The three new bow windows on the parlor-floor level were trimmed in black, and a black wrought-iron gate ran across the front of the building. The bright red front door at the street level was lent importance by a sculpted frame reminiscent of old Dutch New York.

Schmidt's plan for Bessy's house maximized the use of its limited space. With the kitchen and butler's pantry up front, the hall and graceful curved staircase beside them, the dining room could extend the full width of the house with two Dutch doors leading to the terrace and common garden. The dimensions were carefully scaled to contain the small square oak-paneled Charles I room that Elsie had brought from England as a house gift for Bessy. The Dutch doors still had the original leaded-glass panes.

Off a small center hall on the first landing, a drawing room stretched across the front of the house. It would be Elsie's reception room and was furnished accordingly with delicate Louis XVI *bergères,* hardly the sort of chairs to hold the massive Bessy with any degree of safety or comfort. The pine wall stiles framed panels of a very old, softly colored paper. Protected by sheets of clear plastic, it was still up over seventy years later. On the other side of the hall was the library, which was Bessy's domain and increasingly the room in which she lived as she became too incapacitated to venture out in the evenings. It was lined with bookshelves containing well-worn volumes—"no ornate bindings, just practical books to take down and live with." The bulk of them were first editions autographed by clients and friends who were among the most distinguished writers of the previous half-century. Everything in the room was designed for comfort, especially the large chintz-covered chairs and sturdy embracing leather sofa. Morning sun flooded in through the three windows that looked across the garden to the river. Bessy and her neighbors did not consider their community garden "too large until we have to pay our taxes."

By the beginning of 1921, Anne Vanderbilt had made a deal to sell Stepping Stones for $500,000. It was likewise not her wish to live in Alva's Fifth Avenue house amid the grandiloquent contents that had always impressed her as pretentious. Her stepsons shared her distaste for their mother's folly, and, when an offer to option the property for $3,000,000 was received, it was accepted.

Anne Vanderbilt had moved out of 660 Fifth Avenue and was shopping around for a new home even before the original option on the property was taken. What first brought her to Sutton Place was unclear. Very soon after the arrival of the new year, she purchased 1 Sutton Place, which wrapped around Fifty-seventh Street and, with windows on three sides, was the most desirable house in the Square. After seeing Mott Schmidt's plans for Bessy's house, she decided to use him as her architect and hire Elsie to decorate the new house. By the beginning of March, it was clear to Schmidt and Vanderbilt that for him to remodel the existing edifice in accord with her demands would cost more than tearing it down to put up a new building.

The proportions of Schmidt's design for her house were true to Vanderbilt's vision of a Georgian square. The front door would not be on the narrow Sutton Place frontage but in the center of the broad side facing south on Fifty-seventh Street. To give it a feeling of age, the old red bricks that lay under the brownstone facing were saved for use in the new edifice. The Vanderbilt townhouse was a small gem that set the scale and tone for all of the houses on what would be called Sutton Square.

$\mathcal{O}$n March 22, Elsie and Anne Vanderbilt sailed for Europe aboard the *Aquitania*. With hordes of Americans returning to their pre-war European haunts, "half of New York" seemed to be sailing with them. The Berensons were on board and delighted to find that "the ever-resourceful Elsie de Wolfe had secured a table for the three of them and Mrs. William K. Vanderbilt, whose elegant presence assured them an agreeably aristocratic voyage."

Elsie and Berenson were approaching the end of their years of intimacy. Contributing factors could have been that he was suddenly too old for the new Elsie or that visits to Villa Trianon were no longer of interest to him once the caliber of people he met there was not of the intellectual level of a Henry Adams or in possession of the witty *joie de vivre* of a Bessy Marbury. The one known reason for their drifting apart was that Nicky Mariano despised Elsie from the moment she first saw her, when she brought Ogden Codman for a visit to I Tatti.

> This famous Parisian hostess and interior decorator appeared in a huge car with a *cavaliere savente* whose name I have forgotten. . . . To me, she seemed not made of human flesh and blood but of wire and metal and although I met her again and again in Paris and admired her enchanting house I never got over this first impression of her.

Two years earlier, Mariano had accepted a position as Berenson's private secretary and librarian and, over the next forty years, would become the most important woman in his life both professionally and emotionally. Anybody distasteful to her was almost certain to become persona non grata at I Tatti.

$\mathcal{B}$essy's trip to Europe that summer was to be her last. The decision was not made because the effort had proven physically beyond her. Far from it. She traveled three thousand miles around the continent in the back of an automobile with no visible diminution in her energies. The time was profitably spent connecting with old clients, signing up new ones, and re-establishing the American Play Company as the preeminent dramatic and literary agency in the world by opening (or reopening) offices in London (Golding Bright actually had never closed), Paris, Berlin, Budapest, Vienna, Rome, Madrid, and Barcelona, along with entering into affiliations with agents in the Scandinavian countries. Upon returning to the United States, she circularized a letter to all of the leading publishers and producers, informing them that her trip was "successful even beyond my own expectation in establishing live-wire-contact with practically every country in Europe."

Bessy's objective was to become the sole conduit between product and consumer. "We are now in a position to furnish you . . . with all data and information . . . as regards the important plays, successful musical comedies, sensational films, and world famous books" produced in all of the great cultural centers of Europe. With her own list of stars, she was attempting to package and control all aspects of theatrical productions, films, and promotion of books a half-century before it began to be common practice among Hollywood talent agencies.

The trip also served as a sentimental farewell to places in which she had been so happy with Elsie and Anne Morgan for so many years—most of all, to the Villa Trianon. It was no longer a place in which Bessy felt at home. Where once the nymphets had created a society of doers in the arts and politics, engaged in all that was positive and creative, where innovation meant something more vital than simply being new, where good manners were the way of life rather than the rote of form, Elsie was toadying to blasé inheritors unable to feel anything except the latest sensation, looking at tomorrow only as something to replace a today grown stale before the sun set on it.

Bessy's Villa Trianon would soon be rediscovered in the rear library in Sutton Place, overlooking the timeless garden and the swiftly moving river. Set close to the fireplace was a capacious chair, sometimes referred to as her throne. From it she would hold forth to a group of doers old and young, political, artistic, social—attractive in ways that burrowed down beneath their often handsome surfaces, all eager for invitations to Bessy's house, because it was where they met their own kind and opposite numbers, where the action was.

Across the small hall from that often blazing library was Elsie's gemlike salon, where everything was too small, too quiet, too perfect.

Anne Morgan was forty-eight years old that summer of 1921. The time was long overdue for her to move out of the Morgan mansion and have a home of her own. Certainly, her family no longer expected her to remain home until she married, or to marry at all. What brought her to select Sutton Place for her future home could have been Bessy, or it could have been the proximity of Anne Vanderbilt, to whom she always had been enormously attracted. The moment when Anne Vanderbilt admitted a reciprocal feeling remains obscure, for either Morgan stopped keeping a diary during the next decade, or her secretary, Daisy Rogers, later destroyed the volumes from 1920 to 1932, along with most of her personal correspondence.

Morgan acquired both 3 and 5 Sutton Place and hired Schmidt to raze the houses, and build a single residence on the adjacent lots that the De Wolfe team would decorate.

The house's Georgian style related to American Federalist architecture and closely resembled an old New York residence. Next to the Vanderbilt house and extending over the ample southern corner, which allowed the broadest perspective of the block, Schmidt related the two houses in a way that converted Sutton Square into a statement on late eighteenth-century Anglo-Saxon architecture.

At the same time the two Annes and Bessy were setting up homes on Sutton Square, several other women of social standing were taking houses there. These included Mrs. Lorillard Cammann, a member of the family of Elsie's old flame, Pierre Lorillard; Mrs. Chauncey Ollcott, widow of a famous musical star; and Mrs. Francis B. Griswold, a prominent Newporter whose father-in-law had been one of the founders of the Meadow Brook Hunt Club, where Sam Sands was killed. Not only were there these loose links among all of the women, but they were unified by their financial autonomy and the fact that all were either engaged in professions or working regularly in philanthropic services. They were women not only of independent means but of independent minds. As Sutton Square began to take shape, starting with the Schmidt houses, it became clear it would stand alone like a perfect quadrangle, as separated from the rest of the city as if it were an island in the middle of the river that bordered it.

Nothing so threatening to their positions as providers and delineators of the city's shape had ever before happened to the less than sexually secure members of the male upper-class population. As with the Colony Club shortly after the turn of the century, their immediate defense was to strike back in the only way they could—with salacious insinuation. A whispering campaign went the rounds of society to the effect that a sapphic enclave was developing on the eastern fringe of midtown. The women were too proud to indicate they were cognizant of the vicious rumors and too powerful for any individual to dare to take credit for having started them.

On November 13, 1921, the private embarrassment shared by the two Annes during the *Town Topics* trial was rekindled when one of its successors hit the newsstands. *Gossip* was a biweekly magazine that boasted it was "the international journal of society." Lacking the testosterone of Colonel William D'Alton Mann, when he blackmailed Willie K. Vanderbilt and her father, the editor of *Gossip* was content with a more clumsy than titillating attack on Anne Morgan:

> Anne Morgan (as is the case with many of the other women mentioned above) devotes a large part of her time to philanthropic and welfare work and the remainder of it to assisting struggling young girls to attain professional, social, or business recognition. And now that she is to be located in the Sutton Place Colony it is felt among the garrulous element of society that she as well as the remainder of the above named group will continue their various relief and charitable activities to their hearts desire this winter as well as stage many delightful entertainments of one kind or another for the less fortunate but talented young ladies in whom they are intensely interested.

Bessy was among those honored at a dinner given that year for "distinguished Americans who are opposed to government by the Blue Laws." She offered her opinion of the elements of society catered to by publications of the *Gossip* variety:

> This committee is committed to the principle that individual liberty is the most cherished possession of citizens of a free democracy. . . . We challenge the right of any group of citizens to impose their own conception of the manner in which the individual shall live his daily life, pursue his own happiness, regulate his private conduct in so far as those privileges are not abused in a way to offend the ideals which have become characteristic of American rules of conduct.

Bessy remained a staunch adherent of Catholic dogma and occasionally involved in the church's political machinations, but at no point did she indicate that American rules of conduct should be dictated by any single religion or creed. Her warning at the dinner that "this country will be devastated by reformers" referred equally to those of the right and of the left.

CHAPTER FORTY-SEVEN ॐ

When Anne Morgan returned to New York on January 14, her most pressing concern was neither leaving her old home nor building her new one. Before all else came the need to raise two million dollars, if the American Committee for a Devastated France was to continue its work. She was home only three days when she called a press conference to complain of American lack of interest in providing funds to refurbish the French merchant fleet, which was vital to the country's recovery. The United States was indifferent to the struggle to survive of its great ally while permitting their recent common enemy to rebuild its shipping fleet to 60 percent of its pre-war capacity. With little taxation, Germany was able to use its funds to reconstruct its industrial base, while France was burdened with crippling taxation in order to repay its war debt to the United States. Anne was among the few to protest the iniquity that would continue to suppurate inside the French for the remainder of the century. They would not forgive what they deemed American ingratitude for what France had done for it dating back to Lafayette, and would increasingly suspect it of attempting to undermine their language, culture, and economy.

Anne went on a national fund-raising tour, playing to sell-out audiences from coast to coast, averaging two thousand dollars a speech even in the smallest towns. In Chicago, she was among the first to use the radio to solicit contributions. Her voice went into living rooms in the heart of the isolationist Midwest with a message the occupants never heard from politicians pandering for their votes. "The days are over when we can have prosperity in America without prosperity overseas. We must get out of our ancestors' attitudes of taking no active part in European affairs."

As guest of honor at a luncheon given by Chicago's leading merchants and bankers, for whom the Morgan name was still magic, she said: "America is constantly calling for repayment of war debts. There is only one way we will be able to collect from France . . . complete rehabilitation of the country so that the entire nation may resume its pre-war business." She also warned against helping Germany revive its manufacturing and industrial might. Her words were ignored, for it was the investments of men like them (including her brother, Jack) that enabled Germany to have an industrial base in position that would allow Hitler to rearm swiftly and efficiently.

She also criticized the disarmament conference for insisting that France have a smaller navy than Japan. "Japan has never been on the defensive as France must be. France needs a navy to protect herself."

Her words would have a distinct resonance in the late Thirties, when Japan attacked China, and Germany went on the offensive in Europe while defaulting on the loan guaranteed by Morgan & Co.

In addition to her exhaustive fund-raising, Anne Morgan was occupied with plans for an assortment of building projects. Not only was work beginning on her Sutton house, but there was also reconstruction that had to be done at Blérancourt to make it function better in a world in which those who had been devastated by the war would once more become self-sufficient. A third project would prove the most ambitious and the most involving.

There were more workingwomen than ever before in the history of the city, with a concomitant greater deficiency of decent housing for them. Anne's pre-war club, the Vacation headquarters, on West Thirty-eighth and Thirty-ninth streets, had helped in its time but was far from adequate to the needs of the Twenties. By then, the girls of the Vacation Savings Fund had become the women of the American Women's Association. At a meeting on May 23, she inaugurated a campaign to raise $2,500,000 to build a business-women's clubhouse and residence.

In 1922, Bessy found her own cause, the repeal of the Volstead Act, which would continue to concern her for the next decade. She denounced prohibition at a meeting of the Women's Democratic Club, claiming that it contributed to the widening of the gap between the classes, the wealthy able to find and afford the best liquors, the poor endangering resources and health with bathtub gin. Among her conclusions was that being continually forced to break prohibition laws was undermining the morals of young people.

Of the women present, only one thought prohibition was there to stay and a good thing it was, too. Another observed she never drank before the Volstead Act; now she took everything offered to her. The president of the club admitted to having had four glasses of champagne at a dance a few nights earlier. Nevertheless, the women thought it the better part of wisdom for them not to issue any official statement on the prohibition controversy.

Bessy remained undaunted and took her fight to every venue opened to her. She also remained active on every issue affecting Democratic party policy. While attending a meeting of the women members of the Democratic National Committee, she described herself and her function in the party. "I'm a sort of Old Hickory. And when they want resolutions written or something of the kind, they call upon me."

As if playing Joan of Arc to the "wets," Old Hickory to the Democrats, mother to her clients, and moving into a new house were not enough for one aging, ill woman, she decided to take on yet another project. Her friend Horace Liveright, the most distinguished publisher in New York, had convinced her the time had come to write her autobiography for his company, Boni & Liveright. A ghostwriter was suggested to jog her memory and help her to prepare a structure. As a published writer, she refused any professional help and decided the book would take the form of an informal memoir, a ramble through the past, as she recalled it, without being hampered by chronological verisimilitude. The title, *My Crystal Ball*, gave the central image of herself as seeress looking into her clouded ball, which, under her hard gaze, would clear to reveal recollections not so much anchored in time as in the spaces of her mind.

On a late spring afternoon, Bessy went down to have lunch at Keen's Chop House, on West Thirty-sixth Street. It was a place that held memories for her of the days when she was first embarking on her career. Back then, Herald Square was the heart of the theatre district, and the restaurant one of the most popular haunts of actors and playwrights.

Her visit on that May noon had nothing to do with nostalgia. It was for a meeting of a new group, the Anti-Fanatic League of Women, which was set up "to vigorously oppose the nomination and election of all persons who favor prohibition and blue laws." It also called "anti-American" all the successors to Anthony Comstock who were "attempting to regulate by law, frenzy and threats the thoughts, appetites, habits and customs of the individual." Bessy was pleased to be elected its president, for she could not have been in greater concurrence with its goals. From the beginning, her opposition to the Volstead Act had been linked to her abhorrence of all forms of censorship or blue laws. She was often a prude, acting out of a very strict code of morals and behavior on which, with only the slightest provocation, she was quite happy to sound off, but it was a personal code that others were free to accept or reject. She felt that any attempt to legislate it would have been a threat to her right to have it.

*T*he music to which they danced at the Villa Trianon that summer was often provided by Cole Porter, but the tempo was set by Johnnie McMullin. The two were remarkably similar: short, elfin, slender men of a cutting-edge elegance so often achieved when bright effeminate small-town boys were clever enough to live out their dreams in the world capitals of fashion. Theirs was the kind of love of gossip nurtured over rural party and/or clothes lines but raised to a degree of risqué camp bitchiness so often best achieved by those breathlessly pursuing themselves. In Porter's case, it was transfigured by a kind of genius. They filled the villa with the most exotic young beauties of all the sexes. Most important to the extension of Elsie's fame and career, Johnnie brought his publisher, Condé Nast, into her life as Bessy in the past had brought Frohman and the Colony ladies, and like them, he was charmed.

*I*t must have been with quite a bit of frustration that Bessy learned Elsie had joined the three Annes—Vanderbilt, Morgan, and Dike—in the elect group of Chevaliers of the Legion of Honor, among whom she so long and fruitlessly had striven to be numbered. The investiture took place in Strasbourg, on August 24, and Elsie must have spent the sweltering Paris July in fittings for the impeccably tailored Red Cross uniform, cape, and headdress she wore for the event, which were of the length fashionable in the summer collections of 1922 and short enough to reveal a beautifully made pair of double-strap pumps.

One curious aspect of the event was, why Strasbourg, which had not been returned to France until after the war and which had been occupied by Germany for almost fifty years before then. The Alsatian city on the Franco-German border bore no relationship to Elsie or to the ambrine hospital in which she had served. Another curious facet of the occasion was the amount of pomp and circumstance with which the ribbon was bestowed. Chevalier is the lowest of the five classes of the Legion of Honor and generally given in the office of some middle-rank government official or, in some cases, forwarded by mail.

The answer to these mysteries may lie with another of her new young friends, Paul-Louis Weiller, who for over sixty years would sentimentally keep personal photographs of the ceremony. He was not one of the clever homosexuals beginning to cluster around Elsie, but he was an insufferable social climber. Nancy Mitford would later dismiss him as "poor Louis," because his efforts to get "in" were so often to no avail. The famous English beauty Diana Cooper and her husband, Duff, would become dependent on his generosity after Cooper lost his post as British ambassador to France. With a lack of generosity, she would refer to him as "Poor Louis . . . The frog who people can't endure." He gave her a mink coat and, though she did not refuse it, she called it "the coat of shame." Ultimately, she ungratefully complained: "We live free on poor Louis's bounty—and *I could howl!* What shall I do to be saved?"

Elsie would never be similarly troubled about accepting his generosity. Weiller was an air force hero visiting Mathilde de Rothschild when Elsie and he met at Mission Ambrine, to which he had donated a great deal of money.

By 1922, when their friendship actually began, the twenty-nine-year-old Weiller already had acquired the lifelong habit of referring to himself as "commandant" in recognition of his wartime rank. He also was one of the wealthiest young men in France, who was to become still richer by using his flying experience to help start the company that would eventually become Air France.

The Weiller family fortune stemmed from the Gnome et Rhone automotive engineering company, in Alsace-Lorraine. The Weillers were among the most politically influential people in the region, indeed in post-war France, and had everything except social position and, more important, celebrity. Paul-Louis saw in Elsie a means of achieving it.

It was no great feat for a Weiller to have arranged the Strasbourg ceremony for her. A few years later, a member of the family would do something far more impressive. Ever since Bessy bought the Villa Trianon, Elsie had coveted an adjacent strip of land that was actually a part of the Great Park of Versailles. She claimed to have wanted it for a *potager,* but a kitchen garden seemed an unlikely desire in light of the execrable quality of the food she served. What it actually would do was give her access to the grounds of the royal château, something infinitely more valuable to a private residence than its cuisine. Through the influence of Senator Lazare Weiller, the *potager* and right of way were acquired for her. It was all thanks to Paul-Louis and only the beginning of the young man's largesse to her.

The Cole Porters, trying the off season on the Riviera, had leased La Garoupe, a large, airy Mediterranean villa surrounded by terraces and gardens, with bougainvillea climbing up the walls, and adjacent to the pristine beach of Antibes. It was perfectly situated for the new Mediterranean dream.

Their guests that summer included everybody's ideal expatriate American couple, Gerald and Sara Murphy, rich, beautiful, artistic, casually amoral in a way that never interfered with their family life, and possessed of a personal style that had little to do with fashion. Gerald had been at Yale with Cole and the visit that summer would change his life as well as the history of the Côte d'Azur. Cole never returned, but the Murphys did, to establish the French Riviera as a summer resort.

Another Porter guest that summer was Charles Mendl, a gentleman whose English accent was so thick people often could not understand a word he said. That did not matter, for he was so unfailingly good-humored that it was the rare individual who was not charmed by him. He was tall, portly, civilized, and the epitome of Savile Row. Mendl "silly ass" anecdotes abounded, many making him sound like a caricature of the British gentleman, but he never took offense. One of Murphy's favorites concerned the time he was asked what the British meant by a cad. Sir Charles was stumped, and at length sputtered: "Oh, hang it, a cad is just someone who makes you go all crinkly-toes!"

Like Arthur Wing Pinero before him and Leslie Howard after him, this paradigm of the English gentleman was the son of Jewish immigrants. Everything else about him was vague. Depending on who was telling the story, his family was from either Lebanon or Bohemia. His father prospered either as a grain merchant, or as a ship builder, or both. How well he prospered was unknown, but that he did well enough was obvious, for the son's performance as a toff was so flawless, it would appear he had models on which to base it early in life. That his family did not insist he go to university was uncharacteristic of prosperous Jewish immigrants but not unimaginable. He reputedly went to Argentina on family business, where, it was said, he amassed a personal fortune in Argentinian and Paraguayan railroads.

When history caught up with him in the form of Elsie de Wolfe, for it was only because of his relationship with her that anybody recalled he had been there at all, he had a modest flat on the fashionable avenue Montaigne, where he gave small weekly luncheon parties at which he gathered information for British intelligence. Mostly he was an extra man, a walker, a court jester and professional guest at the homes of the wealthy: it is hardly the portrait of a man of means.

Later, it was reputed that Mendl had been a womanizer before Elsie came into his life, but nobody could recall one woman with whom he was involved. His only known close friends were either homosexuals or bisexuals such as Monty Woolley, Gerald Murphy, Johnnie McMullin, and Cole Porter. The one portrait of him remembered from the pre-Elsie days was left by F. Scott Fitzgerald, in *Tender Is the Night*, in which he was depicted as the homosexual Campion.

The portrayal has since been dismissed as "unflattering and highly inaccurate," largely on the basis of the recollections of Gerald Murphy. The latter was sufficiently incensed by the use of Sara and him as partial models for Nicole and Dick Diver in that book to want to cast doubt on the validity of any Fitzgerald character based on one of his friends. Also, Murphy was as discreet about the homosexuality of his friends as he was about his own occasional same-sex dalliances. Nobody has ever come up with a reason that Fitzgerald would portray Mendl as he did were there not some validity in the portrayal.

At the beginning of World War I, Mendl had volunteered as an interpreter and was given the rank of lieutenant, only to be invalided out within five months. He would have to have suffered a severe wound for that to have happened. There was never any sign or mention of such an injury, and he was soon well enough to become an intelligence officer in the British Admiralty. During the peace conference, he was transferred to the British embassy in Paris, but in a capacity that was never specified. He remained there for the rest of his career, officially employed in a news department job that did not exist. When he was knighted, in 1924, the palace issued no formal explanation of why he was being honored. He was an unofficial man of some importance to the English government. In short, he was probably a spy, which would explain the successful obliteration of any information in depth about his past. Did Elsie later know and, perhaps, help him? It was a role she might have enjoyed. For his part, not only was she a good beard, but she gave him access to some of the most powerful Americans during their visits abroad, where they might be a little loose-tongued with an amusing, silly-ass Englishman. That would be another strong motive for his having become involved with her.

*T*he Annes Dike and Morgan were in New York late that autumn to continue their seemingly interminable fund-raising. Morgan found Bessy in fine fettle. She had turned Sutton Place into a latter-day Irving Place, but instead of being one of the bachelorettes, she had become the social lioness of New York. Now they came not to be Bohemian or to meet those they would not meet elsewhere: they came to see Bessy holding court in a capacious antique chair set beside the fireplace in her library, smoking endless cigarettes, issuing edicts, making or breaking reputations, playing the endlessly fascinating temptress and enjoying every minute of it.

That season, John Barrymore was the toast of the town in his brilliant *Hamlet*, but the greatest party boy in the Western world was not stepping out. Having to fit into the tightest tights in the Western world and to give, night after night, what has been called the greatest performance of the legendary part ever seen on Broadway, he was taking no chances on being tempted by rich food and, more lethally, bootleg hooch. The only invitations he accepted were from Bessy, because he knew she would be amused rather than insulted when he brought a small cold chicken for his supper rather than partake of her generous buffet. More important, he could trust the infamously "wet" Bessy Marbury to make certain he remained dry.

*L*ife had been generous to Anne Vanderbilt without ever having been very good to her. The tall fashionably clad figure remained as slender as ever, and though the hair had gone from gold to white, the finely lined skin clung almost seamlessly to the good bones. Although strong enough to withstand the many tragedies, she had been deeply affected by them: Anne Vanderbilt was, in many ways, a lost lady. She continued to pay obeisance to the familiar Protestant God of her youth, who long since had seemed to be overlooking her except in a not inconsequential material sense.

The latest manifestation of her God's desertion was the complete mental breakdown of her daughter Barbara in 1921. It had happened while she was living in Anne's Paris house after obtaining a French divorce. In the early Twenties, Europe offered the most advanced psychiatric treatment available anywhere in the world. Anne sought out all of the great practitioners, but established treatment proved of little help to the unfortunate Barbara. There was nothing to be lost by trying Emile Coué, best described as a Twenties version of a new-age practitioner. She motored to Nancy to consult him at his clinic. Originally a pharmacist, Coué also had studied hypnosis and developed a system of self-mastery through conscious auto-suggestion. In 1920, he invented a mantra and introduced a feel-good psychotherapy based on the repetition of the phrase: "Every day, and in every way, I am becoming better and better."

Anne was not alone in feeling that orthodoxy was failing her. Since the end of the war, the sophistic morality of church and state was proving insufficient to the spiritual and psychic needs of vast numbers of people. Panaceas were being sought in the mystic religions of the Orient, in spiritualism, psychoanalysis, fundamentalist intensifications of Christianity and Judaism, and the new nationalist gods of Fascism and Communism. It was not simply a generation of middle-class expatriates who were lost: a world was lost when one of the bloodiest conflicts in history radically altered it but not, as advertised, for the better. Those who so long had tacitly accepted the will of God were questioning the fate of man and woman.

The comparatively innocuous Coué system apparently was working for a great many of the disaffected. He was among the most successful speakers on the lecture circuit in France and England, and it was becoming increasingly commonplace to find people everywhere muttering: "Every day, and in every way—"

Although there was little this new guru could do for Barbara Hatch, Anne was impressed by him and, toward the end of 1922, was among the prominent people who sponsored his first American lecture tour, with proceeds going to the establishment of Coué training centers in the United States, and to his new Institute Coué d'Education Psychique, in Paris. Sensing something big, the editor of the New York *World*, Herbert Bayard Swope, had a ghostwriter help Coué write daily columns for his newspaper. Syndication made a fortune for both the newspaper and the institute.

Anne Vanderbilt's search for answers for both Barbara and herself took her still further afield when her beautiful and flighty older daughter, Margaret, became involved in a mystic cult having vague connections to Tantric Hinduism and which was presided over by Pierre A. Bernard, who preferred to be known as Oom the Omnipotent.

Her politically ambitious husband and his socially conservative Mills family had always placed constraints on Margaret's unconventional enthusiasms. No longer able to stand it, she had the marriage dissolved in Paris, several months before her sister obtained her divorce there.

Without waiting for her decree nisi to become final, Margaret departed for the small town of Nyack, in Rockland County, New York, where Oom resided over his "Tantrik Order," at the Brae Burn Country Club. Many of its two hundred devotees were socially prominent, wealthy, or both, and were reputed to include the most successful trial attorney of the day, Clarence Darrow, and Fred Upham, the treasurer of the Republican National Committee. Although questions could be raised about the divine inspiration of Oom the Omnipotent or, as he was sometimes called, the loving guru, there could be no doubt of his business and common sense. The shrewd investment of the contributions of his followers had made him a millionaire and enabled him to buy the country club for his headquarters. To keep the goodwill of the citizens of Nyack, he preferred to be known to them by his legal name of Pierre A. Bernard, and in that name gave liberally to local charities. He also was the chief backer of the Nyack Athletic Club, a local baseball team known in the county as "the world champions" for having won twenty-five out of thirty games in its first season.

Bernard made every effort to keep secret the exact nature of the rites practiced by his group. An adaptation of one of the practices of classic Tantrism could have held a great appeal for these 1920s disciples. In an attempt to reach an objective ecstasy, a form of yogic sexual union was practiced in which the act was terminated just before orgasm. The obstruction to supreme pleasure was reputed to bring a mystic sense of oneness with the basic reality of the universe. Margaret never divulged whether or not she met Sir Paul Dukes during the practice of this Hindu form of coitus reservatus, but they did meet and fall in love in Nyack, where he was an ardent devotee of Oom's cult.

Dukes was a strikingly handsome and dashing adventurer well known on the American lecture circuit, where his female audiences thrilled to tales of his exploits as a British agent in Russia. During the war, he had been a British agent who had joined the Soviet army and worked in a Soviet munitions factory to gather information about the Bolsheviks. He was never discovered, and the information he obtained was considered so valuable that Lenin offered a reward for his capture and issued an order allowing any Soviet citizen to shoot him on sight. In those waning days of the British Empire, spies were made knights with the same frequency as contemporary soccer players, and Dukes received his title in 1920.

When Anne Vanderbilt returned to New York with Barbara, she was so disconsolate about her daughter's condition that she was willing to try anything. Margaret brought Bernard to see her, and the two convinced her that a stay at the country club, under the supervision of members of his cult, would do wonders for the unbalanced young woman. Anne agreed, but before Barbara could be admitted, it was indicated that a guaranteed loan of $200,000 be made to the omnipotent Oom. By the chanting of what magical mantras, by the administering of what hallucinogens, by the practice of what arcane method of brainwashing it was achieved, Barbara did seemingly improve and was once more able to cope with the day-to-day problems of ordinary life. Anne was too grateful to complain when only $70,000 of the loan was repaid.

When Margaret married Dukes that October in 1922, Anne was publicly ridiculed for having "given" both a large sum of money and her two daughters to the cult of a man considered by many to be a libidinous charlatan. She would not deign to defend herself. Those who knew her would need no explanation; those who did not, would accept none. Sympathy came from her nearest neighbor, Anne Morgan, who would soon become her dearest friend. It was undoubtedly the ardent nature of Morgan that was most responsible for turning that friendship into a love affair.

Anne Morgan had become so transatlantic that she kept an apartment in Paris, at 22 avenue Montaigne, but much of the ACDF business was conducted from Dike's flat, at 43 rue de Courcelles. Although no longer living together, the two women continued to share a kind of life, but despite their common causes, Morgan was finding the relationship increasingly frustrating. Anne Vanderbilt was then spending a great deal of time in her rue Leroux townhouse. The intimacy between the two women that had begun to develop on Sutton Place blossomed in Paris.

In the summer of 1923, Elsa Maxwell had a blazing success with her assignment from Benito Mussolini's government to turn Venice into a great resort again. Cole Porter, with his clever tunes and naughty lyrics, was the pied piper luring the smart people back to the Jewel of the Adriatic. Linda and he were to lease several palazzi along the Grand Canal before finding their ideal residence in the Rezzonico. Once the Venetian home of Robert and Elizabeth Barrett Browning, it had been described by Henry James as a "great seventeenth century pile, throwing itself upon the water with a peculiar florid assurance."

In the words of a later Porter song, "We open in Venice"—and the party was on. It would last for four years. Actually, there were two parties: the elaborate masquerades attended by both sexes, where some amusing cross-dressing was encouraged; and the drag balls, men only, where the gowns ranged from haute couture to high camp, which, then as now, were often synonymous. It was at one of the latter, given by Porter at the Rezzonico while his wife was out of town, that the great Twenties Venetian summers came to an end. The party became so raucous that the police were called in. Were it not that one of the gorgeously gowned beauties turned out to be the police chief's son, they would all have been hauled off to jail. Instead, Porter was discreetly ordered to leave town, and lights were dimmed all along the Grand Canal.

The stylish set felt it was Venice that had sustained the loss. They returned the city to the Venetians, who would not have such a good time again until after another great war. Elsa Maxwell was hired by the Grimaldis to make a summer resort of their moldering little principality of Monaco, and the next year, everybody worth his weight in publicity would follow her to the South of France, where the Murphys had, so to speak, established a beach-head.

Elsie was also in New York that autumn and dropped a gushing note to Eleanor Robson Belmont, kittenishly addressed to "Eleanore." In it, she mentioned that she was living at 677 Park Avenue during her stay in New York, because she found it "so much more convenient than Sutton Place."

Bessy tried everything she could think of to keep Elsie with her on any terms, even part time. She was responsible for getting her the Sutton Place jobs, had put aside part of her own house for her use when she was in New York, was trying to line up jobs for her as a set designer. It was all to no avail. Elsie was determined to make their physical separation complete and would never again stay under her roof. Perversely, she also refused to release Bessy from her emotional bond. The depth of that bond was proclaimed to the world when *My Crystal Ball* was published the following month with an extravagant dedication.

To

ELSIE DE WOLFE

my friend

Together we sorrowed
Together we rejoiced
Together we failed
Together we succeeded

The distances of life were always bridged because our faith has been large in the skill of that great sculptor Time, who would shape our friendship to a perfect end.

CHAPTER FORTY-EIGHT

Although *My Crystal Ball* had no index, Bessy replaced it with personal notes such as one she sent to Lee Shubert: "Hope you will like the tribute I have paid to you on Page 258." The book did well, receiving generally favorable reviews. The *New York Times* critic called it "a fascinating picture of the men and women of the last fifty years. She has known them all. . . . Her book is a document of her times."

The serial rights were sold to the *Saturday Evening Post,* but the book fell short of being either a best-seller or a major literary document. Bessy was both a professional and a realist. She did not waste energy flogging dead horses. Early that winter of 1924, her interest turned away from her book and to the coming presidential conventions. If the Democrats chose the right man, malfeasance in the Republican executive branch gave them a good chance of victory.

Republican president Warren G. Harding had died the previous summer. His taciturn and incorruptible vice president, Calvin Coolidge, was sworn in as president. He was a man so singularly lacking in charm and personal magnetism that Democratic hopes rose. Bessy felt that if they nominated Al Smith, they would have a candidate to beat Coolidge. He had the personality, the drive, and the vigor to contrast favorably with the Republican. But he was also a Catholic and a New York liberal, neither of which went down well in the vast stretches of the American Bible Belt, which in those days was committed to the Democratic party.

*I*n December 1923, the Equal Rights Amendment was first introduced in Congress. It differed little from the amendment reintroduced and passed by Congress in the 1970s but not ratified by the state referendums in 1982. Both were straightforward, superficially nonthreatening documents encapsulated in one sentence. The original, "Men and women shall have Equal Rights throughout the United States and every place subject to its jurisdiction," sounded more personal and less mulled over by the objective tongue of legalese than its successor: "Equality of rights under the law shall not be denied or abridged by the United States or any state on account of sex."

In 1923, ERA split the women's movement but along no discernible political lines. There were radicals, liberals, moderates, and conservatives on both sides. Those against ERA included Jane Addams; Rose Schneiderman, along with the entire women's labor movement; Carrie Chapman Catt and her League of Women Voters; Lillian Wald; Elisabeth Marbury; Anne Morgan; and Eleanor Roosevelt. They were considered old-fashioned, maternalistic protectionists by the pro-ERA group, which included Elsa Maxwell and the future wife of Henry Luce, young Clare Boothe. In turn, the latter were deemed elitist, bourgeois women who, if not born with sterling silver spoons in their mouths, were at least fed off Sheffield plate. There were no minority or immigrant women in Alva's pro-ERA National Woman's Party, for it addressed none of the problems with which they lived each day of their lives. That party favored revoking as "unequal" those pitifully few laws specifically enacted to protect the female members of the underclasses.

After a meeting with the editor of Alva's magazine, *Equal Rights,* the country's leading specialist in industrial medicine, Dr. Alice Hamilton, wrote to her:

> I could not help comparing you as you sat there ... sheltered, safe, beautifully guarded against even the ugliness of life, with the women for whom you demand "freedom of contract." ... Rescinding all the laws in the country discriminating against women ... at the expense of present and future protective laws ... will have harmed a far larger number of women than you will have benefited and the harm done to them will be more disastrous.

One of Governor Smith's main objectives early that autumn and winter was to bring the Democratic National Convention to New York City. Bessy, a Democratic National committeewoman, was chosen to supervise the activities of New York state and city women. She named a committee to help her that included Harriet May Mills, Belle Moskowitz, Nancy Cook, and Eleanor Roosevelt.

Cook and Roosevelt often worked in tandem in those days. At their first meeting, Eleanor gave Nancy a gift of a bouquet of violets. The symbolism could not have been lost on either of them. So accepted was the gift of violets as a part of the ritual of lesbian courtship that, in 1926, it would be used in that capacity in one of the more controversial plays of the period, *The Captive.* The drama, based on *La Prisonnière,* by Edouard Bourdet, the future head of the austere and government-funded Comédie Française, had opened to excellent reviews but became a cause célèbre when the New York police closed it because its exploration of a lesbian relationship was a danger to public morals.

Bessy was the play's agent and led a group of civil libertarians and respected members of the theatrical profession in its defense. They obtained an injunction to permit the run to be resumed, but after five performances, the producers bowed to reactionary pressure and closed the American production of a play that continued to run in Paris, had been hailed as a masterpiece in the Max Reinhardt representations in Vienna and Berlin, and was being produced all over the world. Two months later, the Republican state legislature banned plays "depicting or dealing with the subject of sex degeneracy or sex perversion." The law forbade the appearance of homosexual characters or discussion of homosexuality on the stage.

Fearing state censorship, the Producing Managers' Association offered to submit all plays of "doubtful propriety" to review by a jury of five members of the American Arbitration Association and two members of the theatrical community. Bessy disagreed with the plan, declaring she did not believe "in either political censorship of plays or in the appointment of a jury composed of any group of citizens." But her own solution was, if anything, worse. Based on the prevailing British system, it called for all plays to be submitted for licensing to one supremely powerful man who would have the authority to forbid their productions or to demand deletions or rewrites of what he considered meretricious scenes. She should have known better from the experiences of her own British playwrights, especially Shaw and Wilde, with the office of the Lord Chamberlain.

Naturally, the West End had joined Broadway in being the only international theatrical centers of any consequence not to have unfettered productions of *The Captive.* The irony was that no play could have greater puritanical morality or be more offensive to homosexual sensibilities than *The Captive,* in which a young woman brings tragedy to herself and all around her by giving in to her lesbian nature and going off with another woman. Its theme was that the wages of homosexuality were degradation and death or something very close to it. It is astonishing that so many members of the allegedly enlightened segment of the theatrical community should have considered the play a break with the prudery of the past and a trenchant, honest, noble work. There was more honesty in Mae West's lubricious *Sex,* a play padlocked during the same season, which also had some homosexual characters but made no moral judgments on their sexual preferences. Unperturbed by being sentenced to ten days in jail, West announced plans to bring another play, *The Drag,* to Broadway. It would be the first play in which openly gay men played gay men onstage.

In many ways, *The Drag* was ahead of its time. In 1927, West gathered a cast of forty gay chorus men, put them onstage, and had them improvise about their lives. The play was developed from what they said and how they said it, with much of the dialogue simply transcriptions of their campy one-liners. Almost a half-century later, *A Chorus Line* would be hailed as a revolutionary musical for doing the same thing. Much of West's later stage persona and dialogue, as personified by her greatest success, *Diamond Lil,* was inspired by the transvestites in *The Drag.* One-liners from that show sound as if they were written for Lil and the other characters West later portrayed in films:

> Listen dearie, I'm just the type that men crave. The type that burns 'em up. Why, when I walk up Tenth Avenue, you can smell the meat sizzling in Hell's Kitchen.

> You should see the creation I'm wearing, dearie. Virginal white in front, no back, with oceans of this and oceans of that, trimmed with excitement in front.

Another boasted of not being able to leave the Navy Yard "without having the flags drop to half mast." Things would later come full circle when Mae West became a homosexual icon and a staple of every transvestite nightclub act.

*W*hen the Democratic state convention met that March, in Albany, it was considered certain that Bessy and Eleanor would be among the eight delegates-at-large selected at the state convention. Eleanor took the lead in demanding the right of women to choose their own delegates and have equal representation on party committees. She won her point and was asked to head and name her own committee to negotiate women's rights within the Democratic party. With that victory, Eleanor became the acknowledged head of the women's wing of the party. It was a position always coveted by Bessy, but her closeness to the male power base was too well-known for her ever to have been selected for it. She managed to retain her position as national committeewoman and delegate-at-large to the convention. The differences between Eleanor and Bessy were political and generational but never personal. They were united not by party or creed but by the many close associations of their old New York families, going back to the McCoun and Roosevelt homesteads, in Oyster Bay.

If Eleanor Roosevelt was troubled by Bessy's ardent commitment to the men of the party, Franklin had no problems with it. When he was made chairman of the New York State Committee for the Nomination of Governor Alfred E. Smith, Bessy was one of the first women to whom he turned for help. She was quite circumspect about an early public endorsement of Smith, because as a member of the National Committee, she would need to "'glad-hand' every candidate," but she did drop a private note to Roosevelt: "I am delighted and will help you in any way I can." Her list of possible committee members included her publisher, Horace Liveright, vetoed by Roosevelt; Richard Madden and Charles Hanson Towne, two executives of the American Play Company, accepted; and William P. Larkin, described at "high in the K. of C. organizations." Roosevelt put a question mark next to his name. Bessy added: "So long as you have Eddie Cantor on the Smith Committee, I suggest that Irving Berlin be asked to join." The phrasing was an example of the sort of coded anti-Semitism often used by one polite member of old New York society to another. The suggestion troubled Roosevelt enough for him to scribble "ok" next to it, then cross it out and write "no," then place a check over that.

Bessy's last recommendation was Mrs. Norman Mack, the wife of a prominent upstate politician. Eleanor or no Eleanor, Franklin Roosevelt delivered the penultimate male politician's attitude toward the position of women in the party by scrawling next to the name "Ask Mack," implying her husband, not she, was the one to ask if her services were available.

To make certain that the convention would take place in New York City, Smith had enlisted the aid of his friend and supporter Herbert Bayard Swope, editor of the New York *World*. The influential and popular Swope raised the then formidable sum of $250,000 to bring the Democrats to Madison Square Garden, on June 24. Even in those days before air-conditioning, that auditorium was known as a sweatbox never intended to be used during the summer. People were hoping for a swift and unseasonably cool convention. The entire edifice had fallen into such decay in the eighteen years since Stanford White was shot there that only a month before the convention, its owner, New York Life Insurance Company, had announced plans to raze it. The convening Democrats were scheduled to be the Garden's last hurrah. As it turned out, it very nearly was the last hurrah of the party.

The hot social ticket for the women delegates was Bessy's Sutton Place party on the last Saturday afternoon before the convention. She had prevailed upon her sixteen neighbors to allow her to give it in their common garden. Her guests were the national committeewomen and women prominent in the Democratic party. Be they important party members or the husbands of important party members, there were to be no men. And that was that. It was to be an old girls' club party.

The women entered through Bessy's house, where, assisted by Mrs. Alfred E. Smith and Mrs. John F. Hylan, she received in the little hallway separating the library and living room, both banked with enough spring flowers to pass for conservatories. Uncharacteristically, she wore a smart and slenderizing black silk dress and a ladylike string of pearls. Access to the garden was through the Dutch doors in the dark-paneled dining room set aglow by great bowls of pink peonies and long-stemmed roses. What the guests beheld when they went into the garden was a great lawn stretching down to the river, its smooth length broken by massive tubs of gay flowers scattered like bouquets on a green velvet gown.

Politics were set aside, as Bessy's neighbors vied with each other in offering hospitality and refreshments on their flower-decked terraces, one of which served as a bandstand for the Ritz Carlton orchestra on leave, for that afternoon, from its palm court. The two Annes, both out of the country, had left orders for garden chairs to be set out on their large adjoining terraces. What Bessy offered on that afternoon was a display of New York aristocracy at its democratic best. She succeeded in her dual intention of sending out the word to every part of the country that women Democrats were true gentlemen, and that her beloved city was one hell of a town. Alas, the convention was to undo all of her good work.

On the morning of June 24, dawn brought a sun wreathed in haze, promising the day would be a scorcher. It was the beginning of a heat wave that would hold the city in its thrall through the coming weeks. All the electric fans in the Garden could not prevent the indoor thermometer from trembling at the 100-degree mark, while unimpeded cigars and cigarettes added stench to humidity. Paper fans were distributed bearing the legend

Ladies and Not-So-Gentle Women

"Keeping Cool Without Coolidge." The promise was in vain, as limp bunting seemed to drip down from the balcony rails.

The heat of politics did little to lower the temperature. As they would be for decades to come, the Democrats were torn by what has comparatively recently become a Republican problem: the dispute between the enlightened Ivy League group and the Bible Belt South. The two factions were polarized over proposed planks to condemn the Ku Klux Klan and to repeal prohibition—a conflict epitomized by the two front-runners, William McAdoo and Alfred E. Smith, with the latter strongly for condemnation and repeal, and McAdoo in the opposing camp. Though a son-in-law of Woodrow Wilson and a member of the northern establishment, McAdoo was courting Dixie in the time-encrusted manner of ambitious politicians corrupting themselves, with no outside help, to win votes.

Both men had to make a lot of deals and do a lot of politicking. They may have been the favorites, but it was an open field in which neither was eliciting any great advance enthusiasm. On that opening day, during an era in which candidates were chosen in the back room and on the floors of convention halls, and state primaries had little to do with the eventual nominee, the call was yet to be made, the battle still to be waged. It would be fought before the entire nation. The liberal wing of the party had insisted that the convention be broadcast on radio for the first time in history. It undoubtedly thought the publicity would help to campaign against a spotless incumbent.

When Franklin Roosevelt was stricken with polio two years earlier, Eleanor went to Swope and other members of the liberal press and begged them not to make too much of it, for it could ruin whatever future career her husband might have. Swope complied by burying the story on one of the inside pages of the *World*. Eleanor's efforts helped to initiate a phenomenal form of journalistic noblesse oblige in which very little was ever made of Roosevelt's affliction during his lifetime. Motion picture newsreel cameras did what television was never to do. If his disability did not interfere with the performance of his duty, they turned their lenses from what might be humiliating to a great man. It was an era in which the more honorable newspapers were as interested in what was fit to read as in what was fit to print and did not excuse their own prurience as a public right to know, which was never defined as such in the Constitution.

One result of what Eleanor had instigated occurred when Roosevelt began his political comeback by delivering the nomination speech for Smith. He hobbled on his crutches toward the microphone with the press making little of his infirmity. Few in his audience had more empathy than Bessy. Her own girth and debility had reached the point where she was physically unable to sit for long periods of time in the narrow Garden seats and had been given permission to bring along a sturdy, leather-covered armchair bearing her name-plate. It would precede her to meetings and conventions for the rest of her life.

Roosevelt sailed through the speech, referring to Smith as "the happy warrior." When he finished, the crowd rose to its feet in cheering acclamation. Bessy tore off the corner of a piece of cardboard and scribbled a note in pencil, which was passed up to Roosevelt on the platform:

> That was a great speech of yours delivered with majesty! No one in the vast auditorium appreciated your courage & effacement of self more than I.

For Eleanor, her husband's speech was the one positive note in the entire convention. The men reneged on all of the promises that had been made about sharing the decision making with representatives of the fifty-three national committeewomen, and locked them out of all of the important meetings. She spent the interminable, breath-grabbing days sitting outside doors barred to her, wishing it was over and trying to retain her composure by knitting. The single-mindedness with which she set about her work put the comedian-politician Will Rogers in mind of Mme Defarge. He asked, "Knitting in the names of the future victims of guillotine?"

Eleanor merely smiled but was "ready to call any punishment down on the heads of those who could not bring the convention to a close." It was to last for a blistering two weeks and go through a record-making 103 ballots before the battle-weary convention finally nominated John W. Davis, a nationally obscure Wall Street attorney with a local reputation for integrity. In striking contrast to the written reports of the refined Republicans, the Democrats being broadcast on the radio were a rude, swearing, backbiting lot who could not seem to agree on anything. Dull cool Cal seemed the essence of the civilized gentleman, and it was later conceded that the radio broadcasts of the Democratic convention did more to elect him than any of the issues.

Bessy was among the few who sat through every hour of every session of the contentious convention. Day after day, she resolutely held high the New York State flag. The policemen placed bets that she would never miss a session. Her appearance on the closing day was hailed by cheering cops, many of them of Irish descent, who had never lost faith in their Mother Casey.

On the weekend after the convention closed, Bessy took her car, chauffeur, and Alice Kuswetter, her faithful maid of some twenty years, and started out on an overnight journey for a stay at the Lakeshore Hotel, which was near Lakeside Farm, the place she had bought the previous year. Her acreage was located on one of the Belgrade Lakes, outside the small village of Mount Vernon, in Kennebec County, Maine. From the first time she had visited the area, three years earlier, it had enchanted her. She would never be returning to Europe, she knew that: the time had come to think of a summer home in the United States. If she originally had thought in terms of her happy childhood summers in Oyster Bay, where she still owned some property, the idea was discarded. The north shore of Long Island had become a high society ghetto, closer than Newport and far less stodgy—a locale replete with polo grounds, foxhunts, and restricted country clubs.

A cottage on a lake in Maine—where she could fish, grow a garden, raise a few cows—suited Bessy far better than the ancestral home. A local realtor had found her the ideal place, and the July after the convention was devoted to supervising the alteration and furnishing. When completed, Lakeside Farm was closer to Morgan's Camp Uncas than to Elsie's Villa Trianon. The walls were paneled in natural bark and much of the furnishings constructed of untreated tree branches and upholstered in animal hides—not Elsie's sleek, chic leopards but those of the fauna of the region. Free of Elsie's restrictions, there was at last a place to put one of her family heirlooms, the rudely carved mahogany pineapple bed in which her beloved grandfather McCoun had been born.

Toward the end of her stay, she looked around and, satisfied with all she found, wrote rather smugly to Ida Tarbell: "I really feel ashamed to have been enjoying the cold weather this last fortnight when New York has been so sweltering."

Before returning to the melee of a hopeless presidential campaign, she took a motor tour of New Brunswick and Nova Scotia. Thoughts of Elsie had to have been particularly vivid, as she traveled through the ancestral homeland of the De Wolfes. For the first time in her life, Bessy owned a house that had been purchased and decorated without consulting her. It was not Elsie's style, but Bessy was looking forward to spending what summers remained to her in it.

That year, Elsie did find a place that was her style. It was the most newsworthy job of her career between the wars. As it was for the most important publisher of style-setting magazines in the world, his satisfaction with it would keep her name in print for the rest of her life. Condé Nast had thrown together three apartments on the top floors of 1040 Park Avenue to form a thirty-room duplex penthouse, and he had hired her to decorate it. As work on the apartment progressed, *Vogue*'s shrewd editor, Edna Woolman Chase, observed: "Elsie kept her friends for many years and considered friendship a very beautiful thing, not to be confused with business, so many of the prices she charged her dear Condé were memorable."

Chase also gave the wisest estimate on both the apartment and Elsie's talents. The decorator could justifiably have been accused of being too elaborate or too addicted to the French styles, but "she never sacrificed practicality to beauty. People were at ease in Elsie de Wolfe rooms. The lighting was suitable to function, whatever it might be, from romantic dinner to reading a good book, and the furnishings were always comfortable." In summation: *"She might sometimes be fancy. She was never foolish."*

The *All about Eve* syndrome has played a part in the lives of many glamorous and celebrated women. The real-life Eve Harringtons are seldom as evil, and the Margo Channings almost never as unpremeditated and guileless, as the ones depicted in Joseph L. Mankiewicz's scenario for the famous film. For the Eves, generally masochistic idolaters, it is a chance to live tangentially to a scintillating world they can never hope to enter by virtue of their own rank, gifts, and looks. The change in their destinies is due to the good fortune of being permitted to become an acolyte in the temple. They use every ounce of their energy and ingenuity (generally, considerable) to achieve and retain this position. On the sadistic idol's part, there is always the flicker of sexuality rarely if ever consummated.

The Eve is a part of the household, family, a friend of the idol's friends. But never is she an equal nor does she wish to be. The idol stands alone. Eve does the correspondence, handles the servants, looks after the wardrobe, takes care of the bills, does all of the nasty work with clients, creditors, debtors, associates, and friends. The idol must not be bothered or sullied by such details. The idol must remain adorable. Ultimately, a transmogrification takes place. Eve becomes so indispensable, so in control of every aspect of Margo's life, that she becomes the alter ego, the second self who assumes supremacy in the relationship.

Elsie de Wolfe found her Eve in the person of Hilda West, nee Wessberg. Hilda was a stocky teenager with no life worth calling her own when Edgar de Wolfe hired her as a stenographer for Elsie's New York office. When his sister came to town, the seventeen-year-old was assigned to follow her around, taking down in shorthand everything the decorator shrieked in her high-pitched, undistinguished voice. The only secretary who could keep up with her, Hilda Wessberg was soon whisked off to France to live until Elsie's death, in easy access to her in the little flat over the garage at the Villa Trianon or in modest furnished digs close to her house in rue Leroux. It was Elsie, not a husband, who changed her name to West. Within a short time, she neutered the newly minted Miss West by dubbing her an asexual "Westy," which she was to remain for as long as her mistress lived. Hilda would become sleeker and more chic with the passing years, but nothing would change the tenor of her connection to Elsie.

An Eve often finds release from the intensity of her life with the idol by being mildly deprecating behind her back with sympathetic souls who either have suffered at the hands of the same idol or are in analogous situations with another. The decorator and ex-wife of Somerset Maugham, Syrie, was Elsie's friendly rival. Her Eve was Olive Cruickshank, known as "Crockie." The four women once crossed the Atlantic together. Crockie recalled running into Westy on deck early one morning and being greeted with: "How's *your* old bitch this morning? Mine's in a hell of a temper."

$\mathcal{A}$nne Vanderbilt returned to Sutton Place after a memorably ignoble summer. Initially, it had seemed as if Oom had worked some sort of miracle by restoring the sanity of her daughter, and her largest cross had been lifted. Barbara had returned to Paris and, to her mother's consternation, immediately plunged into an intense relationship with the Scandinavian opera star Povla Frisch. When she did not get her way, she would throw increasingly alarming temper tantrums. It became apparent Barbara was having another nervous breakdown, and Anne unwisely decided that her unfortunate child should return to Nyack in the hope that Oom could once more work his magic.

Once Barbara was back on the premises of his Brae Burn Country Club, Bernard placed her in the care of his associate, Winfield Jesse Nicholls, who was the calisthenics director at the club and occasionally gave lectures on Tantric philosophy. Her rapid improvement seemed evidence that Anne had done the right thing. Except for the odd fit of rage, her daughter appeared to have cast off her illness by early summer. The sense of relief was cut short when Barbara informed her that she was pregnant by Nicholls. Anne belatedly decided it was time to find out about the backgrounds of these men who held both of her daughters in thrall. Her lawyers were instructed to put some private investigators on the case.

The results of the investigation were hardly reassuring. The only way in which Nicholls and her daughter were a match was that both had ungovernable tempers. Nicholls was known to the police of San Francisco, Seattle, and New York by the aliases of Morton L. Hargis and Arnold W. Kellogg. In 1905, the twenty-one-year-old Nicholls teamed up with Pierre Arnold Bernard, in San Francisco, in pursuit of a profitable scam. Bernard's previous employment record included lemon picking, salmon packing, and being a barber, but he did have a smattering of knowledge of Eastern religions and was sufficiently versed in Tantric Hinduism for them to found the

Tantrik Order. They also founded the Bacchante Club, which would appear to have been a sex club. They were ejected from their premises after complaints that members were smoking opium, and that young people were being debauched there.

Nicholls was arrested late that year for fraud and, early in 1906, was implicated but not charged in hearings on a mother's accusation that he had corrupted her adolescent son. Bernard and Nicholls staged their last west coast operation in Seattle, where they got into trouble with the irate husband of one Daisy Mix and decided less provincial New York City would be more sympathetic to the Tantrik Order.

By May 1910, Bernard had established the Hindu Order of Tantrik, on West Seventy-fourth Street. The premises were raided after two young women charged they had been sexually assaulted there. Bernard spent almost four months in prison before Nicholls could persuade the complainants to leave the city, forcing the district attorney to drop the charges.

Complaints of disturbing the peace kept Bernard moving his Tantric temple-cum-school from address to address on the Upper West Side. Along the way, he managed to garner a group of wealthy and socially prominent adherents who, in 1920, backed him in the purchase of the Nyack country club.

*B*arbara Hatch would not countenance any suggestion of a discreet abortion. She loved her volatile gymnast and wanted to bear his child. Marriage was the only alternative, but Winfield Nicholls would not agree to that before Anne Vanderbilt bought a home for the couple—not simply a home, but a grand residence. As a wedding present, she spent $200,000 to buy them Moorings, a palatial estate high above Tappan Zee.

A week after the wedding, the bride and groom visited the Harriman family bank, where she ordered the sale of a good portion of the securities that were part of the trust fund Willie K. had set up for her. Very soon after, for an undisclosed purchase price, Nicholls transferred the deed for Moorings to Bernard, who would use it as his own residence. Barbara bought a more modest house in Scarsdale. Nicholls abandoned her before their twins were born there shortly after the new year.

*O*n November 12, Fanny Morgan was staying at her country home, Cragston, when she went into a coma after what was described as an attack of "indigestion." No more the majestic sails up the Hudson on their father's *Corsair:* those legendary days of the House of Morgan had ended with the old man's death. Anne, her sisters, Juliet and Louisa, and her brother-in-law, Herbert Satterlee, motored up to Highland Falls and were with Fanny when she died. With Anne living on Sutton Place, there was nobody left to reside in the great somber mansion at 219 Madison Avenue, and it would not be long before it gave way to a white limestone, mausoleum-like extension of the library.

Fanny Morgan was buried in Hartford beside her husband, that mismatched couple together for eternity and, it was to be hoped, finally at peace with one another. It was raining that day just as it had rained on the day Pierpont was buried, and as then, the family stood beneath a temporary canvas shelter during the service. Her favorite child, Jack, broke off three roses from the yellow rose blanket and placed them on top of his beloved mother's coffin. He remained at her graveside after his sisters and the other mourners had withdrawn.

For Anne, there was the trip back to what was now her only home, on Sutton Place, where there waited a warming fire on the grate and the solace to be shared with a loving neighbor equally in need of it.

CHAPTER FORTY-NINE

In 1925, exactly a year after her mother's death, Anne Morgan was seated in a box at the Jolson Theatre, attending a benefit for the American Woman's Association. Her fifty-third year held no dread for her. "A handsome woman, tall and erect with a full figure," she was if anything better looking than she had been as a debutante. Energy, dedication, and loyalty made the difference. A reporter noted, "Indecision is hateful to her." It was doubtful if, in her youth, she had possessed "the magnetic charm" that emanated from her on that evening. "Dressed with an elegant simplicity, her gray hair smartly shingled," she wore her "maturity with distinction."

Morgan's name appeared on the letterheads of dozens of do-good organizations, including several sufficiently left-wing to have brought on an epidemic of dyspepsia in the corridors of the House of Morgan. But in the early Twenties, the AWA had increasingly become her major cause, as had been its pre-war predecessor, the Vacation Fund. She had begun to devote a large part of her energies to the construction of a great clubhouse for the American Woman's Association. She wanted to offer women an ambience rather than merely a decent room of their own, a world of women in which they could grow from the exchange of ideas and intimacies with other women.

What it would not offer was a room for a private heterosexual relationship. The upper-class clubs on which it was to be modeled did not offer it either, but those were places that members frequented to get away from the homes to which they could always return for seclusion and sex. This clubhouse would *be* home without the privilege of utter privacy.

An option was taken on a property at 221 West Twenty-third Street, around the corner from the modest Chelsea row house in which Elsie de Wolfe had spent part of her childhood. The goal was to build an eighteen-story residence at a cost of $4,500,000. The figure had ballooned $2,000,000 in one year, because the plan had grown quite grandiose. In addition to airy well-furnished bedrooms with private baths and maid service, the facility would include a dining room, coffee shop, garden terrace, gymnasium, pool, and bowling alleys. Such amenities as post office, laundry, magazine shop, beauty salon, and infirmary were also planned. There would be a large ballroom for card parties, theatricals, informative lectures, and dances, which would be a source of additional income when rented out to private organizations. The plan was to provide workingwomen living alone on modest salaries with a place to live where they could meet and make friends with others in similar situations, for, next to economics, loneliness was one of the largest problems for single women. It was a visionary scheme, larger in scope than that of any other residence for workingwomen in the world.

Anne had become one of the country's leading exponents of the rights of workingwomen via the radio. Her cigarette-induced contralto tones, vague debutante's drawl, and earnestness made her a popular, if often humorless, talk show guest. Radio enabled her to reach the masses and defuse the demagoguery of those conservatives who found the idea of women living together as threatening as the idea of women living alone, or women living with men in any alliance other than marriage. On NBC, she described the women who would be using the clubhouse.

> Almost every line of endeavor in which women are engaged is represented in the roster. There are secretaries, authors, teachers, editors, explorers, shopkeepers, artists, reporters, sculptresses, accountants, buyers, dieticians, actresses, interior decorators, business executives, trained nurses, social workers, doctors—134 different kinds of jobs in all.
>
> These women vary in age and experience, in interests, tastes, religion, and politics quite as much as they do in their occupa-

*L*adies and Not-So-Gentle Women

tions, but are drawn together by a common desire for social companionship.

By the spring of 1926, the AWA had more than five thousand members and was obviously attracting thousands more than would ever use the clubhouse as a residence. Their backgrounds and professions were as varied as Anne had indicated in her talk. They ranged from Lillian Gilbreth, an industrial psychologist and mother of twelve; to Marie Dressler, the homosexual star of stage and films; to Anita Loos, who in her novel *Gentlemen Prefer Blondes* gave the world a heroine a world away from her AWA associates; to Margaret Sanger, the birth control pioneer. These women wanted a club of their own and were dissatisfied with both the socially elitist Colony and the Cosmopolitan, which did have some professional women but almost none who had to earn their own living to support themselves.

Although Elsie de Wolfe and Elisabeth Marbury were celebrating the fortieth anniversary of their intimate friendship, the fundamental differences that had always existed were deepening. Elsie was pursuing a lost generation in an old world, while Bessy delighted in being in the midst of a new generation of women who were finding themselves heard in the politics, industry, arts of a new world. She trumpeted her oneness with them. "I respond to the sparkle of the present day. I revel in youth. I admire it. I want to be surrounded by it."

It was not long after the 1924 convention that Bessy realized Eleanor Roosevelt and the younger women had been right: the men had not played fair with the women at that fiasco. In a reversal of her original position on suffrage, she warned them that women had the vote and wanted all of the power that went along with it. They were in politics to stay, and her "masculine friends" had best give up their "present obtuse attitude." Her own experience at the convention was finally addressed several months after its close. Unflattering as it was to her vanity, she was forced to admit that she had never had the slightest knowledge of proposals and decisions until informed of the results. Possibly the disaster of the convention might have been averted "had the women really been more than window dressers." The feminine bloc "could not but wonder, even in humility, whether our party would not have been spared at least some of those blunders had the women been conferred with actually and not merely theoretically."

This profound change in perspective was enunciated in 1925, when she demanded that women be given a fair share of spoils. It was no longer adequate for men "grudgingly to concede an office . . . like throwing a bone to a dog." Beyond politics, it was not acceptable to ghettoize women within the professions for which they had been trained.

> So long as they are given equal education, they will insist upon equal opportunity. As lawyers, merely to sit in domestic-relations courts will not satisfy. As physicians, to practice hygiene for babies does not lead them far enough.

By the mid-Twenties, Bessy's weight and infirmities largely confined her to her home except for those hours she put in at the American Play Company. She seldom went out in the evenings except for political engagements, and theatregoing was generally restricted to matinees. Seldom could the opening nights of clients or close friends tempt her to submit to the jostling evening crowds. That meant ordering a dinner party for every evening she spent at home: Bessy could not stand eating alone. Unlike Villa Trianon, where the food was becoming increasingly awful with each passing year, Sutton Place was famous for the quality of its fare. A list was kept of the favorite dishes of her guests, and when they came to dinner, they would find that the cook had been instructed to prepare them.

She was approaching seventy, and the discipline with which she ordered her life lent the illusion of endless vitality. Her bedside light was turned out precisely at eleven-thirty. Once a chain-smoker, she now never smoked before lunch and limited herself to no more than six of her specially blended cigarettes each day. Perhaps for that reason the twinkling blue eyes remained as clear as they had been in her youth. There was an ageless quality to a face never touched by cosmetics: the skin smooth across a broad brow and round cheeks polished to a rosy glow by nothing more exotic than fine soap and water. The still naturally brown hair was piled high in the same pompadour she had been wearing since it was the height of fashion in the Gay Nineties, and that also contributed to the sense of timelessness. What brought a visitor back to the contemporary world was the stream of up-to-the-minute, high-spirited, sometimes caustic, often ribald witticisms that emerged from an almost prissily dainty little mouth.

It was well known among theatre people that Bessy spent much of her time at home, and when Robert E. Sherwood wanted her to read his playscript, he left it at her fire-engine red door. His reputation was such that he could be fairly certain she would read it personally rather than pass it on to one of her assistants.

Sherwood was the editor of *Life*, which was then a humor magazine, a respected film critic, and a member of the Round Table, the group of writers and actors who met for lunch at the Algonquin Hotel to polish quips and boost one another's reputations. He was a bean stalk of a man who shared with the other males at the table an eccentricity of appearance that made them prime subjects for caricaturists. The Round Table was crowded with very talented people whose single approach to minor genius was found in one of its few women, Dorothy Parker. Among the things they had in common was a respect for the commercial theatre, the quality of which they were collectively to improve to a significant degree.

It was generally agreed among the Round Tablers that Bessy Marbury was more than one of the most influential agents in town; she was the one with the keenest sense of how a promising script could be turned into a Broadway hit, which was why Sherwood left his play, *The Road to Rome,* at her house instead of at the office. He did not want Rumsey or Madden to read it. Bessy's opinion was the one that counted. In addition to her eye for success, she was credited with having made George Bernard Shaw commercially viable, and Sherwood had written what amounted to an homage to Shaw.

A fledgling writer's agonizing wait for an important agent's opinion was, in this instance, of amazingly short duration. As soon as her dinner guests departed on the night the script arrived, she read it. Her first opinion was favorable. When she awakened at 4 A.M., she read it again, and her admiration increased. At seven-thirty, when her breakfast and the morning mail arrived, she pushed aside the catalogs and advertisements to have another go at *The Road to Rome.* It still made her laugh aloud.

Sherwood must have been surprised to receive her telephone call less than twenty-four hours after having dropped off the script, amazed to be informed that she had read it not once but three times, and over the moon to hear her affirm that he had written one hell of a play. To Bessy's amazement, the play was rejected by the "class" managements, and at length she optioned *The Road to Rome* to Lee Shubert along with another play, *Fernande.* Shubert was to direct the Sherwood play, and Carlotta Monterey was to play the lead in both plays.

Carlotta was a striking beauty but no star. Her closest approach had come a few seasons earlier playing the small but pivotal role of Mildred Douglas in Eugene O'Neill's *The Hairy Ape.* Bessy had signed her to a personal management contract. Bessy's interest in Carlotta Monterey had begun no earlier than the end of February and would last exactly six months. The period was bracketed by what she must have considered two betrayals: one by Carlotta, the other by Elsie.

On March 10, 1926, Elsie was married to Sir Charles Mendl. It was a step the cautious Elsie probably had been considering for a long time. As she delicately put it: "When one has passed the portals of middle life, one's greatest necessity is companionship."

Elsie had to have informed Bessy when Mendl and she became engaged. It would have been inconceivably callous of her not to have confided her plans to the person who loved her most in the world, to have left it for her to read in the newspapers. Why, Elsie had even made a special trip out to the Villa Trianon to tell the housekeeper who had been with them since Bessy first bought the place. That woman's response was echoed by most of the couple's friends: *"C'est une blague!"*

Elsie took that to mean "It's a joke!" It could be more succinctly translated, "It's rubbish!"

She never pretended to love him. "Charles and I had a deep affection for each other, and mutual respect and admiration." They were married in the British embassy in Paris. Her birth year was given as 1870, and his as 1872. She later admitted to having shaved ten years off her age so as not to make him look ridiculous to his colleagues. Their witnesses were Myron Herrick, once more American ambassador to France; the British ambassador; and Anne Vanderbilt. The Cole Porters were also part of the small party that repaired to a restaurant in the Bois de Boulogne for the wedding breakfast.

They went to Egypt for their honeymoon. It held "little charm" for Elsie beyond the pomp of welcomes at the official British residences that stood sentinel up the Nile from Alexandria to Khartoum. Her attitude toward Egyptian antiquities was the same as it was toward French antiques. Authenticity was welcome: appearance was indispensable. She put it very nicely: "I am in love with life and with living. The past means nothing to me except as experience." Her summation of the entire Egyptian episode was, "I felt that if I ever saw another camel—in a cinema or out of it—I would scream."

Years later, she was reportedly somewhat better disposed toward the Greek antiquities. On first viewing the Parthenon, she was said to have clapped her hands and exclaimed: "Beige—my color!"

Once back in Paris, the Mendls returned to their separate residences. Sir Charles was once more to be found in his comfortable apartment in the avenue Montaigne, where the luncheon parties continued to be of value to British intelligence, and she was once more established in her little house in rue Leroux, with Hilda West, much more indispensable than Sir Charles, close at hand.

If the weather permitted, and they had no engagements in the city, they both went out to Versailles for the weekends, where his knowledge and selection of the wines did much to compensate for Elsie's ghastly cuisine. Johnnie McMullin continued to be part of any arrangements they made.

That inveterate Elsie watcher Edna Woolman Chase described the relationship:

> Charles, Elsie, and Johnnie made a *ménage à trois* that was, by the very nature of things, highly moral. It was the kind of triangle in which Charles, one may imagine, found relief, as Johnnie made a perfect companion, major-domo, and escort for Elsie, leaving her husband free to follow the diplomatic career which best pleased him.

The Mendls were in New York later that spring. They did not stay with Bessy, but Sir Charles met with her privately to give her assurances that, for whatever reason, he had no sexual interest in his wife. He had never been to bed with her in the past nor was he likely to in the future. Theirs was a marriage of convenience. Elsie also came to work her wiles. A peace of sorts was made. Bessy could no more stop loving Elsie than she could stop breathing. The girl could have done a lot worse than Sir Charles. Bessy recognized in him a kindred spirit, a canny one—like herself—shrewdly playing the clown when the script called for it.

$\mathscr{C}$oncealing Carlotta Monterey's inflexible resolve were looks, brains, style, and what passed for breeding. She joined the special group Bessy managed apart from the American Play Company clients. What they had in common was that all were dark-haired, rather exotic-looking, beautiful young women with boyishly slim bodies and, alas, no greater talent in most cases than what met the eye. In addition to Carlotta, the list included Jane Cowl (the exception—truly gifted), Mercedes de Acosta, and Michael Strange (the socially prominent Blanche Oelrichs, who had been married to John Barrymore). The more salacious might think of them as Bessy's harem, but her role was wise and loving parent rather than lascivious pasha.

By securing leading roles for her with Lee Shubert, Bessy indicated that she was sufficiently enamored of Carlotta to take the same gamble on a negligible talent she had taken years earlier on Elsie with Charles Frohman. She invited the actress to spend August with her at Lakeside Farm. Carlotta brought along a daring bathing suit, missing the overskirt that American women modestly wore in those days, consisting only of a white tank top and dark boxer shorts. As she could not swim and professed a terror of the water, the costume could only have been for Bessy's edification. Elsie also had sought to charm Bessy with her wardrobe.

When Carlotta arrived in Maine, Bessy's neighbor, the Broadway star

Florence Reed, recalled that she "took over, and Bess was happy to have her do it. Carlotta ran the servants, ordered the food, supervised the cooking— she took care of everything and did it superbly." Bessy was a superlative household manager. Elsie was the only other person she had ever allowed to run her home. The parallels would have persisted were it not for something that happened that summer none of those involved could have predicted.

Among the uninvolved witnesses, in addition to Reed and her husband, were Bessy's other guests that August, Mercedes de Acosta and a new client sent to her by Golding Bright, John Van Druten, whose first play, *Young Woodley,* had been a big hit and who was to become one of the most successful playwrights of the Forties and Fifties with an impressive list of hits: *The Voice of the Turtle, I Remember Mama, Bell, Book and Candle,* and *I Am a Camera.* Like Ivor Novello and Noel Coward before him and Cecil Beaton after him, Van Druten was one of a succession of young Englishmen for whom the warmth of Bessy's hospitality made New York a far more engaging city.

*D*uring the previous spring, Madden had mentioned to Bessy that Eugene O'Neill was looking for a summer place for his family. It had to have sufficient diversions for his wife and children and be remote enough for him to work without disruption on *Strange Interlude.* She immediately suggested the Belgrade Lakes area and she may even have found Loon Lodge for them, a secluded two-story log cabin surrounded by towering pine trees. Relations between the O'Neills and her were very warm during that summer. When the writer found the noise of a house filled with children too intrusive, Agnes O'Neill brought the problem to Bessy. Her solution was that they put up a primitive studio—no more than four walls and a roof—in which he could work out of earshot of the household. It was the sort of thing a Yankee carpenter could frame out and build in less time than it took to complain.

The summer home of Florence Reed and her husband, Malcolm Williams, was quite close to Loon Lodge, and whenever O'Neill felt the need for some friendly adult company, he would come over, although he never contributed much in the way of conversation. His hostess found him "absolutely the most withdrawn person I've ever known." Mercedes de Acosta agreed after observing him on the fateful afternoon when he first became attracted to Carlotta Monterey. "She was the kind of woman who would make most men shy, and Gene was no exception. He behaved like a nervous schoolboy when she even looked at him."

That afternoon, Agnes and Eugene O'Neill had come over to Bessy's

*L*adies and Not-So-Gentle Women

house for tea. Carlotta later claimed she had not wanted to be there because of unpleasant memories of his behavior during the production of *The Hairy Ape*. When Bessy asked her to stay, as a guest she had no alternative. Agnes would remember Carlotta as being not too bright; Carlotta remembered Agnes as gauchely Bohemian.

O'Neill suddenly decided he had to go swimming, and Bessy dispatched Carlotta to show him the way down to the bathhouse. When they arrived at the lake, he went in to change and emerged looking perfectly ridiculous in one of Bessy's mammoth bathing suits. Carlotta's animosity melted. He suggested she come out on the lake with him. She went in and donned the boyish suit, knowing how well it displayed her figure. "He dived in and swam," she recalled toward the end of her life. "He swam magnificently—and the suit kept billowing up. It was *most* indecent."

The group at Bessy's house was sitting on the porch as their canoe drifted by, the sun red and sinking behind them. They, and the world around them, made a stunning picture. Mercedes glanced at the woman seated near her who, for want of anything else to do with her hands, had begun to do some needlepoint. "Agnes followed them with her eyes and I felt embarrassed and depressed."

Carlotta changed direction in midsummer. Whatever the motivation for her courtship of Bessy—filial, sexual, professional—all that icy intensity, that so resembled a flame, was turned away from her and toward O'Neill. The attraction was more than sex or fame. He incarnated her sense of her own destiny. Edna Woolman Chase's actress daughter, Ilka, had appeared in a play with Carlotta and observed her with the man to whom she was then married. "Carlotta wanted to possess her men and be everything to them. . . . She had a sense of mission and wanted to help him achieve himself." Charlie Chaplin, later O'Neill's son-in-law, thought she wanted "to be all sufficient to a man of genius, to cut him off from everybody and to minister to his genius, while she herself shone in reflected glory." Superficially worldly, Carlotta was the most old-fashioned of women. She wanted to find her identity in her sexual partner, while Agnes spent much of her married life fighting O'Neill's devouring presence to try to preserve an identity of her own.

Florence Reed was much more basic. O'Neill responded so positively to Carlotta because, like so many artists, he needed order around him, and "she was miraculously immaculate and a wonderful housekeeper. There was nobody like her. Agnes' house, on the other hand, always seemed to smell of diapers and lamb stew."

How Bessy reacted is a matter of conjecture. Carlotta left Maine by the end of August, but that could have been the plan before O'Neill came on the scene. Bessy stayed on at Lakeside Farm and dictated the August 30 letter to Shubert from there in which she said Carlotta had decided not to return to the stage. It was unlikely she would have given up all of her ambitions to pursue O'Neill, especially since he had given no indication of being ready to leave his wife. It was more likely that Bessy sent her packing either because she felt her behavior a personal betrayal or because she disapproved of it on moral grounds. Her avowals of both Catholicism and the sanctity of marriage had to have been more than cant.

It would take almost two years for Carlotta to get a firm commitment from O'Neill. It was fortunate that one of her lovers had set up a trust that would pay her fourteen thousand dollars a year for the rest of her life. She did not work during that period nor did she ever work again. Bessy might have had a hand in ending her career, but it would seem implausible since O'Neill continued to trust her. During the difficult negotiations for his divorce, he wrote to his lawyer, Harry Weinberger, about a leak to Swope's influential newspaper: "Never tell Madden anything! Remember that! He's a good guy in his way but a regular old maid for gossip. That's where the World man got his info, you'll find out. Marbury is no fool. They couldn't pump her."

$\mathcal{B}$essy was back from Maine in time to attend the New York State Democratic Convention and again be charmed by the grace and courage of Franklin Roosevelt, who delivered the keynote address. In her own speech, she made a plea for higher wages for state officials. "Today," she said, "they are beneath contempt. A governor receives a salary and is allowed a cook. But the only way he can make any money is to do the cooking himself."

She remained undisputed queen of the quotable quip and, at a dinner for the women's committee, described herself as "a hyphen between the State and National Committees functioning every four years."

That November, when Al Smith was reelected governor of New York by a margin of 257,000 votes, Bessy began looking forward to 1928. It seemed inevitable to many people that he would win the 1928 Democratic nomination for the presidency despite his Catholicism. His advisers deemed it essential to place distance between their candidate and the Tammany Hall political machine. The first step was to appoint Robert Moses as his secretary of state. When word went out that he was considering appointing Herbert H. Lehman to the chairmanship of the Democratic State Committee, Tammany's wrath swelled: it was a post, they felt, that belonged to one of their own. Although a member, Lehman was a Jew, a banker, and a liberal often at odds with the leadership, and Tammany did not trust him to play the game their way.

Lehman did not know what to do. He was reluctant to take the job but anxious to please Smith. His ambivalence continued until one evening, after a concert at Carnegie Hall, he found himself side by side with Bessy. Lehman was a short man, and, such was his esteem of her, he inaccurately remembered her as a head taller than he and looking down as she spoke decisively: "Young man, I understand you're thinking of taking the chairmanship of the State Committee. Let me give you a piece of advice. Don't take it. All you're going to get out of it is a kick in the pants."

That decided him. He rejected Smith's offer, which left him free to maneuver for a more formidable position on the National Committee. It also freed him of any obligation to Smith, allowing him to support Roosevelt in 1932. This ultimately led to his becoming the only Jewish governor in the history of New York State. His gratitude and warm regard for Bessy lasted for the rest of his life. It was misplaced.

Bessy's true role in the incident reflects badly on her. A pernicious letter to the upstate political boss, Norman E. Mack, went beyond the bounds of the accustomed anti-Semitism of her class. There is little justification for dismissing it as an example of her zealous advocacy of Smith. It is a display of bigotry akin to the sort she was condemning in those who would deny a Catholic the nomination. It confirms the suspicion of Eleanor Roosevelt and the more militantly feminists in the party that Bessy too often dishonored herself and her sex by being a minion of Tammany Hall.

> Confidentially, I have been meaning to write to you as I hear that it is practically decided that Governor Smith is to appoint Mr. Lehman as chairman of the State Committee. I am not alone in thinking that this would be a grievous mistake. Jews are not any more popular upstate than are the Catholics. There is an idea here that the Governor is being closed in by the Semitic race due to certain influences.
>
> A great deal of criticism is going around here in high quarters which will not help him in the presidential campaign. Surely there is someone of wealth and position for this state position who is not a Jew! It seems to me that it will be a grave error if Mr. Lehman is selected.

As Carlotta was passing out of Bessy's life, another important woman was entering it and would play a significant role until her death. Mrs. Thomas Lewis, nee Florence Nightingale Graham, world-famous as Elizabeth Arden, was in her early forties and looked years younger. She was a walking advertisement for her own product—a pretty woman with porcelain complexion, honey blond hair, even Anglo-Saxon features rendered interesting by rather too prominent, heavy-lidded blue eyes, and the sturdy, spatulate hands of the nurse and masseuse she once was. Bessy was not remotely interested in the salons, beauty treatment products, and cosmetics on which she had made a fortune. What did intrigue her was that Arden and her leading competitor, Helena Rubinstein, had invented a business that, within a decade of its inception, was grossing over two billion dollars annually, and Arden was earning the lion's share of it. These women were fundamentally industrialists, and every bit as astute as a Henry Ford. When they started, there were no industries that would accept women. They had to create one.

Bessy was soon delighted with Arden. Like Elsie, she was a woman who masked a fine, tough mind in frippery comparable to a feminine lisp. It was the only quality they shared. Arden lacked Elsie's wit and innate taste, just as Elsie lacked, to a large degree, Arden's combination of ruthlessness and provincialism. The cosmetician was a fascinating, complex woman.

During the second half of the Twenties, it was as if Arden could not bear to be away from her dearest new friend. Bessy invited Tom Lewis and her up to Lakeside Farm. The serene beauty of the spot enchanted her. She had never owned or even rented a country home, a retreat from the cares of her business and the mounting social obligations of the world to which Bessy had introduced her. How wonderful it would be to have a place on the lake that was all her own! Whether or not she received a commission, Bessy was ever the agent. There was a 750-acre property available—one of the loveliest sites on the lake—and it adjoined Lakeside Farm.

The Arden house was named Maine Chance. In gratitude and homage to Bessy, henceforth the doors to the Arden salons all over the world were painted the same red as her front door at 13 Sutton Place. Indeed, the red door would become the logo for Arden's empire.

*N*ow that she had her trifling title, Elsie was putting her imprimatur on everything at Villa Trianon. There was to be no mistaking this was the demesne of Lady Mendl despite the fact that Anne Morgan still owned half of the property. Nearly every sofa was festooned by her needlepoint pillows with arch adages: "Today is the tomorrow you worried about yesterday." "There are no pockets in a shroud." "A fool and his money are soon invited everywhere." "Never complain, never explain." Whether she lifted the last saw from Noel Coward or he from her was never clear. Both claimed it for their own and had it stitched or stamped in every conceivable place and possibly a few that were inconceivable.

As was the custom in great houses, the latest best-sellers, or books thought to be of special interest to an overnight guest, were left on his or her nightstand. Elsie's gray bookplate began to appear in them.

> I know all my friends
> Are bad accountants
> But they are
> Very good book keepers.

Villa Trianon   Elsie Mendl

Versailles

*T*he time had come for Anne Morgan to move on. The desire to leave Versailles had been growing since the beginning of her relationship with Anne Vanderbilt. The latter might have represented the Sutton Place contingent as a witness at Elsie's wedding, but she could not abide the bright young things, like Tom Mosley, who were beginning to traipse through the Villa mistaking repartee for communication.

Mosley was among those who insisted that Elsie was twelve years older than her new husband. He described Charles as "a most manly man," Elsie as "distinguished by immense vitality rather than intellectual content," and their union as "a marriage of scent and old brandy." The action around her never ceased to tantalize him. Elsie was a hostess who combined "the hard cutting qualities of a good diamond with the most voluptuous settings it was possible to encounter." It was a "delicate scene of beautiful young women and young men almost as exquisite."

The Sutton Place Annes were much more comfortable weekending with Anne Dike at Blérancourt, where they found the company less smart but more sincere. Morgan was finding the visits to Versailles more of a chore than a pleasure. She wanted to sell out to Elsie and use the money on the clubhouse. The dickering over the price became so acrimonious that it took another world war before Anne Morgan could contemplate being civil to Elsie again. She had not liked Elsie at the beginning of their relationship and liked her less at its end.

CHAPTER FIFTY 🙠

By the end of 1926, the AWA had changed the proposed location of its new clubhouse from Twenty-third Street to a parcel on West Fifty-seventh Street, running through to West Fifty-eighth, between Eighth and Ninth avenues. At first glance, it might have seemed mad to think of housing young women in a neighborhood that lay in the shadow of the Ninth Avenue elevated line and at the northern reaches of notorious Hell's Kitchen. Actually, it made a great deal of sense. Anne Morgan had gotten a wonderful buy on a considerable piece of property in an area that had much more to offer than was immediately apparent. The transportation to the commercial districts was excellent, with a crosstown bus at its door, the Ninth Avenue El at one corner, and Mayor Walker's promised Eighth Avenue subway under construction and scheduled to open at the other corner.

Fifty-seventh Street was becoming a vibrant east–west axis, already dubbed the rue de la Paix of New York. The elegant Jay Thorpe store occupied the site of the old Harriman mansion. Both Bessy Marbury and Anne Vanderbilt had become a part of the AWA project. Vanderbilt's old home served as a midway marker, as she traveled between the extremes of her rewarding life with Anne Morgan on Sutton Place and the site of the new clubhouse.

Although most of the clubhouse block was still occupied by seedy brownstones and apartment dwellings little better than tenements, there were already plans to change it. Across Fifty-seventh Street was the site under consideration for the new home of the Metropolitan Opera. When that project later fell through, the upscale Parc Vendôme apartment complex was built in its place.

The architect Benjamin Wistar Morris had been commissioned to design a new wing for the Morgan Library to replace the mansion in which Anne Morgan had lived for so long. Perhaps because of the connection, she engaged him to do the new clubhouse.

By the late Twenties, Anne Morgan ranked among the best-known women in the United States. The March 1927 issue of *Century* magazine carried an article called "A Woman in the White House." The author, Ida Clyde Clarke, was described by *The New York Times* as "a pioneer in the woman suffrage movement." She advanced the idea that the time had come to investigate the possibility of a woman president.

To the majority of people the idea of a woman in the White House still is unthinkable and yet, since women have successfully aspired to honors as high in the political field as the United States senate, and since, politically speaking, they are not in a state of arrested development, it is not unreasonable to assume that a woman political candidate is at least within the range of possibility.

However, the range of women capable of the job was narrow. Clarke could only think of three: Alice Roosevelt Longworth, Ruth Hanna McCormick, and Anne Morgan. Each of them had "undoubtedly inherited certain rare gifts and striking traits" in addition to "wealth, talent, family name, and position." She added that each had "inherited specific talents from a celebrated father." Although she had reservations, it was apparent from the analogies that Clarke drew that of the women she mentioned, she thought Morgan was the most promising presidential material.

The honors for Morgan were seemingly unending that year. A *New York Times* piece on its editorial page began by comparing her to Helen of Troy and concluded by placing her among the Greek goddesses. She could not escape identity as Pierpont's daughter, but this time the editorialist suggested it was an obstacle she had overcome.

In October 1927, Margaret Leech did a *New Yorker* profile of Anne Morgan, "Lady into Dynamo," in which credit was publicly given to Elisabeth Marbury for turning her from an idle, restless heiress into the dynamo she became. Leech wrote: "Through her friendship with the older woman, she entered for the first time a society in which individualism, self-expression and personal achievement were emphasized."

The interview stimulated the writer's interest in Bessy, and she approached her editor, Harold Ross, with the idea of doing a profile of Marbury. Ross's wife, Jane Grant, a writer and ardent feminist, had been associated with the magazine since its inception two years earlier. Ross tended to treat the publication like a liberal old boys' club but Grant, who was among the first women to refuse to take her husband's name, was a mitigating influence for feminism and probably responsible for the *New Yorker*'s publication of Leech's profile of Elisabeth Marbury, "Seventy Years Young," only two months after the Morgan piece appeared.

In it, the writer observed that although Bessy had great *joie de vivre*, she also had a quality that was "as old as Eve."

> If she wears her decades like a decoration, she has yet withdrawn from them some power that makes her seem a formidable adver-

sary. To attempt to outwit "Bessie" Marbury would be a sporting proposition—something, when one comes to think of it, like her own favorite feat of taking a three-point bass with an eight-ounce trout rod.

Bessy had gone beyond venerable to become a legend and took as much pleasure in it as she did advantage of it. Those early morning hours between four and six were filled by writing regularly for the two monthly Democratic party publications, *The Jeffersonian* and *The Women's Democratic News,* which was edited by Eleanor Roosevelt and where her column appeared under the heading "As Miss Marbury Views It." After her death, it was taken over by Eleanor and retitled "Passing Thoughts." It would later be syndicated by Scripps-Howard as "My Day."

Bessy also began to do regular features for the popular women's magazine, *Delineator,* which paid handsomely for her work—more than could be said for the two political rags. It was in these pieces that Bessy showed her age with homilies that had little relevance for the young, sexually liberated workingwomen of the Twenties. In contrast to Anne Morgan's crusade to better the employment and living conditions of these New Women, Bessy too often sounded as if she was the spokeswoman for the Tammany pols who would have preferred to keep them in their old place than to have to deal with them as voters and a new political force.

To the more progressive women in the party, Bessy was a trial and something of a dinosaur. To those with a more cynical grasp of the practicalities of politics, those willing to compromise with the party as the lesser of two evils, Bessy was a public relations genius totally focused on the virtues of party and candidate, unfailing in the ability to garner national press for her point of view.

The *Delineator* pieces were published under the collective title of *Sayings of a Wise Woman,* with the obvious hope that they would later be collected and released in book form, as had been the case with *The House in Good Taste.* That was to prove impossible. The opinions expressed too often did not relate to modern women. They were arch and condescending, sometimes platitudinous in a style not dissimilar to the one she had used in *Manners,* written forty years earlier. "If the hometown isn't big enough," she wrote, "the world will ultimately be found too small." She added: "We make opportunities, opportunities do not make us."

*S*hortly after construction began on the AWA clubhouse, a conflict began that reflected badly on all involved. Gertrude Robinson Smith had been Anne Morgan's friend and associate since the beginning of the Vacation Fund. On a personal level, she was part of the inner circle that included Vanderbilt and Marbury, and had taken a flat at 1 Sutton Place, immediately after the completion of that first luxury apartment building to be erected on the street they had made fashionable.

As usual, Morgan took over the office of treasurer and allowed somebody else to function as president—in this case, Robinson Smith, who had run it more or less as her own fiefdom during the years when Morgan was occupied with the war and later with almost single-handedly raising the funds to build the clubhouse. In the latter capacity, she had delegated the job of overseeing the sale of stock to Anne Vanderbilt and what was called her "Vanderbilt committee." That was where the problem began. Robinson Smith resented the intimacy of the two Annes. So long as it solely had been Morgan and she, she could accept the terms of the relationship as Robinson Smith herself defined it when she said, "Miss Morgan has, at times, and very properly, enjoyed a power and influence more important that of your President."

There was something to be said for the points of view of both factions. Gertrude Robinson Smith may have lacked a breadth of vision, but she had great compassion for the simple working girl. She wanted anybody who had a job to be able to live at the clubhouse. "Membership in the new clubhouse will be based on one qualification—that the applicant be self-supporting." That had been the purpose of the original Vacation Fund clubhouse. It was assuredly the most magnanimous principle short of turning the place into a shelter for indigent women.

The new clubhouse would be the largest residence for women in the world, but space would still be limited. Times had changed since the founding of the original club, and in the opinion of the professional women and feminists involved with it, the purpose of the new clubhouse could not be merely that of a first-come, first-serve hotel—a residence for decent workingwomen with no consideration given to their aspirations or what they did. It was impossible to ignore the cataclysmic transformation in public perception of them that women themselves had wrought during the previous decade by refusing to accept the limits of convention on their aspirations and accomplishments.

Anne Morgan liked to boast there were more than two hundred occupations represented among the five thousand members of the AWA. She wanted it to be a club to serve their needs and not simply a place in which to warehouse women. It was designed for women wanting to make social and professional contacts, in a later parlance, "to network"—to explore their potentials and brighten their futures.

She defined the new point of view in an article she wrote for the AWA magazine, the *Keynote,* which was entitled "A Democracy of Quality":

We want women to come into this association for what they are going to get out of it, if that is to mean growth. And for that reason, we need those who are the leaders of today in their occupations and the potential leaders of tomorrow.

Ad hoc committees were set up by professional women to formulate future plans and policies that could be set before the board of directors. In the same fashion that indolent wives, mothers, and widows had taken over the old Colony Club, turning it into something restrictively social and other than its original purpose, feminists and professionals were directing the AWA into channels other than that of a self-supporting philanthropy. The new group surrounding the two Annes was exemplified by Virginia Kirkus, who had actually circulated the letter outlining the new intent that forced Robinson Smith to resign. Kirkus headed the children's book department at Harper & Brothers and would found *The Kirkus Report,* one of the most influential insider reports for booksellers in the country.

*W*here Anne Morgan was concerned, neither age nor stated uninterest stopped marital hope from springing eternal in the minds of titled Europeans with an eye on the fabled Morgan fortune. The Prince of Monaco arrived in New York, in January, as the guest of Bernard Baruch. The two men were going down to Baruch's plantation in North Carolina to do some duck shooting. Talk immediately began to circulate that this was only a blind—and not a duck blind. The real purpose of his visit was to bag that rare bird Anne Morgan. She was in the midst of her problems with Robinson Smith and would not take the time to respond. Her secretary, Daisy Rogers, was instructed to make the customary denial for her.

*A*t the annual meeting of the AWA, at the end of February, Anne Morgan was upheld by the membership that elected her president of the organization, a position she would hold for the next fifteen years. On May 5, a crowd of over five hundred witnessed her laying of the clubhouse cornerstone.

Anne Dike's French project continued to have its hold on Anne Morgan. The two women had shared too much at Blérancourt for the place not to have a special meaning for her. She remained secretary of Dike's Les Amis de Blérancourt and, after the ceremony at the clubhouse, went directly to a meeting to raise money to convert the château into a museum of Franco-

American friendship. Elizabeth Lovett was among those present. The wife of Dr. Robert W. Lovett, a prominent Boston orthopedic surgeon and author of several highly regarded books on his specialty, Bessie Lovett was to become one of Anne's best friends and one of the few married women to whom she was very close.

*L*ong periods of peace and happiness were not to be Anne Vanderbilt's lot. Just as she was experiencing a rare serenity in her loving relationship with Anne Morgan, the disorders in the lives of her daughters again intruded. The beautiful Margaret was as flighty as her sister, Barbara, was certifiably manic-depressive. That year, both of them left the husbands they had met in the Oom cult.

In 1927, already in her mid-thirties, Margaret made her debut as a dancer in the ballet *Her Majesty's Escapade* at the Gallo Theatre, which over a half-century later would gain fleeting fame as Studio 54. The stage was striking other members of the Harriman family at the same time. Alice Laidly Harriman, the daughter-in-law of Anne's brother Ollie, announced she intended to star in films. Worse, his son, Borden, became an actor and was appearing in London. That young man was about to become a part of the smart young gay set dominated by Stephen Tennant, Cecil Beaton, and Oliver Messel. He would be exiled by his family and live on in England as a remittance man, ultimately committing suicide.

Fortunately, Margaret's career ended on a happier note. She never danced professionally again but, shortly after divorcing Dukes, she married Prince Charles Murat, a descendent of Napoleon's sister and his favorite general, who had been ennobled upon marrying into the Bonaparte family. Before the wedding, Margaret issued a three-page family tree tracing her lineage back to 1140, in Scotland, and illustrating her kinship to Lord Stirling, Peter Stuyvesant, John Winthrop, Lewis Morris, and the Duchess of Gordon. It indicated that Murat was an upstart, when compared to her, and not to be considered another title purchased by the Vanderbilt connection.

The story of what happened to Barbara Rutherfurd that year was a far sadder one. After Winfield Nicholls abandoned her, so little attention was paid by her to her twins that, three years later, when Nicholls tried to institute an annulment, nobody questioned by the press knew their names, or if they had been christened (they had been; their names were Guy and Margaret). The children were living in Barbara's Scarsdale home in the care of nannies and servants while she was in France. The apparent indifference of their wealthy grandmother reflected badly on her. Unrevealed at the time was that only months after their birth, Barbara had suffered another breakdown and fled to her mother's house in hysterics. Although it might have been a mistake, Anne decided that it would be best for all concerned to say nothing about this latest seizure. Two things were uppermost in her mind, that everything seem normal at the Scarsdale house, and that her daughter be sent to a place where she could not again come under the influence of Oom and his followers. Barbara was returned to the Paris sanitarium, and her house was kept running as if nothing was wrong.

When later criticized, Anne Vanderbilt did not deign to explain that, should she have been needed, she was never more than a short distance away, either in Sutton Place or in nearby Mount Kisco, where Anne Morgan and she shared a weekend place. Moreover, Vanderbilt already had Barbara's older son, Rusty (Rutherfurd) Hatch, living with her. Caring for two additional infants was a bit much to ask of a sixty-five-year-old woman with a heart condition and already wearied by yet another tragedy in the life of one of her children.

Nicholls tried to serve annulment papers on his wife only to find she was in France. He then attempted to serve an affidavit on his mother-in-law, but she refused to see him. His grounds were that he had not been informed of his wife's history of mental illness or of her physical condition at the time he married her and was fraudulently led to believe she was then (and always had been) well in mind and body.

That was untrue. It would have been no problem to establish that Oom and his associate, Nicholls, were aware of Barbara's condition from the moment she arrived at the Nyack compound. Rather than risk a lengthy court case in which he might come away with nothing, Nicholls thought it wiser to go to France and attempt a reconciliation that would give him some control over his wife's income should she be having another breakdown. Barbara was well enough to see him and she refused either to take him back or to acquiesce to an annulment. The press was informed that she would soon be returning to be with her children, at which time she would decide what her next step would be.

Nicholls came back to the States determined to petition the New York Supreme Court for an annulment. He alleged that at the time they married, Barbara was "a lunatic, and was or had been in other respects abnormal mentally and physically." The case was set aside, and the situation dragged on without resolution for another year, when Barbara finally decided she did want a divorce. Her mother paid Nicholls $100,000 plus expenses to go to Reno for a Nevada divorce. His wife was to have the right to resume her maiden name and have full custody of the twins.

$\mathcal{I}$n the late 1920s, Rumsey, Bessy, and Madden had agreed to take a brash young man, Leland Hayward, into the American Play Company. A Nebraskan, still in his twenties and not that long out of Princeton, he had reinvented himself and was Bessy's type to a tee—smooth, intelligent, beautifully dressed, handsome, self-possessed, with enough of the look of a gentleman and heart of a gambler to move easily in any circle. She suggested Hollywood might be the right setting for the young man. He subsequently took her advice and went west to become one of the most successful actors' agents in the world. When he did return to New York, it was as producer of some of the biggest Broadway hits of the post–World War II period.

Hayward was the wave of the future. As such, he had been both fascinating and frightening to Bessy's partners, who were middle-aged and beyond. But she wanted to plug into all that youthful energy and was inspired to take another shot at theatrical production.

In her physical condition, it was a mistake to think she could produce a play, continue as an agent, and work actively for Al Smith's campaign while also serving as a Democratic national commiteewoman and delegate-at-large to the next national convention. Nevertheless, with the idea of turning it into a musical, she took an option on *Love in a Mist,* a light comedy that had been a moderate success the previous season. Bessy was right in thinking that the public was tired of glitzy, big productions, and the time was again right for the intimate musical just as it had been when she conceived the Princess shows. In the words of Gerald Bordman, the distinguished theatrical historian: "All that Miss Marbury misjudged was the quality of her offering."

It was also a question of time and energy: overcommitted and old, she did not have enough of either and was vastly overextended. On June 16, while her show, retitled *Say When,* was floundering during its out-of-town tryout, Bessy boarded the S.S. *Algonquin* in New York to sail to Houston, when the Democratic convention was being held. It would have been faster to take the train, but Bessy was no longer comfortable traveling on trains and, after the exertion of the previous months, could use the rest before facing the rowdy rigors of the convention.

There was no sign of fatigue or slowing of wit in the interview she gave the reporters who came on board to see her. Referring to the speed with which the moderate Republicans had pushed through the nomination of Herbert Hoover, she said she was sailing to make sure there would be no "steamroller" tactic in Houston, as there had been at the Republican convention in Kansas City. "Every candidate . . . will have a chance. The more Governor Smith's claims are investigated, the stronger he will become." She did not believe that prohibition would be a serious issue. "Eight years of trial have proven it does not work."

Although Eleanor Roosevelt had worked tirelessly, along with Belle Moskowitz and Bessy, to get Al Smith nominated, she decided not to go to Houston. The horrible experience of the New York convention, four years earlier, had been as much of that particular form of mania as she wanted. She missed one of her husband's finest hours.

Herself hobbled by braces and canes, Bessy watched Roosevelt heroically put aside his crutches. He leaned on his son Elliott's arm and, with only a cane for support, made his way across the platform to deliver the nominating speech for Alfred E. Smith. It surpassed his "happy warrior" speech at the last convention. Smith was nominated on the first ballot. Bessy had no doubt that should he feel up to the rigors of a campaign, Roosevelt would be his party's candidate in the New York gubernatorial race.

The convention had been so short that Bessy was back in New York by June 25, the night of the disastrous Broadway opening of *Say When*. The show eked out fifteen performances before expiring unlamented by anybody not connected to the production. It was the last production Bessy would ever produce, but she had enough to occupy her that autumn not to have too many regrets.

When Roosevelt did accept the nomination, Bessy worked as wholeheartedly for him as she did for Smith but was finding it difficult to keep up with the demands she was making upon herself. She watched Eleanor and Franklin, admiring both equally. They were the future. Eleanor had such integrity. Despite the fact that Franklin was running for office, Eleanor did not renege on her earlier commitment to Smith and devoted most of her efforts to campaigning for him.

During the grueling campaign, out of the pain of her own exertions, Bessy sent a telegram to Franklin: "No one realizes more than I the great personal sacrifice you have made you will surely be elected Congratulations to the state and may God bless you and care for you."

He replied with a personal note, telling her it was "a mighty nice wire." He added: "Hoping you are much better after the horrid summer that you must have had, and I hope, too, I shall see you very soon."

CHAPTER FIFTY-ONE ॐ

Toward the end of 1928, the construction of the clubhouse was nearing completion. The plans now called for a twenty-seven-story-residence with a basement gym and swimming pool, an arcade of shops, a theatre, a restaurant as well as a cafeteria, a library, a writing room, several lounges, and 1,250 bedrooms, making it the fifth largest hotel in the city. Each bedroom was to have a private bath, ample closet space, and windows looking out on either the street or the hotel patio, which would offer a harmonious vista of fountains, walks paved with multicolored pebbles, huge pots of flowers changed seasonally, and bright-striped awning shading the terrace restaurant. With rates depending on their floor, the rooms were scheduled to rent for from twelve to twenty-five dollars a week, and more than half had been reserved while construction was still under way.

As 1929 began, Anne Morgan had myriad things to do if the club was to be ready in time for the many previews and press receptions that would precede its formal opening. During the first week in February, a telephone call from Paris forced Morgan to reorganize her priorities. Anne Dike had been very ill for some time and was staying in the flat on the rue de Courcelles. When informed that there was every likelihood her old companion would be dead within the week, she dropped everything else and booked passage on the first ship leaving for France.

Dike died on February 8. The funeral service was held in the American Protestant Cathedral, on the avenue George V. Anne wore the uniform of the service the women had co-founded with her many decorations pinned across her breast. The body was transported from there to Blérancourt for burial. People came from all over the Aisne to take part in the funeral procession led by the two great loves of her life, Anne Morgan and André Tardieu, who was to become premier of France before the year was out.

The following week, Anne Dike was the first woman of foreign nationality to be placed on France's National Roll of Honor. The citation listed her many services to the country over the previous dozen years. It ended: "She gave all to France—her heart, her brain, her strength, and she deserves a high place in the gratitude of the nation."

Not long after, Anne Morgan was raised another class in order of the Légion d'Honneur to the rank of Commandeur, a rank held by only one other woman, the Comtesse de Noailles. At the same ceremony, Anne Vanderbilt was raised to the class of Officier of the Légion. There was a sentimental symmetry in this. So often had Anne Dike and Morgan been decorated in tandem that it seemed meet that Morgan and her new Anne should be similarly honored.

*A*t a private reception for the AWA stockholders and board of directors, the patrician Vanderbilt and Morgan were at the head of the reception line. Nobody commented on it, but the physical proximity of the tall and imposing figures said everything. Over the next decade, whenever they were in the city, they would spend one night a week at the club, occupying rooms on the eighteenth floor, fancifully called the Vanderbilt and Morgan suites, although they differed little from the accommodations of the residents. They wanted to experience what the members were experiencing, to chat with them in an informal way, to find out what they thought about the lifestyle and many programs offered to them, if they had any ideas about what else could be done. These two grandes dames were almost girlish in their eagerness to be two of the group and treated just like the others. It was a well-intentioned illusion that never descended to condescension.

*F*or those who were watching, by early September the stock market was signaling that it was in trouble. In the first week in October, several blue chip stocks reached such attractive lows that bargain hunters rushed in, and the market began to climb. Action on the New York Stock Exchange on October 22 was sufficiently spirited for the more optimistic brokers to proclaim the coming of the expected recovery, but the gains were reversed during the last hour of trading, and the market closed down. It was followed by an avalanche of liquidation that began the next day and was nothing compared to what occurred on Thursday, October 24. After the remarkable victories of the great post-war bull market, it was fatally wounded. Years would pass before another bull market proved its mettle in the corrida of the New York Stock Exchange.

The Morgan trusts remained in excellent condition despite the market. The interests of Anne and her sisters were looked after by the Morgan partners, each of whom, including her brother, had suffered losses but remained incredibly rich. Their 1929 Christmas bonuses were less than the million dollars each received the previous year but remained substantial. Anne's nephew moved into a new forty-room mansion on Long Island. Her brother, Jack, continued to draw an annual salary estimated at over five million dollars and spent the early months of the Depression putting the finishing touches on his new boat, *Corsair IV,* the largest private yacht of all time. It would require a crew of over fifty and represent his single most noteworthy effort to stem unemployment.

Anne Vanderbilt's brothers, Oliver and Joe Harriman, were hurt badly by the crash, but she was unaffected by it. With the exception of the Sutton Place and Paris houses, she had sold all of her significant real estate in the boom years of the Twenties. Not wanting to invade the Vanderbilt railroad trusts, Willie K. set up her finances in the gilt-edged securities upon which the running of the country depended. While the railroad shares of other Vanderbilts plummeted, her portfolio remained sound.

On paper, Elsie de Wolfe was a much poorer woman at the end of 1929 than she had been at the beginning of the year. The value of her holdings was almost halved. It did not matter. So long as she was not forced to sell them, continued to collect her dividends in dollars, and resided in France, she was wealthier, in terms of what her money could purchase, then she ever had been in her life. With prices falling on luxuries as well as necessities, the drastic devaluation of the franc made her dollars manifoldly more valuable.

Of the four women, only Bessy Marbury lost the bulk of her fortune in the market. What she did not lose was her spirit. The crippled, obese septuagenarian was not about to be defeated even after it became apparent that she was also going to lose her business. The American Play Company, as she had originally conceived it, might have survived the Depression had it not sold its lucrative stock and amateur rights to the Samuel French Company.

Bessy, Rumsey, and Madden had done well for their clients and themselves with publishing, magazine sales, and film and radio rights, but they were primarily a play agency. Even before the crash, it had been becoming increasingly clear that talking pictures and radio would soon absorb a sizable portion of the legitimate theatre's audience. The crash only ameliorated the death sentence. With money scarce, people could stay home and have the radio bring the biggest stars in the world right into their living rooms. Motion picture palaces were offering a film, stage show, and free piece of china for fifty cents a ticket.

The theatre could not compete. Within five years of the crash six theatres were razed, five became burlesque houses, two were turned into nightclubs, two were taken over by radio stations, and the largest number, sixteen, converted to motion picture houses. Bessy's beloved Princess was rebaptized the Reo Cinema. Thirty-one Broadway houses were lost, with more to follow in the latter half of the 1930s. In that period, not one new theatre was built. It was symptomatic of what was happening across the country. The road was dying, and it was from those national tours that the American Play Company had earned a substantial part of its income.

The big agency business was moving to Hollywood: the wise course would have been to follow Leland Hayward out there. But tough as these three old New York birds were, they could not have survived the trip. Broadway was their natural habitat. The only solution for the American Play Company was to scale back, with the partners doubling their workloads in order to reduce staff. They were getting too old for that.

Madden was the first to leave. He had been longing to devote most of his energies to handling Eugene O'Neill and decided the time was right to make the move. O'Neill was already considered the greatest American playwright in history. The film and world rights to his works would provide the agent with a sufficient income to survive during those dark years.

Even had she wanted to remain, Bessy did not have the physical strength to do what was required. She took a few of her writing and performing clients and with Carl Reed, a young protégé, opened the International Agency in the West Forty-fourth Street building the Shuberts had erected to house Sardi's, the legendary theatrical restaurant. Rumsey was left with the firm—in name only, for the American Play Company would never again be the force it had been during the fifteen years since Bessy had founded it.

*E*leanor Roosevelt was often politically at odds with Bessy but had a genuine affection for her as one might for a great old aunt, a Tartar in her day, but actually rather sweet. They were family in all but blood. Though a generation apart, the Eleanor-Bessy relationship drew on recollections of childhoods spent in neighboring houses in Oyster Bay. They spoke the shorthand of their class and had mastered its ingrained prejudices to assert its best values. Uneasy in the places society assigned to them, they had fought for more independence of intellect and movement than was ordinarily permitted to spirited women whose hereditary position mandated that they behave like proper ladies. Both were skilled politicians and dedicated to the basic tenets of the Democratic party. Much of what separated them was generational.

Born into pre–Civil War old New York society and never a member of the feminist movement, Bessy still had come further in terms of sexual liberation, as well as in personal and professional relationships with minorities, than was conceivable by the vast majority of her contemporaries. That she had not divested herself of all of the bigotry of her class and century was forgiven by many of the younger women with whom she had begun to work once she entered politics. To them she was affectionately "Miss Bessie," a sobriquet she detested—or more editorially, "the grand old lady of the Democratic party," which pleased her.

*O*n the afternoon of July 6, Anne Morgan and Anne Vanderbilt could temporarily forget the bad times when Premier Tardieu opened the Blérancourt château as a national museum of France dedicated to Franco-American friendship. He spoke movingly of the pervasive spirit of Anne Murray Dike having moved Miss Morgan and himself to go forward and make a reality of her dream. A *New York Times* editorial called the museum Miss Morgan's "monument to Mrs. Dike." It concluded: "The friends of Blérancourt are but a few of the friends of France in America, but they represent that friendship in its finest flowering and fruitage."

*W*hen Elsie came to New York in the autumn of 1930, she stayed with Bessy in what was, after all, still considered her room. With the both of them in residence, the evening soirees had at least the semblance of old times. At one of them, Elsie met a young man who was to become one of her dearest friends.

The British photographer-illustrator Cecil Beaton was at the beginning of a brilliant career and had been brought to New York by Condé Nast. It was his first visit, and he had wangled a letter of introduction from Osbert Sitwell to Bessy, who was a legend to the gay young things in the London set, in which he moved. How he longed to sit at her feet "listening to the whole story of Oscar Wilde and his trial . . . to hear about Bernhardt and Lillie Langtry and Mrs. Vernon Castle" from the woman who knew all of them.

In spite of a terrible cold, Beaton presented himself at the house on Sutton Place within a few days of his arrival. When Alice showed him into the library, with its view of the river, he might have been in a house on Cheyne Walk, overlooking the Thames, and he immediately succumbed to its "Chelsea-ish charm of jumbled books, photographs and pictures." Bessy was sitting on a chair heaped with pillows. His first sight of her reminded him of a combination of "a dear, enormously fat Victorian landlady" and a "huge old Buddha." Elsie was among those who later came in. Beaton had a zoomorphic approach to both women. He described Elsie as looking like "a humanly dressed monkey."

Bessy was wearing "a black satin dress that Queen Victoria herself might have worn." The photographer's description of what she looked like was cruel but possibly not too inaccurate:

Surrounded by rolls of fat is the face of a parrot; her arms are as thick as one's own body, and her bolster-like legs have been strapped to iron supports to bear such colossal weight.

From her many years of intimacy with the city, she described "New York life" better than almost anybody else could. She told him what buildings and plays were worth seeing. As she had with Noel Coward, Ivor Novello, and John Van Druten before him, she generously described the many ways in which she could help this stranger to her country. Beaton soon realized she had "a personality as grandiose as her figure" and felt he had "made a new friend as strong as a wall. Soon after, other guests drifted in, among them, the English actress, Irene Browne, Clifton Webb, and one Italian and one English author, both of great renown."

All circled around Bessy in the most sycophantic way, as she told funny stories about, of all things, Arctic explorers. Beaton doggedly outlasted the other guests in order to have another opportunity for a quiet chat with his hostess. Alas, it consisted of her giving him "sound, motherly advice" and laughingly suggesting he tell Sitwell she had become his grandmother. He should not have come out with such a bad cold, and she advised him to go home and get into bed with a very strong cathartic.

Beaton did not know what a cathartic was and wrote to Bessy the next morning to thank her for her friendliness and say he had taken her advice and "gone to bed with a very strong Catholic."

He returned to Sutton Place a few days later to sketch Elsie for *Vogue*. Without losing her pose for an instant, she managed to rattle off a series of orders to Westy, and Beaton knew they would be great friends. She was the sort of "wildly grotesque artificial creature" he adored. Beaton loved playing the transvestite. What he saw in Elsie was an image of all he longed to be. Fashion was Elsie's religion. Everything she did was touched by her devotion to it—her wardrobe as an actress, her grace as a decorator, her élan as a hostess. He considered her "a living factory of 'chic.'"

Except for meeting Beaton, the visit was a failure as far as Elsie was concerned. She had not enjoyed living on the same street as the two Annes, aware that they shared so low an opinion of her. Even Bessy had been unkind. It was apparent the Sutton Place women had become a clique and, as such, were proving a huge disappointment. That was the last time she would ever stay there.

Toward the end of her stay, Elsie was totting up the things that had to be done before she left, and she commented, she thought, quite generously, "And, of course, I want to do something for the older women."

Bessy peered over her granny glasses and responded, "I presume, my dear, that you are speaking of the women of your own age."

Certainly, nothing could be smarter than Elsie's Paris address on the tiny rue Leroux in fashionable Passy, but when she returned to it, she decided the time had come to make a long-contemplated move. She began to complain that the house was too small for the kind of entertaining she envisioned, but there was a more compelling factor to which she would never admit. She was nearing seventy, and it was time to gather together the threads of her support system. A new residence would have quarters for both Johnnie and Charles.

A search was instituted that was confined to the Seizième Arrondissement. It was unthinkable that Elsie would live anywhere but in *les beaux quartiers* that ran along the old river road, now avenue de New York, to St. Cloud through what once had been the country villages of Passy, Chaillot, and Auteuil. On the small mount of Chaillot, overlooking the Seine, Napoleon Bonaparte had intended to build an imperial city. The project was barely begun when Napoleon was deposed. One of the Bonaparte palaces to be completed in Chaillot was at 10 avenue d'Iéna. Its owner, Prince Roland Bonaparte, like many of his class, was feeling the effects of the crash. Unlike his cousin Prince Murat, he had not had the good fortune or good sense to get an infusion of new currency by marrying one of Anne Vanderbuilt's daughters.

Bonaparte's means of replenishing his finances was to convert his palace into flats. The moment Elsie saw the place, she had the same feeling of being at home she had experienced on first sight of the Villa Trianon. The neighborhood was one with which she was familiar.

Chaillot and the park of the Champ de Mars, opposite it on the Left Bank, was the favored locale for the expositions that the French delighted in having every few years. At the time Elsie moved into the neighborhood, it was dominated by two of Paris's most infamous grotesqueries facing each other across the Seine and built a decade apart for different nineteenth-century expositions. In the little over forty years since its construction, the Eiffel Tower had transcended ridicule to become one of the city's most beloved landmarks. The same could not be said for the Palais du Trocadéro. Crowning Chaillot's highest point and only a short distance from Prince Roland's palace, it was universally considered the ugliest building in Paris, the only one in which there was no unity of style, with bits stolen from every architectural period all clashing with each other. The name of its architect,

Davioud, was mentioned with a scorn usually reserved for Landru, Paris's notorious Bluebeard-like serial killer.

Prince Roland's rents took no notice of the Depression. Once it was ascertained that there would be an *ascenseur* in the building, Elsie opted for taking the least expensive and least desirable space—the old servants' quarters in the attic. It was a warren of unattractive rooms with mean dimensions and low ceilings but satisfied her need for air and light, even if being at the top of the *maison* did not automatically confer lovely vistas. The view from what would be her dining room was so ugly that she had the windows blocked with artificially lit garden landscapes, perhaps to recapture for her guests the loveliness of a dinner at the Villa Trianon down to the crepuscular lighting of the end of a summer's day.

When the flat was finished, much of the look was pure Elsie. It was in the decorative leitmotifs that Elsie departed from her traditional self. They derived from Art Deco, a style that had become the rage since its exhibition, in 1925, at the Exposition Internationale des Arts Décoratifs et Industriels Modernes. Without the influence of McMullin and all of the other fashionable young things with whom Elsie was trying so desperately to keep up, it is doubtful that she would been more sympathetic to Deco than she had been to one of its influences, Nouveau, when Minnie Anglesey bought the entire Bon Marché Art Nouveau salon exhibited at the Paris Exposition in 1900.

As with all of the homes she made for herself, her emotional transference was total. Avenue d'Iéna was Elsie serenely at peace with herself and her world.

> Of the several homes I had, none is so faithful a record of the kind of person I am. . . . For those who have a delicate perception it is the symbol of the child of the past and the present that is my true self.

Revealingly, she defined the old as "good" and the new as merely "pleasant to the eyes and the touch." From one point of view, she was correct. Deco made a greater appeal to the tactile than any other style. The viewer was visually drawn to the smooth, glossy surfaces and then reached out to touch them.

Elsie had a way of making news with bathrooms. Thirty years earlier, she had become the talk of Versailles by installing a bathroom for each bedroom in the Villa Trianon. Now, the bathroom she was creating for herself would become the talk of Paris. From the moment the space was gutted, the plans called for a large space at the heart of the apartment to be reserved for her bathroom-boudoir. In its reconstruction and decoration, the practical Elsie insisted upon the latest in plumbing and the use of materials impervious to hot water and steam.

Along with eighteenth-century French furniture, she installed the first mirrored mantel over the bathroom's fireplace. It was destined to be copied often enough to become an Art Deco cliché. There were mirrors and etched glass everywhere. All of the decor and fixtures were in the shells, dolphins, and sea motifs so often found in rococo ornamentation. It was as if René Lalique were one of Louis XIV's master craftsmen. When the room was completed, Elsie was bowled over by what she had wrought.

> Moonshine and glamour, white orchids and rock crystal, silver tissue and white furs, reflected in many mirrors—that is my bathroom. . . . A great many dreams have come true in my life, but none has amused me more than having finally been able to create, live in, and enjoy a bathroom that I myself conceived.

The bathroom took on a celebrity of its own, as it was photographed and written about, admired and ridiculed. It became the favored sight to be seen by the chicest tourists. Coffee was taken in it after one of Elsie's dinner parties. In the afternoon, cocktails or tea was served there to artists, aristocrats, and politicians who dropped in as they might at a private club.

There was life in the old girl yet. Now over seventy years old, Elsie had repeated the magic that had made her famous. She had created something original out of the odd bits and pieces of other people's styles. She was again being copied by decorators on both sides of the Atlantic. The old philosophy held. From her point of view, she was in trouble only during those increasingly frequent periods in which they stopped imitating her.

Commensurate with the deepening of the Depression was the expansion of opportunities for intellectual stimulation offered to members of the American Woman's Association by Anne Morgan, Anne Vanderbilt, and their associates in its leadership. Lectures, debates, seminars, the exchange of information about obtaining and keeping employment during hard times, and the chance to meet the leading women of the day replaced socials, dances, and theatre parties as inducements for joining and taking advantage of its facilities.

In December 1930, Eleanor Roosevelt chaired a seminar on the problems of women over forty in the business or professional world. It appears that not very much has changed since then. An industrial relations counselor, Glenn Bowers, was "forced to admit" that gray hair meant prestige for men but loss of it for women. The psychologist on the panel, Dr. Joseph Jastrow, observed that both men and women were capable of doing their best work "after reaching maturity," but added, "Many employers are still inclined to stress the age factor too strongly, mistaking vivacity for ability and decorative value for service value." Frances Cummings based her talk on a study of fourteen thousand women in business and the professions. The crystal ceiling of that period was age. A woman's salary rose steadily until she reached middle age. At that point, it became stagnant for the remainder of her working life. In summation, Eleanor wryly remarked that the conclusions should be equally "interesting and important to women who have either reached the age of forty or intend to reach it."

In a series of radio addresses on women and the economic realities of the Depression, Morgan said that they were facing them "with a gallantry and understanding that is as amazing as it is admirable." She was filled with praise for their resilience and gave a catalog of survival through compromise that did not sound so much like a list of gallant gestures as it did a sad litany of what was demanded of the innocent by the excesses of the greedy. A well-known actress and a home economics expert were both working in bookshops. A concert singer was giving language lessons, an art director acting as a paid companion, and accountants serving as hostesses in tearooms.

For all of her compassion and experience, Morgan was unable fully to comprehend how difficult it was for a woman to save if she was in a low-income job. Harking back to her years of trying to get workingwomen into savings plans, she concluded with the self-evident observation that "the ability to save contributes something, in addition to the security of the money itself, to a woman's capacity to meet difficulty without the loss of morale."

In attempting to convey her message to the people, Anne Morgan—now immersed in the branch of public relations known as politics—occasionally overstated it. She sometimes sounded ingenuous and at other times, contradictory. She was on a par with, if not the peer of, Roosevelt and Walker and, under Bessy's tutelage, had mastered the politico's craft of the quotable capsule that sank into newsprint never to emerge again. She averred, "God made women. Why should they try to be anything else?" She said, "There is absolutely no purpose in the ridiculous idea of a woman's war for women." She regretted women had not learned what men knew from business—"to be impersonal." Lacking that quality, they assumed men were jealous of them and "trying to shunt them back into the home." What both groups were having trouble reconciling themselves to was that "competition was and is between human beings, not sexes." Despite that noble sentiment, she was proud that men were discovering "with some surprise . . . that women enjoy a good stiff fight."

*I*n 1931, contraception was the right-wing inflammatory issue that abortion was to become by the end of the century. Abortion had been legal in the United States until 1851. It was the newly formed American Medical Association, rather than a religious sect, that started the campaign that led to its illegalization. Its zeal had nothing to do with morality or saving the lives of women or fetuses. It had everything to do with protecting its members, almost all of whom were male graduates from accredited medical schools and had been interns in hospitals. In both sets of institutions, the leaders of the AMA held lucrative positions.

The AMA's feared competition was a group of skilled female midwives who lacked formal educations but could usually deliver a baby or perform an abortion more adeptly and less expensively than many of its members. The organization could not very well make birth illegal, but it could eliminate a sizable portion of the midwife's income by lobbying Congress to outlaw abortion. Through the years, it would continue to erode the rights of midwives until they all but disappeared while infants, currently almost totally remanded to the expensive care of members of the AMA, had a higher morality rate in the United States than in any other industrialized nation in the world.

By 1930, the AMA anti-abortion campaign had proven far more effective than would the later Catholic–Christian Right campaign. Margaret Sanger, the nation's leading advocate of birth control, could not admit officially that abortion was a form of birth control—indeed, the leading form—and what she called birth control was more accurately conception control, but that never had the proper public relations ring to it. It sounded almost religious. *Birth control!* That could grab the attention of a single woman or a mother struggling with more children than she could afford to feed.

A study conducted that year indicated that there were one million abortions performed, which represented 40 percent of all pregnancies. Thirty percent were illegal, and up to 30,000 resulted in the death of the patient. The figures were later adjusted but remained alarmingly high: 700,000 abortions and a conservative estimate of 16,000 deaths.

Sanger's rationale for disassociating herself from abortion was that the practice of what she termed birth control or pregnancy prevention (again avoiding the use of the word *conception*) would obviate the need for it. She was trying to raise money for her controversial Birth Control Clinical Research Bureau during the most difficult of times. The last thing she wanted was to offend the rich and powerful AMA. When in good conscience she could no longer overlook the need for safe abortion, it remained impossible for her group to advocate legalization nor could it officially counsel pregnant women who came for help, although unofficial referrals were occasionally made.

Anne Vanderbilt and Anne Morgan were both members of Sanger's board, along with Mrs. Otto Kahn and Mrs. Thomas Lamont, the wife of the most powerful of the Morgan partners. It was no radical departure for the Morgan family and firm to be involved with family planning and the problems of illegitimacy. Their interest dated back to 1893, when Pierpont contributed one million dollars for the construction of a new building for the New York Lying-in Hospital. Anne Vanderbilt's concern with the need for sex education, contraception, and the prevention of teenage pregnancy began before World War I with her involvement in the Big Sister movement.

Both single and married workingwomen had been freer to admit interest in Margaret Sanger's movement during the more sexually emancipated decade of the Twenties than in the Thirties and Forties. Nevertheless, when the American Woman's Association decided to give an annual award to a woman of "eminent attainment," it was agreed that Sanger should be the first recipient.

Late in November 1931, Eleanor Roosevelt presided at the presentation dinner. Franklin was being mentioned as a possible presidential candidate and, for his sake, the bad press she received for advocacy of birth control would soon force her to give up her public support of the issue. She never disavowed it: she simply refused to state her position.

*A*nne Morgan's life had come together in a most felicitous manner. She had Daisy Rogers to take care of every detail of her professional work. It was said that she kept a filing system that listed every significant person Anne ever met, the circumstances under which they met, and what they discussed, so that should Anne meet them again, she would have a dossier from which to open a conversation. On the domestic side, she had Peacock, an exemplary butler, who saw to it that her house ran to perfection.

The crowning touch came when her sister, Juliet, joined her Sutton Place "family" by buying an apartment at 1 Sutton Place South, where Rogers also kept a modest flat. Anne Vanderbilt also had a sibling in the street: Lillie Havemeyer was living in one of the houses just north of Bessie Marbury's. Vanderbilt's adolescent grandson Rutherfurd Hatch lived with her when not

*L*adies and Not-So-Gentle Women

away at prep school. Bessy had Marbury MacDuffie, a nephew of whom she was fond, living around the corner on East Fifty-seventh Street. Aside from these blood ties, the two Annes and Bessy had become family in the warmest interpretation of the word. At their short remove from the heart of New York, the women of Sutton Place were getting old together with a grace that had been missing from the city and their lives since they were girls.

CHAPTER FIFTY-TWO

The cost of maintaining Lakeside Farm was a drain on Bessy's income. She tried to make the place pay for itself by breeding Guernsey cattle. Although they added a proper pastoral note to the estate's impressive natural beauty, they produced not one cent of income. She said with as much rue as humor: "Milk costs me $1 a quart and butter, $1.05 a pound . . . but I get a lot of fun out of it."

The prices were about ten times the going rate in 1931. But the place did yield a new political base that more than offset her investment in it. She was certain Maine could be made Democratic if Roosevelt would help. An invitation to him revealed the open and unsentimental approach to his infirmity that only a good friend would display:

> I only wish that you could come here. *No steps.* Your bedroom and bath all on the ground floor. Three easy steps up to the piazza with hand rail either side. . . . Why not be a sport and run over? You can take in Portland on the way and make one speech. It would do a lot of good.

He replied encouraging her to keep up the good work in Maine and agreeing they could make a tremendous gain there even if they did not carry the state. As for campaigning, "the best I can do is to send Eleanor to see you about the 20th of July." That was good enough for Bessy, who arranged "a great Democratic *Social* rally" at her farm on which occasion Eleanor would meet the "stars" of the Maine Democratic party.

Eleanor was traveling with Franklin's executive secretary, Missy (Marguerite) LeHand, and wrote to her husband that they arrived at Bessy's in time for lunch. "Miss Marbury has talked politics ever since except for a brief time when Missy & I went in swimming! Molly Dewson is here too for tonight & tomorrow there is a grand jamboree!"

Dewson had been Eleanor's co-chairwoman of the women's committee to reelect Roosevelt in the 1930 gubernatorial race and was to be equally active in the coming presidential campaign. She shared a Greenwich Village apartment with another activist, Polly Porter, that was just across the hall from the one in which Eleanor stayed with the feminist lovers Nancy Cook and Marion Dickerman. Dickerman and Cook may have turned down invitations to accompany Eleanor on the trip to Maine. Dickerman disliked Bessy for condescending to "all of us as novices. We wanted women in the party, because we thought they stood for definite things that we could work for. She was not concerned with those things."

Marion later admitted that there was a more personal side to her dislike of Bessy. "She said to me, 'I feel holy in your presence. You look like a church widow.' I didn't much like that."

*D*r. Max Wolf equaled Bessy and her business as a reason for Elsie's annual sojourns in New York. A Viennese by birth, Wolf was the original Dr. Feel-Good who gave injections of drugs of his own concoction that cured people of whatever it was that ailed them. He did all of his own laboratory work and was not a member of any medical associations. Although he preferred treating writers and painters, his patients ranged from the opera star Feodor Chaliapin to the multi-millionaires Marshall Field and Otto Kahn. For five thousand dollars (a goodly fee in those days), he administered a course of shots designed to do anything—increase stamina, eliminate insomnia, reduce or put on weight—that a patient needed. The critic-author Stark Young recalled a visit to the good doctor's office. "People begin arriving at eight thirty. A monkey show there, from Elsie de Wolfe, Alfred Vanderbilt down or up to me."

Elsie's addiction to Wolf, her erratic eating habits, her weight mania, her nervous energy—indeed, the total personality change that had come over her beginning in the mid-1920s—suggests that she was suffering from an undiagnosed anorexia nervosa that would persist for the rest of her long life. This diagnosis appears confirmed by the quixotic and inadequate recipes given in two articles she wrote (probably with Johnnie McMullin) for the *Ladies' Home Journal* that year, later incorporated into a book, *Recipes for Successful Dining*.

Oddly enough, her cookbook demonstrates that she had lost all sense of food. The Elsie of old knew better, having been no stranger to the kitchen and the proper ordering of meals. Writing the book was her way of saying that she had no problem with food when, in fact, it had become a phobia. Getting fat, like Bessy and their friend Maxine Elliott, who also had become enormous, was getting old, which Elsie feared more than anything else.

Her course of treatments with Dr. Wolf and her business with Edgar completed, Elsie was back in France in time for the *réveillon* parties. She had stayed in a Park Avenue apartment, and as far as the Sutton Place contingent was concerned, it was as if she had not been there. The two Annes had an early dinner on the Sunday before Christmas and went to the AWA club-house for a holiday party. Morgan was not satisfied with the way it was handled, but over 1,200 guests seemed to adore it.

Bessy shared a warm and quiet Christmas Eve at home with the two Annes and drove up to Mount Kisco with them for New Year's Eve. If, after Elsie's desertion, she had some fears about who would look after her should she become seriously ill, they no longer existed. She would always be able to rely on the Annes. And now there was a splendid year coming in which her Democrats would sweep all before them. The only problem was the question of loyalty to her old pal Al Smith, in light of her commitment to Roosevelt. Was it only a matter of class, or did she really believe that the latter was the one for the job? It did not help that people she admired, such as Ida Tarbell, also had their doubts. Ida liked Roosevelt enormously and thought she could trust him but did not know where he stood on important issues.

Bessy attempted to neutralize some of the fears she shared with Ida about precisely where Roosevelt stood on issues vital to the nation's economic survival. She postulated that "Governor Roosevelt, like most of the other candidates, will dodge issues until after the primaries are over." She was certain that once he did reveal his platform, "it would be along the lines of what you want and what we sympathize with." She admitted that, to a large extent, she was working "on faith" and concluded: "He is so much better than anyone else we have in view that I think he can safely be supported."

*O*n June 27, 1932, the Democratic convention opened. Bessy's oversized chair was placed in a prominent position, but she could no longer negotiate the crowds and stairs with only canes or crutches and had to be brought to it daily in a wheelchair.

Had New York State swung in line behind him, Roosevelt undoubtedly would have had a first ballot win, but Tammany Hall was pledged to Smith. The state delegation went 65½ for Smith to 28½ for Roosevelt. Although she believed in Roosevelt and had helped to secure the Maine vote for him, Bessy quixotically voted with the organization for Smith. As she trusted that Franklin would eventually prevail, it would make no difference if she was loyal to those who had been loyal to her. Roosevelt won on the fourth ballot before New York was called. The state then lined up behind its governor.

By the beginning of October, there was little doubt that Roosevelt would be the winner, except among those who were more convinced that the only winner and new world leader was the little man who would undoubtedly become the next chancellor of Germany. That month, Elsie had a party in her new apartment. She had traveled a long distance away from Bessy's influence and opinions. The gathering was of her usual mix of wastrels and tycoons, many of whom were great admirers of Adolf Hitler. Oswald Mosley was among them. His Fascist zeal was kept in check by his first wife, Cynthia, the daughter of Lord Curzon and Mary Leiter, the half-Jewish Chicago heiress. All restraint would be lifted by her death. His second marriage, to Diana Mitford, took place at the home of Joseph Goebbels with Hitler among the guests. But that would be in 1936. In 1932, at Elsie's, Mosley was sufficiently the well-bred product of his upper-class English background to disapprove of the vulgar way that her cronies were "covering Roosevelt with ridicule and obloquy." Only Johnnie McMullin had the courage to speak out. "I think Roosevelt's going to win."

The others thought this preening little queen as silly as he looked. When asked what on earth had led him to that conclusion, Johnnie looked around shrewdly before responding, "Because all our friends think Hoover will win."

That autumn, Bessy was happy to have the two Annes home again. Her summer had been one of fits and starts, good days followed by bad. She had given her annual party for the Maine Democratic bigwigs but had not been up to much more in the way of campaigning. Bessy was one of the few connected with Tammany Hall whom Roosevelt forgave for not supporting him in the primaries and would have gladly used her in the campaign had her health permitted it.

On November 8, he won the election with 57.4 percent of the popular vote. More important to the enactment of his New Deal policies, the Democrats won decisively in both houses. For the first time in history, a woman was named to a cabinet post when Frances Perkins was made secretary of labor. Despite the controversy stirred up by her nomination, in his own party as well as in the opposition, the new president stood by his choice during her difficult confirmation hearings.

$\mathscr{B}$essy had influenza and could not join the two Annes at their Mount Kisco country place for the New Year holiday. Morgan came in to have New Year's Eve lunch with her before departing and was alarmed by the way she looked. But by the following Sunday, Bessy was well enough to have some people in for tea. Vanderbilt came by to help her and among the guests were Hendrik van Loon, an editor of *The New York Times,* and Harold Nicolson, who was visiting New York with his wife, Vita Sackville-West. It was Nicolson's first meeting with her, and he wrote in his diary that night: "Miss Marbury is enormous, emphatic, civilized, gay. She says she is 76 and has never been so happy as in the last fifteen years. All passions spent."

It was fifteen years since the end of the war and Elsie's decision never again to live with her, and so it would seem the peace she ultimately made with the reality of their parting had brought a new happiness. The following Saturday, Bessy went out to Mount Kisco for lunch and appeared to her hostesses "much better," in spite of her legs being in such bad condition that some minor surgery would be necessary to relieve the pressure on the veins.

The operation was performed at home on the following Thursday. By Saturday night, it seemed clear Bessy might not recover from the surgery. If that was to be the case, there was comfort for her in being at home. In all of her seventy-six years of self-indulgent overeating, smoking, and generally abusing her body, she never had been a patient in a hospital. She had not been born in one, and now she was certain she would not die in one. Years in themselves always meant nothing to her. How they were lived was everything. She was prepared to go and had declared only the previous week, "I do not want to die in a state of rust."

For the first Sunday since the war to end all wars, there would be nobody coming in to see her. Not even the two Annes, who were spending the weekend in the country. Her mind could travel back seventy years to the time when her grandfather taught her how to fish on a spot just below where she lay. In those days, Sutton Place and its environs had been an area of spacious plantations that served as the country homes of the city's elite. She had seen so many changes. In her youth, she had believed all change was for the better. It no longer seemed that way.

From her window there was a view of the turreted Queensborough Bridge, with its steady span of headlights like life flashing by. She could recall the festivities marking its opening a quarter of a century before. The river below her was blighted by the dour institutions on Blackwell's Island just as it was in her childhood. Beyond that, above Long Island City, a garish neon mélange flaunted the new era of advertising's triumph over nature. It was not the most inspiring view. As always, the down and outers had that as they gazed from their island prison at the towers of her beloved Manhattan. But there remained a sense of the city's irresistible pace in the vista spread before her, and that was something. At the moment, everything.

There was no way for Bessy to ignore how ill she was. In addition to the operation, she was recuperating from the influenza and she suffered from chronic hypertension due to her enormous weight. Her longtime personal maid and companion, Alice Kuswetter, looked in on her at regular intervals and did not like the way the invalid was breathing. She took it upon herself to send for Bessy's physician, Dr. Archibald Dunn. Together, they kept what they hoped would not become a deathwatch. At 2:30 A.M., Bessy had a coughing spell and lapsed into a coma. It was time to summon her nearest relative, her grandnephew Marbury MacDuffie, who lived around the corner, at 345 East Fifty-seventh Street, and her business associate and co-producer in 1928 of the ill-fated *Say When,* Carl Reed. She died on Sunday January 22, at 5:33 A.M. The cause of death was heart failure.

The river beneath her window flowed swiftly to the sea. Elisabeth Marbury had written that when God in His mercy called her, He would find her ready to embark upon that short journey for which her whole life had been but a preparation, "like the old ship brought into its last port. No more battling with heavy seas, no more fighting with tempestuous waves. . . . As a little child you came into the world. As a little child you will go out from it."

Reed's first call that morning was to the two Annes. His words were "Bessy has passed away peacefully, no suffering." They came back to town immediately to attend to the "first arrangements of all that was possible to do." For Anne Morgan, it was a labor of love. She had adored the older woman for almost thirty years.

No matter what Anne Morgan felt about Elsie de Wolfe, no matter the angers and resentments that might have built up over the years, no matter the disdain in which she held her for Bessy's sake, she knew what her dead friend felt for her adored companion, what she always had felt. Elsie was among the first people she called. If she wanted to be there, the funeral could be postponed until she arrived from Paris. That was unnecessary. Elsie could not or would not disengage herself from whatever commitments she had abroad merely to come home to mourn the woman who had loved her beyond all else for the better part of a lifetime. She sent her brother Edgar to represent her and, more important, look after her interests in Bessy's estate. It was not one of Elsie's better performances.

After all, that Sunday, on which the radio announced her death at every news break, was like all those before it in the house at 13 Sutton Place. Miss Bessy lay in state in her drawing room, while the great and near great of the world came in to pay their respects. When president-elect Franklin Delano Roosevelt heard the news in Warm Springs, Georgia, where he was resting up for the coming inauguration, he said: "I am greatly shocked to hear of the death of my old friend, Miss Marbury. Mrs. Roosevelt and I will miss her very much."

By the next day, messages of condolence were pouring in from all over the world. The leaders of the Democratic party issued statements commenting on her "leadership," "wise counsel," and "genius" for politics as if that rarity in itself was sufficient cause for remorse.

On the floor of Congress, Representative Mary T. Norton, of New Jersey, said: "The death of my dear friend, Elisabeth Marbury, fills me with sorrow and regret. She had an unusual mind and a keen political sense as well as a strict sense of justice. The Democratic women of New York and of the nation have lost not only an able friend and leader but one whose inspiration, vision, and loyalty we shall sadly miss."

She hoped her funeral would be "a bright and rather cheerful event." That was a hope in vain, for it did not reckon with her importance. It would have to be a monumental event, one to echo down the marbled corridors of influence. Upon hearing that Bessy Marbury had passed away on Sunday, Cardinal Hayes asked Monsignor Michael J. Lavelle, the rector of St. Patrick's Cathedral, to celebrate a special mass on Monday, at 8 A.M. Both prelates were among her good friends. The funeral would be held in the great cathedral on Tuesday morning, January 24, 1933, and would undoubtedly be an event of civic, indeed national importance.

Anne Morgan did not attend the first special mass. She was too busy "making all the arrangements for Bessy's funeral." It was like opening a mammoth spectacle without rehearsals, but she was to prove a showman of Ziegfeldian proportions. The Morgan name helped to expedite things. It still had its magic for New York even during the worst depression in the country's history.

The day of the funeral was bright and unseasonably warm. It began quite early for those nearest and dearest with a private ceremony conducted by Father Thomas Graham, of St. Patrick's Cathedral, in Bessy's living room at 13 Sutton Place. They stood around the closed coffin, which was covered with a blanket of deep red roses and lilies of the valley sent by the two Annes, who were present along with a group of public figures who felt close enough to the deceased to want to be part of the inner circle of mourners. Among them were Grover Whelan, Fannie Hurst, a close friend and one of the most popular novelists of the day, and Eleanor Roosevelt.

After the prayers they preceded the coffin down the narrow but graceful staircase and out into Sutton Place. A line of twenty limousines awaited, stretching around East Fifty-eighth Street toward the river. The procession was led by a police motorcycle escort, followed on foot by several rows of men and women representing all of the Democratic districts in the city. Behind them came the hearse, four open cars filled with flowers, and the long column of limousines.

They moved at a slow and stately pace for a distance of almost a half-mile to the grand Fifth Avenue entrance to St. Patrick's Cathedral. Fifty mounted police were fanned out to control the crowd.

People had lined the streets along the route of the cortege, twenty thousand by estimate with another thousand in front of the church. To the press and police, the extraordinary thing was that they all seemed to know who Miss Bessy was and had come only to pay their last respects to "one of the greatest of New York's 'great ladies.'"

The honorary pallbearers formed a double line stretching from the great bronze doors of the cathedral across the broad terrace, down the steps, and along the sidewalk to the curb where the hearse had pulled up. In silk high hats, winged collars, cutaways, and striped trousers, they presented an imposing portrait of the powerful male establishment paying tribute to a woman to whom they collectively owed no small debt. In addition to Al Smith, Governor Lehman, Mayor O'Brien, James Roosevelt (representing his father), and the entire hierarchy of Tammany Hall and the Democratic party, there were the governors of Massachusetts, Maine, Virginia, Rhode Island, and Maryland; the mayors of Jersey City and Chicago; and New York State Supreme Court Justice William Harman Black. There was also the publisher Condé Nast; the writer Hendrik van Loon; the theatrical producers Daniel Frohman, who had given Bessy Marbury her start in the theatre, and Gilbert Miller. Noel Coward made the time to be in their ranks despite the fact that he was opening that night on Broadway, co-starring with Alfred Lunt and Lynn Fontanne in his own play, *Design for Living*. She deserved at least that much. Bessy had been his benefactor, agent, and surrogate mother from the time when he first arrived in New York as an unknown and literally starving young writer-actor.

Bessy's good friend Monsignor Michael Lavelle celebrated the high mass. Pietro Yon, director of music at the cathedral, was at the organ to play his funeral mass, and a male choir of forty sang the responses. Monsignor Lavelle delivered the eulogy, taking his text from *The Book of Wisdom:* "Who shall find a valiant woman? Her price is as things from afar and from the uttermost coasts."

We have just offered holy sacrament for the eternal repose of a lady, an artist, a citizen, and a Christian whose life was like a shining star . . . a strong force for good in every circle in which she moved.

She became interested in government, and it is a question whether any lady of unofficial station ever had a stronger or more uplifting force in the character of those in whose hands the rule of city, state, and nation is held. . . . She associated herself with men highest in government and became their confidante and advisor, and corrector when she thought that correction was necessary.

That Monsignor Lavelle was a practical and worldly man, as befitted a high-ranking prelate in New York City, was obvious from his analysis of the practical way in which Bessy applied her Catholic faith and his recognition of the skepticism it occasionally engendered in others. "Some people have the notion that a spiritual sense interferes with material interests and activity. . . . With her, it acted to purge all her sentiments of dross and put a practical value on all she undertook."

Still, when he went on to describe the facts of Bessy's conversion, a naive wonder crept into the narration.

She had a wonderful spiritual sense. She read and prayed herself into the church without any external help except the grace of God. She told me she had never spoken to a priest until she went to the Church of the Holy Rosary, in 119th Street, and asked for baptism. Apparently, she displayed such knowledge of the Catholic faith that the pastor on duty granted her request on the spot.

Bessy was a prominent Catholic layperson decorated for her services to the church by the Knights of Columbus, loud in her espousal of her religion. Lavelle seemed to have taken her story on faith as did the congregation.

Anne Morgan summed up the feeling of everybody present in a note she jotted down in her diary: "Funeral at St. Patrick's overwhelming—marvelous illustration of her influence and far reaching affection from all sides."

Anne was right. It was overwhelming and an illustration of Bessy's influence that was more than marvelous. It was downright miraculous. After all the masses were ended, and the candles lit in her memory burned down, one religious truth remained unextinguishable: *Elisabeth Marbury was not a Catholic!*

At the time of her alleged conversion, Bessy was living with Elsie downtown in Irving Place. Her affairs rarely took her north of her office in the Empire Theatre Building at the corner of Broadway and Fortieth Street. Between her place of business and her home, there were several Catholic churches. Why had she not applied to one of them for baptism instead of traveling all that distance north to a church close to the banks of the East River in a poor ghetto known as Italian Harlem?

The records of the still-existent Church of the Holy Rosary go back to the church's founding, in 1884, and cover the period that Bessy described to the priest. There is no notation to be found anywhere in them of the baptism of Elisabeth Marbury.

Although it seems unlikely she would have improvised the name Holy Rosary, there is a slight possibility she got it wrong in her conversation with Father Lavelle, which took place years after the event. The description in her memoirs of the church in which she was baptized does not fit the gray granite Holy Rosary in Italian Harlem.

> I was received into the Church by a simple priest whose parish was in the East Nineties. The little wooden structure that served as the place of worship counted as its members only very poor and humble folk. The pastor and his assistants were the volunteer chaplains at North Brother Island on which were the contagious hospitals belonging to the City. These men knew no fear of disease for they regarded their attendance in this plague centre [sic] as merely part of their days work.

The portrait Bessy drew was not unworthy of one of the melodramas on which she made a fortune. A close investigation again leads to a blank wall where the baptismal font should have been. The only Catholic church then existent in the east nineties was Our Lady of Good Council, founded in 1886, at 232 East Ninetieth Street, which is still standing but not constructed of wood. Our Lady is a gray stone building in the Gothic style. It also has no record of Bessy's baptism. There is no mention of it in any of the annals of the Catholic archdiocese.

What private skepticism kept her from being baptized will never be known. Catholicism undoubtedly had a strong spiritual appeal for her and almost as strong a theatrical one. She never explained anything beyond saying she "prayed" herself into the church. Merely saying something with sufficient conviction would seem to have been enough to make it true as far as she was concerned. On the other hand, if her religion was no more than a secret irony, some vast private joke, then this magnificent requiem, this gathering of the great and near great of her city and nation in its grandest Catholic cathedral, was the quintessential punch line.

The final mixed message was her burial in the Protestant Marbury family plot at Woodlawn Cemetery. She had not left instructions to be buried in a Catholic grave.

*F*our days after Bessy's death, Alva Belmont died in Paris. She was among the most complicated women of her day. Voluptuously feminine and passionately feminist, she was an almost sadistically demanding mother whose children adored her. Once she bought her way into society by spending more on parties than anybody previously had, she made it a more amusing place by broadening the list of who were in and who were out to include people as noted for their wit and talent as they were for their bank accounts or old names. Hers was the money that helped to finance the transformation of the suffrage and women's liberation crusades from grassroots to national and then international movements.

Alva had left specific instructions for her funeral. Her body was to be taken back to the United States, where the services were to be held at the Cathedral of St. John the Divine. She wanted a female minister, female pallbearers, and an all-girls' choir to sing hymns of her own composition. Her daughter brought her body home. No woman minister was available, but there were female pallbearers as well as a female guard of honor carrying feminist banners, and a girls' choir to sing a hymn written by her. In one large respect, her wishes were countermanded. The services were not at St. John the Divine but at "the Vanderbilt church," St. Thomas's, the church in which Alva had forced Consuelo to marry the Duke of Marlborough, and one must wonder if perhaps the dutiful daughter had her small moment of revenge.

*B*ecause their deaths came within a few days of each other, the press linked Bessy and Alva as allies in the cause of women's rights, when they could not have been more disparate in their aspirations and their motives for becoming involved in politics. However, there were similarities, and a *New York Times* editorial gave a fair assessment of them:

> The death of Mrs. Oliver Belmont following so closely on that of
> Miss Elisabeth Marbury will recall to many the successive phases

of the fight for woman's suffrage in this country. To that movement both gave an impetus through their personal energy, their indomitable hopefulness, their social position, and their political skill. It is true they took up a cause that had its origins long before they came upon the scene and which was on its way to winning. But it won earlier on account of their persistent and intelligent effort.

CHAPTER FIFTY-THREE

The total value of Bessy's estate came to $109,173, which in 1933 was a respectable amount and would have been several times that sum were it not for her losses in the crash. Her real estate in today's market would have come to between five and ten million dollars. The Sutton Place house alone, valued at $50,033 then, could not be purchased now for less than eight million dollars. To those who knew Bessy, it came as no surprise that Elsie was the chief beneficiary. What was received somewhat more incredulously was the disclosure that she had designated Sir Charles Mendl as one of her executors, but that was undoubtedly done to make things easier for Elsie. Mendl was an honorable man, and whatever pain Bessy had experienced from his marriage was not due to him but to the woman to whom she continued to pledge her worldly goods after death.

To the faithful Alice Kuswetter, she left the income from a $25,000 trust fund, several thousand dollars in German property and securities, and sufficient household goods and furnishings to set her up in an apartment. Five hundred dollars was left to Edgar de Wolfe with comparable sums going to her nieces and nephews.

To her newest good friend, Elizabeth Arden, she left a bracelet with the name *Elisabeth* spelled out in diamonds. Her business, the International Agency, was bequeathed to her associate, Carl Reed. She continued to own a 25 percent interest in the English agency bearing her name and managed by Golding Bright. That was left to Elsie along with Lakeside Farm. There was a provision allowing Anne Morgan and Anne Vanderbilt the use of the Maine estate:

> If said Anne Morgan and Anne Vanderbilt should wish to carry
> out my desire and undertake the maintenance and operation of

said country place for a home for working women then such country place shall be made available to them for such purposes.

The official response came from the board of the AWA, whose members would be the beneficiaries of the bequest. It indicated the direction the organization had taken since its inception in the working girls' Vacation Fund. Although Bessy's desire had been to create a country place for all working-women, the AWA stressed that the farm would become "a country club for business and professional women," in other words, a middle-class environment in which they could rest, swim, and play golf.

Franklin Delano Roosevelt took the oath of office on March 4, and Anne Morgan noted that she was "delighted with Roosevelt speech." Indeed, his impassioned call for a freedom from fear offered the despairing nation a brief rekindling of euphoric belief in its future. During his first year, she was to remain enthusiastic about many of the new president's programs, an enthusiasm that was reflected in her choices of speakers for the Periscope lectures, a series of talks she had initiated at the AWA clubhouse. Their purpose was to enlighten the members on important events of the day. Eleanor Roosevelt would be a frequent speaker at the Periscope meetings as well as at other AWA events. Bernard Baruch already had spoken, and the following week featured Bessy's old client and Roosevelt's future speechwriter Robert E. Sherwood.

As soon as Prohibition was repealed, Morgan asked Anne Vanderbilt to design a bar for the use of clubhouse residents and guests. The result was the festive little Ferris Wheel Bar with its colorful carnival motif. It was such a success that profits from it would later be used to redecorate the lobby and art gallery.

On March 23, Anne Morgan heard from Elsie, via her attorney, that she agreed in principle to allow the AWA to use Lakeside Farm, and that the arrangement could be settled by an exchange of letters. It was not long before it became obvious that the plans for the farm would have to be altered from those suggested by the AWA board.

In early June, a new plan was announced after a meeting in the yellow and white drawing room of Elizabeth Arden's palatial new Fifth Avenue penthouse. In attendance were Eleanor Roosevelt and Lady Mendl, among other prominent women. Before the two Annes sailed for Europe a few days earlier, they had also agreed to be on the committee.

The new plan was to raise fifty thousand dollars, which would be sufficient to both purchase the property and create a permanent endowment that would maintain it in perpetuity as a memorial to Bessy's life and ideals. The proposal was to install a library and museum for the use of the people of Maine. As at Blérancourt, there would be guest facilities, but it would definitely not be run as a country club. Eleanor Roosevelt gave them permission to use her name, but as First Lady was far too busy to give her time. However, she did start the financial ball rolling with a contribution of two hundred dollars.

Elsie was delighted with their decision to purchase Lakeside Farm. She had no interest in the property; had visited Bessy there only once and been so bored she resolved never to return. By all means, let the place become a museum to Bessy. Her extraordinary friend merited one, for there never had been anybody quite like her. Elsie would happily contribute those of Bessy's possessions that she could not sell—what more inspiring way to be rid of them? There was one important collection she would neither sell nor contribute: Bessy's personal correspondence. That, she destroyed, as she later destroyed her own private letters.

*R*eading about the antics of Lady Mendl—her fabled homes, clothes, and parties—few were aware of how badly her business was faring. Things appeared to have hit bottom when she discovered Edgar was doing some creative bookkeeping that resulted in more money in his pocket than in her till. She banished her brother from her business, her life, and her afterlife by cutting him out of her will. Her draconian act eliminated some losses but did not create any new revenue.

That she persisted in the American business for as long as she did was remarkable. Had she decided to retire at the time of Bessy's death, nobody would deny that Elsie had earned her right to play. For all the skills of plastic surgery, her friends—who were mostly younger than she was—thought that she was older than she was, close to eighty, when she was actually some five years younger. The deaths, in rapid succession, of Boni de Castellane, Bessy, and Alva Belmont surely must have given her a disquieting sense of her own mortality.

Elsie had paid her dues, her selfishness nicely counterbalanced by spurts of selflessness, her avarice by generosity. For all her egocentricity, there never had been any meanness of spirit except in her disregard of the feelings of the one person who had loved her more than she had ever thought it possible for anybody to love her. But Elsie had no intention of retiring. The roses at Villa Trianon were very well tended by her gardener, and quitting was not in her nature. When she had arrived in New York well after Bessy's funeral, it was to do the East Side home of Mr. and Mrs. J. Robert Rubin more than to collect her inheritance.

Less than three months later, she closed on the sale of 13 Sutton Place to the film star Miriam Hopkins, for an undisclosed figure that was well over its estimated value. With Lakeside Farm also disposed of, the most significant chapters of Elsie's life had come to an end. All of them had involved Bessy, and none would have happened as they did without her. Elisabeth Marbury had created the tapestry of their life together, and in its cartoon could be found tracings of all that Elsie de Wolfe ever accomplished.

That year, Elsie also made arrangements for the disposal of the Villa Trianon. She quietly sold it to her old friend Paul-Louis Weiller, under terms quite common in France. She was paid immediately but would be allowed to reside in it for as long as she lived with the new owner responsible for its upkeep. Had Weiller known how long that would be, he might have had second thoughts.

When the committee could not raise the relatively modest fifty thousand dollars necessary to create the memorial, Lakeside Farm reverted to Elizabeth Arden who had put up the money to purchase the property for the project. Her business genius again came into play. Arden was almost fifty years ahead of the vogue for them when she combined Bessy's property with her own adjacent estate to create the first health and beauty luxury spa designed exclusively for women. For an average of four hundred dollars a week, a great deal of money in the depths of the Depression, Maine Chance catered to the needs of a maximum of twenty guests with a staff of forty. To create an atmosphere in which her clients would feel at home, Arden allocated $200,000 for the gardens and lavish accommodations. Even Bessy's straight women friends were slow to forgive and forget Elsie's perfidy: she was again rejected for the decorating assignment in favor of Rue Carpenter.

In July, Anne Morgan inaugurated a series of annual fishing trips to Scotland, usually taken in the company of three or four other women. Bessie Lovett was a constant, but the others would change from year to year. Anne would make all of the arrangements with Lady Lovat for cottages on the Lovat Estates. Each year, she would stress that it was going to be "a very feminine group." There were endless cables and letters concerning the number and quality of servants ("We think we can do with less if they are really *good*.")

Typical of the cottages was the one Compton Mackenzie had on long lease and which Anne sublet from the writer for a full year at a rental of 220 pounds. It was a very un-Elsie residence, having six master bedrooms and six servants' rooms but only two bathrooms, one of which had to be reserved for the help. The "household" consisted of a butler, a "good plain" cook, two housemaids, and "an odd man" to help the butler, as well as their personal maids and a chauffeur. That came to 2.5 servants to attend each of four women in a house so primitive, they had to queue for a bath.

*O*n January 30, 1934, Anne Morgan attended a New York exhibition of the work of Malvina Hoffman and was sufficiently impressed with the art and artist to mention the event in her Line-A-Day. The tall and handsome Hoffman was forty-seven and the most celebrated woman sculptor in the country. In 1929, she had received the largest commission ever given to any American artist, when the Field Museum of Natural History in Chicago sent her around the world to do the preliminary studies for 110 bronzes that composed the installation "Races of Mankind." Timed to the opening of the Chicago Century of Progress Exposition, it had been unveiled the previous summer for permanent exhibition in the museum's Hall of Man.

It should have been one of the most exultant periods of Hoffman's life, but instead she was frequently in great pain both physically and emotionally. Nothing seemed to matter, and, as she later recalled, she felt as if she was "a living ghost" when Anne Morgan walked into her exhibition. The attraction was instantaneous. Malvina was a great believer in premonition, ESP, and psychic phenomena, and there were so many points of contact in their lives that it might have seemed their meeting was predestined.

Malvina's first commission had been to do a head of Robert Bacon, then ambassador to France. Soon after, Malvina met her first important sponsor, Mary Averell Harriman, the wife of Anne Vanderbilt's cousin Edward. In 1912, Mrs. Harriman bought a stable from Anne Morgan's sister Juliet on East Thirty-sixth Street, which was converted into a studio for her protégée. It backed onto the fashionable mews Sniffen Court, which is still adorned by the plaster friezes from the Parthenon that Malvina had set on either side of her rear wall.

At the time of the 1934 exhibition, Malvina had a husband, Samuel Grimson, whom she had acquired just before she turned forty, after a twenty-year engagement mostly spent on separate continents and carried on via the mails. There is little doubt that it was a *mariage blanc*. Until the meeting with Morgan, the great passion of her life had been the Russian ballerina Anna Pavlova, adoringly called "my muse," whose nude boyish body she had often sculpted.

No matter what passions Malvina evoked in her, Morgan proceeded with the life she shared with Anne Vanderbilt as if nothing had happened. The two Annes set off on a previously arranged winter holiday in Summerville, South Carolina. Not long after their return to New York, Vanderbilt developed angina and was forced to remain in bed, often for several days at a time, well into the spring. Morgan took charge of Rusty Hatch and began seeing quite a bit of Malvina Hoffman. Consuming though the new affair might be, the two Annes were too entwined personally, politically, and philosophically for Morgan to have contemplated abandoning Vanderbilt. It took neither persuasion nor prior discussion for the two women to find themselves as one on almost every issue. Both had been delighted with Roosevelt during the first months of his administration, but even in the early days of the New Deal, their enthusiasm had never reached the level at which either would have considered resigning from the Republican women's committee. Long after their disillusionment with Franklin, they continued to admire Eleanor. A shared interest in bettering the conditions of the workingwoman often found them allied in support of such organizations as Rose Schneiderman's Women's Trade Union League.

A year later, when Roosevelt announced the formation of the Works Progress Administration (WPA) to create jobs for the unemployed, Morgan was contemptuous of it and the administration that conceived it. She did not believe it was the government's job to create employment; rather, to create the conditions by which American business would be able to stimulate it. In her, there was always the dichotomy between Morgan Republicanism and liberal compassion.

Anne Vanderbilt was plagued by illness throughout the year. By the time she was well enough to get to Mount Kisco for a weekend, it was January, and by then, Malvina was coming up almost every weekend. Vanderbilt apparently accepted her with her accustomed grace and gentleness and was worldly enough to accommodate an infatuation that did not interface with those parts of her relationship with Morgan that she cherished most. Not long after, a friend asked how she defined love, and Vanderbilt replied, "Where Anne is." A seventy-three-year-old with a serious heart condition knew that her life was limited and circumscribed. Malvina was perfect, an independent woman, in a *mariage blanc* that did not inhibit her artistic or emotional freedom. She had come into Morgan's life without threatening Vanderbilt's own position in it. They formed the perfect triangle with none of the difficulties Elsie had created when Morgan and she began to share Bessy's love.

That winter, Malvina started to work on a half-torso of Anne Morgan. The portrait revealed a regal figure with an androgynous head dominated by gentle, wise eyes that had, perhaps, seen too much pain. A double strand of pearls hung over a ribbon from which her Croix de Guerre was suspended. Her other decorations were pinned to the bosom of a lace gown half concealed by a wrap held closed by large, capable, unadorned hands.

Through that season and into the spring, their intimate moments gave Morgan great pleasure, especially one weekend when they were alone in Mount Kisco, and she nursed the sculptor's hand, injured in the course of executing the torso. It was "both fine and cold. M. stayed in bed all day with hand truly painful—wonderful time together good talk."

*I*n August 1935, Malvina joined the two Annes on a motor trip through Germany during which Vanderbilt and she became good friends. This deepened affinity presented a dilemma to a woman of conscience. When they returned to Paris early in September, Malvina invited Morgan to tea. She wanted to discuss the effect of their relationship on the frail Vanderbilt's condition and on her own situation with a husband she did not wish to hurt. Anne observed dolefully that "her plea makes return impossible." But they could not break it off and return she did, two weeks later for lunch. The two Annes lunched two days later, and Vanderbilt's empathy was "a joy." On September 28, Morgan had "an enchanting evening at Miss Hoffman with *Anne*," but two days later, Anne was too ill to go to the country, and Morgan drove out with Malvina for lunch. She was with Anne that evening but noted of their day: "Hoffman most delightful."

As the time to leave for home approached, it became clear Vanderbilt would not be well enough to get on the ship. She was too ill to see Morgan on October 5, but the latter had to admit that this had not prevented it from being "a good day." The next day, she was recovered sufficiently for them to have dinner together. It might have been the gravity of Vanderbilt's condition that made Morgan describe it as "the last, alas," when she was not leaving for another five days. She did manage to see her again, but it was stressful. Fortunately, she could always go to Malvina for solace. After a "bad lunch with Anne," there was a "wonderful eve dinner with M.H." On her last day in Paris, Morgan telephoned Malvina to say goodbye and went to the rue Leroux for "a heartbreaking goodbye" to Anne.

*B*y the summer of 1935, Wallis Simpson's conquest of the Prince of Wales was complete. Diana Cooper went to dine with the couple at

Fort Belvedere and described the prince to their mutual friend Chips Channon as "pretty and engaging." As for Mrs. Simpson, she was dismissed as "glittering . . . dripping in new jewels and clothes." A member of the inner circle did not deign to mention that their future king assuredly had paid for them. What was less well-known was that Elsie assuredly had helped to select them. The center of her life momentarily had moved from the Paris-Versailles-Riviera axis to London, where she was enjoying a renaissance of power by playing Henry Higgins to an Eliza Doolittle who, though not yet divorced from her American husband, might one day become the next Queen of England.

A range of claims were given for Wallis's suzerainty: a knowledge of bizarre Oriental sexual tricks that brought the allegedly inadequate Prince to his first successful orgasms; fellatio turned him on, and she gave the greatest he ever had experienced; she reminded the somewhat retarded royal of a stern nanny who would paddle his bottom if he was naughty; he was a repressed homosexual, and her angular boyish figure, along with her total lack of conventional femininity, was what appealed to him. It could have been any, or none, or all of the above. At the beginning she was doubtless a wonderful mistress who made him feel like a great lover. She had the requisite gifts of a great courtesan: a whore in the bedroom, a lady in the parlor, and a cook (or able to plan a perfect meal) in the kitchen. But more than those gifts, it is likely that she was the first person in his life to make him feel loved for himself rather than who he was, as, in his turn, he was the first in hers profoundly to need her. Whatever the initial attraction, it was a great deal more than sexual fun and games that kept these two undistinguished people not only together but desperately clinging to each other through almost forty years of banality and ridicule.

Soon after they met in 1934, Elsie de Wolfe called on Wallis Simpson at her flat and was a bit disheartened. The interior was as undistinguished as its neighborhood, which was located in the southern part of Marylebone. Mrs. Simpson was from Baltimore, and so was her flat. That alone would have been regrettable, but along the way Wallis had been helped by their mutual friend and Elsie's rival, Syrie Maugham. Mrs. Maugham had made a reputation on the whitewash, with which she covered everything from walls to floor to furniture. Her white rooms had been all the decorative rage of the Twenties. What she did for the Simpsons in the Thirties was to reduce the banal to the boring, and Wallis was clever enough to know it. She turned to Elsie. There was no money to pay her, but if Elsie helped her, she would never regret it.

Elsie sized the woman up, totaling her assets and liabilities, and decided to put common sense aside and go with her instincts. Redoing the flat would have been too costly, but she added the touches—more and more, as money began to be contributed by the prince—that gave the place the De Wolfe imprimatur.

If Elsie was to get any return on her investment, there was more to be done than refurbishing a flat: the woman had to be redone. The head was good enough and the figure fashionably slim, but almost everything else would have to be altered. Whether or not there was a verbal contract and all of this spelled out, both women understood what was necessary and were committed to it. First off, the phony accent would have to go. There was nothing the British aristocracy despised more than Americans trying to sound as if they had been born in England. She advised Wallis to go back to her Baltimore roots. Of all American accents, the southern was the most beguiling to European ears. It tended to soften the harsh edges, and in this case a little softening would go a long way.

At the time they first became friends, Wallis was trying desperately to dress like a Londoner. Unfortunately British clothes of the day were like British food: overcooked. They were either too severely tailored, too casually tweedy, or too flowing, floral, and furbeloved, thus accentuating Wallis's angularity and her severe, almost blunt features. What she needed were clothes with subtle lines, simple but luxurious fabrics, solid colors, and a minimum of adornment. What she needed was Paris, particularly Mainbocher, who would design most of her clothes over the next decade; but also Molyneux, and Schiaparelli (none of them were French). Elsie told the designers they had to dress Wallis Simpson because she was the mistress of the future King of England. She moved in the best circles, wore clothes beautifully, and was certain to be imitated. Moreover, the press gave credit to the designers along with the descriptions of what she wore—especially the American newspapers and Condé Nast. There was a depression, and great competition for those relatively few women who could afford their wares. The right publicity was not easy to come by. Wallis got her Paris clothes, and she got them either at great discounts or free. The arrangement lasted as long as she lived, for almost to the end, she was one of the greatest advertisements the French couture ever had.

What Elsie did for Wallis was to strip away the British upper-class affectations and allow her to be the American woman she was, and would remain, no matter what title she might one day carry. Her critics might not like or approve of her, they might accuse her of destroying the monarchy—but no matter what other epithets they might use, nobody would ever call her a phony. When Elsie was finished, what Diana Vreeland said of her was equally true of Wallis:

> Elsie naturally had wonderful taste. But what Elsie Mendl had was something else that's particularly American—an appreciation of vulgarity . . . a little bad taste is like a nice splash of paprika.

Elsie's rewards for her work were not long in coming. When the prince gave Wallis permission to redo his country home, Fort Belvedere, she naturally called on Lady Mendl to take charge of the job. Doing the residence of the next King of England was a coup for a decorator many considered old-hat. When word got out, there was some initial protest about the choice of an American decorator. Elsie stifled it by pointing out she had renounced her American citizenship to become English when she married Sir Charles.

In November 1935, the leading French couturiers voted on the twenty best-dressed women in the world. Elsie was proclaimed the best dressed of all. They added that, generally speaking, American women were the most elegantly dressed. Though not given in any ranking, nine of the remaining nineteen were American, including three actresses (Kay Francis, Constance Bennett, and Ina Claire) and five millionaires (Anne Vanderbilt, Kitty Bache Miller, Linda Porter, Kitty de Rothschild, and Otto Kahn's daughter). To Elsie's delight, Wallis Simpson was the tenth American on the list.

Elsie already had redecorated the king's country residence, Fort Belvedere, and Wallis's London flat. The great plum was still ripening. It could be the one to secure her immortality as a decorator. No matter how important, other jobs came and went. People redecorated, moved, died; houses were razed or remodeled. Even her beloved Villa Trianon might be changed once she was gone and Weiller took possession. The decorator's art was ephemeral. Only in the great public places did it outlive the artist. Her closest approach had been the Frick mansion, but she had done only the private quarters, which were restricted to the family. The architects, in collaboration with Duveen and the English art critic Roger Fry, had designed the great public rooms. She was on the brink of her last chance.

With his father's death, Edward David was king in all but coronation. Wallis had free access to Buckingham Palace, which he was determined to share with her. For all the riches of art and furniture within its walls, it was a depressing old pile, cold and cheerless even in the royal family's private apartments. From attic to basement, Wallis decreed it needed what, given the situation, the English would snickeringly call "tarting up." And Elsie was the one to do it. Only she could at last give Great Britain what it deserved— its own Versailles. Word, of course, leaked to the press. Could there be any doubt that Elsie would have made sure that it did? The British government was infuriated that this twice-married woman (who it was determined would never be queen) would commission her American friend to make something French out of their proudly English palace. Nevertheless, work reportedly continued on renderings of the proposed changes. Before the entire set could be completed, Edward would no longer be king and the plans canceled. It would take less than a year for him to pass from adored monarch to exiled duke.

*I*n March of 1936, two divorces were being contemplated—one on each side of the Atlantic. In England, the king thought the time had come for Wallis to divorce Ernest Simpson. It would be months before the case could be heard. Her partisans later claimed that she never wanted the divorce, never wanted to be queen, would have been content to continue as the king's mistress. That is doubtful, for she knew the precarious nature of that position from having been involved in the disposal of her predecessors in it. It is unlikely that she would have gone to the trouble of working with Elsie on plans for redecorating Buckingham Palace if she had no intention of living there.

Malvina Hoffman finally decided to divorce Samuel Grimson. Anne Morgan played a large part in that decision. On April 11, Malvina had accompanied Morgan and the ailing Anne Vanderbilt to Summerville. Morgan and she stayed only long enough to get Vanderbilt comfortably settled in and, five days later, were in Philadelphia for the opening of one of her exhibitions. Less than a week later, they flew to Hollywood, where, in movie star fashion, Morgan waited while Malvina went to Reno for the six-week residence required to obtain a Nevada divorce. Once it was final, Malvina rejoined her "devoted and never-failing friend" at the Beverly Hills Hotel for a few days of recreation before flying back to New York. Anne was beside her in the plane as Malvina watched the sun come up and thought: "This was indeed the radiant dawn of a new day such as I had never witnessed before."

*T*hat summer, the Annes flew to Europe for the first time, which Morgan found thrilling. Despite all the cruises on the *Corsair* and the countless transatlantic crossings, she was never a good sailor and had been enamored of flight since a brief time aloft in 1910, when Orville Wright took Elsie and her up, at Le Mans. The season was the pleasant habit of familiar pleasures that it had become over the last few years: time divided between Anne V. and Malvina; fittings at Vionnet; a Scottish fishing holiday; the cure at Marienbad, where she played golf daily with Hollywood's favorite British character actor, C. Aubrey Smith, and beat him every time.

She was home in time to witness Franklin Roosevelt's reelection. His victory was so resounding, her feelings about him so changed, that she felt a "terrible Republican depression" and thought the "only possible future" for her party was "death."

If politics and the economic news were dreary, Anne's social life that autumn was exceedingly enjoyable. She met and was enchanted by Georgia O'Keeffe when Anne Vanderbilt arranged an exhibition of her work at the clubhouse gallery. Malvina brought all sorts of new artistic types into her life. Through them, and despite her own conservative politics, she gave contributions and her endorsement to the decidedly left-wing New School of Social Research. Her new interest in the arts led to sketching trips with Malvina. Anne was again exhibiting that facility for becoming the woman her lovers wanted her to be. She was politically awakened by Bessy, shared a dedication to the French war victims with Anne Dike, approached the best-dressed list with Anne Vanderbilt, and found a dedication to art with Malvina that would have delighted her father, who never had been able to persuade her to share his passion for it.

The King of England signed the instruments of abdication on December 10. By that simple stroke of the pen, he was no longer Edward but again David, the name by which he had been known to his intimates since childhood. The next day, in a broadcast carried around the world, he informed the British people of his decision to resign for the woman he loved. There were no longer any obstacles to his marriage except her divorce. While waiting for it to become final, the future duchess was staying with a wealthy American couple, Charles and Fern Bedeaux, at their Château de Candé, in Tours, where she would later be married. Johnnie and Elsie drove down to have Easter Monday lunch with her. Johnnie later reported that Wallis had given Elsie a photograph Cecil Beaton had taken the month before. It was simply inscribed: "Wallis. May, 1937."

In the years to come, after the Windsors were reduced to being what amounted to professional guests, autographed photographs of themselves would be their customary house gifts. At first, they came in simple sterling silver Cartier frames, but later the duchess discovered a little shop on Madison Avenue that carried plate copies at a fraction of the price, and would order them by the dozen.

The guest list for the wedding was very much abbreviated after it became clear that the duke's brother, the king, was refusing to allow any member of the royal family or its inner circle to attend. The Mendls were not invited because to have asked Charles would have been interpreted as the desperate act of a couple desirous of having a member of the government in attendance, no matter how modest his position.

It was a source of personal gratification to Elsie that Wallis selected Mainbocher to do her wedding dress and most of the sixty-six couture ensembles that made up her trousseau. The duchess atoned for not having asked Elsie by making a present to her of Mainbocher's wedding dress. Realizing its significance as both a Thirties fashion artifact and a piece of social history, Elsie passed it on to the Costume Institute.

That autumn, Wallis again showed her gratitude by allowing Elsie to be the first hostess to entertain the duke and her upon their arrival in Paris. None of the members of the ancien régime Faubourg *gratin* would have accepted an invitation to anything in honor of the déclassé couple, but unlike Edith Wharton and Marcel Proust, Elsie found that segment of society unutterably boring and would not have attempted to crash it even had there been a possibility it would have her. Her career as a hostess had been made with guests from the international celebrity *tout* Paris set, and that crowd considered it a coup to have gotten the Windsors. Elsie's party signaled that the man who once had ruled an empire had become one of her crowd with its many crypto-Nazis. Henceforth, he would be monarch only of the fashion sheets and gossip columns. The duke and duchess were so close to the Mendls that they chose Versailles as a temporary haven and leased the Château de la Maye, not far from the Villa Trianon, to serve as their residence in exile.

CHAPTER FIFTY-FOUR ❧

In 1937, Elsie decided the time had come to liberate Johnnie McMullin from Condé Nast and attach him to her on a full-time basis. She offered him a salary of five thousand dollars a year plus expenses, a roof over his head should he choose to avail himself of it, and the promise of a major portion of her estate when she died. Tired of endless wrangling with Condé Nast editors over his "rococo" style, he accepted. Five thousand dollars a year might not seem a large sum to a woman like Elsie, who spent at least fifteen thousand annually on clothes, but it was much higher than the average salary of the period and, as the glamour magazines were notorious for paying modest salaries, probably not much less than what he earned as a staff writer for *Vogue*.

Ladies and Not-So-Gentle Women

Elsie kept the details of her estate to herself. She had never been above buying loyalty with promissory notes. It was unlikely that Sir Charles Mendl knew a promise of a large legacy had been made to Johnnie, because he had been promised the same thing. On every level, Johnnie was a welcome addition to their ménage: he took all the drudgery out of being with Elsie. Sir Charles was early to bed and early to rise, and when Johnnie was not around, had to wait up until Elsie was ready to retire, for she could not get out of her pearls without help. As well as the wrinkles of age, the gnarled fingers of arthritis were being concealed by the famous little white gloves.

*A*nne Vanderbilt became ill again in January 1938, and was hospitalized by mid-February. When Morgan visited her on the eighteenth, she was "terribly concerned" about her condition, but Vanderbilt seemed to rally during the next week and was "distinctly better on the surface." By March 8, Morgan was able to report a "good visit with Anne at home again and really enjoying it," but the news was not good on any other front.

It was the week in which Hitler invaded and annexed Austria. Anne Morgan was concerned that his actions might eventually lead to another world war. For more than a decade following the first war, she had spoken out time and again about the danger of allowing the German economy to recover more swiftly than that of France and of the necessity of not permitting the Germans ever to rearm. Nobody had listened. People had insisted that Germany was the first line of defense against the Communists. More important to a struggling American capitalism, there was money to be made in Germany, and her own brother had been among the first to claim his share of it.

Anne Vanderbilt remained ill in Paris through most of the summer but by the end of August, when Morgan returned from her annual fishing trip, she was delighted to find Vanderbilt "amazingly like [her] old self [in] spirit and appearance." On September 2, after viewing the Vionnet collection, they went to Blérancourt for the weekend. It was there, among the people who had suffered so dreadfully during the last war, that the fear was highest that they might be dragged into another war over Hitler's intentions toward Czechoslovakia.

Twenty-two percent of the population of the young, small country were quarrelsome ethnic Germans who had established their own strong Nazi party and wanted an independent German state carved out of the prosperous Sudeten region. Since France and England had not made an issue of his annexation of Austria earlier that year, Hitler had been strongly hinting that he was contemplating trying his luck with Czechoslovakia. On September 6, at a mammoth National Socialist rally, in Nuremberg, he told a wildly cheering mob of 150,000 strong that the Sudeten Germans were going to have "a party day of their own" by October 15 in celebration of an autonomous state looking for guidance to Berlin rather than Prague.

On September 13, Hitler officially staked his claim to the Sudeten. The French promised they would march into Germany if Czech territory was violated. Anne noted that on the fourteenth, Paris was experiencing "a terrible day of strain—everyone living in a nightmare." On the fifteenth, the British prime minister, Neville Chamberlain, flew to Munich for the first of three meetings he would have with Hitler that month. Anne found it "a strange day of detente. The world all waiting and listening." While Chamberlain took his dramatic flight, "hope [was] strong & almost belief." She was diverted by a "charming eve [with] Mal."

The two Annes left for Blérancourt on the next morning for what would be a "strange weekend." Vanderbilt, so aware of her mortality, had a very bad night after expressing great unhappiness over the death of a friend after a terrible illness. They awakened the next morning to the news that Hitler was demanding complete secession. He would be satisfied with nothing less than the incorporation of the Sudetenland into the Reich. The two Annes spent the day trying to cheer each other up.

That same afternoon, Bettina Ballard, an editor of French *Vogue*, went out to Versailles for one of Elsie's "glamorous luncheons" and could scarcely believe the table talk on that appalling day. One of the guests asked if anyone had ever known a Czechoslovakian. Another replied that his valet was one "but hardly worth fighting for." Everybody was bewildered by France's pledge to protect a country with so many unknown people in it and agreed that it should simply forget the whole thing. Sir Charles tried to explain with a metaphor he thought they would understand: if one signed a check, it was rather difficult to deny one's signature.

The tall, handsome, impeccably groomed Prince Jean-Louis (Johnny) de Faucigny-Lucinge, a member of both the Faubourg *gratin* and *tout* Paris, quoted Georges Bonnet, the pro-German French foreign minister, as having told him, if Hitler stuck to his bluff, France would back down and accept his terms. (A few months later, Bonnet would sign a non-aggression pact with Germany.) Schiaparelli claimed she knew there would be no war "just by instinct," and Diana Vreeland declared it was all chemical. Hitler became a madman during the full moon. The assemblage anxiously recalled there would be a full moon rising within a few hours.

One fading beauty, compact rudely out to add a fresh coat of powder, observed that Pierre Laval and Anthony Eden had given Italy to Germany. On that subject, Lady Castlerosse was extremely vexed for, if there was a war, she would not be able to get to her recently purchased Venetian palazzo.

One of the older guests recalled a happier time, when Parisians got down on their knees as President Wilson drove by. That reminded Mrs. Douglas Fairbanks, formerly Lady Ashley, how happy she was to be plain Mrs. Fairbanks with an American passport. Another American, Kitty Bache Miller, dismissed the whole thing. It was simply impossible for anything to happen before she finished her fittings and sailed for New York. As for Elsie, she was serenely confident there would be a miracle.

At the same time that the Annes were driving back to Paris the next afternoon, the French premier Edouard Daladier was flying to London for consultations with Chamberlain. That evening, the French radio news broadcast that Czech president Eduard Beneš, "under irresistible pressure from Britain and France," agreed to the secession of the Sudeten provinces.

On September 23, Chamberlain was in Bad Godesberg for a second meeting with Hitler. The Führer knew he had won and applied greater pressure by threatening to march into the Sudeten unless the Czechs declared their intention of withdrawing their troops by October 1. Anne Morgan noted that September 25 was "a terribly strained day—everyone holding their breath—amazingly plucky & quiet—lunched with Anne who was also very wonderful—was herself very quiet and plans made."

The next day, there was "*still* the same strain, the unbelievable useless destruction ahead because mankind had failed to carry through what is real and *true*. It *all* ended in the speech of Hitler. Hatred and a lying justification for his people on one side & the whole world on the other." She found Chamberlain's response that of "a man who had given his best & totally failed." The twenty-eighth was "the hardest morning of all, then came Roosevelt's speech which was magnificent." Of the world leaders, he was the only one who made a plea for the salvation of the Czech people. "Then came news of the Munich meeting and all was changed."

Chamberlain had begged Mussolini to intercede with Hitler, and in return England would recognize him as Emperor of Ethiopia. He was about to go before Parliament and admit the failure of his negotiations when word came that Hitler had agreed to the meeting with Daladier, Chamberlain, and Mussolini. Of course, the fact of the meeting recognized him as the most powerful leader of Europe to whom the others would have to come to plead their case. The glaring omissions were Czechoslovakia, the most concerned party; and Russia, who had joined France and England in guaranteeing Czech sovereignty. Little noted at the time, it was one of Hitler's most brilliant strokes. It proved to Stalin that he could not trust the allies and, for his own safety, had better do business with Hitler.

One week after the signing of the Munich accord, Anne Morgan left for the United States. The delicate Anne Vanderbilt remained in France to be with her daughters during still another disheartening period in their lives. Barbara's mental disease was not responding to treatment, and she continued to be confined in Cannes; while in Paris, Margaret was in the midst of negotiating the terms of her third divorce.

*J*n November, the journalist Dorothy Thompson was the eighth woman to be presented with the annual gold medal of the American Woman's Association. Some maliciously claimed there was some nepotism involved when Malvina Hoffman had won the previous year, but that was unfair. Malvina was an accomplished woman in keeping with the other recipients, who included Amelia Earhart, Margaret Sanger, Frances Perkins, and Mrs. Ogden Reid. New York Republican Assemblywoman Jane E. Todd concluded her introduction of the guest of honor with a remark that elicited a small laugh: "She is the woman journalist standing the best chance of being the first female secretary of state—if the Republican party is returned to power."

Thompson's acceptance speech was a model of the enlightened Republicanism of the day. She warned against exchanging "the tyranny of capitalism for the deeply reactionary tyranny of the State." She hoped she would never see a reversal of the position of women in the face of "a dismaying tendency to resubjugate them."

She stressed that a woman's role in "these genuinely revolutionary times" was that of "the great repository of common sense in the world," more interested in realities than in the enforcement of abstract ideas. "Women would never have allowed Munich. Women know that you don't get peace by betrayal or end war by starting terror."

Anne Morgan's interests continued to be tempered by the women with whom she was most intimately involved. Malvina's influence was reflected in Anne's participation in projects related to the arts. She accepted an appointment to the Municipal Arts Commission, continued to be active on behalf of the New School of Social Research, and, in the late Thirties, joined Abby Aldrich Rockefeller in attempting to establish a museum of American handcrafts. Mrs. Rockefeller was among those women—Gertrude Vanderbilt Whitney, Isabella Stewart Gardner, the Hewitt sisters—responsible for some of America's most striking museums. It was Mrs. Rockefeller's leadership that led to the founding of the Museum of Modern Art, and her collection that provided many of its first and finest pieces.

*G*ertrude Vanderbilt Whitney and Malvina had been commissioned to do major sculptures for the New York World's Fair, which was to open that spring. On a brisk autumn afternoon two years earlier, Malvina had taken Anne Morgan out to tour the site at Flushing Meadows, on the northern edge of Queens. The locals knew it as the Corona Dump, a repository for raw sewage and industrial waste, and a questionable location for "the world of tomorrow." Considering the condition of the world in the year of its opening, the locale was prophetic.

The Germans withdrew from the fair after Mayor Fiorello LaGuardia suggested the creation of a chamber of horrors dedicated to the Nazis. The German press responded by accusing the Italian-American mayor of being "a dirty Talmud Jew." A coalition of anti-Fascist Americans and German exiles suggested a freedom pavilion to exhibit the works of German artists proscribed by the Nazis.

The idea brought a protest from Bessy's eulogist, Monsignor Michael J. Lavelle, who beseeched its supporters to do nothing that might provoke the Germans. "Some of the smallest things cause war between nations." Lavelle was only supporting the ambivalent policy of the mother church in respect to fascism. What really squashed the project was the lack of support from a group of prominent American Jews led by Herbert Bayard Swope and including Governor Lehman, Robert Moses, and Henry Morgenthau.

At first, the Russians had no plans to exhibit at the New York fair, but the American radical community urged them not only to reconsider but also to put on the best show possible. The anti-German feeling could deflect sympathy to the Communist cause. The Russians reconsidered and spent four million dollars to build what was considered "the most effective Classical design" and "probably the most talked about building in the Fair."

Both the Paris International Exposition and the New York World's Fair had been designed to exhibit the world of tomorrow, but in abstraction they more tellingly dramatized the conflicts leading inexorably to World War II. Only the United States remained certain of its ability to stay out of the conflict. That optimism was reflected in the sculptures for the fair created by Malvina Hoffman and Gertrude Vanderbilt Whitney. Malvina's "Dancers of the Races" was a huge relief in the shape of a drum. It echoed the feeling of "Races of Man" in Chicago. Whitney's "To the Morrow" depicted two enormous, youthful male and female nudes borne aloft on the unfurled wings of an eagle. Because of the twenty-four-foot wingspan, it was familiarly called "Wings." LaGuardia described it as a tribute to aviation, but Whitney said its theme was indomitable youth.

The fair was Anne Morgan's major preoccupation that spring. During the week before the fair officially opened, one meal did briefly deflect her attention. Elsie and she made their own peace over lunch at the Empire State Club. They would never be great friends, nor would they ever have been in the past were it not for Bessy, but there need be no more hostility. There already was too much of that in the world. They were both too old—had experienced too much together—for them not to declare a détente. They could laugh and remember together and hope they were setting an example for a world likewise too old and too experienced not to declare a détente.

On a lovely April 30, 1939, the World's Fair officially opened, and Anne found it "a grand and thrilling spectacle." The last great fair before the war, it would remain for the rest of the century the standard by which other international expositions were measured and generally found deficient.

That evening, Albert Einstein threw the switch that was supposed to activate the great night illuminations. Something in the wiring went amiss, and the lights never came on that night. Instead, the world of tomorrow was lit up by a gigantic display of fireworks resembling nothing so much as a fiery, annihilating bombardment.

*T*he two Annes sailed for Europe on June 14, along with Morgan's terrier, Bonzo, who usually went wherever she did. The ship was delayed in port for three hours, which was not a propitious beginning for a summer many feared would end in war. They arrived on the nineteenth, possibly recalling that it was Bessy's birthday, and went to Blérancourt that weekend, where the villagers were in an unsettled mood. Too many remembered what had befallen their homes and families during the last war, and did not trust the elaborate French military barrier, the Maginot Line, to protect them. As the French military did not believe that the enemy would take the same route through Belgium and the Ardennes that had proven so costly during the first war, they concentrated their fortifications along the German-French frontier. The threat to Blérancourt and the entire Aisne province would come if the experts proved wrong and the Boche again attacked through Belgium as was believed by people living in the area.

Anne Morgan agreed with the villagers and decided the time had come to reactivate the relief organization Dike and she had set up in 1917. She was sixty-six years old and knew she would need strong support to run the operation. Rose Dolan had been little more than twenty years old when she

*L*adies and Not-So-Gentle Women

came to work for her during the first war. After the armistice, she remained in France, first working at a private clinic and then establishing her own home for delinquent and orphaned boys. The two women had stayed in touch through the years, occasionally seeing each other during the summers. Anne contacted her to ask if she was ready to come back to work, only to discover that Rose was a few steps ahead of her. She had arranged for her orphanage to be converted to a military hospital within three weeks of mobilization. Anne happily reported: "Rose is fire and flame to work with us in every way."

It was good to have one of her old colleagues back with her. When they started to collaborate again, she added: "Rose is exactly the same steam engine and I can assure you feathers fly when she wants to get something done."

*O*n August 5, Barbara Rutherfurd died at the Château de Veyre, her mother's villa, in Cannes. Anne Vanderbilt had come down from Paris to be with her daughter during those last days. She made the arrangements for Barbara's funeral and saw to it that those of her personal possessions her children might want were sent to them. She put the villa up for sale. It was a lovely property but few of the meaningful times of her life had been spent in the South of France.

*A*nne Morgan heard about the German-Soviet non-aggression pact while touring the Netherlands. She canceled her plans and booked passage to fly back to Paris the following morning. On August 23, she noted: "Plane late starting—discovered [it was] last 'sked' plane as all Dutch aviators to be mobilized on the return of this trip." Once back in Paris, Anne tried in vain to get reliable news in order to make some plans for her people in Aisne. The next day was a Saturday, "the same kind of day." No information. War threat or no, *tout* Paris was out of the city for the weekend. There was little she could do about Blérancourt and she went off to escape at the films. "Ford's *Stagecoach* badly dubbed—then dinner at heavenly peaceful Tour d'Argent."

The entire following week was one in which rumor passed for news. She did manage to get an appointment with General Maurice-Gustave Gamelin, the commander in chief of the French army, and outlined her plan to open civilian relief stations staffed by American and French volunteers and financed by American contributions. The general gave his conditional approval: should there be a war, and should there be a need, etc.— It was all she expected of him and enough to set her off, racing back and forth between Blérancourt and Paris in order to organize her volunteers on a contingency footing.

The declaration of war caught *tout* Paris off guard. Although September, it was actually the last weekend of the August *vacances,* and everybody who was anybody was away. Noel Coward came over to set up an office of propaganda for the British government and "found Paris hot, dusty and deserted, and only the Ritz and Maxim's appeared obstinately open for business." Coward consoled himself by dining at the Ritz on caviare and filet mignon washed down by pink Champagne. He wondered where the war was. The only Royal Air Force bombardments were leaflets dropped over the enemy asking them to do everybody a large favor and lay down their arms.

The "phoney war" had begun. Very shortly, things in Paris improved immeasurably in the eyes of Elsie's set. People came back to town, and there were parties at the Villa Trianon and at the Windsors' new home on the boulevard Suchet. It was during one of those house parties at the Villa Trianon that Coward conceived the idea for what was to be one of his most successful plays. *Blithe Spirit* originally took place in a large French house visited by ghosts of the past. Elsie always claimed that from the first time she entered her villa, she felt the presence of those who had lived there before her.

It would have seemed as if there was no war at all were it not for the number of Elsie's friends in beautifully tailored uniforms and the number of exiles flooding into Paris from beyond the Maginot Line. Judging by the style in which many of the latter were living, they must have entered France via Switzerland, where they had stopped to visit their bank accounts. The couture was booming, the better restaurants booked out days in advance, queues formed at all of the cinemas, and the theatres were doing their best business in a decade. Elsie did her bit by having Cartier copy her Croix de Guerre and Légion d'Honneur in gold and wearing them with the same panache with which her friend the Duchess of Windsor wore the diamond and ruby Prince of Wales feathers given to her by the duke while he was still the Prince of Wales.

The war created a severe shortage of good domestic help. Running the avenue d'Iéna apartment was an impossible chore. Elsie decided to close it and move into a suite at the Ritz, taking with her some of her best pieces of furniture. It would only be for the duration, which she was assured would not be very long. It was obvious that an accommodation would soon be reached with the Germans since there were no battles, and the greatest danger to the boys in the Maginot Line came from boredom.

A great many of her friends had the same idea, and the Ritz was crowded with familiar faces, rather like a large and amusing house party. From the world couture came Schiaparelli and Chanel; from the theatre, the popular playwright-actor Sacha Guitry, and Jean Cocteau; from society, the chronically chic Honourable Mrs. Reginald (Daisy) Fellowes and the Comtesse Minou de Montgomery, the wealthy, ravishingly beautiful editor of *Marie Claire* and keeper of a notoriously right-wing salon.

Owing in part to the presence of some of the members of this group, the Ritz would soon be known as the hostelry of choice of some of the world's most elegant collaborationists and Nazi sympathizers. The decorative Minou would continue to entertain there. It was while in residence at the hotel that both Cocteau and Guitry would be revealed and reviled as alleged collaborationists. In one of its perfumed suites, Coco Chanel would have her last great love affair, with one of the highest-ranking German officers in Paris; while in another, the country's most acclaimed film star, Arletty, would be similarly occupied.

The Ritz was spiritually a world away from the women and children in the frontier provinces. Their men had been conscripted. Few had savings, and suddenly none had incomes. Because of the possibility of invasion, the government was forcing them to evacuate their homes with only those bits of their possessions they could carry in their own hands. They were herded into strange districts with inadequate supplies to care for them although, fortunately, still enough food to feed them. The cool autumn nights came early in the Aisne. The refugees had not been allowed to carry their bedding, and Anne Morgan was furious when she saw these wretched families forced for lack of space to sleep on cold floors, huddling together for warmth.

She sent a desperate plea to AFF in the States asking for donations of money and supplies, and, most of all, for volunteers to help with the work:

> Here one sees no warfare, no excitement, and no enemy. There is only the terribly silent suffering of poor people. Hundreds of women are bearing babies in the roughest of shelters. Some of these mothers were themselves born under similar circumstances twenty five years ago.

When Anne Morgan finally arrived home, on January 12, 1940, she was amused to learn that *Who's Who in America 1938–39* had listed her as having died in 1936. The mistake had not been corrected before the new edition went to the printer, and it was going to have to be recalled. Anne commented it was "pretty funny," and that she was not dead nor was she prepared to die. There was too much work to be done. The frugal millionairess concluded: "It doesn't seem worth while for them to spend so much money to change me from the dead to the living."

The terrible news that awaited her concerned Anne Vanderbilt, who had suffered a severe stroke the day before and been rushed to New York Hospital. She wanted to go directly to the hospital, but no visitors were permitted. The next day, a Saturday, Anne was still too ill to see her, but wanting to stand by for any word of her condition, Morgan canceled her plans to go to the country. On Sunday, she was finally allowed to see her and was too moved to say more than "It's terrible to find her so ill."

Her tour was to begin the next day, and though she wanted to remain on call for Anne, it could not be postponed. The "rather wild days of rush" had her up and down New England for the entire week, speaking to any groups that would have her, sparing herself only enough time to have a short visit with Bessie Lovett, in Boston. The entire week was consumed with "thinking of money and Anne." The next week was no better with stops in Washington, Cleveland, and Chicago, where she stayed over for a big fund-raiser at the Alliance Française. She did not arrive home until the evening of January 31, with only enough time to bathe and change before picking up Malvina Hoffman for an evening of speeches at Town Hall.

It was not until the morning of any given day that she was told whether she would be permitted to see Vanderbilt. During February, all of her energies were spent on raising money, often frustrating work in a country not yet out of the depression and being urged to isolationism by one of its great heroes, Charles Lindbergh. She also had to make time for medical and dental checkups before returning to France, as there was no telling when she would again be able to look after her personal needs. Malvina and she did manage to steal an evening to see New York's biggest hit, *Life with Father,* which for many years would hold the record for being the longest-running play in Broadway history. It was a period piece about a Victorian patriarchal tyrant and his sweet, long-suffering wife told as a warm and affectionate comedy. Anne had grown up with those parents and did not find it amusing. She asked, "Why does everybody adore it so?"

She was able to see Anne again on the eleventh. It was "very heartbreaking." By the twenty-third, Vanderbilt was again unable to see people, but Morgan did manage to get in to see her three days later and noted: "She looks better but far away."

On March 2, Anne Morgan boarded the *Conte de Savoia* to return to Europe. She told the waiting press:

> We have to realize that there will be no country left in this world as a democracy unless things come out right in this war. It is not an exciting war but a deadly war. England and France must be made strong enough to win this war, and we in America must realize how we would benefit from that.

By the beginning of April, there was still no significant land action in the war but, on the ninth, the war began in earnest, when Germany attacked both Denmark and Norway. The news filtering in from the north was most bewildering, but one thing was clear: the situation was dire. Morgan had to continue with her daily rounds in Blérancourt and Paris, once more devoting all her energy to aiding the refugees, arising early each morning, and working unceasingly until too tired to do anything but fall into bed at night.

On Sunday, April 20, there was a short entry in her diary: "Early message Anne passed away peacefully. It so much better for her."

CHAPTER FIFTY-FIVE

During the first spring of the war, Johnnie McMullin wrote to Chase that people rarely discussed the war. It was simply taken for granted that it would last forever, but nobody in the Ritz bivouac was terribly affected by it. "Life," he said, "is very hum-drum but fairly normal."

Anne Morgan's life was neither normal nor "hum-drum." When Elsie's Ritz gang spoke of war, it was as distant thunder informing them it was striking in some distant place. Anne knew of its imminence from the unending, nagging need to stockpile supplies and find dependable womanpower. The latter was immeasurably eased by the arrival from the States of Eva Drexel Dahlgren, a handsome, energetic woman in her mid-thirties who had volunteered in New York and arrived in Paris that April. Drexels and Morgans had been working well together since the early days of Pierpont's career, when the banks of the two families formed an extremely profitable partnership. After their initial meeting, Anne wrote to the AFF committee: "Dahlgren appeared yesterday and seemed to be an ace-high person and, I think, will solve a lot of our problems."

Nearing sixty-seven, Anne remained a vital woman, but she would have been foolish not to be aware of her own mortality. Recognizing Eva's potential, she began to train her to take command when the time came for her to step down. Anne's initial idea was to have Dahlgren and Rose Dolan work as a team, but from the beginning there was an unmistakable antagonism between the glamorous Eva and the pious Rose, a sibling rivalry for Morgan's affections that would have to be put aside for the duration. During the crucial month before the German push to the west, the three women worked brilliantly together.

On May 10, the Germans started their offensive against the Netherlands, Belgium, and Luxembourg, and the war began in earnest. It became obvious to the French army too late that the Germans were circumnavigating the Maginot Line and would cross the Meuse to advance through the Ardennes and Aisne districts to Paris. That afternoon, Anne and her ambulance corps left Blérancourt to journey northeast to Givet. Their mission was to start the evacuation of civilians from the Meuse region. By the light of a brilliant new moon, they shared the road with thousands of French infantry and cavalry troops heading up toward the new German lines. The soldiers would rest every fifteen minutes, impeding the progress of Anne's caravan, and they did not arrive in Givet until ten that evening.

They were awakened at dawn by the roar of a huge Heinkel flying six times around the town. The evacuation of women, children, and the elderly began that day and was slightly inhibited by light bombing. The next day, Whitsunday, three thousand of the evacuees were assembled in front of the town's Grand Palais when twenty-three bombers flew overhead, their objective, the railway station only two hundred meters away. Along with everybody else, Anne flung herself flat on the ground. Railroads were considered legitimate military targets, but the German pilots would leave their formations to strafe defenseless refugees attempting to flee along the road.

They were back in Blérancourt on May 13, the same day that Queen Wilhelmina and her government left Amsterdam for England. In the middle of that night, a French officer arrived at the château to order Anne and her thirty-five volunteers to leave Blérancourt by morning. They were directed to return to Paris but instead headed back toward Givet to pick up more refugees. En route they met the German army, which already had crossed the Meuse. They lost several vehicles in the heavy bombardment and had to make a heartbreaking choice because of the shortage of camions. The elderly were left behind in order to save the women and children.

Blérancourt had not fallen, and Anne was back there by the nineteenth, which was "a day never to be forgotten in its horror." She went out on a scouting trip looking for a missing volunteer, driving down to Château-Thierry and over to Compiègne, which was "desolate." In an empty street, a doctor was frantically searching for a car to evacuate his patient, and she gave them a lift. Amiens was in flames, "the picture of the retreating soldiers with none advancing—a terrible revelation of what is to come." There was nothing to be done except return to Blérancourt and prepare for disaster.

From Blérancourt, they were forced to evacuate to Paris. The next few days were utterly confusing with rumors of the departure of the government, and of the British retreat from France. While Anne was trying to rescue her beloved villagers, Winston Churchill was trying to rescue the whole British Expeditionary Force by evacuating it from the only port left open to the British, Dunkirk. By the end of the week, with the help of private small boats, yachts, and trawlers, the British Navy evacuated to England 198,000 of its own troops and 140,000 French and Belgian soldiers. It was one of the more spectacular feats of the war. On a much more modest level, Anne reported that on "a quiet but very full day" at the end of May, her efforts brought "good news—Blérancourt people were evacuated."

Her group's problem was to move hundreds of refugees, as well as staff, over hundreds of miles from the old centers in the east—all fallen to the enemy—to the new centers that Anne had established in the east: at Bellac, in Haut-Vienne; Mayenne, in Bretagne; and Les Sables-d'Olonne, on the Atlantic coast. When Rose and she were not on the road seeing to it that this vast operation was running with as few glitches as possible, which often meant long and wearying detours, they were foraging for basics in Paris. It was numbing, pride-shattering labor, but Anne was tireless, not even stopping for meals unless they were brought by the staff to wherever she was working.

Throughout this difficult period, Anne had been finding both solace and pain in a relationship with a woman on her staff, Muriel Ames, with whom she shared her hotel room and quarters at Blérancourt. Muriel's price for this intimacy was an insistence upon having a say in all of their activities, which invariably led to difficulties with her colleagues. Three women helped Anne to survive both the personal and professional angst. Eva Dahlgren could always be counted upon to face the worst catastrophes with an unflappable objectivity. Rose Dolan's personal courage was daunting, as she delivered supplies to the Ardennes and Aisne centers, often under enemy fire. Her secretary, Miss Richard, was another version of Daisy Rogers, who was taking care of business in New York.

Anne lived on rumors—elated in the morning by some small success in obtaining materials, fearful by afternoon of air raids and the machine-gunning of refugees on the road. June 7 was "a better day, the line seems holding." Three days later, Anne's world collapsed. The line had collapsed. The Germans crossed the Aisne and were moving to attack the French from the rear of the Maginot Line. The American embassy advised her that if her group intended to leave Paris, they had to get out by no later than the following morning.

On June 13, history repeated itself when the French government moved to Bordeaux. The Germans occupied Paris the next day. It was only a matter of time before they crossed the Loire and were in Niort, where Anne had set up a relief center that served as many as five thousand people at each of three meals a day. She had never dealt directly with the enemy during World War I. If she elected to stay in France now, she would inevitably have to deal with the Nazis, who were far more ruthless than the kaiser's people had been. It was something she was loath to do—it was like giving them comfort—but if she went home, she would be deserting the helpless and devastated French people, who needed her more than ever before. Her decision was to remain. That she might later be criticized for dealing with collaborationists and Germans did not occur to her.

They waited. The week ended with "a strange and terrible Sunday in its quiet with such terrific undercurrents." On the twenty-second, the French-German armistice was signed. By its terms, only two-fifths of the country would be left under French control, to be administered from the new capital, Vichy.

The next day, they listened to the BBC shortwave repeatedly rebroadcast Churchill's speech in which he told of hearing "with grief and amazement" of France's acceptance of terms that would leave her at the mercy of the dictators. He naturally made no mention of how much the complete withdrawal of the British army had contributed to the capitulation. They also heard one of the earliest broadcasts from London of General Charles de Gaulle, an obscure former undersecretary of war, practically unknown in his own country. The British were using him to urge the French people not directly in the line of German guns to continue the struggle.

When Hitler marched up the Champs Elysées two days later, Anne observed: "The Germans are on an 'occupying' visit . . . the nightmare is terrible." She expected two thousand additional evacuees by nightfall. By the end of the week, she had lost most of her volunteers, who had fled south to cross into Spain the moment they heard the peace terms. The displaced people would eventually be permitted to return to their homes, but Anne did not know when or under what conditions. She was forced to see the German commandant about it. He was "too polite" and assured her they were working on their own plan that would be activated the next day.

That ghastly June ended with Anne and her remaining volunteers returning to Paris. The city was a "terrible thing to see." Aside from a few German vehicles, there was not a civilian car on the streets. Little by little, some of the Parisians who had fled abroad began returning to the city, each with a different nightmare to relate, each suffering an awful weariness.

On July 2, the American embassy made an appointment for her with Otto Abetz, the new German ambassador. She donned her best uniform emblazoned with her many decorations, including three levels of the Légion d'Honneur and the Croix de Guerre. Standing almost six feet tall with iron-gray hair and the carriage of a military commander, she made an impressive appearance and managed to persuade him that feeding and resettling the refuges was in everybody's best interest: she must be permitted to continue her work. Abetz was certain there would be no problem in obtaining a laissez-passer for her, which would allow her to travel throughout occupied France. More important to the continued transportation of supplies to the ravaged area was a permit to buy gasoline from the German army. She thought the meeting was "the first good opening for [the] future."

*J*ust before Dunkirk, when the Germans crossed the Belgian frontier, and word reached the British embassy that the British commander, Viscount Gort, was contemplating withdrawing his army by sea, Sir Charles Mendl had resigned his position. He was not about to be the first English Jew left to the mercies of the Nazis.

The Mendl caravan departed from the Ritz led by a chauffeur-driven Rolls-Royce carrying Sir Charles, Elsie, and her two toy poodles dyed to match whatever color their mistress's hair might be that week. Every other inch of space was taken by luggage, which was also strapped to the top of the vehicle. The Rolls was followed by Johnnie's car, in which West and he rode along with their possessions. A Ford station wagon driven by Johnnie's manservant brought up the rear. It carried the remainder of the Mendl baggage, which not only filled the interior but was lashed to the top, rear, and sides of the wagon so that it resembled nothing so much as a moving leather mountain sown with the well-known fleurs de lis and LV monograms.

Their destination was the Spanish border, and their intention to cross Spain to Portugal, where they could board one of Pan American's Yankee

Clippers flying from Lisbon to New York. The roads south were jammed with people with the same objective of getting over the Spanish border before it was closed to refugees.

The following week, the Mendls and McMullin were among the twenty-three passengers disembarking from Pan American's "flying boat" at the La Guardia Airport Marine Terminal. West had been left behind to come by sea with the luggage. Of course, Elsie was the star attraction for the newspaper people. They marveled at the sprightliness of the simian little lady who was seventy according to her passport (the date being one of the perks of having a husband in the embassy that issued it), and closer to eighty according to her friends. She showed few vestiges of the long flight and the harrowing drive that preceded it. When asked about the report that she was the last woman out of Paris, Elsie turned serious and snapped that it was a fairy tale. She described a night she had been forced to sleep in her car. It was at a Portuguese frontier town. Hundreds of people were sleeping on the ground around the car, many of them children with little or nothing to eat. "I had plenty of money," she said, "but the other people had nothing."

By the time they reached Lisbon, she had given all of her cash away. She exclaimed: "I do hope America acts quickly now! Send planes! They are the only things that will win the war. Men don't matter so much. Planes! Planes! Planes!"

One of the reporters asked about the Villa Trianon. She replied: "Shall I tell you about my home? I'm afraid if I tell you I'll cry."

She stared at the ground for a few seconds, and as she looked up, her hand went to her lips to stifle a sob. "But it's foolish to cry for a home when so many are suffering. I didn't take a pin cushion. I left everything—collections, silver, paintings. It's really so little to lose."

At last, Anne Morgan's laissez-passer came through, along with permission to purchase 250 gallons of gasoline per week from the Germans. She was able to attempt to get her relief centers in proper condition for reopening. She also gave interviews and sent home a barrage of letters in an effort to raise money from a recalcitrant American public that had little use for the French after their surrender to the Germans. It tended to equate aid to France with aid to Germany. She could not convince her countrymen that the French were still French: they had not changed their skins since the occupation. Innocent civilians were suffering even more than they had during the war. Her organization would have to cease operations unless there was a change in American attitude. There was no way of carrying on without food and medical supplies.

Anne then went the step too far by adding: "Justice prompts the statement that the Germans are helping us right now." They were supplying the gas "without which our food trucks would be at a standstill." It was enough to start a rumor that she was a collaborationist, when, in fact, the centers were acting as safe houses for French prisoners escaping from prison camps, and the Paris office helped the nascent resistance movement transmit messages in and out of the camps. She could offer no denials without endangering the entire operation: the rumor would dog her through the war into the peace. It was accelerated that autumn when the minister of war for the government of unoccupied France, in Vichy, cited her for her "zeal and generous activity" in helping the refugees. For many, it was impossible to be commended by that government and be on the allied side. For Anne, it was expediency: she had to maintain cordial relations with Vichy in order to gain transit for supplies, refugees, and mail through its territory.

The proliferation of aid groups soon made the Germans less inclined to be cooperative. Anne had never been the easiest person to deal with, never having learned the correct posture for supplication and obdurate in her conviction of the rightness of her causes. Added to that, although they were never caught there were persistent rumors of aid to escaping allied prisoners. The Germans announced that they would work with only one American group, the American Red Cross, and if Anne wished to continue to operate in France, she would have to do so under its umbrella. September 5 was "a tragic day." She was informed that her group would no longer be permitted to work in the Aisne province.

When word came that the Germans were forcing the American Red Cross to move its operations to unoccupied France, Anne knew it was time to go home, where she could be of greater use by raising money for the prisoners of war and displaced persons. Before leaving, Anne turned over the centers, along with what supplies and funds were available, to the local townspeople who had been working with her since the start of the war.

*B*ack home, Anne felt purposeless in a world of peace and plenty and sank into a deep depression. "Everything seems very black," she wrote. "Each day seems worse than last." She found it "terribly hard to pull anything together." All of the causes to which she had devoted her life were foundering. During her absence, the AWA clubhouse had become a losing proposition and, soon after her return, changed its name to the Henry Hudson Hotel and welcomed nonmembers of both sexes.

A little over a week after her arrival, she managed to pull herself sufficiently together to go to Washington on a mission for the American Friends of France. She made the rounds of the State Department and British and Belgian embassies, stopping to lunch at the latter, where, to her extreme irritation, she discovered "the Ambassador doesn't know about his own country." The Roosevelts invited her to visit them at the White House. The president was "most sympathetic," but there was "always [the] same question" about his character. As for Eleanor, the "First Lady [was] just right."

Her days were filled. There were meetings to attend either at the AWA, or Red Cross, or AFF, and she quickly set in motion a fund-raising tour for French war relief, but deeply missed the presence of Anne Vanderbilt next door and the comfort of her gentle nature. It was not until over a month after her return that New York "seemed like home at last." Still, her restlessness persisted. No sooner did she feel settled in than she again began to agitate to be permitted to return to France. If it was impossible to work for the Red Cross, she applied for permission to resume her own group's work but neither the Germans nor the Vichy government would issue a visa to her. An eye infection lingered for three months and kept her from being too persistent. During that period, a new poodle, Dandy by name, became her greatest source of solace and pleasure.

By the time her eye was well, reports made it clear that the constraints Vichy was placing upon American volunteers would make it impossible for her to accomplish anything in France. She would better serve the cause by staying with her original plan to raise money and consciousness in the United States. Her first move was to attempt to gather contributions for food packages to be sent to the 1,500,000 French prisoners of war being held in German concentration camps. It proved difficult, as many Americans persisted in the absurd conviction that it was cowardice that had caused the French defeat, and that the army somehow deserved its fate.

Something unforeseen occurred on June 22. Instead of continuing to concentrate his entire military might on the destruction of England, Hitler turned east and invaded the Soviet Union. It meant a total reversal of mindset for Anne and her colleagues. They suddenly had Communist allies: whether the Russians had the arms and strength of purpose to withstand the Germans could not be determined. If they could hold out until winter, these ardent Francophiles could hope for a replay of what had happened to Napoleon during the fearsome Russian winter.

*N*ew York was not Elsie's town. She once had prospered there, but it never had belonged to her as it had to Bessy Marbury and, in a sense, still did. It was the only place in the world where to many people in high position Elsie remained fundamentally "Bessy's girl." She was astonished by the number of people who continued to hold her in disdain for what they considered her betrayal of Bessy. The theatrical elite, who gratefully accepted her hospitality in France, thought of her in New York in terms of Bessy and wondered how she could ever have left that vital creature for an old duffer like Sir Charles. The society of involved women—Eleanor Roosevelt, Anne Morgan, Consuelo Balsan, Daisy Harriman, Eleanor Belmont, Gertrude Vanderbilt Whitney, et alia—had lost what interest they ever had in Elsie when she opted for the life she had been living for the past two decades, while Bessy remained a vivid and admired memory.

This is not to imply New York was Elsie's Coventry. The members of café society, whom she had been entertaining for years, were eager to return the favor. New York was littered with her fellow exiles from the Riviera, Paris, and London—Somerset Maugham, Baron Alex de Rede, Elsa Maxwell, Syrie Maugham—though none of her set were political or intellectual exiles. They were more aptly described as exiles from an old-world life of comfort and luxury to a new-world life of comfort and luxury. Had there been anything deeply felt in their flight, surely Sir Charles would have gone to London, where he could have been of some service to his country at war and to his people facing a holocaust.

While deciding on her next move, Elsie rented a house in Beverly Hills for the winter and found her refuge, the safe haven for herself and her little band of exiles. She never considered it her final resting place. It was no more than the most pleasant of all available waiting rooms. There was never a thought of any eventuality other than someday returning to France and the Villa Trianon.

All of Elsie's family was very happy to be in Beverly Hills. Johnnie was a native Californian and enjoyed being back among his family and old friends. West could live anywhere so long as she could look after Elsie and have an occasional intimacy with—to everybody's amazement—a member of the opposite sex. For Sir Charles, Hollywood could more appropriately have been named Valhalla. He found nestled in the Hills of Beverly a colony so intensely English that it approached caricature and provided as clear a reflection of himself as any of Elsie's mirrors. It was primarily composed of a group of actors imported to California for roles in the highly successful Thirties American films devoted to the glories of the British Empire in its successful conquest and maintenance of great chunks of India, Africa, and the Near East. They tended to think of California as an outpost of that empire upon which the sun never set and themselves as members of the British Raj who grew increasingly more British with each kilometer they traveled away from Piccadilly Circus. Some built thatched cottages in the canyons and lunched at the Beverly Hill Hotel in plus fours and tweeds no matter how unsuitable the weather. Their contributions to Hollywood's social life included enthusiasms for croquet, lawn tennis, polo, and golf. They attempted to inculcate the attractive American boys next door with an enthusiasm for cricket but failed and had to be content with playing among themselves. Mostly, they tended to treat the natives much as the English army treated the natives of the countries in which they were stationed.

At the time the Mendls settled in Hollywood, the group included Ronald Colman, C. Aubrey Smith, Sir Cedric Hardwicke, Basil Rathbone, Cary Grant, George Sanders, Charles Laughton, and Reginald Gardner. Leslie Howard, David Niven, and Richard Greene were the only original members who went home to join their country's armed forces. The others remained bully-for-Britain to the same degree as Sir Charles but, like him, preferred to do their wartime duty serving in Hollywood. They showed their valor by playing stiff-upper-lip types in early Forties propaganda films exemplified by *Mrs. Miniver.* With his background in the diplomatic corps, Sir Charles was welcomed among them as their new chief of protocol.

*D*uring the summer months, New York City streets were jammed with restless servicemen on passes from the Navy Yard and the many training camps in the region. Anne Morgan decided to host a dance for them on Sutton Place. Many of her neighbors were out of the city for the summer, and those who were in town could hardly object. At eight o'clock on a sultry late August evening, one hundred young soldiers and sailors descended upon the wealthy enclave to be greeted by 150 young women who had been recruited from offices and shops all over Manhattan. The extra fifty had been invited on the premise that not all would come but none stayed home that evening. One of the committeewomen exclaimed: "It's the first time I ever saw that happen!" A call went out to the service centers and, within half an hour, fifty reinforcements arrived, and every young woman had a dancing partner.

The bottom of Fifty-seventh Street in front of the stately house Anne Vanderbilt had built was roped off and became a dance floor where the young people gave rowdy exhibitions of the Big Apple, Susie-Q, boogie, foxtrot, Virginia reel, and conga for an audience watching from the windows of the surrounding apartment buildings.

The front of the Morgan mansion was decorated with red, white, and blue lights. Inside, and in the garden beyond, refreshments were being served. One soldier said: "Nights can be awful low and dull in camp. A shindig like this sure is fun." Another commented a bit more wistfully: "I hope this isn't the last one of these affairs I get to."

Most of the boys agreed that the tall, white-haired old girl dishing up the chow was a doll.

*T*hat autumn, Anne relaxed with her accustomed diversions of golf, movies, and theatre with weekends at Mount Kisco, devoted to house parties with and without Malvina. Bad weather on the morning of December 7 kept her guests from going out of doors. "Then," Anne wrote, "in PM *came* the impossible news—no one can understand—no one can believe— of course, we should have expected just that."

The next day, the entire country was listening to the radio, "still trying to understand," when President Roosevelt addressed a joint session of Congress. Describing the previous day's attack on Pearl Harbor as "a date which will live in infamy," he called for a declaration of war against Japan.

Three days later, Germany and Italy declared war on the United States. Participation by the Free French was considered requisite by the United States and England, which made it easier for Anne's committee to help the French, although there was a great deal of disagreement over whether that included those French nationals still in the homeland and suffering equally at the hands of the German and Vichy governments. How aid was to be distributed in France became considerably clarified when De Gaulle called for the formation of an underground resistance army within the country.

The American entry into the war put an end to any speculation that either Elsie or Anne would be able to return to France until after either an allied invasion or a truce. One desperate hope was that victory would come as swiftly as it had after American entry into the first war. But even the most optimistic observer would have to admit that was extremely unlikely. An indeterminate length of time would have to be bided: while Anne hoped it would be constructive, Elsie hoped it would be amusing.

Anne had never admired Roosevelt and had been opposed to his running for a third term. Nevertheless, a month after the Japanese attack, Anne O'Hare McCormick and she were among those attending a meeting at the Republican Women's Club at which they resolved to forgo dissension and give their full support to the president's wartime policies. Party politics would intervene soon enough, but, for a time, it was an interval of noble gestures, a bipartisan honeymoon dowered by war.

CHAPTER FIFTY-SIX

Fannie Hurst's 1942 novel *Lonely Parade* is about the intimate friendship of three women, Charlotte Ames, Kitty Mulhane, and Sierra Baldwin, modeled respectively on Bessy, Elsie, and Anne Morgan. Not satisfied with mere invasion of the privacy of her friends, Hurst also took a sideswipe in the book's dedication: "To Charlotte Ames, Kitty Mulhane, and Sierra Baldwin who were good but not good enough." Fortunately for them, neither was she, nor was she a Radclyffe Hall, nor, aside from a deliberate similarity of titles, did she have the courage to write a *Well of Loneliness*.

In her book, Hurst described "the structure of the friendship" as "a sort of triptych, its center the spreading friarlike figure of Miss Ames, flanked by the Gothic panels of Sierra and Kitty." Lest anybody get the wrong idea, she had the Bessy character issue the disclaimer:

> "I know what they say of us, that we are ladies of strange feather who flock together. Of course, we do, huddling for warmth, but the rest of the implication is a God damned lie. At least, it's a damned lie so far as we know. It seems to me we're as normal as spinach. What I don't know about my pathology, whatever that is, doesn't bother me."

To make certain nobody got the wrong idea about her heroines, Hurst's "happy ending" had Elsie marrying J. P. Morgan! Bessy would probably have been more distressed by her client's failure as a writer than the implications of the subject. She already had said more about her intimacy with Elsie in the dedication of her memoirs than Hurst did in her whole book. Aside from striking the writer from their address books, it is doubtful that Anne or Elsie gave any thought to her book.

Once the United States entered the war, Elsie decided to settle in for the duration. She persuaded Charles to become her partner in the purchase of a house in Beverly Hills. Elsie found a red adobe house, at 1018 Benedict Canyon Drive. The neighborhood was very good. Elsie called her new home After All, the title of her memoir.

Of Elsie's family, Johnnie McMullin was the only one who was growing dissatisfied with life at After All. He was at that terrible age when he was too young to be Elsie's contemporary and too old to be one of "Mother's boys." She had begun to insist on being called "Mother" by the slew of artistic youths who fluttered around her. Somewhere, Johnnie had lost his function in Elsie's life and the purpose of his own.

In the privacy of After All, Elsie used her age in meaner ways. She was the only one with money and the one most likely to die first. Her will was the weapon with which the others were kept in line. If anybody displeased her, she simply threatened to cut them off. It worked perfectly, for it did not seem possible that this wraith who had become a parody of herself would last much longer. Johnnie could put up with Elsie's caprices but not her cruelty. He packed his things and moved out. Two years later, Johnnie McMullin died of a heart attack in his small apartment, in Beverly Hills. *The New York Times* described him as "an authority on fashion and interior decorating." It also said that he was Lady Mendl's "adopted son."

*S*he called him "Steve," and he called her "Mother." Mother was, of course, Elsie, and Steve was Ludwig Bemelmans. He was both painter and writer, and his most salient quality was sophisticated whimsy. His best work was writing and illustrating the *Madeleine* series of children's books, probably better appreciated by parents than by their offspring. A native of the Austrian Tyrol, he came to Hollywood on a wave of refugees hoping to make their fortunes in a medium to which they condescended. The producer Arthur Freed summed up his talent: "I used to call him a minor Molnar."

Elsie made Bemelmans an offer he could not refuse. She invited him to move into Johnnie's comfortable quarters, told him to feel free to use the butler as his valet, and come and go as he chose. Each recognized what was fraudulent and what was real in the other and, over the next few years, used, abused, and amused each other. It was clear to Elsie he was never going to make it in Hollywood except as a painter, and she urged her wealthy friends to buy his pictures. A measure of her affection was she never asked for a commission. He protested that he did not want to sell his works to Philistines who would not understand them. Elsie had a good enough eye to hang his drawings in her powder room and doubted there was anything in a Bemelmans beyond the comprehension of anybody smart enough to use the facilities.

The two significant "sons" in the coda to "Mother's" long life were Bemelmans and Tony Duquette, an extravagantly gifted furniture, display, and party designer who created the most talked-about settings in her Beverly Hills house. They differed in one significant aspect from the bevy of aging boys that continued to flit around Elsie until the day she died: they were both happily married to wives sufficiently accommodating to allow Elsie access to their husbands whenever it was necessary. More significantly, each man would contribute to a renown that would persist long after her death.

Five years after she died, Bemelmans was to write what purported to be a nonfiction history of his relationship with her, *To the One I Love the Best*. What he was actually attempting to do was what Patrick Dennis (Tanner) did much more successfully that same year with his book *Auntie Mame*, which was also allegedly based on true incidents. In the books, Mame Dennis and Elsie de Wolfe were both larger-than-life characters given to outrageous behavior and statements. The difference was that Mame was portrayed as a woman capable of warmth and love and drawn with affection. Bemelmans's Elsie was egomaniacal, deceitful, obsessive, and as unloving as she was unlovable. By the end of it, the reader felt the author loathed her.

In contrast to Bemelmans's betrayal of her, Duquette would prove his fidelity to his benefactress by becoming head of the Elsie de Wolfe Foundation. It was he who has been largely responsible for keeping the memory of her accomplishments from fading—as has been the case with many more innovative designers—by promoting, supervising, designing, writing, or making invaluable contributions to the stream of exhibitions, articles, and books about her work and life that have appeared regularly over the half century since her death.

*I*n 1942, Anne and Malvina gave a New Year's Eve party, in Malvina's studio, for three hundred servicemen and merchant seamen from allied and occupied nations. The highlight was recording New Year's greetings to their respective countrymen, which Anne had convinced the Office of War Information to shortwave broadcast to their homelands.

The success of the broadcasts gave her a small sense of accomplishment amid endlessly frustrating days of attempting to help a country from which she was cut off. The United States had maintained relations with Vichy France even after its official involvement in the European war. After the allies invaded North Africa, in November 1942, the Germans and Italians overran southern France, forcing a rupture in those relations. All Anne could do was provide aid and comfort to the Free French soldiers, but her strongest commitment would remain to helpless civilian victims of war rather than to the armies fighting it. During the first months of the new year, she displaced that commitment to the helpless black civilians in her own country.

During the previous year, Dr. William Allen Nielsen, president emeritus of Smith College, had recruited Anne for the National Urban League. Black soldiers came back from fighting in World War I to find no improvement in their position in their country. She felt that the injustice should not be allowed to be repeated after the current war. A Morgan, a member of her generation and class, and a Republican: it would have taken extraordinary vision for her to have selected the other great black organization, the National Association for the Advancement of Colored People, whose total dedication to the constitutional extension of complete civil rights must have sounded dangerously leftist to her. With its emphasis on extending employment opportunities and improving housing and living conditions in black ghettos, the Urban League was less threatening and more perfectly suited her approach to social change.

Anne met with the Urban League Executive Board to plan an invitational meeting, to take place at her house in March. She appended a note to each of the invitations sent to the people on her list: "Please, do not think you will be asked to make a contribution. My only hope is that your interest will be aroused in the work of the Urban League." When she was introduced at the meeting, she spoke of the awakening of her own interest and of the necessity of the League's work to the war effort as well as to the peace that would follow it.

The president of the League, William Baldwin, wrote to thank her for "providing so hospitably the opportunity to reach a new and important group of potential supporters." He praised her speech as "forthright . . . the note to challenge both the audience and the speaker." But the meeting was a failure. Of the over seven hundred invitations sent out, only seventy-two accepted, of which nine became members, including Daisy Rogers. Ann Tanneyhill, the secretary of the League's Bureau of Guidance and Placement, was touched by the naïveté of Morgan's genuine disappointment in her own people. Anne later wrote to Lester M. Granger, a member of the board:

> I am not so much concerned with our failure to "sell OPPORTU-
> NITY as I am about the seeming impossibility of enlisting the
> sympathy of what is a very important opinion-making group. It is
> my suspicion that this group is representative of a prevailing opin-
> ion among New Yorkers regarding the "Negro problem." They
> avoid worrying about it by simply ignoring it, and meantime, the
> problem grows tougher and tougher. . . .

Anne was seventy in 1943 and decided the time had come to resign from the American Woman's Association. She had guided it from its inception as the Vacation Savings Fund through the building of the clubhouse to the present time, when a woman's independence and ability to earn a good living made it unnecessary to offer her decent, inexpensive lodgings. Women were free to make their own decisions about where, how, and with whom to live. If the club was to survive, it would have to find a new direction under a younger leader.

June 6, 1944 was an "exhausting D-Day." Anne's feelings ran the gamut from exhilaration over the action and frustration over not being able to get sufficient news from the radio newscasts. The scale and success of the operation were revealed over the next few days, and there was a breathless feeling that the end of the European war was at last in sight. In July, General de Gaulle was in New York to raise funds for both his army and his country, the dreadful condition of which became more and more apparent as the liberation accelerated. His stay started with a reception at the Waldorf, which Anne found "very amusing." During the ten days he was in the city, the very tall woman and the still taller general were often together and became good friends.

The Allied push continued apace, and by August 8, Anne was saying "goodbye to Eva [Dahlgren] who is at last off to France!!!" The news of the liberation of Paris burst upon them on August 24. Anne felt the whole story, with its swiftness of execution, was unbelievable but, strangely, felt no euphoric rush. She was too aware of "trouble ahead just under the surface."

In January 1945, the Office of War Information underwrote a tour of the United States by eight French journalists, including Jean-Paul Sartre. They were free to write anything they liked about the country and its citizens. In the Paris newspaper *Figaro,* the radical Sartre launched an attack against American conservatives who for ideological reasons favored Vichy over De Gaulle. He specifically named Anne Morgan as one of them. Sartre, soon to become one of De Gaulle's severest critics, did not bother to interview Anne and heard only what he chose to hear. The daughter of the arch-villain of capitalism had dealt with Pétain during the early years of the war. That was good enough for him. The fact was that as long as the U.S. government maintained diplomatic relations with Vichy, Anne kept in contact with that government but only in order to find ways to channel aid to the destitute and starving French refugees who had fled south after the occupation.

Although many leapt to her defense, Anne said nothing. The true nature of her relationship with De Gaulle is manifest in a letter from Anne Pleven, an official in his provisional government, that arrived a month after the Sartre attack. It asked for her to do all she could for them and described the dismal conditions of both the army and the civilians. "The lack of everything is beyond description."

*S*trangely, Anne made no note either on Roosevelt's death, April 12, or on the final and complete victory in Europe, May 8. Shortly after, clearance arrived for her to sail for Europe on June 23. She made time to attend a reception at City Hall for her hero, General Dwight Eisenhower. It was only days before her departure, but she could not forgo what would remain a "marvelous, unforgettable day forever and ever."

A group of officials from other relief organizations were sailing with her, and she found the "inside battles very strong and depressing." It was not until she arrived at Blérancourt, on July 8, that her spirits began to lift. The entire village turned out to give her a rousing reception. The local officials gave a luncheon in her honor, and, sensitive to the personal sacrifices entailed in gathering that much food in that time of shortages, the workers from the other centers did not come to greet her until after the meal in order not to embarrass her hosts, who could not have afforded to feed them. This was the first meeting with their revered Miss Morgan in over four years, and once again she had not failed them. Through the auspices of AFF she had brought nine tons of equipment, including automobiles, bicycles, trucks, food, clothing, bedding, and medicine including penicillin. Not all of it was designated for the Aisne—the AFF had many other obligations—but Anne would see to it that a good share of it got there. Medical supplies were especially necessary at the dispensaries at Blérancourt and Vic-sur-Aisne, which were treating returning prisoners of war, deportees, and children suffering from malnutrition as well as tuberculosis.

At first, just being there and seeing so many old friends was enough to fill her with joy. The full scope of the devastation did not come through until she saw what remained of Tergnier, where her group had opened a new community center to deal with the crisis of feeding, housing, and ministering to the survivors. Anne would have to redouble her efforts and get still more supplies allocated to her area. A month slipped by without her noticing that it was gone. She was so busy that not a word was spared for the dropping of the atomic bomb and barely a line devoted to the Japanese surrender, on August 14, which officially ended the war.

On August 25, she took time off to join the rest of the city in celebrating the first anniversary of the liberation of Paris and spent the next month redoubling her efforts to set up the channels through which relief could be filtered to her people in the Aisne. She did not return to New York until September 29, when she disembarked in Staten Island from the troop carrier *Oregon*. On October 4, she wrote one of the last entries in the Line-A-

Day diaries she had been keeping for over forty years: "Everything looks black, too tired & worried & nervous to sleep."

*F*rom the day Paris was liberated, Elsie could think of nothing but Villa Trianon. She had to find out what they done to her beloved house and its contents. Was it repairable? Above all else, she had to get there, to see for herself. She was eighty-six years old; her heart was weak; a fall during her exercises had damaged her spine so severely that she needed a wheelchair; her hair, as thinned from years of dyeing as from age, took all the artistry of great hairdressers to prevent patches of skin from shining through; but the energy was intact, forcing those around her to place themselves in the service of one goal: the return to her house, her testament, her love.

The first report on the condition of the villa came from Cecil Beaton, who had gone out to see it directly after the Germans evacuated Versailles. His vital message to her was that "her pinch beck palace" was still standing, but it had not been completely spared. Sir Charles's magnificent wine cellar had been ransacked. A naked electric lightbulb was dangling where a magnificent rock crystal chandelier once had hung and "modern brothel-furniture" had replaced her signed eighteenth-century pieces. Beaton added bitchily that the looters had shown no interest in "a mountain of Elsie's scrapbooks" still safely lodged in a cupboard.

What Beaton did not know was that many of the best pieces, along with her paintings, had been safely stored in Paris before she left France. The bulk of the rest—tattered, faded, torn—resided in storage rooms in Versailles. Nothing was beyond repair. It awaited only her personal touch, like a magic wand, for all of her precious possessions to live happily ever after.

*I*n the summer of 1946, Anne and Elsie were both in France, each deeply involved in the restoration of their respective monuments. Anne circled the area from Normandie through the Aisne, visiting all of the installations. In addition to the centers in Vire, Tergnier, Blérancourt, and Vic, there were four public health nursing and social service centers in and around Soissons.

In August, Anne's comrades gathered at Blérancourt for what amounted to an "r and r" weekend. Some who knew her best noticed that for the first time in her life, she appeared to be overwhelmed by what remained to be done. She was not feeling up to the chore and was ready to pass the baton to Eva Dahlgren. There were still five million French civilians without homes

*L*adies and Not-So-Gentle Women

and six million acres of farmland lying fallow. Ironically, allied bombs had been responsible for more of the devastation than the enemy.

What was true all across northern France was also true, in miniature, at the Villa Trianon. Elsie was dismayed to find that American soldiers passing through had inflicted more damage than the German occupation. She knew there was not that much time left to her. Skilled in the arts of bribing, bargaining, and begging, she did not take long to have Villa Trianon restored to its former glory even in those desperate days when so many still did not roofs over their heads.

Once the work was completed, Elsie divided her time between Beverly Hills and Versailles. Part of it had to do with climate, part with her own frailty, but mostly it was because of the unequaled level of luxurious frivolity to be found in those locales. They were filled with the kind of people who amused her most and, more to the point, the kind who most appreciated her.

CHAPTER FIFTY-SEVEN ❧

Anne Morgan spent the summer of 1947 in France working on the restoration of the museum at Blérancourt. The château represented the years she had shared with the two other Annes, Dike and Vanderbilt. On July 25, she celebrated her seventy-fourth birthday there and found herself bereft of the energy that once had been so remarked upon. No longer did the strenuous rounds of golf and tennis serve as intervals of relaxation while she ran two or three large organizations at one time. Her colleagues noticed that she was slowing down. Some thought, though not aloud, that the time had come for her to retire to her delphiniums. Her last official act, before returning home that September, was to organize a "Friendship Train" that would tour France at Christmas, distributing gifts of necessities to those still in terrible want.

The first weekend in October, while resting in Mount Kisco, she suffered a severe stroke that resulted in aphasia. The country house was closed, and Anne was moved back to the city, where she was near her specialists and could begin an intensive program of therapy. When capable of understanding that something terrible had happened to her, she was told she had viral pneumonia.

Shortly after Anne became ill, the director of the National Museums of France had requested a bust or portrait of Franklin Delano Roosevelt for display at Blérancourt. Anne wanted to make the request of Mrs. Roosevelt personally but was too ill, and Daisy had to do it for her. Unfortunately, Eleanor did not own one. They were all at the Franklin Delano Roosevelt Library and government property. The best she could offer was a large colored photograph of the Salisbury portrait of FDR, which, she said, "when framed looks very nice but, of course, is not as valuable as a bust or painting."

The request prompted Eleanor to go to Blérancourt during her visit to France the following month. She wrote to Anne:

> I went out to see your Musée de Blérancourt and enjoyed going through it very much. I looked at the outside of your little house and thought it charming. The grounds are so attractive, it must be quite a sacrifice not to spend more time there.
>
> No American could see what you and your group have done for France and not be proud of your work and grateful to you for helping to preserve what is a heritage not only to France but to all those who love beauty.

By September 1949, Blérancourt had a bust of Roosevelt by Jo Davidson. The sculptor was a close friend of Malvina's, and undoubtedly made the gift at her suggestion.

*A*nne lived very well but on a fixed trust fund income. Unlike the other Morgans, she had no financial reserves, having given away every penny of excess income. New medical expenses included two-full time nurses, physicians, therapists, and drugs and caused enormous financial strains. Her nephew Harry Morgan was in charge of her financial affairs, and for a conservative Morgan banker, dipping into the capital of her trust was never an option. Funds to pay for his aunt's expenses would have to come from other sources. With Anne's permission, some of her furniture was sent to French & Co. for sale. The pieces included a daybed purchased from Elsie for which the De Wolfe provenance was offered. French could find no buyer, and the bed was returned. When questioned about it, Anne could only reply; "She [Elsie] thought it old."

When Harry Morgan went over the list of civic and cultural organizations to which his aunt belonged and contributed, he was aghast. Rarely had philanthropies consumed so large a portion of personal income. The range of cultural institutions alone included the Municipal Art Society, the English Speaking Union, the Caramoor Friends of Music, the American Craftsman's Educational Council, and the American National Theatre and Academy (ANTA). Daisy Rogers was instructed to resign from all of them in Anne's name.

By the beginning of 1948, Anne was able to recognize friends and relatives who were allowed to see her for short periods. She was also permitted to be taken for short drives. Anne always loved motor car trips. As is so often the case with stroke victims, her mind dwelled more happily in the past than the present and would go back to those happy pre–World War I days when Bessy and she tooled all over Europe for weeks on end. By the beginning of February, she had recovered sufficiently to go for long winter walks up and down Sutton Place and across Fifty-seventh Street. Daisy did not envy Mrs. Douglas and Miss Williams, the nurses who accompanied her, and who had to put up with both the freezing weather and Anne's temper, which was reviving along with her stamina and flaring up in frustration when her memory failed her.

By mid-February, she was well enough to make reservations for her return to France, sailing on April 23 on the *Oregon*. The *logis* at Blérancourt, on which Anne Vanderbilt had worked so lovingly, was reopening that summer, and she wanted to be there. Douglas and Williams would be accompanying her as would Malvina, who was eager to get back to her Paris studio for the first time since before the war. There were constant communiqués to and from Rose Dolan, who affectionately referred to Anne as "La Patronne," about what medical supplies were needed that could be brought along on the ship.

Anne either actually did or preferred to believe that her ailment was viral pneumonia. On April 8, she took time away from the preparations to drop a note to Bessie Lovett. "I feel today that I am getting the better of my particular bug, although I must say that at times the hole in my head seems only half filled."

At the last moment Anne was forced to cancel the trip. She was simply not yet up to it, and Malvina sailed alone. On the day she was to have departed, she again wrote to Bessie but gave no indication of recalling the canceled plans. "This morning, I am feeling more like a human being." She observed that it was strange to have certain memories coming back, but at least it was an indication of some progress. Her next letter stated: "I am still under the control of my objectionable virus bug as far as forgetting names and my judgment of things." However, her doctor and nurses were assuring her, she was "getting better in many ways."

Now that she was so improved and getting out more often, climbing the stairs to her bedroom a few times a day was proving a bit of a problem. When May brought with it a burst of spring, the Sutton Place house was leased to Arthur Amory Houghton, the president of Steuben Glass, and the house in Mount Kisco was reopened. The chauffeur set up a miniature golf course on the lawn to enable Anne to have some exercise. Her therapist had introduced her to ceramics, which was involving and challenging.

A letter to her sister Juliet in the middle of the month showed great progress in her cognitive powers. She had read Edith Hamilton's *Witness to the Truth* and been impressed by the eighty-one-year-old writer's knowledge of Greece and the Bible. Admitting her own ignorance about "that particular Greek philosopher," she asked what Juliet knew about Socrates. "Incidentally, I am wondering if you ever read our famous great grandfather's sermons and whether he ever alluded to Socrates' teachings which, five hundred years before Christ, seem so amazingly like His."

Slightly more than a month after her sailing on the *Oregon* was aborted, Anne and her nurses were able to depart aboard the *De Grasse*. The country house was rented to help to pay for the trip. In Paris, she checked into the Elysée Park, where her French physician, Dr. Bayon, called to examine her and found her in good physical condition, although he noted the lapses in orientation and memory. Bayon consulted with her New York physician, Dr. Coffin, and they deemed it the wiser course of action to curtail her activities and keep her in Blérancourt for the summer.

In July, Anne suffered a second and more serious stroke. She had to be kept at Blérancourt not only because of her condition but because, with both of her houses leased, she had no place else to go. There was some talk of taking the suites that Anne Vanderbilt and she had occupied at the Henry Hudson Hotel when it was the AWA clubhouse, but it was decided that a hotel could not provide the proper facilities for her.

An old friend, Sally Lockwood, often came out from Paris to see her and would report to Daisy Rogers on her condition. Anne had withdrawn into her own private world, where she was setting up an organization for world peace and to alleviate hunger and poverty. Lockwood wrote: "She seems to have pretty much passed the stage when she *knew* she was ill and was tormented by it and is busy now comparatively happy working on her new committees (imaginary) which of course change from day to day. She has moments of surprising clarity."

Miss Williams was far more concerned about Anne's other interest. In her opinion, she had to be gotten away from the ceramics, which was becoming a "fobia."

The tenants were leaving the Mount Kisco house at the end of August, and Anne was able to sail for home on the *De Grasse* at the beginning of September. Her name was kept off the passenger list. She was confused, bloated, and hesitant in speech. None of her party took meals in the dining room nor did any appear in the public areas, where they might be engaged in conversation by other passengers. When they arrived in New York, on September 10, all requests for interviews were declined. Anne made a supreme effort to walk to the pier elevator under her own power. She entered a waiting limousine that whisked her off to Mount Kisco.

Within a week of settling in at Mount Kisco, Anne had a third stroke. The doctors offered little hope of any real recovery. Houghton renewed his lease, with an option to buy, on the Sutton Place house, and Anne was confined to the country under the care of her nurses. Complete rest was prescribed with no discussions permitted of any of the things that were most meaningful to her. Her butler, Peacock, was in the employ of the Houghtons. On his days off, he faithfully took the train to Mount Kisco to spend the afternoons with Anne, giving her all the latest neighborhood gossip and reassuring her that the townhouse was being maintained in tip-top condition.

For Thanksgiving Day, not knowing whether Anne could comprehend what was being said, Bessie Lovett felt compelled to write before it was too late for words:

> This is just a line, dearest Anne, to tell you again what you already know, how much you have meant to me for many years. Without your friendship, my life would have been empty of so many joys, so much fun and such a deep understanding friendship.
>
> So on this Thanksgiving, when one remembers past happiness, I think of you always.

$\mathcal{E}$lsie's life was in decline. She did manage to make it back and forth from California one more time, but she was dying. She knew it, and so did everybody around her. The public Elsie might have been a fabricator who would deliberately set herself up for caricature if that was the only way to be talked about: the private Elsie was a courageous realist who faced death with the same panache with which she had faced life. She was going. It was time. The last few years had been too filled with pain. But she had to die as she had lived. Nothing haphazard. There had to be style, and she orchestrated the details of her funeral with the same punctilio with which she had decorated a room. Edna Chase, who understood Elsie better than most, summed her up during those last years of her life:

> Entertaining was the breath of life to Elsie, and she did it superlatively well. I don't suppose you could have called her a noble character, but she had her generosities. . . . She was not an intellectual

herself ... but through her salons passed many of the political and literary and artistic figures of her day.

On June 8, 1950, Bernard Berenson came to see her at Villa Trianon. It had been over thirty years since he had last visited, and except for the garden, he found the place unrecognizable—added to, refurbished, if anything more exquisite than ever. Himself eighty-five and repelled by ugliness and intimations of mortality, he never revealed what prompted him to call. He obviously did not know that Anne Morgan was still alive and thought that of the "Trinity" who used to entertain him there, only Elsie still "surexists"—a word that has no meaning except to reveal how unnerved this precise man was. It is as if he had originally written "survives," and like the pentimento familiar to him in painting, it appeared from under the "exists" he wrote over it. It is almost as if he felt that the fact of her still *being* was somehow more remarkable than mere survival.

Berenson viewed her with an amalgam of fascination and revulsion. She was "scarcely alive, a skeleton with a head fantastically dressed up, a pair of dark eyes into which all life has retreated and concentrated, as if for a last, a supreme effort." One could almost see him dance away as this woman, with whom he once flirted so deliciously, suddenly seemed "wild with excitement" to embrace him.

In their last moments together, Berenson's vanity overtook his memory, as he fallaciously recalled that Bessy, Elsie, and Anne had taken him up because they expected he would "shed reflected glory on them." In truth, it was they who had introduced him into a glittering world that ran the gamut from Henry Adams to Marie Lloyd. It was he who cadged invitations to holiday in the supreme comfort and amusement of Villa Trianon, who begged Elsie to take his wife shopping so that she might be presentable to the kind of society he met in Versailles, and who packed her off for cures with Bessy and Anne, hoping she might reduce.

Within a week of Berenson's visit, Elsie took to her bed, too enfeebled any longer to make the effort. On June 30, she was in such agonizing pain that the doctors prescribed morphine and said she could not live for more than another forty-eight hours. She had been ready to die, but perhaps it was the drugs that reopened that portion of her subconscious that still wanted to live. Three days later, she said with perfect clarity: *"Je ne veux pas mourir—je ne veux pas m'en aller."* She lingered for another week in a drugged, painless demi-world and finally died on July 12. As per her own instructions, she was cremated without a funeral service. Sir Charles, a gentleman to the end, purchased the most expensive white marble urn available, in which her ashes were conveyed to a columbarium at the Père Lachaise cemetery.

The amount Elsie ultimately left varied between $1,000,000 and $2,500,000. In her will there was a substantial sum left to the Elsie de Wolfe Foundation, which she already had established to offer scholarships to study abroad to Parsons School students, an income of ten thousand dollars a year to Sir Charles with the capital going to the foundation once he died, and the bulk of her estate to Hilda West. In 1935, she had stated that everything would go to her husband. What happened in the intervening years and what influences might have come into play, nobody will ever know. She did once say, only half in jest, that her only remaining ambition was "to live one day longer than Charles."

If Mendl was bitter, he never showed it. He was not the fool he enjoyed playing and knew Elsie well enough to have observed: "As her generosity is limitless, so is her avarice."

When Mendl died in 1958, he was cremated. His ashes were to be placed in an urn to rest beside those of Elsie. When the urn was brought to Père Lachaise, no sign was found of Elsie's remains. Nobody had bothered to pay the annual cemetery rental, and they had been disposed of—where, nobody knew.

Her authentic remains were not completely lost until Weiller sent the contents of Villa Trianon to auction in 1981, for they were more Elsie de Wolfe than anything to be found in a crypt. As for that beloved house, the joyous, maddening essence of her had departed long before. In 1959, Noel Coward had driven out to see the villa for a last time. It was "a painful experience." Most of her things remained but had been subjected to the mildew of the damp cold. A block of flats had gone up just beyond the garden, shutting out the view. In the old photograph albums he found ghosts of his younger self and of so many fiends who had passed away. "I blew a gentle and loving kiss to Elsie over the years. . . . How she would have loathed to see her *objets* left to die so slowly and so coldly."

$\mathscr{C}$ODA $\mathscr{R}$

The last years of Anne Morgan's life were spent organizing her imaginary peace organization and enlisting as officers in it those few friends she was strong enough to see. Her only recreation was ceramics, which was limited to two days a week because of a tendency to become compulsive.

Many people thought she had already died, and there was a good deal of surprise at the front-page headlines in newspapers across the United States and in France announcing her death on January 29, 1952, at her home in Mount Kisco. The funeral services were held in St. George's, in Stuyvesant Square, where a respectable number of her colleagues and friends attended her obsequies. As had been the case with Elsie, Anne's largest single bequest went to her secretary.

$\mathscr{T}$wo weeks later, a large number of Anne's French and American friends gathered in Blérancourt for a religious ceremony in her memory, conducted by the Bishop of Soissons in the small village church. It was followed by a cortege to the château. Paul Ribeyre, the French minister of health, said: "Miss Morgan will long live in the hearts of those who knew her here. May this simple ceremony prove that she will always retain the title of ambassadress of good will as she was regarded by the French nation."

On March 27, the nation did acknowledge this by dedicating a marble plaque to her in the Court of Honor, near Napoleon's tomb, in the Hôtel des Invalides. It recalled her services to French soldiers and civilians during and between the two wars. It also mentioned her donation to France of the château of Blérancourt, the National Museum of French–United States Friendship. It was the French equivalent of immortality.

$\mathcal{S}$OURCES ℘

Académie Française, Paris

Archbishop Corrigan Memorial Library

Archives of American Art

Association of the Bar of the City of New York

Beineke Library, Yale University

Berg Collection of the New York Public Library

Bibliothèque Nationale, Paris

Bobst Library, New York University

British Library, London

Buffalo and Erie Historical Society

Butler Library, Columbia University

Catholic Archdiocese of New York

Century Club Library

Church of the Holy Rosary

City of New York Municipal Archives

Columbia University Oral Histories

Cooper Union Library

Cooper-Hewitt Museum Library

Elsie de Wolfe Foundation

Fales Library, New York University

Franklin Delano Roosevelt Library, Hyde Park, New York

Frick Collection Library

Harvard Theatre Collection

Houghton Library, Harvard

Humanities Research Center, University of Texas Library

Knights of Columbus, New Haven

Library of Congress

Library of the Boston Atheneum

Lilley Library, University of Indiana

Lincoln Center Library of the Performing Arts

Massachusetts Historical Society

Metropolitan Museum of Art Library

Miami Public Library

Ministère de la Culture et de la Communication, France

Musée des Arts Decoratifs, Paris

Musée National de la Cooperation Franco-Americaine, Blérancourt

Museum of the City of New York Archives

National Academy of Design

National Register of Archives, London

Newport Historical Society

New York City Public Library

New-York Historical Society Library

New York School of Interior Design

New York State Archives

New York State Library

Paley Library, Temple University

Pelletier Library, Allegheny College

Pierpont Morgan Library, New York

Princeton Library, Princeton University

Shubert Archives

Society for the Preservation of New England Antiquities

Theatre Collection at Lincoln Center Library

Trinity Church Parish Archives, New York City

Sources

University Club Library, New York City

University of Pennsylvania Library

Villa I Tatti, Florence

Vizcaya Collection, Miami

William Andrews Clark Library, University of California

William E. Perkins Library, Duke University

$\mathcal{N}$OTES ॐ

Notes Code

AA	Elsie de Wolfe, *After All*.
FDRL	Franklin Delano Roosevelt Library.
FPTP	Mrs. Borden J. Harriman, *From Petticoats to Pinafores*.
KLGA	Elizabeth Drexel Lehr, *King Lehr and the Golden Age*.
LAD	Anne Morgan, *Line-A-Day*.
LHA	Henry Adams, *The Letters of Henry Adams*.
MCB	Elisabeth Marbury, *My Crystal Ball*.
NYHS	New-York Historical Society.
RBL	James Brown Scott, *Robert Bacon: His Life and Letters*.
SPNEA	Society for the Preservation of New England Antiquities.
TAII	Cora Brown-Potter, *The Age of Innocence and I*.
TGTG	Consuelo Vanderbilt Balsan, *The Glitter and the Gold*.
TNYT	*The New York Times*.
TSOAS	Dixon Wecter, *The Saga of American Society*.
TT	*Town Topics*.

Chapter One

p. 2: " . . . *first American McCoun . . . white slave*": Henry Hoff, *Genealogies of Long Is-land Families*.

p. 2: " . . . *grassy way-sides.*": Henry James, *Washington Square*.

p. 4: *descent from King Edward III*: Meredith B. Caskett, Jr., *The English Ancestry of Anne Marbury Hutchinson and Catherine Marbury Scott*.

p. 4: *Comedy in British Museum*: Ibid.

p. 6: " . . . *cowardice, gluttony, and mendacity*": MCB

p. 6: "*strongest passion*": Ibid.

p. 6: "*at one fell swoop*": Ibid.

p. 7: " . . . *truthful through fear*": Ibid.

p. 7: "*Hatred replaced love . . .*": Ibid.

p. 7: *Pro-Union letter:* Grant Wilson, *The Memorial History of New York.*

p. 8: *"Copperhead":* George Strong Templeton, *The Diary of George Strong Templeton.*

p. 8: *"They were packed . . . the capitalists.":* Lloyd Morris, *Incredible New York: High Life and Low Life, 1850–1950.*

p. 9: *"the awful rebels . . . every one.":* MCB.

p. 9: *" . . . other classics.":* Ibid.

p. 10: *" . . . lawn tennis, croquet, and baseball . . .":* Carole Klein, *Gramercy Park.*

p. 12: *"I can recall the joy . . . abounded.":* MCB.

p. 12: *"His livestock . . . crops and fruit trees.":* Ibid.

Chapter Two

p. 17: *"She was not pretty . . . to know.":* AA.

p. 17: *"It's so ugly!":* Ibid.

p. 17: *" . . . poignancy in appreciation.":* Ibid.

p. 17: *" . . . Longfellow's* Evangeline.*":* Ibid.

p. 18: *"Vincit qui patitur":* Galbraith B. Perry, *Charles D'Wolf of Guadeloupe.*

p. 18: *Noel Coward:* Graham Payne and Sheridan Morley, *The Noel Coward Diaries.*

p. 18: *"Baffling charm . . . resistance.":* AA.

p. 19: *"Thrifty . . . solid dimensions.":* Ibid.

p. 19: *"[Georgiana's] chastening.":* Ibid.

p. 19: *"thrifty and practical . . . did securely.":* Ibid.

p. 20: *" . . . I'm a ruined man.":* Ibid.

p. 20: *" . . . teeth were your only decent feature.":* Ibid.

p. 22: *"barometer of the family fortunes . . .":* Ibid.

p. 23: *"In the Valley of the Grand Pré . . . sky.":* Ibid.

p. 23: *"something more than they are today.":* Ibid.

Chapter Three

p. 25: *"to tour Europe . . . never digested.":* MCB.

p. 26: *"the queen and her prime minister":* TSOAS.

p. 27: *" . . . true a gentleman as forty.":* Ward McAllister, *Society as I Have Found It.*

pp. 27–28: *"Why there are . . . editor, artists, and the like.":* Ibid.

p. 28: *"the Bohemian set . . . no brains.":* TSOAS.

p. 28: *" . . . room on the hearth.":* MCB.

p. 28: *" . . . one evening's entertainment?":* Ibid.

p. 29: *"Hostesses . . . fails to fill.":* Ibid.

p. 29: *"divine discontent.":* Ibid.

p. 29: *"She was enormous and amusing . . . outrageous.":* Russell Lynes, *More than Meets the Eye.*

p. 30: *"In order that females . . . employment.":* Ibid.

p. 32: *"fascinating gentleman . . . appearance.":* MCB.

pp. 33–34: *"friendship . . . ambitious publicity.":* William Rounsville Alger, *The Friendship of Women.*

p. 34: *"In the mid- to late eighteenth century . . . valley.":* Ibid.

p. 37: *"I have not said to you . . . loves you so dearly.":* Cited in Carroll Smith-Rosenberg, *Disorderly Conduct.*

p. 37: *"Imagine yourself kissed a dozen times . . . separated.":* Ibid.

p. 38: *"as wives do love . . . for life.":* Ibid.

p. 38: " . . . *the sight of you?*": Ibid.

p. 38: "*essence of you which is like perfume.*": Ibid.

Chapter Four

pp. 39–40: "*It was her habit . . . seen in Paris.*": Edith Wharton, *The Age of Innocence.*

p. 41: "*the rich Englishman.*": George Kennan, *E. H. Harriman, A Biography, Vol. 1.*

p. 42: "*a beautiful soothing voice . . . lovely face.*": FPTP.

p. 46: "*One evening . . . and to him.*": MCB.

Chapter Five

p. 49: " . . . *an Episcopalian sense of sin.*": Andrew Sinclair, *Corsair.*

p. 52: "*When the angels of God . . . Morgan partners.*": Stanley Jackson, *J.P. Morgan.*

p. 52: "*Bob Bacon . . . handsome.*": RBL.

p. 52: "*He was . . . at its best.*": Ibid.

p. 52: "*Mr. Morgan . . . him near always.*": Ibid.

p. 52: " . . . *love you to rejoice in.*": Ibid.

p. 54: " . . . *much richer, to say nothing of more powerful.*": Author's interview of Mabel Satterlee Ingalls.

p. 55: "*Something better . . . fool anyway.*": KLGA.

p. 56: " . . . *Do let her out.*": FPTP.

p. 57: " . . . *medieval steel-stays.*": Ibid.

p. 57: "*Anglo-Saxon Saint George.*": Stanley Jackson, *J.P. Morgan.*

p. 58: " . . . *passed from man to man.*": W.S. Rainsford, *The Story of a Varied Life.*

p. 58: "*The dangerous men . . . quite allow.*": Ibid.

Chapter Six

p. 61: "*It is so true . . . the dear image.*": Margaret Fuller, *Woman in the Nineteenth Century.*

p. 61: " . . . *so common in the New England.*": Cited by Leon Edel in *Henry James.*

p. 62: "*rather austere and frightening.*": MCB.

p. 62: " . . . *wonderful eyes.*": Ibid.

p. 62: " . . . *colorless and unconvincing.*": Ibid.

p. 63: " . . . *who was quite so lovely.*": Ibid.

p. 64: " . . . *an individual bank account.*": Ibid.

p. 65: " . . . *that ever came my way.*": Ibid.

Chapter Seven

p. 66: " . . . *first sovereign of whom this can be said.*": Archibald Hannibal Charteris, *Woman's Work in the Church.*

p. 66: "*rectory was cold and gloomy.*": AA.

p. 66: "*Grecian in style.*": Dr. Duncan Campbell, *Collected Letters,* University of Edinburgh Library.

p. 66: " . . . *a remote heaven.*": AA.

p. 66: " . . . *contend in our day.*": *Woman's Work in the Church.*

p. 67: " . . . *a good number of students . . .*": *Collected Letters.*

p. 67: " . . . *without an effort.*": Ibid.

p. 67: " . . . *a romantic hero.*": AA.

p. 67: " . . . *did not come to his aid.*": *Woman's Work in the Church.*

p. 68: " . . . *a ruined woman.*": AA.

p. 68: "*kid gloves of different lengths.*": Ibid.

p. 68: "*Life began.*": Ibid.

p. 69: " . . . *never be ugly again!*": Ibid.

p. 70: " . . . *attractive if it kills you.*": Ibid.

Chapter Eight

p. 73: "*the end of World War II.*": *Valentine's Manual.*

p. 77: " . . . *what was lost in space.*": Tennessee Williams, *The Glass Menagerie.* (New Directions, New York, 1945).

Chapter Nine

p. 80: " . . . *we began our rehearsals.*": Rita Lawrence, *Amateurs and Actors.*

p. 81: "*Even an objet d'art.*": Related to the author in an interview with Robert Moyer.

p. 81: "*equaled the sum of both.*": TAII.

p. 81: " . . . *fashionable and exclusive club.*": Ibid.

p. 81: " . . . *it's an inspiration.*": Ibid.

p. 82: " . . . *Who in the Four Hundred.*": Ibid.

p. 82: " . . . *Tuxedo Club went for nothing.*": Ibid.

p. 83: "*It was at Tuxedo . . . society.*": AA.

p. 85: " . . . *in demand for private theatricals.*": Ibid.

Chapter Ten

p. 86: " . . . *train stations than homes.*": Robert B. King, *The Vanderbilt Homes.*

p. 87: " . . . *to design the extension.*": Ibid.

p. 87: " . . . *allow him to walk upon them.*": David Sinclair, *Dynasty.*

Chapter Eleven

p. 92: " . . . *under their dimpled chins.*": *The Brooklyn Eagle,* February 18, 1888.

p. 92: " . . . *Stradivarius on her next birthday.*": TT, February 23, 1888.

p. 92: " . . . *you know what charity covers.*": *New York Press,* February 26, 1888.

p. 93: " . . . *place in the Lyceum.*": Ibid.

p. 93: " . . . *endlessly energetic.*": *The Brooklyn Eagle,* February 26, 1888.

p. 93: " . . . *of doing so.*": Ibid.

pp. 93–94: " . . . *Mrs. Arthur M. Dodge.*": Elisabeth Marbury, *Manners.*

p. 94: " . . . *of society and fashion.*": Ibid.

p. 94: *Headings in Manner's:* Ibid.

p. 96: " . . . *of all the great cotillion.*": Moran Tudbury, *Ward McAllister.*

p. 96: " . . . *big or little, young or old.*": Ibid.

pp. 96–97: " . . . *he got very angry.*": Ibid.

p. 97: " . . . *That is all.*": Ibid.

Chapter Twelve

p. 99: " . . . *you have sometimes found out.*": Ron Chernow, *The House of Morgan.*

pp. 99–100: " . . . *taken by my parents to a ball . . .*": Edith Wharton, *A Backward Glance.*

p. 100: " . . . *with Anne Morgan.*": Clarence Barron, *They Told Barron.* Grace Bigelow was the daughter of John Bigelow, the editor of the *New York Post.* Barron was the publisher of the *Wall Street Journal.*

Chapter Thirteen

p. 102: *"failed . . . opportunity.":* Edith Wharton, *The House of Mirth.*

p. 104: *"fast becoming an American city.":* Leon Edel, *Henry James.*

p. 106: *" . . . in long skirts and picture hats.":* Cleveland Amory, *The Last Resorts.*

p. 106: *"a devotion . . . forty years.":* AA.

p. 106: *" . . . grace in the world.":* MCB.

p. 107: *"She's no star to me.":* Ibid.

p. 108: *"Chere amie . . . cordially.":* Alice Lawrence papers. Butler Library, Columbia University.

p. 109: *"Everybody . . . money comes from.":* TT, July 18, 1888.

Chapter Fourteen

p. 109: *"I owe much . . . Presbyterian Church.":* MCB.

pp. 109–110: *"I have . . . soul's best lubricant.":* Ibid.

p. 111: *"inclined [Emma's] wisdom":* Ibid.

p. 111: *"a respect . . . have been denied.":* Ibid.

p. 111: *"Through Emma Lazarus . . . people.":* Ibid.

p. 113: *"I liked . . . that of the sculptor.":* Cited by L.E. Jacob in *The World of Emma Lazarus.*

p. 113: *"Converted Jews . . . purchased.":* Ibid.

p. 113: *"heard . . . about the stage.":* MCB.

p. 114: *"giving an effect . . . New York theatres":* George C.D. Odell, "Annals of the New York Stage," TNYT, January 25, 1903.

p. 115: *"My clients . . . work all over.":* MCB.

p. 116: *"private secretary . . . business agent.":* Ibid.

p. 116: *"In those . . . interstate laws.":* The Lippincott letter is in the B.J. Wendell bequest in the Princeton University library.

p. 117: *Bessy's letter to J.B. Lippincott & Co.:* Ibid.

Chapter Fifteen

p. 119: *"tempestuous voyage, cold and dreary":* MCB.

p. 119: *"Exhilarated . . . mine.":* Ibid.

p. 120: *"meagre [sic] . . . classroom.":* Ibid.

p. 120: *"is an essential in business.":* Ibid.

p. 121: *"a rather conspicuous American stage.":* Ibid.

p. 121: *"perfectly cool and collected.":* Ibid.

p. 122: *"Miss Davenport . . . her productions.":* Ibid.

p. 123: *"mental machinery . . . top speed.":* MCB.

p. 123: *"I knew . . . battle was won.":* Ibid.

p. 125: *"The tender firm . . . Miss Marbury.":* TT, June 19, 1892.

p. 126: *"and I very much . . . ourselves.":* MCB.

p. 126: *"flat so . . . hill-climbing.":* Ibid.

p. 126: *"the hot dusty roads . . . holiday.":* Ibid.

p. 126: *"if you could dignify . . . food.":* Ibid.

p. 126: *"And many a merry outing . . .":* Ibid.

p. 127: *"an enviable . . . amateur actress.":* TNYT, September 26, 1892.

Chapter Sixteen

p. 129: *"His dislike of ostentation . . . him."*: B.A. Gould, *A Memoir of Lewis Morris Rutherfurd, 1816–1892.*

p. 129: *"I'll grant you . . ."*: Edith Wharton, *A Backward Glance.*

p. 130: *"I have heard . . . affairs."*: NYHS. The Rutherford Stuyvesant papers.

p. 130: *"Mrs. Sands . . . family circle."*: Ibid.

p. 131: *"Dear Governor . . . needed."*: Ibid.

p. 131: *"It is nice . . . have it."*: Ibid.

p. 131: *"What wonderful long walks . . . exercise."*: Ibid.

p. 133: *"Please . . . letter."*: Ibid.

Chapter Seventeen

p. 135: *"Of course . . . having talked."*: MCB.

p. 136: *"a prestige beyond words."*: Ibid.

p. 136: *"How I pity you . . . sentiment."*: Ibid.

p. 137: *"Miss Elisabeth Marbury . . . luggage."*: TNYT, August 2, 1891.

p. 137: *"There we were . . . lease is signed."*: AA.

p. 139: *"The success of this drama . . ."*: MCB.

p. 139: *"most generous with me . . . promise."*: AA.

p. 140: *"an error . . . make."*: TNYT, October 14, 1891.

p. 140: *"decidedly limited."*: *Dramatic Mirror,* October 15, 1891.

p. 140: *"for my gratitude . . . for money."*: AA.

p. 142: *"His characterizations . . . concerned."*: MCB.

p. 142: *"A thousand pounds!"*: Richard Ellmann, *Oscar Wilde.*

p. 143: *"his wit scintillated . . ."*: MCB.

p. 144: *"She was always more . . . scripts."*: George Middleton, *These Things Are Mine.*

p. 144: *"With many thanks . . . admirer."*: This letter is in the portion of Wilde's correspondence at UCLA.

p. 144: *"Hope you will be able . . . very good."*: *The Selected Letters of Oscar Wilde,* edited by Rupert Hart-Davis.

p. 144: *"Have wired . . . Wolfe."*: AA.

p. 145: *"an invigorating antipathy."*: George Bernard Shaw, *The Collected Letters of . . . Vol. I.*

p. 147: *"the faintest cause for complaint."*: Ibid.

p. 147: *"I always make my own contracts."*: Ibid.

p. 148: *"This limits . . . good exchange."*: Ibid.

p. 148: *"If you don't like . . . through her."*: Ibid.

p. 148: *"Candida is . . . money would fly somehow."*: Ibid.

p. 148: *"I still play . . . for the part."*: Ibid.

pp. 148–149: *"I couldn't have made love . . . chins."*: Ibid.

p. 149: *"You're a new woman . . . Ibsen."*: Ibid.

p. 149: *"Since you insist . . . manuscript."*: Ibid.

p. 149: *"Offer declined . . . Achurch."*: Ibid.

p. 149: *"quite a foot broader . . ."*: Ibid.

pp. 149–150: *"Rapacious Elisabeth Marbury . . . public."*: MCB.

Chapter Eighteen

p. 152: *Bessy's room:* AA. She may have intended the double entendre. At the time Elsie wrote this, the word "gay" was in parlance in homosexual circles but, at that point, referred only to lesbians.

p. 152: *"Special attention . . . test of time.":* Ibid.

p. 153: *"You never know . . . good time.":* W.A. Swanberg, *Whitney Father, Whitney Heiress.*

p. 153: *"They [Bessy and Elsie] . . . brilliant talk.":* Lloyd Morris, *Incredible New York.*

p. 153: *"society was so snobbish . . . society.":* Geoffrey T. Hellman, *Mrs. De Peyster's Parties and Other Lively Stories from The New Yorker.* (Macmillan, New York, 1963.)

p. 153: *"there is no profession . . . for women.":* Candace Wheeler, *Interior Decorating as a Profession for Women.*

Chapter Nineteen

p. 155: *"the beautiful Daisy White.":* TGTG.

p. 155: *"an equerry than an equal.":* Ibid.

p. 156: *"As Lewis says . . . Van Rensselaers.":* Stuyvesant Papers.

p. 157: *"by breeding and temper. . . society.":* TT, January 11, 1900.

p. 157: *"few personal qualifications . . . hostesses.":* Ibid.

p. 157: *"the literary school . . . priestesses.":* Ibid.

p. 157: *" . . . always coming and going.":* Ibid.

Chapter Twenty

p. 159: *"Editorial writers . . . Jupiter.":* Ron Chernow, *House of Morgan.*

p. 159: *"I'll walk with you . . . loan.":* J.P. Morgan.

p. 161: *"All I really need . . . cemetery.":* Ibid.

p. 162: *"the knots . . . over my head.":* TNYT, June 11, 1992.

Chapter Twenty-One

p. 163: *"to keep . . . desperation.":* Russell Lynes, *More Than Meets the Eye.*

p. 164: *"A bonbonmiere . . . daintiness.":* Henry James.

p. 164: *" . . . earth can dislodge them.":* SPNEA. Letter from Wharton to Codman.

p. 164: *" . . . forbidding coldness of manner.":* AA.

p. 164: *" . . . to dine with me.":* Ibid.

p. 164: *"fat and vulgar.":* SPNEA. Codman letters.

p. 164: *"the brilliant coterie . . . hearth.":* AA.

p. 164: *"I went to see the Marbury salon.":* LHA, letter to Elizabeth Cameron. January 28, 1901. Marbury had hired Adams to translate a French play. Crawford's play, *Francesca de Rimini* would be produced in New York and later in Paris with Sarah Bernhardt. Adams mistakenly thinks de Wolfe is Jewish.

p. 166: *"awfully like a school marm.":* SPNEA. Codman letters.

p. 166: *"making so much money . . .":* Ibid.

p. 166: *"might as well . . . children.":* Ibid.

p. 166: *"too frivolous . . . smart people.":* Ibid.

p. 166: *"Annie Morgan . . . went off well.":* Ibid. The play was *The Man of Genius.* It never got beyond rehearsals.

p. 166: *"the usual embassy people.":* LHA. The quotes in this paragraph come from a letter Adams wrote to Elizabeth Cameron on May 16, 1902.

p. 167: *"It takes a Yankee . . ."*: J.P. Morgan.

p. 167: *"Come now, ye rich . . . resist you."*: TNYT, April 23, 1903.

p. 167: *"Very likely, Andrew."*: J.P. Morgan.

p. 169: *"My God . . . Venus de Milo with arms."*: Diana Forbes-Robertson, *My Aunt Maxine.*

p. 169: *"Of course you're beautiful."*: Ibid.

p. 169: *"the Honorable George Keppel . . ."*: Ibid.

p. 169: *"If Maxine had been a man . . ."*: Ibid.

p. 170: *"Why, you men in Wall Street . . . "*: J.P. Morgan.

p. 171: *"I like it here"*: Ron Chernow, *House of Morgan.*

p. 171: *"He had the cabins."*: Diana Forbes-Robertson, *My Aunt Maxine.*

p. 171: *"The only interest . . ."*: TNYT, August 26, 1908.

p. 172: *"Seems to me the Morgans . . ."*: *New York World,* October 18, 1903.

p. 173: *"Colorado salutes New York."*: Ibid.

p. 173: *"I didn't have any buck fever."*: Ibid.

Chapter Twenty-Two

p. 174: *"She invented the maternal . . ."*: *Metropolitan Magazine.* February 1911.

p. 174: *"associated with Miss Elisabeth."*: TNYT, January 18, 1918.

p. 175: *"The play is all right . . ."*: MCB.

p. 175: *"Oh, that would be fine."*: Ibid.

p. 177: *"Whichever way I looked at it."*: AA.

p. 178: *"The scenic setting . . ."*: TNYT, October 26, 1898.

p. 180: *"Why don't you put on a loose . . ."*: Elizabeth Robins letters, Bobst Library, New York University.

p. 180: *"No woman would do that."*: Frank Harris, *Oscar Wilde: His Life and Confessions.*

p. 180: *"To Oscar Wilde posing as a . . ."*: Ibid.

p. 181: *"If this is how Her Majesty . . ."*: Michael MacLiammoir, *The Importance of Being Oscar.* A one-man show in which the author appeared as Wilde. It opened in New York on March 14, 1961, at the Lyceum Theater.

p. 182: *"had funds . . . debts"*: Frank Harris, *Oscar Wilde.*

p. 182: *"to a sneaking disappointment . . ."*: MCB.

p. 183: *"As I read it . . . existence."*: Ibid.

p. 183: *"There is in New York . . ."*: *The Collected Letters of Oscar Wilde.*

p. 183: *"I fear I have built air castles."*: Ibid.

p. 183: *"Do send a copy at once . . ."*: Ibid.

p. 184: *"As regards to America . . ."*: Ibid.

p. 184: *"Half of the success of Marie . . ."*: Ibid. Marie Corelli was a best-selling novelist.

p. 184: *"Nobody here seems to feel . . ."*: William Andrews Clark collection. University of California.

p. 185: *"he reigned supreme . . ."*: MCB.

p. 186: *"If you can't write your play . . ."*: Frank Harris, *Oscar Wilde.*

p. 187: *"You can see I am asking you . . ."*: The Clark collection.

p. 187: *"It is outrageous . . ."*: *The Collected Letters of Oscar Wilde.*

p. 187: *"You have not only stolen my play."*: Ibid.

p. 187: *"Frank has deprived me of . . ."*: Ibid.

p. 187: *"The contrast was appalling."*: MCB.

p. 187: *"When I first came here . . ."*: The Importance of Being Earnest.
p. 188: *"incessant innuendoes . . ."*: MCB.
p. 188: *"Knowing as I did . . ."*: Ibid.
p. 188: *"It was Wilde's egotism . . ."*: Ibid.
p. 189: *"until the day . . ."*: Ibid.
p. 189: *"Much of my moral obliquity . . ."*: Frank Harris, *Oscar Wilde*.
p. 189: *"He was never able to speak . . ."*: Ibid.
p. 189: *"Catholicism is the only religion . . ."*: Ibid.

Chapter Twenty-Three

p. 192: *"You are not a modern woman . . ."*: AA
p. 193: *"Miss Marbury is magnificently . . ."*: LHA. By the summer of 1900, Adams very much a part of the Marbury de Wolfe set. He considered Marbury the most civilized of the Versailles summer residents.
p. 194: *"I got ashore Sunday afternoon . . ."*: Ibid.
p. 195: *"thrust on me and not solicited . . ."*: Edith Wharton, *A Backward Glance*.
p. 196: *"I love you/I swear to you . . ."*: A typescript of the guest book was graciously sent to me by Frank Liberman.
p. 196: *"Looking back at those days . . ."*: AA.
p. 197: *"it was* l'art nouveau *which . . ."*: Ibid.

Chapter Twenty-Four

p. 197: *"discreetly made not too heavy . . ."*: Montrose G. Moses and Virginia Gerson, *Clyde Fitch and His Letters*.
p. 198: *"the loveliest garden in Versailles . . ."*: AA.
p. 198: *"going to be* awfully good *. . ."*: *Clyde Fitch and His Letters*.
p. 199: *"My dear fellow . . ."*: Mary Cavalita Dunne Bright, *A Leaf from the Yellow Book*.
p. 200: *"read a play over six times . . ."*: MCB.
p. 201: *"probably the most perfect . . ."*: Ibid.
p. 201: *"As we gazed at this . . ."*: Ibid.
p. 202: *"[it] was doubtless regarded . . ."*: MCB.
p. 202: *"My children, I advise you . . ."*: Ibid.
p. 202: *"If you don't buy it . . ."*: Ibid.
p. 202: *"as an artist may look . . ."*: AA.

Chapter Twenty-Five

p. 204: *"Oh, I get all the fun . . ."*: New York World, April 23, 1903. Quoted from London magazine, *Week's End*.
p. 206: *"There were few persons . . ."*: Paris Herald, April 30, 1903.
p. 206: *"So unjust is life that . . ."*: LHA. May 1, 1903.

Chapter Twenty-Six

p. 208: *"But, Bordie, what can women do?"*: FPTP.
p. 209: *"newspaper headlines"*: Ibid.
p. 209: *"a beaver, signifying activity . . ."*: MCB.
p. 209: *"Miss Morgan"*: LAD. Anne Morgan's Line-a-Day diaries are in the Morgan Library. In addition to her day-by-day activities, they provide an unexpectedly revealing portrait of her emotional life.

p. 211: "*All happiness except...*": The daily growth of Anne Morgan's love for Elisabeth Marbury can be found in her Line-a-Day diaries.

p. 212: "*stop talking 'shop'...*": George Tyler and J.C. Furnas, *Whatever Goes Up.*

Chapter Twenty-Seven

p. 212: "*She's not much of an actress...*": Ernest Samuels, *Bernard Berenson: The Making of Legend.*

p. 212: "*I can't bear it.*": LHA, letter to Cameron, February 14, 1904.

p. 213: "*as ever, dying to be approached...*": *Bernard Berenson: The Making of a Legend.*

p. 213: "*talked charmingly of his trees...*": Ibid.

p. 213: "*great gift for words.*": MCB.

p. 214: "*I want the Legion of Honor*": LHA, September 28, 1904. John La Farge (1835–1910). American painter and writer.

p. 214: "*they will always believe...*": Ibid.

p. 216: "*glorious*" and "*heavenly*": LAD.

p. 216: "*partner*": United States Census. 1905.

p. 217: "*Though I know the play...*": *Bernard Berenson: The Making of a Legend.*

p. 218: "*It was my own inner self...*": AA.

p. 218: "*I could not but feel...*": Ibid.

p. 218: "*lift one beyond the nagging...*": Ibid.

p. 218: "*Elsie, that is just your* métier...": Ibid.

p. 220: "*No doubt... an office.*": Ibid.

p. 220: "*Are you all out of your heads?*": Ibid.

p. 220: "*Give it to Elsie...*": MCB.

p. 220: "*sailed for England...*": AA.

p. 221: "*selecting beautiful stuffs...*": Ibid.

p. 221: "*heavenly*" or "*perfect*" evenings: LAD.

p. 221: "*her eye, mouth, and the whole...*": Ibid.

p. 222: "*They all had different ideas...*": AA.

p. 223: "*Ladies, in common fairness I must*": Ibid.

p. 226: "*That valiant spirit was beaming...*": FPTP.

Chapter Twenty-Eight

p. 228: "*... Mann intended to bring a civil suit*": All of the events leading up to the trial as well as Mann's often questionable and occasionally criminal means of gathering information for both *Town Topics* and his lucrative blackmail sideline came out in the course of it. It was all reported on the front pages of every newspaper in the country with no regard for the rights and feelings of the innocent victims: the wives and daughters of the men who purchased Mann's silence and/or good will.

p. 229: "*queer... after his own experience!*": B.H. Gertrude, *Gertrude Vanderbilt Whitney.*

p. 231: "*sense of the irony of life.*": Edith Wharton, *A Blackward Glance.*

p. 231: "*But I never did!*": Ibid.

p. 231: "*So was I.*": Ibid.

Chapter Twenty-Nine

p. 234: *"Of course no nice minded person . . ."*: Ted Morgan, *Maugham*.

p. 234: *"As soon as I had thought . . ."*: FPTP

p. 235: *"Comrades!"*: Ibid.

p. 238: *"a very business-like woman."*: Arnold Bennett, *The Journal*.

p. 238: *"Just like a man."*: Ibid.

p. 238: *"very brilliant, very gossipy . . ."*: The Letters of Bernard Berenson and Isabella Stewart Gardner, edited by Rollin Van N. Hadley.

p. 238: *"He grows more charming . . ."*: Bernard Berenson: The Making of a Legend.

p. 238: *"Miss Marbury and I came across . . ."*: AA.

Chapter Thirty

p. 244: *"It is a strong hint . . ."*: LHA, July 29, 1908.

p. 245: *"It goes on in England . . ."*: FPTP.

p. 245: *"You don't know you took in . . ."*: Archibald Butt, *The Letters of Archie Butt*.

p. 246: *"It was the first luncheon . . ."*: Ibid.

Chapter Thirty-One

p. 246: *"to Anne—Write deserve . . ."*: LAD.

p. 247: *"Charity is not the object . . ."*: TNYT, March 7, 1909.

p. 248: *"I want to say a few words . . ."*: TNYT, January 4, 1909.

p. 249: *"a perfect, metteur en scène,"*: AA.

p. 250: *"If my engagement to 'Papa' were . . ."*: Ibid.

p. 251: *"The sisters with gentle voices . . ."*: MCB.

Chapter Thirty-Two

p. 254: *"The girls took their discharge . . ."*: Nancy Woloch, *Women and the American Experience*.

pp. 255–256: *"I am a working girl . . ."*: Ibid.

p. 256: *"the aloofness of men . . ."*: TNYT, January 3, 1910.

p. 257: *"It is women of your class,"*: Ibid.

p. 257: *"You are on a strike . . ."*: Ibid.

p. 257: *"Delightful. Medieval America . . ."*: Wire to Elizabeth Dutcher, of the WTUL, released to the press in January 1910.

p. 258: *"In many places . . . their lives."*: TNYT, Dec. 16, 1909.

p. 260: *"I am heartily in favor . . ."*: TNYT, January 4, 1910.

p. 262: *"I am a member in good . . ."*: TNYT, January 24, 1910.

p. 263: *"What the hell did . . . shirtwaist?"*: Jeff Kisseloff, *You Must Remember This*.

p. 264: *"I would be a traitor . . ."*: TNYT, April 3, 1911.

Chapter Thirty-Three

p. 265: *"With a very narrow balustrade . . ."*: AA.

p. 266: *"a grimy, four-story . . ."*: Ibid.

pp. 266–267: *"The three estates . . ."*: Metropolitan Magazine, February 1911.

p. 268: *"Do as you please."*: TNYT, October 27, 1910.

p. 268: *"What nonsense!"*: Ibid.

p. 270: *"went away applauding . . ."*: AA.

p. 271: *"time and thought."*: Kathryn Chapman Harwood, *The Lives of Vizcaya*.

Chapter Thirty-Four

p. 273: *"the delicate handling . . ."*: Gilmartin and Massingale Stern, *New York 1900*.

p. 275: *"Like children entranced . . ."*: Robson Belmont, *The Fabric of Memory*.

p. 276: *"to organize and direct . . ."*: TNYT, August 8, 1911.

Chapter Thirty-Five

pp. 277–278: *"A . . . list of boarding houses . . ."*: *New York Evening World*, April 10, 1914.

p. 279: *"the truest qualities of leadership."*: TNYT, May 1, 1914.

p. 279: *"Personality of the most admirable . . ."*: *New York Evening World*, April 10, 1914.

p. 279: *"To acknowledge defeat . . ."*: MCB.

p. 280: *"I am not taking this step . . ."*: A Leaf from the Yellow Book.

pp. 280–281: *"If the manager does not . . ."*: Ibid.

p. 281: *"Whether Shaw was being funny . . ."*: MCB.

p. 281: *"One morning we watched . . ."*: AA.

Chapter Thirty-Six

p. 284: *"But I'm not an anti-suffragist . . ."*: *New York Evening World*, April 10, 1912.

p. 285: *"in spite of Elisabeth's protests,"*: AA.

p. 287: *"The foundering of the Titanic . . ."*: LHA, April 17, 1912.

p. 287: *"splendid."*: LAD, November 4, 1912.

p. 288: *"I believe I could utilize . . ."*: Shubert Archives, Elisabeth Marbury file.

Chapter Thirty-Seven

p. 290: *"sympathetic enthusiasm."*: MCB.

p. 290: *"creeping across the corner . . ."*: Ibid.

p. 291: *"while debauchery and sensuous . . ."*: Ibid.

p. 293: *"If I understand philanthropy . . ."*: *New York Herald*, February 8, 1914.

p. 297: *"He is a dear kid . . ."*: Marbury family correspondence. By the courtesy of Peter and Diana Marbury.

p. 297: *"bright pink all the while."*: Ibid.

p. 298: *"I will finance your lawsuit . . ."*: AA.

p. 298: *"inventories done by 5 experts."*: Victoria Sackville-West Diaries, Lilly Library, Indiana University.

p. 298: *"making himself a nuisance . . ."*: Ibid.

p. 299: *"He went through the house . . ."*: AA.

p. 300: *"It appeared to have been after his . . ."*: Osbert Sitwell in his introduction to *The Frick Collection: An Illustrated Catalogue in Twelve Volumes*.

p. 300: *"All these treasures . . ."*: Ibid.

p. 301: *"You see I plan each day . . ."*: By courtesy of Diana and Peter Marbury.

Chapter Thirty-Eight

p. 302: *"No definite news terrible . . ."*: LAD, August 3, 1914.

p. 302: *"and that all seemed well . . ."*: MCB.

p. 302: *"made us only children of fate . . ."*: Marbury correspondence, August 8, 1914.

p. 303: *"as far removed as possible . . ."*: Ibid., August 15, 1914.

p. 304: *"all enchanted together again."*: LAD, August 18, 1914.

p. 304: *"with lovely stone balustrades . . ."*: Marbury correspondence, August 20, 1914.

p. 304: "*very* precious *responsibility.*": Ibid., August 22, 1914.

p. 306: "*When dark came down . . .*": AA.

p. 306: "*very tired but most interesting.*": LAD, September 19, 1914.

p. 308: "*No modern equipment . . .*": MCB.

Chapter Thirty-Nine

p. 311: "*That modern trade unionism . . .*": Anne Morgan, *The American Girl.*

p. 313: "*I wish for everybody's sake . . .*": TNYT, September 12, 1915.

p. 313: "*We have no new message.*": TNYT, January 16, 1915.

p. 314: "*If Americans knew the imperative.*": TNYT, March 27, 1915.

p. 314: "*I can give you the names . . .*": *New York World,* February 25, 1915.

Chapter Forty

p. 315: "*It was Elisabeth Marbury . . .*": P.G. Wodehouse and Guy Bolton, *Bring on the Girls.*

p. 315: "*produced, costumed, staged . . .*": Florence Yoder, *Washington Times,* November 3, 1915.

p. 316: "*I have never had any ambition . . .*": Elisabeth Marbury, *My Girls As I Know Them.*

p. 316: "*He shows promise.*": *Harper's Bazaar,* August 1917.

p. 318: "*Mrs. W. K. Vanderbilt would glide . . .*": P.G. Wodehouse, *Bring on the Girls.*

p. 318: "*Are there no lifts, Mrs. Vanderbilt?*": KLGA.

p. 318: "*I beg you to announce . . .*": Robson Belmont, *The Fabric of Memory.*

p. 319: "*very lovely*": *Paris Herald,* August 7, 1915.

p. 319: "*by collaborating on the text . . .*": LAD, September 18, 1915.

p. 320: "*Bigelow scores tremendous hit.*": Brendan Gill, *Cole.*

p. 321: *inherited executive ability is responsible*": *Woman's Home Companion,* April 1916.

p. 321: "*It is up to the woman to force . . .*": *Chicago Tribune,* March 5, 1916.

Chapter Forty-One

p. 323: "*inspiring the others with her courage and fortitude*": *Miracles of Surgery on Men Mutilated in War.*

p. 324: "*I was told that I could not stand it . . .*": TNYT, *Sunday Magazine,* January 16, 1916.

p. 324: "*every moment beyond words*": AA.

p. 325: "*I am going to lie like a trooper. . .*": Mrs. W.K. Vanderbilt, "My Trip to the Front," *Harper's Magazine,* January 1917.

p. 326: "*There are many things . . .*": Ibid.

p. 326: "*new nobility, because the scars . . .*": Ibid.

p. 327: "*She is awfully pretty . . .*": KLGA.

p. 327: "*at once struck up a great friendship.*": Ibid.

p. 327: "*Then there was an awful row . . .*": Ibid.

p. 328: "*a talk that meant much.*": LAD.

Chapter Forty-Two

p. 330: "*I made her laugh . . .*": Mercedes De Acosta, *Here Lies the Heart.*

p. 331: "*We walked home together . . .*": Ibid.

p. 331: "*I will work night and day . . .*": MCB.

Chapter Forty-Three

p. 334: *"we need soap, blankets . . .":* Letter from Anne Dike to New York office of American Fund for the French Wounded, dated October 1917, New York Public Library.

pp. 334–335: *"Try as much as we will . . .":* TNYT, December 1, 1917.

p. 335: "Merci, ma bonne dame!": AA. "Thank you, my good lady! Such relief! Such relief!"

p. 335: *"a reward so infinitely touching . . .":* AA.

p. 336: "Je voudrais vous donnez . . .": *Bernard Berenson: The Making of a Legend:* "I would like to give you a smile to thank you."

p. 336: *"they are not a little too . . .":* FPTP.

p. 336: *"real self . . . in the midst . . .":* The Making of a Legend.

p. 337: *"gently but firmly . . .":* Robson Belmont, *The Fabric of Memory.*

p. 337: *"The gay American music . . .":* Dike to AFFW, January 1, 1918, New York Public Library.

p. 338: *"This is a moment of great . . .":* Ibid.

p. 339: *"keeping up the morale . . .":* TNYT, February 16, 1916.

p. 339: *"You cannot separate the welfare . . .":* New York World, March 30, 1918.

p. 340: *"Ah, how handsome he looked, . . .":* MCB.

p. 341: *"Everyone is flying . . .":* TNYT, April 12, 1918.

p. 341: *"Eight o'clock—Paris and the Ritz . . .":* AA.

Chapter Forty-Four

p. 345: *"For thirty years, General, . . .":* MCB.

p. 345: *"Sure we can hear you . . .":* Ibid.

p. 345: *"our negroes staggering back . . .":* Ibid.

p. 346: *"from them I drew a deeper . . .":* Ibid.

p. 347: *"Well! We have signed the . . .":* AA.

p. 347: *"It was one of the greatest days . . .":* Ibid.

p. 347: *"Smooth, smug people . . .":* Sir Oswald George, *My Life.*

p. 348: *" . . . only Jews and Communists were . . .":* Sir Henry Channon, *Chips.*

p. 348: *"Be sure you don't let yourself . . .":* Ron Chernow, *The House of Morgan.*

p. 349: *"All Europe needs help . . .":* New York Herald, November 8, 1919.

p. 350: *"He was a sprite . . .":* Edna Woolman Chase and Ilka Chase, *Always in Vogue.*

p. 350: *"Cancel all my appointments . . .":* Ibid.

p. 351: *"She's not just some démodée old bug!":* Interview with Roddy MacDowell.

Chapter Forty-Five

p. 353: *"Nothing could be more delightful . . .":* MCB.

p. 353: *"the Democratic party had . . .":* TNYT, July 3, 1920.

p. 354: *"for a very simple reason . . .":* Ibid.

p. 354: *"the Court Jester of the Convention":* MCB.

p. 354: *"men whose private lives . . .":* TNYT, July 13, 1920.

p. 355: *"No one in the state . . .":* FDRL, November 1, 1920.

p. 355: *"This is the time . . . New York":* FDRL, November 6, 1920.

p. 355: *"I feel absolutely as you do . . .":* Ibid.

p 355: *"and told them to go to it . . .":* The Berg Collection.

p. 355: *"Rem. Amer. Play Co. . . .":* Sinclair Lewis, *From Main Street to Stockholm.*

p. 356: *"It seems a very long time . . .":* Letter written to Wharton, January 14, 1921, Lilly Library, Indiana University.

p. 359: *"a big, coarse, mannish woman . . .":* TNYT, January 24, 1921. Dr. Daniel L. Marsh, at the Smithfield Methodist Episcopal Church, Pittsburgh, PA.

p. 359: *"Every one regards Miss Morgan . . .":* TNYT, February 16, 1921. Dr. D. Lockrow addressing a Baptist conference, Tremont Temple, Boston, MA.

Chapter Forty-Six

p. 359: *"Beekman Place on the East River . . .":* The Diary of George Templeton Strong.

p. 361: *"no ornate bindings, just practical . . .":* Elisabeth Marbury, "Sutton Place," House Beautiful, November 1930.

p. 361: *"too large until we have to pay . . .":* Ibid.

p. 362: *"the ever-resourceful Elsie de Wolfe . . .":* Bernard Berenson. The Making of a Legend.

p. 362: *"This famous Parisian hostess . . .":* Nicky Mariano, Forty Years with Berenson.

p. 363: *"successful even beyond my expectation . . .":* Letter to Houghton Mifflin, November 25, 1921.

p. 365: *"Anne Morgan (as is the case . . .):* Gossip, November 13, 1921.

p. 265: *"This committee is committed.":* TNYT, April 25, 1921. An address given at a dinner in honor of distinguished American . . . opposed to government by the blue laws. Hotel Commodore, New York City.

Chapter Forty-Seven

p. 366: *"The days are over . . .":* March 26, 1922. NBC national hookup speech.

p. 366: *"America is constantly calling for . . .":* Chicago Tribune, April 6, 1922.

p. 367: *"I'm a sort of Old Hickory . . .":* TNYT, April 29, 1922.

p. 368: *"to vigorously oppose . . .":* TNYT, May 14, 1922.

p. 369: *"poor Louis.":* The Letters of Nancy Mitford and Evelyn Waugh.

p. 369: *" . . . the frog who people can't endure.":* Philip Ziegler, Diana Cooper.

p. 369: *"the coat of shame.":* The Letters of Evelyn Waugh and Diana Duff Cooper.

p. 369: *"We live free on poor Louis's . . .":* Ibid.

p. 376: *"so much more convenient . . .":* Eleanor Robson Belmont file. Butler Library, Columbia University.

p. 377: *"To Elsie de Wolfe, my friend . . .":* MCB. The dedication.

Chapter Forty-Eight

p. 377: *"a fascinating picture . . . her times.":* TNYT, February 10, 1924.

p. 380: *"Listen, dearie . . .":* Lincoln Center Library of the Performing Arts.

p. 381: *"So long as you have Eddie Cantor . . .":* FDRL, May 1, 1924.

p. 384: *"That was a great speech . . .":* FDRL, June 26, 1924.

p. 384: *"ready to call any punishment . . .":* TNYT, July 25, 1924.

p. 385: *"I really feel ashamed to have been . . .":* Ida Tarbell papers. Pelletier Library, Allegheny College.

p. 385: *"Elsie kept her friends for many years. . . .":* Edna Woolman Chase, Always in Vogue.

p. 387: *"How's your old bitch . . .":* Gerald McKnight, The Scandal of Syrie Maugham.

Chapter Forty-Nine

p. 389: "*Dressed with an elegant simplicity . . .*": TNYT, November 20, 1925.

pp. 390–391: "*Almost every line of endeavor . . .*": Radio address, April 12, 1925.

p. 391: "*I respond to the sparkle . . .*": Elisabeth Marbury, "Women in Politics," *Saturday Evening Post*, September 12, 1925.

p. 391: "*could not but wonder . . .*": Ibid.

p. 392: "*So long as they are given equal . . .*": Ibid.

p. 394: "*When one has passed the portals . . .*": AA.

p. 394: "*It's rubbish!*": Ibid.

p. 394: "*Charles and I had a deep . . .*": Ibid.

p. 395: "*Charles, Elsie and Johnnie . . .*": Edna Woolman Chase, *Always in Vogue*.

p. 397: "*He dived in and swam . . .*": Arthur and Barbara Gelb, *O'Neill*.

p. 397: "*Agnes followed them . . .*": Mercedes de Acosta, *Here Lies the Heart*.

p. 397: "*Carlotta wanted to possess her men . . .*": Louis Sheaffer, *O'Neill, Son and Artist*.

p. 397: "*to be all sufficient to a man . . .*": Ibid.

p. 397: "*she was miraculously immaculate*": Arthur and Barbara Gelb, *O'Neill*.

p. 398: "*Never tell Madden anything!*": *The Selected Letters of Eugene O'Neill*, edited by Travis Bogard and Jackson R. Bryer.

p. 398: "*Today they are beneath contempt.*": TNYT, June 24, 1926.

p. 398: "*a hyphen between . . .*": TNYT, September 16, 1926.

p. 399: "*Young man, I understand . . .*": Allan Nevins, *Herbert R. Lehman and His Era*.

p. 399: "*Confidentally . . .*": Buffalo and Erie Historical Society, Norman Mack papers. The remark about influences of the Semitic race refers to Belle Moskowitz about whom Eleanor Roosevelt and she shared an uneasiness that reflected badly on both of them.

p. 401: "*a most manly man.*": Mosely, *My Life*.

p. 401: "*delicate scene of beautiful . . .*": Ibid.

Chapter Fifty

p. 403: "*To the majority . . .*": Ida Clyde Clark, "A Woman in the White House." *The Century*, March 1927. Anne Morgan's renown had been validated in 1922, when the *New York Times* conducted a poll to determine the twelve greatest American women. Morgan had been named along with Carrie Chapman Catt, Jane Addams, Edith Wharton, M. Carey Thomas, Cecilia Beaux, Ida Tarbell, Julia C. Lathrop, Geraldine Farrar, Mary Roberts Rinehart, Katherine Bement Davis, and Evangeline Booth.

p. 403: "*Through her friendship . . .*": Margaret K. Leech, "Lady Into Dynamo," *The New Yorker*, December 12, 1927.

pp. 403–404: "*If she wears her decades . . .*": Margaret K. Leech, "Seventy Years Young," *The New Yorker*, December 12, 1927.

p. 404: "*We make opportunities . . .*": Elisabeth Marbury, "Sayings of a Wise Woman," *Delineator*, June 1927.

p. 405: "*Miss Morgan has, at times . . .*": TNYT, January 19, 1928.

p. 405: "*Membership in the new . . .*": Ibid.

p. 409: "*All that Miss Marbury . . .*": TNYT, June 16, 1928.

p. 410: "*Eight years of trial . . .*": FDRL.

p. 410: "*No one realizes . . . very soon.*": Ibid.

Chapter Fifty-One

p. 415: *"The friends of Blérancourt . . ."*: TNYT, July 8, 1930.

p. 415: *"listening to the whole story . . ."*: Cecil Beaton, *The Wandering Years: Diaries, 1922–1939.*

p. 416: *"Surrounded by rolls of fat . . ."*: Ibid.

p. 416: *"a living factory of 'chic'"*: Cecil Beaton, *The Glass of Fashion.*

p. 417: *"I presume, my dear, . . ."*: AA.

p. 418: *"Of the several homes I had . . ."*: Ibid.

p. 419: *"Moonshine and glamour . . ."*: Ibid.

p. 420: *"Many employers are still . . ."*: TNYT, December 6, 1930.

p. 420: *"interesting and important to women . . ."*: Ibid.

p. 420: *"with a gallantry . . ."*: TNYT, February 4, 1932.

p. 420: *"the ability to save . . ."*: Ibid.

p. 420: *"to be impersonal."*: TNYT, July 3, 1932.

Chapter Fifty-Two

p. 423: *"Milk costs me $1 . . ."*: TNYT, January 27, 1932.

p. 423: *"I only wish that you could . . ."*: FDRL, June 15, 1932.

p. 423: *"the best I can do . . ."*: FDRL, June 29, 1932.

p. 424: *"Miss Marbury has talked . . ."*: Joseph Lash, *Franklin and Eleanor.*

p. 424: *"all of us as novices . . ."*: Ibid.

p. 424: *"People began arriving at eight thirty."*: Stark Young, *A Life in the Arts.*

p. 425: *"He is so much better . . ."*: Ida Tarbell papers, Pelletier Library, Allegheny College.

p. 426: *". . . Hoover will win."*: Sir Harold Nicholson, *Diaries and Letters, 1930–1939.*

p. 427: *"Miss Marbury is enormous . . ."*: Sutherland Derlinger, *New York World Telegram,* January 23, 1933.

p. 427: *"I do not want to die . . . rust."*: MCB.

p. 428: *"like the old ship . . ."*: MCB.

p. 428: *"first arrangements of all . . ."*: LAD, January 22, 1933.

p. 430: *"New York's 'great ladies'"*: "Cholly Knickerbocker," *New York Journal,* January 25, 1933.

p. 431: *"We have just offered . . ."*: Eulogy at St. Patrick's Cathedral, quoted in TNYT, January 25, 1933.

p. 431: *"Funeral at St. Patrick's . . ."*: LAD, January 24, 1933.

p. 432: *"I was received into the church . . ."*: MCB.

pp. 433–434: *"The death of Mrs. Oliver . . ."*: TNYT, January 27, 1933.

Chapter Fifty-Three

pp. 434–435: *"If said Anne Morgan . . ."*: Will of Elisabeth Marbury. Probated in New York State, 1933.

p. 435: *"a country club for business . . ."*: *New York World,* February 29, 1933.

p. 435: *"delighted with Roosevelt speech"*: LAD, March 4, 1933.

p. 437: *"a very feminine group."*: Morgan Library, Anne Morgan papers, 1935.

p. 438: *"a living ghost . . ."*: Malvina Hoffman, *Yesterday Is Tomorrow.*

p. 440: *"both fine and cold . . ."*: LAD. All of the Morgan-Vanderbilt-Hoffman quotes that follow for winter, spring, summer of 1935 from LAD.

p. 441: *"glittering . . . dripping . . ."*: Sir Henry Channon, *Chips.*

p. 443: "*Elsie naturally had wonderful . . .*": Diana Vreeland, *D.V.*

p. 444: "*This was indeed the radiant dawn . . .*": Malvina Hoffman, *Yesterday Is Tomorrow.*

p. 445: "*only possible future.*": LAD, November 4, 1936.

Chapter Fifty-Four

p. 447: "*distinctly better . . .*": LAD.

p. 447: "*amazingly like [her] old self*": Ibid.

p. 448: "*a terrible day of strain . . .*": Ibid.

p. 448: "*glamorous luncheons.*": Bettina Ballard reported the party in French *Vogue* as well as relaying copies of her transcript to Edna Woolman Snow, in New york, and Valentine Lawford, in Paris. All of the quotes of Elsie's guests are from Ballard.

p. 449: "*under irresistible pressure . . .*": LAD, September 17, 1938.

p. 449: "*a terribly strained day . . .*": LAD, September 23, 1938.

p. 450: "*She is the woman journalist . . .*": TNYT, November 15, 1938.

p. 451: "*a dirty Talmud Jew.*": David Gelertner, *1939: The Lost World of the Fair.*

p. 451: "*probably the most talked about . . .*": Ibid.

p. 453: "*Rose is fire and flame . . .*": Lilia Pennant, *Anne Morgan, Eva Dahlgren, Rose Dolan and the Aid They Brought to the French Refugees, 1939–1949.*

p. 453: "*Rose is exactly the same . . .*": Ibid.

p. 453: "*Plane late starting . . .*": LAD.

p. 454: "*found Paris hot, dusty . . .*": *Noel Coward Diaries,* edited by Graham Payne and Sheridan Morley.

p. 455: "*Here one sees no warfare . . .*": *New York Herald Tribune,* September 29, 1939.

p. 456: "*It doesn't seem worth while . . .*": TNYT, January 13, 1940.

p. 457: "*We have to realize . . .*": TNYT, March 3, 1940.

Chapter Fifty-Five

p. 457: "*Life . . . is very humdrum . . .*": Edna Woolman Chase, *Always in Vogue.*

p. 458: "*Dahlgren appeared yesterday . . .*": Lilia Pennant, *Anne Morgan, Eva Dahlgren, Rose Dolan . . .*

p. 459: "*a day never to be forgotten . . .*": LAD.

p. 459: "*good news—Blérancourt . . .*": Ibid.

p. 460: "*a strange and terrible Sunday . . .*": LAD, June 16, 1940.

p. 461: "*the first good opening . . .*": LAD, July 3, 1940.

p. 462: "*I had plenty of money . . .*": TNYT, July 4, 1940.

p. 464: "*always [the] same question . . .*": LAD, January 15, 1941.

p. 466: "*It's the first time . . .*": TNYT, August 22, 1941.

p. 466: " *. . . last one of these affairs . . .*": Ibid.

p. 467: " *. . . the impossible news . . .*": LAD, December 7, 1941.

Chapter Fifty-Six

p. 469: "*an authority on fashion . . .*": TNYT, September 15, 1941.

p. 469: " *. . . a minor Molnar.*": Hugh Fordin, *The World of Entertainment.*

p. 471: " *. . . work of the Urban League.*": Morgan Library.

p. 471: "*providing so hospitably . . .*": Ibid.

p. 472: "*exhausting D-Day.*": LAD.

p. 472: " *. . . everything is beyond description.*": Morgan Library.

p. 473: "*marvelous, unforgettable day.*": LAD, June 19, 1945.

p. 474: *"a mountain of Elsie's scrapbooks.":* Cecil Beaton, *The Years Between: 1939–1948.*

Chapter Fifty-Seven

p. 476: *"when framed looks very nice . . .":* In this chapter, all of the letters to, from, and concerning Anne Morgan can be found in her correspondence boxes in the Morgan Library.

pp. 479–480: *"Entertaining was the breath of life . . .":* Edna Woolman Chase, *Always in Vogue.*

p. 480: *"scarcely alive, a skeleton . . .":* Bernard Berenson, *Sunset and Twilight.*

p. 480: "Je ne veux pas mourir . . .": Jane Smith, *Elsie de Wolfe:* "I don't want to die. I don't want to go away." Cited from a letter sent by Hilda West to Bernard Berenson.

p. 481: *"to live one day longer than Charles.":* Ludwig Bemelmans, *To The One I Love the Best.*

p. 481: *"As her generosity is limitless . . .":* Ibid.

p. 481: *"I blew a gentle and loving kiss . . .":* The Noel Coward Diaries.

ℬIBLIOGRAPHY ॐ

Adams, Henry. *The Letters of Henry Adams,* Vols. I–VI. Cambridge, Mass.: Harvard University Press, 1983–1988.

Adams, Samuel Hopkins. *A. Woollcott.* New York: Reynal & Hitchcock, 1945.

Alcott, Louisa May. *The Journals of Louisa May Alcott,* ed. Daniel Shealy and Joel Myerson. Athens: University of Georgia Press, 1997.

Aldrich, Nelson W. Jr. *Old Money.* New York: Alfred A. Knopf, 1988.

Alger, William Rounsville. *The Friendship of Women.* Boston: Roberts Brothers, 1868.

Allen, Frederick Lewis. *The Great Pierpont Morgan.* New York: Harper & Brothers, 1949.

Amory, Cleveland. *The Last Resorts.* New York: Harper & Brothers, 1948.

———. *Who Killed Society?* New York: Harper & Brothers, 1960.

———, and Frederic Bradlee. *Vanity Fair.* New York: Viking, 1960.

Andrew, A. Piat. *Friends of France.* Boston: Houghton, Mifflin, 1916.

Andrews, Wayne. *The Vanderbilt Legend.* New York: Harcourt Brace, 1941.

Anthony, Carl Sferrazza. *First Ladies: The Saga of the Presidents' Wives and Their Power, 1789–1961.* New York: William Morrow, 1990.

Apcock, A. St. John. *Famous Houses and Literary Shrines of London.* New York: Barnes and Noble, 1993.

Archer, Lieutenant Colonel C. *William Archer.* New Haven: Yale University Press, 1931.

Asquith, Margot. *Portrait of Barrie.* London: James Barrie, 1954.

Auchincloss, Louis. *The Vanderbilt Era.* New York: Charles Scribner's Sons, 1989.

Baker, Paul R. *Stanny: The Gilded Life of Stanford White.* New York: The Free Press, 1989.

Baldwin, Billy. *Billy Baldwin Remembers.* New York: Harcourt Brace, 1974.

Baldwin, Billy, with Michael Gardine. *An Autobiography.* Boston: Little Brown, 1985.

Baldwin, Charles. *Stanford White.* New York: De Capo Press, 1971.

Balsan, Consuelo Vanderbilt. *The Glitter and the Gold.* New York: Harper & Brothers, 1952.

Baltzell, E. Digby. *The Protestant Establishment: Aristocracy & Caste in America.* New York: Random House, 1964.

Banham, Martin. *The Cambridge Guide to Theatre.* New York: Cambridge University Press, 1992.

Barres, Maurice. *The Faith of France,* tr. Elisabeth Marbury. Boston: Houghton, Mifflin, 1918.

Barron, Clarence. *They Told Barron.* New York: Harper & Brothers, 1930.

Barrymore, Ethel. *Memories.* New York: Harper & Brothers, 1955.

Beaton, Cecil. *The Glass of Fashion.* London: Cassell, 1954.

———. *Diaries: 1922–1939.* New York: Holt, Rinehart & Winston, 1965.

———. *The Years Between: 1939–1948.* New York: Holt, Rinehart & Winston, 1965.

———. *Self-Portrait with Friends: 1922–1974.* New York: Times Books, 1979.

Beauchamp, Cari. *Without Lying Down.* New York: A Lisa Drew Book/Scribner, 1995.

Becker, Robert. *Nancy Lancaster: Her Life, Her World, Her Art.* New York: Alfred A. Knopf, 1995.

Beerbohm, Max. *Herbert Beerbohm Tree.* London: Hutchinson & Co., 1918.

Behrman, S. N. *Duveen.* New York: Random House, 1952.

———. *Portrait of Max.* New York: Random House, 1960.

Belmont, Eleanor Robson. *The Fabric of Memory.* New York: Farrar, Straus and Cudahy, 1957.

Bemelmans, Ludwig. *To the One I Love the Best.* New York: Viking, 1955.

———. *Tell Them It Was Wonderful.* New York: Viking, 1985.

Bennett, Arnold. *The Journal.* New York: Viking, 1933.

Benstock, Shari. *No Gifts from Chance.* New York: Charles Scribner's Sons, 1994.

Berenson, Bernard, and Isabella Stewart Gardner. *The Letters of _____,* ed. Rollin Van N. Hadley. Boston: Northeastern University Press, 1987.

Berkman, Ted. *The Lady and the Law.* Boston: Little, Brown, 1976.

Bernier, Olivier. *Fireworks at Dusk: Paris in the Thirties.* Boston: Little, Brown, 1993.

Birmingham, Stephen. *Our Crowd.* New York: Harper & Row, 1967.

———. *The Right People.* Boston: Little, Brown, 1968.

———. *The Grandees.* New York: Harper & Row, 1971.

Black, David. *The King of Fifth Avenue: The Fortunes of August Belmont.* New York: The Dial Press, 1981.

Blaugrund, Annette. *Paris 1889.* Philadelphia: Pennsylvania Academy of the Fine Arts, 1989.

Blum, Daniel. *A Pictorial History of the American Theatre 1900–1950.* New York: Greenberg, 1950.

———. *Great Stars of the American Stage.* New York: Greenberg, 1952.

———. *A Pictorial History of the Silent Screen.* New York: G. P. Putnam's Sons, 1953.

———. *A Pictorial History of the Talkies.* New York: G. P. Putnam's Sons, 1958.

Bordman, Gerald. *American Musical Theatre.* New York: Oxford University Press, 1978.

———. *Jerome Kern, His Life and Music.* New York: Oxford University Press, 1980.

————. *The Oxford Companion to American Theatre.* Oxford: Oxford University Press, 1984.

Bowers, Claude. *My Life.* New York: Simon & Schuster, 1962.

Boyer, M. Christine. *Manhattan Manners.* New York: Rizzoli, 1985.

Boylan, James. *The World and the 20s.* New York: The Dial Press, 1973.

Brady, Kathleen. *Ida Tarbell.* New York: Seaview/Putnam, 1984.

Bright, Mary Chavalita Dunne. *A Leaf from the Yellow Book: The Correspondence of George Eggerton.* London: The Richard Press, Royal Opera Arcade, 1958.

Brinin, John Malcolm. *The Sway of the Grand Saloon.* London: Arlington Books, 1986.

Brody, Iles. *Gone with the Windsors.* Philadelphia: The John C. Winston Company, 1953.

Brough, James. *Consuelo, Portrait of an American Heiress.* New York: Coward, McCann & Geoghegan, Inc., 1979.

Brown, Eve. *Champagne Cholly.* New York: E. F. Dutton, 1947.

Brown, Henry Collins. *New York of Today.* New York: Old Colony Press, 1915.

————. *Book of Old New York.* New York: Old Colony Press, 1920.

————. *Restoring the Century-Old Residential Glories of the East River.* New York: Privately printed, 1925.

Brown, Jared. *The Fabulous Lunts.* New York: Atheneum, 1986.

Brown, John Mason. *The Worlds of Robert E. Sherwood: Mirror to His Times.* New York: Harper & Row, 1965.

Brownell, William C. *Newport.* Illustrated by W. S. Vanderbilt Allen.

Browning, Judith. *New York City, Yesterday & Today.* Conn.: Corsair, 1990.

Brown-Potter, Cora. *The Age of Innocence and I.* Hearst's International-Cosmopolitan. March, April, May, 1933.

Bryan, J. III, and Charles J. V. Murphy. *The Windsor Story.* New York: William Morrow, 1979.

Butt, Archibald. *The Letters of Archie Butt.* Garden City, New York: Doubleday Page & Co., 1924.

Calder, Robert. *Willie.* New York: St. Martin's Press, 1989.

Campbell, Nina, and Caroline Seebohm. *Elsie de Wolfe.* New York: Clarkson Potter, 1992.

Canfield, Cass. *The Incredible Pierpont Morgan.* New York: Harper & Row, 1974.

Caroso, Vincent P. *The Morgans.* Cambridge, Mass.: Harvard University Press, 1987.

Cary, Gary. *Anita Loos.* New York: Alfred A. Knopf, 1988.

Caskett, Meredith B., Jr. *The English Ancestry of Anne Marbury Hutchinson and Katherine Marbury Scott.* Philadelphia: The Magee Press, 1936.

Castle, Irene. *My Husband.* New York: Charles Scribner's Sons, 1919.

————. *Castles in the Air.* Garden City, N.Y.: Doubleday, 1958.

Chalon, Jean. *Portrait of a Seductress: The World of Natalie Barney.* New York: Crown, 1979.

Channon, Sir Henry. *"Chips." The Diaries of Sir Henry Channon.* London: Weidenfeld & Nicolson, 1993.

Chapman, John. *"McKim, Mead & White," Vanity Fair,* September 13, 1919.

Charteris, Archibald Hamilton. "Woman's Work in the Church," *The Presbyterian Review* (London), January 1881.

Chase, Edna Woolman, and Ilka. *Always in Vogue.* Garden City, N.Y.: Doubleday, 1954.

Chauncey, George. *Gay New York.* New York: Basic Books, 1994.

Chernow, Ron. *The House of Morgan.* New York: Atlantic Monthly Press, 1990.

Churchill, Allen. *The Upper Crust.* Englewood Cliffs, N.J.: Prentice Hall, 1970.

Citron, Stephen. *Noel & Cole.* New York: Oxford University Press, 1993.

Clark, Ida Clyde. "A Woman in the White House," *Century,* Vol. 113, March 1927.

Cochran, Charles. *The Secrets of a Showman.* London: William Heinemann, 1925.

Connon, Bryan. *Somerset Maugham & the Maugham Dynasty.* London: Sinclair-Stevenson, 1997.

Cook, Blanche Wiesen. *Eleanor Roosevelt,* Vol. 1. New York: Viking, 1992.

Cooper, Artemis, ed. *The Letters of Evelyn Waugh and Diana Cooper.* New York: Ticknor and Fields, 1992.

Cory, Lewis. *House of Morgan.* New York: G. Howard Watt, 1930.

Coward, Noel. *The Noel Coward Diaries,* ed. Graham Payn and Sheridan Morley. Boston: Little Brown, 1982.

Cowles, Virginia. *The Astors.* New York: Alfred A. Knopf, 1979.

Cox, Anne F. *The History of the Colony Club.* New York: Privately printed, 1984.

Cromley, Elizabeth Collins. *Alone Together.* Ithaca, N.Y.: Cornell University, 1990.

Crowninshield, Frank. "The House of Vanderbilt," *Vogue,* November 15, 1941.

Cruttwell, C.R.M.F. *A History of the Great War, 1914–1918.* London: Paladin Books, 1982.

Custer, Elizabeth B. "The Woman's Club of New York," *Town and Country,* May 1908.

Davenport, Marcia. *Too Strong for Fantasy.* New York: Charles Scribner's Sons, 1967.

Davis, Lee. *Bolton and Wodehouse and Kern.* New York: James Heineman, Inc., 1993.

De Acosta, Mercedes. *Here Lies the Heart.* New York: Reynal & Company, 1960.

Delaney, Edmund T. *New York's Turtle Bay Old & New.* Barre, Mass.: Barre Publishers, 1965.

De Mille, Cecil B. *The Autobiography of Cecil B. De Mille.* New York: Prentice Hall, 1959.

Detmold, Mabel. *The Brownstones of Turtle Bay Gardens.* New York: The East 49th Street Association, 1964.

De Wolfe, Elsie. "Châteaux in Touraine," *Cosmopolitan,* February 1891.

———. "Stray Leaves from My Book of Life," *Metropolitan,* 1901.

———. *The House in Good Taste.* New York: The Century Co., 1913.

———. *Recipes for Successful Dining.* New York: Appleton-Century, 1934.

———. *After All.* New York: Harper & Brothers, 1935.

Dimona, Darcy. *A Biography of Sutton Place, Manhattan.* Unprinted thesis; study of the city 12. New Haven, Conn.: Yale University Press, 1979.

D'ormesson, Jean. *Grand Hotel.* New York: Vendome Press, 1984.

Dorr, Rheta Child. "The Woman's Club of New York," *Harper's,* December 1901.

Drechler-Marx, Carin, and Richard F. Shepard. *Broadway.* New York: Harry N. Abrams, 1988.

Dressler, Marie. *My Own Story.* Boston: Little, Brown, 1934.

Drew, John. *My Years on the Stage.* New York: E. F. Dutton, 1922.

Dunbar, Olivia Howard. "The Newest Woman's Club," *Putnam's Monthly,* May 1907.

Dunlap, David W. *On Broadway.* New York: Rizzoli, 1990.

Duquette, Tony. "Design Classics, Elsie de Wolfe," *Architectural Digest,* September 1996.

Dwight, Eleanor. *Edith Wharton: An Extraordinary Life.* New York: Harry N. Abrams, 1994.

Edel, Leon. *Henry James: A Life.* New York: Harper & Row, 1985.

Edwards, Anne. *The De Milles.* New York: Harry N. Abrams, 1988.

Eels, George. *The Life That Late He Led.* New York: G. P. Putnam's Sons, 1967.

Egan, Maurice Francis, and John B. Kennedy. *The Knights of Columbus in Peace and War,* Vol. I. New Haven, Conn.: Knights of Columbus, 1920.

Ehrlich, Blake. *Paris on the Seine.* New York: Atheneum, 1962.

Eldot, Paula. *Governor Alfred E. Smith.* New York: Garland Publishing Co., 1983.

Ellis, Edward Robb. *The Epic of New York City.* New York: Old Town Books, 1966.

Ellman, Richard. *Oscar Wilde.* New York: Alfred A. Knopf, 1988.

Erlich, Gloria C. *The Sexual Education of Edith Wharton.* Berkeley, Calif.: The University of California Press, 1992.

Etherington-Smith, Meredith, and Jeremy Pilcher. *The "It" Girls.* New York: Harcourt Brace Jovanovich, 1986.

Ewen, David. *The Complete Book of the American Musical Comedy.* New York: Holt, Rinehart & Winston, 1970.

Faderman, Lillian. *Surpassing the Love of Men.* New York: William Morrow, 1981.

———. *Odd Girls and Twilight Lovers.* New York: Columbia University Press, 1991.

Fairfield, Francis Gerry. *The Clubs of New York.* New York: Henry L. Hinter, 1873.

Flanner, Janet. *Paris Was Yesterday.* New York: Viking, 1972.

Forbes, J. Douglas. *J. P. Morgan, Jr. 1867–1943.* Charlottesville, Va.: University Press of Virginia, 1981.

Forbes-Roberston, Diana. *My Aunt Maxine: The Story of Maxine Elliott.* New York: Viking, 1964.

Fordin, Hugh. *The World of Entertainment.* Garden City, N.Y.: Doubleday, 1975.

Foreman, John, and Robbe Pierce Stimson. *The Vanderbilts and the Gilded Age.* New York: St. Martin's Press, 1991.

Fowler, Gene. *Good Night, Sweet Prince.* New York: Viking, 1944.

———. *Beau James: The Life and Times of Jimmy Walker.* New York: Viking, 1949.

Freedland, Michael. *Jerome Kern.* London: Robson Books Ltd., 1958.

Friedman, B. H. *Gertrude Vanderbilt Whitney.* New York: Doubleday, 1978.

Fryer, Jonathan. *Andre and Oscar.* New York: St. Martin's Press, 1998.

Gaige, Crosby. *Footlights and Highlights.* New York: E. P. Dutton, 1948.

Gaines, James R. *Wit's End.* New York: Harcourt Brace Jovanovich, 1977.

Gavin, Terrence. *The Barons of Newport.* Newport, R.I.: Pineapple Publications, 1988.

Gelb, Arthur, and Barbara Gelb. *O'Neill.* New York: Harper & Brothers, 1960.

Gelernter, David. *1939: The Lost World of the Fair.* New York: The Free Press, 1995.

Gilder, Jeanette L. *The Autobiography of a Tom-Boy.* New York: Doubleday Page & Co., 1900.

Gill, Brendan. *Cole.* New York: Holt, Rinehart, Winston, 1971.

Gilmartin, Gregory F. *Shaping the City.* New York: Clarkson Potter, 1995.

Gold, Arthur, and Robert Fizdale. *Misia.* New York: Alfred A. Knopf, 1980.

———. *The Divine Sarah.* New York: Alfred A. Knopf, 1991.

Goodnow, Ruby Ross. "Villa Trianon." *Vogue,* March, 1914.

Gottfried, Martin. *Broadway Musicals.* New York: Harry N. Abrams, 1979.

Gould, B. A. "Memoir of Lewis Morris Rutherfurd 1816–1892," read before the National Academy of Sciences in New York, April 1895.

Gourlie, John H. *The Origin and History of the Century.* New York: William C. Bryant & Co., 1856.

Grafton, David. *Red Hot & Rich! An Oral History of Cole Porter.* New York: Stein & Day, 1987.

Gray, David. "Notes and Pictures," *Metropolitan,* February 1911.

Gray, Christopher. "Neighborhood (Sutton Place)," *Avenue,* September 1980.

———. "Neighborhood (East 57th Street)," *Avenue,* June, July, August, 1985.

———. "History of the Upper East Side," *Avenue,* September 1980.

Green, Martin. *Children of the Sun.* New York: Basic Books, 1976.

Guilgoyle, Timothy S. *City of Eros.* New York: W. W. Norton, 1992.

Hamm, Margherita Alina. *Eminent Actors in Their Homes.* New York: James Pott & Company, 1902.

Hampton, Mark. *Legendary Decorators of the Twentieth Century.* New York: Doubleday, 1992.

Hansen, Arlen J. *Expatriate Paris.* New York: Arcade, 1990.

Hardwick, Joan. *Addicted to Romance.* London: Andre Deutsch, 1994.

Harriman, Mrs. J. Borden. *From Pinafores to Politics.* New York: Henry Holt, 1923.

———. *The Reminiscences of Mrs. Florence Jaffray Harriman.* New York: The Columbia University Oral History Project, April 1950.

Harris, Frank. *My Life and Loves.* New York: Grove Press, 1963.

Hartnoll, Phyllis. *The Oxford Companion to the Theatre.* Oxford: Oxford University Press, 1983.

Harvey, George. *Henry Clay Frick, the Man.* New York: Charles Scribner's Sons, 1928.

Harwood, Kathryn Chapman. *The Lives of Vizcaya.* Miami: Banyan Books, 1985.

Hawes, Elizabeth. *New York, New York.* New York: Alfred A. Knopf, 1993.

Hewitt, Edward Ringwood. *Those Were the Days.* New York: Duell, Sloan & Pearce, 1945.

Higham, Charles. *The Duchess of Windsor.* New York: McGraw Hill, 1988.

Hill, May Brawley. *The Woman Sculptor: Malvina Hoffman and Her Contemporaries.* New York: The Brearly School/Berry Hill Galleries, 1984.

Hoare, Philip. *Serious Pleasures: The Life of Stephen Tennant.* London: Hamish Hamilton, 1990.

———. *Noel Coward.* New York: Simon & Schuster, 1995.

————. *Oscar Wilde's Last Stand.* New York: Arcade, 1998.

Hobhouse, Janet. *Everybody Who Was Anybody.* New York: G. P. Putnam's Sons, 1975.

Hoff, Henry R. *Genealogies of Long Island Families.* Baltimore: Genealogical Publishing Company, 1987.

Hoffman, Malvina. *Heads and Tales.* New York: Charles Scribner's Sons, 1939.

————. *Yesterday Is Tomorrow.* New York: Crown, 1965.

Holroyd, Michael. *Bernard Shaw: The Search for Love.* New York: Random House, 1988.

————. *Bernard Shaw: The Pursuit of Power.* New York: Random House, 1989.

————. *Lytton Strachey: The New Biography.* New York: Farrar, Strauss & Giroux, 1994.

Hone, Philip. *The Diary of Philip Hone.* New York: Dodd, Mead, 1936.

Hovey, Carl. *The Life Story of J. Pierpont Morgan.* Freeport, N.Y.: Books for Libraries Press, 1971. First printing, 1912.

Howard, Jean. *Travels with Cole.* New York: Harry N. Abrams, 1991.

Howe, Irving. *World of Our Fathers.* New York: Simon & Schuster, 1976.

Hoyt, Edwin. *The Vanderbilts and Their Fortunes.* New York: Doubleday, 1962.

————. *The House of Morgan.* New York: Dodd Mead, 1969.

Hughes, Peter. *The Founders of the Wallace Collection.* London: The Trustees of the Wallace Collection, 1981.

Hurst, Fannie. *Lonely Parade.* New York: Harper & Brothers, 1942.

Hyde, H. Montgomery. *Carson.* London: William Heinman & Co., 1953.

————. *Oscar Wilde, the Aftermath.* New York: Farrar, Straus & Giroux, 1963.

Irving, Pierre. *The Life and Letters of Washington Irving.* New York: G. P. Putnam's Sons, 1864.

Irving, Washington. *Letters,* Vols. II and III. Boston: Twayne Publishers, 1982.

Jackson, Kenneth T. *The Encyclopedia of New York City.* New Haven, Conn.: New-York Historical Society/Yale University Press, 1995.

Jackson, Stanley. *J. P. Morgan.* New York: Stein and Day, 1984.

Jacob, H. E. *The World of Emma Lazarus.* New York: Shocken Books, 1949.

James, Henry. *American Scene.* New York: Harper & Brothers, 1907.

————. *A Small Boy and Others.* New York: Charles Scribner's Sons, 1913.

————. *Notes of a Son and Brother.* New York: Charles Scribner's Sons, 1914.

————. *The Middle Years.* New York: Charles Scribner's Sons, 1917.

————. *Washington Square.* Middlesex, England: Penguin Books Ltd., 1984.

Jasen, David A. *The Theatre of P. G. Wodehouse.* London: B. T. Batsford, Ltd., 1979.

Johnson, Walter. *William Allen White's America.* New York: Henry Holt, 1947.

————. *Selected Letters of William Allen White.* New York: Henry Holt, 1947.

Josephson, Matthew and Hannah. *Al Smith, Hero of the Cities.* Boston: Houghton, Mifflin, 1969.

Jullian, Phillippe. *Robert de Montesquiou.* London: Secker and Warburg, 1965.

————. *Dreamers of Decadence.* London: Pall Mall Press Ltd., 1971.

Katz, Jonathan Ned. *Gay American History.* New York: Harper & Row, 1976.

————. *Gay/Lesbian Almanac.* New York: Harper & Row, 1983.

Kellogg, Cynthia. "Decorator of an Era," *The New York Times,* December 9, 1956.

Kennan, George. *E. H. Harriman: A Biography,* Vols. I and II. Boston: Houghton, Mifflin, 1922.

Kessner, Thomas. *Fiorello H. La Guardia and the Making of Modern New York.* New York: McGraw Hill, 1989.

King, Robert B. *The Vanderbilt Homes.* New York: Rizzoli, 1989.

Kirstein, Lincoln. *Mosaic.* New York: Farrar, Straus, & Giroux, 1994.

Kisseloff, Jeff. *You Must Remember This.* San Diego: Harcourt Brace Jovanovich, 1989.

Kleebat, Norman L. *The Dreyfus Affair.* Berkeley: University of California Press, 1987.

Klein, Carole. *Gramercy Park.* Boston: Houghton, Mifflin, 1987.

Knobe, Bertha Damaris. "The New York Women's Colony Club." *Harper's Bazaar,* April 1906.

Kobler, John. *Damned in Paradise.* New York: Atheneum, 1977.

Kotsilibas-Davis, James. *Great Times, Good Times.* New York: Doubleday, 1977.

Lamb, Mrs. M. J. *History of the City of New York,* Vols. I and II. New York: Privately printed, 1877.

Lanton. *Historic Newport.* Newport, R.I.: Newport Chamber of Commerce, 1933.

Lash, Joseph P. *Eleanor and Franklin.* New York: W. W. Norton, 1971.

———. *Eleanor: The Years Alone.* New York: W. W. Norton, 1972.

———. *Love, Eleanor: Eleanor Roosevelt and Her Friends.* New York: Doubleday, 1982.

———. *A World of Love: Eleanor Roosevelt and Her Friends, 1943–62.* New York: Doubleday, 1984.

Lawford, Valentine. *Bound for Diplomacy.* Boston: Little, Brown, 1963.

Lawrence, Rita. *Amateurs and Actors.* Menton: Mentonaise Editions, 1936.

Lehr, Elizabeth Drexel. *King Lehr and the Gilded Age.* Philadelphia: J. P. Lippincott Co., 1935.

Lewis, Alfred Allan. *Man of the World.* Indianapolis: Bobbs-Merrill, 1978.

———, and Constance Woodworth. *Miss Elizabeth Arden.* New York: Coward, McCann & Geoghegan, 1972.

Lewis, R.W.B. *Edith Wharton.* New York: Harper & Row, 1975.

———, and Nancy Lewis. *The Letters of Edith Wharton.* New York: Charles Scribner's Sons, 1988.

Lewis, Sinclair. *Main Street.* New York: Harcourt Brace, 1920.

Liebling, A.J. *Between Meals.* San Francisco: Northpoint Press, 1986.

Lise-Lone, Margaret. *David Belasco: Naturalism in the American Theatre.* Princeton, N.J.: Princeton University Press, 1975.

Littlewood, Joan. *Baron Phillippe.* New York: Crown, 1984.

Lockwood, Charles. *Bricks and Brownstones.* New York: Abbeville Press, 1972.

———. *Manhattan Moves Uptown.* Boston: Houghton, Mifflin, 1976.

Longley, Marjorie, Louis Silverstein, and Samuel A. Tower. *America's Taste, 1851–1959.* New York: Simon & Schuster, 1960.

Longstreet, Stephen. *We All Went to Paris.* New York: Macmillan, 1972.

Lounger, The. *The Critic, An Illustrated Monthly Review.* New Rochelle, N.Y. March, 1903. October, 1903.

Lundberg, Ferdinand. *America's Sixty Families.* New York: Citadel Press, 1938.

Lynes, Russell. *The Tastemakers.* New York: Harper & Brothers, 1954.

———. "What Did They Do Till the Decorator Came?" *House Beautiful,* October 1965.

———. *More Than Meets the Eye.* Washington, D.C: Smithsonian Institution, 1981.

McAllister, Ward. *Society as I Have Found It.* New York: Cassells Publishing Co., 1890.

Maccoll, Gail, and Carol Mcd. Wallace. *To Marry an English Lord.* New York: Workman Publishing, 1989.

McCulloch, David. *Mornings on Horseback.* New York: Simon & Schuster, 1981.

McHenry, Robert, ed. *Famous American Women,* Vols. I, II, and III. Springfield, Mass.: G. & C. Merriam Co., 1980.

MacKail, Denis. *The Story of J.M.B.* TK: Books for Libraries Press, 1941.

McKnight, Gerald. *The Scandal of Syrie Maugham.* London: W. H. Allen, 1980.

MacLiammoir, Michael. *The Importance of Being Oscar.* New York: Dufour Books, 1997.

McNamara, Brooks. *The Shuberts of Broadway.* New York: Oxford University Press, 1990.

Madsen, Axel. *The Sewing Circle.* New York: Birch Lane Press, 1995.

Maher, James T. *The Twilight of Splendor.* Boston: Little, Brown, 1975.

Marbury, Elisabeth. *Manners: A Handbook of Social Customs.* New York: Cassell & Co. Ltd., 1888.

———. "The New Plays: Success in Playwriting." *Harper's Weekly,* December 9, 1905.

———. *Modern Dancing by Vernon and Irene Castle.* Introduction. New York: Harper & Brothers, 1914.

———. "My Girls—As I Know Them," *Harper's Bazaar,* August 1917.

———. *My Crystal Ball.* New York: Boni & Liveright, 1923.

———. *As a Woman Remembers.* Columbia. Volume III. Knights of Columbus. New Haven, Conn. March 1924.

———. "Women in Politics," *Saturday Evening Post,* September 12, 1925.

———. "Where Are Our Manners?" *Colliers,* May 9, 1929.

———. "Sutton Place," *House Beautiful,* November 1930.

Marcosson, Isaac F., and Daniel Frohman. *Charles Frohman: Manager and Man.* New York: Harper & Brothers, 1916.

Mariano, Nicky. *Forty Years with Berenson.* New York: Alfred A. Knopf, 1966.

Marlowe, Derek. *Nancy Astor.* New York: Dell, 1982.

Marshall, S.L.A. *The American Heritage History of World War I.* New York: Simon & Schuster, 1964.

———. *The Simon and Schuster Encyclopedia of World War II.* New York: Simon & Schuster, 1978.

Martin, George. *Madame Secretary: Francis Perkins.* Boston: Houghton, Mifflin, 1976.

Martin, Ralph G. *Jennie, the Life of Lady Randolph Churchill,* Vols. 1 and 2. Englewood Cliffs, N.J.: Prentice Hall, 1969 and 1971.

Matthews, Brander. *These Many Years.* New York: Charles Scribner's Sons, 1917.

Mavor, Elizabeth. *A Year with the Ladies of Llangollen.* Middlesex, England: Penguin, 1986.

Maxtone-Graham, John. *The Only Way to Cross.* New York: Macmillan, 1972.

Maxwell, Elsa. *R.S.V.P.* Boston: Little, Brown, 1954.

Mellow, James R. *The Charmed Circle.* New York: Henry Holt, 1974.

Menkes, Suzy. *The Windsor Style.* London: Grafton Books, 1987.

Merriam, Eve. *Emma Lazarus: Woman with a Torch.* New York: The Citadel Press, 1956.

Metcalf, Pauline C. *Ogden Codman and the Decoration of Houses.* Boston: The Boston Atheneum, 1988.

Middleton, George. *These Things Are Mine.* New York: Macmillan, 1947.

Mikhail, E.H., ed. *Oscar Wilde: Interviews & Recollections,* Vols. 1 and 2. New York: Harper & Row, 1979.

Milbank, Caroline Reynolds. *Couture.* New York: Stewart, Tabori & Chang, Inc., 1985.

Moats, Alice-Leone. "The Elsie Legend," *Harper's Bazaar,* May 1949.

Mooney, Michael Macdonald. *Evelyn Nesbitt and Stanford White.* New York: William Morrow, 1976.

Morella, Joseph, and George Mazzei. *Genius & Lust.* New York: Carroll & Graf, 1995.

Morgan, Anne. "The American Girl," *Woman's Home Companion,* November, December 1914. March, April 1914. In book form: New York: Harper and Brothers, 1915.

———. "Sidelights on the Woman Question" (as told to Mary Margaret McBride), *Saturday Evening Post,* Mar. 26, 1927.

———. "Safety or Adventure in Business," *Good Housekeeping,* May 1932.

Morgan, Ted. *Maugham.* New York: Simon & Schuster, 1980.

Morris, Lloyd. *Postscript to Yesterday.* New York: Random House, 1947.

———. *Not So Long Ago.* New York: Random House, 1949.

Morris, Richard B., and Graham W. Irwin. *Harper Encyclopedia of the Modern World.* New York: Harper & Row, 1970.

Moses, Montrose J., and Virginia Gerson. *Clyde Fitch and His Letters.* Boston: Little, Brown, 1924.

Mosley, Sir Oswald. *My Life.* London: Thomas Nelson & Sons, Ltd., 1968.

Mott, Colonel T. Bentley. *Myron Herrick: Friend of France.* New York: Doubleday, 1929.

Mowat, Robert B. *Americans in England.* Boston: Houghton, Mifflin, 1935.

Muir, John. *Edward Henry Harriman.* New York: Doubleday, Page & Co., 1911.

Mumford, Lewis. *Green Memories.* New York: Harcourt Brace, 1947.

Myers, Gustave. *History of the Great American Fortunes.* New York: Modern Library, 1937.

Neal, Don C. *The World beyond the Hudson: Alfred E. Smith and National Politics.* New York: Garland Publishing Co., 1983.

Nesbit, Evelyn. *Prodigal Days.* New York: Julian Messner, Inc., 1934.

Nevins, Allan. *Henry White: Thirty Years of American Diplomacy.* New York: Harper & Brothers, 1930.

———. *Herbert H. Lehman and His Era.* New York: Charles Scribner's Sons, 1953.

Nicolson, Harold. *Diaries and Letters, 1930–1939.* New York: Atheneum, 1966.

Nicolson, Nigel. *Portrait of a Marriage.* New York: Atheneum, 1973.

O'Connell, Shaun. *Remarkable, Unspeakable New York.* Boston: Beacon Press, 1995.

O'Connor, Richard. *The First Hurrah.* New York: G. P. Putnam's Sons, 1970.

Odell, George C. D. *Annals of the New York Stage,* Vols. XI–XV. New York: Columbia University Press, 1949.

Ogden, Christopher. *Life of the Party.* Boston: Little, Brown, 1994.

Olin, Reuel Keith. *A History and Interpretation of the Princess Theatre Musical Plays: 1915–1919.* Ann Arbor, Mich.: UMI Dissertation Services, degree date, 1979.

O'Neill, Eugene. *Selected Letters of Eugene O'Neill,* ed. Travis Bogard and Jackson R. Bryer. New Haven, Conn.: Yale University Press, 1988.

Parrish, Thomas, ed. *The Simon and Schuster Encyclopedia of World War II.* New York: Simon & Schuster, 1978.

Patterson, Jerry E. *The Vanderbilts.* New York: Harry N. Abrams, 1989.

Payn, Graham. *My Life with Noel Coward.* New York: Applause, 1994.

Pearson, Hesketh. *George Bernard Shaw: A Full-Length Portrait.* New York: Harper & Brothers, 1942.

———. *Oscar Wilde: His Life & Wit.* New York: Harper & Row, 1946.

———. *Beerbohm Tree: His Life & Laughter.* New York: Harper & Row, 1956.

Pennant, Lilla. *Anne Morgan, Eva Dahlgren, Rose Dolan—And the Aid They Brought to French Refugees 1939–1949.* New York: Oliphant Press, 1990.

Perry, Elizabeth Israels. *Belle Moscowitz.* Oxford, England: Oxford University Press, 1987.

Perry, Galbraith B. *Charles D'Wolf of Guadeloupe.* New York Press of T. A. Wright, 1902.

Peters, Margot. *The House of Barrymore.* New York: Alfred A. Knopf, 1990.

Phelps, Alanson Hosmer. *Genealogy and Short Narrative History of One Branch of the Family of George Phelps.* San Francisco: Privately printed, 1897.

Phelps-Stoke, Isaac Newton. *The Iconography of Manhattan Island, 1492–1909.* New York: Robert Dodd, 1926.

Phillips, Cabell. *From the Crash to the Blitz.* New York: Macmillan, 1969.

———. *The 1940s: Decade of Triumph and Trouble.* New York: Macmillan, 1975.

Pine, Carolyn Pryor. *Recollections.* Privately printed, 1943.

Pine, John B. *The Story of Gramercy Park.* Privately printed, 1921.

Porter, Cole. *The Unpublished Cole Porter.* New York: Simon & Schuster, 1975.

———. *The Complete Lyrics of Cole Porter.* New York: Alfred A. Knopf, 1983.

Pound, Reginald. *Arnold Bennett.* New York: Harcourt Brace, 1953.

Purdom, C. B. *Granville Barker.* Cambridge, Mass.: Harvard Universtiy Press, 1956.

Quinn, Arthur Hobson. *A History of the American Drama.* New York: Appleton-Century-Crofts, 1927.

Rainsford, W. S. *The Story of a Varied Life.* New York: Doubleday, Page & Co., 1922.

Real Estate Record & Builders Guide. *A History of Real Estate, Building & Architecture in New York.* New York: 1869–1893.

Reid, Joyce M.H. *The Concise Oxford Dictionary of French Literature.* New York: Oxford University Press, 1976.

Richardson, Nancy. "Elsie de Wolfe," *House and Garden,* April 1982.

Robins, Elizabeth. *Both Sides of the Curtain.* London: William Heinemann Ltd., 1940.

Robinson, Alice M., Vera Mowry Roberts, and Milly S. Barranger. *Notable Women in the American Theatre.* New York: Greenwood Press, 1989.

Robsjohn-Gibbings, T. H. *Goodbye Mr. Chippendale.* New York: Alfred Knopf, 1947.

Rovere, Richard H. *Howe & Hummell.* New York: Farrar, Straus, & Giroux, 1947.

Rowe, Robert R. "Man of Town Topics," *American Mercury,* July 1926.

Saint John, Christopher, ed. *Ellen Terry and Bernard Shaw: A Correspondence.* New York: G. P. Putnam's Sons, 1932.

Salmon, Eric. *Granville Barker: A Secret Life.* Connecticut: Fairleigh Dickenson University Press, 1983.

———. *Granville Barker and His Correspondence.* Detroit: Wayne State University Press, 1986.

Samuels, Ernest. *Bernard Berenson: The Making of a Connoisseur.* Cambridge, Mass.: The Belknap Press, 1979.

———. *Bernard Berenson: The Making of a Legend.* Cambridge, Mass.: The Belknap Press, 1987.

———. *Henry Adams.* Cambridge, Mass.: The Belknap Press, 1989.

Sanger, Margaret. *Autobiography.* New York: W. W. Norton, 1938.

Sante, Luc. *Low Life.* New York: Farrar, Strauss, Giroux, 1991.

Satterlee, Herbert L. *J. Pierpont Morgan.* New York: Macmillan, 1940.

Schwartz, Charles. *Cole Porter.* New York: The Dial Press, 1977.

Scott, James Brown. *Robert Bacon: Life and Letters.* New York: Doubleday & Page, 1923.

Secrest, Meryle. *Between Me and Life.* Garden City, N.Y.: Doubleday, 1974.

Seebohm, Caroline, and Mary Jane Pool. *20th Decorating Architecture and Gardens.* New York: Holt, Rinehart and Winston, 1980.

Seebohm, Caroline. *The Man Who Was Vogue.* New York: Viking, 1982.

Seligman, Germain. *Merchants of Art 1880–1960: Eighty Years of Professional Collecting.* New York: Appleton-Century-Crofts, 1961.

Shand-Tucci, Douglas. *The Art of Scandal.* New York: HarperCollins, 1997.

Shanet, Howard. *Philharmonic: A History of New York's Orchestra.* Garden City, N.Y.: Doubleday, 1975.

Shanke, Robert A., and Kim Marra. *Passing Performances.* Ann Arbor: University of Michigan Press, 1998.

Shaw, George Bernard, and Ellen Terry. *A Correspondence.* New York: G. P. Putnam's Sons, 1932.

Shaw, George Bernard. *Selected Plays,* Vols. I, II, and III. New York: Dodd, Mead, 1948.

———. *Collected Letters,* Vols. I and II. New York: Dodd, Mead & Co., 1965.

Silver, Nathan. *Lost New York.* New York: Weathervane Books, 1967.

Simon, Kate. *Fifth Avenue.* New York: Harcourt Brace Jovanovich, 1978.

Sims, Patterson. *Whitney Museum of American Art.* New York: Whitney Museum of American Art and W. W. Norton, 1985.

Sinclair, Andrew. *Corsair: The Life of J. Pierpont Morgan.* Boston: Little, Brown, 1978.

Sinclair, David. *Dynasty: The Actors and Their Times.* New York: Beaufort Books, Inc., 1984.

Sitwell, Osbert. "Introduction." In *The Frick Collection: An Illustrated Catalogue in 12 Volumes.* Pittsburgh: Printed at the University of Pittsburgh, 1949.

Sloane, Florence Adele, with Louis Auchincloss. *Maverick in Mauve.* Garden City, N.Y.: Doubleday, 1983.

Smith, Harrison. *From Main Street to Stockholm: Letters of Sinclair Lewis, 1919–1930.* New York: Harcourt Brace, 1952.

Smith, Jane S. *Elsie de Wolfe.* New York: Atheneum, 1982.

Smith-Rosenberg, Carroll. *Disorderly Conduct.* New York: Alfred A. Knopf, 1985.

Spann, Edward K. *The New Metropolis.* New York: Columbia University Press, 1981.

Spooner, Walter, ed. *Historic Families of America.* New York: Historic Families Publishing Co., 1907.

Stagg, Jerry. *The Brothers Shubert.* New York: Random House, 1968.

Stasz, Clarice. *The Vanderbilt Women.* New York: St. Martin's Press, 1991.

Steffens, Lincoln. *The Autobiography of Lincoln Steffens,* Vols. I and II. New York: Harcourt Brace, 1931.

Stern, Robert A. M., Gregory Gilmartin, and Thomas Mellins. *New York 1930.* New York: Rizzoli, 1987.

———, and John Massengale. *New York 1900.* New York: Rizzoli, 1983.

Stewart, Henry. "The Playbrokers of New York," *Theatre Magazine,* June 1905.

Stockwell, Fay MacCracken. "Childhood Memories of Irving Place," *Gramercy Graphic,* November 1950.

Stoker, Bram. *The Personal Reminiscences of Henry Irving.* London: William Heineman, Ltd., 1906.

Strange, Michael. *Who Tells Me True.* New York: Charles Scribner's Sons, 1940.

Strong, George Templeton. *The Diary of George Templeton Strong.* New York: Macmillan, 1952.

Strouse, Jean. *Alice James.* Boston: Houghton, Mifflin, 1980.

Strum, Rebecca W. *Elisabeth Marbury, 1856–1933: Her Life and Work.* Ann Arbor, Mich.: UMI Dissertation Services, degree date, 1989.

Sullivan, Edward Dean. *The Fabulous Wilson Mizner.* New York: The Henkle Company, 1935.

Swanberg, W.A. *Whitney Father, Whitney Heiress.* New York: Charles Scribner's Sons, 1980.

Swift, Lindsay. *Brook Farm.* Secaucus, N.J.: The Citadel Press, 1961.

Tanner, Louise. *All the Things We Were.* Garden City, N.Y.: Doubleday, 1968.

Tapert, Annette, and Diana Edkins. *The Power of Style.* New York: Crown, 1994.

Tarkington, Booth. "As I Seem to Me," *Saturday Evening Post.* Six installments, July 5–August 23, 1941.

Tauranac, John, and Christopher Little. *Elegant New York.* New York: Abbeville Press, 1985.

Tellegrin, Lou. *Women Have Been Kind.* New York: Vanguard Press, 1931.

Tharp, Louise Hall. *Mrs. Jack.* Boston: Little, Brown, 1965.

The Forum. "What Must Be Done," *Century Magazine,* May 1918.

Thomas, Augustus. *The Print of My Remembrance.* New York: Charles Scribner's Sons, 1922.

Time-Life Books. *This Fabulous Century: 1900–1910, 1910–1920, 1920–1930, 1930–1940, 1940–1950, 1950–1960.* New York: Time, Inc., 1969.

Tomkins, Calvin. *Merchants and Masterpieces.* New York: E. P. Dutton, 1970.

———. *Living Well Is the Best Revenge.* New York: Viking, 1971.

Tudury, Moran. "Ward McAllister," *American Mercury,* June 1926.

Tyler, George and J. C. Furnas. *Whatever Goes Up.* Indianapolis, Ind.: Bobbs Merrill Co., 1934.

Valentine's Manual: 1841, 1842, 1847–1867, 1868–1870, 1916–1918. New York: Old Colony Press.

Vanderbilt, Anne Harriman. "My Trip to the Front," *Harper's,* January 1917.

———. "Mind the Paint," *Colliers,* March 8, 1930.

Vanderbilt, Arthur T., II. *Fortune's Children: The Fall of the House of Vanderbilt.* New York: William Morrow, 1989.

Vanderbilt, Cornelius. *Farewell to Fifth Avenue.* New York: Simon & Schuster, 1935.

———. *Queen of the Golden Age.* New York: McGraw Hill, 1956.

Van Hoogstraten, Nicholas. *Lost Broadway Theatres.* New York: Princeton Architectural Press, 1991.

Van Rensselaer, May King. *Newport, Our Social Capital.* Philadelphia: J. P. Lippincott Company, 1915.

———. *The Social Ladder.* New York: Henry Holt, 1924.

Vickers, Hugo. *Gladys, Duchess of Marlborough.* New York: Holt, Rinehart and Winston, 1979.

———. *Cecil Beaton.* Boston: Little, Brown, 1985.

———. *Loving Garbo.* New York: Random House, 1994.

Vidal, Gore. *Empire.* New York: Random House, 1987.

Von Eckardt, Wolf, Sander L. Gilman, and J. Edward Chamberlin. *Oscar Wilde's London.* Garden City, N.Y.: Anchor Press, 1987.

Vreeland, Diana. *D.V.* New York: Alfred A. Knopf, 1984.

Warner, Charles Dudley. *Washington Irving.* Boston: Houghton, Mifflin, 1884.

Wechter, Dixon. *The Saga of American Society.* New York: Charles Scribner's Sons. 1937.

Weinreb, Ben, and Christopher Hibbert, eds. *The London Encyclopedia.* New York: St. Martin's Press, 1983.

Weintraub, Stanley. *Shaw,* Vols. I and II. New York: Weybright & Talley, 1969 and 1970.

Wharton, Edith. *The House of Mirth.* New York: Charles Scribner's Sons, 1905.

———. *The Custom of the Country.* New York: Charles Scribner's Sons, 1913.

———. *The Age of Innocence.* New York: D. Appleton & Co., 1920.

———. *Old New York.* New York: Charles Scribner's Sons, 1924.

———. *A Backward Glance.* New York: Appleton Century, 1934.

Wharton, Edith, and Ogden Codman. *The Decoration of Houses.* New York: Charles Scribner's Sons, 1897.

White, William Allen. *Autobiography of William Allen White.* New York: Macmillan, 1946.

Wilde, Oscar. *The Letters of Oscar Wilde,* ed. Rupert Hart-Davis. New York: Harcourt Brace, 1962.

———. *More Letters,* ed. Rupert Hart-Davis. New York: Vanguard Press, 1985.

———. *The Complete Works of _____.* London: The Galley Press, 1987.

Williams, Selma R. *Divine Rebel: The Life of Anne Marbury Hutchinson.* New York: Holt, Rinehart and Winston, 1981.

Wilson, James Grant. *The Memorial History of the City of New York.* New York: New History Company, 1893.

Wineapple, Brenda. *Genet: A Biography of Janet Flanner.* New York: Ticknor & Fields, 1989.

Winkler, John. *Morgan the Magnificent.* Garden City, L.I.: Garden City Publishing Co., 1930.

Wiser, William. *The Crazy Years: Paris in the Twenties.* New York: Atheneum, 1983.

———. *The Great Good Place.* New York: W. W. Norton, 1991.

Wodehouse, P.G., and Guy Bolton. *Bring on the Girls.* New York: Simon & Shuster, 1953.

Wolfe, Garard R. *New York: A Guide to the Metropolis.* New York: McGraw-Hill, 1988.

Woloch, Nancy. *Women and the American Experience.* New York: Alfred A. Knopf, 1984.

Woman's Home Companion. "She Takes After Her Father," April 1916.

Woodress, James. *Booth Tarkington, Gentleman from Indiana.* Philadelphia: Joseph B. Lippincott, 1954.

Woollcott, Alexander. *The Letters of Alexander Woollcott.* Garden City, L.I.: Garden City Publishing Co., 1944.

WPA. *Guide to New York City.* New York: Random House, 1939.

Yeomans, Harry Martin. "A Remodeled City House," *American Homes and Gardens,* December 1913.

Young, Stark. *A Life in the Arts: Letters, 1900–1962.* Baton Rouge: Louisiana State University Press, 1970.

Ziegler, Philip. *Diana Cooper.* New York: Alfred A. Knopf, 1982.

Zim, Larry, Mel Lerner, and Herbert Rolfes. *The World of Tomorrow.* New York: Harper & Row, 1988.

$\mathscr{I}$ N D E X $\mathscr{P}$

Bacon, Martha Waldron Cowdin, 52, 53, 307

Bacon, Robert, 52–53, 57, 215, 306, 307, 318, 321, 438

Baker, Ray Stannard, 237

Baldwin, William, 471

Balfour, Arthur, 347

Ballad of Reading Gaol, The (Wilde), 182–85

Ballard, Bettina, 448

Balsan, Jacques, 203, 229, 347

Barney, Charles T., 208

Barney, Helen, 208

Barney, Natalie, 191

Barnum, P. T., 10–11

Barrès, Maurice, 332

Barrie, James M., 174–76, 221

Barrie, Mary, 175–76

Barron, Clarence W., 100

Barrymore, Ethel, 166, 169, 198, 200, 201, 356

Barrymore, John, 372, 395

Barrymore, Maurice, 144

Bartet, Julia, 104, 120, 134, 136

Bartholdi, Auguste, 112

Baruch, Bernard, 406, 435

Bauble Shop, The, 144–45, 198

Baxter, William, 172–73

Baylor, Frances Courtenoy, 117

Beaton, Cecil, 396, 407, 415–16, 445, 474

Beau Brummell (Fitch), 140–41, 142, 147

Bedeaux, Charles and Fern, 445

Beeks, Gertrude, 235

Belasco, David, 174, 275

Belmont, Alva, xvi, 85–88, 154–55, 157, 164, 165, 204, 235, 256, 261–62, 273, 274–75, 276, 283, 296, 297, 321, 354, 357, 361, 378, 433–34, 436

Belmont, August, 235

Belmont, Eleanor Robson, 275, 277–78, 294, 336–37, 376

Belmont, Oliver H. P., 154, 241

Belmont, Sally Whitney Rives, 241

Bemelmans, Ludwig, 469–70

Benefit of the Doubt, The (Pinero), 176–77

Bennett, Arnold, 237–38

Bennett, James Gordon, Jr., 105, 206

Bennett, James Gordon, Sr., 8

Berenson, Bernard, 212–13, 217–18, 221, 238, 239, 250–51, 267, 336, 362, 480

Berenson, Mary, 212, 362, 480

Berlin, Irving, 85, 310, 381

Bernard, Pierre A., 374, 375, 387–88, 407, 408

Bernhardt, Sarah, 122, 134, 171, 199, 329, 340, 415

Betty's Finish (Fitch), 140

Bigelow, Dorothie, 320

Bigelow, Grace, 100

Big Sisters, 276, 289, 295, 312, 422

Bisson, Alexandre, 124, 134, 135, 139, 142, 143

Blithe Spirit (Coward), 454

Bly, Nellie, 236

Bolton, Guy, 316, 319

Bonaparte, Roland, 417, 418

Boni de Castellane, Count, 100, 249, 250, 436

Booth, Edwin, 73

Booth, Evangeline, 320–21

Bordman, Gerald, 409

Bostonians, The (James), 31, 61

"Boston marriage," xii-xiii, 53, 61–62, 106

Bourbon, Don Jaime de, 268

Bourdet, Edouard, 379–80

Bowers, Glenn, 419–20

Bright, Addison, 174, 199, 200, 233, 268

Bright, Reginald Golding, 199, 200, 233–34, 280, 362, 396, 434

Bronson, Katherine, 35

Brook Farm, 59–61

Brooklyn Navy Yard, 247–49

Browning, Elizabeth Barrett, 376

Browning, Robert, 35, 110, 376

Brown-Potter, Cora, 70, 77–78, 79, 80–82, 93, 102, 127, 135

Brown-Potter, James, 80, 82

Bryan, William Jennings, 159

Buccaneers, The (Wharton), 155

Burden, Mrs. Isaac Townsend, 104–5, 108

Burnett, Frances Hodgson, 113–19, 123, 139, 174, 208

Butler, Eleanor, 34–35

Butt, Archie, 245–46, 286

By the Waters of Babylon (Lazarus), 111

Cameron, Elizabeth, 193, 206, 244

Campbell, Duncan, 66–67

Camp Uncas, 160–62, 172, 385

Candida (Shaw), 148–49

Index